P9-APG-418

Generations of Youth

The United Library
Garrett-Evangelical/Seabury-Western Seminaries
Evanston, IL 60201

Generations of Youth

Youth Cultures and History in Twentieth-Century America

EDITED BY

Joe Austin and Michael Nevin Willard

HQ
796
.G35
US

New York University Press

NEW YORK AND LONDON

NEW YORK UNIVERSITY PRESS
New York and London

© 1998 by Joe Austin and Michael Nevin Willard
All rights reserved

Chapter 6 © 1989, Paula Fass. Reprinted by permission.

Chapter 10 reprinted from James T. Sears. *Lonely Hunters: An Oral History of Lesbian and Gay Southern Life, 1948–1968* (New York: HarperCollins, 1997). © 1996, James T. Sears. Reprinted by permission.

Chapter 17 reprinted from *Ethnomusicology* 39, no. 2 (Spring/Summer 1995). © 1995 by the Board of Trustees of the University of Illinois. Used with permission of the author and the University of Illinois Press.

Chapter 26 reprinted from Stephen Duncombe, *Notes from Underground: Zines and the Politics of Alternative Culture.* © 1997, Verso, The Imprint of New Left Books, Ltd. Reprinted by permission.

Library of Congress Cataloging-in-Publication Data
Generations of youth : youth cultures and history in twentieth-century America / edited by Joe Austin and Michael Nevin Willard.
p. cm.
Includes bibliographical references (p.) and index.
ISBN 0-8147-0645-2 (cloth : acid-free paper). — ISBN 0-8147-0646-0 (pbk. : acid-free paper)
1. Youth—United States—History—20th century. 2. Minority youth—United States—History—20th century. 3. Subculture— United States—History—20th century. I. Austin, Joe, 1957– . II. Willard, Michael Nevin.
HQ796.G4173 1998
305.235'0973'0904—dc21 97-45397
CIP

New York University Press books are printed on acid-free paper, and their binding materials are chosen for strength and durability.

Manufactured in the United States of America

10 9 8 7 6 5 4 3 2

Contents

Acknowledgments *ix*
Contributors *xi*

Introduction: Angels of History, Demons of Culture 1
Joe Austin and Michael Nevin Willard

PART I: Early Twentieth Century

1 Experts and Juvenile Delinquency, 1900–1935 21
Victoria Getis

2 Heroism and the Problem of Impulsiveness for Early Twentieth-Century American Youth 36
Jay Mechling

3 Teenage Girls, Sexuality, and Working-Class Parents in Early Twentieth-Century California 50
Mary E. Odem

4 Rolling with the Punches: Boxing, Youth Culture, and Ethnic Identity at Federal Indian Boarding Schools during the 1930s 65
John Bloom

5 The Deanna Durbin Devotees: Fan Clubs and Spectatorship 81
Georganne Scheiner

6 Creating New Identities: Youth and Ethnicity in New York City High Schools in the 1930s and 1940s 95
Paula S. Fass

7 Brown "Hordes" in McIntosh Suits: Filipinos, Taxi Dance Halls, and Performing the Immigrant Body in Los Angeles, 1930s–1940s 118
Linda N. España-Maram

PART II: War and Postwar

8 The Riddle of the Zoot: Malcolm Little and Black Cultural Politics during World War II 136
Robin D. G. Kelley

9 "Memories of El Monte": Intercultural Dance Halls in Post-World War II Greater Los Angeles 157
matt garcia

10 Growing Up as a Jewish Lesbian in South Florida: Queer Teen Life in the Fifties 173
James T. Sears

11 From Panty Raids to Revolution: Youth and Authority, 1950–1970 187
Beth Bailey

12 "Birth of a New Symbol": The Brown Berets' Gendered Chicano National Imaginary 205
Ernesto Chávez

13 Art and Activism in the Chicano Movement: Judith F. Baca, Youth and the Politics of Cultural Work 223
Jeffrey J. Rangel

PART III: Contemporary Youth Culture

14 Knowing Their Place: Local Knowledge, Social Prestige, and the Writing Formation in New York City 240
Joe Austin

15 ". . . And Tomorrow Is Just Another Crazy Scam": Postmodernity, Youth, and the Downward Mobility of the Middle Class 253
Ryan Moore

16 Dancin' in the Street to a Black Girl's Beat: Music, Gender, and the "Ins and Outs" of Double-Dutch 272
Kyra D. Gaunt

17 Clamor and Community in the Music of Public Enemy 293
Robert Walser

18 Hmong American Youth: American Dream, American Nightmare 311
William Wei

19 Seance, Tricknowlogy, Skateboarding, and the Space of Youth 327
Michael Nevin Willard

20 Teens at Work: Negotiating the Jobless Future 347
Susan Willis

21 What to Make of *Wiggers*: A Work in Progress 358
David Roediger

22 Virtually Out: The Emergence of a Lesbian, Bisexual, and Gay Youth Cyberculture 367
Joanne Addison and Michelle Comstock

23 Gender and Generation down the Red Road 379
Rachel Buff

24 The Hip Hop Hearings: Censorship, Social Memory, and Intergenerational Tensions among African Americans 395
George Lipsitz

25 Nightmares in the New Metropolis: The Cinematic Poetics of Low Riders 412
Brenda Jo Bright

26 Let's All Be Alienated Together: Zines and the Making of Underground Community 427
Stephen Duncombe

Index 453

Acknowledgments

We could not have put this anthology together without the help of our friends. Thanks to Valerie Matsumoto, Stanley Aronowitz, Mary Rothschild, Vicki Ruiz, and Henry Jenkins for their recommendations. Mary Kay Van Sistine and Rachel Buff provided invaluable assistance with editing, critiques, and recommendations. Niko Pfund of NYU Press never let us forget that we had proposed this anthology, now so long ago, and continually encouraged us to follow through on it. Tim Bartlett of NYU Press, our editor, has the patience of a saint. We were continually impressed with his abilities to smooth out the rough edges of this project. Finally, thanks and much respect to the twenty-six authors whose work is included here for their enthusiasm and encouragement with this project.

Contributors

Joanne Addison is Assistant Professor at the University of Colorado-Denver, where she teaches courses in rhetoric and composition. She is currently working on a book entitled *Participatory Research in Basic Writing Classrooms: Cultural Studies, Feminist Postmodernism and Teacher Research at Work*, to be published by Sage Publications.

You can find *Joe Austin's* work at the intersection of popular culture, urban history, and the history of youth-but be careful: the stoplight at that intersection doesn't work. He is the author of *Taking the Train: Youth Culture, Urban Crisis, and the "Graffiti Problem" in New York City*, forthcoming from Columbia University Press.

Beth Bailey is the author of *From Front Porch to Back Seat: Courtship in 20th Century America* (1988) and co-author of *The First Strange Place: Race and Sex in World War II Hawaii* (1992). She is currently writing a cultural and social history of America's post-World War II sexual revolution.

John Bloom is Assistant Professor of American Studies at Dickinson College in Carlisle, Pennsylvania. His work focuses on the relationships between sports, popular culture, and identity. He is the author of *A House of Cards: Baseball Card Collecting and Popular Culture* (University of Minnesota Press, 1997), as well as articles on sports at federally operated boarding schools for Native Americans and on sports fandom and gender identity.

Brenda Jo Bright is a Fellow at the Getty Research Institute for the History of Art and the Humanities in their scholar year, "Perspectives on Los Angeles: Images, Narratives, History." She teaches anthropology as well as Chicano and Latino studies. She is the co-editor of *Looking High and Low: Art and Cultural Identity*, and the author of *Low Rider: Culture in the Time of the Automobile*, forthcoming from the University of California Press in their American Crossroads series.

Rachel Buff is Assistant Professor of History at Bowling Green State University in Ohio. She is currently completing her book manuscript, *Calling Home: Race, Im/Migration and Popular Memory in Caribbean Brooklyn and Native American Minneapolis, 1945–1992* (forthcoming, University of California Press).

Ernesto Chávez is Assistant Professor in the Department of History at the University of Texas at El Paso. He is currently working on a book on the Chicano movement in Los Angeles, 1966–1978.

Michelle Comstock is a doctoral student in rhetoric and composition at Purdue University. She is interested in the connections between postmodern mapping and composing, especially in regard to the development of youth spaces and cultures.

Stephen Duncombe is Assistant Professor of American Studies at the State University of New York at Old Westbury. He co-edits the zine *Primary Documents*, writes regularly for *The Baffler*, and lives in New York City.

Linda N. España-Maram received her Ph.D. in history from UCLA and is currently a chancellor's postdoctoral fellow in the Department of Ethnic Studies at the University of California-San Diego, where she is finishing a book manuscript based on her dissertation, "Negotiating Identity: Youth, Gender, and Popular Culture in Los Angeles' Little Manila, 1920s–1950s." She will join the Department of Asian and Asian American Studies at California State University-Long Beach beginning in fall 1997.

Paula S. Fass, who teaches at the University of California at Berkeley, has written widely in the areas of youth culture, childhood, family, and education. Her most recent book is *Kidnapped: Child Abduction in America* (Oxford University Press, 1997).

matt garcia earned his doctorate in history in 1996 from the Claremont Graduate School, and is currently an Assistant Professor of History and Latina/Latino Studies at the University of Illinois, Urbana-Champaign. His current research focuses on intercultural relations in the citrus-growing regions of Southern California. Selected publications include " 'Just put on that Padua Hills' smile': The Padua Hills Theatre and the Mexican Players, 1931–1974," *California History* (Fall 1995); and "Chicana/o and Latina/o Workers in a Changing Discipline," *Humboldt Journal of Social Relations* 22:1 (1996).

Kyra D. Gaunt teaches ethnomusicology as an Assistant Professor of Music at the University of Virginia. She currently teaches courses on contemporary performance in the African diaspora of the Americas with special interest in U.S. popular "musicking" from girls' game songs to hip hop. Her analysis of music emphasizes the social processes of learning musical styles and identity formation through performance. Her work also appears in *Feminism, Multiculturalism and the Media* (Sage, 1995) and *Language, Rhythm, and Sound* (University of Pittsburgh, 1997). Her forthcoming book, *Music, Body, and "Soul"*, illustrates how the earliest musical games African American girls play challenge the rigid gender distinctions that have been erected as a result of the inattention to women's "musicking."

Victoria Gettis is co-author of *Muddy Boots and Ragged Aprons: Images of Working-Class Detroit, 1900–1930*. She has taught at Keene State College, Western New England College, and Mount Holyoke College.

Robin D. G. Kelley is Professor of History and Africana Studies at New York University. He is the author of *Hammer and Hoe: Alabama Communists during the Great Depression* (1990); *Race Rebels: Culture Politics and the Black Working Class* (1994); *Yo' Mama's Disfunktional!: Fighting the Culture Wars in Urban America* (1997); and *Into the Fire: African Americans since 1970* (1996), a volume in the Young Oxford History of African Americans.

George Lipsitz is Professor of Ethnic Studies at the University of California, San Diego. His publications include *Dangerous Crossroads, A Rainbow at Midnight, Time Passages, A Life in the Struggle,* and *The Sidewalks of St. Louis.*

Jay Mechling is Professor of American Studies at the University of California, Davis. Besides his work on the Boy Scouts, he is writing a book on "Folklore and the Civil Sphere" and another on "Florida in the American Imagination."

Ryan Moore is a graduate student in Sociology at the University of California, San Diego. He is currently working on an ethnographic study of the post-punk music scene in San Diego.

Mary E. Odem is Associate Professor of History and Women's Studies at Emory University. She is the author of *Delinquent Daughters: Protecting and Policing Adolescent Female Sexuality in the United States, 1885–1920.*

Jeffrey J. Rangel is a Ph.D. candidate in the University of Michigan's Program in American Culture and has taught classes in Chicana/o Studies, Latina/o Studies, American Studies, and U.S. History. He is currently completing his dissertation entitled "Gritando al espejo: Artists, Cultural Work and the Politics of Representation in the Chicano Movement, 1965-1981."

Formerly a youth himself, *David Roediger* teaches working-class history at the University of Minnesota. His books include *The Wages of Whiteness, Towards the Abolition of Whiteness,* and the forthcoming anthology of African American writings on whiteness, *Black on White.*

Georganne Scheiner is Assistant Professor of Women's Studies at Arizona State University. Her article is part of a larger manuscript entitled "Signifying Adolescence."

James T. Sears is Professor of Curriculum Studies and Higher Education at the University of South Carolina. Specializing in gay studies in education and the South, he maintains a popular home page at http://www.jtsears.com

Robert Walser is Associate Professor of Musicology at UCLA. He is editor of *American Music,* and author of *Running with the Devil: Power, Gender, and Madness in Heavy Metal Music.*

William Wei teaches modern Chinese history and Asian American Studies at the University of Colorado at Boulder. He is the author of *The Asian American Movement* (Temple University Press, 1993) and *Counterrevolution in China: The Nationalist in Jiangxi during the Soviet Period* (University of Michigan Press, 1985).

Michael Nevin Willard lives in Los Angeles and is completing work on a social and cultural history of youth culture and white racial formation in postwar Los Angeles for the Program in American Studies at the University of Minnesota.

Susan Willis teaches courses in popular culture and literature at Duke University. Her work focuses on daily life and aims to unite theory and ethnography.

Introduction
Angels of History, Demons of Culture

Joe Austin and Michael Nevin Willard

We tune in to daily broadcasts about youth and their place in society, although the messages sometimes arrive under other headlines. "Generation X" is juxtaposed against the aging "boomers" in a struggle for social resources, but we are more likely to watch the conflict, hear it, or read about it in the context of changes in social security or education policy. Implicitly, we are asked to decide which generation is more worthy, but the deck is stacked against the "slackers." In other, more dramatic instances, the practices of young people become occasions for moral panic. Often these incidents are created intentionally to manipulate and hysterically reflect on the contemporary status quo, resulting in calls for social renewal and action. Recurring panics over a "surge" in drug use among high school students, institutionalized in a "war on drugs" that has lasted for over two decades, have been mobilized to justify the incredible explosion in the size of the prison population in the United States, now among the largest in the world. Urban youth, particularly youth of color, inherit cities where employment, adequate education, and the basic necessities of life are increasingly difficult to obtain. These conditions inform contemporary "urban problems," many of which are specifically related to youth: teen pregnancy, gangs, unemployment, drugs. Atrocity tales appearing in newspaper headlines, on magazine covers, and during television newscasts ask us, with alarming regularity, to see young people as animalistic, alien Others. The decline in state education funding is matched by the increase in funding for prisons. We are left to wonder whether the new "Evil Empire" will be located in our schools, streets, and homes, among our friends, siblings, neighbors, and children: "youth".

The public debates surrounding "youth" are important forums where new understandings about the past, present, and future of public life are encoded, articulated, and contested. "Youth" becomes a metaphor for perceived social change and its projected consequences, and as such it is an enduring locus for displaced social anxieties.[1] Pronouncements such as "the problems of youth today," used as a scapegoat for larger social concerns, objectify and reify young people *as the problem in itself.* Young people are approached with the assumption that they are "problems."

The complex conflicts and displaced social anxieties concerning social change, often metaphorized through concerns about "youth," result in contradictions in our understandings of young people. For instance, consider the inconsistent assumptions underlying questions concerning "youth" in the United States during the late 1950s: Were America's individualistic young men being transformed into a herd of complacent, other-directed automatons by preparing for work lives in corporate and government bureaucracies? Was the insidious mixing of races and social classes in the public schools and in popular culture producing a generation of gang members, murderers, sluts, lay-abouts, and delinquents? Were young people the avant garde of a new era of consumer "fun" and sexual pleasure? Were most young people traditional, clean-living, hardworking, "good Americans," unfairly maligned by the actions of a few disturbed members of their generation?[2]

These contradictions, obviously not limited to the late 1950s, highlight the bifurcated social identity of youth as a vicious, threatening sign of social decay and "our best hope for the future." A contemporary television news report on gang violence may be followed by a commercial that challenges muscular youths to "be all that you can be" in the armed forces and another hailing the "Pepsi Generation"—without apparent irony. As Rachel Buff notes in another context, we have all been prepared for this moment of contradiction, and so it seems mundane rather than disorienting.[3]

"Youth" and young people must be understood as more than longstanding metaphors for adult agendas, desires, or anxieties. If youth have so frequently been seen as the demons of culture in the U.S. (when they have been visible at all), perhaps it is because, as George Lipsitz has written, "public records most often reflect the concerns of those in power and only rarely contain evidence of the thoughts, action, or aspirations of teenagers and young adults unless those groups are seen as some kind of threat to people with power."[4]

Over the last thirty years, scholars from a wide range of disciplines have worked to amend those public records, in part by exploring the *historical processes* through which the social identities of young people have been created, transformed, and reproduced. *Generations of Youth* brings together the best recent and new work on youth and youth cultures by social historians and American/cultural studies scholars. We see a new theoretical position emerging from this scholarship that approaches youth (roughly encompassing ages twelve to twenty-four) and youth cultures as specific social-historical formations. Current scholarship calls for an understanding of young people as one particularly important (and frequently neglected) node in a multi dimensional network of social relations, structural forces, and historical developments. The central questions and debates that can guide a broader analysis of youths' singular experiences within these networks have not been articulated, a shortcoming that we hope this anthology will help overcome.

The chapters gathered here are arranged roughly in chronological order within the twentieth century to emphasize the necessity of positioning youth within the larger framework of modern U.S. history. But why limit our view to this century? The early 1900s mark the publication of G. Stanley Hall's monumental work, *Adolescence* (1905), which rendered "scientific" many of the understandings of "youth" that had emerged from the cultural enclaves of the middle class of the previous century.[5] Adolescence was constructed within the medical profession (and later, in psychology) as a separate and particularly fragile stage of physical, emotional, moral, and intellectual development that could be successfully navigated only through the intervention of virtuous adults. This reconceptualization of the life stage between childhood and adulthood in part informed and justified (and often enforced) the new institutional, social, and spatial arrangements that have shaped the lives of twentieth-century youth. This new perception of youth, embedded in the concept of adolescence, influenced schooling, the professionalization of childcare, the juvenile justice system, the rise of adult-supervised youth activities (such as the Boy Scouts), and supported reformers' claims that young people need special consideration in governmental policies.[6] In turn, the growth of mass-socializing institutions such as the public high schools created bonds of common experience based on age within populations that were otherwise quite diverse.

The anthology's timespan is bounded by contemporary suggestions, within the media as well as in academia, that the conceptualization of youth that began with Hall and developed throughout the twentieth century is now under revision, perhaps radically so. Commonly held assumptions about youth are being revised in new state and federal policy initiatives. Declines in state funding for education are matched by increased funding for prison construction and maintenance. Proposed cuts in social welfare will disproportionately effect the lives of young people. These policy initiatives contradict a conception of adolescence as a vulnerable and particularly important period of social and intellectual development, when compassionate adult intervention and supervision are most needed. They assert a cynical (and often racialized) view of youth as dangerous, burdensome "outsiders" rather than valued future citizens; they point toward an important shift in the "place" of youth within the social order of the United States. Issues associated with youth have been a persistent and active site of social contestation throughout the 20th century, but we may be witnessing a renegotiation of the terms of the contests.[7]

In the remainder of this introduction, we offer a summary of the chapters in *Generations of Youth* that emphasizes and makes explicit a historical-formational approach that is also implicit in much of the scholarship on youth and youth cultures that preceded this book. A formational approach addresses the historical specificity of youth, locating young people and the representations of their lives in a complex and changing historical network of institutions, economic structures, state policies, adult initiatives, and youths' self-activities. By engaging this model of an age-formational process, we offer a provisional vocabulary to guide further historical and cultural analyses, and a way of structuring narratives around that vocabulary. Youth, as a social formation, is marked historically by complex processes of continuity, rupture, and transformation. We assume "youth" to be a socially constructed and multiple identity whose relations to other social formations are constantly in flux and only definable temporarily and locally. While the chronological arrangement of the articles suggests the importance of youth and young people within established and emerging historical debates, it leaves out a great deal that might engage a conversation specifically about young people and youth cultures. The formational approach works to bridge that gap.

Age Formation

The basis of our formational model is drawn from the now-classic study, *Racial Formation in the United States.*[8] Michael Omi and Howard Winant define racial formation as

> the *sociohistorical process* by which racial categories are created, inhabited, transformed, and destroyed.... [It] is a process of historically situated projects in which human bodies and social structures are represented and organized.... [W]e link racial formation to the evolution of hegemony, the way in which society is organized and ruled. ... Racial projects connect what race means in a particular discursive practice and the ways in which both social structures and everyday experiences are racially organized, based upon that meaning. (Emphasis added)[9]

The general model of formational processes is applicable to social identities other than race, including youth. We find Omi and Winant's model useful in examining youth culture because it locates important links among discourses, the struggles surrounding representations and social meanings, the distribution of resources, and the actions of the state in its various guises.

The formational perspective put forward here is necessarily provisional, offered as part of an ongoing conversation rather than as a finished project. Although this approach will be drawn out in more detail as we turn to examine specific themes, a rough sketch of three interconnected elements will help to frame our discussion. These elements are best understood as components in an unevenly distributed and constantly shifting formational network.

First, we propose a formational analysis that addresses the changes in the way "youth" is historically constructed and understood as a social identity. That is, the formational approach is concerned with the discourses and meanings that are applied to young people and their lives: how older meanings are sustained, transformed, or supplemented, and how new meanings are produced, circulated, challenged, revised, and reproduced. Actions are guided in part through the understandings we have of ourselves and others, and these understandings are constructed through discourse.

Any interpretation or discourse of youth is, at the same time, an attempt to position youth within a larger social/historical framework. As a second element, we see the formational approach attending to the institutions, processes, practices, and policies that simultaneously shape and reproduce "youth" and young people as social subjects. That is, a formational analysis seeks to understand the ways meanings are deployed, enforced, and realized in concrete, collective social practices and institutions. These would include, among others, the following: the various family systems operative in the United States and their associated child rearing practices; the juvenile-justice system; the social, psychological, and medical professions, and the associated institutions dealing with young people; the multiple institutions and commodities of the consumer marketplace, from advertising and fashion outlets to record stores and radio programs; state laws and policies that restrict and facilitate the actions of youths; and the educational system. A formational analysis impels one to inquire about the connections among bodies, institutions, and languages. For example, what understandings of youth underlie recent policy debates about condom distribution in schools? How does the extension of adult status to juveniles convicted of violent crimes rearrange or reflect commonly held beliefs about young people in general? How do these broadcasts re-form "youth"?

If interpretations of youth and attempts to position youth within a social framework happen simultaneously, then (paraphrasing Omi and Winant) to *recognize the youth dimension in social relationships* is to interpret the meaning of youth.[10] These processes do not happen in a one-way, top-down fashion exclusively. Precisely because interpretations and social framings of youth happen simultaneously, young people themselves have participated in the processes of reinterpreting and reframing the representations of "youth" and its position within social structures.

Thus, the third element of a formational approach considers the way the social identity of youth is practiced, negotiated, refused, and lived by young people in relation to other identities and to other people. These negotiations are carried out as distinct youth formations ("subcultures"), as peer groups, and as individuals, often within those institutions that have been created to manage and socialize youth (schools, the juvenile-justice system, the family). Tactical knowledges used in these conflicts are gained from generational skill funds (techniques of avoiding notice when crossing authority, detailed mental maps of the physical landscape of the city, the construction of identities through self-produced signs, the creation of argots and coded languages) that are circulated, transformed, and deleted at an uneven pace. Included among these skills are tactics used in the marketplace as consumers (e.g., shoplifting), as producers, and as workers.

While it does not exclude an analysis of everyday practices and cultural influences, Omi and Winant's model does little to promote it, focusing instead on mass movements; the model has little to offer in solving "the riddle of the zoot suit," for instance (see Robin Kelley's article in this anthology). Young people have created and been part of important mass movements, some directly related to their status as "youth," but this is only *a part* of the history of youth. Young people, like almost all nondominant groups, negotiate their social position via everyday, "tactical" methods of blunting, avoiding, and, sometimes, transforming the limitations imposed on their lives. For instance, doctors' note pads are stolen and circulated among young people so that "excuse notes" for absences will appear authoritative, just as (adult) workers "call in sick" in order to gain unscheduled vacations. In creating a model of age formation, we are calling for grounded historical scholarship that emphasizes everyday tactics, small social collectivities (peer groups and youth cultures, for instance), and common cultural practices surrounding young people. Here, we borrow from the cultural studies tradition, which more often draws upon ethnographic methods and oral histories to understand current youth subcultures and to reconstruct their pasts. Everyday negotiations are sometimes only visible in the details.[11]

These negotiations of identity and autonomy are carried out *within* the peer culture and its internal segmentations as well; young people bargain for relative statuses and identities within the wider peer culture. The peer group has become one of the major institutions of socialization during the twentieth century, and recent studies indicate that the influence of the peer group for some populations is perhaps greater than any other institution.[12]

In the remainder of this introduction we examine four themes that are closely related to a formational analysis. However, we need to emphasize that *Generations of Youth* stands independent of the age formation model we have provisionally outlined. Our primary intention in the following chapters is to advance the ongoing scholarly discourse among social historians and cultural studies scholars about youth, young people, and youth cultures.

Age, Identity, and Autonomy

Young people in the United States live their lives variously as young Asian American women, as working-class Latino youth, as young Blacks or young whites, as young Southerners, as rural middle-class youth, as young Puerto Ricans, as queer youth, and so on.[13] This fragmentation facilitates both a multiplicity of youth cultures and a wide range of hybrid identities. We can take the implications of this diversity one step further and inquire whether the fragmentation along lines of class, race, ethnicity, gender, sexuality, and location produces *different* "youths." On the other hand, *youth itself reconfigures these social identities* as well as other important categories of social experience such as citizenship and work.

Young people negotiate relative statuses and identities within the wider peer culture as well as within the general population. Differences in age and generation occur along with other social differences and affect them, at times overriding them, at other times being inconsequential.[14] Thus, young people cannot be approached as a homogeneous group; they are neither oppressed as a group, nor are they necessarily a force for progressive social change, although either of those possibilities may appear in specific situations. "Youth" is not constructed or otherwise acted upon through the pure subjection and passivity of young people: they have clearly participated in the processes of differentiation, and their creation of youth cultures speaks to their ongoing negotiations with the multiplicity of their social identities. Nazi youths are no less "youths" for also being white supremacists.

Several articles collected here extend recent scholarship on the differentiations within and among youth culture formations. For instance, gender inequalities produce and reproduce social divisions within youth culture.[15] Ernesto Chávez examines the ways in which contemporary and traditional masculine ideals were employed to construct a new nationalist identity for Chicano youth. But this new identity inadvertently restricted the ability to effectively mobilize young Chicanas; a male-centered ideology pushed out, limited, or lowered the status of those cultural resources related to women. Judith Baca, the subject of Jeff Rangel's article, reflects this gendered limitation through her experiences as a cultural worker associated with another part the Chicano movement during this period. Gender inequalities hindered many of the political youth movements of this period.[16]

Gender reconfigures other youth practices and spaces. Kyra Gaunt addresses the ways in which "musicality" is gendered, performed, and differentially valued as tradition within an African American context. Joanne Addison and Michelle Comstock's collaborative research suggests that young lesbians find it easier to cross generational than gendered boundaries; for instance, gay youth computer websites have difficulty attracting young lesbian audiences, which are often more likely to visit women-only sites.

Building on the important new work on racial identity and hybridity, several chapters examine the ways in which race is negotiated within youth culture. Racial identity is unstable: it is policed for "purity" by adult authorities and peers in one location, while celebrated in its hybrid form in another. David Roediger's work on contemporary *wiggers* explores the fluctuations surrounding racial crossover and cross-racial identification. Roediger historicizes the practice of whites adopting Black cultural codes, and shows the contradictory ways this history reappears among and around *wiggers*. matt garcia describes a more multiracial hybridity taking place in dance and music venues on the outskirts of Los Angeles after World War II. He interprets these crossovers as intentional strategies toward racial harmony among diverse youth populations.

The vast majority of scholarly work on "youth" and youth cultures deals with issues of representation, institutional formation, psychosocial development, or the reflection of adult concerns within the cultural practices of young people. These are valuable studies that help to situate the discursive constructions of youth within a wider social framework, yet they leave us with histories that tell us more about the history of adults than about young people, and reflect an incomplete, if not skewed, record of the ways that youth have achieved a measure of autonomy in the United States. "Youth" is too frequently perceived as a passive and unchanging population subjected and consenting to adult initiatives, mass marketing campaigns, or institutional imperatives.

Several chapters in this collection highlight the ways that youth have challenged, *innovated*, and redirected social and cultural practices. This work emphasizes the semi-autonomy of youth and approaches young people as agents acting in their own behalf: producers of culture, producers of knowledge, producers of new social relations and social understandings. Robin Kelley, in his chapter on the African American hipster subculture during World War II, shows the ways in which marginalized youth recoded and reordered hegemonic ideals of work, play, and masculine display during a period when such ideals were being asserted patriotically. The working class "zoot suit" subculture openly challenged both the racial hierarchy within the United States as well as the class hierarchy within African American communities. Kelley points out the importance of what appear to be minor or ritualistic rebellions during adolescence by highlighting the influence of these resistive acts in the political consciousness of Malcolm X.

Mary Odem calls attention to the ways that young women challenged traditional notions of youthful female subservience and family dependence at the turn of the century. The independence and growing autonomy of young women were helped along by changes in labor and consumer markets during this period, but the markets did not determine the ways in which this autonomy would be expressed. Access to paid employment opened the way for many young women to experience new freedoms, and their examples offered new possibilities to those who were not yet employed. New paychecks and the women's sense of independence did not make significant changes in their parents' views of them, however, and parents resorted to the juvenile court and the age of consent laws to recontain young women within family authority.

Contested Institutions

Youth cultures are often at odds with the interlocking network of social forces, representations, and institutions that attempt to control and guide them. "Socializing institutions," such as schools and churches, as well as adult initiatives, such as curfews and age restrictions on music purchases, have a powerful capacity to shape experiences, and they set many of the structural limitations on the autonomy and identities of young people. Young people, however, are not without power in their interactions with socializing institutions; they reshape and even appropriate such institutions for more self-directed purposes. These institutions provide an arena for shared experiences and/or the creation of shared codes and cultures in schools, in detention centers, or within popular-culture venues.

Victoria Getis identifies the ways in which "delinquent" and "normal" youth were constructed through—and were fundamental to—the academic disciplines of psychology and sociology as they developed in the early twentieth century. Getis tracks the debates concerning the sources of delinquency in youths, situating them in relation to the newly-instituted juvenile-justice system and the urban reform efforts of the period. Her arguments help to locate "youth" within the functionalist ideologies and disciplinary practices of the liberal-therapeutic state generally, and the rise of therapeutic professionals specifically. These ideologies were made concrete in mass-socializing institutions, most notably in the public schools.

Three chapters address conflicts within schools and universities. Drawing on high school records and year books, Paula Fass argues that New York City high school students redirected their schools' intentions of "Americanizing" them through extracurricular activities by forming ethnic peer groups that maintained connections to older immigrant identities. These strategies did not result in cultural nationalisms so much as a hybridized Americanism; public schools were arenas where the second and third generations simultaneously positioned themselves as Americans and as members of specific ethnic communities. Fass shows that these strategies were unevenly distributed and keyed to local conditions. That is, the ways in which ethnic clustering took place were sensitive to the specific contexts of the schools.

John Bloom examines conflicts and anxieties about Native American identity in federal boarding schools during the 1930s. Bloom shows how the sport of boxing caused concerns among boarding school officials but was used to affirm a Native American identity among the sport's participants and audiences in much the same way as Fass's ethnic high school students. Understanding boxing matches as simultaneously athletic events and social events, Bloom shows the ways the matches were appropriated by Native American youths as opportunities for romance and community that were less circumscribed than those available within the schools. Using oral-history sources, Bloom is able to bring to light another, "invisible" history within the official institutions of socialization and discipline.

Beth Bailey turns to young people on college campuses during the 1950s and 1960s. She historicizes the rise of student-life deans during the tremendous expansion of U.S. universities after World War II, part of the process of extending *in loco parentis* authority over an older group of young people—again, with the students' parents in mind primarily. In essence, college students were expected to extend their adolescence until graduation. During the 1960s, students at the University of Kansas, Bailey's case study, challenged women students' imposed dormitory curfews. Bailey shows the divisions between students on the issue, as well as the ways in which students appropriated the therapeutic rhetoric used by the university's administration to justify curfews to challenge the curfew system itself.

Schools are not the only institutions in which age and identity are contested territories. The transposition of adult anxieties into the lives of young people via the Boy Scouts is the topic of Jay Mechling's chapter in this volume. Connecting the history of youth to larger cultural conflicts, he observes the contradiction between the ideology of competitive individualism and the moral sense of shared public responsibility for fellow citizens at the turn of the century. Explaining how this contradiction was worked out within the Boy Scouts, one of the new institutions of masculine socialization at the turn of the century, Mechling demonstrates that "heroism," the selfless rendering of assistance to another while risking one's own person, could not be taught in the same way as other skills and virtues of the Boy Scouts. Rather, selfless heroism was represented to young men as an almost-instinctual impulse, a kind of evolutionary/biological mystery, left for boys (among them Mechling himself, several decades later) to puzzle out, since the contradictions between competition and compassion that it embeds have not be resolved.

Other authors touch on these topics as well. Linda España-Maram examines the contested nature of taxi dance halls and the racist policing of immigrant youth. Kyra Gaunt questions what is lost and what is gained in reconstructing the traditional musical performances of young women's double Dutch games into a "sport" through the creation of the American Double Dutch League. Ernesto Chávez reveals how reformist efforts to integrate Mexican American youths as municipal advisers about their communities were transformed into opportunities for establishing more militant organizations. These chapters articulate the important ways in which a youth-formation approach connects traditional institutional histories with youth and identity. In several instances, the contestations between socializing institutions and the youth they attempt to socialize create a kind of dialectic, a kind of call-and-response between discipline and resistance. The contestations over public institutions in many ways overlap with analyses centered around popular-culture venues and other types of social spaces, which we address separately below.

Popular Culture and the Labor Market

At several historical junctures, adult authorities have diagnosed various "youth problems" through the cultural productions and consumer preferences of young people.[17] George Lipsitz's chapter examines a contemporary example of this phenomenon. Lipsitz argues that conflicts over the "morality" of rap lyrics within the African American community reduce the critiques of historical and structural inequalities that many artists undertake to matters of individual virtue; the brutality and injustice indicted in the music are passed over in debates about rapper's responsibilities as "role models." The historical experiences of many central-city residents who are already marginalized within the public sphere are completely erased and forgotten through censorship initiatives enacted to "protect youth" from *representations of their own lives*; class divisions within the African American community are mobilized to separate those youths supposedly needing "protection" from rap music from those whose lives might be better served by taking the music at its word. Lipsitz shows the importance of understanding young people as useful reporters of contemporary social realities. Rap and other forms of popular culture created by young people are sites for the production of grass roots social theory.

Joe Austin's chapter touches on the ways in which powerful political and economic elites worked to reconstruct a minor transgression, "graffiti" writing, into a symbol of New York City's social decay after the fiscal crises of the late 1970s. In this instance, we see the vilification of "urban youth" by the city-state standing in place of a host of concrete claims that might be made against the city-state itself: cuts in city services, a declining quality of life, and a decaying public transportation system. Building on a long tradition of urban fear mongering aimed at "delinquent youths," an exciting grass-roots (illegal) art movement was represented in ways that have since made it almost impossible to legally integrate into public life.

Despite these examples of hysteria surrounding the popular expressive forms produced by and for youth, it has been more common for U.S. citizens to assume that youth culture is transient, market-based, overly frantic and peer-directed, and without much significance for other populations, so long as it is "harmless." The cultural practices that young people have created (and also what is created *for* young people) are usually considered "entertainment" rather than "serious" culture. Nonetheless, young people and youth cultures have played an important historical role as producers, consumers, and disseminators of new aesthetic forms, new products, new practices, and values.[18] They have also been important in the rise of consumer culture as retail workers, cooks and waiters, and service-sector employees.

Several chapters in this anthology inquire into the ways in which popular culture forms a context of meaning-making for young people. Georganne Scheiner's chapter on early movie star fandom is a study of young people's situated understandings of a popular cultural form at a particular moment in history. Scheiner shows how the "Devotees" of youth star Deanna Durbin selectively interpreted her films, simultaneously accepting certain elements of traditionally proscribed feminine behavior, pushing the boundaries of others, and rejecting other elements altogether. In line with several other scholars working on fan cultures, Scheiner sees fandom and fan clubs as actively negotiated, historical spaces of identity formation, a view that challenges common perceptions of fans as passive and purely imitative.

Linda España-Maram examines the ways that Filipino youth appropriated taxi dance halls as arenas where marginalized identities could be reshaped and asserted through fashion, dance, and public display. Like Robin Kelley, Georganne Scheiner, and several other authors in this volume, España-Maram explores the ways in which popular expressive forms encode and recode wider social meanings. In the case of Filipinos, who were often confined to difficult and demeaning physical labor in their work lives, the taxi dance halls were arenas where they reclaimed their bodies for their own pleasure and display.

Popular culture, of which youth are among the primary producers and consumers, is rarely understood to be invested with the same cultural authority as "established" forms, despite the boundary crossing that constantly blurs the high/low distinction. When popular cultural forms are produced by and/or associated with marginalized groups, particularly urban youth of color, the aesthetic skills and creativity necessary to produce and appreciate their performances are even less likely to be understood. Robert Walser notes the musical gap in discussions of rap; the music, as opposed to the lyrical content, is all but ignored, or if it is recognized, it is often represented as "noise." In a detailed musicological analysis, Walser shows the complexity of Public Enemy's musical constructions and interactions between vocal tracks and samples. Ethnomusicologist Kyra Gaunt makes a similar argument, showing how young African American womens' double Dutch "games" are complex musical performances, although the music is often ignored in favor of the athleticism of rope jumping that is also part of the performance.

As the Durbin Devotees' fandom and the Bomb Squad's sampling make clear, popular culture texts are themselves often an appropriated "raw material" from which other texts and identities are fashioned. Brenda Bright's ethnography of low rider murals reveals how contemporary "nightmare" horror cinema is appropriated to represent the urban experiences and fantasies of Chicanos. Bright's work traces an evolution in these car murals, which had incorporated the Aztec imagery associated with Chicano cultural nationalism during the early 1970s. As Chicano communities have experienced greater unemployment and a reduction of life chances in the face of deindustrialization since that time, the murals, like the lives of many Chicano/a communities, have taken a nightmarish turn.

Ryan Moore follows a similar analysis but directs it toward the fiction and films of Generation X. Moore challenges the common view that the nihilistic aspects of these texts are signs of "degeneracy," "bad choices," or laziness. Situating his analysis within recent history, Moore asserts that the "structure of feeling" in these texts speak to the downward mobility and unemployment experienced by white middle-class youth in a period where film and literature are already marked by a noticeable loss of affect and lack of narrative direction. Thus, the "slackerdom" of contemporary middle-class white youth is both part of a larger historical trend as well as a specifically positioned response from a social group formerly called "the bright hope of tomorrow."

Although the work lives of young people are sometimes mentioned in relation to their importance as consumers, work remains an underexamined experience in the historical and cultural studies scholarship on youth.[19] Correcting this lacuna, Jeffrey Rangel explores the ways in which the political/cultural activism of young people in the early 1970s can be understood as an important kind of work, particularly in the context of the broader political mobilization taking place in Chicano communities during that period. Art making is rarely viewed in this manner, allowing a continuation of the myth that artists and intellectuals do not labor—they magically "create." Judith Baca's organizing for the production of public community murals by local youths demonstrates the importance of cultural work as a mode of integration into community life. In planning meetings where murals were proposed and designs discussed, adult community members contested the participation of gang members in the production of murals, essentially arguing "they are not a valued part of us."

Susan Willis' chapter addresses the work lives of young people more directly. Willis's interviews with working teens indicates that young people have begun to adapt to the boredom and repetitiveness of their working conditions in service industries, in part embracing their limitations as a way of avoiding involvement, identification with, or attachment to the jobs themselves. Most of Willis's interviewees located autonomy in frequent job-changing. Since each job opportunity has roughly the same qualities (no benefits, low pay, low skill level), "benefits" (vacations) are created in the gaps between jobs. But this tactic allows for no collective action as workers; the young people she interviews have a difficult time imagining a strike or a mass action by service workers. Their renegotiation of work identity remains at the individual level.

Michael Willard follows Moore and Willis in considering the implications of global restructuring on the downsized prospects and quality of work for youth. Global restructuring has recuperated youth consumerism and media production—as a means of forming a subcultural community—into a new form of labor. In the emerging global economy, the micro-media practices that youth employ to form subcultures are much more than the "fun consumerism" they would have been considered when youth was understood to be a life stage of postponed adult responsibility. These micro-media practices are part of a new global form of labor: information management. Accordingly, it has become more difficult to clearly identify the boundaries between adult and youth status on the basis of "work." When considered as a form of information labor, skateboarding has given the youth who work in this subculture a somewhat greater voice in the processes of urban restructuring that accompany global economic restructuring.

These chapters, as well as those by Mary Odem, Rachel Buff, and William Wei, among others, demonstrate the important connections and contradictions between young people's work, consumerism, and autonomy throughout the twentieth century. The experiences of young people within these arenas are markedly different from those of adults and carry different cultural meanings. As crucial sites of negotiation between (relative) freedoms and structural limitations, they are important elements of a formational approach.

Communications and Appropriation of Social Spaces

Of the institutions that interactively construct youth cultures, the least studied by historians and American cultural studies scholars are young people's own (often, informal) self-organized institutions, such as peer groups, fan clubs, gangs, friendship networks, and "communities of practice" among youth. In part, the difficulty of writing about these institutions and practices is that historically they have been (and still are) both everywhere and nowhere at all. That is, youth cultures' self-organized institutions and practices are often "invisibly" embedded in social spaces that primarily serve other purposes, or they are located in peripheral spaces, at the edges of adult surveillance.

matt garcia borrows from the work of geographer Edward Soja to understand the locational significance of intercultural dance halls on the metropolitan outskirts. Outside the city limits of Los Angeles, the dance halls were not bound by prohibitive city regulations; the extensive highway system and young people's access to automobiles allowed the dance halls to draw customers from a large geographical area. This encouraged the integration of otherwise dispersed and segregated youth populations, and, as mentioned before, promoted a space of cultural crossover and negotiation. As garcia argues, space, place and identity are inextricably linked.

James Sears uses oral history interviews to retrace the otherwise "invisible" social lives of lesbian and gay youths in 1950s Florida. Sears's informants describe a "map" of the spaces created or appropriated by gay and lesbian youths, ranging from areas within high schools to beaches to apartments to bars. Occupying these spaces required the ability to participate in the culture of gay and lesbian life as well as to "hide in the light" of policing authorities. Since revealing one's homosexuality at that time would have likely lead to institutionalization, there are few "traces" of this history left to interpret, aside from the memories and memorabilia of the gay community itself.

Michael Willard's chapter draws connections between postmodern architectural forms, the "renewal" and "anchoring" of gentrifying areas near downtown Los Angeles, and skateboarders' appropriation and understanding of public spaces. Willard makes a case for youth's creation of "local" knowledges that transform the details of the urban landscape into an alternative social space. Handrails no longer just guide pedestrians and keep them off the lawns, but also are skated pathways available for tricks; the "transparency" which hides everyday disciplinary practices and structures of injustice within the landscape is challenged and rearticulated in skating practice. Like contemporary skaters, "graffiti" writers explicitly claimed a place for themselves in the public spaces and the social order of New York City during the 1970s, but were "visible" in those spaces only through their signatures. Joe Austin argues that writers strategically occupied a set of locations within the 700-mile subway system that allowed them to transform the trains into a kind of communications network, whereby writers' works could circulate across the public spaces of a world city.

A communications network is also a site of community, a space where commonly constructed identities are affirmed and negotiated.[20] Joanne Addison and Michelle

Comstock map out a group of Internet sites that have become spaces of community for lesbian, bisexual, and gay youth. These sites act as institutions that would otherwise be inaccessible—it is only their "virtual" nature that allows them to be used by so many young people. Organizations that might draw together lesbian, bisexual, and gay youth, particularly those under age eighteen, are rare, and recent attempts to defund or deny les-bi-gay student organizations in high schools demonstrate their contested nature.

Stephen Duncombe's chapter on the understudied zine community shows the contradictions that accompany the construction of an "outsider" community during the last fifteen years. Duncombe argues that the zine revolution has allowed contemporary Bohemia to disperse in the wake of gentrification pressures, so that members/participants no longer need to share a common neighborhood or even a common city; the discussions and shared views that help to hold Bohemia together can now take place in the articles, reviews, and letters columns of self-produced zines available through the mail. But the zine revolution has done little to define what "Bohemia" is. A great deal of the discussion in zines reflects the difficulty of constructing a collective identity through an individualist ideology.

Family and Intergenerational Struggles

> Generation conflicts oppose not age-classes separated by natural properties, but habitus which have been produced by different *modes of generation*, that is by conditions of existence which, in imposing different definitions of the impossible, possible, and the probable, cause one group to experience as natural or reasonable practices or aspirations which another group finds unthinkable or scandalous, and vice versa.[21]

The social boundaries between adults and young people are flexible, permeable, and variable. Functionalist analyses would have us believe that such age-based conflicts are "natural" to complex social systems. We affirm the historical reality of social struggles between generations, although these struggles are by no means continuous nor do they arise from conditions of "nature" or necessity. We acknowledge the persistent return of generational moral panics, dating back at least two centuries and recurring in the twentieth century with an increasing frequency that coincides with the rise of "family-centered" social ideologies. But these historical regularities, often cloaked in the rhetoric of "nature," "tradition," and "inevitable" social processes, cannot be allowed to substitute for specific analyses of the complex networks that inform the struggles and experiences of young people. A sense of the historical development of the networks that inform these negotiations is vital.

The conflicts and continuities between generations have appeared in several of the previously mentioned chapters. For instance, the generational conflict between parents and daughters is central to Mary Odem's analysis of gender, sexuality, and the courts during the early twentieth century. James Sears's interviewees point out the generational differences (among others) within the gay and lesbian community of the 1950s, where legal consequences discouraged what might have otherwise been multi generational social gatherings. George Lipsitz argues that the attack on rap from within the African American community is, in part, the result of different historical experiences from one generation to the next.

Two articles look at generational continuities and conflicts in greater depth. William Wei investigates the acculturation experiences of Hmong immigrants, particularly the conflicts between the immigrant parent generation's desires to maintain traditional practices and the U.S.-born children's desires and pressures to replace them with U.S. customs. Although this at first seems like an old story in U.S. history, it is unusual in that the Hmong were first U.S. allies and then long-ignored political refugees from the CIA's secret war in Laos. Many of the immigrant generation had expected to be greeted warmly when they came to the United States; instead, they have been treated with stony indifference and hostility. While the Hmong have understood themselves to be in diaspora for hundreds of years, many of their elders now fear that their culture will disappear in the United States.

Rachel Buff also finds a generational clash over cultural continuity within Native American culture. This clash is focused around contest pow wows, which award prize money (often several thousand dollars) to winning dancers and drum groups. Native American music, dance, and pow wows are in many ways "reconstructed" traditions that became more widespread after the (often forced) migrations from reservations to urban areas beginning in the 1950s. At issue is whether the monetary rewards, which encourage young people to participate and recognize the best practitioners, are not also undermining the spiritual and traditional values that the dances and music convey. In this instance, as in many others, conflicts about the direction of cultural change are fought out around the socialization of youth.

Conclusions

In proposing a formational approach to the study of youth, we are advocating the recognition of age as a fundamental *organizing principal* of social and historical relations. But we do not escape or "stand outside" of the processes we describe. As scholars, we disassemble older, received meanings and assemble new ones; we occupy positions of expertise within powerful institutions where power/knowledge is created and broadcast; we daily involve ourselves with the lives of young people as students, friends, children, citizens, and any number of other social positions occupied by youth. In making this point, we draw attention to the partiality of all knowledge, but we also openly acknowledge our participation in the ongoing process of negotiating the "place" of young people. The self-reflexivity of a formational analysis forces us to recognize the necessity of locating our own positions within its web of connections: as teachers, as parents, as adults. We offer this anthology as one platform for transforming the common understandings about youth.[22]

NOTES

"A Klee painting named 'Angelus Novus' shows an angel looking as though he is about to move away from something he is fixedly contemplating. His eyes are staring, his mouth is open, his wings are spread. This is how one pictures the angel of history. His face is turned towards the past. Where we perceive a chain of events, he sees a single catastrophe. . . . The angel would like to stay, awaken the dead, and make whole what has been smashed. . . . [But a] storm irresistibly propels him into the future to which his back is turned, while the pile of debris before him grows skyward. This storm is what we call progress."

From Walter Benjamin, "Theses on the Philosophy of History," *Illuminations*, trans. Harry Zorn (New York: Schocken Books, 1969), 257–258.

1. This insight is one of the major contributions of the British school of subcultural studies and continues to be a fruitful line of inquiry. See Stanley Cohen, *Folk Devils and Moral Panics* (London: MacGibbon and Kee, 1972); Stuart Hall and Tony Jefferson, eds., *Resistance through Rituals: Youth Subcultures in Post-War Britain* (London: Hutchinson and Co., 1976); Stuart Hall et al., *Policing the Crisis* (London: Macmillan, 1978); Dick Hebdige, "Hiding in the Light: Youth Surveillance and Display," in *Hiding in the Light* (New York: Routledge, 1988), 17–36; Martin Sanchez Jankowski, *Islands in the Street: Gangs and American Urban Society* (Berkeley: University of California Press, 1991); Joel Best, *Threatened Children: Rhetoric and Concern about Child-Victims* (Chicago: University of Chicago Press, 1990); Mike A. Males, *The Scapegoat Generation: America's War on Adolescents* (Monroe, ME: Common Courage,1996); Charles Acland, *Youth, Murder, Spectacle: The Cultural Politics of "Youth in Crisis"* (Boulder, CO: Westview, 1995); James Gilbert, *A Cycle of Outrage: America's Reaction to the Juvenile Delinquent in the 1950s* (New York: Oxford University Press, 1986); Angela McRobbie, "The Moral Panic in the Age of the Postmodern Mass Media," in *Postmodernism and Popular Culture* (New York: Routledge, 1994), 198–219. See also Erich Goode and Nachman Ben-Yehuda, *Moral Panics: The Social Construction of Deviance* (Cambridge, U.K.: Blackwell, 1994), for an excellent treatment of moral panics generally.

2. Among the primary documents to consult about the construction of "youth" in the late 1950s are Benjamin Fine, *1,000,000 Delinquents* (New York: World Publishing, 1955); Bill Davidson, "18,000,000 Teen-agers Can't be Wrong," *Collier's*, January 4, 1954, 12–25; Harrison Salisbury, *The Shook-up Generation* (New York: Harper and Row, 1958); Dwight McDonald, "A Caste, a Culture, a Market," *New Yorker*, November 22–9, 1958, 57–94; Peter Whelihan, "Jack and Jill Fill the Till," *Nation's Business* 36 (October 1948): 42–44+; Betty Betz, "Gold in Them Jeans," *Nation's Business* 41 (January 1953): 27–29+; "A New, $10-Billion Power: The U.S. Teen-age Consumer," *Life*, August 31, 1959, 78–85; Gereon Zimmerman,"U.S. Teen-Agers," *Look*, January 24, 1956, 22–31; William Zinsser, "The Tyranny of the Teens," *Horizon* 1 (January 1959): 137–139; William H. Whyte, *The Organization Man* (New York: Anchor, 1957). Of course, this brief listing in no way exhausts the topic or even addresses all the permutations of "youth" during this period. For secondary sources, see William Graebner, "The 'Containment' of Juvenile Delinquency," *American Studies*,27(1): 84–88; Marty Jezer, *The Dark Ages: Life in the United States, 1945–1960* (Boston: South End Press, 1982); Wini Breines, *Young, White and Miserable: Growing Up Female in the Fifties* (Boston: Beacon, 1992).

3. See Rachel Buff's chapter in this anthology.

4. George Lipsitz, "Who'll Stop the Rain: Youth Culture, Rock 'n' Roll and Social Crisis," in David Farber, ed., *The Sixties: From Memory to History* (Chapel Hill, NC: University of North Carolina Press, 1994), 206–234.

5. G. Stanley Hall, *Adolescence: Its Psychology and Its Relations to Anthropology, Sociology, Sex, Crime, Religion and Education*, 2 vols. (New York: 1905). The major biography of Hall is Dorothy Ross, *G. Stanley Hall: The Psychologist as Prophet* (Chicago: University of Chicago Press, 1972). Joseph F. Kett, in *Rites of Passage: Adolescence in America, 1790 to the Present*

(New York: Basic Books, 1977), locates Hall within the history of youth in the United States more broadly. See also Gail Bederman, *Manliness and Civilization* (Chicago: University of Chicago Press, 1995).

6. These issues have been explored in a number of key texts. Along with Kett, mentioned above, see Mary P. Ryan, *Cradle of the Middle Class* (New York: Cambridge University Press, 1981); Howard Chudacoff, *How Old Are You? Age Consciousness in American Culture* (Princeton, NJ: Princeton University Press, 1989); Neil J. Smelser and Sydney Halpern, "The Historical Triangulation of Family, Economy, and Education," and Anne Foner, "Age Stratification and the Changing Family," in John Demos and Sarane Spence Boocock, eds., *Turning Points: Historical and Sociological Essays on the Family* (Chicago: University of Chicago Press, 1978), S288–S315 and S340–S365, respectively; Roberta Wollons, "Introduction," and Hamilton Cravens, "Childsaving in Modern America, 1870s–1990s," in Roberta Wollons, ed., *Children at Risk in America: History, Concepts, and Public Policy* (Albany, NY: SUNY Press, 1993), ix–xxv and 3–31, respectively; David Nasaw, *Children of the City* (New York: Oxford University Press, 1985); Margo Horn, *Before It's Too Late: The Child Guidance Movement in the United States, 1922–1945* (Philadelphia: Temple University Press, 1989); Viviana A. Zelizer, *Pricing the Priceless Child: The Changing Social Value of Children* (New York: Basic Books, 1985); Susan Tiffin, *In Whose Best Interests? Child Welfare Reform in the Progressive Era* (Westport, CT: Greenwood Press, 1982).

7. Christine Griffin, *Representations of Youth: The Study of Youth and Adolescence in Britain and America* (Cambridge, MA: Polity Press, 1993); Susan M. Ruddick, *Young and Homeless in Hollywood: Mapping Social Identities* (New York: Routledge, 1996); Males, *The Scapegoat Generation*; James E. Cote and Anton L. Allahar, *Generation on Hold: Coming of Age in the Late Twentieth Century* (New York: New York University Press, 1996).

8. A formational model has been implicit in much of the literature on the social history of childhood, youth, and the family and the history of social policy. This literature has shown the important connections between the various understandings of the "nature" of youth (grounded in religion and morality, psychology, medicine, etc.), the institutions, social policy, and practices that "form" youth, and changes in economic structure, religious affiliation, ethnicity and race, and other structures of social relations. See the works by Ryan, Chudacoff, Smelner and Halpern, Wollons, Craven, Nasaw, Horn, Zelizer, and Tiffin cited above. Also see Elliot West and Paula Petrik,eds., *Small Worlds: Children and Adolescents in America, 1850–1950* (Lawrence, KS: University of Kansas Press, 1992); N. Ray Hiner and Joseph M. Hawes, eds., *Growing Up in America: Children in Historical Perspective* (Chicago: University of Illinois Press, 1985); Selma Cantor Berrol, *Growing Up American: Immigrant Children in America Then and Now* (New York: Twayne Publishers, 1995); John R. Gillis, *Youth and History: Tradition and Change in European Age Relations, 1770–Present* (New York: Academic Press, 1981); Michael Mitterauer, *A History of Youth* (London: Blackwell, 1992); Paula Fass, *The Damned and the Beautiful: American Youth in the 1920s* (New York: Oxford University Press, 1977); Joseph M. Hawes and Elizabeth I. Nybakken, eds., *American Families: A Research Guide and Historical Handbook* (New York: Greenwood Press, 1991); Joseph M. Hawes and N. Ray Hiner, eds., *American Childhood: A Research Guide and Historical Handbook* (Westport, CT: Greenwood Press, 1985); Tamara K. Hareven, "Historical Changes in Children's Networks in the Family and Community," in Deborah Belle, ed., *Children's Social Networks and Social Supports* (New York: John Wiley and Sons, 1989); Peggy Pizzo, "Slouching toward Bethlehem: American Federal Policy Perspectives on Children and Their Families," in Edward F. Zigler, Sharon Lynn Kagan, and Edward Klugman, eds., *Children, Families, and Government: Perspectives on American Social Policy* (New York: Cambridge University Press, 1983), 10–32.

The scholarship on the rationalization of the European and American life course and on age segmentation within institutions defines a second important source for a formational perspective. We see the life course perspective as important not only because of its contributions to understanding the ways in which the boundaries of "youth" have been transformed over time, but also because it allows a more general model of age formation to emerge. One could easily imagine a formational approach to "middle age" or "old age" as well as "youth"; this places age as an ongoing formational process that allows analyses both historically and biographically. See Chudacoff *How Old Are You?* Also, see Panel on Youth of the President's Science Advisory Committee, James S. Coleman, chair, *Youth: Transition to Adulthood* (Chicago: University of Chicago Press, 1974); Glen H. Elder, John Modell, and Ross D. Parke, eds., *Children in Time and Place: Developmental and Historical Insights* (New York: Cambridge University Press, 1993); John Modell, *Into One's Own: From Youth to Adulthood in the United States, 1920–1975* (Berkeley: University of California Press, 1989); Martin Kohli, "The World We Forgot: A Historical Review of the Life Course," in Victor W. Marshall, ed., *Later Life: The Social Psychology of Aging* (Beverly Hills, CA: Sage Publications, 1986), 271–303; David A. Stevens, "New Evidence on the Timing of Early Life Course Transitions: The United States, 1900 to 1980," *Journal of Family History* 15, no. 2 (1991) 163–178; Don C. Charles, "Historical Antecedents of Life-Span Developmental Psychology," in L. R. Goulet and Paul B. Baltes, eds., *Life-Span Developmental Psychology: Research and Theory* (New York: Academic Press, 1970), 23–52; John Modell, Frank F. Furstenberg, Jr., and Theodore Hershberg, "Social Change and Transitions to Adulthood in Historical Perspective," *Journal of Family History* 1, no. 1 (Autumn 1976): 7–32.

Cultural studies is a third source for our formational model, particularly the extremely important body of work produced within British subculture studies. We are interested in building upon the multidimensional analysis developed by this tradition, which seeks to combine the analysis of economic structures, institutional practices, the role of media, and young people's own self-activity in explaining the creation of subcultures. See Ken Gelder and Sarah Thornton, *The Subcultures Reader* (New York: Routledge, 1997); Sarah Thornton, *Club Cultures: Music, Media and Subcultural Capital* (Hanover, NH: Wesleyan University Press, 1996); Andrew Ross and Tricia Rose, eds., *Microphone Fiends: Youth Music and Youth Culture* (New York: Routledge, 1994); Vered Amit-Talai and Helena Wulff, eds., *Youth Cultures: A Cross-Cultural Perspective* (New York: Routledge, 1995); Mike Brake, *The Sociology of Youth Culture and Youth Subcultures* (Boston: Routledge and Kegan Paul, 1980); Raymond A. Calluori, "The Kids Are Alright: New Wave Subcultural Theory," *Social Text* 12 (Fall 1985): 43–53; Hilary Pilkington, *Russia's Youth and Its Culture: A Nation's Constructors and Constructed* (New York: Routledge, 1994).

9. Michael Omi and Howard Winant, *Racial Formation in the United States*, 2d ed. (New York: Routledge, 1994), 55–56.

10. Ibid., 66–67.

11. Although much abused, Michel de Certeau's *The Practice of Everyday Life* (Berkeley: University of California Press, 1988) is useful in understanding the micropolitics of everyday life. See Susan Willis's critique of the ways this work is put to use in "Hardcore: Subculture American Style," *Critical Inquiry* 19 (Winter 1993): 379–381.

12. See S. N. Eisenstadt, *From Generation to Generation: Age Groups and Social Structure* (New York: Free Press, 1956), for an older, functionalist approach to the rise and importance of peer cultures that is still worth reading. For more recent work on the peer culture and its role in gender socialization, see Donna Eder, with Catherine Colleen Evans and Stephan Parker, *School Talk: Gender and Adolescent Culture* (New Brunswick, NJ: Rutgers University,

1995), and Elijah Anderson, *Streetwise: Race, Class and Change in an Urban Community* (Chicago: University of Chicago Press, 1990).

13. Many of the early critiques and revisions within British subcultural studies were devoted to demonstrating the impossibility of reducing youth cultures to a singular negotiation of class status. See Angela McRobbie and Jenny Garber, "Girls and Subcultures," and Angela McRobbie, "Settling Accounts with Subcultures: A Feminist Critique," both in *Feminism and Youth Culture* (Boston: Unwin Hyman, 1991); Dick Hebdige, *Subculture: The Meaning of Style* (London: Methuen, 1979); Angela McRobbie, "Different, Youthful, Subjectivities: Towards a Cultural Sociology of Youth," in *Postmodernism and Popular Culture* (New York: Routledge, 1994), 177–197.

14. That youth formation intersects with other social formations is readily evident in federal policy: the laws applying to children adopted in the Social Security system were written so that control of the programs was located at the state level, to appease the "states' rights" opposition to the laws. This allowed the individual states to maintain racist policies that offered reduced services to people of color and to female-headed households, or to exclude some or all of these groups from the programs altogether. Here we see an intersection of racial formation, gender formation, class formation, and age formation simultaneously.

15. See Eder, *School Talk*.

16. See Sara Evans, *Personal Politics: The Roots of Women's Liberation in the Civil Rights Movement and the New Left* (New York: Vintage, 1979).

17. See Gilbert, *A Cycle of Outrage*. Also, Herman Gray, "Popular Music as a Social Problem: A Social History of Claims against Popular Music," in Joel Best, ed., *Images of Issues: Typifying Contemporary Social Problems* (New York: Aldine de Gruyter, 1989), 143–158; Graebner, "The 'Containment' of Juvenile Delinquency"; Linda Martin and Kerry Segrave, *Anti-Rock: The Opposition to Rock'n'Roll* (New York: Da Capo Press, 1993); Donna Gaines, *Teenage Wasteland: Suburbia's Dead End Kids* (New York: Pantheon, 1990). For a current example of this phenomenon, see Jeffrey Jensen Arnett, *Metalheads: Heavy Metal Music and Adolescent Alienation* (Boulder, CO: Westview Press, 1995)

18. Grace Palladino, *Teenagers: An American History* (New York: Basic Books, 1996).

19. On the other hand, the "youth unemployment problem" has been given more attention, particularly after the mid-1960s. See Melvin Herman, Stanley Sadofsky, and Bernard Rosenberg, eds., *Work, Youth, and Unemployment* (New York: Thomas Y. Crowell, 1968); Stephen F. Seninger, "Postwar Trends in Youth Unemployment," in Arvil V. Adams and Garth L. Mangum, eds., *The Lingering Crisis of Youth Unemployment* (Kalamazoo, MI: W. E. Upjohn Institute for Employment Research, 1978), 19–49; Norman Bowers, "Young and Marginal: An Overview of Youth Employment," *Monthly Labor Review* 102, no. 10 (October 1979): 4–18; Morris J. Newman, "The Labor Market Experience of Black Youth, 1954–1978," *Monthly Labor Review* 102, no. 10 (October 1979): 19–27.

20. See Lisa A. Lewis, *The Adoring Audience: Fan Culture and Popular Media* (New York: Routledge, 1992); Marc Libarle and Tom Seligson, *The High School Revolutionaries* (New York: Random House, 1970).

21. Pierre Bourdieu, *Outline of a Theory of Practice*, p. 95, as cited in James M. Ostrow, "Culture as a Fundamental Dimension of Experience: A Discussion of Pierre Bourdieu's Theory of Human Habitus," *Human Studies* 4 (1981): 289.

22. Several useful and important works dealing with youth in various contexts have appeared in the last five years. Although this list is in no way intended to be exhaustive, we would include Barry Shank, *Dissonant Identities: The Rock 'n' Roll Scene in Austin, Texas* (Hanover, NH: Wesleyan/University Press of New England, 1994); Sojin Kim, *Chicano Graffiti*

and Murals: The Neighborhood Art of Peter Quezada (Jackson: University of Mississippi Press, 1995); Lawrence Grossberg, *We Gotta Get out of This Place* (New York: Routledge, 1992); Stephanie Coontz, *The Way We Never Were: American Families and the Nostalgia Trap* (New York: Basic, 1992); Rinaldo Walcott, "Performing the Postmodern: Black Atlantic Rap and Identity in North America," Ph.D. diss., University of Toronto, 1996; Raul Villa, "Tales from the Second City: Social Geographic Imagination in Contemporary Urban California Chicana/Chicano Literature and Arts," Ph.D. diss., University of California Santa Cruz, 1993; David McBride, "The Counter Culture in 1960s Los Angeles," Ph.D. diss., University of California Los Angeles, forthcoming; Laura Helper, "Whole Lot Of Shakin' Going On: An Ethnography of Race Relations and Cross-Over Audiences for Rhythm & Blues and Rock & Roll in 1950s Memphis," Ph.D. diss., Rice University, 1997; Leerom Medovoi, "Bad Boys: Masculinity, Oppositional Discourse, and American Youth Culture in the 1950s," Ph.D. diss., Stanford University, 1995; Nan Enstad, "Compromised Positions: Working-Class Women, Popular Culture and Labor Politics, 1890–1920," Ph.D. diss., University of Minnesota, 1993; Dionne Espinoza, "Pedagogies of Nationalism and Gender: Cultural Resistance in Selected Representational Practices of Chicana/o Movement Activists, 1967–1972," Ph. D. diss., Cornell University, 1996; John Wrathall, "American Manhood and the Y.M.C.A., 1868–1920," (Ph.D. diss., University of Minnesota, 1994.

PART I: EARLY TWENTIETH CENTURY

Chapter One

Experts and Juvenile Delinquency, 1900–1935

Victoria Getis

Between 1899 and 1932, graduate students at the University of Chicago turned out more than twenty master's theses and doctoral dissertations on the subject of juvenile delinquency.[1] Even though juvenile delinquency had been recognized as an urban problem during the mid-nineteenth century, the topic did not earn any student's attention in the years before 1899. After the establishment of the nation's first juvenile court in 1899, juvenile delinquency began to capture scholarly attention. This interest stemmed from a number of sources: an increase in juvenile crime as cities grew; the legitimation and facilitation of research on the topic by the establishment of a juvenile court; and efforts of scholars in many fields to understand adolescence.

While Americans had long recognized that the teenage years were somehow different from early childhood and adulthood, the early part of this century witnessed a concerted attempt to define adolescence. As children lost their roles as economic assets in middle-class families, adults in those families enshrined a new idea of adolescence as an important stage of life. Adolescents, experts like G. Stanley Hall told wide audiences, experienced the transition from childhood to adulthood as a period of stress and turbulence; but it was also a period of great promise, the years in which the future of the individual was determined. Progressive reformers used the protection of youth as the basis for legislation, such as child labor laws, that helped to institutionalize adolescence as a life stage and expand government power.[2]

That institutionalization took many forms. In *Rites of Passage* (1977), Joseph Kett noted that during the 1910s and 1920s, clubs, high schools, and vocational guidance all changed shape to accommodate and reflect—and some would say impose—the middle-class and expert concept of adolescence. According to Kett, the period encompassing the shift from childhood to adulthood became one of increased dependency as it became increasingly regulated.[3] The regulations were both positive and negative. Many states passed labor laws to protect children (up to fourteen years old). Other laws provided for compulsory education, mothers' pensions, and pure milk, and prevented the sale of alcohol to children. On an institutional level, the expansion of boys' and girls' clubs, church youth-group activities, and high schools promoted the health and education of children. To keep adolescents in check, laws were passed to create juvenile courts, raise the age of consent, create probation, and provide for the inspection of institutions housing children. On an institutional level, these laws were reflected in a flurry of institution building—homes for delinquent boys, wayward girls' homes, training and reform schools—and the separation of children from adults in almshouses, hospitals, and asylums.

The legislative and institutional construction of adolescence occurred as scholars in many disciplines "discovered" adolescence; the scholarly, regulatory, and institutional endeavors were linked as experts tried to create a science of man. Scholars in psychology, psychiatry, sociology, social work, and anthropology investigated the so-called normal child.[4] At the same time, some social scientists—notably sociologists and psychologists—worked from the other end of the same question, defining an abnormal adolescence. In Chicago, these efforts centered on the Cook County juvenile court, the first court established for children under age sixteen. Founded in 1899, the court threw open its doors to social scientists, making the records of the youths who passed through the court available to those who would help in the effort to understand the causes of juvenile delinquency. By taking advantage of the court's accessibility, Chicago social scientists made the court and the data it generated the centerpiece of studies of abnormal adolescence. In this chapter, I argue that the social scientists in Chicago used a body of data generated by the court—a disciplinary institution—to arrive at different definitions of juvenile delinquency; in the process of doing so, juvenile delinquency became an important cornerstone of each discipline. Sociologists and psychologists differed on the causes of juvenile delinquency and hence the importance of different aspects of human behavior and what, in fact, was meant by a "normal youth." Such differences had important implications for the possibility of attaining the progressive reformers' goal: a moral, just, society.

A Science of the Mind

Psychology evolved as an academic discipline during the late nineteenth and early twentieth centuries. The Harvard philosopher William James offered the first course in psychology in the United States in 1876. For many years thereafter, psychology was taught under the rubric of moral philosophy. Philosophers grappling with Kantian questions of knowledge and reality were drawn to the prestige of natural science. Science could deal with the problem of knowledge, they believed, and philosophers employing science could study the mind in the same way biologists could study natural physical processes.[5]

Psychologists did not lose their broader interests in questions of religion, morals, and education as the focus of psychology turned from the exclusively philosophical questions posed by Kant to the study of the mind's operation. In the 1880s, G. Stanley Hall, a psychologist who had trained with William James, conceived an original approach to educational reform. Education, he hypothesized, should be based on a scientific study of child development. His call for "child study" coincided with German scientific efforts to study children and the development of the mind.[6]

The movement to study children's development flourished in the 1890s and early 1900s. Hall and his students at Clark University in Worcester, Massachusetts, collected data from teachers and parents. They generalized about developmental changes in the young: children progress through stages dominated by the instincts, then "mentalize" those instincts to more rational behavior. At the same time, children begin to display a growing memory and the ability to think abstractly.[7] The child study movement gained proponents nationwide as Hall helped to generate popular interest in the topic; in the 1890s, many states—including Illinois—boasted societies for child study.[8] A few years later Hall turned his attention to older children.

In his two-volume *Adolescence* (1904), Hall described the teenage years as stress-filled, emotional, and turbulent. It was that period of life, he held, that determines the future of the individual as the child assumes the sexual and moral responsibilities of adulthood. During adolescence, a youth should aspire to virtue and upright living; these would help an adolescent become an upstanding adult.[9] Adolescence, therefore, was a dangerous time, but also a special one, one that needed the utmost help an adult or all of society could provide—protection, guidance, and supervision. To Hall, the normal adolescent was a person undergoing momentous changes, both emotional and physical, but one who could fulfill his or her promise and become a virtuous adult.

It was a wealthy scion of Chicago's upper class who helped psychology's child study movement make the transition to an institutionalized endeavor. Ethel Sturges Dummer's consuming interest was reform, and she spent most of her life and much of her money working for reform causes. In 1894, her mother, noticing her daughter's overabsorption in her first child, suggested a diversion: setting up a lunch club for working women.[10] From the luncheon club, Dummer's activities grew to include work with the National Child Labor Committee and the Juvenile Protective Association (JPA), where she furthered her education in how the other half lived.[11] Her work with the JPA and contact with the poor convinced Dummer that the juvenile court alone could not solve juvenile delinquency. Studying JPA cases, she became convinced that "the children were not to blame; that we adults, having leisure, should see to it that the environment was improved. Prevention is better than cure." A large proportion of the cases she read indicated substantial feeble-mindedness among juvenile delinquents. Some children were "so abnormal that I urged scientific research concerning the causes," she recalled. She persuaded the JPA of this need, and a group of reformers, psychologists, and philosophers met at Dummer's house to discuss the matter. The group agreed to hire a psychologist to carry out such research.[12]

After considering various candidates, the group hired Dr. William Healy, a former student of William James already in Chicago. The son of English immigrants, Healy had lived and worked in Chicago as a youth. Coming under the tutelage of several academically-minded fellow clerks, and becoming the protege of the leader of Chicago's Ethical Culture Society, Healy had won admission to Harvard. He finished his degree in 1899, then received a medical degree at Rush Medical School in Chicago one year later. He worked in Chicago and Wisconsin in various medical specialties for a number of years, becoming increasingly interested in neurology.[13] Then he met Ethel Dummer.

Dummer sent Healy on a tour across the United States to meet other psychologists whose interests touched on delinquency and children. She also established the Juvenile Psychopathic Institute (JPI) with a five-year endowment (1909–1914). Three staff members—Healy, psychologist Grace Fernald, and a secretary—were given office space near the juvenile court. Four years later, Augusta Bronner replaced Fernald; she had studied with Edward L. Thorndike, an educational psychologist, at Columbia University's Teacher's College.[14] Together, the team set out to understand the psychological roots of delinquency.

In the late nineteenth century, psychologists held two general theories about delinquency. The anthropometric school, following the Italian Cesare Lombroso, held that delinquency was hereditary. Criminals, Lombroso hypothesized, showed distinct physical markings: a small or an abnormally large head, heavy lower jaw, receding forehead, deformities of the face, and so forth.[15] The second school believed that delinquency signaled the presence of a defective or feeble-minded person. The psychologists at the JPI tested the two dominant theories about delinquency.

Even though he was skeptical about Lombroso's work, Healy tested the Italian's theories, looking for the physical markings and determinants of delinquency. By 1915, he felt he had laid Lombroso's theories to rest. His studies at the JPI, Healy told the American Academy of Medicine, provided no proof of the existence of hereditary criminal traits. He also tested his subjects to find physical causes for their delinquencies—infected tonsils, impacted teeth, etc.—but refuted this as a possible cause of delinquency, as he did the anthropometric school. Human behavior, Healy believed, must have deeper roots: his 1910 article about studies performed at the JPI noted a plethora of causes for youngsters' misdeeds, then concluded that the very number of factors involved precluded only one explanation for behavior. He finally dismissed physical stigmata of criminal tendencies in *The Individual Delinquent*, published in 1915. "Our experience," he wrote, "is simply that we found the facts too much for the theories." Classifications by trait, he went on, contributed little to understanding the delinquent; Lombroso and his followers had mistaken incidentals for essentials.[16]

Healy's colleague Augusta Bronner waged the main battle against the theory that most delinquents were feeble-minded. Soon after she reached Chicago, Bronner began giving delinquents the intelligence tests that H. H. Goddard had pioneered at the Vineland Training School in New Jersey. As early as 1914, she refuted the popular theory, writing that only a small proportion of the delinquents she tested were also feeble-minded. Her study of five hundred cases at the JPI, she said, proved that only about ten percent of the delinquents could be classified as feeble-minded; the rest were of normal intelligence.[17]

In the years following their refutations of traditional notions about the causes of delinquency, Healy and Bronner focused on refining the study of and finding the causes of delinquency. They attempted to create a rigorous, scientific method for understanding deviance that incorporated some sociological ideas and some Freudian approaches but that steered a course between sociology and Freud.

In almost every article or book they wrote, Healy and Bronner emphasized the need for intensive, comprehensive study of the individual child. Like sociologists (see below), they gathered information about the child's environment, the conditions of the home, and so forth. Contrary to general sociological practice, however, Healy and Bronner warned against the seductiveness of "general causation theories." Many works on delinquency, Healy wrote, attempt "to establish geographical, climatological, economic and many other correlations." Much of this is valuable, he conceded, but many suggested correlations contain only half-truths. General theories should be avoided, Healy and Bronner believed, because individuals do not always conform to them: conditions in the home may seem to be the decisive factor in an individual case, but then one finds others in the same family, with the same friends on the street, who do not become criminals. Similarly, the most upright family might produce a delinquent youth, while a vicious drunkard's family might produce none.[18]

The individual, Healy felt, was the key to the problem. The psychologist *must* study individuals, not groups, and since he had found no single cause of juvenile delinquency, there could be no generalizations. One must study the whole person, Healy said in 1911, and the only way to understand delinquency was through careful, but comprehensive, individual study.[19] In *The Individual Delinquent*, Healy listed the schedule of data he and Bronner gathered about children at the JPI. The list included a family history, especially aspects of heredity; a developmental history of the child, including antenatal conditions; the child's environment; the child's mental and moral development; a medical examination; a psychological examination, including mental testing and psychological analysis; the histories of the delinquencies; a diagnostic and prognostic summary; and follow-up records. Under the heading of the psychological exam, Healy and Bronner included psychological tests and the recording of the delinquent's own story.[20] Healy and Bronner recommended gathering information from parents and other family members, teachers, neighbors, police and probation officers, and religious leaders.[21] Healy's method of acquiring the child's own story became his weapon in a battle against the Freudian approach to psychoanalysis.

Healy first dealt with Freud's theories to any great extent in *The Individual Delinquent* (1915). In that book, he cited Freud's lectures at Clark University (1909) and his *Three Contributions to the Sexual Theory* (1910), in addition to various expositions of Freud's theories appearing in both German and English. Healy's next book, *Mental Conflicts and Misconduct* (1917), also referred to Freud and cited more recent essays by Freud, Jung, and American psychologists. "The psychoanalytic method," Healy explained, "first and foremost, invokes retracing the steps which progressively formed the whole character; hence it bespeaks utmost value for students of social misconduct."[22]

Even though he found the psychoanalytic method useful, Healy did not adopt Freud's theories outright. Healy's objections to Freudian theory focused mainly on the methods of analysis, but his first objection to it centered on sex. Freud's emphasis on the sexual was shocking to many turn-of-the-century Americans; Healy attributed Freud's discussion of it to the "open" Viennese environment. In *The Individual*

Delinquent, Healy reserved judgment about the importance of sex in causing mental problems: "We are not at all convinced that the sole source of mental conflict is some experience with the sex instinct; there are other causes of emotional disturbance which strike deeply into the mental organism."[23]

The emphasis on sex was not Healy's only misgiving about Freudian theory, however. He also objected to Freud's method of psychoanalysis, including his reliance on dreams, and the treatment of psychoanalysis as an end in itself. In 1917, Healy dismissed the interpretation of dreams and symbols. "Then, although we have made many inquiries about significant dreams," he said, "it is rare indeed that we found the slightest suggestion of anything that would warrant analysis of them."[24]

One of the reasons Healy and Bronner found little use for dreams was the age of their subjects. Children, Healy believed, were easier to "analyze" than adults; their experiences were not as thoroughly buried or hidden in the subconscious, and children often wanted to help the psychologist discover the roots of their troubles. Healy described his methods as comprising quietness and good will, questioning without suggestion, and overall sympathy. He found that the important facts about young miscreants were easily obtainable. In fact, Healy and Bronner found that a few interviews with the child, not the long-term work prescribed by Freudian psychoanalysts, were all that was needed to get the necessary information. The best results, Healy believed, could be obtained through "working with misdoers at a time not far from the beginnings of their misbehavior."[25]

At bottom, Healy and Bronner preferred their own methods of studying delinquents to Freudian analysis because they felt their methods appealed more to common sense about juvenile delinquency. While Freudian psychoanalysts presented analysis as an end in itself, Healy and Bronner used their psychological analysis as merely a step in the process of solving the delinquent's problems and ending the child's misconduct.[26]

As Healy and Bronner moved beyond the two common theories of delinquency, steering between the generalities of sociological explanation and the theorization of Freudianism, and developing their own methods of study, they evinced as much interest in a child's mental and emotional life as in his or her intelligence and environment. At first, Healy and Bronner seemed slightly at sea, lost in a welter of environmental, hereditary, or mental causations. In 1913 and 1914, Healy wrote repeatedly that there was no simple cause of delinquency. He held that causation could be found in a variety of sources: outer influences, congenital conditions, mental defects, mental habits or conflicts, or in any combination of these sources.[27]

Amidst this confusion, Healy always held to the belief that the basis for all behavior was in the mind. "Crime is conduct," he told one audience, "and that conduct is an attribute of mind. . . . When directly considered, conduct, and therefore crime, is a psychological matter."[28] By 1917, Healy had focused his attention on one psychological cause of delinquency—mental conflicts, a term he used to denote an inappropriate reaction to external events—which he and Bronner had found to be the source behind about seven percent of the delinquencies of some two thousand recidivists in the juvenile court in Chicago.[29]

In 1917, the backers of Boston's Judge Baker Foundation, a new psychological clinic attached to the city's juvenile court, wooed Healy and Bronner away, and the two left Chicago while still very much unsure as to the exact psychological causes of delinquency.[30] In the years after their departure, the JPI, now led by psychiatrist Herman Adler, continued the work of the institute but generally halted research into the causes of delinquency. Gradually, a perspective woven out of the strands of social work, Healy and Bronner's work, and 1920s normalcy took hold: juvenile delinquents, it held, were unadjusted to society.[31] Instead of plumbing the depths of that difference, JPI workers attempted to integrate the children into "wholesome" activities—clubs, scouting, etc.—to keep them from repeating their transgressions.

In their years at the JPI, Healy and Bronner established the method of psychological examination of children, the centerpiece of which was intense concentration on the individual. The individual delinquent, they believed, displayed mental conflicts, mental defects, or defective mental habits. Delinquency, Healy and Bronner argued, had no simple cause: it was not a result of physical abnormalities, feeblemindedness, or sublimated sex instincts. Crime is an attribute of the mind, they insisted. Although they did not phrase it in Hall's terms, what the Chicago psychologists seemed to be arguing was that the normal adolescent could withstand the turbulence and stress of adolescence, succeeding in his or her aspirations to achieve the virtue and integrity necessary in adulthood; the abnormal adolescent, the juvenile delinquent, could not withstand the stress of adolescence nor achieve virtue. The abnormal adolescent instead gave into the stress and deviated from social norms. Studying juvenile delinquency became one way for psychologists to examine the mind of the adolescent who had misbehaved and these experts elevated one aspect of adolescence—the mind—as a symbol for all of adolescence. In this, they differed from other scholars who studied the same children who passed through the same court, during the same years.

A Science of Society

While psychologists like Healy and Bronner argued that delinquency was a psychological matter, sociologists at the turn of the century saw the roots of crime in the environment. During the years between the founding of the University of Chicago (1892) and World War I, professors of sociology at the university taught their students that the city itself was a great source of information about society. The professors urged their students to use the city as their "sociological laboratory," collect data through participant observation, and map the results of their studies.[32] (As a descriptive method, mapping the incidence of certain phenomena—the location of churches and saloons, for instance, alongside the location of various ethnic groups—was unparalleled in making social traits or trends visible.[33]) These investigations, they hoped, would reveal the sources of delinquency and other social problems in the city and urban society.

As part of their effort to explore the city, Chicago sociologists and their graduate students examined the juvenile court and juvenile delinquents early in the century. Generally, sociologists' studies rejected the popular notion that criminality could be inherited. Instead, they emphasized the importance of delinquents' families, home conditions, environment, and poverty.[34]

Sociology graduate student Mabel Carter Rhoades's 1907 study of boys in the juvenile court stemmed both from her academic interests in sociology and criminology and from her year's employment with a charitable agency in Syracuse, New York. It demonstrated the common sociological understanding of delinquency and abnormal adolescents early in the century. For her data, she relied on statistics gathered by Cook County juvenile court officials. She affirmed that the "leading cause of delinquency would seem to be the loss or absence of parents. Poverty, bad neighborhoods, and bad homes take practically equal rank in the list; often, of course, they occur together."[35] A normal adolescent, in other words, was the product of an intact, middle-class family living in a non-poverty-stricken neighborhood. The delinquent was the product of the bad environment. These admittedly biased and often ethnocentric views shaped sociology for the first decades of the century.

The general consensus in sociology on the causes of delinquency began to change in the 1920s. Chicago sociologists began to understand the environment—the city—in a more nuanced fashion, differentiating the city into zones and finding the cause of crime to be the interplay between the individual and his or her environment. In fact, sociologists began to incorporate a psychological approach like that practiced by Healy and Bronner into their studies of delinquency. By the early 1930s, some psychological concepts had become common currency among sociologists.[36]

During the 1920s, students at the University of Chicago produced a number of studies on delinquency that used data from the juvenile court. In general, these studies focused on the environment and the individual's place within it, but they also paid some attention to the individual's psychological constitution. They analyzed the function played by the city, mapping the distribution of delinquency and related it to various areas of the city that were marked by certain characteristics. They included some quantitative work—usually a few tables—and some qualitative evidence, such as interviews or letters.

For example, in his 1926 Ph.D. dissertation (published as a book in 1927) and in an article on gangs, Frederic Thrasher emphasized the importance of studying delinquency in a social context. He conceded that Healy and Bronner's studies of delinquents were well rounded, but argued that they left something to be desired because they neglected the "group approach." The juvenile delinquent must be studied as a person, but the subject should be treated as an individual in society, not in a social vacuum. The sociologists must understand the community, the social groups, *and* the individual. Bowing to psychology, he stated that the study of the juvenile delinquent should follow the principle of Gestalt psychology, in which the meaning of an event is relative to its setting or background.[37]

Thrasher included maps of the distribution of gangs in the city and tables displaying the ethnic backgrounds of various gangs. Describing the attractions of gang life in great detail, he blamed delinquency on society, not on the boys. Delinquency, he held, was created by the disorganizing forces of current American life and slum life, which created family and social disorganization.[38] ("Social disorganization" became the sociologists' catch-all phrase to describe urban ills.)

Reviewers of *The Gang* praised its vivid descriptions. They understood that Thrasher's evidence pointed to social explanations of delinquency, exculpating various immigrant groups and the feeble-minded from blame for delinquency.[39] *The Gang*, they felt, was the sort of project that led to a better understanding of the social and political structure of the city.[40] Thrasher included few suggestions for addressing juvenile delinquency in Chicago, perhaps a sign of sociologists' increasing recognition that delinquency was not easily solved.

Perhaps the best-known example of Chicago sociology's investigation into juvenile delinquency is Clifford R. Shaw's body of work. Shaw started graduate work in sociology at the University of Chicago after serving in World War I. He also worked as a parole officer to supervise children released from the state training schools and as a probation officer of the Cook County juvenile court.[41] Shaw's first venture in the sociological description of delinquency was *Delinquency Areas* (1929). With the aid of maps, Shaw demonstrated that delinquency rates were highest in the center of the city and lowest at the edges.[42]

During his employment as a parole officer, Shaw began to collect delinquents' life histories. His best-known book, *The Jack-Roller* (1930), is a personal document, a life history written by a young delinquent called "Stanley" who had been recently released from the Cook County House of Correction. Stanley's story began as a short narrative of his delinquent acts; Shaw pointed out areas he would like to know more about, either through more writing or interviews, and Stanley expanded his tale.[43] Choosing events and shaping the narrative, Shaw eventually produced Stanley's "own story."

Building on *Delinquency Areas*, Shaw also included maps of the incidence of juvenile delinquency to provide background in *The Jack-Roller*. Focusing his explanation of delinquency on the environment, Shaw interpreted Stanley's story to demonstrate the importance of the uncongenial home life and the influence of companions in causing delinquency. Shaw believed that delinquency was not caused strictly by the environment, but that it flourished in certain areas of the city with high levels of social disorganization.[44]

Shaw included a discussion of Stanley's personality and psychology in tracing the roots of his delinquency. He pointed out that Stanley did not get along with his family, he pitied himself, and tended to justify his misconduct. For example, Shaw wrote of Stanley, "[He] . . . makes a rather definite attempt to place the responsibility for his misconduct upon fate . . . and other persons. Regardless of the justifiability of this attitude, it reflects a fundamental aspect of his personality." In terms of treating the delinquent, Shaw felt that it was essential to understand the delinquent's attitudes, values, and interests. Nonetheless, Shaw emphasized the primacy of sociological, not psychological, explanations and methods. Shaw was empathetic to Stanley, it was clear, but this method was certainly *not* psychoanalysis. Attention to personality was one thing, plumbing the depths of the unconscious was another.[45]

The text of Stanley's narrative is told in the boy's own words. It is a tale of poverty, a wicked stepmother, evil companions, and wrongful imprisonment. Upon release, Stanley came under Shaw's guidance. Shaw found him a foster family and a succession of jobs and lent him a willing ear. By the end of the narrative it seems that

Stanley was finally doing well, a change that Stanley, Shaw, and Shaw's adviser credited to Shaw. They agreed that Stanley's separation from his old neighborhood, family, and companions was especially important in his transformation. Environmental causes, environmental treatments.[46]

The sociological studies of delinquency by Thrasher and Shaw point up two differences between Chicago sociology before the war and after the war. First, sociologists' understanding of the city had become more nuanced. No longer was the entire environment of an individual to blame for his or her delinquency: the environment was differentiated into zones that were conducive to social disorder. Second, sociologists' understanding of delinquency, taking advantage of insights in the works of William Healy and Augusta Bronner, had also become more sophisticated. Sociologists in the 1920s and 1930s considered the individual in his social environment, not merely the incidence of delinquency in the urban environment, as the proper object of research.

The changed methods of sociological research indicated changed understandings of the abnormal and normal adolescent. To sociologists at the turn of the century, the normal adolescent was middleclass, living in an intact family in a good neighborhood. By the early 1930s, sociologists had decided through their research on juvenile delinquents that the delinquent was formed by both an interaction between the individual and the environment. The normal adolescent, reacting to his environment, social disorganization, and family stress, could even be a child who joined a gang. Unlike Hall and Healy, who centered on adolescence as a time of stress, the sociologists understood adolescence as a period in which the individual was likely to be affected by both his formative experiences and living conditions. Indeed, as Thrasher and Shaw showed in their work, given the experiences of some children, it was a wonder that any adolescents escaped delinquency at all.

Conclusion

In the years between 1900 and 1930, psychologists and sociologists analyzed juvenile delinquency to help them define an abnormal adolescence. In the process, sociology and psychology established their claims to juvenile delinquency as an area of each field's expertise. In juvenile delinquency, these scholars hoped to find a key to human behavior, a building block in the construction of a science of man, echoing Hall's insistence on the importance of adolescence, the time in which a boy is "born a man." Social scientists centered their methods on the study in the early part of the century, building a therapeutic worldview that they soon expanded to include adults as well.

Psychologists William Healy and Augusta Bronner studied the juvenile delinquents brought before the juvenile court. First, they disproved the two reigning theories about the causes of juvenile delinquency. Next, they dispensed with the generalities provided by those who looked to the environment as wholly the cause of deviance. Acknowledging that the environment generally did play a role in delinquency, but insisting on the careful study of the individual, Healy and Bronner argued that deviance had its roots in the mind. For children, however, Freudian analysis went too far, insisting on too much theorization, concentration on dreams and symbols, and long-term work for the psychologists' taste. The psychologists defined the abnormal adolescent as one who succumbed to the stresses of adolescence, the normal as one who could withstand them and become a virtuous adult.

Sociologists and graduate students at the University of Chicago also scrutinized the children appearing in the juvenile court. Dispensing with popular theories that blamed deviance on heredity and ethnic background, the sociologists first concentrated on delinquents' environments. In the years after World War I, however, the scholars' understanding of the city became more nuanced. In addition, they began to incorporate some of the insights of Healy and Bronner, theorizing that deviance could be understood only by examining the individual and his or her environment. Shaw and Thrasher's studies of gangs and delinquents typified this approach, building an analysis based on understanding of the individual and the environment in which he or she found himself. While the psychologists emphasized the mind in their study of deviance, the sociologists concentrated on the environment and secondarily on the individual and his or her psychology. The normal adolescent, to the sociologists, reacted to his or her environment and formative experiences: if these included stress and social disorganization, the adolescent might become abnormal.

The interest displayed by Chicago's psychologists and sociologists in defining the cause of juvenile delinquency, in essence defining an abnormal adolescent, was a reflection of the national scholarly interest in adolescence that Kett detected occurring from 1900 to 1920. As experts debated the cause of delinquency, the role of environment and individual psychology, they could not agree on the cause or the cure. This group of experts, using the rubric of science, defined the abnormal adolescent by assuming that there was a normal adolescent, a normal mind in a normal environment. In subsequent years, those children and adults who deviated from the norm were inspected, examined, and "adjusted" to society. The disciplines of science and the social sciences had become agents of regularization, normative behavior, and discipline.

NOTES

1. Robert E. L. Faris, *Chicago Sociology, 1920–1932* (Chicago: University of Chicago Press, 1967), 135–150.

2. Joseph M. Hawes and N. Ray Hiner, "Introduction," in *American Childhood: A Research Guide and Historical Handbook*, ed. Joseph M. Hawes and N. Ray Hiner (Westport, CT: Greenwood Press, 1985), 7–9; Howard P. Chudacoff, *How Old Are You? Age Consciousness in American Culture* (Princeton, NJ: Princeton University Press, 1989), 66; John R. Gillis, *Youth and History: Tradition and Change in European Age Relations, 1770–Present* (New York: Academic Press, 1974), 104–105, 133.

3. Joseph F. Kett, *Rites of Passage: Adolescence in America, 1790 to the Present* (New York: Basic Books, 1977), 215–244. Kett was probably influenced by Philippe Aries's *Centuries of Childhood*, as they both discovered the "invention" of a life stage. Many scholars have since modified Kett's argument in one way or another, but none have denied the enormous amount

of attention paid to adolescence in the years 1900–1920. Gerald Moran, for instance, states that there was an "adolescent" period as far back as the 1400s. Susan Juster and Maris Vinovskis write that colonial Americans understood "youth" to mean adolescence, but had no fixed ideas as to its experience or span. Other scholars, such as Paula Fass and John Modell, take another tack, arguing that the definition of adolescence was not merely performed by experts and adults, but also by adolescents themselves. Gerald F. Moran, "Adolescence in Colonial America," in *Encyclopedia of Adolescence,* ed. Richard M. Lerner, Anne C. Peterson, and J. Brooks-Gunn (New York: Garland, 1991), 157–171; Susan M. Juster and Maris A. Vinovskis, "Adolescence in Nineteenth-Century America," in *Encyclopedia of Adolescence,* ed. Richard M. Lerner, Anne C. Peterson, and J. Brooks-Gunn (New York: Garland, 1991), 698–707; Paula Fass, *The Damned and the Beautiful: American Youth in the 1920s* (New York: Oxford University Press, 1977); John Modell, *Into One's Own: From Youth to Adulthood in the United States, 1920–1975* (Berkeley: University of California Press, 1989).

4. Hamilton Cravens, "Child-Saving in the Age of Professionalism, 1915–1930," in *American Childhood: A Research Guide and Historical Handbook,* ed. Joseph M. Hawes and N. Ray Hiner (Westport, CT: Greenwood Press, 1985), 415–488. For a good overview of literature on child-saving, see Ronald Cohen's article in the same volume, "Child-Saving and Progressivism, 1885–1915," 273–310.

5. Dorothy Ross, *G. Stanley Hall: The Psychologist as Prophet* (Chicago: University of Chicago Press, 1972), 66–67.

6. Ibid., 124–126; Sheldon H. White, "Child Study at Clark University: 1894–1904," *Journal of the History of the Behavioral Sciences,* 26 (1990), 145.

7. White, "Child Study",.135–147.

8. Ross, *G. Stanley Hall,* 281; Club Minutes, 1893–98, Box 20, vol. 90, Chicago Woman's Club Papers, Chicago Historical Society, Chicago, Ill.; Chicago Woman's Club, *Annals of the Chicago Woman's Club for the First Forty Years of Its Organization, 1876–1916,* compiled by Henriette Greenbaum Frank and Amalie Hofer Jerome (Chicago: Chicago Woman's Club, 1916), 241.

9. Chudacoff, *How Old Are You?,* 66; Louise J. Kaplan, *Adolescence: The Farewell to Childhood* (New York: Simon and Schuster, 1984), 51, 79.

10. Ethel Sturges Dummer, *Why I Think So: The Autobiography of an Hypothesis* (Chicago: Clarke-McElroy, 1937), 21.

11. Ibid., 34–39, 45; Ethel Sturges Dummer to Mrs. Louis de Koven Bowen, 6 Jan. 1949, Box 27, File 460, Dummer Papers, Schlesinger Library, Cambridge, Mass.; Sophonisba Breckinridge to Ethel Sturges Dummer, 13 Dec. 1906, Box 27, File 462, Dummer Papers, Schlesinger Library. Dummer already had a solid background in social and political thought, as she had read the works of Lester Ward, E. A. Ross, John Commons, and Simon Patten. Ethel S. Dummer, *The Evolution of a Biological Faith* [Chicago Dummer Library, 1938], 10–11.

12. Dummer, *Why I Think So,* 35, 45, 50; Ethel Sturges Dummer, "Life in Relation to Time," in *Orthopsychiatry 1923–48: Retrospect and Prospect,* ed. Lawson G. Lowrey (Menasha, WI: American Orthopsychiatric Association, 1948), 9; "Mental Hygiene," n.d., Box 30, File 378, Dummer Papers, Schlesinger Library; Cook County (Ill.), Board of County Commissioners, *Charity Service Reports,* Cook County, Illinois (1907), 30.

13. George Gardner, "William Healy, 1869–1963," *Journal of the American Academy of Child Psychiatry,* 11:1 (1972), 8; oral history interview with William Healy and Augusta F. Bronner, 21 January 1960, Chicago Historical Society, 12.

14. John C. Burnham, "Bronner, Augusta Fox," *Notable American Women, the Modern Period* (1980); Healy and Bronner oral history, pp. 137–147.

15. Charles R. Henderson, *Introduction to the Study of the Dependent, Defective, and Delinquent Classes* (1893; rpt. Boston: Heath, 1908), 225–228.

16. Edith R. Spaulding and William Healy, "Inheritance as a Factor in Criminality: A Study of a Thousand Cases of Young Repeated Offenders," *Journal of Criminal Law and Criminology*, 4:6 (1914), 857; Roy Lubove, *The Professional Altruist: The Emergence of Social Work as a Career, 1880–1930* (Cambridge, MA: Harvard University Press, 1965), 65; William Healy, "Present Day Aims and Methods in Studying the Offender," *Journal of Criminal Law and Criminology*, 4:2 (1913), 208; William Healy, "The Individual Study of the Young Criminal," *Journal of Criminal Law and Criminology*, 1:1 (1910), 61–62; William Healy, *The Individual Delinquent: A Text-book of Diagnosis and Prognosis for all Concerned in Understanding Offenders* (1915; rpt. Boston: Little, Brown, and Co., 1917), 16–17.

17. Augusta Bronner, "A Research on the Proportion of Mental Defectives among Delinquents," *Journal of Criminal Law and Criminology*, 5:4 (1914), 566. Carl Degler credits Healy with repudiating the idea of a connection between intelligence and criminality, between heredity and delinquency. Of course, Bronner had a hand in this, too. See Carl Degler, *In Search of Human Nature: The Decline and Revival of Darwinism in American Social Thought* (New York: Oxford University Press, 1991), 140.

18. Healy, *Individual Delinquent*, 23–24; Healy, "The Contribution of Case Studies to Sociology," *Publications of the American Sociological Society* 18 (1923), 149.

19. Joseph M. Hawes, *Children in Urban Society: Juvenile Delinquency in Nineteenth-Century America* (New York: Oxford University Press, 1971), 207; G. Stanley Hall, *Adolescence: Its Psychology and Its Relations to Physiology, Anthropology, Sex, Crime, Religion, and Education*, vol. 1 (1904; rpt. New York: D. Appleton and Co., 1928), 393; Illinois State Conference of Charities and Correction, "Proceedings," *Institution Quarterly*, 3:4 (1912), 112.

20. Gardner, "William Healy," 28; Healy, *Individual Delinquent*, 53, 60–61.

21. Healy, *Individual Delinquent*, 39–40.

22. Ibid., 116. Ironically enough, Healy was advised by other German psychologists not to bother visiting Freud during his trip to Europe in 1906. Healy and Bronner oral history, 53; William Healy, *Mental Conflicts and Misconduct* (1917; rpt. Boston: Little, Brown, and Co., 1923), 35; Healy, *Individual Delinquent*, 116.

23. Healy and Bronner oral history, 207, 296; Healy, *Individual Delinquent*, 120.

24. Healy, *Individual Delinquent*, 118. Barry Krisberg posits that Healy's early work was heavily influenced by the theories of Freudian psychology. The evidence, it seems to me, points in exactly the opposite direction. Elizabeth Lunbeck points out that prior to 1915 or 1920, no one in the United States really counted himself as a Freudian. See Barry Krisberg, *The Juvenile Court: Reclaiming the Vision* (San Francisco: National Council on Crime and Delinquency, 1988), 5; Elizabeth Lunbeck, *The Psychiatric Persuasion: Knowledge, Gender, and Power in Modern America* (Princeton, NJ: Princeton University Press, 1994), 23; Healy, *Mental Conflicts*, 63.

25. Healy, *Individual Delinquent*, 118–119; Healy, *Mental Conflicts*, 21.

26. Healy, *Individual Delinquent*, 45, 121. On this, I agree with Levine and Levine's point that Healy emphasized the child's potential rather than his psychopathology. The Levines see this as evidence of the progressive faith in every person's potential. Murray Levine and Adeline Levine, *A Social History of Helping Services: Clinic, Court, School, and Community* (New York: Appleton-Century-Crofts, 1970), 182–183.

27. Frank J. Bruno, *Trends in Social Work as Reflected in the Proceedings of the National Conference of Social Work, 1874–1946* (New York: Columbia University Press, 1948), 172; William Healy, "Present Day Aims and Methods in Studying the Offender," *Journal of Criminal*

Law and Criminology, 4:2 (1913), 208, 209; Healy, "Medicopsychological Work in Courts," *Institution Quarterly*, 5:4 (1914), 102.

28. Illinois State Conference of Charities and Correction, "Proceedings," *Institution Quarterly*, 3:4 (1912), 110–114, 117.

29. Healy, *Individual Delinquent*, 32; Healy, *Mental Conflicts*, 7–8.

30. Healy and Bronner oral history, 72, 202; William Healy and Augusta F. Bronner, "The Child Guidance Clinic: Birth and Growth of an Idea," in *Orthopsychiatry, 1923–1948: Retrospect and Prospect*, ed. Lawson G. Lowrey (Menasha, WI: George Banta Co., 1948), 29.

31. For a very interesting discussion of psychologists and assumptions about adjustment in adolescence, see Cravens, "Child-Saving in the Age of Professionalism, 1915–1930."

32. L. L. Bernard, "Some Historical and Recent Trends of Sociology in the United States," *Southwestern Political and Social Science Quarterly*, 9 (1928), 291; Ruth Cavan, "The Chicago School of Sociology, 1918–1933," *Urban Life*, 11 (1983), 411; Dennis Smith, *The Chicago School: A Liberal Critique of Capitalism* (New York: St. Martin's Press, 1988) 119; Faris, *Chicago Sociology* 12; Jonathan H. Turner, "The Mixed Legacy of the Chicago School," *Sociological Perspectives*, 31 (1988), 331, 332; Jim Thomas, "Toward a Critical Ethnography," *Urban Life*, 11 (1983), 393, 389, 480–482.

33. Faris, *Chicago Sociology* 52.

34. See, for example, Charles R. Henderson, "The Prevention of Crime, Not Merely Its Punishment," *Journal of Criminal Law and Criminology*, 1:2 (1910), 9–12; Charles R. Henderson, "Prevention of Delinquency," *Journal of Criminal Law and Criminology*, 4:6 (1914), 798–800; Charles R. Henderson, "Juvenile Courts: Problems of Administration," *Charities*, 12 (7 Jan. 1905), 340–343; Charles R. Henderson, "The Theory and Practice of Juvenile Courts," *Proceedings of the National Conference of Charities and Corrections*, 15–22 June 1904, 358–369; A. P. Drucker, "A Study of 100 Juvenile-Adult Offenders in the Cook County Jail, Chicago, Illinois," *Journal of Criminal Law and Criminology*, 4:1 (1913), 47–57; B. H. Clark, "Reaching the Adult Responsible for the Delinquent and Neglected Child," *Journal of Criminal Law and Criminology*, 8:5 (1918), 782.

35. Mabel Carter Rhoades, *A Case Study of Delinquent Boys in the Juvenile Court of Chicago* (Chicago: University of Chicago Press, 1907), 3–4, 20.

36. See, for example, Maurice Krout, "The Sociological Meaning of Wholesome Adolescence," *Welfare Magazine*, 17:8 (1926), 53–55; F. E. Haynes, "The Individual Delinquent," *Journal of Criminal Law and Criminology*, 18:1 (1927), 68.

37. Frederic M. Thrasher, "The Group Factor: An Element to be Reckoned With in the Causation and Treatment of Juvenile Delinquency," *Welfare Magazine*, 18:2 (1927), 141–142, 143.

38. F. Emory Lyon, review of *The Gang: A Study of 1,313 Gangs in Chicago*, by Frederic M. Thrasher, in *Journal of Criminal Law and Criminology*, 18:1 (1927), 138; Frederic M. Thrasher, "The Group Factor," 318; Frederic M. Thrasher, *The Gang: A Study of 1,313 Gangs in Chicago* (1927; rpt. Chicago: University of Chicago Press, 1963), 20; Robert M. Mennel, *Thorns and Thistles: Juvenile Delinquents in the United States, 1825–1940* (Hanover: University of New Hampshire Press, 1973), 188.

39. Lyon, review of *The Gang*, 139; Arthur J. Todd, review of *The Gang: A Study of 1,313 Gangs in Chicago*, by Frederic M. Thrasher, *Welfare Magazine*, 18:3 (1927), 398; Kimball Young, "Frederic M. Thrasher's Study of Gangs," in *Methods in Social Science*, ed. Stuart A. Rice (Chicago: University of Chicago Press, 1931), 511–516.

40. Ernest W. Burgess, "Studies of Institutions," in *Chicago: An Experiment in Social Sci-*

ence Research, ed. T. V. Smith and Leonard D. White (Chicago: University of Chicago Press, 1929), 171; Todd, review of *The Gang*, 398.

41. "Cooperation in the Parole of Boys and Girls from Correctional Schools," *Institution Quarterly*, 14:3 (1923), 19; Jon Snodgrass, "Clifford R. Shaw and Henry D. McKay: Chicago Criminologists," *British Journal of Criminology*, 16:1 (1976), 4–5.

42. James Bennett, *Oral History and Delinquency: The Rhetoric of Criminology* (Chicago: University of Chicago Press, 1981), 169.

43. Martin Bulmer, *The Chicago School of Sociology* (Chicago: University of Chicago Press, 1984), 107; Faris *Chicago Sociology*, 75.

44. Bennett, *Oral History and Deliquency*, pp. 168, 169; Clifford R. Shaw, *The Jack-Roller: A Delinquent Boy's Own Story* (1930; rpt. Chicago: University of Chicago Press, 1938), 10, 34–39, 165.

45. Shaw, *Jack Roller*, 165, 47, 18, 8, 14, 195–196.

46. Ibid., 187, 196.

Chapter Two

Heroism and the Problem of Impulsiveness for Early Twentieth-Century American Youth

Jay Mechling

This inquiry begins with my memory of the mild frustration I felt when, in 1956 as a freshly minted Boy Scout at age eleven, I pored through my new *Handbook for Boys* and came across the description of the medal to be awarded "for saving life." I gazed longingly at that medal and read carefully the description of the circumstances under which the medal was to be awarded: "This is awarded by the National Court of Honor to Scouts who save life or attempt to save life at the risk of their own, and show heroism, resourcefulness and skill."[1] The medal was unique; it felt strangely inaccessible to me. Every other badge, every other medal could be earned. In this organization that directly rewarded individual hard work and accomplishment, every badge and every rank (including the pinnacle, Eagle Scout) was within my grasp. But the medal "for saving life" could not be "earned" in the usual sense of that word. The medal was bestowed as recognition of a certain act that could not be planned, an act that would be construed as revealing a truth about my inner character. True, as a Scout I could "be prepared" (as the motto told it); I could acquire all the lifesaving and first-aid skills I would need to draw upon if I were faced with the occasion to save a life, and a comic strip in the *Boy's Life* magazine that arrived every month illustrated actual cases where a Scout drew upon those skills and rescued other people. But I could not know for sure, until confronting the event, that I also had the internal something I needed to draw upon in order to save a life. I knew how to be a good son, how to be a good student in school, and how to be a good Scout. Here, though, was something I could not acquire through hard work and conformity, and it made me nervous. Despite my subsequent success as a Boy Scout, I never lost my ambivalent feelings about that medal, and I have never faced a situation where I had the opportunity to save a life. So, still, I wonder.

I begin with this memory because it captures the puzzle this essay aims to solve. I know now that my middle-class male anxiety over the heroism medal in the late 1950s had its origins in the cultural conditions and ideological responses to those conditions motivating the youth movements in the late nineteenth century, movements that led (among other things) to the founding of the Boy Scouts of America in 1910. The heroism medal condenses a number of cultural themes, contradictions, and anxieties present in the United States in the transition from the nineteenth- to the twentieth-century world; and, as so often happens, the socialization of young people became a prime site for adults to play out these cultural dramas. I believe the continuity between the "problem of heroism" at both ends of the twentieth century signals an important, ongoing cultural dilemma for Americans.

Put most simply, I argue that the twentieth-century socialization of children and adolescents around the issues of courage and "heroism" unwittingly unmasks two cultural contradictions. First, the discourse shows Americans the dangers of defining the self in a public culture built on competitive individualism. The "dirty secret" of the egalitarian, individualistic, achievement-oriented society is that we really do rely more upon others than our public ideologies would have it. Thus, narratives about heroism, and especially about heroism in young people, provide reassuring proof of altruism as a basic instinct that will provide a safety net in a modern society of strangers. Second, the discourse's emphasis on "impulse," that is, on the spontaneous rather than calculated performance of service to others, creates a new dilemma, for early discourse that valorized impulse in heroism could not distinguish very well the society-serving impulse from the selfish impulse that would serve commodity capitalism in the grand change from an economy based on production to one based on consumption. Grounding the meanings of the self in an ever-changing commodity culture leaves the individual with an "identity project" that never can be completed, a point made elegantly by Christopher Lasch in his diagnosis of the culture of narcissism.[2]

In what follows I look first at the ways the Boy Scouts of America dealt with the problems of fear, courage, and heroism as the adults created an institution meant to socialize adolescents in the early decades of this century. I then sketch the web of larger cultural discourses and other contexts within which these socialization efforts took place, extracting certain themes from the larger cultural discourse about heroism and noting the tensions present in those themes. Having established the official (one might say hegemonic) discourse aimed at socializing youth on these matters, I next ask how might the young men themselves have received, accepted, or resisted the official discourse? Finally, I want to connect these early-twentieth-century patterns with the present, showing how this history helps serve cultural criticism nearly a hundred years later.[3]

The Boy Scouts Institutionalize Heroism

The Boy Scouts of America (BSA) is merely the best known of a large number of youth movements begun in the late nineteenth and early twentieth centuries.[4] The BSA had obvious connections with the movement founded slightly earlier in England by Lord Baden-Powell, but in truth the American organization was from the outset a syncretic creation of several American movements.[5] Ernest Thompson Seton, the famed naturalist, artist, and author brought to the BSA in 1910 nearly twenty years' worth of experimenting with a youth organization—Seton's Woodcraft Indians—

organized around American Indian lore.[6] Daniel Carter Beard, who shared with Seton a respected status as author and illustrator, had been experimenting with his own organization, the Sons of Daniel Boone, created in 1905.[7] Added to this mix were men such as John L. Alexander who were veterans of YMCA work.

These nineteenth-century founders were trying to find a successful formula for socializing young men for the twentieth century, and in the organization they created lie clues to the cultural transformation they were trying to understand. All of these youth movements were responding to demographic changes in the final decades of the nineteenth century, as increasing numbers of young people were living in cities, came from the working class, and were either first- or second-generation immigrants. The attention given to the urban gang in public discourse was a signal that most middle-class Americans were alarmed by the increasing evidence of unruly boys in the streets. Another fundamental change was economic, as the United States began to enter a stage of capitalism where consumption would replace production as the key challenge. At the same time, science—from Darwinism to the new physics—was working to destroy the old verities, and scientific psychology was emerging to challenge religion as the intellectual system explaining who we are and why we act the way we do, both individually and in groups. These changes created an ideological crisis that spawned antimodern revitalization movements, among which we must count Seton's Woodcraft Indians, Beard's Sons of Daniel Boone, and the BSA.[8] These movements were attempting to create new institutions that would undo the harm done to boys by the modernization of consciousness and by other assorted changes in economic and social relationships. A symptom of the problem was the felt crisis of masculinity for white, middle-class men in the late nineteenth century, a crisis that the BSA was meant to help solve.[9]

Understanding the crisis these men were experiencing helps us to see why the earliest discourse in the BSA stressed nineteenth century concepts such as honor, duty, courage, and heroism. The Scout Oath established the centrality of honor and duty. In introducing the twelve points of the Scout Law, John L. Alexander explains in the first *Handbook for Boys* that the Scout Law has its origins in the "unwritten laws coming down from past ages." He then lists a veritable inventory of sources, from the Middle Ages to America's "Red Indians," for revitalizing American values.[10] The first point of the Scout Law is "A Scout is Trustworthy." "A Scout's honor is to be trusted," explains the text, and earlier in this section of the *Handbook* Alexander warns the boy reader that the "honor of a scout will not permit of anything but the highest and the best and the manliest."[11] A Scout virtue related to honor is courage. The tenth point of the Scout Law is "A Scout is Brave," and the *Handbook* explains what it means for a Scout to be brave: "He has the courage to stand up to danger in spite of fear and has to stand up for the right against coaxing of friends or the jeers or threats of enemies, and defeat does not down him."[12] In a later chapter on "Chivalry," Alexander makes the point even more directly. "It is horrible to be a coward," he writes there. "It is weak to yield to fear and heroic to face danger without flinching."[13] The *Handbook* also makes it clear that the will to act bravely is not enough; the boy must prepare his mind and body to be able to respond to situations.[14]

Toward solidifying these values and expectations, the BSA founders established the Honor Medals that could be awarded to Scouts and to adult leaders for heroic acts. The Bronze Medal was awarded to a scout who had saved a life, the Silver Medal to a scout "who saves life with considerable risk to himself," and the highest medal, the Gold Medal, was to be awarded only "to a scout who has saved life at the greatest possible risk to his own life."[15] Moreover, the act could not stem from doing one's duty: "In no cases, however, shall a medal be awarded where it appears that the risk involved, was merely in the performance of duty or the meeting of an obligation because of responsibility to supervise and give leadership to the person whose life was saved."[16]

Having the will and the skill to respond heroically, then, are twin goals of the Scout program. But there is a dilemma buried in this simple formula, a dilemma of which the Scout leaders themselves were mindful. Each boy could have all the lifesaving skills that Scout instruction had to offer, and still only some boys would act heroically in given circumstances. Everyday heroism, it seemed, remained a mysterious quality of self that could not be learned, as could lifesaving skills. To see the power of this dilemma for the boys and men of the early twentieth century, we must turn to some of the larger contexts for this Boy Scout discourse on duty, courage, and heroism.

Other Discourses about Heroism

The BSA's discourse about heroism, courage, and honor took place among broader contexts in which Americans were talking about the nature of children's fears, the role of instincts in adolescence, the puzzle of altruism, and the evidence of "everyday heroism." The effort to socialize children for everyday heroism began at a particularly ambivalent moment in the socialization of children's fears. As historians Peter Stearns and Timothy Haggerty explain, "Middle-class Americans became increasingly aware after 1900 of fear's unpleasantness and replaced an emphasis on mastery with one on avoidance in their implicit definitions of the desirable emotional life."[17] Until 1900, control over fear was, for boys at least, a moral test, a "masculine badge," whereas girls were "essentially advised not to be more fearful than necessary."[18] From 1900 until about 1925, however, the advice to middle-class parents was to help children of both sexes overcome fear "not through direct mastery but through benign evasion."[19] Gone by 1920 was the notion that overcoming fear was a moral challenge; fear now was a "bad emotion" that needed to be "talked through" in "a placating and supportive environment."[20] The socialization of fear from 1900 to 1925, then, was filled with the ambivalences and ambiguities of a transitional period from the Victorian view of fear as a moral test, to the twentieth-century "scientific" view of fear as an unpleasant emotion to be talked through. Child-rearing advice manuals were trying to move away from the Victorian ideology, but other discourses around adolescence—the age group that would become Boy Scouts—still spoke of bravery, duty, and heroism.

The BSA position had its own foundation in the Victorian era's instinct psychology of G. Stanley Hall. Hall's writings had pervasive effects on youth movements, and his 1904 work, *Adolescence*, virtually invented that stage in the life cycle. Ernest Thompson Seton's papers make clear his debt to Hall, and the first *Handbook for Scoutmasters* is full of talk of boys' "instincts."[21] Hall's recapitulation theory suggested that the problem for boys' work was taking the boys' natural instincts—the basis for gang behavior—and turning them to socially useful purposes. Hall's romantic view of the male adolescent led him to see these boys as ripe for programs that would appeal to their instinct to serve others.[22] Dorothy Ross argues persuasively that Hall's writings reveal his own crisis of masculinity, and much of what she says about Hall could as easily be said about Seton and Daniel Carter Beard. All three men embodied the strong ambivalences surrounding masculinity and modernity at the end of the nineteenth century.[23]

From the beginnings of scientific psychology in the United States, with Hall and William James, "altruism" posed a special challenge. Since instincts as well as organs supposedly were subject to the laws of natural selection, it was necessary for the Darwinians to explain how an instinct, altruism, which could easily lead to the death of an organism, had some competitive advantage in the dynamics of natural selection. One version of the debate was that between Thomas Henry Huxley and Prince Kropotkin. In response to Huxley's well-known defense of Darwin's view of the role of competition in natural selection, Russian anarchist Kropotkin wrote eight articles ultimately gathered together into the book, *Mutual Aid as a Factor of Evolution*.[24] Where Huxley argued for competition as the fundamental rule of nature and of natural selection, Kropotkin and others argued that the evidence of nature more clearly pointed to cooperation within the individuals of a species as the potent source of adaptation and survival. Perhaps best known in this vein is John Fiske, whose *Outline of Cosmic Philosophy*, published in 1894, argued that altruism was the fundamental evolutionary stimulus for progress in human civilization.[25]

The fascination of the Victorians with altruism also spilled over from scientific literature into the relatively new genre, the nature story. Ernest Thompson Seton had established his naturalist's credentials with work that culminated in his *Life Histories of Northern Animals*, but it was for his animal stories that he became known.[26] Seton brought to these stories his considerable expertise as an ethologist and as an artist. Seton was no Spencerian; he viewed animal behavior from Kropotkin's perspective on mutual aid. He believed strongly that sociability was a powerfully adaptive behavior.[27] He brought this belief to his youth work, designing games and badge requirements that featured cooperation or "competition against standards" rather than competition between people.[28]

It was not only the biologists and naturalists who seized upon altruism as a compelling puzzle. Still another American who worried about the state of heroism at the turn of the century was the industrialist Andrew Carnegie. On the evening of March 12, 1904, Carnegie read a story in the newspaper about an act of lifesaving heroism by an ordinary citizen of poor means. Carnegie mused aloud to his wife that there ought to be some way to honor and assist these everyday heroes. Taking pen in hand, he wrote out a deed of trust establishing the Carnegie Hero Fund.[29]

The fund provided for medals and even cash awards for heroes or their widows and next of kin.[30]

Carnegie's fascination with the notion of a heroism of peacetime rather than wartime was not an isolated eccentricity of a wealthy man. Quite the contrary, Carnegie's philanthropic act of 1904 merely institutionalized a growing American interest in what the press at the end of the nineteenth century called "everyday heroism." News stories of the sort that prompted Carnegie's largesse were rather common at the turn of the century. An article by Gustav Kobbe in *Century* magazine was typical. Kobbe tells the stories of "every-day people" who "were suddenly confronted with the question whether or not they would risk death to save the lives of others; and the manner in which they met, without preparation or forethought, that supreme moment."[31] He hopes to read in the details of these stories "evidence of a heroic strain in our every-day humanity, often latent, yet likely to flash up, when a crisis comes, even in the humblest of those we daily pass."[32] A few years later, another *Century* article gave readers an idea of the scale of everyday heroism in the United States. The author was a physician, S. Weir Mitchell, best known to historians for helping construct the nineteenth-century "nervous disease" called "neurasthenia," especially "male neurasthenia," a syndrome marked by "insomnia, tension, depression, and (especially) fatigue accompanied by an utter lack of energy."[33] Mitchell engaged a clipping service to send him a year's worth of reports of heroism in newspapers.[34] He was especially surprised to find so many accounts of heroic acts (fifty-three) by children. Many of the rescuers were injured themselves, and of the 717 rescuers, "one in every eleven lost his life in trying to save that of another, and usually that of one strange to him."[35] Mitchell sees in these accounts "an ever-enlarging conscience as to the duty man owes to man."[36] But the spirit of duty is not sufficient; everyday heroes need courage as well, and Mitchell reads in these stories evidence that "civilized life" has not dampened the courage of everyday Americans. Moreover, these qualities seem to be instinctual, for most everyday heroes have no time to reflect upon the danger.

The articles by Kobbe and Mitchell represent a much larger body of press coverage of everyday heroism at the turn of the century, and we see in their ruminations most of the themes running through the public discourse. We might note, first, that these accounts describe urban, industrial America at the turn of the century as an especially dangerous environment.[37] Second, these accounts emphasize the heroic acts of people other than uniformed police officers, firemen, and soldiers. Heroism in uniform is expected, especially in wartime, but uniformed professionals are not always present. A corollary of this point is an oft-mentioned contrast between heroism in wartime and heroism in peacetime. Thus, by the time William James wrote on "The Moral Equivalent of War" in 1910, American readers of newspapers and magazines had already had James's question posed to them as authors reflected on the meaning of acts of everyday heroism. The worry was that the combination of prolonged peace and the blossoming of a consumer economy would lead to the "degeneration" of the qualities Americans prized in themselves. As James put it, "The transition to a 'pleasure economy' may be fatal to a being wielding no powers of defence against its disintegrative influences. If we speak of the *fear of emancipation from the fear regime*, we put the whole situation into a single phrase; fear regarding ourselves is now taking the place of the ancient fear of the enemy."[38] Tales of everyday heroism confirmed for readers that it was possible for people to act heroically without the enabling condition of war.

A third theme evident in the accounts of everyday heroism is that heroism seems to know no boundaries of age, gender, race, or social class. Many of the accounts comment that the heroes are in no way out of the ordinary except for the singular act of heroism. Writers seemed especially fascinated with heroic acts by women, children, and "negroes." Fourth, the journalists and others writing about everyday heroism made special note of the spontaneous nature of the heroic act. Carnegie himself said, "I do not expect to stimulate or create heroism by this fund, knowing well that heroic action is impulsive."[39] Mitchell quotes one hero's response to the question why he risked his life to help another: "I had a sense of queer mental confusion, and then I did it. I have never been able to feel that I had any conscious motive."[40]

Especially illuminating to the writers on everyday heroism were the cases where a hero saved the life of an enemy.[41] Everyday acts of heroism were all the more remarkable in light of the fact that American law held that citizens have no duty to rescue. Several legal commentators agree that the strong ethos of individualism in the United States has been largely responsible for the unwillingness of the courts to impose upon the person a duty to assist others.[42] Clearly, acts of heroism permitted no premeditation, no calculation of comparative benefits and risks, no rational assessment of future gain, and the defenders of the Carnegie Hero Fund made this argument to reassure the critics who worried that rewarding everyday heroism was about to become part of the capitalist, commercial system of exchange.[43] The talk of spontaneity and impulse carried a critique of the rampant, calculating self-interest inherent in capitalism.[44]

The BSA discourse about heroism, bravery, and honor, therefore, was part of a larger American public conversation exploring the effects of modernity upon the American character. Popular novels between 1880 and 1920 increasingly pictured urban individualism as selfish, and it was only in the occasional act of everyday heroism in these novels that "individual heroism and city culture [seemed] compatible."[45] For Americans worried about living in an increasingly urban world surrounded by strangers, the evidence of everyday heroism by children and others reassured citizens that spontaneous altruism was still alive. If one sort of social safety net, the closely knit rural community, was gone, a fundamental, instinctual human quality was there to take its place. The selfish, competitive individualism of the bourgeois, capitalist society was not undoing the self-sacrifice Americans were willing to extend to strangers. The loss of a "fear regime" in peacetime was not jeopardizing, after all, the "manly" qualities of character represented by brave acts of everyday heroism. In all, the discourse about heroism reassured adult Americans that the effects of modernity need not destroy the duty we have toward one another.

But if boys of Scouting age were among those targeted in the campaign to encourage both the motives and the skills for heroism in everyday life, how did they "read" this adult discourse? Since we lack direct evidence of the ways the boys understood the adult narratives about heroism, popular fiction read by the boys might provide us with indirect evidence of the power of the boys to read the official discourse in different ways.[46] The Boy Scout novels, of which there are hundreds of titles, are formula fiction that use two hundred or so pages of narrative to work through the meaning of key Scout terms, such as "courage" and "heroism" and "honor." Many of the Scout novels appearing after 1910 were simply syndicate-written adventure and mystery novels of the Rover Boys genre. But a few novelists knew something about the Scout movement and wrote novels that complemented and reinforced the official literature of the organization. One of these authors was Percy Keese Fitzhugh, whose complex and thoughtful novels won the imprimatur of the BSA. Fitzhugh's fictive world contains a troop of Boy Scouts whose stories he weaves through dozens of novels. The Tom Slade series of nineteen novels appearing between 1915 and 1930 begins with *Tom Slade: Boy Scout of the Moving Pictures*.[47] Three other characters from the troop received their own series treatment from Fitzhugh—Roy Blakely for eighteen novels (1920–1931), Pee Wee Harris for thirteen novels (1922–1930), and Westy Martin for eight novels (1924–1931). These interconnected series permit Fitzhugh to develop more complex stories that eschew the quick-and-easy solutions most other Boy Scout novels offered in their two hundred pages of adventures and mystery. Fitzhugh could allow his characters to change and mature over the course of fifteen years, and he felt less compelled to resolve every problem or ambiguity in a single novel.

For the historian, the fiction might provide resources for the boys' understanding of the cultural contradictions disguised by the simple formula of everyday heroism. Fitzhugh's novels, especially, are "friendly" toward young readers in that they don't "preach" to them. His novels assume a vernacular voice closer to the oral cultures of adolescents, and they present life as having more complexities, more dilemmas and gray areas, than seem in the official literature. Yet none of these novels really undermines the official BSA view of heroism. Fitzhugh's *Tom Slade at Temple Camp* (1917), for example, deals quite explicitly with everyday heroism, and Fitzhugh raises the possibility (which we would never hear in the *Handbook* or elsewhere) that a boy can be calculating in his approach to winning a medal. But the plot finally declares heroism to be a spontaneous, unselfish act.[48] The boys' fiction, in short, may have provided a more nuanced view of boys' character-building, but it did not provide resources for boys' resisting the official understanding of heroism. If the boys constructed their own meanings of courage or even altruism apart from the official discourse provided by adults, we see no evidence of it.

All of the public discourses about heroism and altruism, then, provided a context for understanding a boy's heroism as an instinctual, impulsive act that displayed the selflessness embodied in the Scout virtues of honor, duty, and courage. But this official view still had not resolved a fundamental dilemma—namely, how to reconcile the impulsive nature of heroism with the deliberate decision to act manly by fulfilling social obligations through the performance of duty.

Boys' Heroism and the Problem of Impulse

In trying to sum up the great changes going on in American culture at the turn of the century, from the economic changes to the effects of physics and psychology, historian Thomas Cochran settled on the term "the inner revolution" and proposed 1910 as the watershed year for understanding the culture's transition from the nineteenth century to the twentieth.[49] Warren Susman, writing about the same transition, notes that talk about "character" in the nineteenth century gave way to talk about "personality" in the twentieth.[50] The BSA has always seen itself as an organization for "building character" in American boys, belonging very much to the world in which production-oriented capitalism and a "muscular," Protestant Christianity reinforced each other (had an "elective affinity," as Max Weber put it). The founding of the BSA in 1910 nicely fits this view, for I have been arguing that the founders were nineteenth-century men struggling with creating an organization that would socialize young men for the new century. Theirs was a revitalization movement, an attempt to hold back the ill effects of "the inner revolution" on youngsters. But the discourse and strategies they adopted laid bare the cultural contradictions of a generation that had not yet entered the twentieth century world and had not quite jettisoned the nineteenth.

The recurring emphasis upon spontaneity in these accounts of everyday heroism may be the single best clue to the meanings of the period's discourse about altruism, courage, and heroism. Everyday heroes act spontaneously, impulsively. They take no time to judge their obligation to the victim or to calculate the relative costs and benefits of endangering themselves to rescue another. Their act of heroism is pure and authentic.

The keyword "impulsive" carries all of the ambiguities signaling a fundamental dilemma in late capitalism.[51] For the BSA leaders attempting to preserve the nineteenth-century (or earlier) world in the twentieth, the "impulsiveness" of children and of the act of heroism spoke of a better, premodern world. The word's use in, say, 1910 assured William James and other Americans that good instincts would survive despite the "pleasure economy" so evident in emerging commodity capitalism. This impulsiveness served the altruistic instinct, which the adults of 1910 saw as an ever-present corrective to the worst effects of selfish, competitive individualism.

But at the same time, impulsiveness also had its meanings and uses in that new, consumer-driven economy. The creation of the ideal consumer required a person who would act impulsively in the pleasure economy. The "expressive individualism" described by Robert Bellah and his colleagues, for example, or the "impulsive" conception of the self described by Ralph Turner, serve commodity capitalism by valorizing the self-serving impulsiveness of late capitalism rather than the group-serving impulsiveness read into acts of everyday heroism by a generation experiencing a fundamental transition in the society.[52]

Americans still celebrate "everyday heroism" nearly a hundred years after the concept became common in public discourse. The Carnegie Hero Fund still awards medals and cash stipends, the Boy Scouts of America still award medals for bravery, and we find in modern reports by the Carnegie Hero Fund the same sense of wonder that initially impelled Carnegie. "Nobody really knows why some people are moved to action on behalf of their fellows," wrote the president of the fund in his introduction to the 1979 report. "Carnegie recognized the impulsive in some kinds of heroism; the psychologists refer to heroic behavior as 'pro-social' or 'altruistic.' But neither they, nor we, can explain why some people possess this divinely-directed quality, while others do not."[53]

These are reassuring narratives, islands of altruism and caring in an ocean of urban haste and indifference. Despite the striking continuities between Americans' fascination with everyday heroism in the 1890s and 1990s, acts of heroism and the public discourse about them mean something different. Altruism takes on shades of foolishness in a period of expressive individualism untempered by notions of duty, obligation, and social connectedness. Our historical moment both resembles and is dramatically different from that of 1910, when Americans had lost a world and were casting about frantically for signs that caring and unselfishness still existed. Those Americans created socializing organizations like the Boy Scouts in an attempt to hold off the deleterious effects of "the pleasure economy," but they never resolved the ways that the act of creating medals and honoring an impulse like heroism actually might reinforce the other uses of impulse that were emerging with commodity capitalism.

That I felt the twinges of the unresolved dilemma as a pubescent Scout immersed in the consumer economy of the mid-1950s shows how, at mid-century at least, the socialization of middle-class children still had not adequately explained how to achieve a balance between competitive individualism and obligations to others, especially within a society that uses the consumption of goods as the means for constructing a self. There is still no sign of that solution in the adult discourse, though children and adolescents may be using their own folk cultures to discover a solution that the adults either cannot or will not offer.[54]

NOTES

Research for this essay received support from the Research Committee of the Davis Division of the Academic Senate of the University of California, for which I am grateful. I also extend thanks to Walter F. Rutkowski, executive vice president of the Carnegie Hero Fund Commission, who in 1991 generously made available to me the historical archives of the Commission. Volume editors Mike Willard and Joe Austin provided a very helpful critique of an earlier draft of this essay, for which I give them thanks.

1. Boy Scouts of America, *Handbook for Boys* (5th ed.; New Brunswick, NJ: Boy Scouts of America, 1948), 446.

2. Christopher Lasch, *The Culture of Narcissism* (New York: Norton, 1978).

3. I realize the gender limits of this inquiry. The Girl Scouts and the Camp Fire Girls (both founded in 1912) were responding to changes in the cultural "scripts" for women in the first few decades of this century, yet it remains an open question whether men and women were experiencing the same cultural transformation described by historians, whether what was so problematic for boys in 1910 was at all at the center of girls' worries.

4. For an excellent historical account of these movements, including the BSA, see David

I. Macleod, *Building Character in the American Boy: The Boy Scouts, YMCA, and Their Forerunners, 1870–1920* (Madison: University of Wisconsin Press, 1983).

5. The protagonists themselves and later historians disagree on how much the American movement borrowed and how much it invented. Seton and Baden-Powell had heated exchanges of correspondence, each accusing the other of having stolen ideas for their movements (Seton Papers, Seton Village, Santa Fe, New Mexico). On the English movement, see Michael Rosenthal, *The Character Factory: Baden-Powell's Boy Scouts and the Imperatives of Empire* (New York: Pantheon Books, 1986). For a rather controversial biography of Baden-Powell, see Tim Jeal's *The Boy-Man: The Life of Lord Baden-Powell* (New York: William Morrow, 1990).

6. Jay Mechling, "The Manliness Paradox in Ernest Thompson Seton's Ideology of Play and Games," in G. A. Fine, ed., *Meaningful Play, Playful Meaning* (Urbana, IL: Human Kinetics Press, 1987), 45–59. See John Henry Wadland, *Ernest Thompson Seton: Man in Nature and the Progressive Era, 1880–1915* (New York: Arno Press, 1978), and Betty Keller, *Black Wolf: The Life of Ernest Thompson Seton* (Vancouver: Douglas and McIntyre, 1984).

7. Allan Richard Whitmore, "Beard, Boys, and Buckskins: Daniel Carter Beard and the Preservation of the American Pioneer Tradition" Ph.D. diss., Northwestern University, 1970.

8. Jay Mechling, "The Collecting Self and American Youth Movements," in Simon J. Bronner, ed., *Consuming Visions: Accumulation, Display, and Goods in America, 1880–1920* (New York: Norton, 1989), 255–85. On revitalization movements, see Anthony F. C. Wallace, "Revitalization Movements," *American Anthropologist* 58 (1956): 264–81, and T. J. Jackson Lears, *No Place of Grace: Antimodernism and the Transformation of American Culture, 1880–1920* (New York: Pantheon, 1981).

9. Jeffrey P. Hantover, "The Boy Scouts and the Validation of Masculinity," *Journal of Social Issues* 34:1 (1978): 184–95. There is a similar "crisis of masculinity" felt a century later, probably responding to similar social and economic dislocations, as evidenced by the various new men's movements, including the mythopoetic men's movement, the Promise Keepers, and the Million Man March. See Elizabeth Walker Mechling and Jay Mechling, "The Jung and the Restless: The Mythopoetic Men's Movement," *Southern Communication Journal* 60 (1994): 97–111.

10. Boy Scouts of America, *The Official Handbook for Boys* (Garden City, NY: Doubleday, Page, 1911), 15.

11. Ibid., 9.

12. Ibid, 16.

13. Ibid., 248.

14. Ibid., 7.

15. Ibid, 44.

16. Boy Scouts of America, *Handbook for Scoutmasters*, 2d ed. (New York: Boy Scouts of America, 1924), 179–80.

17. Peter N. Stearns and Timothy Haggerty, "The Role of Fear: Transitions in American Emotional Standards for Children, 1850–1950," *American Historical Review* 96 (1991): 64.

18. Ibid., 71–72. On the gender gap, see also Peter N. Stearns, "Girls, Boys, and Emotions: Redefinitions and Historical Change," *Journal of American History* 80 (1993): 36–74.

19. Stearns and Haggerty, "The Role of Fear," 75.

20. Ibid., 76–77.

21. See, for example, Chap. 10, entitled "Boys," of the second *Handbook for Scoutmasters* (1924), 263–91.

22. See the discussion by Joseph F. Kett, in *Rites of Passage: Adolescence in America, 1790 to the Present* (New York: Basic Books, 1977), esp. Chap. 8.

23. Dorothy Ross, *G. Stanley Hall: The Psychologist as Prophet* (Chicago: University of Chicago Press, 1972).

24. Peter Kropotkin, *Mutual Aid a Factor of Evolution* (London, 1902).

25. Peter J. Bowler, *Evolution: The History of an Idea* (rev. ed., Berkeley: University of California Press, 1989). Altruism continues to be a central "problem" addressed by sociobiologists, since the argument for the adaptive advantage of the altruistic act seems counterintuitive at best. Sociobiologists invented the concept of "kin selection" to account for seemingly nonadaptive traits (such as altruism). Individual organisms act unselfishly, even sacrificing themselves, to protect their kin because such behavior increases the survivability of the genes shared with the protected offspring, siblings, and other kin. To explain the more challenging case of altruism toward strangers, one sociobiologist (R. Trivers) has posited the notion of "reciprocal altruism," a sort of microeconomic exchange in which an altruistic act toward a stranger amounts to an inducement for the stranger to return the favor at some future time.

26. Ernest Thompson Seton, *Life Histories of Northern Animals* (New York: Charles Scribner's Sons, 1909). Seton's autobiography is entitled *Trail of an Artist-Naturalist* (London: Hodder and Stoughton, 1951).

27. Wadland, *Ernest Thompson Seton*, 15. See also Ralph H. Lutts, *The Nature Fakers: Wildlife, Science and Sentiment* (Golden, CO: Fulcrum Publishing, 1990).

28. On Seton's games, see Mechling, "The Manliness Paradox."

29. Andrew Carnegie, "Deed of Trust—Carnegie Hero Fund Commission," in *Annual Report of the Carnegie Hero Fund Commission* (Pittsburgh, PA: Carnegie Hero Fund Commission, 1930), 9–11.

30. The Carnegie Hero Fund is still in business. In the report celebrating the fund's seventy-fifth anniversary, president Robert W. Orff noted that the fund had honored 6,400 men women and children, averaging about eighty-five awards each year. *Carnegie Hero Fund Commission, Seventy-Five Years, 1904–1979* (Pittsburgh, PA: Carnegie Hero Fund, 1979), 3.

31. Gustav Kobbe, "Every-Day Heroism," *Century* 55 (1897–98): 401.

32. Ibid.

33. E. Anthony Rotundo, *American Manhood: Transformations in Masculinity from the Revolution to the Modern Era* (New York: Basic Books, 1993), 186. Also see the discussion by Michael Kimmel, *Manhood in America: A Cultural History* (New York: Free Press, 1996), 134–35.

34. S. Weir Mitchell, "Heroism in Every-day Life," *Century* 65 (1902–1903): 217.

35. Ibid., 219.

36. Ibid.

37. Viviana A. Zelizer discusses the urban dangers for children in her *Pricing the Priceless Child: The Changing Social Value of Children* (New York: Basic Books, 1985).

38. William James, "The Moral Equivalent of War," in *William James: The Essential Writings*, ed. Bruce W. Wilshire, 349–361 (Albany: State University of New York Press, 1984). James wrote this essay as a leaflet for the pacifist organization, the Association for International Conciliation, but the essay also was published in *McClure's Magazine* (August 1910) and the *Popular Science Monthly* (October 1910). James's proposal in this essay was for a peacetime conscription of youth to public service jobs, a proposal now being resurrected for high school and college students.

39. Quoted in "Awards to the Brave," *Ha-per's Weekly* 57 (May 17, 1913), 17.

40. Mitchell, "Heroism in Every-day Life," 220.

41. Frank Marshall White, "Man's Humanity to Man," *Harper's Weekly* 53 (June 12, 1909): 8, and "Heroes and Heroism," *The Outlook* 44 (October 27, 1906): 444–45.

42. Leon Shaskolsky Sheleff, *The Bystander: Behavior, Law, Ethics* (Lexington, MA: Lexington Books, 1978), 102, 104, 105, 112–13. Only in the 1940s, with the accumulation of social change, the creation of the modern welfare state, and the social psychology of the war did legal commentators begin an aggressive critique of the narrow conception of the duty to assist. And it was not until the infamous 1964 case of Kitty Genovese, who was savagely assaulted and killed within earshot of thirty-eight neighbors in New York City, that Good Samaritan Laws became part of the public agenda. In her book, *Rights Talk: The Impoverishment of Political Discourse* (New York: Free Press, 1991), Mary Ann Glendon draws out the cultural implications of the lack of a duty to rescue in American jurisprudence. Given the American principle of the "lone rights-bearer" who holds individually the right of privacy, and given the complementary American silence on responsibilities, it makes sense that American law does not recognize the duty to rescue. Glendon finds an "impoverished" language of "duties" altogether in American legal thinking, a view of "duty" that holds "an unexpressed premise that we roam at large in a land of strangers" (77).

43. Oddly contradictory of this general principle was the case wherein the Carnegie Hero Fund denied a medal to a five-year-old boy who had saved a playmate from drowning. A boy that age, explained fund manager F. M. Wilmot, had "not reached the age of discretion." See "Too Young to Get a Hero Medal," *The Literary Digest* 47 (October 18, 1913), 725–26.

44. Not everyone thought the Carnegie Hero Fund was a good idea. See George Gladden, "To Encourage Heroism," *Current Literature* 36 (June 1904), 591–92.

45. Arthur Margon, "Changing Models of Heroism in Popular American Novels, 1880–1920," *American Studies* 17 (1976), 74, 83.

46. See Emily Cahan, Jay Mechling, Brian Sutton-Smith, and Sheldon H. White, "The Elusive Historical Child: Ways of Knowing the Child of History and Psychology," in *Children in Time and Place*, ed. Glen H. Elder, Jr., John Modell, and Ross D. Parke (New York: Cambridge University Press, 1993), 192–223. All of the essays in this book illustrate both the problems of writing the history of childhood and some creative solutions to the problems.

47. Percy Keese Fitzhugh, *Tom Slade: Boy Scout of the Moving Pictures* (New York: Grosset & Dunlap, 1915). The subtitle of this novel apparently refers to a silent-moving-picture version of the novel, for this novel (unlike Fitzhugh's others) is illustrated by still photos from the movie. I have been unable to find any evidence that this film has survived to the present.

48. Percy Keese Fitzhugh, *Tom Slade at Temple Camp* (New York: Grosset & Dunlap, 1917). Another fiction forum in which the adult leaders could explain the nature of bravery and heroism to young men was the magazine *Boys' Life*, acquired by the BSA in 1912. Short stories were a regular feature in the magazine. Boy Scout librarian Franklin K. Mathiews collected and published several of these stories under the title *Boy Scouts Courageous* in 1918. Though the stories are considerably less sophisticated than Fitzhugh's novels, they reinforce the point that heroism includes both the dramatic lifesaving act and the less dramatic willingness "to do the right thing."

49. Thomas C. Cochran, *The Inner Revolution: Essays on the Social Sciences in History* (New York: Hill and Wang, 1967).

50. Warren Susman, *Culture as History: The Transformation of American Society in the Twentieth Century* (New York: Pantheon, 1984).

51. My strategy here, of course, is to follow Raymond Williams's strategy. See Raymond

Williams, *Keywords: A Vocabulary of Culture and Society* (New York: Oxford University Press, 1976).

52. Robert N. Bellah, Richard Madsen, William M. Sullivan, Ann Swidler, and Steven M. Tipton, *Habits of the Heart: Individualism and Commitment in American Life* (Berkeley: University of California Press, 1985), and Ralph H. Turner, "The Real Self: From Institution to Impulse," American Journal of Sociology, 81(1976): 989–1016. Turner observes that the dynamics of "deprivation and desire," a cardinal Freudian principle but also to be found in George Herbert Mead, may have created a tension between the late nineteenth-century requirements of urban, industrial civilization for the suppression of impulse on the one hand, and the increasing sense that impulse may be more real, more authentic, than socially sanctioned control.

53. Goff, "President's Report," *Carnegie Hero Fund Commission, Seventy-Five Years, 1904–1979.*

54. I have addressed this quality of children's folklore elsewhere; see, for example, Jay Mechling, "Children's Folklore," in Elliott Oring, ed., *Folk Groups and Folklore Genres* (Logan: Utah State University Press, 1986), 91–120, and Jay Mechling, "Children and Colors: Children's Folk Cultures and Popular Cultures in the 1990s and Beyond," in Marilyn F. Motz et al., eds., *Eye on the Future: Popular Culture Scholarship into the Twenty-First Century* (Bowling Green, OH: Popular Press, 1994), 73–89. Other essays in the present volume likewise strive at discovering to what extent children and adolescents can use their folk cultures to resist the adult discourse aimed at socializing them.

Chapter Three

Teenage Girls, Sexuality, and Working-Class Parents in Early Twentieth-Century California

Mary E. Odem

The social and sexual autonomy of daughters was a major source of conflict in working-class families in the early twentieth century and led many parents to seek the assistance of the legal system. Working-class parents made use of recent changes in statutory rape laws to control their rebellious teenage daughters. Middle-class purity reformers had carried out a successful national campaign to make sexual intercourse with teenage girls a criminal offense by raising the age of consent in rape statutes. Their demand was based on the belief that sexual exploitation by adult men was the major cause of moral ruin among young working-class women and girls. When the campaign began in 1885, the age of consent in most states was ten or twelve years; by 1920, nearly every state in the country had raised the age of consent to sixteen or eighteen years. Through this campaign, reformers aimed to control both male sexual license and the social and sexual behavior of working-class teenage girls that conflicted with middle-class moral standards.[1]

Middle-class reformers may have been responsible for raising the age of consent, but once this legislation was in place, working-class parents used it for their own needs and purposes. In the California counties of Alameda and Los Angeles, working-class parents initiated approximately half of the prosecutions for statutory rape in the early decades of the twentieth century.[2] They, along with middle-class reformers, were greatly disturbed by their daughters' assertions of social and sexual autonomy. As traditional forms of moral regulation proved less effective, some parents turned to the courts to control teenage daughters and their male partners. This chapter explores the struggles over teenage sexuality in working-class families through an analysis of statutory rape prosecutions in the Alameda County Superior Court for the decade 1910 to 1920 (112 cases), and in the Los Angeles County Juvenile Court for the years 1910 and 1920 (31 cases).[3] (See the Appendix for more information on these case records.)

Like many urban areas in the rest of the country, Alameda and Los Angeles counties witnessed tremendous population growth and economic development in the late nineteenth and early twentieth centuries. The principal cities of the two counties, Oakland and Los Angeles, grew at a rapid pace. Between 1880 and 1920, the population of Oakland increased from 34,555 to 216,261, and the population of Los Angeles grew from 11,183 to 576,673.[4] The great expansion of transportation, trade, and industry in California drew a succession of native-born and foreign-born workers to both cities. In the late nineteenth century, native-born white Americans and northern Europeans made up the bulk of the working-class population in these cities. After the turn of the century, thousands of southern and eastern Europeans, Mexicans, Asians, and African Americans joined these earlier migrants to California.[5]

This diverse population of working people in Alameda and Los Angeles counties exhibited a range of sexual norms and practices. Many adhered to strict moral codes that placed great importance on the chastity of daughters. Some of the parents eventually turned to the legal system to enforce these moral codes and to punish rebellious daughters and their male partners. Virtually all of the parents who filed statutory rape complaints in these counties were working class; that is, they and/or their spouses were employed as skilled, semiskilled, or unskilled workers. This group of parents reflected the diversity of the working-class populations of the two counties. They included native-born whites and blacks; skilled workers and common laborers; rural migrants and seasoned urban dwellers; and immigrants from Germany, Ireland, Italy, Portugal, Russia, and Mexico.

Historians have usually associated the emphasis on female sexual purity with bourgeois Protestant culture and have drawn clear distinctions between the sexual behavior and norms of middle-class and working-class people. They have shown that middle-class Americans in the nineteenth century developed an ideology of sexual restraint that emphasized female purity and male continence and relied on individual self-control to regulate the passions.[6] We know far less about the sexual mores of white, immigrant, and black working-class people during this period, but it is generally assumed that they were not bound by middle-class moral reticence. They supposedly had more fluid definitions of licit and illicit behavior, were more tolerant of sex outside of marriage, and did not stigmatize children born out of wedlock.[7]

Although there clearly were important differences between middle-class and working-class expressions of sexuality, one has to be careful not to overgeneralize about the working-class experience or to neglect the strict moral codes that operated within many working-class and immigrant communities. Concern with female chastity was not rooted in middle-class Protestant culture alone. It was also based in the patriarchal family structure of preindustrial societies, in various religious traditions, and in a code of honor that linked family reputation to the morality of wives and daughters. Many of the migrants to California came from rural communities and small towns in Europe, Mexico, and parts of the United States in which fathers had controlled the labor and sexual lives of wives, children, and servants in ways that best supported the family economy. The stability of the patriarchal household demanded particularly close control of the sexuality of wives and daughters. Out-of-wedlock births threatened the limited economic resources of the family and the need to insure "legitimate" male heirs.[8]

Religious teachings reinforced the importance of premarital chastity in preindustrial communities. According to the Judeo-Christian ideal, sexual intercourse before marriage, and after marriage except with one's spouse, was sinful. The Catholic Church, in particular, placed great value on virginity. Catholic doctrine forbade sex outside of the bonds of marriage and held that sex between married partners was strictly for the purposes of reproduction.[9]

In theory, religious strictures on chastity applied to both sexes, but religion competed with a popular ethos that expected moral purity in women yet tolerated and even encouraged male sexual license. This double standard of morality was deeply rooted in Anglo-American culture and shaped both law and social custom in Britain and the United States.[10] The insistence on female chastity was particularly pronounced in the Mediterranean societies from which Italian and Portuguese immigrants came, and also in Mexico, where a code of honor linked a family's status and reputation to the sexual purity of its daughters and wives. Here again, though, the double standard was in operation, for whereas sexual promiscuity destroyed a woman's honor, it enhanced a man's prestige and status in society.[11]

Other working-class and immigrant groups came from communities that were somewhat less vigilant about guarding female chastity. In some small towns and rural villages of northern and western Europe and the United States, families tolerated sexual play and sometimes intercourse among young couples in the context of betrothal. Such courting practices were permitted because it was expected that marriage would follow, particularly if pregnancy resulted. Families and community leaders could usually pressure a reluctant father to marry his pregnant girlfriend.[12]

To regulate the sexual behavior of youth, preindustrial and rural societies relied on external methods of control that operated best in relatively small, close-knit communities. Family, community, and church worked together to monitor young couples and to channel sexuality into marriage. In the small towns and rural villages of the United States, Europe, and Mexico, most daughters worked in farm households or small workshops and family businesses, under the close supervision of their parents or other relatives.[13] The familial context of such work not only insured that parents retained control over their daughters' labor and services, but also enabled them to monitor the young women's social activities and relations with men. Families generally were well acquainted with the young men who courted their daughters. Couples usually met at the young woman's home or at community events and celebrations under the watchful eyes of neighbors. In southern European and Mexican villages, daughters were usually chaperoned by family members whenever they left home to go to the market, attend religious services, or take part in social events.[14]

Even among experienced urban workers, as well as among migrants from rural areas and small towns, a preoccupation with female morality was evident. By the late nineteenth century, certain sectors of the American working class had embraced standards of sexual respectability that resembled those of the middle class. This was particularly true of the aristocracy of skilled laborers—made up primarily of native-born Americans and workers of Canadian and northern or western European backgrounds—and of the small elite in African American society. However, this development should not be read as a passive acceptance of bourgeois values, the end result of decades of moralizing by middle-class reformers and ministers. Rather, these white and African American workers reformulated dominant standards of respectability in response to their particular needs and social experiences. Many skilled workers and their wives embraced values of female domesticity and moral purity, yet at the same time mounted a radical critique of industrial capitalism which, in their view, destroyed the home by forcing women and children to work for wages, thereby threatening their physical and moral well-being. These workers and their unions fought for a "family wage" that would enable them to keep their wives and young children out of the paid labor force. This strategy aimed both to protect male wages and the family's standard of living and also to preserve the moral respectability of wives and daughters.[15]

For a range of economic, cultural, and religious reasons, then, diverse groups of native-born and immigrant working people in Alameda and Los Angeles counties valued female chastity and used various means to enforce it. Traditional expectations of daughters and controls over their social interactions and relations with men, however, were seriously challenged in the rapidly growing and changing urban environments of Oakland and Los Angeles. In such large cities, earlier methods of regulating the sexuality of youth through family, community, and church were far less effective than they had been in villages and small towns. The great geographical mobility of workers, the crowded, ethnically diverse neighborhoods, and the growing number of young people living away from home made it difficult for parents or community leaders to ensure that marriage would automatically ensue when young women engaged in sex or got pregnant. Religious and communal sanctions did not have the same power to control deviant sexual behavior in large, heterogeneous cities as they had in small, face-to-face communities.

Compounding the problem, working-class daughters began to challenge familial expectations and roles as a result of new forms of work and recreation that drew them increasingly into the public sphere, where they experienced greater freedom from family constraints. Daughters continued to play a vital role in the family economy, for most working-class fathers did not earn enough to support the whole household on their wages alone. But the context of women's labor had changed dramatically. Instead of domestic work or industrial home work in family settings, the principal forms of female employment in the nineteenth century, daughters now worked in department stores, offices, factories, canneries, and restaurants. In Los Angeles some also had access to a variety of jobs in the burgeoning movie and entertainment industry.[16] Most of these changes in employment opportunities did not apply for African American women, who were barred from the higher-status female jobs and compelled to work mostly in domestic service. But even young black women experienced greater social autonomy during this period as they left their families and farm households in the rural South to live and work in new urban environments.[17]

Working out from under the supervision of family members, young women formed casual acquaintances with men they met on the streets and in the workplace. They used their status as wage earners to assume privileges such as staying out late, going to dance halls, and using part of their earnings to buy stylish clothes, makeup, or movie tickets. Some daughters took advantage of their new economic power to move away from home and live with friends or coworkers. Although most wage-earning daughters continued to live with parents or relatives, a growing number boarded in apartments and rooming houses with their peers.[18]

The expansion and commercialization of leisure activities in Oakland and Los Angeles at the turn of the century created a youth-oriented, mixed-sex world of amusement that altered courtship patterns and further undermined family control of daughters. Urban youth spent many of their leisure hours with peers in the dance halls, movie theaters, and cafes that sprang up in the downtown areas, and they also flocked to the amusement parks built in the early years of the twentieth century in both cities. Opened in 1903, Oakland's Idora Park covered seventeen acres and offered numerous attractions to the thousands who visited daily: a carousel, a roller-coaster, a vaudeville theater, a dance pavilion, and a skating rink featuring a Tunnel of Love. In Los Angeles, young men and women could ride the trolley from almost anywhere in the county to the beachside amusement parks at Venice and Long Beach, which featured roller-coasters, merry-go-rounds, penny arcades, shooting galleries, and brightly lit promenades with cafes and dance pavilions. These new recreational facilities provided social spaces for unsupervised flirtation and intimate encounters with members of the opposite sex.[19]

In response to these changes, immigrant and working-class families pursued various strategies to monitor their adolescent daughters as they worked and played in American cities. Mexican and Italian families attempted to maintain a system of chaperonage by having a relative, often an older brother, accompany daughters when they left home. Some parents also tried to supervise their wage-earning daughters by having them work in establishments with other family members.[20] In the rapidly growing cities of Oakland and Los Angeles, however, such careful supervision was difficult to maintain. Over the objections of their families, daughters still went out in the evenings on their own and formed intimate relationships with young men they met at work, on the streets and beaches, and in the various amusement centers.

When familiar methods of sexual regulation proved ineffective in modern urban environments, some working-class parents turned to the courts for assistance. They used the statutory rape law to restrain daughters and their male partners who violated traditional moral codes. Numerous working-class parents sought legal intervention to end intimate relationships their daughters had formed with male companions. In one case, a fifteen-year-old Portuguese girl left home and stayed in a hotel for several days with a young man she had been dating. When her father found out, he confronted the man in his place of employment and then had him arrested for statutory rape. He explained to court officials, "You know how I felt towards him, what I wanted to do when he ruined my home."[21] One working-class mother called on the court when she learned that her fifteen-year-old daughter, Louise, was involved in a sexual relationship with a young man nineteen years of age. The couple first met at the Majestic Dance Hall in Oakland and had been seeing each other for several months without the mother's knowledge. When the mother discovered a letter from the young man that revealed the nature of the relationship, she beat her daughter, reported her to juvenile authorities, and had the young man arrested for statutory rape.[22]

In numerous cases, parents used the law to retrieve runaway daughters and their male companions. During the late nineteenth and early twentieth centuries, female runaways presented a serious problem to families in Oakland and Los Angeles, as well as other urban areas in the country. The local newspapers contained daily notices about teenage girls missing from home. Parents and police often suspected that the girls had been kidnapped and forced into prostitution by white slavers. A typical notice in the *Oakland Tribune* read: "Grace Logan goes to pay a visit to friends in Alameda and drops from sight. . . . It is the opinion of the girl's brother that she was either 'spirited away or has been the victim of white slavers.' "[23]

Court records and newspapers, however, reveal that the young women and girls had more complex reasons for leaving home. Some were seeking greater independence and freedom from strict parental supervision. The *Oakland Tribune* reported that the mystery surrounding one seventeen-year-old girl's disappearance was solved when her friend reported "she was tired of restrictions placed on her by parents and planned to leave home and seek employment to make her own way in the world."[24] There was great conflict in many families over how late daughters remained out at night, whom they dated, and where they spent their leisure time. Such a dispute led to the case of two female cousins who, frustrated with strict familial control of their behavior, ran away one Sunday afternoon. They headed immediately for the dance pavilion in Oakland's Idora Park, where they met a young man who worked as a sales clerk at a local store. After spending the evening with them at the amusement part, the man invited the teenagers to stay in his room for the night. The next evening, as the girls were on their way to another dance, they were apprehended by the police.[25]

A number of other cases involved teenage girls who had run away to escape unhappy or abusive home situations. One Russian Jewish girl left her father's house because of his constant beatings. She moved in with her boyfriend, a young man who had previously boarded in her home until he was kicked out of the house because he tried to prevent the father from beating his daughter. The parents sent the police after the couple and had the young man arrested.[26] Other young women also left home without parents' permission to live with their boyfriends. In one such case, sixteen-year-old Sara Gardner, who worked as a sales clerk, met a young Frenchman, a musician, at a dance pavilion in San Francisco. Over the next few weeks, the man visited her home, met her parents, and took her out several times to the movie theater and ice-cream parlor. Then he persuaded her to leave home and live with him in his Oakland apartment, and helped her find a job in the same theater where he worked. Within a week Sara's mother, uncle, and the police tracked down the couple at the theater and had the man arrested for statutory rape.[27]

A number of parents turned to the court when confronted with a daughter's out-of-wedlock pregnancy, a problem which threatened both the economic stability and the social standing of many working-class families. Parents also worried about the humiliation and limited marriage prospects their daughters would face as unmarried mothers. Such were the concerns of Mrs. Alvarez, when she learned of her teenage daughter's pregnancy. Attempting to salvage her daughter's reputation, Alvarez enlisted several female relatives and neighbors to confront the suspected father where he worked and urge him to marry the girl. When he still refused, Alvarez had him arrested. As she explained in court, "I did it because I didn't want my daughter that way, because when a girl is that way, nobody thinks good of her . . . I told him I wanted him to marry the girl just to give her a name."[28]

As working-class parents turned to the court to enforce traditional moral codes, their daughters struggled to assert their own social and sexual autonomy. The sexual encounters they described in court did not fit the image of male lust and female victimization described by purity reformers in the age-of-consent campaign. Instead of being the helpless victims of evil men, most of the young women were willing participants in a more complicated sexual drama. In 72 percent of the Alameda cases prosecuted between 1910 and 1920 and 77 percent of the Los Angeles cases in 1920, young women said they had consented to sexual relations with their male partners.[29] The desire for pleasure, adventure, companionship, marriage, and economic support all figured in young women's decisions about their sexual choices. Most of their male partners were young working-class men. Seventy-three percent of the defendants in Alameda County were between the ages of eighteen and twenty-nine, the bulk of them between eighteen and twenty-four.[30] Seventy-four percent of those whose occupation is known were skilled or unskilled laborers.[31] The young men charged with statutory rape in the Los Angeles Juvenile Court were between thirteen and nineteen years of age, with 74 percent between the ages of fifteen and seventeen.[32] They were employed in various working-class occupations such as store clerk, agricultural laborer, and teamster.

The young women in these court cases also challenged prevailing conceptions of female sexual innocence through their dress, language, and behavior. Many had flirted openly with young men on the street, dressed in the latest fashions, and attended dance halls, movie theaters, and amusement parks unchaperoned, often "picking up" young men once they arrived. In so doing, working-class daughters undermined the rigid classification of women as good and bad, angels and prostitutes, a division that was a staple of Victorian culture. They adopted many of the manners associated in the public's mind with prostitution—wearing makeup, smoking cigarettes, going out at night alone, and engaging in sex outside of marriage—yet they clearly distinguished themselves from prostitutes. The young women had not accepted money for sexual favors, and several expressed their clear disapproval of that type of exchange. Yet they acknowledged women's sexual agency and condoned sexual relations in certain circumstances.

Numerous young women had taken an active role in their romantic encounters. Out on the streets, in movie theaters and in dance halls, they encouraged and sometimes initiated contact with young men. When asked how she met her sexual partner, one teenage girl explained to court officials: "A flirtation . . . I turned the corner and looked back and he was standing outside smoking, then I went down a little ways and I looked around again and he was standing on the corner, then he followed me."[33] Another teenager who appeared in court had apparently invited her boyfriend on several occasions to visit her in her bedroom at night without her parents' knowledge. Her family had learned of the relationship when they discovered the following note she wrote to the defendant: "Dear Joseph, I am sleeping in that little room and

I felt rather lonesome and cold. I wonder if you couldn't come over to see me tonight about 11:00 . . . From the one that loves you."[34]

Eighteen-year-old Margaret Emerson explained in court how she and her girlfriends met the defendant, George Cheney, and his friends when they went to the "moving picture show" in downtown Oakland one Sunday afternoon. Wearing stylish dresses for the occasion, the girls attracted the attention of the young men, gave out their addresses in East Oakland, and made a date to go to Lincoln Park the following weekend. Margaret explained to the court that "Mama would never let me talk to any fellows unless she saw them." Nevertheless, she went out with George twice before introducing him to her mother. After dating for several months, the couple decided to move in together and made plans to marry once George secured a divorce from his wife. To get Mrs. Emerson's approval for this arrangement, they told her they had already married and did not mention George's previous venture into marriage.[35]

Like Margaret Emerson, many young women formed intimate relationships with their "steadies," men they had been dating and planned to marry. Yet the expectation of marriage was not always a precondition for engaging in sex. One teenage girl of Mexican descent, Edna Morales, fell in love and became intimately involved with a nineteen-year-old man whom she met at the store where she worked in Los Angeles. When questioned by court officials, Edna plainly stated that she had engaged in sex not because of a promise of marriage, but because of the affection she felt for her partner. The probation officer assigned to the case reported that when she asked the young woman about her sexual relations, "she very boldly said, yes . . . She did not seem to think there was anything wrong about it but refused to give me the young man's name."[36]

For other young women, sex was not necessarily linked to marriage or even to love, but was simply a form of pleasure, part of an evening's entertainment and adventure. Julia Townsend, who lived with her parents in southern California, made occasional weekend trips to Los Angeles with her two girlfriends to visit dance halls and cafes. On one of these trips, she and her friends arrived in Los Angeles on a Saturday evening, registered at a downtown hotel, and headed for Solomon's Dance Hall. Julia, who was employed as a stenographer, used her own money to pay for the trip and her share of the room. The young women met several young men at the dance hall and invited them to their hotel room. That night the police raided the hotel and arrested the three couples. Julia was charged with "visit[ing] hotels with men to whom she is not married, sleeping and staying in the same room and apartment with these men."[37] Another young woman expressed a liberal sexual standard similar to Julia Townsend's. According to the probation officer who handled her case, "She told me in talking with her that she did not believe there was any wrong in having sexual intercourse with boys, if she would not take money and if she did not become pregnant."[38]

Other young working-class women had exchanged their sexuality for an evening's entertainment, a ticket to the amusement park, a meal, or a place to stay for the night. In a society that severely restricted women's access to economic independence and self-support, it is not surprising that many young women chose to barter with sex. Even though employment opportunities had expanded for women during this period, they earned only approximately 60 percent of the standard men's wages, and women workers typically earned less than the "living wage," estimated to be $9 or $10 dollars a week in 1910.[39] Young women discovered early on that their sexuality was a valued commodity which they could trade for things they wanted or needed. Because of their low wages, working girls often depended on men to "treat" them if they wanted to take part in urban recreations or enjoy a night on the town. In return, men expected sexual favors, which could range from affectionate companionship to sexual intercourse.[40]

When sixteen-year-old Annie Wilson was asked in court how she became sexually involved with the defendant, she explained that she and her sister had skipped Sunday School to go to the skating rink at Idora Park in Oakland. There they met Andrew Singer, who treated them to refreshments and rides in the park. Later that night Annie returned with the young man to his hotel room and stayed the night. In the meantime her family notified the police, who located her the next morning. When asked by the court why Annie behaved this way, her sister responded, "She didn't like to turn him down, he had given us lunch and paid our way into the rink and she didn't like to turn him down."[41]

Fifteen-year-old Agnes Farrell and her friend Amelia made a similar exchange with sailors they met at the train station in downtown Los Angeles or at the navy dock in San Pedro. They accompanied the sailors to dance halls and the amusement park at Long Beach and on several occasions spent the night with them in hotels along the beach. Agnes explained to court officials that they did not expect to receive money from the sailors but were merely interested in being taken out and shown a good time.[42]

A number of girls used their sexuality as a strategy for survival after running away from home. Runaways often relied on boyfriends or men they met along the way to pay for meals and hotel rooms. In return for such support, the young women engaged in sexual intercourse with their male companions, following an arrangement that was often unspoken. A teenage runaway with no viable means of economic support often had only her sexuality to trade. One teenage girl left home to escape the heavy domestic duties her family demanded of her. She had no money with which to rent a room, but she met a young man in downtown Los Angeles who found and paid for a hotel room and later helped her to find a job at a nearby cafeteria. In return, she had sexual relations with him.[43] A fifteen-year-old African American girl found herself in a similar situation when she left her aunt's home in a small town in northern California, where she had been living ever since her mother died. She ended up stranded in Oakland with no means of support until she ran into a young black man she knew. He offered to pay for her room and board and the two lived together for several days until they were arrested by the police.[44]

Other young women had exchanged their sexuality, not for entertainment or shelter for the night, but for a promise of marriage. Some hoped marriage would offer a way out of tedious employment or an unhappy or overly strict home. Such was the situation of Louise Howard, who met her boyfriend, Robert Camarillo, at an Oakland dance hall. After they had dated for several weeks, Louise suggested that they get married. She desperately wanted to leave home because of the constant fights she had with her stepfather. Robert promised to marry her once he received the approval of his father. In the meantime, he wanted her to prove her love by having sex with him. Louise agreed to his request, but whenever she brought up the question of marriage, Robert claimed he was still waiting for his father's approval. Eventually Louise's mother learned of the couple's relationship, reported her daughter to juvenile authorities, and had the young man arrested.[45] In another case a fifteen-year-old Portuguese girl, who worked in a telephone office, agreed to spend the night with a young man she had been dating after he promised to marry her. She was eager to leave her own home because she did not get along with her parents and was particularly distressed by their plan for her to marry a Portuguese man they had selected for her.[46]

Sexuality was a means of rebellion for young women, but it was also clearly an area in which they were exploited. Engaging in sex outside of marriage involved serious risks for them—pregnancy, disease, abandonment, social ostracism. Although they were far from the helpless victims of reformers' accounts, young women nevertheless entered the sexual relationship from a greatly disadvantaged position compared to their male partners. They had far more restricted access to economic independence and faced greater condemnation for their sexual transgressions. Despite the purity reformers' campaign against the double standard, families and society still punished women more harshly than men for illicit sexual activity. Young women also encountered a popular male culture that viewed them as sexual bait, yet ostracized those who acquiesced as "loose," not fit to be wives and mothers. One young man refused to marry the pregnant teenage girl he had been dating, because, as he told court officials in Los Angeles, she was "a girl of easy morals."[47]

One of the greatest risks of sexual experimentation for working-class daughters was out-of-wedlock pregnancy. Margaret Emerson found herself unmarried and pregnant after she agreed to have sex with her boyfriend, George Cheney. George had persuaded her to move in with him and promised they would marry as soon as he secured a divorce from his wife. After continually delaying the marriage, George finally moved out when Margaret became pregnant a year and a half later. Alone and with few resources, Margaret filed a rape complaint against him and told the court she thought he should marry her and help support the baby.[48]

The social and economic costs of out-of-wedlock pregnancy led some young women to resort to illegal abortion, a dangerous and sometimes deadly procedure. One young woman in Los Angeles nearly died from blood poisoning after a botched abortion she received from a local doctor.[49] Another pregnant teenage girl died from an "operation" shortly after her unsuccessful attempt to make her boyfriend marry her by taking him to court in Alameda County.[50]

Young women's increased social autonomy could also make them vulnerable to forcible assault. At times, the boundaries and limits of the system of sexual exchange were not entirely clear. In some cases girls who were reluctant to comply with the expectation of sexual favors were forcibly raped.[51] This was the case with Ruby Haynes, a teenage girl who accepted a date with a young man she met at the movie theater in Oakland. The night they met, Jason Strand took her to the beach, walked her home that night, and made a date to go to the nickelodeon a few days later. As they were walking home after the show, Jason took Ruby into a vacant lot and urged her to have sex with him. When she refused, he threw her to the ground and raped her.[52]

The cases discussed in this chapter demonstrate the complex meanings that sexuality had for working-class teenage girls. As they explored romantic relations and heterosexual pleasures in new urban environments, teenage girls rebelled against traditional family expectations of daughters. Some were seeking intimacy with boyfriends; others were looking for adventure and excitement; a number sought escape from unhappy or overly strict homes; and still others used sex as a strategy for survival in the face of economic hardship and family abuse. As a result of gender and class discrimination, sexual experimentation involved serious risks for teenage girls. They encountered both pleasure and danger as they navigated the complicated sexual terrain of early-twentieth-century cities.

Appendix: A Note on Court Records

The analysis of statutory rape prosecutions in this chapter are based on two bodies of court records: (1) all prosecutions for statutory rape in the Alameda County Superior Court for the decade 1910–20 (112 cases); (2) all prosecutions for statutory rape in the Los Angeles County Juvenile Court for the years 1910 (8 cases) and 1920 (23 cases).

The unusually rich and complete body of felony trial court records from the Alameda County Superior Court are particularly fruitful for examining the enforcement of age-of-consent legislation. The two major sources of information are the register of actions and the case files. The register lists the defendant's name, case number, charge, and a summary of the legal processing of each case. The case files contain the official complaint and verbatim trial transcripts from the preliminary hearings that took place in the lower courts.

For the Los Angeles County Juvenile Court, case files of delinquent youth for each decade year beginning with 1910 have been preserved on microfilm. A complete case file contains a verbatim trial transcript, detailed probation report, and summary of the legal processing of the case. Most of the 1920 case files are complete, but many of the 1910 files are not. I have therefore relied on the 1920 case files alone for statistical analyses, but have used both sets of records for qualitative descriptions of the cases.

Not all of the Alameda and Los Angeles County court records that I have used for statistical analyses contain full information on each case. I have therefore indicated in the footnotes the number of case records (N) that have information on the particular subject under discussion and have made the calculations on the basis of this number.

NOTES

1. On the age-of-consent campaign in the United States, see Mary E. Odem, *Delinquent Daughters: Protecting and Policing Adolescent Female Sexuality in the United States, 1885–1920* (Chapel Hill: University of North Carolina Press, 1996), chaps. 1–2.

2. Parents and relatives initiated close to half (46%, N = 92) of the statutory rape cases that appeared before the Alameda Court from 1910 to 1920; another 13% were initiated by the young women themselves, and 38% by law enforcement officials. Families initiated more than half (57%, N=23) of such cases before the Los Angeles County Juvenile Court; the remaining 43% were reported primarily by law enforcement officials. See the Appendix for further information on the statistical calculations in this chapter.

3. When discussing individual cases, I have changed the names of the young women, male partners, family members, and others involved in the cases, but have attempted to retain their ethnic distinctions.

4. U.S. Bureau of the Census, *Tenth Census of the United States, 1880: Population* (Washington, D.C.: GPO, 1883), 1:416; U.S. Bureau of the Census, *Fourteenth Census of the United States, 1920: Population* (Washington, D.C.: GPO, 1922), 3:118; Marilynn S. Johnson, *The Second Gold Rush: Oakland and the East Bay in World War II* (Berkeley: University of California Press, 1993), 13–15; Robert M. Fogelson, *The Fragmented Metropolis: Los Angeles, 1850–1930* (Cambridge, Mass.: Harvard University Press, 1967), chap. 4.

5. U.S. Bureau of the Census, *Twelfth Census of the United States, 1900: Population, Pt. 1, California* (Washington, D.C.: GPO, 1904); *Thirteenth Census of the United States, 1910, Population*, vol. 2, *Reports by States, California* (Washington, D.C.: GPO, 1913); *Fourteenth Census of the United States, 1920: Population*, vol. 3, *Composition and Characteristics of the Population by States, California* (Washington, D.C.: GPO, 1922); Beth Bagwell, *Oakland: The Story of a City* (Novato, CA: Presidio Press, 1982), 81–90; Johnson, *The Second Gold Rush*, 16–17; Fogelson, *Fragmented Metropolis*, 75–83.

6. On middle-class sexuality, see John D'Emilio and Estelle Freedman, *Intimate Matters: A History of Sexuality in America* (New York: Harper and Row, 1988), 66–72; G. J. Barker-Benfield, *The Horrors of the Half-Known Life: Male Attitudes toward Women and Sexuality in America* (New York: Harper and Row, 1976); Barbara Welter, "The Cult of True Womanhood, 1820–1860," *The American Family in Social-Historical Perspective*, ed. Michael Gordon (New York: St. Martin's Press, 1973), 224–50; Nancy Cott, "Passionlessness: An Interpretation of Victorian Sexual Ideology, 1790–1850," *Signs* 4(Winter 1978): 219–36.

7. For this interpretation of working-class sexuality in nineteenth-century New York City, see Christine Stansell, *City of Women: Sex and Class in New York, 1789–1860* (Urbana: University of Illinois Press, 1987), 85–101, 175–80. Freedman and D'Emilio also posit a sharp distinction between the sexual norms and attitudes of middle-class Americans and those of immigrants, workers, and African Americans in *Intimate Matters*, 74–75, 183–88.

8. Louise A. Tilly and Joan W. Scott, *Women, Work and Family* (New York: Holt, Rinehart, and Winston, 1978), 31–42; Susan Glenn, *Daughters of the Shtetl: Life and Labor in the Immigrant Generation* (Ithaca, NY: Cornell University Press, 1990), 8–16, 79–89; Virginia Yans-McLaughlin, *Family and Community: Italian Immigrants in Buffalo, 1880–1930* (Ithaca, NY: Cornell University Press, 1977), 82–98.

9. D'Emilio and Freedman, *Intimate Matters*, 4–5; Ramon A. Gutierrez, *When Jesus Came, the Corn Mothers Went Away: Marriage, Sexuality, and Power in New Mexico, 1500–1846* (Stanford, Calif.: Stanford University Press, 1991), 241–43; Lawrence Stone, *The Family, Sex, and Marriage in England, 1500–1800* (New York: Harper and Row, 1977), 498–501; John T. Noonan,

Jr., *Contraception: A History of Its Treatment by the Catholic Theologians and Canonists* (Cambridge, Mass.: Belknap Press, 1965), 36–46, 131–39.

10. Christopher Smout, "Aspects of Sexual Behavior in Nineteenth-Century Scotland," in *Bastardy and Its Comparative History*, ed. Peter Laslett, Karla Oosterveen, and Richard M. Smith (Cambridge, Mass.: Harvard University Press, 1980), 192–216; Keith Thomas, "The Double Standard," *Journal of the History of Ideas* 20 (April 1959): 195–216.

11. Richard Griswold Del Castillo, *La Familia: Chicano Families in the Urban Southwest, 1840 to the Present* (Notre Dame, Ind.: University of Notre Dame Press, 1984), 26–29; Gutierrez, *When Jesus Came, the Corn Mothers Went Away*, chaps. 5–7; John G. Peristiany, ed., *Honor and Shame: The Values of Mediterranean Society* (Chicago: University of Chicago Press, 1966); Julian Pitt-Rivers, "Honor," in *International Encyclopedia of the Social Sciences* (New York: Macmillan, 1968), 503–11; Jane Schneider, "Of Vigilance and Virgins: Honor, Shame, and Access to Resources in Mediterranean Societies," *Ethnology* 10 (January 1971): 1–24; Yans-McLaughlin, *Family and Community*, 82–84, 92–94.

12. Ellen K. Rothman, *Hands and Hearts: A History of Courtship in America* (New York: Basic Books, 1984), 46–49; Smout, "Aspects of Sexual Behavior in Nineteenth-Century Scotland," 210–13; Tilly and Scott, *Women, Work and Family*, 38–40.

13. Micaela DiLeonardo, *The Varieties of Ethnic Experience: Kinship, Class, and Gender among California Italian-Americans* (Ithaca, NY: Cornell University Press, 1984), 48–54; George J. Sanchez, *Becoming Mexican American: Ethnicity, Culture and Identity in Chicano Los Angeles, 1900–45* (New York: Oxford University Press, 1993), 26–27, 33–35; Yans-McLaughlin, *Family and Community*, 52–54, 170–74; Glenn, *Daughters of the Shtetl*, 16–26.

14. Dino Cinel, *From Italy to San Francisco: The Immigrant Experience* (Stanford, Calif.: Stanford University Press, 1982), 189; Griswold del Castillo, *La Familia: Chicano Families in the Urban Southwest*, 29, 76; Elizabeth Ewen, *Immigrant Women in the Land of Dollars: Life and Culture on the Lower East Side* (New York: Monthly Review Press, 1985), 208–209; Glenn, *Daughters of the Shtetl*, 82, 147, 157; Sanchez, *Becoming Mexican American*, 31–35.

15. Susan Levine, *Labor's True Woman: Carpet Weavers, Industrialization, and Labor Reform in the Gilded Age* (Philadelphia: Temple University Press, 1984), 129–53; Jeffrey Weeks, *Sex, Politics and Society: The Regulation of Sexuality since 1800*, 2d ed. (New York: Longman, 1989), 75–76. On sexual respectability among African Americans, see Dorothy Salem, *To Better Our World: Black Women in Organized Reform* (New York: Carlson Publishing, 1990), 20–31, 44–51; Linda Gordon, "Black and White Visions of Welfare: Women's Welfare Activism, 1890–1945," *Journal of American History* 78 (September 1991): 568–70, 578–79. On the family wage, see Martha May, "The Historical Problem of the Family Wage: The Ford Motor Company and the Five-Dollar Day," in *Unequal Sisters: A Multi-Cultural Reader in U.S. Women's History*, ed. Ellen Carol DuBois and Vicki L. Ruiz (New York and London: Routledge, 1990), 275–91.

16. Joseph A. Hill, *Women in Gainful Occupations, 1870–1920* (Washington, D.C.: GPO, 1929), p. 45; Joyce Loranger and Mary Tyler, "Working Women in the Los Angeles Area, 1920–39," Master's thesis, California State University, Dominquez Hills, 1984; California, Industrial Welfare Commission, *Biennial Report*, 1913–14 and 1919–20.

17. Jacqueline Jones, *Labor of Love, Labor of Sorrow: Black Women, Work, and the Family from Slavery to the Present* (New York: Basic Books, 1985), chaps. 3–5; Teresa L. Amott and Julie A. Matthaei, *Race, Gender, and Work: A Multicultural History of Women in the United States* (Boston: South End Press, 1991), 157–70.

18. For a discussion of similar changes among wage-earning daughters in New York and Chicago, see Ewen, *Immigrant Women in the Land of Dollars*, 106; Kathy Peiss, *Cheap Amuse-*

ments: Working Women and Leisure in Turn-of-the-Century New York (Philadelphia: Temple University Press, 1986), chap. 2; Joanne Meyerowitz, *Women Adrift: Independent Wage Earners in Chicago, 1880–1930* (Chicago: University of Chicago Press, 1988), 1–20.

19. Bagwell, *Oakland: The Story of A City*, 148; Carey McWilliams, *Southern California: An Island on the Land* (1946, Rpt., Salt Lake City, Utah: Gibbs M. Smith/Peregrine Smith, 1985), 129–33; Sanchez, *Becoming Mexican American*, 171–87; Long Beach Municipal Convention and Publicity Bureau, "Long Beach Amusement Zone" (no date), Long Beach Public Library, Pike file. For an excellent discussion of working-class women's leisure, see Peiss, *Cheap Amusements*. See also Ewen, *Immigrant Women in the Land of Dollars*, 208–217; Glenn, *Daughters of the Shtetl*, 159–66.

20. Alice Kessler-Harris, *Out to Work: A History of America's Wage-Earning Women in the United States* (New York: Oxford University Press, 1982), 137–38; Vicki L. Ruiz, *Cannery Women, Cannery Lives: Mexican Women, Unionization, and the California Food Processing Industry, 1930–50* (Albuquerque: University of New Mexico Press, 1987), 11, 33; Yans-McLaughlin, *Family and Community*, 171.

21. Alameda Case no. 5558 (1913).

22. Alameda Case no. 7550 (1920).

23. *Oakland Tribune*, August 26, 1911, clipping located in Oakland Police Department Scrapbooks, Oakland Public Library, Oakland, Calif.; Mark Connelly, *The Response to Prostitution in the Progressive Era* (Chapel Hill: University of North Carolina Press, 1980), 125–126.

24. *Oakland Tribune*, February 9, 1912, clipping located in Oakland Police Department Scrapbooks, Oakland Public Library.

25. Alameda Case no. 5501 (1913); Alameda Case no. 5502 (1913).

26. Alameda Case no. 5023 (1911).

27. Alameda Case no. 7595 (1920).

28. Alameda Case no. 6081 (1915).

29. For the Alameda cases, N = 106; for the Los Angeles cases, N = 22. The remaining 28% of the Alameda cases and 23% of the Los Angeles cases were forcible assaults. For a detailed discussion of these cases, see Odem, *Delinquent Daughters*, 58–62.

30. For these cases, N=105.

31. For these cases, N=86.

32. For these cases, N=23.

33. Alameda Case no. 5732 (1914).

34. Alameda Case no. 5201 (1912).

35. Alameda Case no. 6153 (1915).

36. Los Angeles Case no. 1937 (1910).

37. Los Angeles Case no. 16190 (1920).

38. Los Angeles Case no. 2184 (1910).

39. Kessler-Harris, *Out to Work*, p. 230; Leslie Woodcock Tentler, *Wage-Earning Women: Industrial Work and Family Life in the United States, 1900–30* (New York: Oxford University Press, 1979), 19; Peiss, *Cheap Amusements*, 52.

40. For an analysis of the practice of "treating" among working-class youth in New York City in the early twentieth century, see Peiss, *Cheap Amusements*, 108–114. On a similar practice in nineteenth-century New York, see Stansell, *City of Women*, 97–100.

41. Alameda Case no. 5564 (1913).

42. Los Angeles Case no. 16266 (1920).

43. Los Angeles Case no. 16059 (1920).

44. Alameda Case no. 6672 (1917).
45. Alameda Case no. 7550 (1920).
46. Alameda Case no. 7678 (1920).
47. Los Angeles Case no. 16196 (1920).
48. Alameda Case no. 6153 (1915).
49. Los Angeles Case no. 16077 (1920).
50. Alameda Case no. 6882 (1918). On the practice of abortion during this time period, see Leslie Reagan, "When Abortion Was a Crime: The Legal and Medical Regulation of Abortion, Chicago, 1880–1973," Ph.D. diss., University of Wisconsin, Madison, 1991.
51. For an insightful analysis of the system of sexual exchange among working-class youth and its consequences for young women in nineteenth-century New York, see Stansell, *City of Women*, 97–100.
52. Alameda Case no. 5657 (1914).

Chapter Four

Rolling with the Punches

Boxing, Youth Culture, and Ethnic Identity at Federal Indian Boarding Schools during the 1930s

John Bloom

In late October of 1933, the Bureau of Indian Affairs received an anonymous letter postmarked from Arkansas City, Kansas, expressing concern over the popularity of boxing at the Chilocco Indian School in northern Oklahoma, a federally operated vocational institution for Native Americans. The letter writer asserted that boxing was "made more than a school activity," that the school print shop was used to print publicity posters, and that revenue from the bouts might have been tampered with. The letter ends with a thinly veiled accusation: "Large crowds [*sic*] are always present and what becomes of the gate receipts?" (National Archives, Chilocco).

The commissioner's office responded to this letter, sending investigators to Chilocco. They uncovered no evidence of embezzlement or larceny. However, the prominence of the boxing team did cause concern at the Bureau of Indian Affairs. Director of Education W. Carson Ryan, worried about professionalism creeping into boarding-school athletics and asked if there was a need to review athletic policy at these schools. Two years later, Commissioner John Collier, responding to an article published in an Oklahoma newspaper, voiced his criticism of boxing at the school. He wrote to Chilocco superintendent L. E. Correll that year, "Newspaper clippings and other information coming to this office relative to your boxing team would lead me to believe that perhaps you are over-emphasizing this sport" (National Archives, Chilocco).

By the early 1930s, sports had become a central part of life at boarding schools like Chilocco, institutions that the federal government established at the turn of the century to educate and assimilate Native American youths. From the time that the Carlisle Indian School in Pennsylvania first fielded a nationally ranked, college-level football team in the 1890s, sports grew to become one of the most significant programs of the boarding school movement, generating revenue for schools, fame for coaches and athletes, and publicity for proponents of federal assimilationist policies for indigenous American people. The case of boxing, however, reveals another side of sports at Indian boarding schools, a side characterized by institutional uncertainties, ideological contradictions, and, most importantly, by the passions and expressions of boarding school-students. Most of the highly visible, revenue-generating sports that were practiced at boarding schools also generated controversy, but boxing proved to be the most controversial of all, and, for students, one of the most memorable.

Created at the behest of a loose coalition of reformers, cattle ranchers, homesteaders, oil companies, and politicians, boarding schools were designed to foster the immediate assimilation of all American Indian tribes and nations. The motives of these groups were diverse, but generally all opposed Native American sovereignty and saw any occupation of tribes upon North American soil as an obstacle to social progress and financial gain. The most idealistic members of this group, like Carlisle Indian School founder Richard Henry Pratt, felt that, as human beings, Native Americans deserved not to be the victims of genocide, but instead needed to be eliminated culturally through a broad-based, institutionalized program of assimilation and education. Pratt initially hoped to complete this process in a single generation (Olson and Wilson 1984, 60–61).

Between 1880 and 1930, boarding school students, both girls and boys, experienced an extremely regimented life at boarding schools that included a rigidly enforced universal course of study, military marching, and uniforms, and an often brutal system of discipline. Students had their hair cut to standardized lengths, were sometimes given new names, and were allowed to speak no other language but English. Punishments for breaking rules were often harsh, involving heavy labor and sometimes physical beatings.

Recently, however, a number of scholars have used oral histories and documents generated from students to explore how Native Americans, in response to the specific contexts and conditions they experienced at boarding school, struggled to create their own cultural lives and identities. Brenda Child, Sally Hyer, Alice Littlefield, Tsianina Lomawaima, and Sally McBeth have created a body of scholarship that delves into the complex memories and emotions that former students have toward their boarding school lives. In spite of the brutality they faced, students often managed to negotiate and create new understandings of tradition and cultural autonomy while at school and often remember their lives as students with a complex set of mixed emotions (see Child 1993; Hyer 1990; Littlefield 1989; Lomawaima 1994; McBeth 1984).

School Sports and Youth Culture

The existence of relatively autonomous cultures among students at boarding schools constitutes one of the most significant findings by this group of historians. Lomawaima (1994)and Child(1993), for example, explored how students at Haskell in Lawrence, Kansas, and at Chilocco organized their own cultural lives around pranks, gangs, and the breaking of rules. Their research reveals insidious folklore among female students, male gangs that dominated peer relations, students fermenting and drinking their own alcohol, and even outright student rebellion.

Sports comprised a concrete site at boarding schools where students negotiated these cultures within the boundaries of their institutionalized lives. Alice Littlefield, in her oral history of students who attended the Mt. Pleasant Indian School in Michigan, argues that the historical position that American Indian students faced in boarding school made sports an important source of pride, one that ran counter to federal assimilationist ideologies. Through interviews, Littlefield found that former students, particularly males, had vivid memories of Mt. Pleasant competing successfully on the high school level in football and basketball, particularly of times when they beat non-Indian opponents. "Given the assimilationist aims of the BIA educational system, athletic prowess became a symbol of Indian identity and Indian pride." (Littlefield 1989, 438).

Littlefield's conclusions suggest that sports were a complex part of boarding school life, one that posed specific possibilities for Native American students to creatively reimagine their cultural memories, traditions, and identities. Given the institutionalized racism and ethnocentrism that guided boarding school policies, it is likely that students found ways to resist. At the same time, Littlefield's observations about sports being a site for expressions of resistance are unique, for they tend to conflict with what other scholars have observed about the relationship of school sports to youth and social reproduction.

School-sponsored athletics have been a vitally important part of the cultural construction of youth in the United States for over a century. Yet high school and college-level athletics have also not been a place that most cultural studies scholars have looked to find meaningful expressions of young people about their lives. Instead most critical work that has explored the relationships between school sports and youth cultures has illuminated how athletic competition fosters conservative values and behavioral norms. In his exploration of contemporary working-class culture, for example, Stanley Aronowitz argues that school operates as an institution of socialization for young people in capitalist societies, and that officially sponsored sports are part of this process. Analyzing working-class culture from a macrosocial perspective, Aronowitz associates school sports with high school, a stage in the educational process that replicates work. In contrast to the warmer, homelike atmosphere of elementary school, where creative play is more encouraged, high school classes are more regimented, there is no single home classroom, and students learn more instrumentalized ways of thinking and behaving. As part of this educational stage, play becomes serious competition in sports, and more voluntary forms of recreation, like intramurals, "are denigrated"(Aronowitz 1973, 76).

The process of transforming play into school sports is an important one, according to Aronowitz. Play is the one realm of life in capitalism that people can regard as their own, in which "the person sees him or herself in the object produced." Officially sponsored high school sports teams, however, alienate most people from participation in the game. Most students experience a high school sport as passive spectators. Aronowitz writes, "There can be no doubt that the process of maturation from childhood/youth to adulthood is signaled by people taking the role of spectator with increasing frequency, so much that they 'forget' that their activities produce all of social life" (Aronowitz 1973, 62–67).

Aronowitz's analysis provides an important interpretation of how school sports operate to regiment and rationalize the lives of young people within the broadly experienced structures of capitalist life. This was particularly important in the case of Indian boarding schools, where student life was highly oriented around discipline and regimentation. Aronowitz does not, however, account for the kind of responses to sports that Littlefield mentions, in which ethnic allegiance plays a role in the way an audience member identifies with a team.

Like Aronowitz, Douglas Foley has carefully examined school sports as an important cultural form in which young people "learn capitalist culture." Unlike Aronowitz, however, he approaches the topic from a microsocial perspective of a community study in which ethnicity plays a major role. In his ethnography of high school youth culture in a small town in southwestern Texas, Foley pays close attention to the high school football game, interpreting it as a community ritual. He carefully explores in detail the varying experiences that different peer groups and community members have with high school football—including band members, Anglo and Mexicano athletes, students considered "nerds" and "nobodies," business leaders, and rebellious male Mexicano subcultures. Although these groups interpret the football game in different ways, Foley sees it as more important to understand the event as a community ritual that ultimately reinforces patriarchal norms, race and class hierarchies, and militaristic values. By focusing on the event at that level, Foley exposes the limitations of sports as a vehicle for cultural resistance and instead reveals "the durability of the politically unprogressive cultural traditions that 'the people' find pleasurable and self-serving" (Foley 1990, 28–62, 200).

Foley's research provides an important interpretation of school sports, one that is sensitive to the multiple lines of gender, race, and class along which power relations are sustained in a community. He describes in detail how local businesses, Anglo community leaders, local boosters, and male citizens all invest heavily in making the football game a symbolic centerpiece of local life. As a cultural site for the expressions and emotions of young people, Foley understands sports as more of a rehearsal for proscribed adult roles than an imaginative vehicle through which alternatives are explored. He certainly documents moments when Mexicano athletes are able to express pride and strength through their sport in ways that express dissatisfaction with their social condition, just as Littlefield discovered such expressions among Indian boarding school students. However, as his quote illustrates, Foley also concludes that the ritual of the football game itself limits the extent to which such expressions might be translated into meaningful change.

Aronowitz and Foley provide discussions of high school athletics that call into question the extent to which, as Littlefield claims, memories of boarding school sports constitute resistance. Yet these authors also make it difficult to imagine how sports might have played a role in the lives of Native American boarding school students beyond that of social reproduction or assimilation. Such perspectives do not adequately explain the ways that Littlefield observed expressions of ethnic identity and pride being associated with memories of boarding school athletic heroics. Littlefield's oral histories reveal cultural codes that seem to support assimilation (sports like football) being used to express anti-assimilation sentiments. April Schultz has argued in her work on immigrant ethnicity that "historical evidence that seems to embrace Americanization can sustain alternative interpretations." In her study of ethnicity and assimilation among Norwegian immigrants, Schultz concludes that ethnic identities are a "process of identification at a particular moment to cope with historical realities," rather than fixed items that are either maintained or lost (Schultz 1991, 1267).

Patricia Albers and William James also have argued in their study of the Santee (Sioux) that ethnic identity is dynamic and changes over time. Albers and James see ethnic identity as a dialectic process in which people "differentiate and label themselves in relation to others" within the "concrete circumstances and dynamics of social relationships" that are present at a moment in history and that help define how groups are differentiated from one another (Albers and James 1986, 12). Popular culture is a location where this kind of dialectic process often takes place. George Lipsitz suggests that popular culture forms, of which one can include popular sports activities and events, are contradictory and multilayered, and can be understood as vehicles for recalling alternative memories from the past that exist in dialogue with the concrete conditions and possibilities that subjugated people face at any historic moment (Lipsitz 1990).[1]

Boxing became popular at Indian boarding schools during the 1930s. For many students it was a new sport, yet through it they developed a youth culture that made anti-assimilationist expressions of Native American identity possible.

Boxing and Life at Indian Boarding Schools during the 1930's

Early in the history of boarding schools, many Native American parents actively resisted sending their children away. By the 1930s, however, economic depression led many American Indian families to send their children to boarding school as a way of obtaining relief (McBeth 1984). Ironically, those who did end up at places like Chilocco or Haskell discovered a set of circumstances and possibilities for autonomous youth cultures that were freer than any others that had existed before at these institutions. In part, this had to do with reforms taking place within federal Indian educational policy.

In 1928, the Meriam Commission investigated life at boarding schools and issued a scathing report that expressed dismay over their conditions and curriculum. The report cited malnutrition due to lack of funds for food, and criticized the military routine, lack of time for free play and recreation, and the uniform curriculum that defined boarding school life. With the appointment of W. Carson Ryan as BIA director of education in 1930, and John Collier as Commissioner of Indian Affairs in 1933, the agency initiated many of the changes recommended by the report. Among other things, Ryan, advocated more respect for Native American cultures, more time for free recreation at schools, an outlaw of corporal punishment, and less emphasis on discipline. Ultimately, Collier focused the attention of federal Indian education policy upon building day schools located on reservations, and he hoped eventually to phase out the boarding school system altogether (Szasz 1977).[2]

Sports were an important institution that the Collier administration set out to reform within the system of off-reservation boarding schools. After the Meriam report, the Bureau of Indian affairs had begun to discourage boarding schools from using sports as a source of public relations. Earlier in the century, the Carlisle Indian School and Haskell Institute had fielded football teams that had competed successfully against the best college teams in the country. They had trained some of the greatest athletes of the early twentieth century, including Jim Thorpe, Hall of Fame baseball pitcher Charles Albert "Chief" Bender, and distance runner Louis Tewanima (Oxendine 1988). Other schools also competed successfully in sports such as track, girls basketball, and lacrosse. At the same time, however, sports were a source of controversy and embarrassment for boarding schools. Accusations of professionalism and corruption, for example, tainted the reputation of Carlisle's football team on a number of occasions between 1907 and 1918 (Bloom 1997). In 1932, on the eve of Collier's reign over the BIA, officials in Washington had begun to draw a stark contrast between a collegiate-level athletic system they saw as costly and exploitative, and a high school level athletic system that they saw as more in line with the goals of federal Indian educational policy. In a report to the Office of Indian Affairs on athletics at the Albuquerque Indian School, Harold Bentley used the occasion to contrast what he saw as a favorable high school system at Albuquerque with a more corrupt system that existed at Haskell (National Archives, Albuquerque). Collier went even further, discouraging school sports teams altogether in favor of more participatory recreational activities. The 1941 *Manual for the Indian School Service*, for example, states that "intramural athletics and games in which everybody has a chance to play shall be encouraged, rather than formal gymnastics or calisthenics or interscholastic athletic competition" (Bureau of Indian Affairs 1941, 26).

The reforms initiated by the Collier administration, as well as the changes in boarding schools brought about because of the Meriam Report, seem to have had an effect on football programs. Institutional changes, for example, that lowered the average age of boarding school students severely undercut the ability of highly visible teams to win against college competition. However, such policy changes did not eliminate interscholastic sports. In fact, they provided an institutional context for boxing to become a prominent sport at boarding schools, one that involved fewer costs than football and brought schools local, and even national, notoriety.

Boxing began at Chilocco in 1932 when a sports promoter from Wichita, Kansas, persuaded Superintendent Correll to field a team from Chilocco for an American Legion Tournament. Chilocco's team performed well even though it had been hastily trained. Only one year later, boxers from the school traveled to amateur tournaments as far away as Boston, and were celebrated on the pages of *Ring* magazine (Bradfield 1963, 122–123).

Boxing was popular not only at Chilocco, although it undoubtedly had the best and most famous team. Other Indian boarding schools also created popular boxing teams during the 1930s. Teams from Albuquerque, Haskell, Phoenix, and Santa Fe were quite successful, sending boxers to regional and national Amateur Athletic Union tournaments. Boarding schools fought against one another, but also competed with local colleges, high schools, and amateur boxing clubs.

In a relatively short time, one that coincided with a decline in the status of football, boxing emerged during the 1930s as one of the most important sports on Indian school campuses and a prominent aspect of boarding school life. Institutional changes partly explain why such a sport would grow in stature, but they offer an incomplete explanation. Boxing was also a sport that resonated with the lives of boarding school students. Changes in federal policy, school funding, and economic climate all were important to introducing boxing to boarding schools, but students developed and made meaning of the sport as an important part of their cultural lives. For example, Lomawaima writes that violent play, fights, and gangs were common at Chilocco among the male students. She argues that such behavior was, in fact, an expression of a more pervasively violent culture of discipline and authority that existed at boarding school. She writes: "Fighting to settle differences was common, an accepted method of working things out. Not surprisingly, the boxers were foremost among Chilocco's athletic teams. They won Golden Glove status and traveled to fights in Chicago and Madison Square Garden" (1994, 112–113). Oral history interviews that I conducted with former boarding school students support Lomawaima's observations. A Navajo man whom I interviewed who fought for the Santa Fe Indian School during the 1930s recalled that such an atmosphere motivated him to take up boxing. He remembered how the boys' adviser, a man named Stein, would beat the children with a strap for violating rules: "I used to think about the time when I grew up. I said, I'm going to be a fighter. I'm going to tangle with that Mr. Stein, the boys' adviser. But he left before then." If male students readily took to boxing as it became introduced into the boarding school athletic curriculum, then it is also true that the symbols and structures of amateur boxing during the 1930s helped to shape the kind of cultural expressions students would make through the sport. As Lomawaima indicates in her discussion of Chilocco's boxing team, boarding school fighters often competed at national amateur tournaments sponsored by the Amateur Athletic Union. In oral history interviews, former fighters and boarding school students often highlighted these events, even more than they did boxing matches that took place between boarding schools. Amateur Athletic Union tournaments usually took place in big cities, beginning with elimination matches in places such as Albuquerque or Wichita with winners advancing to a more general set of regional bouts in Kansas City or Denver, and ultimately to a national gathering in Chicago, New York, or Boston. These fights received national attention in newspapers. This particular structure of amateur boxing in the United States during the 1930s made the sport a particularly meaningful one, for it offered fighters an opportunity to get off campuses within which many former students often report feeling isolated. At AAU tournaments, fighters I interviewed told of the excitement they experienced performing upon a public stage. The man previously quoted, for example, told me of his experience fighting at an AAU tournament held in Chicago Stadium during the 1930s.

> *A:* It looked like Chicago was almost spending full time in the gymnasium hoping to . . . to . . . boys and men that were interested in boxing because they had one, two, three, four rings going all at one time.

> *Q:* Wow. And a lot of people watching.
> *A:* A lot of people watching, yeah . . . I think it is a big stadium there.

For some, such national tournaments provided a forum in which they could express a strong sense of pride, and within the sport of amateur boxing, this pride was often understood in terms of race. The urban contexts of AAU tournaments tended to blur together distinctions within groups, and fighters were often categorized within broadly defined terms of national identity. For example, when I asked the man previously quoted about ethnic groups against whom he fought, he replied, "The majority I think were black, with here and there Caucasians and very few Spanish." A different Navajo man who also fought for the Santa Fe Indian School during the 1930s expressed a sense of racial combat more explicitly. When I asked him why he was a successful fighter, he replied:

> I fought many a different people, like Anglo people, black people, you know, and boy I'm telling you, you put me in the . . . put my gloves on, I know for what I'm doing. You got the pride . . . if there's any race that's speaking different languages you got the pride to demonstrate that you going to be in there fighting . . . because you're an Indian, you going to show what an Indian can do. So that was always my intention, 'cause when I fought against a black, man, well . . . I fought.

Both Elliott Gorn and Jeffrey Sammons have written about the important symbolism that national and racial pride has had within the field of professional prize fighting. The idea that a fighter is a representative of one's race comprises a deep thread within the history of boxing in the United States (See Gorn 1986, Sammons 1988). Such ideas were also a part of the amateur boxing culture of the 1930s and early 1940s. One particularly ironic example appeared in the February 13, 1941, edition of the *Santa Fe New Mexican,* which reported that a "negro from Denver" and an "O'jibway Indian" would meet for the " 'white hope' trophy offered the heavyweight champion in the Rocky Mountain AAU Regional boxing tournament" ("Indian Meets Denver Negro" 1941).

At the same time, this kind of racial discourse surrounding boxing resonated with historically particular aspects of boarding school life that students experienced, especially the ideological contradictions that were an inherent aspect of the assimilating labor assigned to these institutions. The very notion of assimilation that had guided boarding school policies from their beginning had tended to connote the erasure of European ethnicity that would allow immigrants and their children a common privilege of white racial identity in American culture. Yet boarding schools, in their very definition of "Indian," constructed Native Americans as a "racial" category. Entry qualifications at schools had little to do with cultural background, but instead were based upon blood quantum. In this manner, boarding schools simultaneously forced assimilation while denying its possibility. This contradiction characterized the earliest uses of athletics at Carlisle and Haskell. Their teams provided schools with a visible source of public relations that validated the government-run boarding school mission for white audiences. Football and track teams that competed successfully allowed boarding school advocates to show that Indians could be successfully "Americanized." At the same time, sports drew heightened attention to the players themselves as biologically defined racial "others" (Churchill, Hill, and Barlow 1979; Malmsheimer 1985).

Amateur boxing during the 1930s provided a stage upon which racial identities could become appropriated by boarding school students as a source of pride. However, this is not necessarily to say that it erased cultural differences between students. As Lomawaima points out, students at Chilocco were very conscious of their tribal languages and identities. In addition, they divided themselves along a variety of other lines, including race (all students, she writes, were aware of those who had African lineage), geographical origin, gender, religion, age, vocation, and even athletic skill (Lomawaima 1994, 125). In fact, the Navajo man who was previously quoted as framing his own involvement in boxing in terms of racial pride also associated prowess in different sports with particular tribal identities. He drifted into this discussion during our interview after I asked if he was ever allowed to speak his native language at school.

> Different tribes of Indians came to school here, and any number of, say like over twenty different-speaking Indians, languages are spoken here that represent different, from different parts of the United States. So that's what they were. Why they have, some are interested in playing basketball . . . well they used to have a basketball team, they travel different places, you know. And they play good teams. . . . And then again there are these track teams at, some of those Indians, oooh my. They get some of the fastest runners. You know, like, they have, uh, the state record. There was, uh, that would represent them, like, uh, Kia Begay, no Key Begay. . . . He was a Navajo. He was a fine runner. Nobody could beat that man.

Historian Joe Sando, a Santa Fe Indian School graduate, echoed this relationship between athletic skill and tribal origin during an interview I conducted with him. He told me, "I guess some of the basketball players came from South Dakota because they were taller and there were mixed breeds" (Sando 1995). These testimonials suggest that boxing provided a context for the prideful expression of pan-Indian identities among boarding school students that were made possible because of the particular circumstances that surrounded amateur fighting during the 1930s. However, it also suggests that such expressions coexisted alongside a continued awareness of diversity among students, and did not necessarily represent a stage within a linear process of assimilation.

In addition, not all students experienced the sport of boxing at Indian schools primarily as a vehicle through which they expressed racial pride. The pleasures associated with boxing matches as social events are also important for understanding their significance to students, administrators, and government officials. Students who were not boxers recall how fights were exciting, fun-filled events that people looked forward to each week. Importantly, they were events that girls and boys could attend together, and at which they could intermingle and express excitement.

This type of social event was particularly important to students, in part because sexuality was highly regulated at boarding schools. Females and males were often segregated at meal times, in their curriculum, and in classrooms, and dating was often carefully monitored. During the 1930s, schools tended to allow more time for free interaction between boys and girls, but there were still important gender boundaries that remained in place. For example, the Haskell Institute's information bulletin for the 1940–41 school year reflects a heavy emphasis upon vocational labor for both females and males. However, the school selected very different vocational tracks for each. For girls, the school offered courses in home economics, secretarial skills, and child care. Their education reflected powerfully a Victorian ideology of domesticity in which women were responsible for the moral character of the family and home. For example, an entire section of the curriculum, entitled "Social and Personal Development," was directed entirely at female students. Under this category of courses, girls took classes in "Hygiene" and "Family Relationships" that were intended to prepare them for their domestic role. Under "Hygiene," the bulletin reads,

> This course purports to give the student a clear understanding of the relationship of good health to attractiveness and success, to show her the responsibility she must accept in helping her family to realize good health habits, and to train her in the care of the sick and to give her a knowledge of simple first aid methods. (*Information Bulletin* 1940–41, 59)

Similarly, the course entitled "Family Relationships" instructed female students in, "correct family relationships from the standpoint of individual development and adjustment in the home. The traits which go to make up good family citizenship are studied. The emphasis falls on the girl's responsibilities and duties in creating a happy home of her own after her marriage" (*Information Bulletin* 1940–41, 59–60). This kind of curriculum illustrates how important a domestic ideology was to the education that Native American students received in boarding school. Wendy Kozol, in her study of *Life* magazine, illustrates that female domesticity would become a central component of national ideology during the Cold War, associating heterosexist norms, privatism, and a gendered division of labor where a woman's primary responsibilities would rest within the home along with patriotism and national loyalty (Kozol 1994, 53). The curriculum revealed by this document from Haskell espouses these values by assuming women will become married, locating values and duties of citizenship in the home, placing responsibility for family and home entirely upon females, and associating all of these behavioral norms with assimilation.

In oral history interviews I have conducted, both female and male former students often have discussed regulations placed upon the behavior of female students. They also report how they engaged in mischievous behavior that surrounded dating, or the breaking of rules related to the regulation of sexuality (Bloom 1997). Weekly boxing matches on campus were an opportunity for the interaction between girls and boys during their leisure time. They were events that involved excitement and intense emotional expression. A woman who attended the Santa Fe Indian School during the 1930s, interviewed for the documentary *Santa Fe Indian School: A Remembrance*, remembered the boxing team fondly: "These boys were very good. Our boys were very good. And I never thought I'd like boxing, but I really enjoyed it then. The whole school attended" (Reyna and SFIS students 1990). It is appropriate that the woman quoted in the Santa Fe Indian School video should feel somewhat contradictory about boxing. On the one hand, the sport itself is a brutal one that elevates violence and masculine power in ways that translate to real oppressions women face at the hands of men. Simultaneously, however, the social atmosphere that boxing provided mirrors what Kathy Peiss describes as the turn from homosocial private spaces to heterosocial public spaces associated with urban popular culture forms for women at the turn of the century. The Victorian family model of the nineteenth century allowed for very little public interaction between men and women, relegating public space a male "homosocial" arena, and private spaces of the home predominantly female homosocial locations. Commercial popular culture forms, however, allowed women to gain access to public space, albeit in ways that were dependent upon commerce and male companionship (Peiss 1986).

For both male and female students, boxing matches were public events. Even when they took place on campus, they sometimes attracted fans from surrounding communities. This was perhaps most true at Chilocco. A man who attended Chilocco during the 1930s, and later went on to coach there, remembered:

> At Chilocco, the people would come from miles around for that boxing. There's something about it, about boxing. It's kind of like gambling, I guess, people were *crazy* about it! Boy, they just packed that gym. Just packed it up. . . . It was just those ranchers from over around Powhuska, and people from Wichita, Kansas, and people from Tulsa would come up for it. That's a hundred miles, you know. Back then, that was about a three or four hour drive. But they'd come up there and just pack that gym.

The first man quoted who fought for Santa Fe remembered that the atmosphere at the Chilocco gym was especially electric. He recalled that the arena was so filled with smoke that his lungs hurt after the fight. At other schools, mostly students and faculty were in the stands, but as the testimony from the Santa Fe Indian School graduate illustrates, they were no less enthusiastic in their support for their team. The crowd, however, was not only something that created pleasure for students and townspeople, and undoubtedly revenue for promoters and school administrators, it was a source of concern for federal officials throughout the history of boxing at Indian boarding schools.

The BIA long opposed boxing as a sport for boarding schools, and eventually banned it as a form of athletic activity in 1948. Their rationale included a discussion of the crowd. In an article published in *Indian Education* announcing the ban, BIA director of health, Fred Foard, and the agency director of education, Willard W. Beatty, wrote, "There is still an animal-like ferocity in many of us, which accounts for attendance at prize fights, wrestling matches, midget auto races and other spectacles where life is endangered or where sadistic punishment is inflicted" (Foard and Beatty 1948). The authors of this statement importantly align boxing with a range of working-class amusements popular during the 1930s, 1940s, and 1950s. Such a concern is appropriate, for the educational curriculum at boarding schools trained students for working-class occupations. According to Joe Sando,

> The policy of the Bureau was that our parents did not have the financial standing to afford college for us. Consequently college was never promoted or we were never told that here was such a thing as a chance to go to college, so they taught us the trades because they figured that instead of becoming farmers when we went home, we would be able to use some of the things that we learned there back home you know as cabinet

> makers, carpenters, electricians, plumbers, and cement finishers. (Reyna and SFIS students 1990)

In his 1935 letter to Chilocco superintendent Correll in criticizing the school's emphasis on boxing, John Collier defined the mission of Indian boarding schools in a way that confirms Sando's observation. Collier wrote:

> I believe in athletic training of all sorts for the students in our vocational schools, but you must keep in mind that their vocational education is the primary object of their attendance and that athletic contests with teams from various parts of the country are of secondary importance and must not be permitted to interfere with their vocational training. (National Archives, Chilocco)

The language of concern in both the announcement of the boxing ban and in Collier's letter suggests that some officials in the BIA considered the kind of pleasure gained at a boxing match a misuse of leisure time that, at best, was unproductive and, at worst, evoked images of savagery. Certainly, officials in Washington were concerned about their liability with regard to the health of students. As the man who used to coach at Chilocco said to me, "It is kind of a peculiar sport. It's the only sport they have where you're trying to hurt your opponent." Yet this same man also remembered from his days as a student that the crowd, while enthusiastic, never was violent or out of control: "There never was any, any problems that I ever heard of. You know, anybody ever getting in scrapes or anything. They just enjoyed it, and then they, when it was over they went home. And the kids all went back to the dorms. But we never had any problems." Rather than being based on actual incidents of unruly behavior by boxing crowds at boarding school fights, the institutional rhetoric against boxing suggests that BIA officials were very concerned with controlling and making "productive" the culture that students generated during their leisure time. The reforms of the 1930s gave students a great deal more time to themselves than they had ever had at boarding schools, but this also created possibilities for autonomous cultures, mischief, and actions by students outside the direct supervision of teachers and administrators. Students at Indian boarding schools like Chilocco constantly received messages and lessons about using their leisure time productively in and out of the classroom. Whether they were female and therefore learning domestic labor skills, or male and learning a vocation, the overall lesson they were learning was how to live in a "modern" society. Chilocco's school newspaper, *The Indian School Journal*, contained numerous articles advising students on proper behavior at movie theaters or at plays, on how best to spend leisure time, and on how to select a good movie.

Often, articles discussed sports in this manner. Editorials, for example, heralded the virtues of sportsmanship and teamwork. A 1939 column even associated boxing with "productive" virtues. It reads:

> A boxer's life is not all limelight and glory. In fact it is hard work in training for a bout, that carries him through. . . . It takes stamina, pluck, and perseverance to go through those hard rounds of fighting. When he steps into the ring he not only thinks of himself but of the color under which he is fighting. Red and White of Chilocco! (*Indian School Journal* 1939, 8)

Even though this writer defends boxing as productive and consistent with the most conservative values associating sports with a Protestant work ethic and school patriotism, she or he acknowledges the other, pleasurable, decadent side of boxing by writing, "A boxer's life is not all limelight and glory."

In fact, concerns over the control of student cultural expression led to a number of programs initiated as reforms during the 1930s that showed a respect toward Native American cultures in ways that had not been seen before. At boarding schools and in Native American communities, this new attitude took a number of different forms. At the Santa Fe Indian School, for example, art educator Dorothy Dunn began an Indian arts program in which students were encouraged to explore their histories through traditional expressions such as pottery and weaving, as well as other artistic forms like painting (Hyer 1990). Narcisco Abeyta, the well-known Navajo painter (and, incidentally, Golden Gloves boxer) was but one student who was able to take advantage of this program and build an art career as a result of his education.

Yet it is important to keep in mind the conservative implications of many such programs when considering the popularity and problems that boxing generated during this decade. Before the Meriam Report, boarding school administrators tended to favor a strict assimilationist approach to education, in large part cutting students off completely from their ethnic traditions and cultural memories. Although programs such as the Indian arts school at Santa Fe contrast with this approach, they also attempted to recuperate Native American traditions in the service of a progressive set of assimilationist goals. In other words, if boarding schools had been built at the turn of the century to assimilate Native American children by eradicating their memory of Native American ethnicity and history, federal policy during the 1930s attempted to use cultural memory to enlist and legitimate a nationalist ideology.

An example of this strategy was the Gallup Indian Ceremonial in August 1938. The ceremonial consisted of exhibits featuring "authentic Indian-made goods" from the southwestern Pueblos that the BIA had encouraged Indians to develop into marketable products. The agency's monthly magazine, *Indians at Work*, featured a photo of one such exhibit which illustrated the uses of such items in the decor of the "modern home." This represents a significant change from earlier policies that positioned Native American culture and traditions as incompatible with middle-class norms and values. In this case, the Indian ceremonial presented Pueblo arts and traditions as entirely compatible with middle-class tastes, commodity buying, and family living. The Bureau seemed to be enlisting one form of Native American cultural memory to establish federal leadership and commodity capitalism as legitimate markers of progress, as represented by the "modern home" ("Pueblo Art in the Modern Home" 1939).

George Lipsitz has argued that, within popular culture, ethnic memories have often been used to establish the legitimacy of new social arrangements built around consumption, making individualistic acquisition and consumption seem consistent with "traditional values." Yet he also argues that evoking such memory invites counterinterpretations of the present drawn from the textured experiences of the past. There is always the potential that drawing from memory might not transform values, but instead recall a past that can be used to understand the present and future critically rather than ahistorically (Lipsitz 1990, 39–75). Although the Bureau of Indian Affairs was ultimately conservative in the way that it encouraged expressions of ethnic memory, such memories created the possibility for critically understanding the present. For example, the Indian arts program at the Santa Fe Indian School would, in 1962, become the Institute for American Indian Arts in Santa Fe, a training ground for a number of Native American artists who would provide a strong critical vision of contemporary Native American life in the United States by drawing upon the histories experienced by indigenous peoples in the Americas (Mellick and Shutes 1996).

Whether or not boxing drew upon historical memory for its appeal among students is open to argument. However, it did grow to become a popular sport, one seemingly at odds with federal aims to direct productively the cultural life of students, at the very time that the Bureau of Indian Affairs was allowing students to express themselves as ethnically connected to diverse and historically significant nations. The huge popularity of the sport among students, as well as its strong association with pride and pleasure rooted in the common historic experiences of Native American people, suggests that for some, boxing made it possible to understand expressions of cultural memory in diverse ways.

At the very least, BIA policies themselves during the 1930s often invited critical interpretations. In an essay in the May 15, 1933, edition of *Indians at Work*, Collier criticized "planless individualism" that guided allotment policies of the previous generation. He advocated "planned cooperative use of the land and its resources." Yet this was also placed within the context of a more general patriotic agenda. Such policies on reservations, wrote Collier, "unquestionably will blaze the way on many tracks for the vaster experiment and readjustment, now being started, which is intended to bring about a rebirth of the American people—a rebirth in spirit, even more than the rebirth of a more fairly distributed prosperity" (Collier 1933, 3). This early statement evokes a radically egalitarian vision of social relations drawn from the historical memory of many Native American groups even as it places this vision ("more fairly distributed prosperity") into secondary importance to the national pride that Collier hoped it would foster.

Collier's early criticism of boxing is somewhat typical of other elitist criticisms of sports and popular culture as nonproductive and nonserious. Perhaps at stake with the passions boxing evoked, however, were some very serious issues regarding the control that the federal government could expect to have over Native Americans in the future. The popular appeal of boxing matches drew upon historical memory and identity in ways that were not entirely consistent with the productive, progressive ideology that continued to guide boarding schools through the 1930s and into the 1940s and much of the 1950s. Even when they encouraged the expression of Native American identities and cultures on campuses, the Bureau of Indian Affairs portrayed indigenous life as a static heritage, something that was a part of the past but no longer relevant in the present.

Through the youth culture that students experienced and created within boxing, however, their cultures, histories, and identities came alive in ways that spoke to their conditions in the present, be they continuing tribal differences or common experiences of racial discrimination and disenfranchisement. In addition, the culture surrounding boxing spoke to the ways that gender and class identities intersected with those of race and ethnicity. Boxing may have been a violent and exploitative sport, but it was one that students also took and of which they made meaning for themselves in ways that spoke to the conditions they experienced. In the words of the Santa Fe boxer whom I interviewed who successfully fought his way to the national AAU tournament, "When you're in condition for boxing, you sway with the punches. That's a skill that you develop as a fighter."

NOTES

Primary research for this article was conducted under a year long fellowship from the American Council of learned Societies during 1994–1995. I also would like to thank Julia Renquist for helping to arrange an important group interview with graduates of the Pipestone and Flandreau boarding schools, as well as all of the others who shared their memories and time with me during interviews, but wished not to be identified.

1. Lipsitz understands rock and roll music during the early post-World War II era as an example of popular culture's dialogic possibilities at a given historic moment. Rock and roll became a cultural forum through which a new, multi-ethnic, youth culture emerged. It certainly spoke to the alienation that many white, middle-class youths experienced in newly built suburbs, but it also was made possible because of specific historic conditions of poorer and non-white Americans: migrations of African Americans and Latinos to urban areas in the United States who infused their music and cultural expressions into popular music, the rapid growth of a consumer economy, an expanding recording industry aided by new technologies, and the increasingly central position of commercial broadcasting through television and radio in the daily lives of young people. These conditions not only allowed white, middle-class youths to enjoy a new form of entertainment, they created a diverse alternative to mainstream culture in the United States that was in dialogue with the textured experiences and histories of African-Americans, Latinos, and other underrepresented ethnic groups.

2. It is important to note that Collier was not successful at ending boarding schools, and in fact some remain open today. The BIA was successful during this time period, however, in shifting the emphasis of Indian education toward on-reservation day schools.

REFERENCES

Albers, P. C. and W. R. James. 1986. "On the Dialectics of Ethnicity: To Be or Not to Be Santee (Sioux)." *Journal of Ethnic Studies* 4 (1), 1–27.

Aronowitz, Stanley. 1973. *False Promises: The Shaping of American Working Class Consciousness.* New York: McGraw-Hill.

Bloom, John. 1997. " 'Show What an Indian Can do': Sports, Memory, and Ethnic Identity at Federal Indian Boarding Schools." *Journal of American Indian Education.* Forthcoming.

Bradfield, Larry. 1963. "A History of Chilocco Indian School." Master's thesis, University of Oklahoma.

Bureau of Indian Affairs. 1941. *Manual for the Indian School Service.* Washington, D.C.: U.S. Government Printing Office.

Child, Brenda. 1993. "A Bitter Lesson: Native Americans and the Government Boarding School Experience, 1890–1940." Ph.D. diss., University of Iowa.

Churchill, Ward, N. S. Hill, and M. J. Barlow. 1979. "An Historical Overview of Twentieth Century Native American Athletics." *The Indian Historian* 12 (4), 22–32.

Collier, John. 1933. "At the Close of Ten Weeks." *Indians at Work*, 15 September, 1–5.

Foard, F, and W. Beatty. 1948. "Boxing Not an Approved Sport." *Indian Education 171*, 15 November.

Foley, Douglas. 1990. *Learning Capitalist Culture: Deep in the Heart of Tejas*. Philadelphia: University of Pennsylvania Press.

Gorn, Elliott. 1986. *The Manly Art: Bare Knuckle Prize Fighting In America*. Ithaca, NY: Cornell University Press.

Hyer, Sally. 1990. *One House, One Voice, One Heart: Native American Education at the Santa Fe Indian School*. Santa Fe: Museum of New Mexico Press.

"Indian Meets Denver Negro." 1941. *The Santa Fe New Mexican*, 13 February.

Indian School Journal. 1939. 27 January.

Information Bulletin for Haskell Institute. 1940–41. Kansas Collection.

Kozol, Wendy. 1994. *Life's America*. Philadelphia: Temple University Press.

Lipsitz, George. 1990. *Time Passages: Collective Memory and American Popular Culture*. Minneapolis: University of Minnesota Press.

Littlefield, Alice. 1989. "The BIA Boarding School: Theories of Resistance and Social Reproduction." *Humanity and Society 13(4)*, 428–441.

Lomawaima, K. Tsianina. 1994. *They Called it Prairie Light: The Story of Chilocco Indian School*. Lincoln: University of Nebraska Press.

Malmsheimer, Lonna. 1985. " 'Imitation White Man': Images of Transformation at the Carlisle Indian School." *Studies in Visual Communication 11*, 54–75.

McBeth, Sally J. 1984. *Ethnic Identity and the Boarding School Experience of West-Central Oklahoma American Indians*. New York: University Press of America.

Mellick, Jill, and Jeane Shutes. 1996. *The Worlds of P'otsunu: Gernomima Cruz Montoya of San Juan Pueblo*. Albuquerque: University of New Mexico Press.

National Archives, Record Group 75. Decimal Classification 750 for Albuquerque.

———. Record Group 75. Decimal Classification 750 for Chilocco, Letters Received.

Olson, James, and Raymond Wilson. 1984. *Native Americans in the Twentieth Century*. Champaign, IL: University of Illinois Press.

Oxendine, Joseph. 1988. *American Indian Sports Heritage*. Champaign, IL: Human Kinetics Books.

Peiss, Kathy. 1986. *Cheap Amusements: Working Women and Leisure in Turn-of-the-Century New York*. Philadelphia: Temple University Press.

"Pueblo Art in the Modern Home." 1939. *Indians at Work*. April.

Reyna, D., and SFIS students (producer and director). 1990. *Santa Fe Indian School: A Remembrance*. Film. (Available from the Santa Fe Indian School, 1501 Cerrillos Rd., Santa Fe, New Mexico 87502.)

Sammons, Jeffrey. 1988. *Beyond the Ring: The Role of Boxing in American Society*. Urbana: University of Illinois Press.

Sando, Joe. 1995. Interview. Albuquerque, New Mexico, 10 January.

Schultz, April. 1991. " 'The Pride of the Race Had Been Touched': The 1925 Norse-American Immigration Centennial and Ethnic Identity." *Journal of American History 77 (4)* 1265–1295.

Szasz, Margaret Connell. 1977. *Education and the American Indian: The Road to Self-Determination since 1928*. Albuquerque: University of New Mexico Press.

Chapter Five

The Deanna Durbin Devotees
Fan Clubs and Spectatorship

Georganne Scheiner

In 1941, Hedwig Federowicz of Rhode Island wrote to *Deanna's Diary*, the official magazine of the Deanna Durbin fan club: "Like millions of girls I have grown to love Deanna more than just a child star . . . but now as a grown actress . . . I have attended operas, balls, visited an emperor, worn beautiful clothes . . . not in reality, but by living through each and every Durbin picture."[1] Durbin's fans found comfort and meaning in her screen characterizations. Her films presented them an opportunity to make sense of the depression, of World War II, and more often, of their own identities as young women in relation to normative definitions of gender that prescribed a narrow range of legitimate female behavior.

While often depicted as a savior in her films, Durbin actually played that role in real life. Deanna Durbin has been credited with single-handedly saving Universal Studios from bankruptcy. Although that claim is exaggerated, her film grosses accounted for 17 percent of the studio's entire revenue in the late thirties, and her presence attracted some major stars to Universal. Within a year of her screen debut in 1937, Durbin had completely eclipsed the other major stars of the period, including Shirley Temple and Jane Withers, to become one of the biggest box office stars of the period. In 1939, at the eleventh annual Academy Awards, Durbin received a special, miniature Oscar for "bringing to the screen the spirit and personification of youth, and as a juvenile player, setting a high standard of ability and achievement."[2]

Like an earlier "America's Sweetheart," Mary Pickford, Durbin was really a Canadian. She was born Edna Mae Durbin in 1921 in Winnipeg, Canada, to British parents. The Durbins moved to Los Angeles when Edna Mae was a baby. Her singing talent was apparent from an early age. While performing in a recital in 1936, she was spotted by an MGM talent scout and signed to an optional contract. While at MGM, her name was changed to Deanna and she was teamed with newcomer Judy Garland in a short, *Every Sunday*. Her option was dropped, and it was soon picked up by Universal. Her early film career at Universal was guided by producer Joe Pasternak and director Henry Kosters, who oversaw her first feature film in 1937, *Three Smart Girls*. Her film career was relatively brief, spanning the next eleven years.[3] In 1948, when her contract with Universal was up, Durbin embarked on an extended stay in France. She was only twenty-seven but already had two failed marriages behind her and an infant daughter. In France, Durbin refused all film offers, choosing instead to live modestly in Paris. In 1950 she married French film director Charles Henri David. Madame David and her husband settled in a Paris suburb, had a son, and she has lived with her family in relative obscurity ever since.[4]

Durbin's career spanned the depression and the Second World War, and her screen characterizations not only register the conflicts of both periods but they also begin to explain her appeal to both adolescent girls who would join her fan clubs, and their parents. For young girls, her portrayals of independent young women during the depression may have communicated an expanded and empowered definition of teenage femininity. For adults her portrayal of family devotion and filial piety during the war may have assuaged fears of juvenile delinquency and simultaneously promoted consensus for the war effort. There is an important change in her film roles from the thirties to the forties, partly owing to her own maturation. I will return to these changes later by focusing on two representative films, *100 Men and a Girl* (1937) and *It Started with Eve* (1941).

The Deanna Durbin Devotees, which was begun in 1937 after Universal had released only one of her feature films, *Three Smart Girls*, became one of the largest international fan clubs, with over three hundred chapters around the world. There are still active chapters today, particularly in Great Britain, where they are known as the Deanna Durbin Society. The original Deanna Durbin Fan Club was founded by four teenaged girls, Marguerite Slaney, May Blockwell, Ann Inman, and Marian Jentz. Shortly after its inception, the fan club had enough support to publish *Deanna's Journal*, a mimeographed newsletter that featured biographical notes, editorial comments by its founders, and profiles of Durbin's family members. In 1938 a *Life* magazine feature on Durbin generated a number of enthusiastic fan letters. One of the letter writers, Jay Gordon, became somewhat of a celebrity himself when he wrote to the editors, "Thanks a million for the liveliest picture ever printed in life—that full page photograph of Deanna Durbin. I'm framing it and redecorating my room around that picture." Gordon received hundreds of letters and decided to form his own fan club, the Deanna Durbin Devotees, which eventually merged with the original club. Because of Gordon's promotional skills, the Devotees soon enjoyed their own feature article in *Life* in a profile that detailed club activities.[5]

Universal Studio was very supportive of the undertaking, including supplying funding for the publication of the fan club's journal, and giving a small stipend to Gordon and other club officers. The studio also gave club officers and reporters unlimited entree to Durbin and often allowed them on the set to watch her work. This was a real change from the 1920s in the studio's attitudes toward fan clubs, which had been quite unpopular with studio administrators and were generally considered a nuisance. Fan mail was a costly burden in terms of having to answer and to send back photos. Fan club organizers were not even allowed within the studio gates. By 1934, the situation began to change as studios realized that fans constituted useful pressure groups on local theater owners through which to sell their films via block bookings. Fan clubs were also a free form of publicity. One of the Devotee's most important contacts at Universal was Kathleen Ehlen, who was the head of the fan mail department. She gave the club assistance in securing possible names for membership as well as fan letters, photographs, and other publicity material. Ehlen estimated that Durbin generated about three thousand letters a week.[6]

Although she is largely forgotten in the United States today, Deanna Durbin was one of the major box office stars of the late thirties to late forties.[7] She is unique in that she was one of the few stars to bridge the gap successfully between adolescence and young adulthood on screen. Moreover, adoration of Deanna generated a huge number of fan-driven texts. She is also significant, because, unlike other adult film stars with huge fan followings, Durbin was the same age as many of her fans. She was not only a role model, but a cohort. The age factor is important in examining her appeal and in the role fandom played in identity formation. The Devotees and the cultural texts they produced become a useful venue for examining the historical discourse of fandom. Being members of fan clubs was not only a way in which adolescent girls organized their social lives, but fan membership also constituted a specific form of cultural expression. This chapter will focus on adolescent fans and their cultural texts, specifically the journals published by the Deanna Durbin Devotees. I am primarily interested in the social aspect of fandom, in the girls' relationships not only to the star, but to one another. Fan clubs comprise communities of spectators, joined together by a particular pleasure in consumption, a pleasure that extends beyond the moviegoing context. Female fans created cultural products through which they could explore dimensions of female identity that went beyond societal definitions of gender.

Deanna Durbin and the Historical Spectator

Before examining the meanings that adolescent fans created around Durbin, it is important to understand that her characterizations spoke to the specific material conditions of the 1930s and 1940s. Durbin's film portrayals complicate ideas about female spectators advanced by feminist film critics. Her appeal cannot be explained by theories of spectatorship that conceptualize the female spectator as ahistorical and passive. In fact, Durbin's appeal might have been so great precisely because her screen characterizations were often bold, assertive, autonomous young women in control of their circumstances and actively participating in civic life.

One of the most contentious debates among feminist film theorists has been how to conceptualize the female spectator. Laura Mulvey began the debate in 1975 in her essay, "Visual Pleasure and Narrative Cinema." Drawing on Freudian, psychoanalytic theory and Lacanian structuralism, Mulvey argued that in classical Hollywood cinema, the female object is positioned to be voyeuristically consumed by the male spectator. Women in film exist to be looked at, thus spectatorship is essentially a male prerogative. In the 1980s, using Mulvey's work as a springboard, theoreticians began to conceptualize the female spectator. Most theoretical paradigms offer a model of a passive, fixed, female spectator who is controlled by the text.[8] The debate persists, but there is still no real agreement as to what actually constitutes the female spectator. Mary Ann Doane distinguished between this ambiguous, psychologically constructed spectator and the "real" spectator when she argued, "I have never thought of the female spectator as synonymous with the woman sitting in front of the screen, munching her popcorn. . . . The female spectator is a concept, not a person." Yet it seems to me that historians must be primarily concerned not with concepts, but with the women sitting in darkened Bijous, munching their popcorn. As Judith Stacey argues:

> Devoid of sociality and historicity, the spectator has often been seen to be a subject position produced by the visual and narrative conventions of a film text, and assumed to respond to it in particular ways due to the universal workings of the female psyche. The women in the cinema audience have been virtually absent from consideration within much feminist film theory, and the model of female spectatorship has been criticized for its ahistoricism and lack of details to contextual specificities.[9]

Before we consider the spectating positions of Durbin's fans, perhaps it would be useful to examine two of her representative screen characterizations of the thirties and forties, because these characterizations do not portray women as passive and therefore do not position women spectators as passive, either.

A typical Durbin film is *100 Men and a Girl*, released in 1938. Durbin plays Patsy Cardwell, the daughter of an unemployed musician (Adolphe Menjou), who must convince the noted conductor, Leopold Stokowski, to conduct her father's orchestra of unemployed musicians. Early in the film, Patsy stumbles into a society party, where she instructs the rich folks about the plight of the out-of-work musicians. The hostess, Mrs. Frost (Alice Brady), makes an off-hand comment that she will ask her industrialist husband (Eugene Palatte) to sponsor an orchestra of the unemployed on his radio show, but she leaves for Europe without informing her husband of her promise. In the meantime, Patsy has assembled the musicians, giving them hope of employment. She becomes the organizer, agent, manager, and promoter. Frost initially refuses to honor his wife's promise, but he later concedes that he might reconsider if they can get a famous conductor. Patsy must overcome numerous obstacles to convince the great Stokowski to conduct, including assembling the orchestra in his foyer, where, moved by their playing, he begins to conduct them in Liszt's *Second Hungarian Rhapsody*. Patsy, the adolescent girl, has single-handedly engineered the employment of one hundred men. During the concert finale of the film, Stokowski brings her on stage for an "impromptu and unrehearsed" aria from *La Traviota*, thus insuring not only the orchestra's success, but her own as well.

I would like to situate this film in relation to the work of Lary May, who has challenged the dominant view of historians who argue that a "constant commitment to liberal capitalism and consumerism informed the popular arts from the 1930s through the 1950s." Instead, May concludes that the "American Way" was really not formed until World War II. May challenges the vision of Hollywood as a monolithic entity that produced a "classic American cinema." Instead, May sees Hollywood as part of a "competitive civic sphere" where myths, symbols, and national ideologies were contested. When Hollywood films are explored as an arena of competing ideologies, May finds a significant number of films critical of the "American Way." But films critical of the status quo were not the only films made during the 1930s. Certainly, there were numerous other films that "promoted escapism and reinforced the myths and symbols of liberal individualism and conformity." Yet, as May posits, films critical of the "American Way" were films that featured coalitions of class, ethnic, and sometimes racial difference. Such films did not champion an American consensus, an overriding deference to authority, business, or the state. Films of the thirties that preserved class and ethnic differences showed groups "tied together in reciprocal social environments." Films of the 1930s that challenged established "American" values did not privilege authority, but rather portrayed mutual cooperation and reciprocity, which in turn preserved class, ethnic, and regional differences.[10]

100 Men and a Girl was clearly critical of the status quo, particularly the role of big business. The gravelly voice of Palatte is in sharp contrast to the melodious tones of Durbin and her orchestra. He is the heartless industrialist motivated by money, with little thought for human suffering. Moreover, he remains unmoved by the entreaties of the darling Patsy, further proof that he is not worthy of deference. *100 Men and a Girl* features a reciprocal cross-ethnic coalition of musicians who meld together to form an orchestra, and a cross-class alliance between the unemployed and the rich. Patsy is an empowered, autonomous adolescent girl who asserts her independence not in the domestic sphere, but in the public sphere. Durbin's film characterizations of the late thirties have much in common with those of Shirley Temple in terms of her being a savior who fosters cross-class coalitions, which either implicitly or explicitly critique the rich, the state, or big business. The difference is that Durbin employs high culture, while Temple employs popular culture, whose characters were more often associated with the vernacular.[11]

There does appear to be a change from cross-class alliances to consensus in Durbin's films of the 1940s. Perhaps it was her high culture status which made a switch to patriotic support of consensus possible. By the early forties, Durbin's roles also began to change as she matured from a child star to an ingenue, and though she could no longer be depicted as a child savior, she was still working miracles. A representative film is *It Started With Eve*, made in 1941. Although the film was released shortly before the United States entered World War II, there are still signs of a change toward consensus. As May argues, films of the forties labeled thirties' counternarratives of difference as subversive. Many 1940s films featured plots where a character underwent a conversion from an animosity toward the state/big business to a deference for authority and organized institutions that subordinated "class and ethnic consciousness," on the one hand, to patriotic effort in service to the nation, on the other. There was a shift from the critical stance of reciprocity to a rejection of that stance in favor of patriotic conformity. Although these forties films of consensus still featured ethnic, racial, class, and regional differences, these differences were melted into a common American consensus.[12]

Such is the case in *It Started With Eve*, whose plot turns on a case of mistaken identity. As rich industrialist Jonathan Reynolds (Charles Laughton) lays dying, his last request of his playboy son, Johnny (Bob Cummings), who has been in Mexico on vacation, is to meet his new fiancee. Unfortunately, she is not immediately available, and with time at a premium, Johnny finds a quick replacement in the hatcheck girl at the hotel, Anne Terry (Durbin). The elder Reynolds is instantly taken with the young woman, and instead of dying, he makes a full recovery, forcing Johnny and Anne to continue the charade.

Anne is initially disdainful of the upper-class patrons who frequent her hotel, as she complains that they are "diming her to death." She is clearly not intimidated or impressed with the wealth of the Reynoldses. Yet, unlike Eugene Palatte in *100 Men and a Girl*, Laughton's Reynolds is the industrialist without the sting. Inside this gruff curmudgeon is a pussycat, whose role is simply to show Johnny and Anne they were made for each other. From Anne's initial disdain for the rich there is a conversion to a deference for authority. Early in the film, Anne is focused on manipulating Reynolds to further her own career as an opera singer. Her continued participation in the charade is motivated not only by her sincere kinship with Reynolds, but by the fact that Reynolds is good friends with Leopold Stokowski (the constant references to the invisible Stokowski serves as a sort of inside joke for Durbin aficionados.) Yet by the end of the film, Anne's self-aggrandizing behavior gives way to altruism as she is no longer motivated by personal gain, but by her love for both of the Reynolds men. Big business, in the guise of the lovable Jonathan Reynolds, is rendered benign, paternal, and all-knowing. Father really does know best. Class lines are blurred in *Eve*. Although Anne initially appears to be working class, this is no ordinary hat-check girl. Her work is simply a means to an end, earning money for singing lessons so that she can achieve of goal of becoming an opera singer.

Although Durbin's screen characterizations changed according to the material conditions of the 1930s and '40s, both Durbin's adolescent and young adult film characterizations appear to go against the dominant ideology of femininity. Durbin's comedic skills have been overlooked by film historians in favor of her singing talent. Yet the Durbin persona was funny, sarcastic, mischievous, outspoken, argumentative, and bossy. In *100 Men and a Girl*, grown men are rendered impotent by the economic crisis, but the depression simply makes Patsy more capable and effective. She has no compunctions about standing up to the adults in her life. Cab drivers, butlers, society matrons, industrialists, symphony orchestra conductors, fathers—all are leveled by her determination. She demands to be taken seriously. That same single-mindedness of purpose is apparent in *It Started with Eve*, as she bulldozes Reynolds into arranging an audition with Stokowski and foils Johnny's efforts to get her out of his father's life. She is more agile physically and mentally than Johnny, and even though they are the romantic leads, it is clear that Anne and the elder Reynolds are the true soul mates, and Anne will never be a docile wife. Durbin's films did not position spectators as passive objects of the male gaze. Instead, spectators were given agency, an agency that corresponded to their fan activities.

If Durbin's screen characterizations portrayed empowered women in the 1930s and '40s, her female fans also enjoyed newfound independence. Just as there have been few attempts to theorize the historical spectator, so too have there been few attempts to situate fandom in its historical context. The milieu of the depression and the war affected adolescents in specific ways. In their fictional study of Muncie, Indiana, the Lynds argued that high school girls felt the depression less than any other group in Middletown, less than their parents and male counterparts.

> Although there has been less money to play with, cars have not been so new, more dresses have been made at home, in fact . . . the social pace has continued. High school enrollment was almost universal for adolescents of the period as the depression forced many teens to remain in school because unemployment rates were so high. In many ways, the depression actually served to reinforce adolescent subculture.[13]

The same could be said of adolescents during the Second World War, as they remained one of the few segments left virtually intact. Adult men were drafted and many women entered the work force. Teenagers began to have an increased market visibility. Before the 1940s, the film industry had catered primarily to the female adult audience. This trend began to change in the forties as filmmakers recognized the market power of teens. Many adolescents began to take part-time jobs. In 1943, the United States Children's Bureau said that the increase in the numbers of adolescent workers was nearly as great as the increase in women over the age of thirty-five. Between 1940 and 1943, the percentage of adolescents in the labor force rose 300 percent. From slightly less than a million in 1940, by 1943 there were three million adolescents between the ages of fourteen and seventeen employed.[14] Adolescent girls were in particular demand as babysitters for women in war industries. By 1948, the *Saturday Evening Post* would report that babysitting had become "a craft dominated by a militant minority of high school girls extracting $750 million a year."[15] One contemporary observer noted:

> Most of the teenagers work at odd jobs after school hours in war factories, soda fountains, department stores, etc. . . . and hundreds of thousands of them have left school entirely in order to work full time. This means that they, like many adults, have more money to spend than they enjoyed before; and they can indulge themselves by seeing more movies, flocking to dance halls . . . and collecting records for private jive sessions.[16]

Fan activity remained an affordable, easily accessible diversion during the depression and the war. Being a member of an organized fan club allowed teens a space to create texts for personal consumption outside the official, market economy, and thus outside the realm of the dominant ideology regarding gender. The Deanna Durbin Devotees found a sphere of cultural production in which they could explore dimensions of female identity that went beyond parental and mass media definitions of femininity. We can begin to flesh out the historical spectator through teenage consumer behavior because consumers were engaged in identity formation through consumption. Consumption itself can be a political act, and as much a process of identity formation and meaning making as is production.[17] Fan club activity was one way girls structured their leisure activities, and in this sense, can be read as constituting a specific subculture.

The Cultural Economy of the Devotee Subculture

Subculture theorists treat youth subcultures as a distinct phenomenon of the historical and material conditions of the working class in post-World War II Great Britain. There is little recognition of the existence of subcultures before the war and certainly no recognition of the cultural life of girls. In fact as Angela McRobbie and Jenny Garber have pointed out, girls may have become invisible because the term "subculture" has such strong masculine connotations.[18] Jeff Bishop and Paul Hoggett argue that hobby groups constitute distinct subcultures organized around leisure activates. They note that "collective leisure offers opportunities . . . to reassert values related not to passive consumerism, but to production for one's own use and enjoyment," and refer to this as "mutual aid."[19] The same can be said of fandom and spectatorship. Spectatorship has most often been conceptualized in terms of consumption. Looking at fans might allow us to think of spectatorship in terms of production, and the ways in which fans negotiate the two. Spectators not only produce meanings, but also cultural texts and practices outside the moviegoing context. Moreover, the concept of "mutual aid" becomes even more significant when considered in relation to the dominant ideology of gender, which constructs female identity as the object of male pleasure. The Deanna Durbin Devotees used fandom to construct alternative gender identities that went against the dominant cultural perception of fandom—even Durbin's own perception of her fans—and the dominant cultural perception of femininity for young girls.

Joli Jensen has noted what she calls "the stigma of fandom," the tendency to construct fandom as pathological and deviant. Fans are often seen as cultural dupes, totally lacking in critical skills and easily manipulated.[20] Fan activity is most often associated with marginal groups, those for whom identity formation and conflict are most intense, particularly adolescents. According to audience researchers, 75 to 90 percent of all fans in the 1930s and 1940s were younger than twenty-one, and approximately 80 percent were female.[21] It is reasonable to assume that the pathologizing of fandom also constructed fans as female. The feminization of fandom further delegitimized and trivialized fan activity. Durbin herself negatively stigmatized not only her fans but her persona as well. In a 1967 interview, Durbin said, "I never had any feeling or identity with the 'Deanna Durbin' born from my early pictures, and from a mixture of press agents, publicity, and fan worship. . . . The fact that even today with the world's terrifying problems, people are still interested in the synthetic old Durbin of the thirties only shows what escape from reality I must have meant."[22] Her disdainful attitude is further illustrated:

> My fans sat in the dark, anonymous and obscure, while I was projected larger than life on the screen. Fans took home an image of me and studio and press agents filled in the personal details. They invented most of them, and before I could resist . . . this worldwide picture of me came back stronger than my real person and very often conflicted with it. . . . I was a typical thirteen year old American girl. The characters I was forced into had nothing in common with myself—or with other youth of my generation for that matter.[23]

While much of what fans were responding to in the Durbin persona was totally artificial, according to Durbin, who disavows her own characterizations, fans were still able to derive enormous pleasure from the representations. Perhaps this illustrates that fans were able to create alternative meanings and thus alternative identities from Durbin's screen characterizations as well. *Deanna's Diary*, in attempting to pinpoint Durbin's appeal, gave voice to the adolescent fans themselves when it noted, "Deanna Durbin owes much of her popularity to the fact that she always has portrayed on screen girls who do the things most girls dream of doing." What she rarely did on screen was to defer to the adults or other figures of authority. Instead, she was often brash, impudent, impertinent, sarcastic, and independent, hardly the qualities touted for female adolescents in prescriptive literature that targeted youth and offered guidelines for teenage feminine behavior.[24] Fans might have transposed Durbin's agency on screen to their own fan activities.

Using Pierre Bourdieu's model of culture as an economy, John Fiske has described what he calls the "shadow cultural economy" of fan culture. That is, fans create a culture with its own system of production and distribution that lies outside official culture yet appropriates certain values and characteristics of that culture. Fiske has isolated three major characteristics of fandom: discrimination and distinction, productivity and participation, and capital accumulation.[25] I will look specifically at the cultural economy of the Devotee subculture.

One form of productivity noted by Fiske is textual productivity, fan-produced texts that circulate among and help to define the fan community. These texts are created outside the official market economy for consumption among the fan community. Unlike products produced by the official culture, these texts are not produced for profit and thus often lack technical merit or a certain sophistication. The *Diary,* however, was fairly glossy for a fan publication. It usually had a studio photo on the cover, and a number of publicity and fan-generated photos inside. A typical issue consisted of contributions from Jay Gordon and other club officers, Branch Club News, a personal letter form Durbin, a selection of fan letters sent to Durbin from all over the world, a Correspondence Club, fan poetry or prose, and a profile of Durbin's latest film or a biographical note. The overwhelming majority of the content was fan generated, allowing adolescents a forum to express their cultural tastes publicly.[26]

An important form of textual productivity among fans, not meant for public consumption, was the scrapbooks. Making a scrapbook was a very individualized activity and a creative aspect of fandom that has often been overlooked as a source of historical investigation. These are tangible artifacts that illustrate the participatory nature of fandom. Scrapbooks created opportunities for creative expression and the chance to develop a sense of achievement and pride in one's personal collection. Scrapbooks might contain photos clipped from newspaper or periodicals, film programs, and even a fan's own creative expression through poetry and drawings. Collections might be contained in store-bought scrapbooks, notebooks, or a box; sometimes they were made by pasting pictures onto a telephone book or magazine. Scrapbooks are also, as Lisa Lewis points out, a way for fans "to chronicle or represent their own histories" by including a program from a Durbin film the fan had attended, a letter or photo from Durbin, or a correspondence letter with another fan, all of which might reflect a particular sense of time and place for a collector. Scrapbooks became a venue through which fans could organize the cultural resources of fandom. Moreover, the pleasure of consumption could be repeated any time a fan worked on or looked at her scrapbook. Many branch clubs of the Devotees required members to produce collections of memorabilia. As Fiske points out, the capital accumulation of fandom tends to be inclusive rather than exclusive. The goal is to collect as much as possible, and the objects are often those that lack value according to the standards of the official culture. One adolescent girl, Loraine McGrath, attained prominence among Devotees because she had the largest collection of "Durbiniana" in the world, with four scrapbooks full of clippings and an additional fifteen hundred photos of Durbin. The pleasure, histories, and personal memories associated with scrapbooks are a tangible artifact of identity formation, and the pride of creating a collection was an alternative arena of achievement. Instead of concentrating on their man-pleasing and catching skills, girls could take pride not only in their unique creative endeavors, but in displaying their expertise.[27]

Devotees tried to draw distinctions between themselves and other spectators. Their mission statement underscores their desire for a more intimate connection with Durbin, "[The Devotees] was formed by a group of sincere admirers . . . in order to provide for Miss Durbin's followers the world over a closer contact than is possible through ordinary channels." Devotees also publicly proclaimed and signaled membership. They were given membership cards and official pins, while some branch chapters had jackets with a special insignia. Fans might also signal membership by appropriating Durbin's appearance. Female fans often adopted her hairstyle, mannerisms, or attire. Many issues of the *Diary* featured the Durbin look-alikes: "There are a few girls on earth who not only pattern their conduct after Deanna's, but actually resemble her physically—one or two actually possessing singing voices of high quality." As Lisa Lewis points out, dressing like the star represents the acquired textual knowledge of fans: "Female culture based knowledge and textual knowledge join to create a field of authority that is both gender and fan specific."[28] It is in this area that female fans in the pages of the *Diary* come the closest to appropriating normative definitions of femininity. Yet the Deanna look-alikes strove for emulation of the star as an end in itself rather than as the way to attract a date.

The discourse of the *Diary* is much like the private writings of adolescent girls, full of superlatives and dramatic, flowery, romantic, and sometimes full of anguish. On Devotee wrote: "The photos you sent me are lovely—every time I get one from you I just squeal with delight—honest! And isn't the new Diary simply grand?" The *Diary* stressed that as Devotees, they had access not only to her public persona but her private life as well, a special kind of insider's knowledge. For example, Devotees were well versed not only on the names of her dog and her immediate family, but her maternal grandmother, her secretary, her manager, her directors, and even the various studio administrators through the articles that were written by or about them in the *Diary*. Durbin fans in the *Diary* often position themselves as being more culturally refined and discriminating than the fans of other popular stars because of Durbin's association with "highbrow" instead of popular music. In the case of the Devotees, there is a blurring of distinction between high and pop culture. Her fans often mention not only a preference for classical music, but a vast knowledge of opera and a proficiency in a musical instrument. The *Diary* turns on a celebration of talent and achievement, both Durbin's and that of the fans themselves.[29]

Many of the fan letters published in the *Diary* are very chatty, gossipy letters full of personal news, the kind of letters that are exchanged with a friend or confidante. Lisa Lewis posits that these letters "suggest a reciprocity between fan and textual persona, a pattern of identification, a relationship not unlike girls' friendships in which secrets and wishes are exchanged." Many of the letters are informational; for example, a fan in Paraguay wrote to tell Durbin the names of her films in Spanish, and a fan in Egypt wrote about the pyramids. Many letters simply recorded the uneventful occasions of daily life, such as the antics of a pet. Sometimes a fan wrote to give Durbin advice. One fan in New York suggested that she request a clause in her contract prohibiting placement of her films on a double bill. There is a feeling of familiarity about her fan letters. Fans seemed to gravitate to Durbin, because she represented a friend, a confidante, someone who would care. Such exchanges are also an example of the ways in which same-sex relationships are formed and maintained.[30]

Bourdieu's metaphor of the cultural economy is characterized by struggle and competition between class factions whose interests are often in conflict. Yet I would argue that the cultural economy of fandom is marked by community and support. The values of the fan's cultural economy are radically different from those embedded within the formal economy. As Bishop and Hoggett argue, "They are the values of reciprocity and interdependence as opposed to self interest, collectivism as opposed to individualism, the importance of loyalty and a sense of 'identity' or 'belonging' as opposed to the principle of forming ties on the basis of calculation, monetary or otherwise."[31] In addition, the ways in which female fans constructed understandings of gender identity can also be considered a communal value. Club activities emphasized alternative conceptions of female behavior and female identity, such as talent, expertise, achievement, creativity, and a knowledge of current events. Within the ideology of romantic love, women were encouraged to view other women as their competitors. However, with Durbin fans there seems to be evidence of girl-girl solidarity, both in their identification with Durbin and in their friendships with each other. This solidarity was fostered by the Devotee Correspondence Club, which essentially functioned as a pen-pal service. Each issue of the *Diary* featured about fifteen to twenty letters from correspondents looking for a fellow Durbin fan, with whom to share their hobbies, interests, fill gaps in their Durbin collections, or to learn about a specific geographical location. Moreover, during World War II, war news from soldiers and European fans was an integral part of the *Diary*.[32] Writing to other fans was a tangible way in which adolescent girls constructed a community of spectators and created friendships with diverse people they might not, otherwise, have had the opportunity to meet. Getting mail from all over the world probably heightened the pleasure of fandom, and collecting such letters became a part of the capital accumulation of fandom.

Bishop and Hoggett argue that leisure activities "consistently offer enthusiasts the opportunity to develop a sense of value and identity . . . through their creations and collections," or simply through their involvement in discussion and debate. Fan club activity constituted not only a space "to do," but also a space "to be."[33] In the uncertain days of the depression and the Second World War, adolescent girls could structure their leisure activities and create new forms of meaning, enjoyment, and identity by being fans. Fandom also provided girls with alternative areas of expertise and legitimacy—and their own cultural capital. The Devotees produced cultural texts outside of the market setting for personal consumption. Fan-produced texts, such as scrapbooks and *Deanna's Diary*, contained fan-produced meanings sometimes at odds with normative definitions of gender. Studying the Devotees allows us to think about spectatorship as both a process of production and consumption, and to look at the ways in which the two are negotiated. It also allows us to examine the ways in which spectatorship can occur outside the moviegoing context. Being Devotees allowed girls a specific form of cultural expression that offered them a public forum for what normally has been private discourse. It also gave them not only a form of cultural authority, but enabled them to acquire and construct knowledge in their own way. The Deanna Durbin Devotees allowed female adolescents autonomy, agency, and a uniquely creative voice.

NOTES

1. "Correspondence Club," *Deanna's Diary* 5, no.1 (1941): 29. Thanks to Mary Rothschild and Barry Schenck for their comments on a draft of this article presented at the Maple Leaf and Eagle Conference in Helsinki, Finland, 1996. I would also like to acknowledge Michael Willard for getting me to think more about identity formation and fan behavior in the context of the Depression and World War II.

2. Anthony Slide, "A Tribute to Deanna Durbin," *Academy of Motion Picture Arts and Sciences Program*, 9 December 1978.

3. Her filmography includes: *Three Smart Girls* (1937), *100 Men and a Girl* (1937), *Mad about Music* (1938), *That Certain Age* (1938), *Three Smart Girls Grow Up* (1939), *First Love* (1939), *It's a Date* (1940), *Spring Parade* (1940), *Nice Girl?* (1941), *It Started with Eve* (1941), *The Amazing Mrs. Halliday* (1942), *Hers to Hold* (1943), *His Butler's Sister* (1943), *Christmas Holiday* (1944), *Can't Help Singing* (1945), *Lady on a Train* (1945), *Because of Him* (1946), *I'll be Yours* (1946), *Something in the Wind* (1947), *Up in Central Park* (1948), and *For the Love of Mary* (1948).

4. For biographical sketches of Durbin, see Norman Zierold, *The Child Stars* (New York: Coward McCann, 1965); Gene Ringgold, "Deanna Durbin," *Screen Facts*, no. 5 (1963): 3–22; "Notes on a Songbird," undated and unsourced, Clipping files of the Academy of Motion Picture Arts and Sciences (AMPAS).

5. See Jay Gordon, "A History of Deanna's Diary," *Deanna's Diary* 4 no.1 (1940): 25. For Gordon's letter, see "Letters to the Editor," *Life* (4 April 1938): 6. The Devotees were profiled in "Deanna's Fans Have a Devotee Club," *Life*, 3 October 1938, 33–34.

6. For a discussion of fan clubs, see Alexander Walker, *Stardom: The Hollywood Phenomenon* (London: Michael Joseph, 1970), 250–251; and Margaret Thorpe, *America at the Movies* (New Haven: Yale University Press, 1939), 39. For Universal's role, see Jay Gordon, "Editor's Last Word," *Deanna's Diary* 5, no.1 (1941): 31.

7. Although her appeal was and continues to be enormous among fans, Durbin has virtually been ignored by film scholars. Durbin is particularly useful to study because her career is so self-contained and finite. She literally walked away from films never to return. She is forever frozen in celluloid as a young woman.

8. Laura Mulvey, "Visual Pleasure and Narrative Cinema," *Screen* 16 (1975): 6–18. Mulvey

revisited her argument in "Afterthoughts on 'Visual Pleasure and Narrative Cinema' Inspired by *Duel in the Sun*," *Framework* 6 (1981): 12–18. The special issue of *Camera Obscura* 20/21 (1989) summarized the debates on spectatorship. See also Judith Stacey, *Stargazing: Hollywood Cinema and Female Spectatorship* (London: Routledge, 1995), 19–24, for an excellent critique of spectating positions.

9. Mary Ann Doane, untitled entry, *Camera Obscura* 20/21 (1989): 142–147, quoted by Stacey, *Stargazing*, 22–23, 36. For similar criticism of spectating positions, see Janet Staiger, *Interpreting Films: Studies in the Historical Reception of American Cinema* (Princeton: Princeton University Press, 1995), and Teresa de Lauretis, *Alice Doesn't: Feminism, Semiotics, Cinema* (London: Macmillan, 1984). As Stacey points out, psychoanalytic, feminist film theorists have often privileged textual analysis with little attention given to the audience or the discourse of stardom. While cultural studies approaches have been more fruitful in examining the role of the audience, these investigations have largely focused on television, video, and popular fiction. One notable exception is Stacey's *Stargazing*, an ethnographic study, which looks at how British female spectators found meaning in Hollywood stars of the forties and fifties. For other ethnographic studies of female spectators, see Janice Radway, *Reading the Romance* (Chapel Hill: University North Carolina Press, 1984); Lisa Lewis, *Gender, Politics and MTV* (Philadelphia: Temple University Press, 1990); and Henry Jenkins, "Startrek: Rerun, Reread, Rewritten: Fan Writing as Textual Poaching," Critical Studies in *Mass Communication* 5 (1989): 85–107.

10. Lary May, "Making the American Consensus: The Narrative of Conversion and Subversion in World War II Films," in *The War in American Culture: Society and Consciousness during World War II*, ed. Lewis Erenberg and Susan E. Hirsch (Chicago: University of Chicago Press, 1996), 72–79. I would like to acknowledge Michael Willard for making me see this connection.

11. See Charles Eckert, "Shirley Temple and the House of Rockefeller," *Jump Cut* 2 (July/August 1974): 17–20. Eckert positions Temple's early films within the competing political argument over depression relief programs. Temple's films emphasize the healing power of love, but it is a love precipitated by need: "Shirley turns like a lodestone toward the flintiest characters in her films—the wizened wealthy, the defensive unloved, figures of cold authority. . . . She assaults, penetrates and opens them, making it possible for them to give of themselves" (19). *100 Men's* Mr. Frost is not capable of redemption through love, while the industrialist in Durbin's film *It Started with Eve* is.

12. May,"Making the American Consensus," 72.

13. Robert S. Lynd and Helen Merrell Lynd, *Middletown in Transition* (New York: Harcourt Brace and World, 1937), 171; Joseph Kett, *Rites of Passage: Adolescence in America 1790 to the Present* (New York: Basic Books, 1977), 264. See also Grace Palladino, *Teenagers: An American History* (New York: Basic Books, 1996), 3–16.

14. James Gilbert, *A Cycle of Outrage: America's Reaction to the Juvenile Delinquent in the 1950s* (New York: Oxford University Press, 1986), 19.

15. Cited by Marjorie Rosen, *Popcorn Venus* (New York: Avon, 1973), 251.

16. Mary H. Hinant, "Paging Miss Bobby Sox," *Library Journal* 70 (15 September 1945): 803.

17. Angela McRobbie and Jenny Garber, "Girls and Subcultures," in *Resistance through Rituals*, ed. Stuart Hall and Tony Jefferson (London: Hutchinson, 1976), 211–213.

18. Ibid, 211. Subcultural theorists such as Stuart Hall, Michael Brake in *Comparative Youth Culture* (London: Routledge and Kegan Paul, 1985), and Dick Hebdige in *Subcultures and the Meaning of Style* (London: Routledge, 1979) have consistently marginalized girls. McRobbie

and Garber point out that much of female subcultural activity has taken place within the private space of the home, rather than the public space of the street or the clubs. Another reason that girls' subcultural forms might have been marginalized is because they appear to lack political intent and are often not subversive or in opposition to the dominant culture.

19. Jeff Bishop and Paul Hoggett, *Organizing around Enthusiasms: Mutual Aid in Leisure* (London: Comedia, 1986), 43–44.

20. Joli Jensen, "Fandom as Pathology," in *The Adoring Audience: Fan Culture and Popular Media*, ed. Lisa Lewis (London and New York: Routledge, 1992), 9–27. For a further discussion of some misconceptions of fans, see Lawrence Grossberg, "Is There a Fan in the House?: The Affective Sensibility of Fandom," in Lewis, *The Adoring Audience*, 50–65.

21. Edgar Morin, *The Stars* (New York: Grove Press, 1960), 102.

22. Quoted by Slide, "Tribute to Deanna Durbin."

23. Quoted by Zierold, *Child Stars*, 203.

24. "Durbin Doubles," *Deanna's Diary*, no. 1 (1941): 28. See Palladino, *Teenagers*, 20–33 for a discussion of prescriptive sources in the 1930s and 1940s.

25. Pierre Bourdieu, *Distinction, A Social Critique of the Judgement of Taste* (Cambridge, Mass: Harvard University Press, 1984); John Fiske, "The Cultural Economy of Fandom," in *The Adoring Audience*, ed. Lisa Lewis (New York and London: Routledge, 1991), 30–48.

26. See Fiske,"Cultural Economy," 42–43. For this study, I looked at issues of *Deanna's Diary*, the official journal of the Devotees, between 1937 and 1943, as well as fan letters published in popular periodicals and fan-created artifacts, such as scrapbooks, poetry, drawings, and other personal memorabilia created by fans themselves.

27. Lisa Lewis, *Gender Politics and MTV* (Philadelphia: Temple University Press, 1990), 157. I have a child's scrapbook from the 1930s that was, in fact, created by pasting pictures onto a local telephone directory. I would like to thank Kimberly Cooper of Twentieth Century Fox for sharing her personal antique scrapbook collections, and Adele Droll and Val Finhert for sharing their Durbin memorabilia. For a discussion of capital accumulation see Fiske, "Cultural Economy," 42–44. McGrath was profiled in *Life* magazine in October 1938.

28. "Apologia," *Deanna's Diary* 5, no. 1 (1941): 1; "Durbin's Doubles," *Deanna's Diary* 5, no. 1 (1941): 28. Lewis, *MTV*, 168.

29. "Deanna's Own Letters," *Deanna's Diary* 4, no.1 (1940): 22. For examples of "insider's knowledge," see "Introducing Granny," *Deanna Journal* 1 (1937): 5; "Informal Chat with a Proud Mother," *Deanna's Diary* 4, no.1 (1941): 28; Nelson Blair, "Meeting Members," *Deanna's Diary* 4, no. 1 (1940): 13. For discussions of musical proficiency, see "Correspondence Club," *Deanna's Diary*, no. 1 (1941): 29, and Jay Gordon, "Editor's Last Word," *Deanna's Diary* no. 1 (1941): 31.

30. Lewis, *MTV*, 169. See Eunice Blair, "Branch Club News" and "Correspondence Club," *Deanna's Diary*, no. 1 (1943).

31. Bishop and Hoggett, *Organizing around Enthusiams*,2.

32. For Correspondence Club, see "DDD Correspondence Club," *Deanna's Diary* 5, no. 1 (1941): 29, or "Eunice Blair, Correspondence Club," *Deanna's Diary* 5, nos. 2 & 3 (1942): 10. For examples of the ways in which the *Diary* was informed by the war, see James R. Stannage, "Hands across the Sea," *Deanna's Diary* 4, no. 1 (1940): 11–12, and "Deanna's Own Fan Letters," *Deanna's Diary*, nos. 2 & 3 (1941): 9.

33. Bishop and Hoggett, *Organizing around Entusiasms*, 53, 127.

Chapter Six

Creating New Identities

Youth and Ethnicity in New York City High Schools in the 1930s and 1940s

Paula S. Fass

In the early years of the twentieth century, educators moved vigorously to expand and rationalize schooling, and to extend the age of attendance well beyond childhood into adolescence. "The period of adolescence," the famous progressive educator, Elwood Cubberly, noted, "we now realize is a period of the utmost significance for the school." This period, newly encoded as a life stage and coincident with high school age, was increasingly viewed as a strategic period for socialization as well as education.[1] The new emphasis on adolescent schooling was in good part a response to the immense growth of the immigrant population in cities and the social issues this presented. The possibilities that schooling offered for assimilation were not new, of course, but in the first two decades of the twentieth century schooling was newly viewed as the solution to various social problems, making its urgency among immigrant youth seem ever more obvious and necessary. As schooling expanded to incorporate the children of immigrants during their important transition from childhood to adulthood, indeed as it helped to create this transition,[2] a genuinely new kind of educational environment was created, one in which young people contended within schools for control over student behavior, allegiance, and identification. Indeed, by the 1930s, and certainly by the 1940s, the attendance at high school of large numbers of the progeny of the great early twentieth-century migrations marked the arrival of a new common school era. In contrast to its nineteenth-century predecessor, the common school era of the early twentieth century concerned adolescents, not children, and in large cities it replaced the pious air of Protestant respectability with a complex cosmopolitanism.[3] In cities like New York and Chicago, the high schools, like the neighborhoods in which they flourished, became ethnic (often multiethnic) enclaves. In this context, the high school as a fundamental agency of socialization became both more important and different than its planners had anticipated.

By the 1920s and 1930s, educators looked to the developmental significance of adolescence, especially to the special aptitudes for self-direction and the clannishness of youth as a potent force for citizenship and assimilation, and with this in mind they tried to construct a broadly conceived school program. Integral to their new programs was a range of activities in which students, although under adult auspices, exercised their own forms of self-direction in social, civic, athletic, and academic affairs. Through these extracurricular activities, Earle Rugg of Columbia's Teachers College noted, "The school may well make itself the laboratory for training pupils for efficient citizenship." Various informal school activities had existed at the fringes of the academic curriculum since the twentieth century, but it was not until after World War I that educators made a concerted effort to align them with the expanded concerns and "progressive" developmentally oriented pedagogy of the modern school. "Largely within the past decade, and wholly within the past two," Elwood Cubberly noted in 1931, "an entirely new interest in the extra-curricular activities of youth has been taken by the school. In part this change in attitude has been caused by the new disciplinary problems brought to the school through the recent great popularization of secondary education."[4] That popularization, it hardly needed to be said, now included vast numbers of young people from neighborhoods and urban enclaves who scarcely dreamed of attending school some decades earlier.

Educators and school administrators who hoped to adopt extracurricular activities to the purpose of socialization had to walk a fine line that balanced adult supervision with student initiative. Although they hoped to use the activities for their own purposes, too much control would undermine the usefulness of the activities as theaters for training in genuine citizenship and voluntary cooperation. The activities were thus both an obvious and tricky realm for educational efforts. It is clear, moreover, that school systems and individual schools differed in their treatment of the activities, especially in the degree to which they were directed by adults and integrated into the curriculum.[5]

With this variation fully in mind, it is still possible to reconstruct certain dimensions of students' social experience as registered in their participation in extracurricular activities. In fact, as an area of youth semiautonomy, the activities had the potential to be pivotal locales in which the plans of school officials and the social needs of students clashed. In light of the assimilationist aims of the schools, the extracurriculum also provides us with an unusually important vantage for observing how immigrant youth became Americans during the strategic decades of the thirties and forties, and how the young affected this process.

The following analysis is based on the extracurricular participation of fifteen thousand New York City high school graduates between 1931 and 1947 as these experiences were recorded in high school yearbooks. It was my aim to determine if and how ethnicity influenced extracurricular choices in order to evaluate the place of ethnicity among students in high school. Obviously, partly because my tabulations are based on name identification and because all activities were self-reported, these conclusions are only near approximations of what took place. The results may also have been skewed by the fact that all the students were seniors, and the different ethnic groups were unevenly represented in graduation rates. The seeming precision of numbers should not be allowed to obscure the imprecision of the method. Still, given how underexamined schools have been as lively arenas of youth culture and how very difficult it is to peer into the process of Americanization from below, even this kind of inexact portrait can begin the serious process of understanding how youth culture intersected the historically critical issue of Americanization.

New York was in no way a representative environment, but it was the preeminent immigrant city and an investigation of the city's schools is especially illuminating. Students in New York came from a very wide variety of nationality groups; I have selected six for analysis—native white, Irish, German, Italian, Jewish, and black.[6] The schools varied greatly in ethnic, class, and even gender composition and in their neighborhood setting. These differences mattered. Wherever possible, therefore, I have based my conclusions not only on the overall pattern but on the behavior of groups within specific schools and I have defined ethnic tendencies only when there were compelling similarities among several schools.[7]

For the high school graduates of the thirties and forties, extracurricular activities had become a regular part of their school experience.[8] Four-fifths of all students participated in some club or activity, although the extent of their participation varied from a high of 99 percent at Bay Ridge High School to a low of 56 percent at Theodore Roosevelt, and women were everywhere more active than men. Given that these were seniors, this high rate is not surprising, since seniors, as the most successful of all students, were probably most involved in all aspects of school life. But certain groups were more active than others and engaged in a wider range of activities. Jews and native white students were the most active. Table 6.1 summarizes the experiences of the various groups.

A student's ethnicity clearly influenced the extent of his or her participation in the extracurricular world of high school. More significantly, ethnicity had a powerful effect on the kind of activity a student was likely to elect. Sometimes the ethnic variations depended on a specific school environment, but at other times there were uniformities across schools that suggest strong ethnic preferences.[9] Taken as a whole the yearbooks point to the strategic role of ethnicity in determining student choices among extracurricular offerings and help to define the continuing significance of ethnicity in the lives of high school students.

TABLE 6.1.
Participation in Some Activity by Sex and Ethnicity
(Each box signifies overrepresentation in designated school.)

	Men						Women					
	1	2	3	4	5	6	1	2	3	4	5	7
Jewish	■	■	—	■	■	■	■	■	■	■	■	■
Italian	—	—	—	—	—	—	—	—	—	—	—	■
Black	—	■	■	■	a	—	—	—	■	—	—	■
Irish	—	—	b	■	■	—	—	—	—	■	■	■
German	—	—	■	■	—	—	—	—	—	■	—	—
Native	■	—	■	■	—	■	■	■	—	■	■	—

Note: School Key
1. George Washington High School
2. Evander Childs High School
3. Seward Park High School
4. Theodore Roosevelt High School
5. New Utrecht High School
6. High School of Commerce
7. Bay Ridge High School

a. No blacks at Utrecht High School
b. Not enough Irish at Seward Park to be meaningful.

Members of some ethnic groups rarely or never joined in certain activities. Irish men only rarely joined science clubs or participated in the orchestra or in dramatics. Jews and blacks participated in religious clubs very infrequently. Indeed, blacks were the most consistently absent from a wide range of activities;[10] they almost never participated in dramatic clubs or in the sciences; no black woman or man was ever elected president of the senior class or the student body; no black was ever editor in chief of the newspaper. The fact that blacks were the group most frequently absent from a range of activities suggests a strong exclusionary bias against them. Blacks joined only certain activities and almost never others; no other group was absent in so many categories in so many schools. Blacks who were eager to participate in school activities—and three-quarters of blacks did participate—chose carefully and judiciously, consistently sidestepping activities in which they either had no interest or were clearly not welcome.

In one activity, black men were dominant in an unparalleled way. In every school with a meaningful population of black men, they conspicuously chose the track team. Indeed, track was the activity most consistently associated with blacks: almost one-third of all black men in the entire population were on the team. At George Washington High School, where blacks were scarcely 5 percent of the male population, eleven of forty-four track men were black. At Seward Park, where blacks constituted slightly more than 1 percent of the male population, three of thirteen runners were black in a population of only thirty-one black men. Half of all black men at Evander Childs (six of twelve) and one-sixth (ten of sixty) of all black men at the High School of Commerce were on the track team. Although these were small numbers, because the number participating in track was small and because the number of black seniors was small, it was stunningly clear that the chances of a black man electing track as one, and possibly his only, high school activity was very great.

The same concentration of black men was present in no other sport. Although black men were also active in basketball, they almost never played football and rarely participated in other sports. These sports were dominated by white natives, Italians and, Germans, and, to a lesser degree, the Irish. Jews, like blacks, were not drawn to football. When Jews participated in sports, they strongly favored basketball. Italians showed the opposite tendency, choosing basketball only rarely, but inclining strongly toward football. Native whites participated most heavily in football and in the "other sports" category, but very infrequently in track.

The pattern in sports choices is clear and illuminating. Members of different ethnic groups made significant distinctions among the sports offered at school. They divided the sports among themselves as each group chose several of the sports categories and bypassed the others. We can only guess at how these preferences were established. Track, a highly individualistic sport that required little team cooperation or body contact, may have served as an ideal outlet for blacks against whom discrimination would preclude strong group involvement. Native white men may have been particularly drawn to football with its collegiate aura. It is possible that the example of some sports hero, like Jesse Owens or Red Grange, helped to orient different groups to sports in a selective manner. Once the preferences were set, however, they most likely defined a clear status and prestige hierarchy and created ethnic associations that, in turn, differentially attracted members of various groups. The strong symbolic meanings that divided men among the sports apparently did not affect women. Sports never played the ethnically differentiating role for women that they did for men. In the end this may mean that women simply did not invest sports with the same social meaning as men.

In general, even though ethnic patterns were less sharply etched for women, certain preferences were notable. Jewish women tended to elect literary activities of all kinds in all schools. Wherever women were editors of the student newspaper, they were almost certain to be Jewish. At Theodore Roosevelt, all three female editors were Jewish; at George Washington, both women were Jewish; at New Utrecht, the one female editor was Jewish, and at Evander Childs two of the three women editors were Jews. Only at Bay Ridge High School, where Jewish women were a very small group in an all female school, was there a much broader ethnic distribution. Overall, Jewish women were 60 percent of all female editors but only 48 percent of the female population, a disproportion that would have been far greater if the special case of Bay Ridge were excluded. (See table 6.2.)

In the 1930s and 1940s in New York high schools, literary activities for women took on a distinctly ethnic cast. German and native white women were also quite active on the school newspaper, but Italian, black, and Irish women were consistently underrepresented, as they were in the "other publications." Jewish men were active in literary activities as well, but far less consistently than Jewish women.[11] The yearbook was an exception to the ethnic patterns in literary activities. Jewish women were not as conspicuous on the yearbook staff while Irish and native women were far more heavily represented in this than in other literary activities. Native women and especially native men tended to be disproportionately active on the yearbook. Irish men also expressed a unique interest in the yearbook, contrary to their usual reticence to join publications activities. A major reason for these differences was due to the fact that the yearbook was a political tool. In documenting senior class activities, the yearbook played a strategic role as the publicity vehicle of dominant senior personalities.

In fact, student politics attracted a different constituency than literary activities. Overall, Irish men were the most disproportionately represented among presidents

TABLE 6.2.
Participation of Jewish High-School Women in Literary Activities by School and Activity

			Activity*			
School	Total # Jewish Women	% of Women Who Are Jewish	Editor	Other News	Other Publications	Yearbook
George Washington	(525)	40.4%	(2) 100.0%	(19) 38.3%	(4) 80.0%	(9) 20.0%
Evander Childs	(858)	46.8	(2) 66.7	(23) 57.5	(20) 58.8%	(31) 57.4
Seward Park	(770)	75.9	-	(29) 85.3	(25) 86.2%	(20) 76.9
New Utrecht	(1026)	60.7	(1) 100.0	(73) 79.3	(33) 73.3	(55) 76.4
Theodore Roosevelt	(575)	43.4	(3) 100.0	(21) 63.7	-	(41) 50.0
Bay Ridge	(88)	6.4	(1) 16.7	(8) 13.3	(4) 18.2	(15) 9.7
All schools	(3842)	44.8	(9) 60.0	(173) 56.0	(86) 63.2	(171) 39.5

*In each column, the number in parentheses represents the number of Jewish women in the activity in each school during four years of my sample. The percentage is the proportion of all women in each activity who were Jewish.

of the senior class and student body. Eleven percent of all male presidents were Irish, although the Irish made up only a little more than 4 percent of male seniors. Native men were also very active, and German men, usually the least active of all the groups, appear to have been especially drawn to student politics. Native and German men were nearly twice as likely to be presidents than their population would warrant. Jewish men were somewhat underrepresented, and Italians had fewer than one-half of the presidents warranted by their numbers. No black ever achieved this coveted position.

The strong showing of the Irish is somewhat misleading. In fact, it was the natives, not the Irish, who usually dominated presidential offices. Whenever native whites composed a significant part of the school population, they disproportionately controlled presidential offices, except at the High School of Commerce. It was the presence of three Irish presidents at Commerce, in the absence of any native presidents, that exaggerated the Irish presence. Elsewhere, though the Irish were very active in politics, as shown by their frequent election to "other political" offices, it was natives who were most frequently elected to the highest offices. At George Washington, four of five presidents were natives, although natives were only one in five senior men. At Evander Childs, where natives composed one-sixth of the male population, two of six presidents were native. At Theodore Roosevelt, one-half of all male presidents were native, but natives were less than one-fifth of the male population. If we think of the president as a symbol of aspiration, the conspicuous position of natives among presidents becomes more explicable and significant. Only at Seward Park and New Utrecht, in each of which Jews were more than 50 percent of the population, were Jewish men consistently chosen. All the male presidents at Seward Park were Jews, and at New Utrecht, located in a heavily ethnic neighborhood which grew from the outmigration of Jews and Italians from the Lower East Side, four of the five male presidents were Jewish. In these two schools, the president was of course a direct expression of electoral realities. But if the presidency was also symbolic, as I have suggested, then the pattern at these schools indicates an alternative social environment and another ideal. Both Seward Park and New Utrecht were heavily ethnic schools, with Jews the dominant ethnic group. Within an overwhelmingly ethnic setting, Jews set their own standard of success, as natives did in schools which were middle class and status was defined by native whites.

The Irish were heavily involved in the lesser offices. Fifteen percent of all Irish men held some political office, compared with slightly more than 10 percent of Jews, natives, and Germans. Irish men, not especially active in the clubs generally, tended to gravitate toward political activities in high school, choosing political office over many other kinds of endeavors. Irish women were likewise more frequently elected to political office than either Jewish or native women. Neither Italians nor blacks were represented up to their proportion of the population.

Students interested in politics were forced to seek and to get peer approval. Native men seem especially to have benefitted from this, at least at the highest political level. One other measure of popularity and esteem was contained in the category "celebrity status," which was not strictly an activity but an expression of school prominence. A celebrity could be the man or woman chosen most likely to succeed, prettiest, handsomest, best athlete, best musician, and so on. Although some of these designations suggest special talent, they all depended finally on prominence in school affairs and required peer approval.

Among female celebrities, Irish and native women were far ahead of women from all other groups, while Jewish women were frequently selected at only one-half of their proportion in individual schools and were represented at just 66 percent of their population overall. This was the case despite the strong involvement of Jewish women in a wide range of extracurricular clubs and activities. Black women were *never* chosen. Among men, natives found the most approval, with twice the proportion of celebrities as the native population and they were especially conspicuous in three schools. Jewish men did better than Jewish women, but lagged behind natives. Italian men, like Italian women, were favored in only one school, while Irish men, unlike Irish women, were uniformly underrepresented. Two black men made the list.

The discrepancies between male and female celebrities, most obvious between Jewish men and women and the Irish, are revealing. Men appear to have been accorded celebrity status for their achievements, such as sports, politics, and editorships, which explains the fairly good showing of Jews and even the special instances of black success. Women appear to have been differently evaluated, often, in light of the preferred celebrity categories, on measures of beauty, grace, and popularity. Irish, native, and to some degree German women, not Jews, Italians, or blacks, most consistently embodied idealized versions of these attributes. In other words, if this designation was anything more than a quirky and humorous yearbook game, Jewish men appear to have approximated peer criteria of success better than Jewish women. Irish and German women did far better approximating a female ideal. But, overall, native men and native women were the most popular. (Table 6.3 compares the celebrity status of four ethnic groups.)

The achievement of Jewish men in the extracurricular realm was impressive, but they were especially prominent in academically related activities. Most conspicuously,

TABLE 6.3.
Celebrity Status by Sex, School, and Ethnicity (in percentages)

	Jewish		Italian		Irish		Native	
Men	Population	Celebrities	Population	Celebrities	Population	Celebrities	Population	Celebrities
George Washington	39.2	40.9	4.0	4.5	4.8	0.0	21.0	45.5
Evander Childs	39.7	50.0	19.5	0.0	4.8	0.0	16.7	0.0
Seward Park*	-	-	-	-	-	-	-	-
New Utrecht	55.9	73.7	24.2	21.1	1.2	0.0	7.8	0.0
Theodore Roosevelt	32.9	31.8	23.3	13.6	5.3	4.5	17.3	45.5
Commerce	20.2	29.3	17.8	14.6	11.7	2.4	18.6	29.3
Totals	44.9	40.4	17.4	12.8	4.4	1.8	13.4	29.3
Women								
George Washington	40.4	27.3	4.3	9.1	2.8	22.7	20.1	18.2
Evander Childs	46.8	14.3	15.1	0.0	1.5	0.0	20.0	57.1
Seward Park*	-	-	-	-	-	-	-	-
New Utrecht	60.7	47.4	15.7	10.5	0.7	0.0	9.9	31.6
Theodore Roosevelt	43.4	20.0	20.5	5.0	2.9	10.0	14.5	30.0
Bay Ridge*	-	-	-	-	-	-	-	-
Totals	44.8	29.4	15.9	7.3	2.7	10.3	16.4	29.4

*At these schools, celebrities were not indicated in the yearbook.

Jewish men dominated the science clubs. The pattern in the sciences was repeated with only small variations in the category of "other academic clubs." Native men also participated substantially, while the Irish, Germans, and Italians were only weakly involved. Black men were least active.

A glance at the representation of men in Arista, the National Honor Society, brings the academic pattern home. Arista was not a voluntary activity; students were honored by election to Arista on the basis of their school record. But the parallel between academic standing and personal choice among the activities makes clear how cogent the club choices of high school students could be. Only Jews were elected to the honor society disproportionately to their numbers in every school and by very wide margins.

Whatever it was that drew Jewish men toward the science and other academic clubs—college and professional ambitions, cultural preferences, or association with members of their own group—did not exert the same influence on their sisters. The number of women in the physics clubs was very small, and Jewish women failed to participate strongly in either physics or chemistry, and they showed only a weak interest in the "other science" clubs. Irish and native women showed a strong interest in chemistry and also made an impressive showing in the other sciences. Jewish women were also far less active than Jewish men in the "other academic" clubs. Italian women, on the other hand, made the strongest showing overall. Their special interest in academic clubs, in sharp contrast with Italian men, requires some explanation: it may lie in the selective attendance (and graduation) of Italian women in the 1930s and 1940s. Unlike other groups, such as the Jews and the Irish, who began to send female children to school much earlier and kept them there longer, Italian preconceptions about woman's place and the limited expectation of women's ambitions meant that only the most academically inclined and wealthiest attended high school at all, and still fewer graduated.[12] Those who did may have chosen academic clubs as a further expression of their seriousness of purpose and possibly even to legitimate their extracurricular participations to themselves and to their parents.

Men and women often behaved differently. Native women were much more likely than Jewish women to join Jewish men in the chemistry club. Jewish women were not drawn to academic clubs to the same degree as Jewish men or Italian women. Ethnicity at school was often differently expressed by men and women and this suggests that whatever culture students brought to high school, it was shaped and refashioned in gender-specific ways. In general, however, when we look at each

TABLE 6.4.
Participation by Men in Science, Other Academic Clubs, and Arista by Ethnicity, across all Schools

	Chemistry		Physics		Other Sciences		Other Academic		Arista		Percent of All Men
Jewish	(46)	54.8%	(30)	60.0%	(58)	52.7%	(288)	52.7%	(273)	56.4%	44.9%
Italian	(6)	7.1	(3)	6.0	(11)	10.0	(81)	14.8	(59)	12.2	17.4
Black	(0)	-	(0)	-	(1)	0.9	(4)	0.7	(3)	0.6	2.0
Irish	(2)	2.4	(0)	-	(0)	-	(10)	1.8	(11)	2.3	4.4
German	(4)	4.8	(2)	4.0	(5)	4.5	(22)	4.0	(16)	3.3	5.3
Native	(14)	16.7	(8)	16.0	(17)	15.4	(72)	13.2	(62)	12.8	13.4

school individually, men and women from the same ethnic groups tended toward the same choices among the performance clubs—orchestra, glee club, and drama. In fact, the similarity in the school-specific choices of ethnic men and women appear more striking than any marked consistency in ethnic choices across schools. This was probably because dramatic and musical performances were social events as well as arenas for aesthetic expression, and the strong resemblance between men's and women's choices suggests that these clubs and activities provided important occasions for heterosexual socializing.

The service category was the weakest ethnic differentiator, and, not coincidentally, this was the activity least dependent on peer acceptance or approval. Service did not require a heavy commitment of time or a demonstration of strong interest. Usually rendered during a free period in the regular student schedule, work in the dean's office, on the projector squad, or at any one of the myriad other services that students performed was least peer intensive and peer dependent. Since Jews engaged most extensively in extracurricular activities in general, it is not surprising that they were the most active in service in most schools, but every group of men and women was overrepresented in service in at least one school. Blacks often made quite a good showing in service, and this strongly confirms what might have been expected: in their desire to participate in school affairs, black men and women often chose just activities that involved few group events, little team work, and few potentially exclusionary practices by other students.

The absence of a strong relationship between service activities and ethnicity places the other patterns into even sharper relief. Certain of these patterns are especially notable. Despite the generally high level of Jewish participation, Jews did not gravitate equally to all parts of the extracurricular network. Instead, Jewish men moved into literary activities, science and academic clubs, and to service. The opposite tendency is evident among the Irish, who were rarely engaged in scientific, literary, or academic clubs except the yearbook, but were very active in politics, religion, and many of the sports. Italians also chose religion, but much more rarely politics. They were much more selective among the sports, choosing football above all. The Germans were less selective than the Irish, participating more broadly in literary and academic clubs without marked prominence, but like the Irish they chose politics frequently. Black choices were the most limited of all—track, basketball, service, and, to some extent, the orchestra. Native men were least restricted in their choices and were very frequently overrepresented in a wide range of clubs and activities, but they were particularly conspicuous in the most prominent positions and those that were socially most strategic—the presidencies, editorships, and the yearbook. And they were most often chosen as school celebrities.

The pattern among women was less sharp but still revealing. Jewish women were almost as active overall as Jewish men, but far less prominent among the celebrities. Despite their disproportionate election to Arista, Jewish women bypassed the academic and science clubs consistently to choose literary activities. Native women also chose literary clubs, but not to nearly the same degree. When they did, they chose the yearbook. Native women were also very active in the performance clubs and in social activities, which may explain their special prominence among the celebrities.

Weakly involved in most areas, Italian women made a clear and specific decision to join academic clubs and religious activities. Irish women were far more dispersed among the activities than Irish men, but like Irish men they chose politics and religion very frequently. Unlike Irish men, they were active in the science clubs. Whatever the reason for these strong and clear expressions of preference, men and women from various ethnic groups made definable choices in selecting extracurricular activities, choices that describe a complex and busy social system in which ethnicity affected what students did and how they viewed each other.

It is important to remember that the ethnic patterns, which we reconstruct with difficulty today, were at that time visible, palpable, and meaningful for young men and women. It helped them to define who they were, where they belonged in the extracurricular world, and where others were in that world. It not only set groups apart but provided individuals with effective networks of peers, establishing a competitive universe with hierarchies of power and status that provided tangible lessons in Americanization. This was, in many ways, the core of high school assimilation, a process defined not merely by incorporation and cultural diffusion but through the very process of differentiation, stratification, and group identification.

Overall ethnic patterns provide only partial insight into the lively social environments that youth peers created at high school. A fuller and more focused view results when we examine the ethnic patterns at specific schools. A closer look at the environments in which the second and third generations learned about America and an understanding of the consequences of their diversity offer an important means for understanding the multivalent nature of assimilation. The seven schools can be crudely described as illustrating three different paths to assimilation: schools where native patterns dominated; schools in which one ethnic group was especially powerful; and finally schools in which there was vigorous contention among ethnic group. While this tripartite division only begins to suggest the intricacy of school life, it provides a significant basis for grasping how the societies young people created influenced their experience of Americanization in the 1930s and 1940s.

Manhattan—symbolic center of New York's urban primacy—contained a variety of vocational and academic high schools throughout the twentieth century. Two of the borough's comprehensive schools, Seward Park High School and George Washington High School, illustrate the enormous range of the borough's social and ethnic experiences. Situated at the very top of Manhattan Island, George Washington was located in a luxurious building in a solidly middle-class neighborhood of prosperous and up-to-date apartment buildings, although the school drew from a larger and somewhat more heterogeneous area.[13] Yearbook pictures documented the well-to-do appearance of students, who were usually elegantly dressed, many of them wearing fashionable furs even during the depression decade. Paul Robeson, Jr., was among the one hundred twenty blacks who graduated from George Washington in this period, and black students, like students from other groups, were among the most economically privileged of their community. Seward Park, on the opposite end of the island, was unlike George Washington in almost every respect. Drawing its students from the tenements and alleys of New York's lower East Side, the classic

American ghetto-slum, students at Seward Park could depend on the similarity in the economic circumstances of their families, whatever their ethnic origins. Poor Italians, Jews, Germans, and others attended Seward Park in the twenties and thirties, and gradually, in the forties and later, more and more blacks and Puerto Ricans.[14]

The most heavily Jewish of the seven schools (74 percent), Seward Park was in many ways a Jewish city. No other group had even 10 percent of the remaining population. Instead, at Seward Park, Germans, natives, Italians, and blacks contributed only small spices to a homogeneous stock. At Seward Park, black men played football as well as basketball and track, held minor political offices, and were even duly represented in "social activities." They seem to have been welcomed to an extent that was unusual in New York schools in the thirties and forties. Black women were even more widely involved in activities; proportionately they were the most active group of women. Unlike black men, who were totally absent from academic activities, sciences, and Arista, black women were represented to some degree in each of these activities. For black women certainly, Seward Park proved to be a hospitable environment for the expression of a broad range of interests and talents.

The experience of blacks at Seward Park is illustrative of the mixed ethnic character of the activities. Most clubs were ethnically heterogeneous, although, of course, most were also overwhelmingly composed of Jews. Despite their ubiquity, however, Jews seem not to have participated as strenuously at Seward Park as in most other schools. The one exception was politics. Jews were politically very much in control at Seward Park. Their numerical superiority showed itself in this one activity that explicitly represented power and required election by peers. In a Jewish school, Jews could depend on other Jews for very large voting majorities. All presidents, male or female, at Seward Park were Jewish. Of all male groups, only Jews were disproportionately represented in political office holding.

It is worth thinking about the lackluster performance of Jews at Seward Park in the context of the record Jews made elsewhere. Bearing in mind that Seward Park catered to an overwhelmingly working-class population (those poorest members who had not yet made the trek to satellite areas of Brooklyn and the Bronx) it is still revealing that where the Jews were most at home, they were the least competitive. Jews could assume their social acceptability (and political control) at Seward Park, and in that context they seem to have exerted themselves least. At the same time, their overwhelming presence did not exclude other groups, including blacks, from active participation in the extracurricular life of the school.

Jewish experience at George Washington was very different. Jews were disproportionately active in general and especially conspicuous in certain areas: orchestra, drama, "other political" offices, and the whole range of academic clubs. But the strenuous involvement which seems, on the surface, a demonstration that Jews had arrived may well have been the reverse. If Seward Park provides a yardstick of Jewish activity in a largely Jewish context, then Jewish hyperactivity at George Washington may well suggest a kind of restlessness produced by a lack of manifest status and assured social position. Significantly, Jewish men were underrepresented as presidents and as editors of the newspaper, the most prominent positions a student could hold. In both, Jews took second place to native men, who captured far more presidencies and editorial chairs than was warranted by their numbers. Unlike Seward Park, where Jews were the occupants of these positions but were not conspicuously active in most other activities, Jews were active participants at George Washington but failed to capture the positions with the most power and prestige.

Native men held these positions to a very marked degree. They did well in general at George Washington, but they were even more prominent than is apparent from a quick perusal of their overall level of participation, since they were especially strong in certain areas of strategic and visible importance—presidencies, editorships, yearbook staff, news staff, football—and they contributed almost one-half of all "celebrities." The conspicuousness of native men in these areas, despite the fact that they were only half as large a group as the Jews, suggests a great deal about the relationship between ethnicity, prestige, and power at George Washington.

Jewish restlessness and achievement in extracurricular life as well as in academic activities seem to have been especially strong at George Washington. In part, this was a function of the largely middle-class composition of its student body—it was full of students whose parents had already gained considerable economic success. This may also explain the strong showing made by Italians. Usually a quiescent group elsewhere, Italian men at George Washington were unusually active. Their choices were selective to be sure, but their high level of activity is notable nevertheless and underscores how class structure affected participation. Italians completely, and uncharacteristically, ignored football at George Washington. Instead, they concentrated on social activities: the yearbook, orchestra, glee club, track, and "other sports." Italian men and even Italian women avoided the academic clubs where Jews were extremely dominant. The weak showing made by Italian women in academic clubs may well have reflected the great prominence of the Jews. Academics, formal and informal, at George Washington were even more than elsewhere an arena for Jewish achievement.

The social texture of student life at George Washington is best understood in the fact that while all groups participated actively, power and status belonged to native whites. It is worth considering the possibility that "native" names at George Washington may have hidden ethnic roots, that is to say, the parents of ethnic students changed their names along with their increasing prosperity. This would only underscore the conclusion that at George Washington, native standards and interests defined student culture. George Washington illustrated an archetypical pattern of assimilation in which standards were set by native whites who held the most visible campus offices and were selected as representatives of student values and ideals.

The experience of students at Seward Park is less easily definable. Most students at Seward Park were Jewish. That they were not unduly active in most clubs hardly affected the social environment of these activities or the school since Jews were influential by their sheer numbers and they held the important political offices and ran the newspaper. The Jewish presence did not seem to dampen the enthusiasm of other groups for participation, but it did mean that Jews, not natives, set the standards for other Jews and probably for other groups. The behavior of the eighty-nine senior natives (in four years) could not have meant much in a place like Seward Park. But Seward Park also represented a form of Americanization, although one in which it was possible for Jewish men and women to go through adolescence and graduate from high school without making significant contact with students outside their own ethnic group, either in class or out. As significantly, for non-Jews at Seward Park, Jews, not natives, defined the host society. For students at Seward Park, American urban culture and assimilation were a very different experience than for those who attended George Washington. Both, of course, were thoroughly exposed to American values and ideals in the classroom, but neither the meaning of those values nor their practice in the context of daily school experience was the same for students from the two schools.

George Washington and Seward Park capture two different geographic and economic corners of Manhattan. Evander Childs in the Bronx and New Utrecht in Brooklyn were suburban. Overwhelmingly, white and lower middle to middle class, New Utrecht in Bensonhurst and Evander Childs in the Pelham Parkway section of the Bronx serviced two of the many satellite immigrant communities growing up all over the greater city in the 1920s and 1930s.[15] At Evander Childs, Jews and Italian newcomers (44 percent and 17 percent of the senior classes) met a large contingent of natives (19 percent) in an area previously dominated by natives. Also present were small groups of Germans, Irish, and an even smaller number of blacks. New Utrecht was less complex and more Jewish. It had no blacks, few Irish, and fewer than 10 percent natives. The Jews were a substantial majority, comprising 58 percent of the population; the Italians were the largest minority with 20 percent.

The Jews were very active in both schools; but while they dominated at New Utrecht, they were far less prominent at Evander Childs. Italians also had different experiences at the two schools. At New Utrecht, Italians were underrepresented in the social world of politics, dramatics, publications, and the yearbook, which were controlled by Jews. Italian men tended to cluster in the glee club, in religious clubs, and in football, and they showed an unusual interest in academic clubs. They were joined in these activities by Italian women, who also joined religious clubs and academic clubs in very disproportionate numbers and substituted "other sports" for the male interest in football. This patterning of extracurricular clubs effectively describes a social world in which Jews exercised power and enjoyed prestige. Although Italian men, and especially Italian women, did join Jews in some activities, Italian and Jewish separation suggests both marked distinctions in choices and the probable exclusion of Italians from the most sensitive political and social areas. This conclusion is amplified by the fact that natives had less trouble joining Jews in politics, the newspaper, and on the yearbook. Not surprisingly, Jewish men at New Utrecht dominated the celebrity categories. Even at New Utrecht, however, Jewish women were denied celebrity status commensurate to their numbers while native women, here as elsewhere, represented ideals of beauty and popularity.

Italians also showed no special prominence at Evander Childs, but they engaged more extensively in sensitive areas and were the most disproportionately active of all groups in the category of social activities. At Evander, Italian men also held one of three editorships and one of six presidencies. They were disproportionately represented on the yearbook staff. Blacks, on the other hand, were almost invisible in the activities. Besides service and track, which absorbed three-quarters and one-half of all the black men, respectively, they were scarcely represented in extracurricular activities at Evander Childs. While blacks were physically absent from the New Utrecht population, they were effectively socially absent from Evander Childs, as well.[16]

In contrast, native men were everywhere at Evander Childs. They were especially active as editors and in all publications, in the presidencies, in football and other sports, Arista and other academic clubs, and in social activities—their involvement was both far-ranging and intense. Jews also fanned out into most activities, but they rarely dominated them here as they did at New Utrecht. As was true at George Washington, Jews were bested by natives in the most prestigious posts, the presidencies and editorships. Even though there were more than twice as many Jewish as native men at Evander Childs, there were twice as many native presidents and as many native editors.

Jewish women at Evander took first place in a long list of activities, including membership in Arista and "other science" clubs, as editors-in-chief, and in social activities, "other publications," and "other news." As at George Washington, Jewish women did relatively better than Jewish men, and they did so in a similar social setting—a middle class school with a substantial native population. In this context, native men tended to capture and hold strategic positions while Jewish and native men appear to have been in continuous competition, with their interests similarly focused. While Jewish and native women were active in similar activities, Jewish women were usually more active and more readily assumed prominent posts. Despite these achievements, native women still overwhelmed Jews in celebrity status.

The differences in the experiences of Jews and Italians at Evander Childs and New Utrecht had less to do with the economics than with the demographics of the schools and their surrounding neighborhoods. Evander Childs, like its Pelham Parkway neighborhood, was more recently developed and changing rapidly as it became increasingly populated by newer ethnic groups.[17] Between 1933 and 1945, the proportion of natives in the senior class at Evander was cut in half, from 26 percent to 14 percent, while the proportion of Italians more than doubled, from 10 percent to 23 percent. This growing Italian presence may help to explain the substantial participation of this ethnic group. Sensing their developing role in the school, Italian men moved more smoothly into the social life of Evander Childs than they could or were allowed to do at New Utrecht, where they were a constant minority, with Jews in the majority. The other groups were too small to matter. In that context, Italians were an outgroup and their status in the activities testified to that position. Though Italians were active in a broad range of clubs, status and influence were exercised by Jews. Seventy percent of all male celebrities at New Utrecht were Jewish. At Evander Childs, Jews had to compete with a large and active native group and a growing Italian population. In that context, Italians were not an outgroup but only one of several minorities. This kind of complex and changing ethnic situation was also part of Americanization in the city's schools. It affected not only the experience of growing up in the neighborhoods but the structure of social relationships in the schools. Young men and women from the city's ethnic groups often reacted as much to each other in their development as they did to any specific and stable native norm.

At Theodore Roosevelt High School in the Bronx, Jews experienced an even sharper set of constraints than at Evander Childs. An ethnically mixed school with a substantial Jewish minority, Theodore Roosevelt had very clearly defined patterns of ethnic participation. Despite the school's relatively small Irish population (4 percent), its location in the old Irish bailiwick of Fordham Road (directly across the street from Fordham University) meant that the extracurricular world at Theodore Roosevelt reflected the specific ethnic pressures of its location. During the 1920s, '30s and '40s, parts of the old Irish neighborhood rapidly filled with Jews and Italians, and the area witnessed heightened frictions between the Irish and Jews in the context of the depression and the city's political coalitions. Antisemitism became a familiar experience for Jewish youths, who were frequently harassed by the Irish on the streets. Even the churches became embroiled in the controversies.[18]

At school, too, Jewish men appear to have been on the defensive. At Theodore Roosevelt, Jewish men were far less prominent in the extracurricular realm than elsewhere. The small group of Irish men and the larger group of native men made a remarkable showing in the activities.[19] The strength of the combined influence of the Irish and natives may have intimidated Jews, or more likely the two groups actively excluded Jews from participation. It is significant that many Irish and a good number of native men belonged to religious clubs. Elsewhere, religious clubs were largely female preserves, but at Roosevelt, one-fifth of all the Irish men and one-tenth of all native men were members, and almost one-third of all Irish women. Italians, though they were Catholics, did not participate significantly. Religion may have become especially important at a school like Theodore Roosevelt as the Irish were forced to define themselves in the context of a growing group of new immigrants.

The Irish and natives were the most active groups in general, and both groups were especially prominent in politics. Native men were three times as likely to be presidents than was warranted by their population and twice as likely to hold other political offices. The yearbook staff, with its strong social and political influence, also had a disproportionately large Irish and native presence. The Irish were unusually active on the newspaper staff as well as in drama clubs, a situation unlike that at most other schools, where Jews tended to be dominant in both. Election to the presidency highlighted the pattern: the Irish and natives together controlled two-thirds of the male presidencies but scarcely one-fifth of the population.

Although the pattern of ethnic exclusiveness and separation is not as clear for women as for men at Roosevelt, there remain strong indications of a prestige hierarchy in which the Irish and natives were strongly dominant. The only woman ever to be elected president was native, and the other political offices were disproportionately in the hands of Irish women. But even here, the strong tendency for Jewish women to participate in literary activities was evident and sharply distinguished them from Jewish men. All three women who ever became editor-in-chief of the newspaper were Jewish, and Jewish women were also much more prominent than Jewish men on the news staff. Although not quite so consistently or strongly as the men, Jewish, Italian, and German women tended to cluster in activities not interesting or important to Irish and native women. Overall, however, Jewish women were more active than Jewish men. Jewish men, far more than Jewish women, apparently were overpowered by the natives and Irish in the school's extracurricular world.

High schools exist within the broader context of the neighborhoods they serve. In the 1930s and 1940s, they reflected not only the economic realities of those locations but also their special social and cultural pressures. At Roosevelt, the Irish made a strong showing in activities, just as they were also a powerful presence in the community. Schools do not operate in isolation from the pressures experienced by young people at home and in the streets, and these are often brought into the school. This was the case despite and possibly even in response to the assimilationist pressures exercised by the planned school program.

New York City was also full of special schools, defined not by neighborhood but by vocational or other goals. Some of these were sexually restricted. Bay Ridge High School and the High School of Commerce were two such schools. Although quite different from each other, both were sexually exclusive; Bay Ridge was a women's academic school in Brooklyn, while Commerce, as its name implies, emphasized business. During the war, Commerce became coeducational but throughout the thirties and most of the forties it was exclusively a men's school.[20]

Located in Brooklyn's southwest corner, Bay Ridge High School drew its students from a wide geographic area. Though it was noted for its academic excellence in the 1930s and 1940s, Bay Ridge's most prominent feature was social: as a woman's school, Bay Ridge was considered "safe," a factor of some consequence for parents, many of them first- or second-generation immigrants who hoped to protect their daughters from daily association with men.[21] This seems to have been especially important to Italians, who sent large numbers of their female children to Bay Ridge. Italians with 31 percent and natives with 26 percent (the school was situated in a heavily native enclave) were the two largest population groups. There were far fewer Jews, only 6 percent.

At Bay Ridge, Italian women participated more widely and actively in extracurricular activities than elsewhere, a fact that may explain why Italian women were reluctant to participate in coeducational schools and restricted their extracurricular participation largely to academic clubs. It may also reflect the sheer size and greater confidence of the Italian population. At Bay Ridge, Italian women were unusually active in politics, winning one of four presidencies. Italian women also landed two of the editors' posts; two others went to natives and one each to an Irish and a Jewish woman. At the same time, and despite being a small part of the population, Jewish women were very active in a large number of activities, and especially prominent in literary ones. Indeed, Jewish women expressed their literary interests regardless of specific environment. Italian women, on the other hand, were not especially drawn to any of the literary activities—yearbook, news staff, or other publications. Native women at Bay Ridge were also very active, but it was the Italians, not the natives, who dominated the social activities.

Bay Ridge was hospitable to all of the ethnic groups. Indeed, its most prominent characteristic was the extraordinarily high, practically universal, participation of students in extracurricular activities. Despite having clear preferences for certain activities, the ethnic groups seem less marked for their differences than for universal participation. This is well illustrated by the experience of blacks. The number of black women was small, only four, but they were involved in a surprisingly wide range of activities, in sharp contrast to a comparably small number of black men at Evander Childs and Theodore Roosevelt. Ethnically heterogeneous, Bay Ridge provided all groups with substantial access to activities and encouraged different groups to mix in the clubs. It is significant that Bay Ridge had only women students. Women, as we have seen, tended to demonstrate fewer sharply defined ethnic patterns. In addition, at Bay Ridge the social functions of the extracurricular clubs in the dating-and-rating games of adolescence were missing, and therefore some of the reasons for ethnic associations were absent. The very high level of participation also suggests that clubs at Bay Ridge were probably closely monitored by a faculty that encouraged universal involvement and may well have discouraged too much ethnic clustering.

The High School of Commerce, like Bay Ridge, was a unisex school, in this case male, and it had an even more ethnically balanced population. Of the 1,138 senior men, 20 percent were Jewish, 18 percent Italian, 5 percent black, 12 percent Irish, 7 percent German, and 19 percent native. Unlike Bay Ridge, Commerce was a vocational school, one of the many located in Manhattan. The extracurricular pattern at Commerce demonstrates and amplifies the tendency for Jews and natives to take the lead in student activities. Except for sports, the orchestra, and social activities, Jews were almost always the most active group. Most surprising was the Jewish absence in the science categories. The tiny number of science club members and the business orientation of commercial students probably explains this. Jewish students with clear academic and professional interests went elsewhere than to Commerce. Among the other groups, the Irish showed considerable activity. In addition to their control of one-third of the presidencies, the Irish were heavily involved in "other political" offices, the yearbook, other news, and all the sports. But the Irish did poorly on various measures of academic interest—Arista, "other academic" clubs, "other publications." Indeed, Irish interests and avoidances in general are well illustrated at Commerce. Wherever the Irish attended in any number, they concentrated in sports, politics, and the yearbook staff, as well as in social and religious clubs. They rarely took an interest in the sciences, "other academic" clubs, and they usually made a poor showing in Arista. This pattern was no doubt related to the peculiar pattern of attendance of Irish Catholics at public high schools in the 1930s and 40s, when the most ambitious and academically talented attended Catholic rather than public schools. Indeed, the unusually large proportion of Irish at Commerce already points to this, since the less academically oriented were often enrolled in the city's vocational programs.[22]

The Germans, like the Irish, were very selective among the activities at Commerce, as they were in most schools, and they tended to cluster markedly. They were lowest ranked of all the groups in general activity level and in service. Though completely absent from basketball, they were especially active in "other sports." Germans ignored the orchestra, but joined the glee club and drama. For Germans at Commerce, this noticeable clustering seemed more significant than the choices themselves.

Native whites joined Jews at Commerce to take the lead in campus activities. Jews and natives were designated celebrities to about the same extent at Commerce, the usual native preeminence in schools with a substantial native population. Above all, natives were largely absent from the newspaper staff, and had neither editors nor presidents. In these categories of symbolic prestige, the absence of natives is curious. Perhaps this anomaly can be explained by the different ambitions of students attending the High School of Commerce from those attending the usual comprehensive high school. Unlike most high schools, Commerce had fewer students with college plans, and thus the extracurricular world did not serve as leverage for college entrance. To some extent, extracurricular participation everywhere reflected the different college-going ambitions of various ethnic groups. At a time when college admissions committees began to evaluate students according to nonacademic or marginally academic criteria, the college-oriented were far more likely to covet the plums of the extracurricular arena such as editor-in-chief of the newspaper or a presidency.[23] In this context, the special propensity for extracurricular participation of Jewish students and those of native white background at most schools becomes more comprehensible, since they were most likely to have college plans or ambitions. Their prominence in the choicest positions of the extracurricular world as well as on the Arista rolls substantiates this.

It would be a mistake, however, to attribute the complex patterns in extracurricular activities to selective college-going ambitions of different ethnic groups alone. These ambitions could intensify the pattern and might explain certain features, but they are inadequate to explain the many patterns we have been finding. Far more students participated in activities than could or would attend college. Moreover, the diversity in school experiences and the specificity of choices made by different ethnic groups cannot be understood by reference to college ambitions. One example will suffice. Although both editorships and presidencies were prominent and attractive positions, native men were much more likely to be presidents, while Jews were more frequently editors. The elaborate patterning of extracurricular participations in New York high schools must be understood at least in part as the effects of ethnic preference and evidence for the continuing significance of ethnic group association at school.

As the child of immigrants, Leonard Covello understood that school life was a shared group experience. "Whatever problems we had at school or in the street, we never took up with our parents. These were our personal problems to be shared only by companions who knew and were conditioned by the same experience."[24] Certainly the lives of the children were unlike those of their parents, but they shared them with others of their own group, and high school students still existed in a world strongly shaped by ethnic bonds and identities. Even at school, where assimilation was an educational objective, and among adolescents who could be expected to view their parents' old-fashioned world with disdain, or with pain, ethnicity was a significant fact of social experience.

The ethnic experiences of high school students were not like those of their parents. Indeed, that experience differed even for students of the same group among the different schools in the city of immigrants. A Jew at Theodore Roosevelt did not have the same experiences as one at New Utrecht or at George Washington. An

Italian at Evander Childs had different school experiences than an Italian at New Utrecht or at Bay Ridge. The specific mix of ethnic groups, the neighborhood context, the size of the native population, as well as traditions specific to the school's history all influenced the nature of high school extracurricular and social life. So too, ethnicity often affected men and women differently. Women often made different choices than their ethnic brothers. Italian women placed a heavy emphasis on academic clubs, a choice much more rarely made by Italian men. Jewish women chose literary activities more consistently than Jewish men but hardly ever joined Jewish men in the science clubs. Irish women chose science clubs while Irish men almost never made the same decision. These were strong variations and they remind us that ethnicity, like culture in general, is not homogeneous but operates in a socially differentiated universe strongly marked by gender. Ethnicity seems also not to have been as consistently expressed by women as by men, and one sees the ethnic patterns across schools and within schools much more clearly by looking at men only. Male ethnics divided their activities more regularly among themselves, as each group emphasized different kinds of interests. Participation in extracurricular activities and successful competition especially may have had status resonances and possibly relationships to future goals that appear not to have influenced women to the same degree as men. Some of this was no doubt the result of differences in college-going plans between men and women. But women may have been more accepting of other groups and less exclusionary in general.

The class composition of a school population also mattered. Except for service activities, the ability of students to engage in many extracurricular activities was dependent on the time available to them after school hours. Some groups, like Italians and blacks, probably had less leisure because they were poorer. At a prosperous school like George Washington, Italians and blacks were far more active across the board than at a lower-middle-class school like New Utrecht.

It is also important to remember that even where activities were ethnically stratified, students from different groups did meet. That mixing was most notable at a school like Bay Ridge, but it was true almost everywhere that, except for blacks, students from different groups had overlapping interests in a range of activities. Since I have made conclusions about ethnic participation on the basis of group disproportions, it is easy to overlook or discount the degree to which individuals from all the groups made contacts with those from other groups in the social life of the school. Even at Theodore Roosevelt, Jews met Irish as well as Italians, Germans, and natives on the yearbook staff. These exchanges were mediated by considerations of status, prejudice, and even hostility, as well as shared interests and friendship, but that only meant that the activities reflected the larger realities of American society.

In this sense, the high schools and the social and extracurricular activities exposed students to various critical features of American social and civic life. This was certainly what theorists and administrators had in mind when they developed the activities as allies in socialization and Americanization. But Americanization and assimilation were never neat or uniform. At different schools, students began to grasp the complex features of the society differently. While they met students from other groups, they did so in ways that were mediated by ethnic bonds and stratifications.

The prestige of natives, the ambition and drive toward success of Jews, the exclusion of blacks were variously experienced, and these experiences introduced students to the broad features of American urban life in which ethnicity was as much a part as voting, caucusing, and the ability to change one's name. The cliquing and selecting of friends, the preferences for certain activities, and the inclination to attribute power, popularity, and even beauty to some and not to others were fundamental experiences of adolescents in school and out. Those who theorized about the potential of the extracurricular activities in socialization were correct to this extent.

In the end, however, one is left with the sharp and clear impression of a high school society divided along ethnic lines of which assimilation-minded educators would not have approved. On the simplest level, this meant that it was more likely for men and women of the same group to associate together in performance clubs and in social activities at individual schools. Beyond that, groups became identified with different talents and characteristics. Some groups, notably the natives and Jews (and the Irish in politics and sports), usually captured the limelight and strategic posts. Certain activities, like science, track, and football for men and literary clubs for women, were disproportionately selected by members of some ethnic groups over others. Wherever females were appointed editors, they were almost certain to be Jews. In schools with a native white population, males of this background were the most likely to be elected to high office. The track team was likely to contain a good portion of the male black population. And almost everywhere, Jews were the academic achievers.

While the data provide us with provocative and compelling patterns, they are less yielding in giving insights to the causes of this variation. It would be tempting but unwise to ascribe the differences to cultural traditions pure and simple. It is also important to avoid stereotyping the groups as they adapted to American circumstances that can be read into the Jewish interest in science and the Irish fascination with politics. It is probably safe to conclude, however, that extracurricular life and student society at school generally encouraged continued reliance on group bonds.

Beyond this, the regularity of certain patterns across schools suggests that student society helped to create new American identities, identities which resulted from a strategic interaction between inherited traditions that shaped perceptions initially, functional patterns of adaptation, and forces of imitation in a youth environment that rewarded imitation. If imitation of natives was important, as I believe it was in light of their extraordinary popularity as registered in celebrity status, the distribution of natives among almost the full range of extracurricular activities (they were far more distributed than other groups) meant that various groups attached themselves to different areas of the school's social world in the process of imitation. Once they did, however, each group created coherent and meaningful ethnic patterns at school, patterns strongly mediated by ethnic peers. In other words, youth society shaped ethnicity for the second and third generations. This peer-mediated ethnicity provided an important form of differentiation in the schools of the thirties and forties, and it was a potent ingredient in the status and prestige hierarchy among students at most schools. Despite the rhetoric and plans of educators who hoped to loosen students from their ethnic pasts, students refashioned their immigrant traditions into American identities. Throughout the most significant period of Americanization, ethnic peers continued to provide students in high school with a source of group bonds within the mass culture and the massive impersonality of the schools.

NOTES

1. Editor's Introduction to Elbert K. Fretwell, *Extra-Curricular Activities in Secondary School* (Boston: Houghton, Mifflin, 1931), vi. For adolescence, see Joseph F. Kett, *Rites of Passage, Adolescence in America: 1790 to the Present* (New York: Basic Books' 1977). The development of the high school is discussed in William Reese, *The Social History of American Education* and Edward A. Krug, *The Shaping of the American High School*, 2 vols. (Madison: University of Wisconsin Press; 1964, 1972); Theodore R. Sizer, *Secondary Schools at the Turn of the Century* (New Haven: Yale University Press, 1964); Lawrence Cremin, "The Revolution in American Secondary Education, 1893–1918," *Teachers College Record*, 56 (March 1955), 295–308.

2. For an important discussion of the role of schooling in creating new age categories among immigrants, see Stephen Lassonde, "Learning and Earning: Schooling, Juvenile Employment, and the Early Life Course in Late Nineteenth Century New Haven," *Journal of Social History*, 29 (Summer 1996), 839–870.

3. As early as 1911, almost 50 percent of the secondary school students in thirty-seven of the largest cities were of foreign-born parentage. See Francesco Cordasco, *Immigrant Children in American Schools: A Classified and Annotated Bibliography of Selected Source Documents* (Fairfield, N.J.: A. M. Kelly, 1976), 27.

4. Earle Rugg, "Special Types of Activities: Student Participation in School Government," *Twenty-Fifth Yearbook of the National Society for the Study of Education* (Bloomington, Ill.: Public School Publishing Co., 1926), 131; Cubberly, "Editor's Introduction," v. For a brief history of the activities, see Galen Jones, *Extra-Curricular Activities in Relation to the Curriculum*, Contributions to Education, Teachers College, Columbia University (New York: Teachers College, 1935), 13–29. See also the discussion in Elbert Fretwell, *Extracurricular Activities in Secondary Schools* (Boston: Houghton-Mifflin, 1931). Fretwell was a premier exponent of extracurricular activities and socialization.

5. Fretwell, *Extracurricular Activities*. Some have argued that by the 1920s, the aim of most school principals was toward maximum control; see Thomas W. Gutowski, "The High school as an Adolescent-Raising Institution: An Inner History of Chicago Public Secondary Education, 1856–1940," Ph.D. diss., University of Chicago, 1978, 221–238.

6. "Native white" was defined for the purposes of this study to include all students whose surnames were either British (exclusive of Ireland), Dutch, or French. I have included these non-British groups in this category because historically both the French and Dutch were long settled in New York. It is certainly true that some Germans, Jews, and Irish were also long established in the city, but their numbers were small compared to the large migrations of the late nineteenth and early twentieth centuries. Obviously, even those students of French or Dutch ancestry who were part of the newer immigration were included among the natives.

Because many individuals of Irish descent have native-sounding names (for example, White), there was probably some undercounting among them. This was probably greatest at Theodore Roosevelt High School, where the proportion of Irish was lower than might have been expected from the demographics of the neighborhood.

All German-surnamed individuals, except those who were most probably Jews, were included as Germans. The "other" category was composed of a very large variety of individuals, including Hispanic surnamed, Scandinavians, Chinese, Japanese, Middle Easterners, and Russians and Poles who obviously were not Jews. Chinese, Japanese and Middle Eastern.

7. Readers are directed to the Appendix tables in Paula S. Fass, *Outside In: Minorities and the Transformation of American Education* (New York: Oxford University Press, 1989), Appendix 2 240–253, for tables detailing the evidence for the following discussion.

8. Gutowski argues that in Chicago, extracurricular participation had become almost a requirement by the 1930s because it was an important part of the way in which high school education was conceived by educators. Moreover, some extracurricular participation was necessary for election to the honor societies. See, Gutowski, "High School as an Adolescent-Raising Institution," 211–221. While participation among seniors in New York was generally very high, it was not uniform across schools and therefore does not appear to have reflected across-the-board policy. At the same time, individual school principals may have made participation almost mandatory.

9. For the purpose of analysis, student activities were divided into twenty-three categories. Although these did not exhaust the range of activities available to students in all schools, they were generally representative of the most important activities in which students engaged.

10. The reader should note that small population groups, like blacks and Irish, may be absent from some activities within a school more often than larger population groups like Jews or Italians.

11. Only at Seward Park were black women overrepresented in "other publications," but this was a statistical fluke, since only one black woman was in fact involved. (See Appendix 2, Table 2). In literary activities, Jewish men were in fact less conspicuous than native men. This is best seen by looking at the editors. Of twenty-one male editors, thirteen were Jews, although Jews made up only 45 percent of the male population. But native men held four of the twenty-one editorial chairs and were more disproportionately represented (13 percent of the male population). Indeed, the apparent success of Jewish men among editors was inflated because of their control of the editorial posts at New Utrecht, where all the editors were Jewish.

12. For the attitudes of Italians toward women, see Virginia Yans McLaughlin, *Family and Community: Italian Immigrants in Buffalo, 1880–1930* (Ithaca, N.Y.: Cornell University Press, 1977), 147, 149–151, and passim.

13. Students were admitted to high schools in New York in the 1930s and 1940s technically on the basis of open admissions, that is, students could choose what school they wished to attend. In practice, however, except for those who elected to go to the academically exclusive schools, where admission was by test, most students attended high schools in their general neighborhood.

14. For the remarkable ethnic diversity in today's Seward Park, see Samuel G. Freedman, *Small Victories: The Real World of a Teacher, Her Students and Their High School* (New York: Harper and Row, 1990).

15. Deborah Dash Moore, *At Home in America: Second Generation New York Jews* (New York: Columbia University Press, 1981).

16. In a memoir of Evander Childs during the depression, Shirley Jacoby Paris notes that black students were hardly noticed at Evander Childs because "they were students, integrated with the rest, meeting the same standards as the whites, and given neither adverse nor preferential treatment." "Evander Childs High School," *Bronx County Historical Society Journal*, 21 (Spring 1984), 5. In fact, whatever their equality in the classroom, blacks were unnoticed in the busy club and activity life because they were largely absent from them. Blacks probably came to Evander Childs from outside the neighborhood.

17. Moore, *At Home in America*, 24, 66.

18. Ronald H. Bayor, *Neighbors in Conflict: The Irish, Germans, Jews, and Italians of New York City, 1929–1941* (Baltimore, Md:, John Hopkins University Press, 1978).

19. Some of the natives may in fact have been Irish with English surnames. The high proportion of natives in religious clubs makes this likely, as does the low number of Irish at the school.

20. I used the June 1947 class at Commerce, which was co-ed, in order to try to get a glimpse of the patterns when the school contained women, but the numbers were simply too small and the range of activities women joined too limited to be very useful.

21. At Bay Ridge, the secretaries in the principal's office, who had themselves attended the school in the forties, made clear that parents usually chose to send their daughters to Bay Ridge because it was an exclusively female school and considered safe. This, they told me, was especially true for Italians. Many Catholic families may have used Bay Ridge as a substitute for parochial schools.

22. For Catholic schools, see Paula S. Fass, *Outside In,* chapter 6.

23. Harold S. Wechsler, *The Qualified Student: A History of Selective College Admissions in America* (New York: John Wiley and Sons, 1977).

24. Leonard Covello and Guido D'Agostino, *The Heart Is the Teacher* (New York: McGraw-Hill, 1958), 47.

Chapter Seven

Brown "Hordes" in McIntosh Suits

Filipinos, Taxi Dance Halls, and Performing the Immigrant Body in Los Angeles, 1930s–1940s

Linda N. España-Maram

taxi dance
8 p.m.–2 a.m.
blondies
seven days a week

"I forgot
my labors
for awhile
at the taxi dance"

the hand around
your waist
feels good

is nothing
but my own

belonging to nobody
but you
if you want it

"they're all blondies
most of the women
all *mataba* [plump] from the south"

but the goddamn tickets
for you
went so fast

into three minutes
ten-cent squeezes

—al robles, "taxi dance"
in *rappin' with ten thousand carabaos in the dark*, 1996

In October 1935, the Los Angeles Police Department conducted a series of surprise raids on all of the city's taxi dance halls for two consecutive Saturday nights. The police claimed to have received an anonymous tip that a murder was to take place in one of the recreation centers. Interrupting the busiest evening in the dance halls, the LAPD thoroughly searched the premises and the male patrons, confiscating a number of weapons, including knives, guns, and ice picks. Before the end of the week, after the second raid, the police announced that patrons caught with lethal weapons in dance halls faced the possibility of deportation.[1]

Because immigration policies were (and still are) under federal jurisdiction, the local police department did not have the authority to carry out the threat. But in the midst of the Great Depression, with repatriation campaigns directed against Mexicans and Filipinos in full swing, issuing such a decree suggests that the police sought to cloak a racist policy in the mantle of local "peace-keeping" tactics. Further, the LAPD's full-scale response to a single anonymous tip and the consequences aimed specifically toward the immigrant male patrons of the taxi dance halls speak volumes about the relationship among the city's regulating agencies, ethnic Angeleños, and commercialized recreation centers.

This chapter traces how popular culture practices among members of a working-class immigrant community facilitated the negotiation of identity politics through an examination of the leisure activity arguably most closely associated with Filipinos of the 1920s and 1930s: the taxi dance halls where they paid to dance with women in timed, ritualized sequences. Some observers from the period decried these centers as nothing more than gathering places for working-class brown "hordes," particularly what one young woman described as the "sensuous, gaudily dressed, almost fierce-looking young Filipinos on the East Side of L.A."[2] But for the participants, these taxi dance halls became important sites for creating a vibrant subculture. Fueled by the intense nativism and racist and sexist legislation of the Great Depression and New Deal eras, these leisure centers provided opportunities for young, poor immigrant men like Filipinos to create identities that allowed them to be something other than what their ethnicity, class, or national origin dictated.

Conflicts emanating from issues related to the taxi dance halls indicate the effectiveness of commercialized leisure as conduits to fostering an alternative culture among marginalized populations. Within the Filipino community itself, issues related to taxi dance halls exposed the class distinctions between the small, self-described "adjusted group" of Filipino students who "cannot afford to waste much of their time in terms of the pleasures of their brothers," and the workers, whom the students argued comprised the "bewildered group, [whose] most outstanding characteristic . . . is the lack of any tangible aim in life."[3] On another level, the competition in the dance halls evinces the struggle among Filipino workers themselves as they sought to create viable individual and group identities. Finally, the controversies elucidate tensions between the dance halls' largely youthful, largely working-class participants and the dominant society's policing agents, including the LAPD and a number of reform societies. Reformers conducted campaigns against taxi dance halls in part because the centers presented a visible threat to the dominant culture's construction of youth, morality, and gender relations, but also because the commercialization represented the uneasiness they felt about the expansion of capitalism into the area of leisure. In a broader sense, then, this chapter analyzes the struggles over the issues of ethnicity, class, and popular culture not only within immigrant and working-class communities but within the larger American society as well. In forging a collective sense of ethnicity and building a viable community, Filipino immigrants challenged the host society over the nature of "American" values. By displaying "improper" behavior, they sought to carve niches of autonomy for self-definition, fought against imposed restrictions on space, and sought to expand the boundaries of alternative expressions.

Filipinos constitute one of the largest Asian/Pacific Island immigrant groups in the United States today. Despite their numerical significance, however, few researchers have explored this immigrant community and the Filipino-American experiences.[4] This chapter focuses on Filipino immigrants from the 1920s until the late 1930s, a period when young, single, unskilled males made up the vast majority of the group. Agents of United States agribusinesses went to the Philippines to recruit Filipinos as an additional pool of exploitable labor, first for Hawaii's sugar plantations and then for California's fields, since U.S. immigration laws barred Chinese and Japanese laborers.[5] In addition, as a result of the Spanish-American War of 1898, American imperialism, and the defeat of large-scale Filipino resistance to United States occupation, the Philippines became a colony of the United States. The United States government thus considered Filipinos as "nationals," and as such they were not subject to immigration restrictions or quotas; like other Asian immigrants, however, neither could they vote, own land, buy homes, nor apply for citizenship. The immigration of this wave of Filipinos virtually stopped by the mid-1930s, largely because of the Tydings-McDuffie Act which, among other things, significantly reduced the number of Filipino immigrants to the United States mainland through a quota of fifty per year.

The first large group of more than 2,000 Filipino laborers arrived in California by 1923. This figure represents a threefold increase over the number of Filipinos in California in the previous year. Single young men formed the bulk of these immigrants, with 84 percent in their teens to mid-twenties. By 1930, men made up 94 percent of the Filipino immigrant population. In that same year, more than 45,000 Filipinos resided in the continental United States, 67 percent of whom lived and worked in California.[6] By 1933, an estimated 65,000 Filipinos had arrived in the continental United States, with about one-fifth of that population (about 12,000) residing in Los Angeles County. Of these, about 4,000 lived in the city's downtown area on a year-round basis.[7]

In part because of racism and in part because of the requirements of an industrialized economy, the bulk of these laborers found employment only in the lowest ranks of some of the most exploitative sectors, including agribusiness, the canning industries, and service-oriented jobs. The vast majority (80 percent) became migratory laborers, routinely traveling between farms, ports, and urban areas. Other Filipinos, including full-time students on scholarships, students who worked part-time, and workers employed full-time in domestic service as houseboys, dishwashers, or bellboys, settled in cities. Studies of these Filipino laborers have often failed to explore

Fig. 7.1. Town mates Romy Madrigal (top row, second from right), Dodo Zamorano (top row, second from left), Bonifacio Libre (sitting center), others unknown, pose for a group picture in Los Angeles' harbor area during the 1930s. Photographs like this linked the immigrants with their families and friends across the Pacific Ocean. This posed photograph of workers at the fish canneries of Terminal Island attired in their fashionable McIntosh suits, no doubt delighted and fired the imagination of the recipients of the picture. (Courtesy of "Shades of L.A." Archives, Los Angeles Public Library.)

this fluidity associated with creating an ethnic, working-class identity among such a young, geographically mobile population. While earlier theses have acknowledged the migrant lifestyle, they nevertheless tend to look at Filipinos only as rural agricultural hands, only as cannery workers, or only as urban laborers.[8]

Filipinos earned meager wages for tedious, hard work in often closely supervised positions. One study estimated that Filipino migrant workers in California's fields earned between 30 to 50 cents per hour or between $2.50 to $5 a day in the late 1920s.[9] These already marginal salaries plummeted during the Depression. Toribio Castillo, who worked in Stockton's agricultural fields before settling in Los Angeles, recalled that during the 1930s, Filipinos felt "lucky" if they earned $2 for a 12–hour day cutting celery or picking peaches.[10] Celendo La Questa and his cohorts, however, remember making only one dollar a day for 15-hour days performing back-breaking stoop labor like hoeing cabbage in the Salinas Valley.[11] The economic slump affected Filipinos in urban areas just as dramatically. Johnny P. Rallonza, who worked as a dishwasher in Los Angeles, recalled that his weekly salary fell from $45 to $10, while his work day increased from 9½ to 15 hours. Rallonza expressed discontent, but quickly added that "I *had* to work. Too many people were out of jobs and had no place [even] to sleep."[12] Indeed, one study estimated that in Depression-era Los Angeles County, about 75 percent of the more than 12,000 Filipinos lost their jobs.[13]

As laborers in some of the most exploitative sectors, Filipinos sought to create meanings in their lives by developing cultural practices and oppositional strategies to mitigate the harsh circumstances of their lives and to foster some semblance of ethnic solidarity. The taxi dance halls and other recreational centers which dotted the migratory routes and the downtown areas where Filipinos lived became significant rendezvous points for calling the community into being, where Filipinos could cement and rejuvenate personal bonds, share food, swap stories, and surely gossip about the *kababayan* (countrymen) along the migration circuit. Barred from buying homes and forced to rent small shoddy rooms in the rundown sections of cities by a combination of legislation, poverty, racism, and segregation, Filipinos invested instead in clothing and activities that showcased a vibrant public life in and around Los Angeles's Little Manila. From the 1930s until World War II, this ethnic enclave flourished in the downtown area, roughly demarcated by San Pedro Street on the east, Sixth Street on the south, Figueroa Avenue on the west, and Sunset Boulevard on the north.[14]

Filipinos eagerly frequented the taxi dance halls near the community, including Danceland and the Hippodrome Palace on Main Street, the Liberty Dance Hall on Third, Roma Hall on Figueroa, and the Orpheum and the Red Mill Dance Hall on Broadway. Many of the dance halls were within easy walking distance, sometimes even next to each other, or at least along the route of the red cars, the city's public transportation system in the 1930s. The dance halls were part of the effervescent street culture of the downtown scene, blending in with the various restaurants, cafes, barbershops, and pool halls ardently patronized by the Filipino residents. Walkways leading to these leisure centers were strategic meeting points in the Filipinos' social lives. Indeed, Filipino foot traffic was so brisk that at least one researcher observed how "Filipino arrests in Los Angeles for blocking the sidewalk alone run proportionately high. In 1928–1929, 46 of the total 80 arrested under this ordinance were Filipinos."[15]

Clearly, street culture and commercialized leisure activities represented sites that nurtured an important alternative lifestyle. In their search for places that afforded them some sense of dignity and relative freedom of expression, Filipino workers flocked to taxi dance halls to tout young brown bodies not as exploited workers but as sources of enjoyment, style, and sensuality.[16] Living in a world where their work time was dictated by cycles of crops, migration patterns of fish, and demands of service-oriented industries, dance halls provided the spaces for Filipinos to be what they also were: young men in search of the proverbial wine, women, and song. Ray Corpuz, for example, who emigrated when he was fourteen years old, recalled that in the Filipino community of the 1930s,

> we were all males at that time, from L.A. to Seattle . . . so what do we have to do? We were young so we go to Chinatown because there are a lot of, ah, things going on there. Taxi dances, prostitution, whatever, they were there. And of course young people

like me at the time, I like to try everything to see what it looks like as opposed to, you know, [reading about] it in the books.[17]

In the dance halls, Filipino workers developed a dynamic subculture, where they celebrated the body attired in McIntosh suits, expensive formal attire with padded shoulders and wide lapels worn by some of Hollywood's most famous leading men like William Powell. This desire for a form-fitted McIntosh in turn provided opportunities for some entrepreneurs in Little Manila. When Vincent Bello, for example, tired of the migratory lifestyle, he opened the Bello Smart Tailor Shop on Main Street, where he made a living in custom fitting, and sometimes designing, clothes for his compatriots.[18] Felix Pascua remembered that Bello "made the best McIntosh suit around town in those days."[19] Bello never had to return to migrant labor to make a living.[20] Oscar F. Huck's tailor shop on 706 South Hill Street also thrived on a brisk business due to a "large Filipino clientele."[21] The Calderon Company on 105 East First Street, capitalizing on the appeal of the McIntosh suit to Filipinos, advertised that the shop specialized in "custom-built Hollywood clothes."[22]

Dressed to the hilt, Filipinos flocked to L.A. leisure halls to dance to music ranging from sentimental love songs to more rousing numbers like the swing, the jitterbug, and the fox trot. Entrance fees usually ranged from ten cents to a quarter. Some dance halls, like the Red Mill on Broadway, offered free admission up to a certain hour. Others charged a dollar upon entering, but patrons received tickets good for ten one-minute dances. Various establishments offered a spectrum of incentives, including the "lucky number" lottery, where the owners hid numbers amid the decorations in the ceiling. At certain intervals, the house would call out a "lucky" number, and the patron standing under, or closest to, that number received free dance passes.[23]

Other dance halls provided "free" entertainment like dance shows and musical recitals before or after the regular taxi dancing. The Hippodrome Dance Palace, for example, regularly sponsored a Sunday midnight program that featured an "all girl show" led by "Big" Rita Gaythorne. One such line-up included Spanish dances performed by Betty Bernard and a rumba number by Billie Wallace. But if "Big" Rita, Betty, and Billie were not enough for the patrons, the Hippodrome promised that all "other girls will be called on demand."[24] A Filipino observer noted that during these shows, "the Filipino patrons cannot refrain from participation when watching the dancing or listening to the singing. When a dancing couple performs a 'blues' or a 'moonlight waltz,' voices from the crowd will be raised time and again. . . . Also, when there is a popular song, voices occasionally join in a wild exultant shout at certain intervals."[25]

The key to participating in the games and dances, of course, was the continual purchase of tickets. "If you wanted to dance you had to buy a roll of tickets in advance," a Filipino laborer recalled, "then you would dance with a woman until all your tickets were gone. . . . Each ticket was 10 [cents] and you were lucky if your salary was even $5 a day then. So your whole salary might last for only an hour if you liked to dance."[26] For some Filipinos, this price was too high for one night's pastime. Johnny Garcia remarked that "if they [Filipino patrons] would work and save their money now instead of hanging around dance halls and going out with the girls they would be better off. I like to dance but I don't like to well enough to throw all my earnings on it."[27] Indeed, even Carey McWilliams quipped that taxi dancing "is about the costliest [entertainment] to be found in California: ten cents for a dance that lasts exactly one minute."[28] Still, most Filipinos bought rolls of tickets in the dance halls. Severely restricted by racism and segregation in other aspects of their lives, they reveled in the night clubs which accepted, indeed encouraged, their participation. Felix Pascua recalled that Filipinos faced rejection in most social institutions, and that "the only places that welcomed us with open arms were the gambling houses and dancing halls."[29]

While the tickets frequently represented the bulk of their wages, for some Filipinos taxi dancing remained a popular diversion because it paid off in another way: it enhanced their prestige as "sporting men" among their compatriots. Frank Coloma, for example, bragged that "there were four main dancing cabarets in Los Angeles and I had a girlfriend in every hall."[30] Miguel Lawagan also frequented taxi dance halls in Los Angeles, going to the Hippodrome Dance Palace, the self-proclaimed "rendezvous of sportsmen," almost every night. For him, taxi dancing "is cheaper than a date—for one dollar you can have, say, ten different girls."[31]

While most dance halls remained open every evening, Saturday and Sunday were the busiest nights, when young, working-class immigrant men like Filipinos and Mexicans cruised these leisure centers in pursuit of some night moves.[32] Inside the crowded dance halls, one anxious observer described "dancing that was thoroughly immoral. Couples dance or whirl about the floor with their bodies pressed tightly together, shaking, moving, and rotating their lower portions to rouse their sex impulses. Some even engage in 'biting' one another on the lobes of the ears and upon the neck."[33] The sexual overtones in part reflected how workers took control of their own bodies and actions in these commercialized centers. Regarded by many Anglo employers primarily as exploitable "stoop labor" in the fields, Filipinos and Mexicans proclaimed their sensuality and virility in ways denied them as workers. Under the guise of performing modern dance movements, overworked brown bodies reveled in a charged atmosphere of raw sexuality. Through public displays of simulated sexual intercourse, workers seized moments of gratification absent from other aspects of their lives. Working for farm owners who pitted them against each other during often bitter labor disputes, taxi dance halls encouraged an interethnic working-class culture based on the body's ability to express, or at least effectively suggest, passion, arousal, and sexual bravado.

While promoting a shared, decidedly heterosexual masculine experience, confrontations were also frequent enough among the young Filipino and Mexican regulars and the Anglos who occasionally attended the dance halls that the police had a convenient reason to raid the clubs regularly.[34] Sammy R. Lopez, a migrant worker who came to the United States in 1929, recalled how "Filipinos, Americans, Mexicans ... get jealous ... [of] one another [because] they think somebody [is] fooling around with their sweetheart.... I see actually shooting, too, in Los Angeles in front of the [taxi dance hall]."[35] Rivalry over accouterments and the affection, or at least the availability, of taxi dancers appear to be the overwhelming causes of these skirmishes. One Mexican observer noted how a number of the Mexican immigrant men in the dance halls were "very poorly dressed . . . [and] many of them dance Mexican style."[36] This aspect of clothing and dancing style among Mexican patrons contributed to the competition with the customarily impeccably groomed, and periodically flashy, Filipinos who routinely frequented the same leisure centers. Frank Coloma recalled that whenever he went out, "I always wore the very best suit—a McIntosh suit."[37] Vicente Elequin remembered interethnic tensions also based on clothing in San Diego, where "the Mexican and Anglo guys did not like us [Filipinos] because we got all the girls at the dance halls. We wore the best clothes in the market and entertained the girls well."[38]

Bursts of interethnic tensions among the youthful male patrons notwithstanding, amicable relations developed between some taxi dancers and their Filipino partners, suggesting that the attraction between brown men and white women was mutual. Alida C. Bowler, director of the Delinquency Unit of the U.S. Children's Bureau, noted that a number of Anglo taxi dancers preferred Filipino customers. When she worked as the LAPD's director of public relations, Bowler recalled that

> from the Filipino youth, she [the taxi dancer] will tell you, she usually receives treatment greatly superior to that accorded her by the average American frequenter of the dance-hall. The Filipino is a natty fellow, almost always immaculately groomed, well garbed, with a flair for that style of dress described by these girls as "classy". . . . And he has manners. His approach to the girl is habitually marked by a courtesy practically non-existent among the more or less uncouth American white men to whom she has already been or has become accustomed. The girls are by no means indifferent to these qualities.[39]

Not all taxi dancers, however, shared these sentiments regarding Asian patrons of the leisure centers. Intense interethnic prejudices often had to be overcome before dancer and client ever stepped onto the dance floor. In some of Los Angeles's dance halls, a Mexican observer noted how "the majority of the Mexican [taxi dancers] do not like to dance with the Chinese, Japanese, or Filipinos who, for their part, generally prefer American or Mexican women who are very light-skinned and can easily pass as Americans."[40] Slang terms among Filipino workers reflected some of these pervasive racial tensions—for example, "staying white" referred to taxi dancers who danced with Filipinos but dated only Anglo men, while a "nigger lover" was a white taxi dancer who accepted dates with Filipinos.[41]

Thus the dance hall culture was neither inherently utopian nor even democratic. The only acceptable sexual mores, for example, were based on heterosexual desires. Further, hand in hand with the emergence of the male youth subculture was the patrons' objectification of women in the dance halls. The gendered arrangements of the public space underscored this principle. Unless they were dancing with clients, all of the taxi dancers were required to stand in a line, in full view of potential customers. While waiting, women were supposed to attract the interests of any male patrons.[42] Slang expressions among Filipinos reflected the sexism within the largely male population. A number of them generally referred to taxi dancers and female Anglo companions, no matter how old, as "*bata*," a Tagalog word for, literally, baby or a very young child, not necessarily always a term of endearment.[43] These condescending attitudes may in part be what the taxi dancers perceived as "manners" among the Filipino patrons.

Despite the male-centered subculture of the taxi dance halls, for some women, especially young women, working in the leisure centers provided one way of making a living. Generally, dancers earned one-half of the ticket price per dance, but whatever else the patrons gave them as "tips" or gifts were theirs to keep. For some unemployed women, working as taxi dancers seemed to offer a relatively more profitable alternative job. One study estimated that taxi dancers could potentially earn between $35 to $40 per week, a figure representing at least twice or even three times the salaries offered by factories and department stores.[44] Income and other benefits from taxi dance halls became especially crucial to single young women during the Great Depression and the New Deal decades, when men received preferential treatment from federal programs like the Works Progress Administration (WPA) on the assumption that men were the principal breadwinners. This policy squeezed not only single women from federally funded jobs, but wives and female heads of household as well.[45]

The predominance of young men paying to dance with women in these taxi dance halls suggests how, on one level, entertainment industries began to take seriously working-class youth, immigrant or not, as consumers.[46] Some of the most popular recreation centers, like the Orpheum and the Hippodrome, were originally built as luxurious theaters for quality vaudeville acts for the largely middle-class Midwesterners and their families who migrated to Los Angeles beginning at the turn of the century.[47] When vaudeville ceased to be profitable, a few theater owners sold their properties to entrepreneurs, some of whom catered to an emerging population of consumers, young working people with discretionary incomes.

On another level, however, popular culture practices represented sites where workers, marginalized by class, race, age, or gender, took back what they felt was rightfully theirs: their bodies, their time, and the freedom to construct, affirm, or reject identities in their own fashion and among their own peers. Historian Robin D. G. Kelley understands the urgency of this need within communities of exploited laborers. Writing about oppositional strategies among workers of color in general and African Americans in the Jim Crow South in particular, Kelley eloquently argues that the

> search for the sonic, visceral pleasures of music and fellowship, for the sensual pleasures of food, drink, and dancing was not just about escaping the vicissitudes of southern life. They went with people who had a shared knowledge of cultural forms, people with whom they felt kinship, people with whom they shared stories about the day or the latest joke, people who shared a vernacular whose grammar and vocabulary struggled to articulate the beauty and burden of their lives."[48]

Like these black workers, Filipinos went to dance halls because they not only liked to dance, but also to share experiences and formulate a collective memory in addition to those in the work place.

To the broader American society and its policing agencies, however, the combination of youth, flagrant displays of sexuality, and bursts of violence among working-class men in the taxi dance halls represented the close association they had always assumed existed among vice, prostitution, and commercialized entertainment. In 1929, for example, the Los Angeles Police Commission embarked on an impassioned crusade against taxi dance halls when a newspaper's unsubstantiated "exposé" alleged that "white girls [are] 'sold' to Oriental Men as Partners for 'Taxi-Dance.' "[49] But because of poverty, restrictive covenants, and brute force from neighboring Anglo residents, ethnic communities were usually segregated in neighborhoods that were crime ridden even before the arrival of immigrants or poor people of color in the area.[50] Filipino immigrant author Carlos Bulosan wrote how, in 1930s Los Angeles, he, his brother, and many compatriots were forced to live on Hope Street, "where pimps and prostitutes were as numerous as the stars in the sky. It was a noisy and tragic street, where suicide and murders were a daily occurrence, but it was the only place in the city where we could find a room. There was no other district where we were allowed to reside."[51]

For numerous reasons, including recreation, possible employment, and varying degrees of protection from a hostile dominant society, immigrants often congregated in ethnic neighborhoods like Sonoratown, Chinatown, and Little Manila. Thus, the police associated violence particularly with the activities of Angeleños of color, despite the fact that arrest rates for Filipinos under twenty-five years old in Los Angeles during the Great Depression were lower than those among Anglo men of the comparable age group.[52] Furthermore, these statistics were typical throughout California where Filipinos and Anglos worked and lived, including San Francisco and Stockton.[53] Nevertheless, Manuel Buaken, who worked as a houseboy in Los Angeles in the 1930s, remembered that he and his friends constantly faced harassment by police officers. Strolling along his employer's affluent residential street during a break from his domestic duties one evening, Buaken recalled how an officer barked at him to "move along, you appear like a questionable and suspicious character."[54]

In addition to localized attempts at controlling the Filipinos' use of public spaces, campaigns for restrictive legislation regarding Filipino immigration became typical responses among associations like the Native Sons of the Golden West and the Commonwealth Club. Members aggressively lobbied for exclusionist policies based on the presumed unbridled "sexual passions" of Filipinos for Anglo women. David T. Barrows, a former president of the University of California, testified before the House Committee on Immigration and Naturalization that the Filipino "usually frequents the poorer quarters of our towns and spends the residue of his savings in brothels and dance halls, which in spite of our laws exist to minister to his lower nature."[55]

Competition over the regulation of taxi dance halls, however, was not restricted to the impulses and racist attitudes of the dominant society. Divisions within the Filipino community illustrate the competing agendas and visions of what a Filipino ethnic identity should incorporate. Campaigns to discipline and "correct" the behavior of the young Filipino workers came not only from the host society's policing institutions and reform associations but also from small groups of self-appointed guardians of Filipino "morality" within the community. Controversies associated with the leisure activities of fellow countrymen reveal tensions, including interethnic class struggles and differences over the image of Filipinos in the United States, among the immigrants. Mutual-aid societies like the Filipino Federation of America (FFA), for example, renounced the workers' many "immoralities," and actively discouraged Filipinos from drinking, gambling, and dating white women, activities which its members argued contributed to disparaging stereotypes of Filipinos.[56]

Some Filipino fraternal organizations also routinely organized dances for the "boys" as alternative recreational activities to commercialized dance halls, but these gatherings were generally not popular. The groups served no liquor, they kept the dance floor well lit, and the only female dance partners available were the wives of the organizers. As one young Filipino laborer explained, "I wouldn't want to go there and dance with them. They're married and they're too old and they don't dance very well."[57] Still other Filipino leaders appealed to the business owners of nearby commercialized centers to close the dance halls part of Sunday evenings in the hopes that Filipino workers would come to community-based socials and events instead. Danceland and Hippodrome Dance Palace complied with the request, but Liberty Dance Hall remained open early on Sundays, and with free admission to boot. This issue evoked strong reaction among the small Filipino elite. Johnny Samson, chairman of the Filipino Unity Council, charged that Liberty Dance Hall's owner, "Jack Goldberg [,] is not a human being. He is only interested in what he gets from Filipinos—their MONEY, their hard earned MONEY!"[58]

Conflicts related to taxi dance halls were also often intense among the Filipino workers themselves. One old-timer recalled that tensions among the youthful patrons occasionally ran high, and the

> boys used to get jealous with each other because those girls would dance with anyone with ten cent ticket[s]. And some guys have more money than others and [the] boys think he's trying to outshine him. Naturally, the fight start[s] ... Filipinos are really hot-tempered when it comes to things of that sort. ... It happened everywhere[,] ... Los Angeles, Stockton, everywhere where they have [taxi] dances.[59]

In part, these anxieties depict the importance of, and the urgency to maintain, an image of desirability among themselves. The competition, however, also evinced an internal code of behavior among Filipino workers which allowed them to define what was acceptable or unacceptable on their own terms. Living in a world that classified all of their leisure activities as "deviant," the workers themselves formulated ways of discouraging conduct which threatened the community and communal experiences beyond a tolerable level. While they considered dressing in vogue for a night out proper behavior, monopolizing all the dances clearly was not.

The biggest and by far the most turbulent confrontations at the taxi dance halls, however, were between Filipino and Anglo laborers. On one occasion, an Anglo migrant worker seethed about losing jobs to Filipinos because they worked longer hours and accepted lower wages. Included in this bitter complaint was that when Anglos went to the taxi dance halls, they found that

> Filipino boys are good dancers. They can dance circles around these "white" boys, and the "white" boys don't like that—especially when the Filipinos dance with "white" girls. It's no telling what these Filipinos will do if they keep comin'; and it's no tellin' what the "white" man will do either. Something is liable to happen.[60]

In January 1930, something *did* ensue in what is arguably the largest and most vicious display of anti-Filipino sentiment in California. In Watsonville, crowds of white workers and residents stormed a new taxi dance hall in a nearby town because, as one participant declared, "taxi-dance halls where white girls dance with [Filipinos] may be all right in San Francisco or Los Angeles but not in our community. We won't stand for anything of the kind."[61] In the days that followed, the mob, at times numbering up to seven hundred men, roamed Watsonville's streets, beating or shooting all Filipinos on sight. A Filipino laborer recalled that "the mob came into the pool halls and with clubs bludgeoned all of us and followed us until we were out of the city. Then residences where Filipinos were quartered were ransacked and burned to the ground. Automobiles that contained Filipinos were fired upon, and many of the boys were wounded."[62]

In the following month, the Los Angeles correspondent for the *Baltimore Sun* explained that the ferocious attack on Filipinos occurred in part "because [Filipinos] wore 'sheikier' clothes, danced better, and spent their money more lavishly than their Nordic fellow farmhands and, therefore, appealed more than some of the latter to the local girls."[63] This commentary underscores how the counterimage of Filipino workers created by the Filipinos themselves unsettled the dominant culture's assumptions about the brown "hordes." In sporting quality, fashionable attire like McIntosh suits, Filipinos disrupted the stereotypes of asexual laborers in the dirty, tattered overalls of the agricultural fields and the seemingly docile attendant in the uniforms issued by the service-oriented industries. In effect, Filipino laborers subverted the icons of white middle-class American masculinity, including the ability to dress stylishly, dance well, and exhibit manners appreciated by white women.[64]

Despite the intricate intra- and especially interethnic conflicts which at times erupted into violent confrontations, Filipino workers continued to frequent taxi dance halls. By the 1940s, however, reformers and church groups opposed to "our blondes dancing with Filipinos and Orientals" finally succeeded in getting legislation that barred Filipinos and all Asian men from taxi dance halls.[65] In Los Angeles, regulatory agencies, including the police commission, the fire department, and the health department, implemented this restriction by stricter licensing requirements, exorbitant fees for infractions, and threats to suspend or revoke a license. In September 1940, for example, the police commission launched a zealous investigation of business owners suspected of continuing to operate "mixed" dance halls within the city. A commission spokesperson declared that "the past city administration might have felt that the Oriental and white halls were proper, but I think this administration should take another stand."[66] In addition, guidelines to obtain permits shifted the internal regulation which had rested with the dance hall owners and dancers themselves to the police department, which assigned female officers to the newly formed Dance Hall Detail of the Juvenile Control Division. To further curtail interethnic youth relations, this department supervised the hiring and work schedules of the Anglo women who predominantly worked as taxi dancers.[67]

For Filipinos, legal exclusion from the taxi dance halls created yet another hurdle on one of their favorite leisure activities. This consequence, however, did not mean that Filipinos readily abandoned or forgot the alternative youth culture and community nurtured in the dance halls. Some Filipinos shed their outdated McIntosh suits of the 1930s for the new craze, the zoot suit. Dressed in their drapes and reet-pleat trousers, these Filipinos went instead to the segregated black-and-tan cabarets in Los Angeles, dressing up and dancing to the rhythms of a myriad sounds.[68]

The persistence displayed by Filipinos in negotiating a viable identity in the context of complex race, class struggles reveal the crucial role that popular culture practices played in the formulation of a collective memory and coping strategies among immigrant working-class youths. Looking at the activities deeply embedded in the daily lives of members of aggrieved populations broadens our understanding of the effectiveness of resistance and complicates the questions associated with work, leisure, popular culture, and acculturation.

NOTES

I would like to thank the *manongs* whose oral testimonies enriched this work, and editors Joe Austin and Michael Willard for their comments and suggestions on drafts of this essay. Critiques and encouragement provided by Sheldon Maram, George Lipsitz, Norris Hundley, George Sánchez, Don Nakanishi, Jeffrey Rangel, Theodore Gonzalves, and Dorothy and Fred Cordova helped polish this work. Many thanks to Carolyn Kozo-Cole of the Los Angeles Public Library for sharing visual images from the "Shades of L.A." photo collection. A research grant from the Institute of American Cultures at UCLA allowed me to examine and collect materials from the libraries of the University of California, Berkeley, the University of Washington at Seattle, and the Pinoy Archives of the Filipino American National Historical Society, Seattle.

1. *Philippines Review* (Los Angeles, California), 31 October 1935.

2. Interview of R. K., an "American girl," by Emory Bogardus, in "American Attitudes toward Filipinos," *Sociology and Social Research* 14, no. 1 (September-October 1929): 68.

3. D. F. Gonzalo, "Social Adjustments of Filipinos," *Sociology and Social Research* 14, no. 2 (November-December 1929): 171–172.

4. Some Filipinos had immigrated and settled in the Americas by the late sixteenth century as a result of the galleon trade between the Spanish colonies of Mexico and the Philippines. A number of these "Manilamen," or Spanish-speaking Filipino sailors, jumped ship and settled in Mexico and Louisiana. The first significant wave of Filipino immigrants, however, consisted of *pensionados*, government-sponsored students who came to the United States under the U.S. colonial administration of William Howard Taft in the Philippines. Groups of these students arrived between 1903 and 1938 to study in American institutions, including Harvard, Stanford, Yale, and the University of Southern California. About 14,000 pensionados completed their education between these years, and the vast majority returned to the Philippines. The second biggest wave of Filipino immigration began in the 1920s and lasted until the 1940s. Unlike the preceding wave of pensionados who came from the most privileged families in the Philippines, poor, unskilled laborers from rural provinces constituted the bulk of this group. During World War II, a number of these immigrants joined the United States armed forces and returned to the Philippines to fight against the Japanese. Postwar immigration represented a shift in the composition of Filipinos coming to the United States. For the first time, Filipinas, many of them war brides, began to constitute the greater portion of immigrants from the Philippines. The liberalization of United States immigration laws in 1965,

which gave preference to professionals and family reunification, facilitated the immigration of the latest wave of Filipinos, the majority of whom are middle class, professionals, and their families. See Fred Cordova, *Filipinos: Forgotten Asian Americans* (Seattle: Demonstration Project for Asian Americans, 1983); Royal Morales, *Makibaka: The Filipino American Struggle* (Los Angeles: Mountainview Publishers, 1974); H. Brett Melendy, *Asians in America: Filipinos, Koreans, and East Indians* (Boston: G. K. Hall and Co., 1977); Sucheng Chan, *Asian Americans: An Interpretive History* (Boston: Twayne Publishers, 1991); and Ronald Takaki, *Strangers from a Different Shore: A History of Asian Americans* (New York: Penguin Books, 1989). On the "Manilamen" and their legacy in Louisiana, see Marina E. Espina, "Filipinos in New Orleans," *Proceedings of Louisiana Academy of Sciences* 37 (December 1974): 117–121; and Cordova, *Filipinos*, 1–7. On pensionados, see Catherine Ceniza Pet, "Pioneers/Puppets: The Legacy of the *Pensionado* Program" (B.A. thesis, Pomona College, 1991). On Filipino laborers in the continental United States during the Great Depression, see, for example, Linda Nueva España-Maram, "Negotiating Identity: Youth, Gender, and Popular Culture in Los Angeles's Little Manila, 1920s-1940s" (Ph.D. diss., University of California, Los Angeles, 1996); and Barbara M. Posadas, "Mestiza Girlhood: Interracial Families in Chicago's Filipino American Community since 1925," in *Making Waves: An Anthology of Writings by and about Asian American Women*, ed. Asian Women United of California (Boston: Beacon Press, 1989), 273–281. Some Filipino students wrote about their working-class compatriots. See, for example, Severino F.Corpus, "An Analysis of the Racial Adjustment Activities and Problems of the Filipino-American Christian Fellowship in Los Angeles" (M.A. thesis, University of Southern California, 1938); and Benecio T. Catapusan, "The Filipino Occupational and Recreational Activities in Los Angeles" (M.A. thesis, University of Southern California, 1934). On struggles for unionization, see Craig Scharlin and Lilia Villanueva, *Philip Vera Cruz: A Personal History of Filipino Immigrants and the Farmworkers Movement*, memorial edition, ed. Glenn Omatsu and Augusto Espiritu (Los Angeles: UCLA Labor Center, Institute of Industrial Relations, and the UCLA Asian American Studies Center, 1994); Chris Friday, *Organizing Asian American Labor: The Pacific Coast Canned Salmon Industry, 1870–1942* (Philadelphia: Temple University Press, 1994); Howard A. de Witt, *Anti-Filipino Movements in California* (San Francisco: R and E Research Associates, 1976); and Arleen Garcia de Vera, "A Case Study of the Cannery Workers and Farm Laborers Union, 1948–1955" (M.A. thesis, University of California, Los Angeles, 1990). On Filipinos and World War II, see Manuel Buaken, "Life in the Armed Forces," *New Republic* (30 August 1943): 279–280; Bienvenido Santos, "Filipinos in War," *Far Eastern Survey* 11, no. 24 (30 November 1942): 249–250; and Theodore Sanchez Gonzalves, " 'We hold a neatly folded hope': Filipino American Veterans of World War II on Citizenship and Political Obligation," *Amerasia Journal* 21, no. 3 (Fall 1995): 155–174. On Filipina war brides, see Dorothy Cordova, "Voices from the Past: Why They Came," in *Making Waves*, 42–49. On post-1965 Filipino immigrants, see Fred Arnold et al., "Estimating the Immigration Multiplier: An Analysis of Recent Korean and Filipino Immigration to the United States," *International Migration Review* 23 (1989): 813–838; Richard E. Joyce and Chester L. Hunt, "Philippine Nurses and the Brain Drain," *Social Science and Medicine* 16, no. 12 (1982): 1223–1233; and *Amerasia Journal* 13, no. 1 (1986–87), which focused on Filipinos. See especially Tania Azores, "Educational Attainment and Upward Mobility: Prospect for Filipino Americans," 39–52; Pyong Gap Min, "Filipino and Korean Immigrants in Small Business: A Comparative Analysis," 53–71; and Madge Bello and Vincent Reyes, "Filipino Americans and the Marcos Overthrow: The Transformation of Political Consciousness," 73–83. See also Bangele Alsaybar, "Satanas: Ethnography of a Filipino American Brotherhood" (M.A. thesis, University of California, Los Angeles, 1993).

5. The Chinese Exclusion Act of 1882 prevented the immigration of Chinese laborers, while the 1908 "Gentlemen's Agreement" targeted Japanese workers. The National Origins Act of 1924 completely banned Asian immigration, including Asian spouses of U.S. citizens.

6. State of California Department of Industrial Relations, *Facts about Filipino Immigration*, Special Bulletin No. 3 (San Francisco: State Building, 1930), 16. See also Harry H. L. Kitano and Roger Daniels, *Asian Americans: Emerging Minorities* (Englewood Cliffs, N.J.: Prentice Hall, 1988).

7. See Corpus, "An Analysis of the Racial Adjustment Activities and Problems of the Filipino-American Christian Fellowship"; and Casiano Coloma, "A Study of the Filipino Repatriation Movement" (M.A. thesis, University of Southern California, 1939). All figures related to Filipinos are estimates, since the vast majority of these immigrants were migratory laborers.

8. The work (mostly sociological theses) by students in the 1930s that focused on Filipino Angeleños include Catapusan, "The Filipino Occupational and Recreational Activities in Los Angeles," and Corpus, "An Analysis of the Racial Adjustment Activities and Problems of the Filipino-American Christian Fellowship." Relatively more recent studies by Edwin B. Almirol, for example, focus on Salinas in "Filipino Voluntary Associations: Balancing Social Pressures and Ethnic Images," *Ethnic Groups* 2, no. 1 (1978): 65–92; Herminia Quimpo Meñez focuses on Delano in *Folklore Communication among Filipinos in California* (New York: Arno Press, 1980); and Howard de Witt focuses on Watsonville in *Violence in the Fields* (Saratoga, Calif.: Century Twenty One Publishing, 1980). Barbara M. Posadas's studies examine the urban Filipino-American experience in Chicago. See, for example, "Ethnic Life and Labor in Chicago's Pre-World War II Filipino Community," in *Labor Divided: Race and Ethnicity in United States Labor Struggles, 1835–1960*, ed. Robert Asher and Charles Stephenson, 63–80 (New York: State University of New York Press, 1990).

9. State of California Department of Industrial Relations, *Facts about Filipino Immigration*, 23–24.

10. Toribio Castillo, interview by author, 1 March 1992, Los Angeles.

11. Celedonio La Questa, Jacinto Sequig, and Florentino Mendoza, "A Dollar a Day, Ten Cents a Dance: A Historic Portrait of Filipino Farm Workers in America," produced by George Ow, Jr., Geoffrey Dunn, and Mark Schwartz, directed by Mark Schwartz, 40 min., Impact Productions, 1984, videocassette.

12. Johnny P. Rallonza, interview by author, 23 April 1992, Downey, California.

13. See Coloma, "A Study of the Filipino Repatriation Movement."

14. References to Little Manila are valid only until World War II. This geographical location for the ethnic community no longer exists. Most of the original buildings were demolished in the postwar gentrification of Los Angeles's downtown and Little Tokyo's expansion. Information on Little Manila for this study came from advertisements in the *Philippines Review* (Los Angeles); Corpus, "An Analysis of the Racial Adjustment Activities and Problems of the Filipino-American Christian Fellowship"; Tania Azores, "Filipinos in the Los Angeles Labor Force: Placemaking in Little Manila," unpublished paper, 1983; and Rosemarie D. Ibañez, "Birds of Passage: Filipino Immigrants in the 1920s and 1930s," unpublished paper, 1990. On the postwar Filipino Angeleño community, see Valentin R. Aquino, "The Filipino Community in Los Angeles" (M.A. thesis, University of Southern California, 1952). On recent struggles to create a Filipino Town in downtown Los Angeles, see Augusto Fauni Espiritu, "The Rise and Fall of the Filipino Town Campaign in Los Angeles: A Study of Filipino American Leadership" (M.A. thesis, University of California, Los Angeles, 1992).

15. James Earl Wood, "Field Notes Regarding Filipinos," James Earl Wood Papers, Bancroft Library, University of California, Berkeley (hereafter cited as Wood Papers).

16. Robin D. G. Kelley touches on these themes in relation to leisure activities of African Americans in " 'We Are Not What We Seem': Rethinking Black Working-Class Opposition in the Jim Crow South," *Journal of American History* 80, no. 1 (June 1993): 75–112. See also the collection of essays in idem, *Race Rebels: Culture, Politics, and the Black Working Class* (New York: Free Press, 1994). On class, gender, and alternative notions of sexuality fostered through participation in urban leisure centers, see Kathy Peiss, *Cheap Amusements: Working Women and Leisure in Turn-of-the-Century New York* (Philadelphia: Temple University Press, 1986). On popular culture and oppositional strategies among aggrieved populations, see George Lipsitz, *Time Passages: Collective Memory and American Popular Culture* (Minneapolis: University of Minnesota Press, 1990); Stuart Hall, "Notes on Deconstructing 'The Popular'," in *People's History and Socialist Theories*, ed. Raphael Samuel (London: Routledge and Kegan Paul, 1981), 227–239; Kelley, "Notes on Deconstructing 'The Folk'," *American Historical Review* 97, no. 5 (December 1992): 1400–1408. See also James C. Scott, *Domination and the Arts of Resistance: Hidden Transcripts* (New Haven, Conn.: Yale University Press, 1990); and C. L. R. James, *Beyond a Boundary* (New York: Pantheon Books, 1963).

17. Ray Edralin Corpus, interview by Bob Antolin, 22 September 1981, Tacoma, Washington, interview PNW81-Fil-028ba, transcript, Pinoy Archives, Filipino American National Historical Society (hereafter cited as FANHS).

18. Castillo interview. Bello adamantly refused to be interviewed for this project, insisting that Filipino/a-American students should concentrate less on the past and more on promoting the achievements of contemporary Filipino/a Americans. By 1938, the Vincent Bello Smart Tailoring Shop had moved to 238 East Second Street. See Corpus, "An Analysis of the Racial Adjustment Activities and Problems of the Filipino-American Christian Fellowship," 67.

19. Felix Pascua, interview by author, 21 May 1995, Los Angeles.

20. Castillo interview.

21. See *Philippines Review* (Los Angeles), 6 April 1935, and passim.

22. See *Ang Bantay* [*The Guardian*] (Los Angeles), 7 December 1929, and passim.

23. On the "lucky number" and "lucky door ticket," see Benecio T. Catapusan, "Leisure Time Problems of Filipino Immigrants," *Sociology and Social Research* 24, no. 2 (July-August 1940): 548.

24. *Philippines Review* (Los Angeles), 13 November 1935.

25. Catapusan, "Leisure Time Problems," 548.

26. Joan May T. Cordova and Alexis S. Canillo, eds., *Voices: A Filipino-American Oral History* (Santa Rosa, CA: Northwestern Graphics, 1984).

27. Johnny Garcia, interview by Lundy, 18 January 1937, transcript, "Racial Minority Survey: Filipinos," Federal Writers' Project, box 142, folder 1086, University Research Library, University of California, Los Angeles (hereafter cited as FWP).

28. Carey McWilliams, *Brothers under the Skin* (Boston: Little, Brown and Company, 1942; reprint, 1964), 238 (page reference is to reprint edition).

29. Felix Pascua, interview by Dante Ochoa, in "Little Manila Revisited," *Philippine Beat Magazine* 1, no. 2 (January-February 1989): 15.

30. Frank Coloma, interview by Roberto V. Vallangca, *Pinoy: The First Wave* (San Francisco: Strawberry Hill Press, 1977): 96.

31. Miguel Lawagan, interview by author, 26 June 1993, San Francisco.

32. On Mexican immigrants and dance halls in La Placita, see George J. Sánchez, *Becoming*

Mexican American: Ethnicity, Culture and Identity in Chicano Los Angeles, 1900–1945 (New York: Oxford University Press, 1994), especially chapter 8.

33. Clyde Bennett Vedder, "An Analysis of the Taxi-Dance Hall as a Social Institution, with Special Reference to Los Angeles and Detroit" (Ph.D. diss., University of Southern California, 1947), 183.

34. Conflicts were also common between Filipinos and the white ethnic patrons of Chicago's taxi dance halls. See Paul Cressy, *The Taxi Dance Halls: A Sociological Study in Commercialized Recreation and City Life* (New York: Greenwood Press, 1932).

35. Sammy R. Lopez, interview by Cynthia Mejia, 24 November 1975, interview FIL-KNG 75-36cm, transcript, Washington State Oral/Aural History Project, Olympia, Washington (hereafter cited as WSOAHP).

36. Luis Felipe Recinos, "Observaciones—Los Salones de Baile," Los Angeles, 15 April 1927. Manuel Gamio Collection, Bancroft Library, University of California Berkeley (hereafter cited as Gamio Papers). Spanish passages translated by author.

37. Coloma interview in Vallangca, *Pinoy*, 87.

38. Vicente Elequin, in Adelaida Castillo-Tsuchida, "Filipino Migrants in San Diego, 1900–1946" (M.A. thesis, University of San Diego, 1979), 52.

39. Alida C. Bowler, "Social Hygiene in Racial Problems—The Filipino," *Journal of Social Hygiene* 18, no. 8 (November 1932): 455.

40. Recinos, "Observaciones," Gamio Papers.

41. See collection of slang among Filipinos in Corpus, "Analysis of the Racial Adjustment Activities and Problems of the Filipino-American Christian Fellowship."

42. *L.A. Express* (Los Angeles), 16 April 1929. Thanks to Michael Willard for pointing out this source and photocopying the clippings relevant to this study.

43. Ibid.

44. See Cressy, *Taxi-Dance Hall*, 12.

45. See, for example, Lois Scharf, *To Work and to Wed: Female Employment, Feminism, and the Great Depression* (Westport, Conn.: Greenwood Press, 1980).

46. See, for example, the collection of essays in *Small Worlds: Children and Adolescents in America, 1850–1950*, ed. Elliott West and Paula Petrik (Lawrence: University Press of Kansas, 1992).

47. Stan Singer, "Vaudeville in Los Angeles, 1910–1926: Theaters, Management, and the Orpheum," *Pacific Historical Review* 61, no. 1 (February 1992): 103–113.

48. Kelley, " 'We are not what we seem'," 84–85.

49. See the *Los Angeles Express* (Los Angeles), 16 April 1929.

50. See, for example, Neil Larry Shumsky, "Tacit Acceptance: Respectable Americans and Segregated Prostitution, 1870–1910" *Journal of Social History* 19, no. 4 (Summer 1986): 664–679. See also Donald Teruo Hata, Jr., and Nadine Ishitani Hata, "Asian-Pacific Angelinos: Model Minorities and Indispensable Scapegoats," in Norman M. Klein and Martin J. Schiesl, eds, *Twentieth-Century Los Angeles: Power, Promotion, and Social Conflict* (Claremont, Calif.: Regina Books, 1990), 61–99.

51. Carlos Bulosan, *America Is in the Heart* (New York: Harcourt, Brace, 1943; reprint, Seattle: University of Washington Press, 1973), 134 (page reference is to reprint edition).

52. See *Annual Report of the Los Angeles Police Department*, 1936–1937 and 1937–1938.

53. See Honorante Mariano, "The Filipino Immigrants in the U.S." (M.A. thesis, University of Oregon, 1933).

54. Manuel Buaken, *I Have Lived with the American People* (Caldwell, Idaho: Caxton Printers, 1948), 89.

55. David P. Barrows, quoted in Takaki, *Strangers from a Different Shore*, 329.

56. On the FFA, see Steffi San Buenaventura, "Nativism and Ethnicity in a Filipino-American Experience" (Ph.D. diss., University of Hawaii, 1990).

57. Interview by James Earl Wood, n.d., but almost certainly in the 1930s, when he conducted his fieldwork. Wood Papers, folder no. 3.

58. *Associated Filipino Press* (Los Angeles), 15 February 1939 (emphasis in original).

59. Alfronso Perales Dangaran, quoted in Cordova, *Filipinos*, 215.

60. Interview by James Earl Wood, n.d., but almost certainly in the 1930s, when he conducted his fieldwork. Wood Papers, folder no. 3.

61. Ibid.

62. Buaken, *I Have Lived with the American People*, 103. Amazingly, only one Filipino, Fermin Tovera, died in the riot.

63. Duncan Aikman, quoted in "Causes of California's Race Riots," *Literary Digest*, 15 February 1930, 12.

64. On subverting and inverting icons of the dominant culture, see, for example, George Lipsitz, "Mardi Gras Indians: Carnival and Counter-Narrative in Black New Orleans," in *Time Passages*, 233–253.

65. Quoted in Vedder, "An Analysis of the Taxi-Dance Hall," 48.

66. *L.A. Express* (Los Angeles), 18 September 1940.

67. See Los Angeles Police Department, "Rules Governing Taxi Dance Halls, 1943."

68. For a preliminary examination of Filipino zoot suiters in Los Angeles, see España-Maram, "Negotiating Identity," 225–269. On the explosion of nightclubs in war time Los Angeles, see Stephen J. Loza, *Barrio Rhythm: Mexican American Music in Los Angeles* (Urbana and Chicago: University of Illinois Press, 1993).

PART II: WAR AND POSTWAR

Chapter Eight

The Riddle of the Zoot

Malcolm Little and Black Cultural Politics during World War II

Robin D. G. Kelley

But there is rhythm here. Its own special substance:
I hear Billie sing, no good man, and dig Prez, wearing
the Zoot
suit of life, the pork-pie hat tilted at the correct angle,
through the Harlem smoke of beer and whiskey, I
understand the
mystery of the signifying monkey,
in a blue haze of inspiration, I reach to the totality
of Being.
I am at the center of a swirl of events. War and death.
rhythm. hot women. I think life a commodity
bargained for
across the bar in Small's.
I perceive the echoes of Bird and there is a gnawing in
the maw
of my emotions . . .

—Larry Neal, "Malcolm X—An Autobiography,"
In *For Malcolm*, 1967

Much in Negro life remains a mystery; perhaps the zoot suit conceals profound political meaning; perhaps the symmetrical frenzy of the Lindy Hop conceals clues to great potential power—if only Negro leaders would solve this riddle . . . —Ralph Ellison, 1943

"Like hundreds of thousands of country-bred Negroes who had come to the Northern black ghetto before me, and had come since," Malcolm X recalled in his autobiography, "I'd also acquired all the other fashionable ghetto adornments—the zoot suits and conk that I have described, the liquor, cigarettes, the reefers—all to erase my embarrassing background."[1] His narrative is familiar; the story of a rural migrant in the big city who eventually finds social acceptance by shedding his country ways and adopting the corrupt lifestyles of urban America. The big city stripped him of his naivete, ultimately paving the way for his descent from hipster to hustler to criminal. As Malcolm tells the story, this period in his life was a fascinating but destructive detour on the road to self-consciousness and political enlightenment.

But Malcolm's narrative of his teenage years should also be read as a literary construction, a cliche that obscures more than it reveals.[2] The story is tragically dehistoricized, torn from the sociopolitical context that rendered the zoot suit, the conk, the lindy hop, and the language of the "hep cat" signifiers of a culture of opposition among black, mostly male, youth. According to Malcolm's reconstructed memory, these signifiers were merely "ghetto adornments," no different from the endless array of commodities black migrants were introduced to at any given time. Of course, Malcolm tells his story from the vantage point of the Civil Rights movement and a resurgent Pan-Africanism: the early 1960s when the conk had been abandoned for closely cropped hairstyles, when the zoot had been replaced with the respectable jacket and tie of middle-class America (dashikis and Afros from our reinvented Mother Country were not yet born), and when the sons and daughters of middle-class African Americans, many of whom were themselves college students taking a detour on the road to respectability to fight for integration and equality, were at the forefront of struggle. Like the movement itself, Malcolm had reached a period in his life when opposition could only be conceived as uncompromising and unambiguous.

The didactic and rhetorical character of Malcolm's *Autobiography*—shaped by presentist political concerns of the early 1960s and told through the cultural prism of Islam—obscures the oppositional meanings embedded in wartime black youth culture. None of Malcolm's biographers since have sought to understand the history and political character of the subculture to which he belonged.[3] This chapter rethinks Malcolm's early life, and to reexamine the hipster subculture and its relation to war time social, political, economic, and ideological transformations.

World War II was a critical turning point not only for Malcolm but for many young African Americans and Latinos in the United States. Indeed, it was precisely the cultural world into which Malcolm stepped that prompted future novelist Ralph Ellison to reflect on the political significance of the dance styles and attire of black youth. Ironically, one would think that Malcolm, himself a product of the wartime black youth culture, was uniquely situated to solve the riddle posed by Ellison in 1943. Nevertheless, whether or not Malcolm acknowledged the political importance of that era in his own thinking, it is my contention that his participation in the underground subculture of black working-class youth during the war was not a detour on the road to political consciousness but rather an essential element of his radicalization. The zoot suiters and hipsters who sought alternatives to wage work and found pleasure in the new music, clothes, and dance styles of the period were "race rebels" of sorts, challenging middle-class ethics and expectations, carving out a distinct generational and ethnic identity, and refusing to be good proletarians. But in their efforts to escape or minimize exploitation, Malcolm and his homies became exploiters themselves.

"I Am at the Center of a Swirl of Events"

The gangly, red-haired young man from Lansing looked a lot older than fifteen when he moved in with his half-sister, Ella, who owned a modest home in the Roxbury section of Boston. Little did he know how much the world around him was about to change. The bombing of Pearl Harbor was still several months away, but the country's economy was already geared up for war. By the time United States troops were finally dispatched to Europe, Asia, and North Africa, much of the black community restrained their enthusiasm, for they shared a collective memory of the unfulfilled promises of democracy generated by the First World War. Hence, the Double-V campaign, embodied in A. Philip Randolph's threatened march on Washington to protest racial discrimination in employment and the military, partly articulated the sense of hope and pessimism, support and detachment, that dominated a good deal of daily conversation. This time around, a victory abroad without annihilating racism at home was unacceptable. As journalist Roi Ottley observed during the early years of the war, one could not walk the streets of Harlem and not notice a profound change. "Listen to the way Negroes are talking these days! . . . [B]lack men have become noisy, aggressive, and sometimes defiant."[4]

The defiant ones included newly arrived migrants from the South who had flooded America's northeastern and midwestern metropolises. Hoping to take advantage of opportunities created by the nascent wartime economy, most found only frustration and disappointment since a comparatively small proportion of African Americans gained access to industrial jobs and training programs. By March 1942, black workers constituted only 2.5 to 3 percent of all war production workers, most of whom were relegated to low-skill, low-wage positions. The employment situation improved more rapidly after 1942: by April 1944, blacks made up 8 percent of the nation's war production workers. But everyone in the African American community did not benefit equally. For example, the United Negro College Fund was established in 1943 to assist African Americans attending historically black colleges, but during the school year of 1945–46, undergraduate enrollment in those institutions amounted to less than 44,000. On the other hand, the number of organized black workers increased from 150,000 in 1935 to 1.25 million by war's end. The Congress of Industrial Organization's (CIO) organizing drives ultimately had the effect of raising wages and improving working conditions for these black workers, though nonunion workers, who made up roughly 80 percent of the black working class, could not take advantage of the gains. The upgrading of unionized black workers did not take place without a struggle; throughout the war, white workers waged "hate strikes" to protest the promotion of blacks, and black workers frequently retaliated with their own wildcat strikes to resist racism.[5]

In short, wartime integration of black workers into the industrial economy proceeded unevenly; by war's end most African Americans still held unskilled, menial jobs. As cities burgeoned with working people, often living in close quarters or doubling up as a result of housing shortages, the chasm between middle-class and skilled working-class blacks, on the one hand, and the unemployed and working poor, on the other, began to widen. Intraracial class divisions were exacerbated by cultural conflicts between established urban residents and the newly arrived rural folk. In other words, demographic and economic transformations caused by the war not only intensified racial conflict but led to heightened class tensions within urban black communities.[6] For Malcolm, the zoot suit, the lindy hop, and the distinctive lingo of the "hep cat" simultaneously embodied these class, racial, and cultural tensions. This unique subculture enabled him to negotiate an identity that resisted the hegemonic culture and its attendant racism and patriotism, the rural folkways (for many, the "parent culture") that still survived in most black urban households, and the class conscious, integrationist attitudes of middle-class blacks.

"The Zoot Suit of Life"

Almost as soon as Malcolm settled into Boston, he found he had little tolerance for the class pretensions of his neighbors, particularly his peers. Besides, his own limited wardrobe and visible "country" background rendered him an outsider. He began hanging out at a local pool hall in the poorer sections of Roxbury. Here, in this dank, smoky room, surrounded by the cracking sounds of cue balls and the stench of alcohol, Malcolm discovered the black subculture that would ultimately form a crucial component of his identity. An employee of the poolroom, whom Malcolm called "Shorty" (most likely a composite figure based on several acquaintances, including his close friend Malcolm Jarvis), became his running partner and initiated him into the cool world of the "hep cat."[7]

In addition to teaching young Malcolm the pleasures, practices, and possibilities of hipster culture, Shorty had to make sure his homeboy wore the right uniform in this emerging bebop army. When Malcolm put on his very first zoot suit, he realized immediately that the wild sky-blue outfit, the baggy punjab pants tapered to the ankles, the matching hat, gold watch chain, and monogrammed belt were more than a suit of clothes. As he left the department store he could not contain his enthusiasm for his new identity. "I took three of those twenty-five-cent sepia-toned, while-you-wait pictures of myself, posed the way 'hipsters' wearing their zoots would 'cool it'—hat dangled, knees drawn close together, feet wide apart, both index fingers jabbed toward the floor." The combination of his suit and body language encoded a culture that celebrated a specific racial, class, spatial, gender, and generational identity. East Coast zoot suiters during the war were primarily young black (and Latino) working-class males whose living spaces and social world were confined to Northeastern ghettos, and the suit reflected a struggle to negotiate these multiple identities in opposition to the dominant culture. Of course, the style itself did not represent a complete break with the dominant fashion trends; zoot suiters appropriated, even mocked, existing styles and reinscribed them with new meanings drawn from shared memory and experiences.[8]

While the suit itself was not meant as a direct political statement, the social context in which it was created and worn rendered it so. The language and culture of zoot suiters represented a subversive refusal to be subservient. Young black males created a fast-paced, improvisational language which sharply contrasted with the passive stereotype of the stuttering, tongue-tied sambo, and in a world where whites commonly addressed them as "boy," zoot suiters made a fetish of calling each other "man." Moreover, within months of Malcolm's first zoot, the political and social context of war had added an explicit dimension to the implicit oppositional meaning of the suit into an explicitly un-American style. By March 1942, because fabric rationing regulations instituted by the War Productions Board forbade the sale and manufacturing of zoot suits, wearing the suit (which had to be purchased through informal networks) was seen by white servicemen as a pernicious act of anti-Americanism—a view compounded by the fact that most zoot suiters were able-bodied men who refused to enlist or found ways to dodge the draft. Thus when Malcolm donned his "killer-diller coat with a drape-shape, reat-pleats and shoulders padded like a lunatic's cell," his lean body became a dual signifier of opposition—a rejection of both black petit bourgeois respectability and American patriotism.[9]

The urban youth culture was also borne of heightened interracial violence and everyday acts of police brutality. Both Detroit and Harlem, two cities in which Malcolm spent considerable time, erupted in massive violence during the summer of 1943. And in both cases riots were sparked by incidents of racial injustice.[10] The zoot suiters, many of whom participated in the looting and acts of random violence, were also victims of, or witnesses to, acts of outright police brutality. In a description of the Harlem Riot, an anonymous zoot suiter expressed both disdain for and defiance toward police practices:

> A cop was runnin' along whippin' the hell outa [*sic*] colored man like they do in [the] slaughter pen. Throwin' him into the police car, or struggle-buggy, marchin' him off to the jail. That's that! Strange as it may seem, ass-whippin' is not to be played with. So as I close my little letter of introduction, I leave this thought with thee:
>
> Yea, so it be
> I leave this thought with thee
> Do not attempt to fuck with me . . .[11]

The hipster subculture permeated far more than just sartorial style. Getting one's hair straightened (the "conk" hairdo) was also required. For Malcolm reflecting backwards through the prism of the Nation of Islam and Pan-Africanism, the conk was the most degrading aspect of the hipster subculture. In his words, it was little more than an effort to make his hair "as straight as any white man's."

> This was my first really big step toward self-degradation: when I endured all of that pain, literally burning my flesh to have it look like a white man's hair. I had joined that multitude of Negro men and women in America who are brainwashed into believing that the black people are "inferior"—and white people "superior"—that they

will even violate and mutilate their God-created bodies to try to look "pretty" by white standards.[12]

Malcolm's interpretation of the conk, however, conveniently separates the hairstyle from the subculture of which it was a part, and the social context in which such cultural forms were created. The conk was a "refusal" to look like either the dominant, stereotyped image of the Southern migrant or the black bourgeoisie, whose "conks" were closer to mimicking white styles than those of the zoot suiters. Besides, to claim that black working-class males who conked their hair were merely parroting whites ignores the fact that specific stylizations created by black youth emphasized difference—the ducktail down the back of the neck, the smooth, even stiff look created by Murray's Pomade (a very thick hair grease marketed specifically to African Americans), the neat side parts angling toward the center of the back of the head.

More importantly, once we contextualize the conk, considering the social practices of young hepcats, the totality of ethnic signifiers from the baggy pants to the coded language, their opposition to war, and emphasis on pleasure over waged labor, we cannot help but view the conk as part of a larger process by which black youth appropriated, transformed, and reinscribed coded oppositional meanings onto styles derived from the dominant culture. For "the conk was conceived in a subaltern culture, dominated and hedged in by a capitalist master culture, yet operating in an 'underground' manner to subvert given elements by creolizing stylization. Style encoded political 'messages' to those in the know which were otherwise unintelligible to white society by virtue of their ambiguous accentuation and intonation."[13]

"But There Is Rhythm Here"

Once properly attired ("togged to the bricks," as his contemporaries would have said), sixteen-year-old Malcolm discovered the lindy hop, and in the process expanded both his social circle and his politics. The Roseland Ballroom, and in some respects the Savoy in Harlem, constituted social spaces of pleasure free of the bourgeois pretensions of "better class Negroes." His day job as a soda fountain clerk in the elite section of black Roxbury became increasingly annoying as he endured listening to the sons and daughters of the "Hill Negroes," "penny-ante squares who came in there putting on their millionaires' airs." Home (his sister Ella's household) and spaces of leisure (Roseland's Ballroom) suddenly took on new significance, for they represented the negation of black bourgeois culture and a reaffirmation of a subaltern culture that emphasized pleasure, rejected work, and celebrated a working-class racial identity. "I couldn't wait for eight o'clock to get home to eat out of those soul-food pots of Ella's, then get dressed in my zoot and head for some of my friends' places in town, to lindy-hop and get high, or something, for relief from those Hill clowns."[14]

For Malcolm and his peers, Boston's Roseland Ballroom and, later, Harlem's Savoy, afforded the opportunity to become something other than workers. In a world where clothes constituted signifiers of identity and status, "dressing up" was a way of escaping the degradation of work and collapsing status distinctions between themselves and their oppressors. In Malcolm's narrative, he always seemed to be shedding his work clothes, whether it was the apron of a soda jerk or the uniform of a railroad sandwich peddler, in favor of his zoot suit. At the end of his first run to New York on the "Yankee Clipper" rail line, he admitted to having donned his "zoot suit before the first passenger got off." Seeing oneself and others "dressed up" was enormously important in terms of constructing a collective identity based on something other than wage work, presenting a public challenge to the dominant stereotypes of the black body, and reinforcing a sense of dignity that was perpetually being assaulted. Malcolm's images of the Roseland were quite vivid in this respect: "They'd jampack that ballroom, the black girls in wayout silk and satin dresses and shoes, their hair done in all kinds of styles, the men sharp in their zoot suits and crazy conks, and everybody grinning and greased and gassed."[15]

For many working-class men and women who daily endured back-breaking wage work, low income, long hours, and pervasive racism, these urban dance halls were places to recuperate, to take back their bodies. Despite opposition from black religious leaders and segments of the petit bourgeoisie, as well as some employers, black working people of both sexes shook and twisted their already overworked bodies, drank, talked, engaged in sexual play, and—in spite of occasional fights—reinforced their sense of community. The sight of hundreds moving in unison on a hardwood dance floor unmistakably reinforced a sense of collectivity as well as individuality, as dancers improvised on the standard lindy hop moves in friendly competition, like the "cutting sessions" of jazz musicians or the verbal duels known as the dozens. Practically every Friday and Saturday night, young Malcolm experienced the dual sense of community and individuality, improvisation and collective call and response. "The band, the spectators and the dancers, would be making the Roseland Ballroom feel like a big rocking ship. The spotlight would be turning, pink, yellow, green, and blue, picking up the couples lindy-hopping as if they had gone mad. '*Wail, man, wail!*' people would be shouting at the band; and it *would* be wailing, until first one and then another couple just ran out of strength and stumbled off toward the crowd, exhausted and soaked with sweat."[16]

It should be noted that the music itself was undergoing a revolution during the war. Growing partly out of black musicians' rebellion against white-dominated swing bands, and partly out of the heightened militancy of black urban youth—expressed by their improvisational language and dress styles, as well as by the violence and looting we now call the Harlem Riot of 1943—the music that came to be known as "bebop" was born amid dramatic political and social transformations. At Minton's Playhouse and Monroe's Uptown, a number of styles converged; the most discerning recognized the wonderful collision and reconstitution of Kansas City big band blues, East Coast swing music, and the secular as well as religious sounds of the black South. The horns, fingers, ideas, and memories of *young* black folk like Charlie Parker, Thelonius Monk, Dizzy Gillespie, Mary Lou Williams, Kenny Clarke, Oscar Pettiford, Tadd Dameron, Bud Powell, and a baby-faced Miles Davis, to name only a few, gave birth to what would soon be called "bebop."

Bebop was characterized by complex and implied rhythms frequently played at blinding tempos, dissonant chord structures, and a preelectronic form of musical "sampling" in which the chord changes for popular tin pan alley songs were appropriated, altered, and used in conjunction with new melodies. While the music was not intended to be dance music, some African American youth found a way to lindy hop to some remarkably fast tempos, and in the process invented new dances such as the "apple jack."

Although the real explosion in bebop occurred after Malcolm began his stay at Charleston State Penitentiary, no hip Harlemite during the war could have ignored the dramatic changes in the music or the musicians. Even the fairly conservative band leader Lionel Hampton, a close friend of Malcolm's during this period, linked bebop with oppositional black politics. Speaking of his own music in 1946, he told an interviewer, "Whenever I see any injustice or any unfair action against my own race or any other minority groups 'Hey Pa Pa Rebop' stimulates the desire to destroy such prejudice and discrimination."[17] Moreover, while neither the lindy hop nor the "apple jack" carried intrinsic political meanings, the social act of dancing was nonetheless resistive—at least with respect to the work ethic. Cultural critic Paul Gilroy insists that black working people who spent time and precious little money at dance halls and house parties regarded "waged work as itself a form of servitude. At best, it is viewed as a necessary evil and is sharply counterposed to the more authentic freedoms that can only be enjoyed in nonwork time. The black body is here celebrated as an instrument of pleasure rather than an instrument of labor. The nighttime becomes the right time, and the space allocated for recovery and recuperation is assertively and provocatively occupied by the pursuit of leisure and pleasure."[18]

"War and Death"

From the standpoint of most hep cats, the Selective Service was an ever-present obstacle to "the pursuit of leisure and pleasure." As soon as war broke out, Malcolm's homeboys did everything possible to evade the draft (Malcolm was only sixteen when Pearl Harbor was attacked, so he hadn't yet reached draft age). His partner, Shorty, a budding musician hoping to make a name for himself stateside, was "worried sick" about the draft. Like literally dozens of young black musicians (most of whom were drawn to the dissonant, rapid-fire, underground styles of bebop), Shorty succeeded in obtaining 4F status by ingesting something which made "your heart sound defective to the draft board's doctors"—most likely a mixture of benzedrine nasal spray and coke.[19] When Malcolm received notice from the draft board in October 1943, he employed a variety of tactics in order to attain a 4F classification. "I started noising around that I was frantic to join . . . the Japanese Army. When I sensed that I had the ears of the spies, I would talk and act high and crazy . . . The day I went down there, I costumed like an actor. With my wild zoot suit I wore the yellow knob-toed shoes, and I frizzled my hair up into a reddish bush conk." His interview with the army psychiatrist was the icing on the cake. In a low, conspiratorial tone, he admitted to the doctor, "Daddy-o, now you and me, we're from up North here, so don't you tell nobody . . . I want to get sent down South. Organize them nigger soldiers, you dig? Steal us some guns and kill up crackers [sic]!" Malcolm's tactic was hardly unique, however. Trumpeter John "Dizzy" Gillespie, a pioneer of bebop, secured 4F status and practically paralyzed his army recruitment officer with the following story:

> Well, look, at this time, at this stage in my life here in the United States whose foot has been in my ass? The white man's foot has been in my ass hole buried up to his knee in my ass hole!... Now you're speaking of the enemy. You're telling me the German is the enemy. At this point, I can never even remember having met a German. So if you put me out there with a gun in my hand and tell me to shoot at the enemy, I'm liable to create a case of "mistaken identity," of who I might shoot.[20]

Although these kinds of "confessions" were intended to shake up military officials and avoid serving, both Malcolm and Dizzy were articulating the feelings of a great majority of men who shared their inner cultural circle—feelings which a surprisingly large number of African Americans identified with. The hundreds, perhaps thousands, of zoot suiters and musicians who dodged the draft were not merely evading responsibility. They opposed the war altogether, insisting that African Americans could not afford to invest their blood in another "white man's war." "Whitey owns everything," Shorty explained to Malcolm. "He wants us to go and bleed? Let him fight." Likewise, a Harlem zoot suiter interviewed by black social psychologist Kenneth Clark made the following declaration to the scholarly audience for whom the research was intended: "By [the] time you read this I will be fighting for Uncle Sam, the bitches, and I do not like it worth a dam [*sic*]. I'm not a spy or a saboteur, but I don't like goin' over there fightin' for the white man—so be it."[21] We can never know how many black men used subterfuge to obtain a 4F status, or how many men—like Kenneth Clark's informant—complied with draft orders but did so reluctantly. Nevertheless, what evidence we do possess suggests that black resistance to the draft was more pervasive than we might have imagined. By late 1943, African Americans comprised 35 percent of the nation's delinquent registrants, and between 1941 and 1946, over two thousand black men were imprisoned for not complying with the provisions of the Selective Service Act.[22]

While some might argue that draft dodging by black hipsters hardly qualifies as protest politics, the press, police, and white servicemen thought otherwise. The white press, and to a lesser degree the black press, cast practically all young men sporting the "drape shape" (zoot suit) as unpatriotic "dandies."[23] And the hep cats who could not escape the draft and refused either to submerge their distaste for the war or discard their slang faced a living nightmare in the armed forces. Zoot suiters and jazz musicians in particular were the subject of ridicule, severe punishment, and even beatings. Civilian hipsters fared no better. That black and Latino youth exhibited a cool, measured indifference to the war, as well as an increasingly defiant posture toward whites in general, annoyed white servicemen to no end. Tensions between zoot suiters and servicemen consequently erupted in violence; in June 1943, Los Angeles became the site of racist attacks on black and Chicano youth, during which white soldiers engaged in what amounted to a ritualized stripping of the zoot. Such tensions were also evident in Malcolm's relations with white servicemen. During a rather short stint as a sandwich peddler on the Yankee Clipper train, Malcolm was frequently embroiled in arguments with white soldiers, and on occasion came close to exchanging blows.[24]

"I Think Life a Commodity Bargained For"

Part of what annoyed white servicemen was the hipster's laissez-faire attitude toward work and their privileging of the "pursuit of leisure and pleasure." Holding to the view that one should work to live rather than live to work, Malcolm decided to turn the pursuit of leisure and pleasure into a career. Thus, after "studying" under the tutelage of some of Harlem's better-known pimps, gangsters, and crooks who patronized Small's Paradise, Malcolm eventually graduated to full-fledged hustler.

Bruce Perry and other biographers who assert that, because Malcolm engaged in the illicit economy while good jobs were allegedly "a dime a dozen," we should look to psychological explanations for his criminality betray a profound ignorance of the wartime political economy and black working-class consciousness.[25] First, in most northeastern cities during the war, African Americans were still faced with job discrimination, and employment opportunities for blacks tended to be low-wage, menial positions. In New York, for example, the proportion of blacks receiving home relief *increased* from 22 percent in 1936 to 26 percent in 1942, and when the Works Progress Administration shut down in 1943, the percentage of African Americans employed by the New York WPA was higher than it had been during the entire Depression.[26] Second, it was hard for black working people not to juxtapose the wartime rhetoric of equal opportunity and the apparent availability of well-paying jobs for whites with the reality of racial discrimination in the labor market. Of the many jobs Malcolm held during the war, none can be said to have been well paying and/or fulfilling. Third, any attempt to understand the relationship between certain forms of crime and resistance must begin by interrogating the dominant view of criminal behavior as social deviance. As a number of criminologists and urban anthropologists have suggested, "hustling" or similar kinds of informal/illicit economic strategies should be regarded as efforts to escape dependency on low-wage, alienating labor.[27]

The zoot suiters' collective hostility to wage labor became evident to young Malcolm during his first conversation with Shorty, who promptly introduced the word "slave" into his nascent hipster vocabulary. A popular slang expression for a job, "slave" not only encapsulated their understanding of wage work as exploitative, alienating, and unfulfilling, but it implies a refusal to allow work to become the primary signifier of identity. (This is not to say that "hustlers" adamantly refused wage labor; on the contrary, certain places of employment were frequently central loci for operations.) Implied, too, is a rejection of a work ethic, a privileging of leisure, and an emphasis on "fast money" with little or no physical labor. Even Shorty chastised Malcolm for saving money to purchase his first zoot suit rather than taking advantage of credit.[28]

Malcolm's apprenticeship in Boston's shoeshine trade introduced him to the illicit economy, the margins of capitalism where commodity relations tended to be raw, demystified, and sometimes quite brutal. Success here required that one adopt the sorts of monopolist strategies usually associated with America's most celebrated entrepreneurs. Yet, unlike mainstream entrepreneurs, most of the hustlers with whom Malcolm was associated held on to an anti-work, anti-accumulation ethic. Possessing "capital" was not the ultimate goal; rather, money was primarily a means by which hustlers could avoid wage work and negotiate status through the purchase of prestigious commodities. Moreover, it seems that many hustlers of the 1940s shared a very limited culture of mutuality that militated against accumulation. On more than one occasion, Malcolm gave away or loaned money to friends when he himself was short of cash, and in at least one case "he pawned his suit for a friend who had pawned a watch for him when he had needed a loan."[29]

Nevertheless, acts of mutuality hardly translated into a radical collective identity; hustling by nature was a predatory act that did not discriminate by color. Moreover, their culture of mutuality was a male-identified culture limited to the men of their inner circle, for, as Malcolm put it, the hustler cannot afford to "trust anybody." Women were merely objects through which hustling men sought leisure and pleasure—prey for financial and sexual exploitation. "I believed that a man should do anything that he was slick enough, or bad and bold enough, to do and that a woman was nothing but another commodity." Even women's sexuality was a commodity to be bought and sold, though for Malcolm and his homeboys selling made more sense than buying. (In fact, Bruce Perry suggests that Malcolm pimped gay men and occasionally sold his own body to homosexuals.)[30]

At least two recent biographies suggest that the detached, sometimes brutal manner with which Malcolm treated women during his hipster days can be traced to his relationship to his mother.[31] While such an argument might carry some validity, it essentially ignores the gendered ideologies, power relationships, and popular culture that bound black hipsters together into a distinct, identifiable community. Resistance to wage labor for the "hep cat" frequently meant increased oppression and exploitation of women, particularly black women. The hipsters of Malcolm's generation and later took pride in their ability to establish parasitical relationships with women wage earners or sex workers. And jazz musicians of the 1940s spoke quite often of living off women, which in many cases translated into outright pimping.[32] Indeed, consider Tiny Grimes's popular 1944 recording featuring Charlie Parker on alto:

> Romance without finance is a nuisance,
> Mama, mama, please give up that gold.
> Romance without finance just don't make sense,
> Baby, please give up that gold.
>
> You're so great and you're so fine,
> You ain't got no money, you can't be mine,
> It ain't no joke to be stone broke,
> Honey you know I ain't lyin'.[33]

Furthermore, the hustler ethic demanded a public front of emotional detachment. Remaining "cool" toward women was crucial to one's public reputation and essential in a "business" that depended on the control and brutal exploitation of female bodies. In the words of black America's most noted pimp scribe, Iceberg Slim, "The best pimps keep a steel lid on their emotions."[34]

These gendered identities, social practices, and the discursive arena in which pimping and hustling took place were complicated by race. As in the rest of society, black and white women did not occupy the same position; white women, especially those with money, ranked higher. Once Malcolm began going out with Sophia, his status among the local hipsters and hustlers rose enormously:

> Up to then I had been just another among all the conked and zooted youngsters. But now, with the best-looking white woman who ever walked in those bars and clubs, and with her giving me the money I spent, too, even the big important black hustlers and "smart boys" . . . were clapping me on the back, setting us up to drinks at special tables, and calling me "Red."[35]

As far as Malcolm and his admirers were concerned, "Detroit Red" conquered and seized what he was not supposed to have—a white woman. Although some scholars and ordinary folk might view Malcolm's dangerous liaison as an early case of self-hatred, the race/gender politics of the hustling community and the equally cool, detached manner with which they treated white women suggests other dynamics were operating as well. White women, like virtually all women (save one's mama), were merely property to be possessed, sported, used, and tossed out. But unlike black women, they belonged to "Charlie," the "Man," "whitey," and were theoretically off limits. Thus, in a world where most relationships were commodified, white women, in the eyes of hustlers at least, were regarded as stolen property, booty seized from the ultimate hustle.

Hustling not only permitted Malcolm to resist wage labor, pursue leisure, and demystify the work ethic myth, but in a strange way the kinds of games he pulled compelled him to "study" the psychology of white racism. Despite the fact that members of this subaltern culture constructed a collective identity in defiance of dominant racist images of African Americans, the work of hustling "white folks" often required that those same dominant images be resurrected and employed as discursive strategies. As a shoeshine boy, for example, Malcolm learned that extra money could be made if one chose to "Uncle Tom a little," smiling, grinning, and making snapping gestures with a polishing rag to give the impression of hard work. Although it was nothing more than a "jive noise," he quickly learned that "Cats tip better, they figure you're knocking yourself out." The potential power blacks possessed to manipulate white racial ideologies for their own advantage was made even clearer during his brief stint as a sandwich salesman on the Yankee Clipper:

> It didn't take me a week to learn that all you had to do was give white people a show and they'd buy anything you offered them. . . . We were in that world of Negroes who are both servants and psychologists, aware that white people are so obsessed with their own importance that they will pay liberally, even dearly, for the impression of being catered to and entertained.

Nevertheless, while Malcolm's performance enabled him to squeeze nickels and dimes from white men who longed for a mythic plantation past where darkeys lived to serve, he also played the part of the model Negro in the watchful eye of white authority, a law-abiding citizen satisfied with his "shoeshine boy" status. It was the perfect cover for selling illegal drugs, acting as a go-between for prostitutes and "Johns," and a variety of other petty crimes and misdemeanors.[36]

In some respects, Malcolm's initial introduction to the hustling society illumined the power of the trickster figure or the signifying monkey, whose success not only depended on cunning and wiles, but knowing what and how the powerful thought. Yet the very subculture that drew Malcolm to the hustling world in the first place created enormous tension as he tried to navigate between Sambo and militant, image and reality. After all, one of the central attractions of the zoot suiters was their collective refusal to be subservient. As Malcolm grew increasingly wary of deferential, obsequious behavior as a hustling strategy, he became, in his words, an "uncouth, wild young Negro. Profanity had become my language." He cursed customers, took drugs with greater frequency, came to work high, and copped an attitude that even his coworkers found unbecoming. By war's end, burglary became an avenue through which he could escape the masking of petty hustling, the grinning and Tomming so necessary to cover certain kinds of illicit activities. Although burglary was no less difficult and far more dangerous than pulling on-the-job hustles, he chose the time, place, and frequency of his capers, had no bosses or foremen to contend with, and did not have to submit to time clocks and industrial discipline. Furthermore, theft implied a refusal to recognize the sanctity of private property.

Malcolm's increasingly active opposition to wage labor and dependence upon the illicit economy "schooled" him to a degree in how capitalism worked. He knew the system well enough to find ways to carve out more leisure time and autonomy. But at the same time it led to a physically deleterious lifestyle, reinforced his brutal exploitation of women, and ensured his downward descent and subsequent prison sentence. Nevertheless, Malcolm's engagement with the illicit economy offered important lessons that ultimately shaped his later political perspectives. Unlike nearly all of his contemporaries during the 1960s, he was fond of comparing capitalism with organized crime and refused to characterize looting by black working people as criminal acts—lessons he clearly did not learn in the Nation of Islam. Just five days before his assassination, he railed against the mainstream press's coverage of the 1964 Harlem riot for depicting "the rioters as hoodlums, criminals, thieves, because they were abducting some property." Indeed, Malcolm insisted that dominant notions of criminality and private property only obscure the real nature of social relations: "Instead of the sociologists analyzing it as it actually is . . . again they cover up the real issue, and they use the press to make it appear that these people are thieves, hoodlums. No! They are the victims of organized thievery."[37]

"In a Blue Haze of Inspiration, I Reach the Totality of My Being"

Recalling his appearance as a teenager in the 1940s, Malcolm dismissively observed, "I was really a clown, but my ignorance made me think I was 'sharp.' " Forgetting for the moment the integrationist dilemmas of the black bourgeoisie, Malcolm could reflect: "I don't know which kind of self-defacing conk is the greater shame—the one you'll see on the heads of the black so-called 'middle class' and 'upper class,' who ought to know better, or the one you'll see on the heads of the poorest, most downtrodden, ignorant black men. I mean the legal-minimum-wage ghetto-dwelling kind of Negro, as I was when I got my first one."[38] Despite Malcolm's sincere efforts to grapple with the meaning(s) of "ghetto" subculture, to comprehend the logic behind the conk, the reat pleat, and the lindy hop, he ultimately failed to solve Ralph Ellison's riddle. In some ways this is surprising, for who is better suited to solve the riddle than a former zoot suiter who rose to become one of America's most insightful social critics of the century?

When it came to thinking about the significance of his own life, the astute critic tended to reduce a panoply of discursive practices and cultural forms to dichotomous categories—militancy versus self-degradation, consciousness versus unconsciousness. The sort of narrow, rigid criteria Malcolm used to judge the political meaning of his life left him ill-equipped to capture the significance of his youthful struggles to carve out more time for leisure and pleasure, free himself from alienating wage labor, survive and transcend the racial and economic boundaries he confronted in everyday life. Instead, "Detroit Red" in Malcolm's narrative is a lost soul devoid of an identity, numbed to the beauty and complexity of lived experience, unable to see beyond the dominant culture he mimics.

This is not at all to suggest that Malcolm's narrative is purposely misleading. On the contrary, precisely because his life as a pimp, prostitute, exploiter, addict, pusher, and all-purpose crook loomed so large in his memory of the 1940s, the thought of recuperating the oppositional meanings embedded in the expressive black youth cultures of his era probably never crossed his mind. Indeed, as a devout Muslim recalling an illicit, sinful past, he was probably more concerned with erasing his hustling years than reconstructing them. As bell hooks surmises, Malcolm's decision to remain celibate for twelve years probably stems from a desire to "suppress and deny those earlier years of hedonistic sexual practice, the memory of which clearly evoked shame and guilt. Celibacy alongside rigid standards for sexual behavior may have been Malcolm's way of erasing all trace of that sexual past."[39]

In the end, Malcolm did not need to understand what the zoot suit, bebop, the lindy, or even hustling signified for black working-class politics during the war. Yet his hipster past continued to follow him, even as he ridiculed his knob-toed shoes and conked hair. His simple but colorful speaking style relied on an arsenal of words, gestures, and metaphors drawn in part from his street-corner days. And when he lampooned the black bourgeoisie before black working-class audiences, he might as well have donned an imaginary zoot suit, for his position had not changed dramatically since he first grew wary of the "Hill Negroes" and began hanging out in Roxbury's ghetto in search of "Negroes who were being their natural selves and not putting on airs."[40] There, among the folks today's child gangstas might have called "real niggaz," fifteen-year-old Malcolm Little found the uniform, the language, the culture that enabled him to express a specific constellation of class, racial, generational, and gendered identities.

What Malcolm's narrative shows us (unintentionally, at least) is the capacity of cultural politics, particularly for African American urban working-class youth, to both contest dominant meanings ascribed to their experiences and seize spaces for leisure, pleasure, and recuperation. Intellectuals and political leaders who continue to see empowerment solely in terms of "black" control over political and economic institutions, or who belittle or ignore class distinctions within black communities, or who insist on trying to find ways to quantify oppression, need to confront Ellison's riddle of the zoot suit. Once we situate Malcolm Little's teenage years squarely within the context of wartime cultural politics, it is hard to ignore the sense of empowerment and even freedom thousands of black youth discovered when they stepped onto the dance floor at the Savoy or Roseland ballrooms, or the pleasure young working-class black men experienced when they were "togged to the bricks" in their wild zoot suits, strolling down the avenue "doin' the streets up brown." Whatever academicians and self-styled nationalist intellectuals might think about Malcolm Little's teenage years, the youth today, particularly the hip-hop community, are reluctant to separate the hipster from the minister. Consider, for example, W.C. and the Maad Circle's sampling of Malcolm's voice to open their lyrical recasting of the political economy of crime, "If You Don't Work, You Don't Eat," in which Los Angeles rapper Coolio asserts, "A hustle is a hustle, and a meal is a meal/that's why I'm real, and I ain't afraid to steal." Or consider Gangstarr's (rap group now defunct) video, "Manifest," in which the lead rapper, Guru, shifts easily between playing Malcolm—suit, rimmed glasses, and all—rapping behind a podium before a mosque full of followers, to rollin' with his homeboys, physically occupying an abandoned, deteriorating building that could have easily been a decaying Roseland Ballroom. Not coincidentally, beneath his understated tenor voice switching back and forth between sexual boasting and racial politics, one hears the bass line from Dizzy Gillespie's bebop classic, "A Night in Tunisia." Through an uncanny selection of music, an eclectic mix of lyrics, and a visual juxtaposing of young black men "hanging out" against Malcolm the minister, Guru and D. J. Premier are able to invoke two Malcolms, both operating in different social spaces but sharing the same time—or, rather, timelessness. While some might find this collapsing of Malcolm's life politically and intellectually disingenuous, it does offer a vehicle for black (male) youth to further negotiate between culture as politics and culture as pleasure.

But "collapsing" the divisions Malcolm erected to separate his enlightened years from his preprison "ignorance" also compels us to see him as the product of a *totality of lived experiences.* As I have tried to suggest, aspects of Malcolm's politics must be sought in the riddle of the zoot suit, in the style politics of the 1940s that he himself later dismissed as stupidity and self-degradation. This realization is crucial for our own understanding of the current crisis of black working-class youth in urban America. For if we look deep into the interstices of the postindustrial city, we are bound to find millions of Malcolm Littles, male and female, whose social locations have allowed them to demystify aspects of the hegemonic ideology while reinforcing their ties to it. But to understand the elusive cultural politics of contemporary black urban America requires that we return to Ellison's riddle posed a half century ago and search for meaning in the language, dress, music, and dance styles rising out of today's ghettoes, as well as the social and economic context in which styles are created, contested, and reaccented. Once we abandon decontextualized labels like "nihilism" or "outlaw culture," we might discover a lot more Malcolm X's—indeed, more El Hajj Malik El Shabazz's—hiding beneath hoods and baggy pants, Dolphin earrings and heavy lipstick, Raider's caps and biker shorts, than we might have ever imagined.

NOTES

1. Malcolm X, with Alex Haley, *The Autobiography of Malcolm X* (New York: Grove Press, 1964), 56.

2. A number of scholars, from a variety of different disciplines and standpoints, have illustrated the extent to which the *Autobiography* depended on various rhetorical strategies and literary devices (i.e., conversion narrative). See especially Thomas Benson, "Rhetoric and Autobiography: The Case of Malcolm X," *Quarterly Journal of Speech* 60 (February 1974), 1–13; Werner Berthoff, "Witness and Testament: Two Contemporary Classics," *New Literary History* 2 (Winter 1971); Nancy Clasby, "Autobiography of Malcolm X: A Mythic Paradigm," *Journal of Black Studies* 5, no. 1 (September 1974), 18–34; David Demarest, "*The Autobiography of Malcolm X*: Beyond Didacticism," *CLA Journal* 16, no. 2 (December 1972), 179–87; Carol Ohmann, "*The Autobiography of Malcolm X*: A Revolutionary Use of the Franklin Tradition," *American Quarterly* 22, no. 2 (1970), 131–49; John Hodges, "The Quest for Selfhood in the Autobiographies of W. E. B. DuBois, Richard Wright, and Malcolm X" (Ph.D. diss., University of Chicago, 1980); Stephen Whitfield, "Three Masters of Impression Management: Benjamin Franklin, Booker T. Washington, and Malcolm X as Autobiographers," *South Atlantic Quarterly* 77 (Autumn 1978).

3. Part of the reason for this, I believe, has something to do with the unusual proclivity of most Malcolm biographers to adopt a psychobiographical approach in place of an analysis that places the subject within specific historical and cultural contexts. Examples include Bruce Perry, *Malcolm: The Life of a Man Who Changed Black America* (Barrytown, NY: Station Hill Press, 1991), and Perry's three articles: "Malcolm X in Brief: A Psychological Perspective," *Journal of Psychohistory* 11, no. 4 (Spring 1984), 491–500; "Malcolm X and the Politics of Masculinity," *Psychohistory Review* 13, nos. 2 and 3 (Winter 1985), 18–25; and "Escape from Freedom, Criminal Style: The Hidden Advantages of Being in Jail," *Journal of Psychiatry and Law* 12, no. 2 (Summer 1984), 215–30; Lawrence B. Goodheart, "The Odyssey of Malcolm X: An Eriksonian Interpretation," *The Historian* 53 (Autumn 1990), 47–62; Frederick Harper, "Maslow's Concept of Self-Actualization Compared with Personality Characteristics of Selected Black American Protestors: Martin Luther King, Jr., Malcolm X, and Frederick Douglass" (Ph.D. diss., Florida State University, 1970); Cedric J. Robinson, "Malcolm Little as a Charismatic Leader," *Afro-American Studies* 3 (1972), 81–96; Eugene Victor Wolfenstein, *The Victims of Democracy: Malcolm X and the Black Revolution* (Berkeley and Los Angeles: University of California Press, 1981). The worst example thus far is clearly Bruce Perry's massive psychobiography. Ignoring African American urban culture in general, and black politics during World War II in particular, enables Perry to treat Malcolm's decisions and practices as manifestations of a difficult childhood, thus isolating him from the broader social, cultural, and political transformations taking place around him. Throughout the book Perry betrays an incredible ignorance of black culture and cultural politics; the fact that standard works are omitted from the notes and bibliography further underscore this point. On the other hand, Wolfenstein does make some reference to black politics during the war, but his very thin

discussion focuses almost exclusively on organized, relatively mainstream black politics such as A. Philip Randolph's March on Washington Movement. The cultural politics of black zoot suiters, for all its contradictions and apparent detachment from social struggle, is ignored. See also George Breitman, *The Last Year of Malcolm X: The Evolution of a Revolutionary* (New York: Pathfinder Press, 1967); George Breitman, *Malcolm X: The Man and His Ideas* (New York: Pathfinder Press, 1965); John Henrik Clarke, ed., *Malcolm X: The Man and His Times* (New York: Macmillan, 1969); James Cone, *Martin and Malcolm and America: A Dream or Nightmare* (Maryknoll, NY: Orbis Books, 1991); Peter Goldman, *The Death and Life of Malcolm X* (New York: Harper and Row, 1973); William Moore, "On Identity and Consciousness of El Hajj Malik El Shabazz (Malcolm X)" (Ph.D. diss., University of California, Santa Cruz, 1974).

4. Roi Ottley, *New World A-Coming: Inside Black America* (New York and Boston: Houghton and Mifflin, 1943), 306. On black politics during the war, see Richard Dalfiume, *Fighting on Two Fronts: Desegregation of the Armed Forces, 1939–1953* (Columbia, MO: University of Missouri Press, 1969), and "The 'Forgotten Years' of the Negro Revolution," *Journal of American History* 55 (June 1968), 90–106; Herbert Garfinkel, *When Negroes March: The March on Washington Movement in the Organizational Policies for FEPC* (Glencoe, IL.: Free Press, 1959); Lee Finkle, "The Conservative Aims of Militant Rhetoric: Black Protest during World War II," *Journal of American History* 60 (December 1973), 692–713; Peter J. Kellogg, "Civil Rights Consciousness in the 1940s," *The Historian* 42 (November 1979), 18–41; Neil A. Wynn, *The Afro-American and the Second World War* (New York: Holmes and Meier Publishers, 1975); John Modell, Marc Goulden, and Magnusson Sigurdur, "World War II in the Lives of Black Americans: Some Findings and an Interpretation," *Journal of American History* 76 (December 1989), 838–48; Harvard Sitkoff, *A New Deal for Blacks: The Emergence of Civil Rights as a National Issue* (Oxford and New York: Oxford University Press, 1978), 298–325, and "Racial Militancy and Interracial Violence in the Second World War," *Journal of American History* 58 (December 1971), 661–81; Robert Korstad and Nelson Lichtenstein, "Opportunities Found and Lost: Labor, Radicals, and the Early Civil Rights Movement," *Journal of American History* 75 (December 1988), 786–811; Herbert Shapiro, *White Violence and Black Response: From Reconstruction to Montgomery* (Amherst: University of Massachusetts Press, 1988), 301–48.

5. Manning Marable, *Race, Reform, and Rebellion: The Second Reconstruction in Black America, 1945–1990* (Jackson and London: University Press of Mississippi, 1991, 2 ed.), 14–17; Philip Foner, *Organized Labor and the Black Worker, 1619–1981* (New York: International Publishers, 1981), 239, 243; Daniel R. Fusfield and Timothy Bates, *The Political Economy of the Urban Ghetto* (Carbondale: Southern Illinois University Press, 1984), 48; William H. Harris, *The Harder We Run: Black Workers since the Civil War* (New York and Oxford: Oxford University Press, 1982), 113–22; George Lipsitz, *Class and Culture in Cold War America: "A Rainbow at Midnight"* (New York: Praeger, 1981), 14–28; Nelson Lichtenstein, *Labor's War at Home: The CIO in World War II* (New York and Cambridge, U.K.: Cambridge University Press, 1982), 124–26.

6. Wolfenstein (*Victims of Democracy*, 175–76) makes a similar observation about the intensification of intraracial class divisions, although we disagree significantly as to the meaning of these divisions for the emergence of black working-class opposition. Besides, I am insisting on the simultaneity of a heightened intraracial class struggle and racist oppression.

7. Perry, *Malcolm*, 48–49; Malcolm X, *Autobiography*, 38–41; Wolfenstein, *Victims of Democracy*, 154–57.

8. I'm making a distinction here between African American zoot suiters and the Chicano zoot suiters in the Southwest. In predominantly Mexican-American urban communities, es-

pecially Los Angeles, the zoot suit emerged about the same time but it also has its roots in the pachuco youth culture, an equally oppositional style politics emerging out of poverty, racism, and alienation. They reappropriated aspects of their parents' and grandparents' Mexican past in order to negotiate a new identity, adopting their own hip version of Spanish laced with English words and derived from a very old creolized dialect known as Calo. For more on Chicano zoot suiters and pachuco culture, see Stuart Cosgrove, "The Zoot-Suit and Style Warfare," *History Workshop Journal* 18 (Autumn 1984), 78–81; Mauricio Mazon, *The Zoot-Suit Riots: The Psychology of Symbolic Annihilation* (Austin: University of Texas Press, 1984); Marcos Sanchez-Tranquilino and John Tagg, "The Pachuco's Flayed Hide: Mobility, Identity, and *Buenas Garras*," in Lawrence Grossberg, Cary Nelson, and Paula Treichler, eds., *Cultural Studies* (London: Routledge, 1992), 566–70; Marcos Sanchez-Tranquilino, "Mano a mano: An Essay on the Representation of the Zoot Suit and Its Misrepresentation by Octavio Paz," *Journal of the Los Angeles Institute of Contemporary Art* (Winter 1987), 34–42; Ralph H. Turner and Samuel J. Surace, "Zoot Suiters and Mexicans: Symbols in Crowd Behavior," *American Journal of Sociology* 62 (1956), 14–20; Octavio Paz, *The Labrynith of Solitude: Life and Thought in Mexico* (New York: Grove Press, 1962), 5–8; Arturo Madrid-Barela, "In Search of the Authentic Pachuco: An Interpretive Essay," *Aztlan* 4, no. 1 (Spring 1973). The best general discussions of the zoot in African American culture are Cosgrove, "Zoot Suit," 77–91; Bruce M. Tyler, "Black Jive and White Repression," *Journal of Ethnic Studies* 16, no. 4 (1989), 32–38; Steve Chibnall, "Whistle and Zoot: The Changing Meaning of a Suit of Clothes," *History Workshop* 20 (Autumn 1985), 56–81. Malcolm's own description of his zoot suits can be found in *Autobiography*, 52, 58.

9. Cosgrove, "Zoot Suit," 78, 80; LeRoi Jones, *Blues People: Negro Music in White America* (New York: William Morrow, 1963), 202; Eric Lott, "Double V, Double-Time: Bebop's Politics of Style," *Callalloo* 11/3 (1988), 598, 600; Ben Sidran, *Black Talk* (New York: Holt, Rhinehart and Winston, 1971), 110–11; Tyler, "Black Jive and White Repression," 31–66.

10. Dominic J. Capeci, Jr., *Race Relations in Wartime Detroit* (Philadelphia: Temple University Press, 1984), and *The Harlem Riot of 1943* (Philadelphia: Temple University Press, 1977); Harvard Sitkoff, "The Detroit Race Riot of 1943," *Michigan History* 53 (Fall 1969), 183–206; Shapiro, *White Violence*, 310–37.

11. Clark and Barker, "The Zoot Effect," 146; and for a broader discussion of police brutality in Harlem during the late 1930s and 1940s, see Cheryl Greenberg, *Or Does It Explode: Black Harlem in the Great Depression* (New York and Oxford: Oxford University Press, 1991), 193–94, 211.

12. Malcolm X, *Autobiography*, 54.

13. Kobena Mercer, "Black Hair/Style Politics," *New Formations* 3 (Winter 1987), 49; also see Lawrence Levine, *Black Culture and Black Consciousness: Afro-American Folk Thought from Slavery to Freedom* (New York and Oxford: Oxford University Press, 1977), 291–92. For a general discussion of the ways oppositional meaning can be reinscribed in styles that are essentially a recasting of aspects of the dominant culture, see Dick Hebdige, *Subculture: The Meaning of Style* (London: Methuen, 1979), 17–19. Although Wolfenstein does not completely accept Malcolm's description of the conk as an act of self-degradation, he reduces his transformation to hipster entirely to a negation of waged work, ignoring the creative construction of an ethnic identity that celebrates difference as well as challenges the hegemonic image of the black male body. In Wolfenstein's schema, oppositional identity becomes merely caricature. Thus he writes, "he was trying to *be* white, but in a black man's way" (Wolfenstein, *Victims of Democracy*, 157).

14. Malcolm X, *Autobiography*, 59–60.

15. Ibid., 72 (first quote), 49.

16. Ibid., 51; and for a description of the Savoy in Harlem, see Jervis Anderson, *This Was Harlem: A Cultural Portrait, 1900–1950* (New York: Farrar Straus Giroux, 1981), 307–14.

17. Quoted in Lott, "Double V, Double Time," 603. Lott's essay is by far the best discussion of the politics of bebop. See also Ira Gitler, *Swing to Bop: An Oral History of the Transition in Jazz in the 1940s* (New York and Oxford: Oxford University Press, 1985); Jack Chambers, *Milestones 1: The Music and Times of Miles Davis to 1960* (Toronto and Buffalo: University of Toronto Press, 1983); Ira Gitler, *Jazz Masters of the 1940s* (New York: Collier Books, 1966); Jones, *Blues People*, 175–207; Frank Kofsky, *Black Nationalism and the Revolution in Music* (New York: Pathfinder Press, 1970), chapter 1; Robert Reisner, *Bird: The Legend of Charlie Parker* (New York: Citadel Press, 1962); Sidran, *Black Talk*, 78–115; John Wilson, *Jazz: The Transition Years, 1940–1960* (New York: Appleton-Century-Crofts, 1966).

18. Paul Gilroy, "One Nation under a Groove: The Cultural Politics of 'Race' and Racism in Britain," in David Theo Goldberg, ed., *Anatomy of Racism* (Minneapolis: University of Minnesota Press, 1990), 274; see also discussions of the social meaning of dance-halls black life in Tera Hunter, "Household Workers in the Making: Afro-American Women in Atlanta and the New South, 1861–1920" (Ph.D. diss., Yale University, 1990), 92–93; and Katrina Hazzard-Gordon, *Jookin': The Rise of Social Dance Formations in African American Culture* (Philadelphia: Temple University Press, 1990).

19. Malcolm X, *Autobiography*, 71; Gerald R. Gill, "Dissent, Discontent and Disinterest: Afro-American Opposition to the United States Wars of the Twentieth Century" (unpublished manuscript, 1988), 166–67; Gitler, *Swing to Bop*, 115–16; Tyler, "Black Jive," 34–35. It is interesting to note that in Germany a subculture resembling black hipsters emerged in opposition to "Nazi regimentation." They wore zoot suits, listened to jazz, grew their hair long, and spent as much time as possible in the clubs and bars before they were closed down. The "swing boys," as they were called, faced enormous repression; jailings and beatings were common for merely possessing jazz records. Earl R. Beck, "The Anti-Nazi 'Swing Youth,' 1942–1945," *Journal of Popular Culture* 19 (Winter 1985), 45–53; "Hans Massaquoi," in Studs Terkel, ed., *The Good War: An Oral History of World War Two* (New York: Pantheon Books, 1984), 500–501; Michael H. Kater, "Forbidden Fruit? Jazz in the Third Reich," *American Historical Review* 94 (February 1989), 11–43; Michael H. Kater, *Different Drummers: Jazz in the Culture of Nazi Germany* (Oxford and New York: Oxford University Press, 1992).

20. Malcolm X, *Autobiography*, 104–7; Dizzy Gillespie, with Al Fraser, *To Be or Not . . . to Bop: Memoirs* (Garden City, NY: Doubleday, 1979), 119–20. Malcolm's later speeches returned to this very theme. The military was initially reluctant to draft African Americans, Malcolm explained to his audiences, because "they feared that if they put us in the army and trained us in how to use rifles and other things, we might shoot at some targets that they hadn't picked out. And we would have." George Breitman, ed., *Malcolm X Speaks: Selected Speeches and Statements* (New York: Pathfinder Press, 1965), 140; "Not Just an American Problem, but a World Problem," in Bruce Perry, ed., *Malcolm X: The Last Speeches* (New York: Pathfinder Press, 1989), 176.

21. Malcolm X, *Autobiography*, 71; Kenneth B. Clark and James Barker, "The Zoot Effect in Personality: A Race Riot Participant," *Journal of Abnormal and Social Psychology* 40, no. 2 (April 1945), 145.

22. Gill, "Dissent, Discontent, and Disinterest," 164–68; George Q. Flynn, "Selective Service and American Blacks during World War II," *Journal of Negro History* 69 (Winter 1984), 14–25. Ironically, one of the most widely publicized groups of black conscientious objectors happened to be members of the Nation of Islam. About one hundred of its members were

arrested for resisting the draft—even its spiritual leader, Elijah Muhammad. Yet, despite the fact that a number of jazz musicians had converted to Islam and even adopted Arabic names (e.g., Sahib Shihab, Idris Sulieman, and Sadik Hakim) during the war, Malcolm claims complete ignorance of the Nation prior to his prison stint. On the Nation of Islam during the war, see Gill, "Dissent, Discontent, and Disinterest," 156–57; E. U. Essien-Udom, *Black Nationalism: A Search for Identity* (Chicago: University of Chicago Press, 1962), 80–81; Sidran, *Black Talk*, 82.

23. See especially Tyler, "Black Jive," 34–39 passim.

24. Tyler, "Black Jive," 38; Mazon, *Zoot Suit Riots*, 54–77; Cosgrove, "Zoot-Suit," 80–88; C. L. R. James, George Breitman, Edgar Keemer, et al., *Fighting Racism in World War II* (New York: Pathfinder Press, 1980), 254–55; Malcolm X, *Autobiography*, 77.

25. Bruce Perry, for example (who characterizes Malcolm's entire family as a bunch of criminals), not only suggests that theft is merely a manifestation of deviant behavior rooted in unfulfilled personal relationships, but he naturalizes the Protestant work ethic by asserting that Malcolm's resistance to "steady employment" reflected a reluctance to "assume responsibility" (*Malcolm*, 57–61 passim).

26. Greenberg, "*Or Does It Explode?*" 198–202; Fusfield and Bates, *Political Economy*, 45–46.

27. Carol B. Stack, *All Our Kin: Strategies for Survival in a Black Community* (New York: Harper and Row, 1974); Betty Lou Valentine, *Hustling and Other Hard Work: Life Styles in the Ghetto* (New York: Free Press, 1978) For comparative contemporary and historical examples from Britain, see the brilliant book by Peter Linebaugh, *The London Hanged: Crime and Civil Society in the Eighteenth Century* (London: Allen Lane, The Penguin Press, 1991); Steven Box, *Recession, Crime, and Punishment* (Totowa, NJ: Barnes and Noble Books, 1987); Jason Ditton, *Part-Time Crime: An Ethnography of Fiddling and Pilferage* (London: Macmillan, 1977); Richard C. Hollinger and J. P. Clark, *Theft by Employees* (Lexington: Lexington Books, 1983); and for a general discussion of the informal economy and working-class opposition, see Cyril Robinson, "Exploring the Informal Economy," *Crime and Social Justice* 15, nos. 3 and 4 (1988), 3–16.

28. Malcolm X, *Autobiography*, 44, 51; Wolfenstein, *Victims of Democracy*, 157. For a discussion of the "hustler's ethic" as a rejection of the "Protestant work ethic," see Julius Hudson, "The Hustling Ethic," in Thomas Kochman, ed., *Rappin' and Stylin' Out: Communication in Urban Black America* (Urbana: University of Illinois Press, 1972), 414–16.

29. Wolfenstein, *Victims of Democracy*, 155; Perry, *Malcolm*, 72. Horace Cayton and St. Clair Drake found numerous examples of poor black residents in Chicago's Southside mutually supporting one another while simultaneously engaged in the illicit economy. *Black Metropolis: A Study of Negro Life in a Northern City* (New York: Harper and Row, 1962, 2 ed.), vol. 2, 570–611 passim.

30. Malcolm X, *Autobiography*, 134; Perry, *Malcolm*, 77–78, 82–83. The evidence Perry provides to make this assertion (which includes simplistic Freudian interpretations of later speeches!) is slim, to say the least. But even if the hearsay Perry's informant passed on is true, it would not contradict my argument. For the manner in which Malcolm allegedly exploited gay men positioned them as Other, and in the cases Perry cites obtaining money was far more important than sexual pleasure. He apparently did not identify with an underground gay community; rather, it was merely another "stunt" in the life of a hustler.

31. Perry, *Malcolm*, 51–52; Wolfenstein, *Victims of Democracy*, 162–63.

32. See, for example, Miles Davis with Quincy Troupe, *Miles: The Autobiography* (New York: Simon and Schuster, 1989), 87–189 passim; Charles Mingus, *Beneath the Underdog* (Har-

mondsworth, U.K.: Penguin, 1969); and for some postwar examples beyond the jazz world, see Elliot Liebow, *Tally's Corner: A Study of Negro Streetcorner Men* (Boston and Toronto: Little, Brown, 1967), 137–44; Christina Milner and Richard Milner, *Black Players: The Secret World of Black Pimps* (New York: Little, Brown, 1973).

33. "Romance without Finance," *Bird/The Savoy Recordings [Master Takes]* (Savoy, 2201).

34. Iceberg Slim [Robert Beck], *Pimp: The Story of My Life* (Los Angeles: Holloway House, 1969), vi.

35. Malcolm X, *Autobiography*, 68.

36. Ibid., 47–48, 75. A number of scholars have suggested that pimps and hustlers, at least in black folklore, were more like modern-day tricksters than "bad men." See, for example, Levine, *Black Culture and Black Consciousness*, 381–82; Milner and Milner, *Black Players*, 242.

37. "Not Just an American Problem, but a World Problem," in Perry, ed., *Malcolm X: The Last Speeches*, 161.

38. Malcolm X, *Autobiography*, first quote, 78: second quote, 55.

39. bell hooks, "Sitting at the Feet of the Messenger: Remembering Malcolm X," in *Yearning: Race, Gender and Cultural Politics* (Boston: South End Press, 1990), 84.

40. Malcolm X, *Autobiography*, 43.

Chapter Nine

"Memories of El Monte"
Intercultural Dance Halls in Post-World War II Greater Los Angeles

matt garcia

With great anticipation, the staff at Rainbow Gardens, Pomona's famed dance palace, prepared for another night of ballroom dancing in 1950. This evening's dance, however, differed substantially from any other function held by the club since its opening in the mid-1940s. For one, concerts usually occurred on the weekends at Rainbow; this event was happening on a Wednesday. Second, and perhaps most noticeably, this evening's attraction drew Mexican Americans, not the white patrons who usually frequented the establishment.

"You're gonna lose your shirt," cautioned the wary owner, Gertie Thomas, to a young, confident local disc jockey, Candelario Mendoza.[1] Mendoza, host of a local, early-morning, Spanish-language radio program, knew that many Latin American *orquesta* and Mexican American *conjunto* bands frequently passed through Southern California. This fact, combined with the presence of a significant Mexican American community, presented the potential for hosting Latin American music concerts in San Gabriel Valley.[2]

Still, Gertie and Ray Thomas, owners and operators of Rainbow Gardens, had little confidence that a midweek dance could make a profit. Fearing imminent failure, the Thomases opened only one of three bars, scheduled just a few employees, and permitted Mendoza to use the facilities without charge. Mendoza graciously accepted their gift and proceeded to advertise the event on his radio program.

As a large crowd gathered in front of the door, Gertie Thomas immediately realized she had underestimated both the number of Mexican people living in the San Gabriel Valley and the drawing power of Latin American music. Beto Villa, the popular Tejano bandleader, Rainbow's first Latin American act, drew over 750 people that evening. Admitting her error later, Gertie Thomas told Mendoza: "How can this be? Who is this guy? He must be the greatest around. I cannot get that many people [for] Les Brown, Harry James, or even Count Basie on a Saturday night."[3] A new era for Latin American music had begun in eastern Los Angeles county.

The emergence of Rainbow Gardens as a venue for Latin American music represented the beginnings of a renegotiation of public space in Southern California during the 1950s. Consisting primarily of Mexican Americans and whites, but also African Americans and Asian Americans/Pacific Islanders, Southland communities engaged in a degree of intercultural communication that increased over time. In this chapter I evaluate this evolutionary process through the interethnic history of two dance halls: Pomona's Rainbow Gardens and El Monte's American Legion Stadium. Following the leads of Steven Loza and George Lipsitz, I consider music and dance of the 1950s and 1960s to be reflective of the intercultural conflict, exchange, and convergence prevalent in Southern California society.[4] To their studies I hope to contribute an understanding of the geographic, aesthetic, and cultural importance of the dance halls in the creation of this predominantly youth-oriented culture.

Informed by the theories of Edward Soja, I employ "an interpretive balance between space, time, and social being" in analyzing this history, taking into account the unique "multi-nucleated" physical and cultural geography of the region.[5] "The formative spatiality of social life" shaped by parkways and freeways, radio and television, and residential segregation provides a "template of critical insight" into intercultural relations in Southern California throughout the post-World War II period.[6] While economic and social structures of inequality segregated Mexican Americans and other ethnic/racial minorities, their historical presence, employment, and resistance provided the potential for transformations in Southland race relations. Furthermore, their determination to claim equal access to public space, their manipulation of Greater Los Angeles's unique physical and cultural geography, and their preservation of distinctive cultural forms contributed to the ongoing social development of Southern California.

Although spontaneous music and dance events occurred throughout the Southland in church halls, local armory auditoriums, and high school gymnasiums, a few men and women involved in the burgeoning music industry invested in night clubs and ballrooms and promoted regular weekly dances in "civic" buildings.[7] I have chosen to focus on Rainbow Gardens and American Legion Stadium as a vehicle for analyzing musical importation and hybridization in Greater Los Angeles because their stories represent the kind of cultural transference, transformation, and creation that took place in the L.A. suburbs between World War II and the student movements of the late 1960s.

Rainbow Gardens

Before 1950, Rainbow Gardens had an established reputation as one of the premier venues for big band music in Southern California. In spite of big bands' cross-cultural appeal, Latinos did not appear at Rainbow Gardens as either audience members or performers.[8] In fact, when asked whether Mexican Americans attended Rainbow Gardens' dances in the 1940s, Cande Mendoza commented: "Oh, no. Absolutely not. In fact, and I hesitate to say this, but I think that even before [1950] a Mexican American had to be *extremely* well dressed and not even look too much like a Mexican in order to get into Rainbow Gardens on a Saturday night."[9] Soon after the success of Beto Villa's concert, Gertie and Ray Thomas made Cande Men-

Fig. 9.1. Rainbow Gardens' exterior on a Saturday night in the 1950s. (Courtesy of Candelario Mendoza.)

doza the permanent music consultant, booking manager, and emcee at the club in an effort to boost business. Although Mendoza mixed white acts with Latin American bands, once Mexican Americans began to frequent the club, whites ceased to patronize Rainbow Gardens. Therefore, a predominantly Latino audience enjoyed performances by such varied entertainers as Les Brown, María Victoria, Harry James, Luis Arcaráz, Lou Castello, Ray Touzet, Machito, Tito Puente, and Dámaso Pérez Prado.

Local groups also appeared on the Rainbow stage as intermission bands. While most headline acts consisted of a twelve- to fourteen-piece orquesta, intermission bands were often much smaller, and represented the more working-class genre of music known as "conjunto." Consequently, a trip to Rainbow Gardens on Saturday nights exposed patrons to a full range of Latin American music: small, local working-class bands, to large, internationally known orquestas.[10]

Although Mendoza began his tenure at Rainbow Gardens as a champion of the Latin American big band sound, he also recognized the generational cleavages within the Latino community. In response to the growing popularity of rock 'n roll in the mid-1950s, Mendoza began Friday night dances at Rainbow Gardens to accommodate large numbers of Mexican American teens interested in the "new" American popular music. As with his big band shows, Mendoza successfully attracted notable recording stars, including Little Richard and a young, Mexican American rock 'n roller named Ritchie Valens.

The emergence of rock 'n roll represented an important change in the direction of Mexican American/Chicano music. Although young people of the late 1950s and early 1960s shared an appreciation for mambo, conjunto, and orquesta, many viewed these forms as the music of their parents. According to Jerry Castellano, a veteran of the music scene and founding member of two Pomona bands, The Velveteens and The Royals, "we appreciated [Latin American music], but we were into another bag."[11] For him and his peers, Mexican music occupied a space on the kitchen table in the form of a transistor radio.

> Like any other person, all [Mexican] families did this—the father would get up early and eat breakfast before going to work, and the wife would get up and make breakfast for him—and they had a little radio with a *soft* Mexican station on so it wouldn't wake up the kids. That was the only time we heard Mexican music.... But, it wasn't the "in" thing to listen to Mexican music, because [Spanish] was a second language.[12]

In addition to the language barriers, generational gaps also played a part in separating young Chicanos from music of a previous generation. For example, although Pérez Prado's popularity reached its highest level in the mid-1950s across a very diverse audience, a young, new generation of Latinos with a growing interest in rock 'n roll mostly regarded him as an elder icon of the Latin American big band scene.[13] Jerry Castellano explains his generation's impressions of Prado:

> Everybody had their own taste, but mainly all the groups—the Latin groups and the big band groups—they were much older, much much older than us. Pérez Prado, when he was popular, he wasn't a young man. He was already... mid-30s or 40s already. And the reason for this was because it took so long for them to get exposure. You know, T.V. wasn't in that much, and you couldn't get into radio [Latin American musicians on English speaking radio]. It was very difficult to get the word out. So they had to travel a lot to get exposure.[14]

Rainbow Gardens served as an important venue for bands such as Prado's and helped disseminate and popularize the music among the Mexican population of Southern California. However, for a younger generation of Mexican Americans (many second and third generation), born, if not raised in a predominantly English-speaking, mass-culture-based, multicultural society, this music did not have the same appeal. These youths increasingly validated artists' fame with their appearances on mainstream radio stations and television programs, while Rainbow Gardens' Saturday night dances and entertainers became associated with an older crowd.

For Castellano and other young aspiring rock 'n rollers, generational as well as ethnic/racial affinity represented an equally important factor in encouraging young Mexican Americans to take up music as an expression of their culture. For example, Castellano recalled the importance of seeing Ricky Nelson weekly: "We grew up with him on T.V. And I remember every time he sang or played, it was like 'if he can do it, so can we!' "[15] Such enthusiasm translated into increased record sales for rock 'n roll artists and encouraged record companies to focus more attention on the emerging youth market.[16]

The success of Ritchie Valens, a local artist from Pacoima in the San Fernando Valley, galvanized other Mexican American youths. As Castellano remembered: "Especially when we saw someone like Ritchie Valens make it to the top. Wow! That means that we can do it. . . . Chicanos that made it!"[17] Although Valens had the good fortune of succeeding on a national level early in his career, the rock 'n roll music culture of Southern California mostly developed in the dance halls and small auditoriums throughout the Southland. Music groups, whose proliferation easily surpassed the number of recording companies willing to sign them, depended mostly on exposure at local venues such as Rainbow Gardens.

As the 1950s came to a close, the musical tastes of a younger generation influenced the kind of music featured in the dance halls. While Mendoza adjusted his focus to incorporate rock 'n roll music into Rainbow Gardens' weekend repertoire, the change did not accommodate the enormity of rock 'n roll's following. Rainbow Gardens' reputation as a site for Latin American music and Mendoza's allegiance to the big band genre and an older generation of Mexican American patrons did not permit him to commit Rainbow's stage to the exclusive production of rock'n roll shows.

El Monte's American Legion Stadium

El Monte's American Legion Stadium, on the other hand, developed directly out of the youth subculture which seized the mainstream during the 1950s. Located in the heart of the San Gabriel Valley, Legion Stadium drew a diverse, multicultural audience from all ends of the Southland. Art Laboe, a popular local radio disk jockey and concert promoter, remembered: "White kids from Beverly Hills, black kids from Compton, and local Chicano kids used to come out to our shows every weekend."[18]

El Monte's American Legion Stadium, a cavernous auditorium which was the sight of wrestling matches for the 1932 Olympics and roller derby matches for the Los Angeles Thunderbirds, proved to be the perfect place for rock 'n roll concerts. Initially, Laboe attempted to organize these shows within the Los Angeles city limits; however, a city ordinance restricted gatherings of people under the age of eighteen. According to Laboe, "Concerts started at El Monte because the laws were different in the county than they were in the city [of Los Angeles]."[19]

Angelenos' experience of life in Greater Los Angeles—a network of suburbs connected first by parkways, and then by freeways—encouraged young people to drive from their homes to county dance hall sites.[20] The appeal of radio to teenagers during this period created "imagined communities" based on equal access to programs and generational affinity.[21] Although young people may have lived in a particular geographical region segregated by race and class, the common experience of listening to music broadcasted across the Southland on KRLA and other radio stations prefigured the interethnic popularity of the halls. Moreover, Laboe and other disk jockeys assembled an attractive array of popular performers including Jerry Lee Lewis, Ray Charles, and Sam Cooke whom fans could not resist.

The commute gave rise to an emergent car culture. According to one faithful El Monte patron, Richard Rodríguez, "Lowriders were early fifties, and everybody was lowriding."[22] To lower their cars, teens would either heat the suspension springs underneath their wheel base or load their trunks with sand or cement bags.[23] Often, lowriders played music from *within* their cars as a way to prepare for the night's

Fig. 9.2. A typical weekend crowd at El Monte's American Legion Stadium in the late 1950s. Disk jockey, concert promoter, and emcee Art Laboe stands in the foreground. (Courtesy Original Sound Record Co., Inc.)

entertainment. As Rodríguez remembered, "You had your record player that was made by Craig. The actual 45 rpm record inside the car! If you hit a bump in the street, there went the record."[24]

In addition to the cars, clothes shaped the world of the teen dance halls. Unlike Rainbow Gardens, which maintained a dress code, American Legion Stadium allowed young patrons to wear whatever they desired. This condition led to an eclectic, nonconformist fashion at El Monte, reflective of the cultural diversity extant in rock 'n roll audiences. Khaki pants and a "Sir Guy" brand, plaid shirt were particularly common among many local Chicanos, while Chicanas frequently wore a short sleeved blouse with a tight-fitting, short skirt, usually cut about six inches above the knee. These fashion statements expressed subtle acts of rebellion on the part of Mexican American youths who consciously broke with the "classy" suit and gown look of their parents.[25]

White, Mexican American, black, and Asian/Pacific Islander youths shared styles that contributed to the development of "fads." Richard Rodríguez remembered: "The black guys . . . would *dress* all the time!"[26] Many African American men dressed in suits that imitated the look of popular black performers such as Don Julian, Brenton Woods, and Richard Berry. Wearing tailored suits trimmed with velvet or satin along the sleeves and lapels, audiences adapted these fashions to their material means and aesthetical tastes to create "the Continental" look. Rodríguez explained: "That would be narrow lapels, narrow pant legs, [and] Continental pockets meaning . . . kind of your western cut."[27] These styles would make their way back to the stage as performers simultaneously influenced and incorporated changes in fashion by contributing their own regional tastes in clothing and appropriating styles worn by audiences. Occasionally, clothing fads informed the themes of songs, as represented in Hank Ballard's tune, "Continental Walk." Similarly, the car culture inspired many songs such as Thee Midnighters' "Whittier Blvd." or for a later generation, WAR's classic 1975 hit, "Lowrider."[28]

The music and groups best represented the degree of intercultural exchange and ethnic/racial diversity present at rock 'n roll shows. Several bands consisted of musicians from a variety of cultural backgrounds, including African American, Mexican, white, and Asian/Pacific Islander. The racial/ethnic intermixing facilitated a blending of cultural influences within a musical genre already distinguished by its hybridized origins of African American rhythm and blues, jazz, gospel, and white country and rockabilly.[29] Created within the context of the ethnically diverse environment of Southern California dance halls, music emerging from this scene possessed a broad-based, cross-cultural appeal, which facilitated understanding among a racially diverse audience. Recalling how music effected his life and the lives of people of his generation, Jerry Castellano remembered:

> The music of the fifties kind of helped because everybody got into it . . . the blacks were popular entertainers, the whites were popular entertainers. . . . It helped bring generations—not generations—but cultures together and understand. We took that same road, and we tried to do the same thing as far as bringing people together. That's all we did in our music.[30]

Following these tenets, Castellano recalled adding a Jewish pianist with a "classical" background to his group, *The Royals*, as much for his musical contributions as for the message it delivered to audiences. "We did not want to keep it just a Chicano band."[31]

Such was the case with Rainbow Gardens' house band, The Mixtures. The self-conscious, iconographic title of the group epitomized the intentions of many bands and artists who sought to reflect the multicultural world of Southern California's dance halls. Led by the Mexican American pianist Steve Mendoza and the African American saxophonist Delbert Franklin, the group also included a Chicano drummer (Eddie de Robles), a Purerto Rican bass player (Zag Soto), a black horn player (Autry Johnson), a white guitarist (Dan Pollock), and an American Indian/West Indian percussionist (Johnny Wells). Although they never achieved national fame, The Mixtures possessed an "aural and visual" appeal that garnered favor from Southern California's diverse audiences and radio personalities such as Bob Eubanks and Dick Moreland.[32]

That The Mixtures gained popularity as a live band but never as recording artists also reflects the importance of place in the formation of Los Angeles's interethnic music culture. Although many youths respected the "commercial" success of Ritchie Valens or Ricky Nelson, Southern California bands could also achieve significant notoriety from their live performances. Noting the unique qualities possessed by The Mixtures on their only record album (not surprisingly, a live album recorded at

Rainbow Gardens), Dick Moreland wrote, "California has discovered them [The Mixtures] to be the most exciting act which has ever provided in-person entertainment in their area."[33] The emphasis on the live, or "in-person" quality of the band accurately reflects the significant connection between audience and performer, and music and dance which made the dance halls the center of an emerging youth culture. Moreover, it demonstrates the egalitarian or democratic nature of musical production during this period. Although recording deals came to precious few bands, aspiring musicians could seek affirmation and acceptance outside the recording industry in the dance halls.

The multiethnic dance halls also provided youths the unique opportunity to challenge racial/ethnic prejudices in Southern California. A tradition of cooperation in multicultural communities and multiethnic organizations such as the Community Service Organization competed with persistent discriminatory attitudes to shape the larger society's response to intercultural mixing at rock 'n roll shows.[34] Prejudices against intercultural courtship and dating, particularly between non-blacks and African Americans, persisted in the minds of many parents of the 1950s. Richard Rodríguez recalls his experience living in Duarte during the early fifties: "You see, back in the fifties, if you dated a black girl, your parents would probably move out of the area. If you were even seen walking with a black girl, [and you were] Mexican, your old man would probably take a switch [blade] to you."[35] Living next to African American families in a community segregated because of racial restrictions in housing, Rodríguez recalled: "[My parents] rented a house to black people, [but] I was not allowed to date a black girl. My mother didn't want it, my uncles and aunts didn't want it. . . . And it was like I better not do this."[36]

The experience of growing up in a racially mixed community, however, provided a basis of familiarity that presented the potential for breaking down color and cultural barriers. Through exposure to multiethnic music and contact with a racially diverse audience in the dance halls, a new generation realized some of this potential. As Rodríguez recalled: "When I went to El Monte, I felt that I could date anybody I wanted to; I could dance with anybody I wanted to. But, I was a little shy yet at El Monte because I was trying to understand the crowd, and why the girls would dance with black guys, and nobody's fighting over it."[37] Eventually, such interethnic mixing on the dance floors and in the parking lots at rock 'n roll shows broke down youths' ambivalence toward intercultural romance. During the late 1950s, Rodríguez remembered seeing "more blacks dating white girls and Chicana girls." He added, "Every now and then you might see a white man with a black girl or a white man with a Mexican girl, or vice versa. . . . El Monte was a melting pot!"[38]

Political decisions and demographic realities in Southern California suburbs facilitated the blossoming of intercultural cooperation among youths in the 1950s. The combination of a growing youth population and the failure of the educational infrastructure to address such growth led to a high degree of race and class mixing in local schools. For example, in the heart of the San Gabriel Valley, the cities of Monrovia, Arcadia, and Duarte maintained just one high school for the three townships. Arcadia contained a white, affluent, middle-class population, while Monrovia and Duarte had a cross-section of black, white, and Mexican working-class families.

Although this clash of cultures initially resulted in conflict, administrators, out of necessity, actively sought ways of facilitating understanding and tolerance by holding "get-acquainted dances" and naming the school mascot the "M.A.D. Wildcats" [Monrovia, Arcadia, and Duarte].[39]

Music and dance served as a bridge between cultures and helped to ameliorate racial tensions on Southland campuses. Playing at a similar high school function in Pasadena, Jerry Castellano recalled how music forged a link between him and a mostly white audience:

> We went thinking we were going to be playing to a lot of Latinos. Wrong! They were all white. So we thought, "What are we going to do, what are we going to play?" So we decided we'll mix it up. We'll play their music, and we'll throw in ours once in a while. And, as it turned out, we played our own stuff and they loved it![40]

Although Castellano and other Mexican Americans played a hybridized music composed of a variety of cultural influences, many still acknowledged distinctions between mainstream rock 'n roll and "their" music. Much of this can be attributed to the regional development of a unique "Eastside Sound" characterized by the presence of Mexican/Latin American influences. Although African American rhythm and blues formed the basis of this music, Chicanos had their own variation of R&B. Mexican teens emphasized a more "intense" rhythmic pattern. According to Castellano, "We didn't use a bass player; we used rhythm guitar."[41] In addition, the presence of a brass section, particularly a saxophone, often set Southern California, Mexican-influenced bands apart from other rock 'n roll groups. "We always had a saxophone, a rhythm section, and a brass section. It was part of the makeup of our music," commented Castellano.[42] Moreover, these bands maintained contact with their audiences throughout a show so that patrons could often call out to the performers, "Play that song," or "We want to do this dance."[43] This made for a particularly "raw" or "primitive" quality, in which audiences' hoots and hollers figured prominently in the Southern Californi' musical aesthetic.[44] Audience "contributions" were recorded on many albums such as The Mixtures' "Stompin' At the Rainbow," or the more popular hits of the period such as Thee Midnighters' "Whittier Blvd." and Handsome Jim Balcolm's "Corrido Rock."

The popularity of the latter song (which also served as El Monte's theme song) demonstrates the important influence of Mexican/Latin American rhythms on Southern California bands and the acceptance of this music by a multiethnic community. Although the traditional *corrido* typically contains words and a distinguishable rhyme scheme, rock musicians probably used the title "corrido" not as a literal description of the song but rather as a reference to the Latin American origins of its musical arrangement.[45] "Corrido Rock" contains all of the above-mentioned influences, such as a strong rhythmic guitar beat with a saxophone lead, that harken back to a previous generation. This dance hall "standard" represents an adaptation of the instrumental music enjoyed by a mostly Mexican American audience at places like Rainbow Gardens on a Saturday night. Moreover, the recording of this song by a white artist exemplifies the cross-cultural appeal of this music.

Music from a previous generation, however, was not as remote as the separation of these two worlds might suggest. For example, Latin American big band venues continued serving adult audiences through the 1960s. At Rainbow Gardens, where rock'n roll and Latin American big band "shared" the stage, though on different nights, teens could keep up with the popular trends in Latin American music. In addition, youths commonly began their musical education at home. Jerry Castellano recalled: "I learned [music] from [home] . . . my dad taught me or my uncle had taught me. . . . They were all Mexican chords. Then I used them in rock'n roll and then as the years went by, I learned the seventh chord . . . the jazz chords . . . but they all came from the Mexican chords that my dad used.[46] The experience of performing in church, at family functions, and in the community also shaped the tastes and attitudes of many young musical artists. María Elena Adams-González, for example, recalls how she got her start in music by singing at the fiesta held every year in the Arbol Verde barrio in Claremont: "It was right next to grandma's [house] at the hall of the Sacred Heart Church in the community. Cecilia [her younger sister] and I would sing every year there."[47] "Discovered" by Frank Zappa who lived in the Pomona Valley during the late 1950s and early 1960s, Adams-González went on to perform with the popular local band, Ronnie and the Casuals, and later recorded and performed as a solo artist under the name "Gina Terry."

Frequently, the origins of artists' music and the inspiration for their participation conflicted with the emerging "commercial" mentality of the industry. Ultimately, record producers and promoters came to dominate the rock'n roll scene and soured many musicians' interest in pursuing a professional career in popular music. For example, Adams-González remembers singing for pleasure and to express her culture and feelings through song; however, "when Frank [Zappa] heard me for the first time at the Ontario Music Center, all I remember is him telling me he saw dollar signs."[48] Although Adams-González mentioned that "Frank was a very nice man," she did not view her talents as a vehicle to fame and fortune. After a short teen career, recording and performing at local venues, Adams-González chose to leave the profession and pursue music in less commercial venues.[49]

Similarly, Jerry Castellano remembered: "We didn't do it for money. It was something else to do, to stay out of drugs, to stay out of trouble."[50] For Castellano and his partners, forming a band represented another option for gathering with friends. Their popularity, however, attracted an agent, who imposed a new mode of relating to their music and to one another:

> When the agent came in, he did get us a lot more interest, and bookings, and stuff like that. But what we later found out was that he was doing it for his own purposes. Things were beginning to happen, like little small arguments between us because of him. . . . To make a long story short, he took over the whole thing and we had no say-so in it anymore.[51]

Despite achieving some local success, Castellano and two original members eventually broke off from their first band The Velveteens and formed new groups.

Ultimately, the infiltration of the music industry by self-interested recording executives and predatory music promoters changed the complexion of the rock'n roll.

Although the "Eastside" sound created in the 1950s and early 1960s continued to the present in the music of groups such as El Chicano, Malo, WAR, and more recently Los Lobos, the number of bands and the interest in live performances at small, intimate venues waned toward the end of the sixties and the early seventies. Frequently artists would record original material and send it to a recording company for consideration. Often, the band or artist would never receive a reply; however, the music, or some portion of it would manifest itself in the sounds of groups already signed by the label.[52]

In addition, a small number of large recording companies bought out many of the over four hundred local recording labels of the 1950s and significantly consolidated the industry by the early seventies. This consolidation resulted in a concomitant concentration of varied musical expressions into the music of select groups and artists. Although musicians such as Jerry Castellano continued to perform and create music, access to radio airwaves and dance hall stages became increasingly difficult. By the late 1960s, radio stations and recording companies attempted to ensure their profits and market share by highlighting particular artists or supergroups.[53]

The world of the dance halls and the message of the music also changed during the late 1960s and early 1970s as a result of the social, political, and economic turmoil of the period. In addition to the Vietnam War and its dramatic effects on teen-aged populations, material inequalities and persistent social injustice contributed to a fracturing of Southern California society. As the 1950s boom economy slowed and industries began to relocate in right-to-work states, black and Latino communities were the first to be hurt by growing unemployment.[54] Although the intercultural mingling at places like El Monte's American Legion Stadium and Rainbow Gardens familiarized blacks, Latinos, Asians, and whites with one another, it also tended to accent the growing material inequalities among Southern California's residents. Moreover, as rebellions developed in Latino and black communities in response to the deepening economic and social crises, whites tended to recoil from the intercultural understanding of another age back to their secure white, middle-class neighborhoods. The construction of new schools and the further development of Homeowners' Associations that supported de facto segregation along racial and class lines facilitated such retrenchment.[55] Moreover, with the "refinement" of commercial radio and the promotion of particular popular music stars and supergroups, a local music scene lost its appeal for many teens, including blacks and Latinos.

Conclusion

By the early 1960s, the mambo craze that swept the United States in the fifties had subsided, thus reducing Rainbow Gardens' Saturday night audiences. Although the Pomona dance hall remained a viable and profitable business, both the Thomases and Cande Mendoza chose to leave the music business. Gertie and Ray Thomas retired, while Mendoza, inspired by his early activities in community organizing and journalism, pursued a successful career in education and politics.[56] In 1963 the Thomases sold Rainbow to the owners of Virginia's, another Latin American venue operating in downtown Los Angeles. Somewhat mysteriously, the facility burned down the following year, never to be rebuilt.

El Monte's American Legion Stadium continued to host dances through the 1960s on the strength of rock'n roll's popularity. Initially, as the industry grew, so did El Monte's stature among fans. Toward the end of the 1960s, however, changes in both the music business and society made El Monte a less suitable place for live shows. Ultimately, promoters moved performances elsewhere as laws changed and demographic, geographic, and economic circumstances reshaped the location of entertainment. El Monte's American Legion Stadium was destroyed in 1974.

Compilation albums of that period, retrospective collections recently assembled, reunions such as the annual "Memories of El Monte" show, and the many "oldies" radio stations throughout the Southland preserve some of the memories of the musical culture extant in Greater Los Angeles between the end of World War II and the tumult of the 1960s. The evolution from exclusively white big band ballrooms of the 1940s, to predominantly Latino clubs in the 1950s, to multiethnic teen music dance halls in the 1950s and 1960s demonstrated the degree to which public space opened for a greater number of Southern California residents and cultural influences after World War II. Although material inequalities and persistent racial/ethnic prejudice continued to shape social relations throughout this period, people of diverse cultural backgrounds were able to discover some common ground in the music culture and dance halls.

The creation of such a place required a respect for, or at least tacit acceptance of, predominantly non-Euroamerican-based music by a larger, white-dominated society. The market for Latin American music concerts and recordings provided Mexican Americans a cultural foothold and a sense of belonging in United States society. Equally important, it presented the potential for Latin American culture to influence and transform dominant culture *and* public space by making both more receptive to non-Euroamerican influences.

Eventually, mambo and other forms of Latin American music garnered favor from a predominantly white American listening audience.[57] This popularity, however, did not dramatically alter whites' perceptions of Latinos within their immediate surroundings, nor did it inspire them to reconceptualize and reorganize public space. As the above history suggests, whites may have listened to the music, but places like Rainbow Gardens on a Saturday night remained mostly Latino.

The creation of shared, multiethnic public spaces and cross-fertilization among various cultures in music depended on a new generation of Angelenos. Although de facto segregation and material inequalities persisted, young people of various cultural backgrounds voluntarily chose to enter the multicultural environment of the dance halls and enjoyed the culturally hybridized sounds of Southern California rock'n roll. Shaped by radio, television, and freeways, the "postmodern" social geography of Greater Los Angeles facilitated the convergence of Southland youths in places like El Monte's Legion Stadium.

Finally, the intentional mixing of cultural forms, the use of symbolic iconography, and the incorporation of environmental influences in the music and dance hall culture of the 1950s and 1960s suggests that many youths had more on their minds than just "good time" rock'n roll. The music and experiences of these teens represent what Paul Gilroy calls a "politics of transfiguration." Communicating through non-traditional means, using nonlinguistic communicatory mediums such as rhythms, body motion, and fashion, these youths projected "an alternative body of cultural and political expression that considers the world critically from the point of view of its emancipatory transformation."[58] Although their exchanges were often restricted to the dance halls, youths, nevertheless, quieted the dissenting voices implanted in their heads by a larger society to forge relationships across racial/ethnic and class lines. Moreover, performers successfully transcended divisions in society to create a hybridized music influenced by the many cultures present throughout Greater Los Angeles. The intentional blending of musical forms; the purposeful cultural diversity in bands such as The Mixtures; the cross-cultural exchanges that took place on the dance floors among African Americans, Asian Americans/Pacific Islanders, whites, and Latinos; and the sharing of fads and fashions across ethnic/racial lines all provide evidence of this alternative vision of human relations considered by these young Angelenos. Like other cultural historians who have accepted popular music as a serious indicator of social change, I believe that, while musical expression constitutes "dangerous crossroads" of cultural influences and interpretations, its unpredictability and fluidity grants music the potential to transfigure society in positive ways.

NOTES

1. Candelario Mendoza, interviewed by the author, February 17, 1995.

2. The San Gabriel Valley sits at the foot of the San Gabriel/San Bernardino Mountains, which frame the northeastern boundaries of the Los Angeles basin. The valley extends from Pasadena eastward toward San Bernardino and composes a portion of the expansive Los Angeles metropolis (referred to here as "Greater Los Angeles"). Although Pomona geographically lies in another (though connected) valley of its own, culturally, politically, and economically it constitutes the eastern "fringe" of Greater Los Angeles and is often included as a part of the San Gabriel Valley. For a discussion of this concept of "Greater Los Angeles," see Richard E. Preston, "The Changing Form and Structure of the Southern California Metropolis," *California Geographer*, vols. 12 and 13 (1971 and 1972).

3. Ibid.

4. George Lipsitz, "Land of a Thousand Dances: Youth, Minorities, and the Rise of Rock and Roll," in Lary May, ed., *Recasting America: Culture and Politics in the Age of Cold War* (Chicago: University of Chicago Press, 1989) 267–284; and Steven Loza, *Barrio Rhythm: Mexican American Music in Los Angeles* (Urbana and Chicago: University of Illinois Press, 1993).

5. Edward Soja, *Postmodern Geographies: The Reassertion of Space in Critical Social Theory* (London: Verso, 1989), 23. For ideas on "multi-nucleation," see Richard E. Preston, "The Changing Form and Structure of the Southern California Metropolis."

6. Ibid., 31.

7. These institutions, to name just a few, included Los Angeles's Palladium and Zenda Ballroom, East L.A.'s Paramount Ballroom, Long Beach Municipal Auditorium, Fullerton's Rhythm Room, San Bernardino's Orange Show and Valley Ballroom, El Monte's American

Legion Stadium, and Pomona's Rainbow Gardens. Candelario Mendoza, interviewed by the author, February 17, 1995. Also see Steven Loza, *Barrio Rhythm*; and George Lipsitz, "Land of a Thousand Dances."

8. For an understanding of the significant development of Latin American music in the 1940s, see John Storm Roberts, "The 1940s: The Watershed," in *The Latin Tinge: The Impact of Latin American Music on the United States* (New York: Oxford University Press, 1979), 100–126.

9. Candelario Mendoza, interviewed by the author, February 17, 1995, 5.

10. Manuel Peña has written the most thorough analysis of Latin American music in the American Southwest. *Norteño* was a type of music developed in Monterrey, Mexico, during the nineteenth century, which consisted of the accordion-based sound brought to the country by Eastern European immigrants combined with the indigenous music of Mexico. Later, this music migrated with Mexican immigrants to Texas and became known as *conjunto*, a working-class music reflective of the socioeconomic status of Tejanos. *Orquesta* was a merging of the big band sounds popular in the United States during the 1930s and 1940s with Latin American rhythms of Puerto Rico, Cuba, Mexico, and the American Southwest. Peña argues that this was a "status" music created by and for the Mexican American middle-class to differentiate themselves and their tastes from the Mexican American working-class. See Manuel Peña, *The Texas-Mexican Conjunto: History of a Working-Class Music* (Austin: University of Texas Press, 1985).

11. Jerry Castellano, interviewed by the author, May 11, 1995.

12. Ibid.

13. Lipsitz, "Land of a Thousand Dances," 267–268. Lipsitz explains African Americans' and Chicanos' break with the music of a past generation and their creation of a new rock'n roll aesthetic, particularly in Southern California.

14. Jerry Castellano, interviewed by the author, May 11, 1995. In addition to providing Latin American entertainers exposure, the emergence of Latin American music shows at Rainbow Gardens established the dance hall within the cultural geography of "Greater Mexico/Latin America." As Américo Paredes has argued, places such as the San Gabriel Valley and the entire United States Southwest represent a cultural area of "Greater Mexico" that transcends geopolitical boundaries. See Américo Paredes, *Folklore and Culture on the Texas-Mexican Border*, ed. Richard Bauman (Austin: Center for Mexican American Studies, 1993), 129–142. Lisabeth Haas applies this concept to her study of Mexican communities in Santa Ana/Orange County. See Lisabeth Haas, *Conquests and Historical Identities in California, 1769–1936* (Berkeley: University of California Press, 1995),11. Finally, Rubén Martínez's recent book suggests that this Greater Mexico could be widened and redefined as a Greater Latin America, including such cities as Havana, Mexico City, San Salvador, Los Angeles, El Paso, and New York City. See Rubén Martínez, *El Otro Lado, The Other Side* (London: Verso Press, 1993).

15. Ibid.

16. When Ricky Nelson's 1958 hit, "Poor Little Fool," unseated Pérez Prado's "Patricia" for the number one spot on the Top 100, it represented just one example of a move on the part of the greater listening public to rock'n roll oriented music during the late 1950s. See Peter Grendysa, liner notes for "Mondo Mambo," 13.

17. Jerry Castellano, interviewed by the author, May 11, 1995.

18. Art Laboe, interviewed by the author, May 15, 1995.

19. Ibid.

20. For a history of freeways and car culture in Los Angeles, see Reyner Banham, *Los Angeles: The Architecture of Four Ecologies* (London: Penguin Books, 1971); and Scott L. Bottles,

Los Angeles and the Automobile: The Making of the Modern City (Berkeley: University of California Press, 1987).

21. Benedict Anderson, *Imagined Communities: Reflections on the Origin and Spread of Nationalism* (London: Verso, 1983).

22. Richard Rodríguez, interviewed by the author, May 26, 1995. Mr. Rodríguez attended shows regularly at Legion Stadium throughout its existence and helped Art Laboe with the production of El Monte's reissued compilation album entitled *Art Laboe's Memories of El Monte: The Roots of L.A.'s Rock and Roll.* Today, Mr. Rodríguez serves on the board of directors for the Doo Wop Society and is a part-time organizer of concerts and music events.

23. Most youths did not have the luxury of owning their own cars and could not make permanent alterations to their parents' vehicles. Consequently, placing sand bags in the trunk was the most popular option among cruisers. Richard Rodriguez, interviewed by the author, May 26, 1995.

24. Richard Rodríguez, interviewed by the author, May 26, 1995.

25. Ibid. Not all youth, however, made such radical breaks with the past. Some men wore the traditional "pegger" slacks with a shirt and tie, and occasionally a sport coat, while many women opted for the conservative look of a full skirt or party dress.

26. Richard Rodríguez, interviewed by the author, May 26, 1995.

27. Ibid.

28. George Lipsitz identifies the process of fashion and youth culture influencing the themes of rock'n roll music coming out of Southern California. The "pachuco" style and subculture in particular had an early effect on Southland music, manifested in Don Tosti's 1948 hit, "Pachuco Boogie." Chuck Higgins's 1952 hit, "Pachuko Hop" (popular with El Monte's audiences), demonstrated a continuing influence of the pachuco in the fifties. According to Rodríguez, Castellano, Mendoza, and Lipsitz, however, the pachuco subculture gave way to what Lipsitz called a cholo style in the 1950s. See Lipsitz, "Land of a Thousand Dances," 271–272. Also, Richard Rodríguez, Candelario Mendoza, and Jerry Castellano, interviewed by the author.

29. Lipsitz, "Land of a Thousand Dances," 267–284.

30. Jerry Castellano, interviewed by the author, May 11, 1995.

31. Ibid.

32. Dick Moreland, liner notes to The Mixtures' album, "Stompin' at the Rainbow" (Los Angeles, CA: Linda Records, 1962).

33. Ibid.

34. Lipsitz, "Land of a Thousand Dances," 270. The experiences of such labor and community organizers as Bert Corona and Hope Mendoza Schechter, who married non-Mexicans demonstrates the affect activism had on breaking down cultural barriers in courtship and dating of this period. See Bert Corona, interviewed by Mario T. García, *Memories of Chicano History: The Life and Narrative of Bert Corona* (Berkeley: University of California Press, 1994); Margaret Rose, "Gender and Civic Activism in Mexican American Barrios in California: The Community Service Organization, 1947–1962," in Joanne Meyerowitz, ed., *Not June Cleaver: Women and Gender in Postwar America, 1945–1960* (Philadelphia: Temple University Press, 1994), 188. For issues surrounding interracial marriage, see Peggy Pascoe, "Race, Gender, and Intercultural Relations: The Case of Interracial Marriage," *Frontiers: A Journal of Women Studies*, 12, no.1 (1991).

35. Richard Rodríguez, interviewed by the author, May 26, 1995.

36. Ibid.

37. Ibid.

38. Ibid.

39. Ibid.

40. Jerry Castellano, interviewed by the author, May 11, 1995.

41. Ibid.

42. Ibid.

43. Ibid. Castellano mentioned that the appropriation of artists' material by record executives was a common occurrence in the 1950s and 1960s. For example, he composed a song entitled "Jerry's Jump" with his first group, The Velveteens. After Castellano left the band, however, the agent had the bandleader record the song under a new title, "Johnny's Jump."

44. Rubén Guevara, interviewed by the author, July 22, 1997. See also Lipsitz, "Land of a Thousand Dances," 280.

45. For a description of the *corrido* and its importance in Mexican/Mexican immigrant culture, see María Herrera-Sobek, *Northward Bound: The Mexican Immigrant Experience in Ballad and Song* (Bloomington: Indiana University Press, 1993), xxii-xxv, and *The Mexican Corrido: A Feminist Analysis* (Bloomington: Indiana University Press, 1990).

46. Jerry Castellano, interviewed by the author, May 11, 1995.

47. Maria Elena Adams-González, interviewed by the author, August 28, 1995.

48. Ibid.

49. Adams-González chose to sing for her local Catholic Church parish. She still participates in the church choir. Ibid.

50. Jerry Castellano, interviewed by the author, May 11, 1995.

51. Ibid.

52. Ibid. Also, Candelario Mendoza, interviewed by the author, February 17, 1995.

53. For a thorough analysis of how commercial motives transformed the rock "business" during the late 1960s and early 1970s, see Peter Wicke, trans. by Rachel Fogg, " 'We're Only in It for the Money': The Rock Business," in *Rock Music: Culture, Aesthetics and Sociology* (Cambridge, U.K.: Cambridge University Press, 1987), 113–134.

54. Mike Davis explains how many corporations in the 1960s adopted General Electric's 1950s strategy of moving production to the "Sunbelt" (i.e., Arizona), where labor organizing was discouraged and legislated against. Mike Davis, *Prisoners of the American Dream* (London: Verso Press, 1986) 127–138. In his book, *City of Quartz*, Davis examines how the white Los Angeles power structure directed redevelopment money into ventures that benefited white Angelenos while abandoning black and Latino communities. The 1965 Watts Rebellion and the 1970 Chicano Moratorium in East Los Angeles represented just two climatic events in an ongoing struggle against such civic neglect. See Mike Davis, "Chapter Two: Power Lines," in *City of Quartz: Excavating the Future in Los Angeles* (London: Verso Press, 1990), 101–149.

55. For a history of how Homeowners' Associations helped sculpt the segregated landscape of greater Los Angeles, see Mike Davis, "Chapter Three: Homegrown Revolution," in *City of Quartz*, (London: Verso Press, 1990), 152–219.

56. Mendoza served as the president of the Pomona Unified School District twice, and started his own bilingual (Spanish/English) newspaper, *La Voz*, in the 1980s. Mendoza interview, February 17, 1995.

57. John Storm Roberts, "The 1940s: The Watershed," 100–126.

58. Paul Gilroy, *The Black Atlantic: Modernity and Double Consciousness* (Cambridge, Mass: Harvard University Press, 1993), 39.

Chapter Ten

Growing Up as a Jewish Lesbian in South Florida
Queer Teen Life in the Fifties

James T. Sears

During the past dozen years, an impressive volume of gay and lesbian history has emerged. These groundbreaking works have provided new insights about the construction of sexual identity, illustrated novel approaches in historiography and oral history, chronicled a long-forgotten history of a queer nation as it struggled for visibility, respect, and equality, and forged a culture against the onslaught of homophobia and heterosexism.[1] Regrettably, gay history, like the movement itself, has had a bicoastal bias. If you were to rely on the many books found in lesbian and gay bookstores, you would assume that the South was irrelevant to the contemporary lesbian and gay movement. Even in the post-Stonewall histories, Southerners have been marginalized; the ways in which we and past generations have authored our lives have been ignored.[2]

For Southerners born between the Great Depression and World War II, events of the Cold War and Civil Rights Movement became their generational anvils. Aliens—be they from Mars or Moscow, Washington or Fire Island—were poised ready to invade the South. In a span of a generation, however, Southern society and Southerners' image of themselves would alter as persons clinging to the certainties of small-town community life felt assaulted by a revolution of politics, popular culture, technology—and sexuality. Insular and inward in their thinking, homosexual Southerners would also undergo a change that would only become obvious a generation later.

During the Cold War era, lesbian and gay Southerners began to transform themselves as well as the South. Following what oral historian Studs Terkel has called "the good war," men and women were anxious to return to the normalcy of prewar life: marriage and families; movies, dances, and maltshops; factory worker and homemaker; the family automobile and nylon hose. Although from hindsight, such a view may appear hopelessly romantic, in postwar America it was the zeitgeist of the times.

Most Southern towns and cities had their "wrong-side of the tracks," variously populated by the working poor and people of color. Largely invisible in everyday social life, each person understood his or her role defined against the taken-for-granted symbols and rituals of American life: the flag and the Bible, Fourth of July parades and barbecues, Southern Baptist and Colored Methodist Episcopal steeples, the courthouse square and the county fair, "colored" and "white" facilities.

Though Florida entered the Union as a slave state, south of its cotton-growing counties like Leon, Jackson, and Gadsden, Northern sentiments ran strong.[3] In the absence of a dominant planter class, state politics was largely free-for-all. This was an era of powerful county officials and demagogic state politicians, "pork-chop" appointments and gutter-level politics between individual personalities. While the Florida Klan, though active since the twenties, never assumed the powerful role it did in other Southern states, South Florida was very much part of the Old South. Blacks sat at the rear of Miami buses: beaches, parks, and sporting events were strictly segregated: and there was only token integration of public schools.

Although Jewish Southerners comprise less than one percent of the region's population, their presence has always been felt in the South. From the founding of Montgomery by Abraham Mordecai to the founding of one of the largest department store chains by the Rich brothers, Southern Jews have served with distinction from Confederate regiments and cabinet positions up to contemporary mayoral and gubernatorial positions. While reform-minded Jews emigrated to the seaport communities of Charleston and Savannah in the late eighteenth century, Jewish migration to Miami was a twentieth-century phenomenon.

History is full of ironies. Developers, like Indianapolis Speedway founder Carl Fisher, had built Miami Beach as a Gentile alternative to the "Jew-ridden" Atlantic City. On the southern tip of Miami Beach, however, the Lummus brothers, having less personal capital, had welcomed Jewish money, resulting in the first Jewish-American settlements south of Fifth Street. Following the land bust of 1926, local realtors were more willing to sell properties in other parts of the Beach. As the Depression ended, there was a small but vibrant community of five thousand Jewish Americans networked by two synagogues, delicatessens, and a private Hebrew school. Anti-Semitism, though, was still prevalent. Many Beach hotel brochures in the thirties included a warning that accommodations were reserved for "Christian Gentiles."

At the time of Pearl Harbor, 40 percent of American Jews lived in New York City, with many others scattered in cities like Chicago, Boston, Cleveland, and Philadelphia. Following the war, Los Angeles and Miami were the major destinations for Jewish migration. By 1950, about six hundred fifty Jews were migrating each month to Miami, and the Jewish population had already increased sevenfold.

The influence of the Miami Jewish community, while it did not eliminate discrimination, made the Beach more friendly to the growing Jewish population. Despite the disclosure of Nazi death-camp atrocities in Europe, anti-Semitism was still far from dead in South Florida. There were still plenty of "Gentile Only" hotels: even Arthur Godfrey's swank hotel, The Kenilworth, was "restricted"—a euphemism for "no Jews allowed."

Immediately after the war, a group of Jewish veterans, wearing their service uniforms, began a direct assault on these restrictions by visiting each business and discussing the need to rid the Beach of anti-Semitism in a world just rid of Hitler. In 1949, a Miami Beach ordinance, eventually approved by the state legislature, banned signs and advertisements that publicized discrimination on the basis of religion and creed as well as race. Most of the offending signs quietly disappeared. Nevertheless, by 1953, the year Ethel and Julius Rosenberg were electrocuted for espionage, the Anti-Defamation League found that more than one-half of the tourist hotels in Florida still discriminated against Jews, though only one in five did so on the Beach.

By the late fifties, Miami Beach included an estimated eighty thousand American Jews. Kosher restaurants and shops abounded, orthodox and progressive Jews gathered in Flamingo Park, the public beach at 14th Street became known as "bagel beach," and Jewish-Americans held municipal and county offices. There was, though, a "5 o'clock shadow," when contact between Jew and Gentile ended. Jewish-Americans were not allowed membership in prestigious clubs, and some communities included restricted covenants (declared by the Supreme Court as unenforceable in 1948, but still widely observed). Jews, like blacks and gays, were subjected to intimidation, discrimination, and harassment. In the spring of 1951, the Klan dynamited an uncompleted section of the Northside Jewish Center. In 1958, the Orthodox Temple Beth El, Miami's oldest synagogue, was damaged by a dynamite explosion.

South Florida, then, was not immune to the bigotry, racism, and hatred that characterized much of the South and the nation in the fifties. Like most Southerners, many Miamians were preoccupied with communism, integration, corruption—and perversion. In 1954, the army television hearings, led by Senator Joseph McCarthy, were in the news, as was the Supreme Court's groundbreaking decision declaring an end to "separate but equal" education with all "deliberate speed." Floridians—already in a frenzy over McCarthy's allegations of communists in government, the Warren Court's judicial activism, and political stirrings of the National Association for the Advancement of Colored People and the Congress of Racial Equality—voiced their support for the purge of homosexuals or simply remained silent.

The Purge of '54

A year before the witch-hunt against the "boys from Boise,"[4] the Miami *Daily News* launched a series of articles and investigative reports on the "homosexual menace." Roused by the Hearst-like reporting of the *Daily News*, the city's competing morning newspaper, the Knight-owned Miami *Herald*, printed more restrained stories charging that "shoulder-shrugging by police is the cause of Miami's reputation as a comfortable haven for homosexuals."[5] Headlines blazed across the two dailies: "$200,000 Outlay Urged for Center to Treat Deviates"; "Police to Harass Pervert Hangouts"; "How L.A. Handles Its 150,000 Perverts"; "Clean This Place Up!"[6]

Newspaper stories disclosing Miami as a deviate Disneyland of juke joints, drag queens, and cruising grounds was a political opportunity to link perversion and corruption to the powerful police chief. Local politicians with ambitions for higher office or hopes of discrediting opponents in the Metro-Dade consolidation battle quickly initiated a highly publicized crackdown. Police vigorously enforced vagrancy laws, fined owners of "homosexual hangouts," arrested "femmics" (female impersonators); judges committed "sexual psychopaths" to the Chattahoochee state hospital and sentenced homosexual felons to stiff prison sentences; politicians conducted hearings, drafted new ordinances and legislation, while criticizing opponents for being soft on deviates.[7]

Miami Police Chief Headley promptly formed a special squad—known variously within the department as the "Powder Puff Brigade" and "Fruit Pickers." Beginning September 2, 1954, a dozen or so bars ranging from Leon and Eddies to the Echo Club were raided nightly—sometimes twice a night. The immense prepublicity, of course, yielded few arrests as many bars closed or were deserted.[8]

Other local law enforcement agencies also participated in the "purge." Miami Beach Police Chief Romeo Shepard raided bars, swarmed parks, and plucked suspicious swimmers from the 22nd Street public beach. On Friday the 13th of August, Shepard's beach raid was "executed with all the advance planning and secrecy of an amphibious landing." Thirty-five "men who act like girls" were questioned; six were charged with disorderly conduct for failing to give a "good account of their reasons for being in Miami Beach." According to the chief, some of these men sported "bikini" swimsuits that were "little more than a strip of cloth fore and aft" ranging from "shocking pink, and daring cerise to a leopard skin pattern."[9] Arrest and harassment extended to lesbians as well as persons of color. During the first week of September, for example, six women were arrested at one bar, questioned, and then released.

The purge of '54 was not a simple manifestation of homophobia but part of the larger political milieu where the homosexual became a convenient whipping boy for aspiring politicians and corrupt officials, as well as useful political fodder for proponents of municipal consolidation. The purge, however, marked a turning point in Miami's benign neglect of homosexuals and police acceptance of drag queens like Jackie Jackson of the Jewel Box Revue, who had performed six years earlier at the Policeman's Ball.

Breeding Homosexualism and Recruiting Youth

New Jersey Senator Robert Hendrickson and his subcommittee investigating "juvenile delinquency" paid a winter visit to Miami in 1954 and again the following fall. Much of the subsequent testimony focused on the "recruitment by adult perverts" of teenagers into "homosexual practices." In testimony ending the day of hearings, Abraham Aronovitz, Miami's reform-minded, Jewish mayor and an ardent supporter of the Metro-Dade consolidated plan, described himself as "just a country lawyer ... who don't have any scientific knowledge on this subject." However, he made it clear that neither the menace of homosexuality nor police laxity would be tolerated in his reformed city:

> We have accumulated ... up to about a month or two ago, about seven or eight thousand perverts, which was amazing and astounding to our decent church-going and

church-loving people. But they did not come to Miami and the Greater Miami area merely because they wanted to sojourn amongst us. They came... because they were welcomed here and enticed here.

Giving our chief of police the best of credit for having good intentions, he repeatedly announced that we ought to congregate them, those who are here, in a few places, where the police could observe and watch them. Unfortunately, that appeared in magazines published by pervert organizations and operated as a welcome.

Unfortunately, too, some of the bar owners, being a part of this greedy faction that I am talking about, violated all kinds of laws in the books. They even... invited certain types of people, who went out in our city as roamers to entice other young people to get into Cadillac automobiles to take them out for a good time, and to take advantage financially of their conditions.[10]

The Senate subcommittee returned the following November for a three-day hearing. One day was again devoted to problems of juvenile delinquency. Mayor Aronovitz continued his campaign against deviates and those, like Headley, who "coddled them." Proposing amending the white slavery act to include homosexuals, he lashed out at the police chief:

We have political, official, and perhaps some parental delinquency because we have too much complacency toward the wrong things of life.... perversion, nude modeling schools, pornographic literature... How much confusion is there in the minds of young people when they read that Miami's chief of police has stated the perverts ought to be corralled in six or seven bars where they can be better watched by police?... Some young people have learned the whereabouts of the locations which used to be the gambling rooms but have now been turned into plush parlors with lace curtains and lounge chairs.[11]

Two years later, the Miami *Daily News* returned to pervert-bashing with a series of articles, "Profits in Perversion." In the first of the exposé stories, reporters Bob Hardin and Dom Bonafede penned: "A three-week survey by the *Daily News* showed that the pervert colony is flocking back in the same places raided consistently during the 'purge' of 1954."[12] In the second installment of the series, "Deviate Hangouts' Owners Prosper," the two reporters described the "lucrative business" of Miami's "pansy palaces." Listing the bar owners, their home addresses, and their police records, they quoted "law enforcement bigwigs" who proclaimed no increase in the "resurgence of homosexuals." Such statements, the skeptical reporters concluded, were "in direct variance with lower-ranking officers who admit to a fresh wave of perverts."[13] The next day, this reporting duo chided police and described the ineffectiveness of current laws against homosexuals. An article featuring full pictures of the tavern owners' homes led off with the provocative statement: "It's no secret that Greater Miami's 'queer haunts' are operating wide open. But, the police lament, there is not much they can do about it.... This is in the face of 180 sex offense cases involving juveniles in Miami... [including] homosexualism and child molestation"[14] Focusing on the homosexual menace, the *Daily News* readers were dutifully informed: "Psychiatrists call homosexuality a social disease. In another sense, it is a communicable disease, as the psychiatrists generally agree that early exposure to homosexualism breeds perversion." Two other stories featured comments from a prominent judge, and an anonymous psychiatrist who pronounced:

> Many people are struggling with homosexualism, or some other form of perversion; they can go either way. These pervert hangouts balance the scales against them. . . . The open exhibitions may actually throw them into a panic or lead them into that type of life. . . . The only hope for a cure that a homosexual has is within the medical profession. The less the law has to do with him the better he is. . . . [It] is a hard, unhappy life; most of them, consciously or unconsciously, wish they were not what they are.[15]

Generally, though, the police and the courts had much to do with the "hard, unhappy life" of the homosexual. Dade County Judge Ben C. Willard handled most of the "pervert" cases as he had since assuming the bench in the thirties. In compliance with the 1955 Chattahoochee criminal sexual psychopath law, he routinely appointed psychiatrists—at $100 a case—to examine those so charged.[16] A year later the judge remanded a sixteen-year-old "confirmed homosexual" and "wrecked human being" to the state prison for fifteen years for "molesting" other boys his age.[17]

In the midst of these media-whipped, politically motivated, and government-led efforts to purge perverts from city life, a new generation of homosexual Southerners like Merril Mushroom entered adolescence.[18]

Merril

In 1952, Merril began her first year at Miami Beach High School, where Jewish families had replaced the Gentile families of a decade earlier. Jewish students often socialized among themselves in a patio area know as "LJ" (Little Jerusalem). Most of the teachers, though, were Gentile, and the influence of Christianity pervaded the high school as it did other schools in the county: a required five minutes of daily Bible reading (generally from the New Testament), Christmas and Easter celebrations.

Not fitting into the "popular set," Merril turned the collar of her blouses up to be "real cat," wore tights, smoked, and hid her brunette eyes behind sunglasses. At school she hung out with the motorcycle group for whom James Dean was "the be all and end all" and with the GAA (Girls Athletic Association) comprised of "sporty girls" with a strong undercurrent of lesbianism. She reminisces:

> I was hanging around the gay girls and guys a good bit of the time maintaining I was "straight." We didn't use the "L word" back then; it was one of the dirty words. At Beach High, there were the sporty PE lesbians who hung together. There was also a flamboyant student, Eddie, a drag queen who was very popular; a lot of kids who were coming out followed his lead. There was an undertone of being "cool" at the school which meant not getting too academic or condemning those things that were real outrageous—being gay was certainly outrageous. Some of the kids even went to the 22nd Street Beach!
>
> At high school, you had to be either butch or femme. The role models we had for coupling were male/female heterosexual images with no alternative lesbian and gay role

models. At first, I wasn't sure so I became a "ki-ki"—meaning you could be either. But some of us thought in our hearts that anyone who was ki-ki, like my friends Dotty and Joan, was really either butch or femme. The advantage of being ki-ki was that you could go with someone who was either.

I soon rejected that, though. It didn't feel right. Being a femme equated too much to being a girl: weak, lacking privilege, and unable to do what you want. The destiny of being a wife, a mother, a teacher, a servant to a man never appealed to me. Who the hell wanted to do that? By being butch I could swagger and strut; I could be abrupt and assertive. I wore my hair in a DA [duck's ass] with a flat-top. When I went to school I combed it into a brush-up so it looked vaguely feminine. I also wore men's clothes—since I was big, they fit me better than women's clothes.

Like most homosexual Southerners of the times, Merril and her friends were isolated from the emerging homophile movement on the West Coast:

Of course, *The Ladder* had just gotten started. But, that was really not accessible to us because we were just kids. Most of us didn't know how to get a copy of the magazine even if we would have had the courage to do so. But, we knew the names: Daughters of Bilitis, Del and Phyllis. This kind of stuff was the height of radical. We were all so closeted and it was so illegal to be queer. You could be put in jail, put in mental hospitals!

They, too, were largely isolated from the purges of '54 and '56. During this era of bar raids and beach arrests, tabloid exposés and sordid headlines, harsh and lenient sentences, shake-downs and robberies, suicides and murders, there was a sense of "normality" within the lesbian and gay Greater Miami community. *Tea and Sympathy*, starring Linda Darnell, was playing to rave reviews at the Coconut Grove Playhouse, and Leonard Sillman released the popular musical revue *New Faces* of 1956 that included local female impersonator T. C. Jones.

Coming out just before her high school graduation, Merril was aware of the risks associated with being gay but felt little personal vulnerability. "We were just kids. We didn't have jobs to lose. We didn't have families to support. And, of course, when you're a teenager you're immortal; nothing is going to ever happen to you."

Merril formed relationships with other lesbians, some of whom became short-term lovers but remained longtime friends.

Penny was my first love, and she brought me out well, carefully teaching me the rules, roles, and lingo of the gay subculture. I learned how to "read" another gay person and also reveal myself through an intricate language of signals and subtleties and how to camp and carry on. I learned to use conversational gay slang terms and to sprinkle my conversation liberally with gay innuendo. My lesbian friends and I practiced developing masculine movements, aping and emulating the men we professed to despise. To be a man meant to be strong and to have power. The best we could do as women was to be like men, since we had not yet learned of women strength and women power.

The lesbians and gay men I hung out with were really close. Some bars were primarily men's bars and others primarily women but there was a lot of crossing over and the bars were pretty mixed. We partied together; we went to the beach together; we danced together; we "fronted" for each other if someone needed a date for work or family.

Now the people in their thirties, forties, fifties, and sixties were cordial and friendly when we were out. But they primarily stayed away from us. It was very dangerous—not so much for us but for the adults who befriended us in any way. For them, in addition to being busted for being homosexual they could also be booked for "contributing to the delinquency of a minor"—a very, very serious charge.

Although there were a few professional-type people in the bars, it would be unusual to see teachers, social workers, or nurses. They had too much to lose if they were found out. Generally, folks who hung out at the bars were working-class people, students, those who owned their business or who were simply too wealthy to care. In Liberty City there was also the Sir John Club—a black rock 'n roll club where some of the gay kids would go.

But, there was no mixing between the two races on the beach or in the bars. There was some gay overlap, though, between the Anglo and Cuban cultures which was very vivacious and ostentatious. And, although there was still a tremendous amount of anti-Semitism in the Miami community, the Jews and Gentiles mixed pretty well within the gay scene. But I was mainly a queer who just happened to be Jewish.

There also was the Coconut Grove set: older, arty, rich, chi-chi set. They didn't mix with the rest of us. We weren't invited to their house or yacht parties. If one of the parties at a private home was raided, of course, everyone would go to jail. It would be horrendous for them. There was a middle-aged "bisexual" woman who was very wealthy and had phenomenal parties attended by other wealthy persons, professional, show people, and some gangsters. I knew her. She explained to me once how she wished she could include us in her parties but "it's just too dangerous."

Despite Miami's social class, racial, and religious divisions, there was a realization by Merril of her common bond with other women. "From the high-class call girls to the diaper-truck driving diesel dykes, from the wealthy property owners to the high school and college girls, from the professional lady to the lady wrestler, we were essentially all the same under the skin—we all could be, and many of us were, socially persecuted and criminally prosecuted."

Despite the difficulties of the times, Merril focused on bars, not bombings, fun not fear.

It was difficult to be an underage dyke back then. If you didn't have phony proof of age, there weren't many places to go. If you had the three required pieces documenting that you were 21, those who owned or tended the bar would let us inside. But, if they anticipated any problems they wouldn't.

There were a handful of older men who lived in a small apartment complex known as The Manor—we called it the Sex Manor. They would let some of the underage kids use their apartments for trysting. Back then, there was no place for a gay kid to go where you could be yourself. It was especially difficult to find a place to make love when you're both in high school and living with your parents. So, some of the people who lived at The Manor would give a couple the use of their bed for a few hours. This was very brave of them, because adults involved in any way with underage kids could get busted, especially if the kid was an undercover cop.

Even meeting a woman in a bar could be dangerous. Back then there were "teases"—a straight woman who liked to get a lesbian to make a pass at her and then say, "Oh! I don't do that. I'm straight." For those who were really straight, it was an ego trip: "I may have to submit to men but I can put down lesbians." For those with lesbian tendencies it was kind of a double ego trip: "I'm better than you, because I have sex with men. I am found attractive by other women, but I'm really heterosexual." These women would appear in lesbian bars, befriend a lesbian, and go on dates with us. When the lesbian finally made the sexual pass, she would be slapped down. It was not only worrisome because of the rejection, the humiliation, and the degradation but because of the undercurrent of danger: What if she turns me in? There was always this fear of disclosure and arrest which brought further humiliation and sometimes actually incarceration or loss of a job.

The bars—ranging from the most seedy to the classiest—were Merril's principal haunts. Four decades later, pouring another glass of herbal ice tea in the living room, streaks of gray hair glistening as the afternoon sunshine streamed through the windows of her Tennessee farmhouse, Merril called to mind those youthful times:

> In the 22nd Street beach area there were a number of bars. On Alton Road there was the Hi Room, primarily a women's bar. The Hi Room adjoined the Red Carpet much . . . like the lesbian auxiliary of the faggot contingent. I remember my first visit to the bar. I was terrified. I was all dressed up, with my hair combed back looking real butch. I kept walking past the bar's entrance, up and down the street. I just knew my phony proof of age wouldn't work and that I would be thrown out or Mom would be driving down the street and see me walking inside. I finally went home.
>
> The next time, after walking back and forth for a while, I pushed the door open. Behind the bar was Mikki Marr. She was every dyke's dream of a drag butch. Mikki was tall and broad-shouldered, wearing black pants and a white dress shirt. Her short dark hair was combed back in a DA. Her skin was pale and her eyebrows were dark. She had these great cheekbones and a fine strong jawline with a sensitive mouth and chin.
>
> The Hi Room was dark with a velvety look, immaculate and cool. The air conditioning lifted up every hair on my arms. It was wonderful; I was in fairyland; it was my dark ice palace. Soft music played over the jukebox: Johnny Mathis, Ella Fitzgerald. I went there often after that, drinking stingers and staring at Mikki for hours.

Further up Alton Road were other bars. There was the Onyx Room, a swank, hot touristy club featuring female impersonators like Charles Pierce and Jackie Jackson. Well ventilated with a designer stage, it was "always crowded, the bartenders were always terrific, and the male drag shows were always excellent." Mondays were open talent night where, as Merril recounts: "The queens who were not in the regular show would get up and do their numbers. Sometimes they were wonderful; sometimes they were terrible. But, their makeup was always divine and their costumes spectacular."

One day Merril and two of her lesbian friends, Connie and Penny, were talking about the Onyx shows and wondering why they never saw any male impersonators. Sometimes a New Yorker would come down to perform, but there never was a Southern woman doing male drag, although there were plenty of drag butches in the bar.

> After rejecting various performance schemes, we decided to go on as a rock 'n roll male group. We called ourselves the Tongueston Trio. We practiced and rehearsed at Connie's apartment and got our three numbers together. It was more difficult for me because I was still living at home and underage. I had to sneak out for rehearsals posing

as a typical fifties teenager going out to do homework and listen to records with a girlfriend. I took my school books and records—and, hidden in my book bag, my brother's loafers, borrowed with his consent, and my father's tie, borrowed without his knowledge.

Well, when the big night arrived, I gave the usual teenage story about girlfriends, homework, and records, and left the house. I really wanted to say, "I'll be late tonight; I'm competing in the drag show at the Onyx. Wish me luck." I didn't dare. Meanwhile, word had gotten around that we were going to perform. Every lesbian in town must have showed up to cheer us on. The club was jammed.

The fellow who did the lighting was a friend of ours; he did an especially great job for us. We fancied up our usual duck's ass hairdos with pompadours, and we wore black pants, white shirts, black neckties, white socks, black loafers, and sunglasses. Backstage, Penny, Connie, and I paced and fidgeted, trying to keep quiet while the drag queens went through their numbers. Then they were done, and it was our spot.

"And now," we heard the emcee announce, "The Onyx Room is proud to present a brand new act—The Tongueston Trio!" The curtain parted, and hot red and blue lights moved over us as we trotted on-stage in perfect step, waving and smiling. Three separate spotlights came on each of us merging into one big spot. All the girls in the room screamed—the faggots, too! Penny, Connie and I bunched together, ready to start. The lights went down, all throats hushed, and out over the speakers came the opening instrumental notes of our first number, "Bad Boy," by the Jive Bombers:

> I'm just a bad boy,
> la-la-la-la-la-la-la-la-la-la-la-la-la,
> all dressed up in fancy clothes . . .

Then we did "Why Don't You Write Me Darling?" by The Jacks, and ended with "Come Go with Me" by the Del Vikings.

When we came off the stage and into the barroom, people hugged us, mobbed us, bought us drinks. "You were wonderful!" they all said. Of course we had been! Everyone went crazy over us and we won first prize.

I had to go home before my curfew. The management wanted us to come back and do our numbers again for the second show, but I couldn't. It was a real struggle just doing it that one time with my living at home, my mother's scrutiny, and being underage. I suppose if I had been independent we might have gotten it together as a regular act. I was really bummed out to be so restricted.

On the weekends, however, Merril frequented the 22nd Street Beach. Here memories of fun are mixed with those of fear:

On the 22nd Street side was the Sea Isle Hotel and a long pavilion with a juke box and snack bar on the 22nd Street side. We would all dance to six plays for a quarter on that pavilion—it wasn't more than a pier with a roof over the snack bar and a seawall jutting out into the Atlantic where we danced: mambo, pasa doble, cha-cha-cha, fox trot, Panama City bop, chicken, lindy, and the hully-gully. We would do mixed gender dancing and group dancing. If you could get two guys and two girls together and dance in a foursome you could look like you were dancing cross gender and really not be. That was our kind of passing—doing what we really wanted to do in a way that we could get away with it.

There was some occasional brave same-gender couples fast dancing, but never slow!

There was a lot of Cuban music and black music; not much of American Bandstand. Johnny Mathis, of course, was the all-time favorite as well as Frances Faye. There was also a lot of bluesy, jazzy, slow kind of music: Perry Como, Della Reese, Roy Hamilton, Ray Charles, Diana Washington, Ella Fitzgerald, Ray Charles, Dave Brubeck.

There were also lots of plainclothes police. Normally, they had a "cop" look about them. Sometimes they were wearing swimsuits; other times cotton pants. I remember a friend giving me the elbow: "There's a cop." I looked to see an ordinary fellow with a mustache smoking a cigarette with one foot propped up on a bus stop bench leaning on his knee gazing over the beach as though he was cruising.

In reading the news stories of bar busts, precinct bookings, and criminal convictions, one might conclude that lesbians were generally immune from this hate, harassment, and homophobia. Merril cautions against such a brash assessment:

The police hated us; they hated us. They were cruel, vicious, and loved nothing better than catch a lesbian in the act and make her blow him. This was second only to catching a queen and raping him or beating him up.

Sometimes, as we ate our hot dogs and hamburgers, drank our beer and soda [at the pavilion], we would be pulled up by police and thrust toward the street, leaving our food behind. We would be pushed all together—the dancers, the swimmers, the diners, the sunbathers—into paddy wagons which lined the road, shoved in the back, herds of half-naked bodies pressed into the vans until the space was filled and the doors, with mesh-barred windows, would be slammed and locked. Then off we would go to the local precinct house, there to be finger printed, booked, and thrown into a cell, with the promise of public humiliation yet to come. . . .

Women were simply not reported on. Women weren't important; lesbians were invisible. After all, who cared about women anyway? There may have been an underlying belief that if they reported about lesbians then they were acknowledging lesbians—and if they acknowledged us they'd have to think about the possibility of the women they owned loving one another.

But we were harassed, we were arrested, and we were subjected to that same bullshit as the men—but not in the same numbers. At the bars, paddy wagons would pull up to the doors, police would enter the premises, alert for any sign of same-sex relating from dancing to hand-holding. We paired off to appear heterosexual ("Oh, heh, heh, officer, I just came in here with my boyfriend to have a drink, I mean I had no idea . . ."). They would read the contents of wallets carefully, make lewd comments over photographs, ask personal questions. Anyone who appeared to be too much in drag was immediately hustled off to the precinct house to be physically inspected for three articles of sex-appropriate clothing as required by law. Anyone else the police chose to bust was held "on suspicion." Sometimes lesbians—drag queens, too—were beaten up or raped by the cops.

Of course, the cops weren't the only ones we had to worry about back then. All it took to be put in a mental hospital was for your husband or parents to bring you in. If you were a woman, of course, you were a possession. You'd show up to the bar one night and ask, "Where's Diane?" A person would reply matter-of-factly: "Oh, she's in a mental hospital. Her mother committed her." Again, this was not that unusual. If you were a lesbian then you were inflicted with "homosexualism." You needed to be purged of this illness through electro-shock therapy and lots of medication.

Lesbians were an easy target. I remember my friend Lynn once coming in late to

> the bar. She was a mess. "What happened?" we asked. "Oh, Officer so and so caught me again. I had to go and blow his dick. He messed me up a bit." No one got too incensed. There was nothing we could do and this was not that unusual. No one ever considered filing a complaint! These were the police. They could do whatever they goddamned well pleased. We were queers. We just tried to keep out of other people's way. If we were harassed, well, that was just part of queer life.

Concluding Remarks

Growing up as a "homosexual," "fairy," "dyke," "pervert," "bull-dagger," or "faggot" from the gay nineties of the nineteenth century through today's postmodern nineties has always been difficult. From the nationally publicized trial and insanity defense of Alice Mitchell, who murdered her separated lover Freda Ward on a Memphis street as her parents whisked her away,[19] to the coming-out courage of first Cuban-American generation Pedro Zamora, who challenged Hialeah homophobia and championed HIV-awareness on MTV's *The Real World*, growing up gay in the South has been tough.

As a Jew in the Baptist-drenched South and a dyke in a television world of happy homemakers, Merril was different. In the South Florida of the fifties, the emergence of the homophile movement on the West Coast was little more than a rumor as she struggled to make sense of her emerging sexual identity within an environment where being queer was, at best, an illness and, at worst, a felonious act or sinful transgression. During an era when being a woman was defined by her subordinate relationship to a man, acting like a man and preferring female intimacy was radical.

From today's vantage point, we may view the fifties as an era when life was simpler. In fact, queer life for adolescents living in the South has always been complex. Despite talk-show discussions about lesbianism, television shows featuring gay characters, and websites for queer youth, there remains a sense of isolation and differentness.[20] Like Merril and her friends living during the hate-plagued era of blacklists, police harassment, and racial as well as religious prejudice, queer adolescents growing up in the nineties still confront Southern prejudice, violence, and loneliness—in some ways more insidious than two generations ago.

Then as now, there are few homosexual adults willing to support a new generation of gay Southerners. Few public schools or social agencies in the South provide supportive services for queer adolescents, and gay bars or social activities within the gay community are generally age-segregated. Thus, teens of the nineties, like those of generations past, must largely re-create communities of difference and construct sexual identities from cultural material available to them. Growing up different in a region that prizes sameness and coming out within a culture that values discretion is different but no less difficult today than it was yesterday.

NOTES

This chapter is an edited excerpt from my book, *From Lonely Hearts to Lonely Hunters* (New York: HarperCollins-Westview, 1997). © James T. Sears. Additional information can be found at http://www.conterra.com/jsears.

1. These range from oral histories such as Marcus, E. 1992, *Making History: The Struggle for Gay and Lesbian Rights, 1945–1990*. New York: Harper Perennial and Nestle, J. 1993, "Excerpts from the oral history of Mabel Hampton." *Signs* 19(4), 925–935; to detailed studies of specific communities such as Chauncey, G. 1994, *Gay New York*. New York: Basic and Kennedy, E., and Davis, M. 1993, *Boots of Leather, Slippers of Gold: The History of a Lesbian Community*. New York: Routledge; and events such as Bérubé, A. 1990, *Coming Out Under Fire: The History of Gay Men and Women in World War Two*. New York: Plume; Duberman, M. 1993, *Stonewall*. New York: Dutton; as well as more sweeping historical studies such as D'Emilio, J. 1983, *Sexual Politics, Sexual Communities. The making of a homosexual minority in the United States, 1940–1970*. Chicago: University of Chicago Press and Faderman, L. 1991, *Odd Girls: A History of Lesbian Life in Twentieth Century America*. New York: Columbia University Press; also historical documentation such as Duberman, M., Vicinus, M., and Chauncey, Jr., G., eds., 1989, *Hidden from History: Reclaiming the Lesbian and Gay Past*. New York: New American Library and Katz, J. 1992, 2d ed., *Gay American History*. New York: Crowell.

2. The local histories of lesbians and gay men are only now being documented. With few exceptions, though, the South has not been the focus. Currently, no book recounts the oral histories of gay and lesbian Southerners. There are, however, a number of other excellent books such as the autobiographical *Memoirs of a Race Traitor* (Segrest, M. 1995, Boston, MA: South End Press), the edited letters of Lillian Smith entitled *How Am I to Be Heard?* (Gladney, R. 1993, Chapel Hill: University of North Carolina Press), and the historical essays in *Carryin' On* (Howard, J., 1997, ed. New York: New York University Press), and the contemporary ethnographic narratives of young people found in *Growing Up Gay in the South* (Sears, J. 1991, New York: Haworth Press). A variety of articles have also appeared in both scholarly journals, such as Duggan, L. 1993, "The Trials of Alice Mitchell: Sensationalism, sexology, and the lesbian subject in turn-of-the-century America." *Signs* 19(4), 791–814; or the subject of thesis or dissertations such as Remington, B. 1983, "Twelve Fighting Years: Homosexuals in Houston, 1969–1981." Masters thesis, University of Houston.

3. Material on the history of South Florida was gleaned from the following sources: Dunn, M., and Stepick, A. 1992, "Blacks in Miami," in E. Grenier and A. Stepick, eds., *Miami Now*, 41–56. Gainesville: University Press of Florida; Gannon, M. 1993, *Florida: A Short History*. Gainesville: University Press of Florida; George, P. 1986. "Brokers, Binders and Builders: Greater Miami's boom of the mid-1920s." *Florida Historical Quarterly*, 55(1), 27–51; Kagnoff, N., and Urofksy, M., eds., 1979, *Turn to the South: Essays on Southern Jewry*; Moore, D. 1994. *To the Golden Cities: Pursuing the American Jewish Dream in Miami and L.A.* New York: Free Press; Portes, A., and Stepick, A. 1993, *City on the Edge: The Transformation of Miami*. Berkeley: University of California Press; Railey, H., and Polansky, L. 1994, *Old Miami Beach*. Miami Beach: Miami Design Preservation League; Redford, P. 1970, *Billion Dollar Sandbar*. New York: Dutton; Rothchild, J. 1985, *Up for Grabs*. New York: Viking; Seemann, S. 1961, *A Report on Politics in Greater Miami*. Cambridge, MA: Joint Center for Urban Studies of the Massachusetts Institute of Technology and Harvard University.

4. This 1955 Idaho homosexual male prostitute scandal involving prominent citizens was later chronicled by John Gerassi (1966) in *The Boys from Boise: Furor, Vice and Folly in an American City*. New York: Macmillan.

5. Pedersen, L. (aka Jim Kepner), "Miami Hurricane," *One*, November, 1954, 5.

6. Collier, B. (August 1954), "$200,000 Outlay Urged for Center to Treat Deviates," *Miami Herald*; "Clean This Place Up!" *Miami Herald*, 11 August 1954; Roberts, J. (15 August 1954), "How L.A. Handles Its 150,000 Perverts," *Miami Daily News*.

7. See, for example: "Hypnotist Offers to Help Deviates," *Miami Herald*, 31 August 1954, 1; "Stiff Laws Urged on Perversion," *Miami Herald*, 8 September 1954; "Ordinance Would Kill Pervert Bars' Permits," *Miami Herald*, 10 September 1954.

8. Voltz, L. (31 August 1954), "Police to Harass Pervert Hangouts," *Miami Herald*; Voltz, L. (1 September 1954), "Evans Sets Thursday as D-Day," *Miami Herald*; Voltz, L. (4 September 1954), "Perverts Disperse But Drive Goes On," *Miami Herald*.

9. "Six Suspected Perverts Held in Beach Raid," *Miami Daily News*, August 1954; Flynn, S. (13 August 1954), "Beach Police Round up 35 in Pervert Crackdown," *Miami Herald*; Miller, J. (13 August 1954), "Perverts Seized in Bar Raids," *Miami Herald*.

10. Hearing Before the Subcomittee to Investigate Juvenile Delinquency of the Committee on the Judiciary. (1955) United States Senate, Eighty-third Congress, Second Session, Pursuant to S. Res. 89, Investigation of Juvenile Delinquency in the United States 16 December 1964. Washington, DC: U.S. Government Printing Office, 103–104.

11. Collier, B., and Thompson, L. (17 November 1955), "Deviates, Minors' Drinking Spur Call for Federal Laws," *Miami Daily News*; Hearing before the Subcommittee to Investigate Juvenile Delinquency of the Committee on the Judiciary, United States Senate, Eighty-Fourth Congress, First Session, Pursuant to S. Res. 62 as extended, *Investigation of Juvenile Delinquency in the United States*, 16 November, 1955. Washington, DC: US Government Printing Office, 1956, 49.

12. Hardin, B., and Bonafede, D. (27 February 1956), "Homosexuals Return, Find Heat's Off Again," *Miami Daily News*, 1A, 6A.

13. Hardin, B., and Bonafede, D. (28 February 1956), "Homosexuals Return, Find Heat's Off Again," *Miami Daily News*.

14. Hardin, B., and Bonafede, D. (29 February 1956), "Let Deviates Alone, Police View," *Miami Daily News*.

15. Hardin, B., and Bonafed, D. (1 March 1956), "Police Policies on Deviates Hit by Psychiatrist," *Miami Daily News*.

16. "Experts at Odds on Deviates Law," *Miami Daily News*, 7 March 1956.

17. "He Get 15 Years as Sex Deviate," *Miami Herald*, 29 September 1957.

18. Interview with Merril Mushroom, Dowelltown, TN, 1 October 1995, by James Sears. Tapes and related materials are located in the author's papers located at the Special Collections Library of Duke University. Other sources used to amplify Mushroom's description of 1950s Miami, written by her and used with her permission, are as follows: "The True Tale of the Tongueston Trio—1959," *Common Lives/Lesbian Lives*, no. 18, Winter 1985, 9–12; "Womonwrites 1988: Memories of the '50s," *Common Lives/Lesbian Lives*, no. 18, Winter 1985, 67–71; "dykeling merril meets dykeling penny," in J. Penelope and S. Valentine, eds., 1990 *Finding the Lesbians*, 188–190, Freedom, CA: Crossing Press; "Letter," in S. Wolfe and J. Stanley, eds., 1980, *The Coming Out Stories*, 135–138. (1st ed.). Watertown, MA: Persephone Press. "Dear Julia," 1990, *The Original Coming Out Stories* (2d ed.). Freedom, CA: Crossing Press, 55–58; "Gay Girls and Gay Guys," in J. Nestle and J. Preston, eds., 1994, *Sister and Brother*. San Francisco: Harper.

19. Duggan, L. 1993, "The Trials of Alice Mitchell."

20. Sears, J. 1991, *Growing Up Gay in the South*.

Chapter Eleven

From Panty Raids to Revolution
Youth and Authority, 1950–1970

Beth Bailey

In the spring of 1952, as the police action in Korea dragged on and as support for Eisenhower's candidacy grew, college campuses throughout the nation erupted into violence. Windows were smashed, buildings were briefly occupied, and in the most extreme case, Governor Forrest Smith of Missouri called out the National Guard.

The panty raids—for that is what they were—attracted a great deal of attention and prompted a spate of articles on the problems posed by the younger generation. The media, both national and local, chronicled the raids in great detail. At the University of Wisconsin, 5000 male students had charged the women's dorms, urged on by bugle calls. At the University of Alabama, women's lingerie had been locked in trunks in anticipation of a raid, while at the University of Indiana the director of women's residence halls sent out a "barrelful of female undergarments in the hope that the males would help themselves and go home quietly." At the University of Oklahoma, two thousand students "battled" state police in what was politely referred to as a "lingerie raid." In one of the several raids at the University of Kansas, only a single pink brassiere was taken.[1]

The outbursts on college campuses in the spring of 1952 were not politically motivated, as so many of those in the following decade would be, but that does not mean that they were without significance or without political content, broadly defined. They embody a politics of sexuality, a politics of age and of gender. Some involved real violence, the destruction of property, physical injuries. And ultimately they were, in the long tradition of student riots, about power.[2]

Alfred Kinsey, when asked his opinion of the panty raids, said simply, "All animals play around."[3] The dean of men at the University of Kansas was willing to go along with that analysis: youthful high spirits, springtime, the end of the semester.[4] But he, and every other college administrator who saw his or her job as controlling these youthful energies, recognized the danger of the riots. Panty raids, these administrators believed, were a contest for power between the young and their elders. They challenged authority. When University of Alabama president John Gallalee appeared at a women's dorm that was under siege, gallantly shouting up to the girls hanging out the windows, "Don't worry, everything will be all right," they threw eggs at him.[5]

But even more importantly, the panty raids linked this challenge to authority to the potentially explosive power of sexuality. When Princeton students rioted through town in the spring of 1953 and then marched on Westminster Choir College screaming, "We want girls! We want sex! We want panties!" you can be sure that most adults understood how potentially dangerous this rite of spring was.[6]

University administrators, charged with supervising the sexual behavior of youth, had a difficult job. They were faced with the growing autonomy and power of teenagers and young adults in postwar American society. They were faced with what they and others understood to be the great—and dangerous—power of sexuality. And they were left with increasingly tenuous justifications for restraining sexual conduct as absolute moral sanctions were replaced with arguments based either on a sexual economy or on psychological or psychoanalytic theory.[7] Despite contemporary condemnation of passive, conformist youth in the 1950s, these images of panty raids, produced and reproduced, suggested nothing so much as barbarians at the gates. And those who were the first line of defense, it appeared, lacked the cultural authority to stop them.

One might argue that these panty raids, more or less contemporaneous with the Kinsey report on women and the introduction of *Playboy*, are opening salvos—at least for college youth—of what we call "the sexual revolution." We see youth arrayed against age, challenges to authority, the centrality of sex. (The gender politics of panty raids are problematic, but that was true of much of what we claim as revolutionary during the following decade.)

However, campus unrest about sex and its governance on college campuses in the 1960s did not develop from the same trajectory as the panty raids of the 1950s. Panty raids were in the tradition of carnival, not of revolution. While panty raids enacted power relations and challenged and denied the mores of their society, those involved did not seek to alter the hierarchies of power or the existing institutional controls over sexual behaviors. In the 1960s "revolution," college and university students *directly* challenged the systems of sexual controls and supervisions that governed their lives and questioned the legitimacy of the authority to which they were subject. They sought permanent change. These direct challenges were very different from the eruptions (panty raids, whether drunken rampages or fraternity highjinks) and evasions (furtive fumblings in back seats, climbing through dormitory windows after curfew) in which the struggles of "the fifties" were more typically embodied. In a fashion that was rarely evasive, students in the 1960s and early 1970s questioned authority and demanded rights. Yet in many ways, the sexual revolution on campus was often *less* confrontational than the panty raids of the previous decade. Our commonly told story of youth storming the barricades, of freedom challenging repression in the 1960s, is neither complete nor accurate.

To complicate our story, first—and obviously—we must acknowledge that bipolar constructions of "youth" and its opposite, "the Establishment," are just that: constructions, which demand attention. We also need to complicate our picture of administrative resistance on college campuses; too often administrators appear as little more than cardboard villain backdrops for the play of youth.[8] And we need to pay more attention to the multiple positions and sites of power that participants assumed in their battles over sexual behaviors and boundaries. Their struggles must be understood as a process of cultural negotiation, not simply as an uprising of "youth" against "authority." Actors on all fronts were seeking new bases of power and authority and new languages of legitimacy.

Second, we must look beyond the agency of youth to larger structural and cultural reconfigurations of the role of the university in the postwar era. In the years following World War II, universities grew at an unprecedented rate and students were drawn from an increasingly broad swath of the American population. Growth alone made changes in university structure and management necessary. But universities (partly in appealing for funding) also rearticulated their sense of mission, claiming new importance in the postwar, cold war world. These changes helped to create a generation of student activists, but they created a new generation of administrators first. The new administrators of "student life" in the vastly enlarged universities of the 1950s and 1960s claimed the task of fostering "growth" and "maturity" in students, preparing them for life in their democratic nation. The professional ideologies that legitimated the new administrators' positions created openings for student claims that were less oppositional than they were logical extensions of the premises espoused by administrators. In the confrontations over sex on the college campuses of the 1960s, youth and the administrators who sought to manage them often met on common discursive ground. Frequently, debates were enjoined from "both" sides in the language of liberal humanism and a therapeutic ethos. In the negotiations over rules governing sexual behaviors (and opportunities), sex itself was often decentered, attached to or subordinated to concepts of civility, responsibility, citizenship, and individual growth.

Of course, this language does not contain sex entirely; the topic erupts inconveniently and unpredictably. And despite the fact that those involved spoke of responsibility and individual growth more than of sex itself, it is clear that all participants understood that they were also talking about sex: its proper manifestations, its governance, its changing context. Clearly, for both administrators and students, the language they used was at least partially strategic. Administrators were not likely to promote their increased role in "student life" by stressing Foucaultian models of sexual discipline; students were not likely to argue for an end to parietals by noting that one can do "it" before 11 P.M. just as well as after. The specific position of each group shaped its discursive strategy. But our understanding of language as strategic should serve to reemphasize the point that social change takes place in relation to existing power relations, often as embodied in large and powerful institutions. The changes which we identify with the sexual revolution took place in specific places, within specific spaces, and many of them were possible because of institutional changes that had nothing to do with sex. Instead, the defeat of *in loco parentis* and other forms of sexual supervision on college and university campuses was possible because of major changes in the role of the university in postwar America, especially those related to the increased importance of national culture and to the demands of the postwar version of corporate capitalism. These large-scale changes establish the ground on which specific negotiations take place.

In the remainder of this chapter I will follow my own advice about specificity by analyzing the struggles over *in loco parentis* at a Midwestern state university in the mid-1960s. I am focusing on the University of Kansas rather than on one of the nation's most prominent sites of student activism because I want to demonstrate that change did not simply trickle down from East and West Coast centers of radical activity, but instead was forged on interlocked university campuses throughout the nation. Moreover, I want to emphasize that change took the shape it did because the United States was, in the postwar era, ever more effectively tied together by the increased activism of the federal government and by the extension and elaboration of national systems of economy and culture. That the struggles I analyze took place in the heartland state of Kansas, the state so often positioned in "the" American imagination as the antithesis of bicoastal sophistication, shows the extent to which the changes we call "the sexual revolution" were national phenomena and indicates how important national systems were to the social-change movements of the 1960s.[9]

In the summer of 1946, more than likely reeling under the administrative demands of a student population that was more than doubling from one academic year to the next, the chancellor of the University of Kansas wrote to the state's former governor, Alf Landon. Kansas parents, the chancellor claimed, were no longer "satisfied to send their youngsters off to shift for themselves, relatively unsupervised, in rooming houses of various and assorted types and standards, or to the garret and basement rooms where students too often eke out a lonely and unsatisfying existence." Faced with an explosion of student numbers, the university not only had to arrange for students' academic education, but also to provide opportunities for "gracious living together . . . wholesome food, proper chaperonage," and a "better-regulated existence." Despite the logistical nightmare, KU's Chancellor Mallot was not opposing the trend. In fine political style, with an eye toward the financial costs of the trend he chronicled, Mallot wrote Landon that the "increasing accent on the modern university" is to offer students a "well-rounded experience." "Experiences of the college environment outside of the classroom and laboratory," he continued, "are perhaps as important in developing the character and personality, the curiosity and imagination, and energy of the future citizen, as the hours spent each day under the various professors and teachers."[10]

The University of Kansas, like other American universities, changed dramatically in the postwar era. With enrollments swollen first by the G.I. Bill and later by rising expectations and affluence among America's growing middle classes, more and more students, from more diverse backgrounds, were going to college. In postwar America, the rapidly expanding universities were charged with educating students to function in a new order. The new technocrats and bureaucrats and corporate employees the universities were producing needed to be mobile, to be less invested in a local or regional culture, to be less provincial, less *narrowly* religious, less *culturally* ethnic, even less prejudiced against those unlike themselves. They were to be socialized into the norms of the postwar white middle class. As the dean of students at KU wrote in a long newspaper article in the early 1960s, "discipline" was sometimes necessary "to correct or modify in individuals or groups attitudes brought to the campus from other cultures."[11]

The socialization of the college student had further purpose in cold war America. Students frequently figure as "future citizens" in whom the values of responsibility, maturity, and citizenship must be fostered. Kansas University's 1958 Annual Report claimed that the university oriented itself in a "humanistic philosophy of the dignity of the individual; avoiding coddling but assisting students to a more responsible, self-directing and productive end."[12]

When Lawrence C. Woodruff, dean of students at KU for a decade already, wrote an article on student discipline in the local newspaper in 1963, he emphasized the unique expectations Americans had of their universities. Unlike European universities, where "staff" is "appalled" at the suggestion of responsibility for students beyond the classroom, the American public expects the university to serve "not only in *loco parentis* [*sic*] for their students but as 'all things to all people.'" Building steam, Woodruff catalogued those expectations: to "house the student, feed him, watch his finances, oversee his moral and social development, provide a broad recreational and cultural program, and be concerned with his emotional and physical health problems as well as his intellectual development and maturity." The "inevitable result," he concluded, was the "phenomenon of the personnel dean."[13]

With large and still growing student bodies, with immense and expanding expectations of university functions, the old administrative structures became insufficient. New administrators—professionals—were required to manage the logistics of student life and to oversee the process of "assisting students to a more responsible, self-directing and productive end." One can see the changes in university structure clearly: in 1953, an administrative reorganization created a new position, "dean of Students." This dean supervised the deans of men and women, as well as the Housing and Aid and Awards offices. A Committee on Student Personnel Practices was established the same year.[14] These new administrators were part of an increasing professionalization of student services. As newcomers, they had to claim status and authority within the university community—including within the administration itself. This they did by stressing their professionalism and expertise. In a major policy document produced by the Council on Student Affairs (formerly the Committee on Student Personnel Practices), committee members emphasized that the "educational experience" of the student was not solely academic, but consisted of "all of the impacts of the University upon the student throughout the twenty-four hour day." In order to "fulfill the complete educational responsibility to the student," this statement continues, the chancellor relies on "professional specialists" who are "fully as competent professionally in their areas as are the faculty members employed to assist the student in achieving academic growth."[15] Insisting that university education was a "twenty-four hour a day growth process," not just "academic stimulation," the new student-services administrators positioned themselves as parallel to—and equal in importance to—the faculty.

And so, justified both by structural demands resulting from the postwar student population explosion and by an ideological conjunction of cold war and therapeutic cultures, which combined to define the proper end of education as "maturity" and "personal growth," personnel administrators carved out a significant domain within the university. But in claiming their importance within the university, they were also asserting the centrality of students. The university they spoke of was not the faculty-oriented institution with twin missions of teaching and research, but an institution organized around the complete education of the nation's youth—a mission in which they claimed equal status with the faculty. And while these administrators attempted to meet a myriad of student needs, the overarching rationale they claimed (fostering personal growth and responsibility) quite logically led them to encourage students to take greater roles in the governance of the university, most especially their own lives outside the classroom.

Thus, while KU's women students were subject to carefully detailed and often stringent rules governing their comings and goings during the 1950s and early 1960s, these rules increasingly were both made and implemented by the women students themselves. The Associated Women Students met biannually to determine the rules under which they would live; a student disciplinary committee heard cases and punished infractions. Students often disciplined their peers more harshly than administrators would have, taking away weekend privileges from women students who arrived a minute or two past curfew.[16] The students who had obtained such power tended to use it. To some extent, student oversight was a front for administrative control, in which the dirty work of day-to-day discipline was distanced or displaced from administrators to student proxies. But in the case of women students, administrators also pushed them to assume more individual responsibility for their daily lives.

The University of Kansas, for example, was the second university in the nation to begin a "senior key" program. As of fall semester 1960, senior women had no official "closing hours," but could sign out keys to their residences and return when they wished. The Associated Women Students had passed the senior key plan at their rules convention, but the initiative behind it, as well as the clout to get it approved by the chancellor and board of regents, came from the dean of women, Emily Taylor. Throughout her eighteen-year tenure as dean of women, Taylor advocated equal rights for women and publicly stated that her job was to promote independence and responsibility among her women students.[17] Her sales pitch for senior keys was in keeping with these goals. In a letter to the parents of senior women, she emphasized student and administrative confidence that "senior women were sufficiently mature to accept personal responsibility" for their actions. The new senior key system implied no change in "standards of propriety," she said bluntly, attempting to deflect the most predictable criticism. Instead, it reflected the university's faith (a royal "we") in the "maturity and judgment of our senior women," who have given "every reason to believe that they will use their freedom of decision judiciously."[18]

Such initiatives, couched in such language, decentered the "moral" justifications for oversight (controlling sexual behavior) and presented greater freedom of action as a positive step toward the larger educational goal of social maturity. Certainly all parents did not accept the paradigm shift: one mother wrote Taylor that peer pressure would certainly lead daughters to request a "very dubious moral permission," for in the case of senior keys, "such unrestrained liberty can well become license, and will definitely impair the reputation of K.U."[19] But over and over again, with successive classes of students and their parents, the issue of closing hours was presented through the paradigm of personal responsibility, not behavioral control.

It was in the fall of 1965, five years after the inauguration of the senior key program, that student protest about parietals—and about the other ways the university exercised control over students' nonacademic lives—began in earnest. While the students who formulated demands for abolishing parietals and ending all extracurricular supervision of students wanted to decrease the role of the student life administrators, they made their arguments in much the same terms as those administrators had used to justify *increasing* their role and power. In many ways, these student demands were more a logical extension of the doctrines of personal maturity so popular among student life administrators than a rejection of them. Perhaps ironically, the first storming of the barricades at the University of Kansas was with the battle cry, "Responsibility!"

On November 12, 1965, the *University Daily Kansan* ran a front-page article under the headline, "Student Freedom Movement Gains Momentum at Meeting." The first sentence of the article, in a breathtaking conflation of terms, read: "A push for greater student responsibility at KU was sparked last night at an open meeting of Students for a Democratic Society." The cartoon illustration that accompanied the article portrayed a mass of students, women with lacquered I-sleep-in-curlers mid-1960s hair, men in coats and ties. Their features were uniformly serious, even grim, and to the back of the crowd we get only faceless suggestions of human beings. Across the top flies a banner: "Student Responsibility." A placard to the left proclaims: "*WE HAVE THE RIGHT TO BE CITIZENS TOO*"; a placard to the right demands: "*ABOLISH CLOSING HOURS.*"[20]

Unlike national SDS, the fledgling local chapter of SDS at KU focused on the relation of the university to students' private lives—most particularly parietal rules for women.[21] KU's SDS chapter, in its position papers, its journal, and its public meetings, worked to equate the terms "freedom" and "responsibility," arguing that the university's *in loco parentis* stance hindered "the individual's quest for maturity in a free society." Arguing specifically against parietals for women at the first SDS assembly, a senior from Garden City, Kansas, asked the rhetorical question: "Are they going to be adults, or are they going to be cripples, plodding along on the crutches of the University? Are they going to be citizens now, or are they going to be thrust upon a complex world at the sudden moment when the sheepskin is placed in their hands and told: 'Now—you're an adult.' "[22]

The arguments of KU's SDS are couched in existentialist language—"the role of moral agent"; "genuine independence"; "choice." This language combines well with the administrative language of responsibility and shares with it some basic assumptions. However, the language of the "Student Responsibility Movement" betrays its roots in the philosophy department, whose graduate students and junior faculty (and at least one faculty spouse) were, at least initially, the most visible members of the movement. They pushed the debate over parietals (one that most students very much understood as a debate about the sexual freedom and conduct of women students) toward a discussion of the role of the individual in the larger world. Writing in the second issue of *The Kansas University Students for a Democratic Society Journal*, graduate student John Garlinghouse leapt quickly to a larger canvas. Noting, somewhat disingenuously, that he did not intend to address the fact that "a high school dropout selling cabbage in a supermarket" has rights and freedoms denied university students, he shifted ground to argue that the problem was not with the rules in specific, but with the "whole atmosphere they create":

> Ours is a complex world, fraught with dangers and inconsistencies. It has its Vietnam ... its Budapest, its Algeria. ... To cope in any way with these problems, the universities must produce independent, responsible human beings. If an individual entering a university is socially a fetus, another four years in an incubator will not help him. He will be no more than a senseless automaton. ... [The university] only defeats itself when it attempts to incubate its students. Both our society and we, ourselves, sell ourselves cheaply when we allow it to do so. If we do not act soon, and constructively, to remedy this situation, we can pass into history confident that our children and our children's children will be set upon by our very same problem. In some form. At some time. With progressively more horrible implications.[23]

In passages such as this one, written by a male graduate student, the issue of gender tended to disappear. This tendency is worth noting for, after all, the local issue that led to such global speculation was parietals—a set of rules that applied to women students only, not to their male counterparts. However, the women who spoke or wrote for the record kept gender front and center, even to the point of shifting focus from the individual to the collective. "I have a dream," one female undergraduate told a *Kansan* reporter, positioning herself in those four words, of seeing hundreds of KU women massed together at the hour of curfew "in plain sight for the University to see, but refusing to be herded [inside] like cattle."[24] But the most visible woman in this initial debate, the one who wrote key articles for the *Journal* and gave the lead speech at the SDS meeting, centered her arguments in existential philosophy and psychology. Identified only as "Mrs. Donald Emmons," she was the wife of a young assistant professor in the philosophy department. "At the very core of becoming a human being is assuming the role of moral agent," she wrote in the *SDS Journal*. "Women," however, "are not encouraged to think of themselves as persons with lives to choose. They are regulated in the most minute aspects of everyday existence—a method well used in Nazi concentration camps to disintegrate the personality." Conceding that closing hours for women were "generous" ("I should think that most could not keep them and stay in school"), she nonetheless concluded: "The thing that is wrong with them is that they are imposed." The University, she continued, prepared women better for lives as "cocker spaniels" than for "self-actualizing" adulthood.[25]

As gender was only inconsistently visible in these movement writings, it is not surprising that the issue of sex—the control of which most students, parents, and administrators had traditionally assumed to be the point of women's hours—was almost invisible. In discussions of "moral choice" we sometimes catch a glimpse of it, but the subject of such moral choice might just as well be cheating on exams for all the articles specify. In so doing, these writers refused to treat sexual mores as a separate and more important category of moral choice, instead implicitly arguing that individuals face a whole array of moral choices in their everyday lives, and that sexual behavior is not necessarily the most significant of those. Nonetheless, much of the opposition to their demands centered on the issue of sex, so proponents of "responsibility" occasionally attempted to counter such charges. In "A White Paper on Student Rights," circulated by the new "University Party" before the 1966 spring student elections, the undergraduate candidates tried to make the issue appear ridiculous: " 'Bacchanalia!' comes the cry to the background chorus of 'How Ya' Gonna Keep 'Em Down on the Farm after They've Seen KU?' The obvious assumption is that, freed of restrictions other than those of law, the average student will become some kind of satyr." Instead, they asserted, more freedom would lead to "*less* bacchanalia."[26] Such comments were relatively rare, however, for both the administration and members of the Student Responsibility Movement avoided discussions of sexual morality. The dean of women stated categorically that parietals were "not related to moral issues," a statement the *Kansan* rendered as "Rules Not Meant to Curb Morals."[27] However, while the shared language of individual maturity and responsibility shaped much of the debate among one set of students and administrators, the issue of sex control continued to structure the unfolding events.

The "Student Responsibility Movement" got a lot of attention on KU's campus. While the KU SDS chapter could claim only a few dozen members in the mid-1960s, its focus on parietals engaged a large number of students. And as the movement appealed to student life administrators on their own terms, they could not ignore or easily refute the movement's logic. As a sign of how seriously the administration took the protests, when a small group of students drafted a lengthy list of questions about university policy, KU provost James Surface, who received the questions (with no prior warning) on a Friday, worked through the weekend to provide detailed answers by the beginning of the following week. This exchange, which was chronicled in great detail by the *Kansan*, focused on the legitimacy of university authority over students. The questions suggest a more legalistic turn of mind than the earlier philosophically based demands: "What is the University's definition of '*in loco parentis*'?" "What is the legal justification for discrimination against women?" "What are the 'accepted standards of social conduct' to which students are expected to adhere" and are they "codified in state law?" After meeting with Surface, the students told the *Kansan* reporter they were "deeply impressed" with Surface's "candidness and apparent sincerity," but found the university policies he described disturbingly "arbitrary." They followed up with a second set of questions devoted to pointing out legal and logical inconsistencies.[28]

But even before this exchange, beginning soon after the Student Responsibility Movement's opening salvos, the chancellor's office and board of regents had begun seeking clarification of their own positions, checking legal precedents and requesting the Council on Student Affairs to draft a report that laid out not only the sorts of authority exercised by the university over its students, but explained from whence that authority derived. Both documents, the legal (based on a 1956 statement from Kansas's attorney general) and the administrative, traced power back through the chancellor to the board of regents to the "people" or "taxpayers" of the State of Kansas.[29] Such advice had limited utility for administrators, who more and more self-consciously based their claims to authority upon their professional expertise and on the national mission of "the university." Few administrators in postwar America believed that the local knowledge of state taxpayers should dictate university policy so directly. And in the case of Kansas, most students, faculty, and administrators at the state university were less socially conservative than the majority of the "people" who constituted the state. Thus questions of legitimacy generated by the Student Responsibility Movement were not easily resolved.

It was in this climate of uncertainty—and possibility—that the Associated Women Students met in March 1966 to draft the rules under which women students at KU would live for the following two years. The AWS was largely responsible for the proliferation of rules about women's hours that was so typical of the latter stages of parietal systems. At each biannual convention, the AWS voted progressively more freedoms for women students but anchored them in an ever-more complicated system of rules, penalties, and exceptions. This AWS rules convention, following close upon the highly visible actions of the Student Responsibility Movement, would break with that tradition.

What is most striking about the Associated Women Students meeting that convened on March 12, 1966, is how far from agreement these young women were.[30] It's not simply that they disagreed on what rules were appropriate or how to implement them; rather, different groups approached the issue from what seem today radically different paradigms. The "responsibility" faction was well represented, mainly by delegates from the "scholarship halls" that housed students attending KU on academic scholarships, and by married women who had only limited representation in the rules convention. Activists in the Student Responsibility Movement had lobbied hard in advance of the meeting, writing signed editorials in the *Kansan* and circulating a copy of Tom Hayden's 1962 article,"Student Social Action," to which they added a handwritten title, "IN LOCO PARENTIS," and the request: "PLEASE PASS THIS ON SO THAT MORE KU WOMEN WILL *STOP* AND *THINK* ABOUT *THEIR AWS* CONSTITUTION & THE REGULATIONS UNDER WHICH WE LIVE." (A copy was passed on to the chancellor's "Student Protest" files.)[31]

A second group, drawn primarily from the large and powerful network of sororities on campus, insisted—*unlike* the administration—that the purpose of women's hours was to control sexual behavior. While the rhetoric and actions of both administrators and student protestors had decentered sexual mores in this debate, these delegates insisted that the key issue *was* the sexual morality, or "standards," of women students. They strongly supported a system of administrative supervision to help women "set their standards." Finally, a third group (sometimes overlapping with the "morality" delegates) skirted the "standards" argument but held to a gender-specific line: hours were necessary for the safety of women students; because women were different from men they required different regulations from their male peers.

A complete transcript of the convention exists, in the garbled language of actual speech. The convention fairly quickly came to a boil around one question: Should closing hours be abolished for all women students? Delegates argued the intricacies of rules and programs all day, and the language of their (sometimes heated) arguments tells us as much—if not more—than the outcome of the convention.

The "responsibility" argument presented no surprises to anyone who'd read the *Kansan* in the preceding weeks and months. It was less elegantly argued, certainly ("We are responsible to our actions for ourselves," stated one delegate), and lacked philosophical and legal foundations. Sometimes the "responsibility" argument sounded like a simple claim: we're old enough/mature enough to take care of ourselves. But all concerned heard these assertions in the context of a continuing public debate.

The motions of these delegates to abolish closing hours were countered by delegates working with highly gendered notions of sexuality. The antiprogressive, sorority-dominated faction raised the issues most explicitly. They insisted that the rules and regulations *were* about morality, real or perceived. Arguing that KU must not adopt "open closing" for all undergraduate women, the Gamma Phi Beta delegate explained: "When you come to the university, your freshman and sophomore years, you are away from your folks and this is when you truly determine your standards. I truly believe that we need to impose some rules on freshmen and sophomore women. It is too easy to disregard whether things are right or wrong." A Chi Omega delegate urged other delegates to think of the "philosophy involved": hours are necessary so that women can "set their standards."[32] In direct opposition to the "responsibility" argument, these women portray rules as the *means* to moral grounding and responsible conduct.

Scholarship hall delegates rejected this line of reasoning, venturing to "suggest the idea that closing hours do not determine the moral standards on campus." But the "morality" delegates were working with another concern that was still a reasonable one in 1966: reputation. "Public image," the Gamma Phi Beta delegate sputtered, incoherently. "Run around free or do whatever we would like to." The Pi Beta Phi delegate, in more measured tones, argued: "To go to this extreme now is hurting not only ourselves but it is hurting the other women we go to school with."[33] In much of American society, a woman's "reputation" still determined, in significant ways, the sort of life she could expect to lead, for it made a difference in her marriage prospects. While this seems the most antediluvian of arguments here, it is worth noting that the most progressive "responsibility" delegate capped her argument by claiming that "many women are contemplating marriage . . . if you are contemplating marriage you are capable of deciding your own hours."[34]

Most of the morality delegates were willing, in a form of compromise, to go along with the arguments of the third group, which took the position that the very term "closing hours" should be changed to "security hours" to "get rid of a lot of connotations" and emphasize the protective aspect of the regulations.[35] Personal security was an important issue in the debate. Delegates worried about maintaining security in residence halls and sorority houses with so many keys floating around. Some were concerned that no one would notice when a coed failed to come home, and thus no one would check to be sure she was safe until it was too late. But the language in which many of these delegates made their points is convoluted and betrays tensions within their seemingly coherent reasoning. The Pi Beta Phi delegate argued, in a paragraph that fairly deconstructs itself:

> We have to realize what we are talking about. If we continue to pass these proposals, we will find ourselves with NO closing hours. We are here to learn, and the reason women have closing hours is because there is a difference between men and women. Women must be protected. A woman cannot be out on the streets at night . . . I feel

> women have no place being out on the streets at night. Two women were attacked by men. Therefore, I think this brings us to the point that if we do vote on no closing . . . the sophomores have no place [in this "open closing" plan].[36]

In the end, the delegates took decisive action: they voted to completely eliminate parietals for seniors, juniors, and second-semester sophomores. While not complete, this was the most significant step in the overthrow of the parietals system, which would end entirely within three more years.[37] Coverage in the *Kansan*, while "objective," clearly supports the liberalization of rules and the actions of the convention.[38] But it also highlights the level of disagreement among students. Under the headline, "Student Opinion Varies," the reporter quotes Sara Paretsky, a scholarship hall delegate to the convention, who flatly states that KU women "need more freedom," and Linda Adamson, a sophomore from Lawrence, who argued: "Students are here to get an education, and hours can only help you. Most girls don't know how to regulate their lives. That's why there are so many illegitimate births."[39] No matter how much some spoke of "responsibility," the subtext remained sex.

Further complicating this story of social change, the rules passed by the convention were altered (closing hours were reinstituted for second-semester sophomores) in secret meetings of the AWS Senate, a small group of women students with close ties to the administration. In the context of the raging debate over university control of students' lives, some AWS delegates had believed that the AWS charter allowed them to *make* the rules, not simply to fine-tune them. The senate's action provoked much anger and a more generalized sense of betrayal, but it was clearly legal, for according to the written regulations, the convention was to make "recommendations" to the senate, which would then make "recommendations" to the administration.[40] The sense of frustration on campus was increased because it was not clear who was really responsible for the changes. Was it fellow students? Or was it the administration?

A partial and indirect answer appears in the new University Party's platform for student elections that term. Calling upon "our University community" to "establish the University of Kansas as a national leader in the recognition of students as free, mature individuals who yearn to be responsible for their own acts, and who seek the experience of full citizenship as the best education of all," they praised the AWS convention as "courageous" and further critiqued the practice of *in loco parentis* at KU. But in a brief preface signed by the candidates, this oppositional document (which found its way into the chancellor's "Student Protest" files), offered an interesting *caveat* to their strongly worded call for change. While some important administrators "fully sympathize" with their demands for freedom from supervision, the candidates wrote, these administrators are "constrained" and thus remain "publicly unresponsive."[41]

The chancellor's "correspondence" file for that year is crammed with letters from parents and other citizens of the state of Kansas. Many are accompanied by clippings of highly negative articles from local newspapers about the doings at KU. Virtually all treat women's hours as a means for controlling sexual behavior, and *every* letter opposes change.[42] A state university ignores such sentiments at its own peril. "Youth" and "Authority" were not the only actors in struggles over sex control at the University of Kansas. Another major player—as the legal and administrative memos emphasized—was "the people," or "the taxpayers," or what I could call in more general terms, democracy. And when it comes to social issues, in twentieth-century America democracy generally has been a conservative, not a progressive, force.

So: to what extent do we see "youth culture" in these struggles over women's hours at the University of Kansas in the mid-1960s? Certainly "youth" was the key to the entire set of events. The struggle, as all participants agreed on a level so basic it was rarely discussed, was about how America's college youth should be educated. Because it dealt with the conjunction of youth and sex, the debate was highly charged. But while there was intense disagreement over means (strict rules? complete freedom?), everyone involved stated the same goal: that "youth" become mature, responsible, "self-actualizing" adults.

Unlike the panty raids of the previous era, the struggle over women's parietals did not simply pit students against administration. Lines of agreement and alliance were significantly more complicated. Young people were divided over these issues, as were their elders. We know that it is reductionist to expect that any social category—race, class, gender, age—will be fully determinative of belief or behavior. But what is more significant is that the students who sought this significant social change at KU did not use a language of youth. They never positioned themselves strategically within a youth culture, never claimed the singularity of their experience or knowledge, never defined themselves as youth in opposition to an adult world. *None* of the students who participated in this debate, whether they claimed the right to freedom or the need for rules, claimed their legitimacy from their youth.

This episode, as I read it, serves as a corrective to the romanticized histories that too easily posit "youth" as the key agent of social change. Young people acted here—but they were not in concert, and they did not frame their actions primarily through the construct of youth.[43] Instead, these students were participating in a larger struggle over the shape of American society, one that pitted concepts of individual growth against traditional moral strictures in the search for a citizenry capable of sustaining democracy in an increasingly complex world.

This would change. Well before the end of the decade, "youth" had become the key discursive paradigm through which many young activists (at the University of Kansas and elsewhere) negotiated social change. The slogan, "Don't trust anyone over thirty," somewhat awkwardly embraced by twenty-nine-year-old Jerry Rubin, drew lines in the sand that have hardened in our historical consciousness, obscuring earlier and equally influential paradigms of social change. In the struggles of the 1960s, "youth" is a changing and contested construct, used in different ways and to different ends—including by young people themselves. Thus, the debate over women's hours at the University of Kansas stands as a reminder of the importance of historical specificity and historical context in the practice of cultural studies.

NOTES

1. Accounts of panty raids are drawn from the following: "Manners and Morals: Girls! Girls! Girls!" *Time*, 26 May 1952, 27; [No title preserved], Chicago *Sun Times*, 23 May 1952, clipping

in AEO, Box 1, folder 2, Northwestern University Archives; "Men Students Raid Women's Dorms," newspaper clipping (probably from the Lawrence *Journal World*) in "Problems and Discipline, 1951/52" files (P&D), Dean of Men's papers, University of Kansas Archives (KUA); "7 Women's Houses Invaded by 1,500 Raiding Students," *University Daily Kansan* (*UDK*), 21 May 1952, 1; "Murphy Speaks Up to Halt Raiding," Lawrence *Journal World* (*JW*), 21 May 1952; "Romeos, Juliets—But No Balcony," *JW*, 21 May 1952; "Panty Raids," Dean's Memo, 30 May 1952, and "Trouble Report," KU Police Dept., 20 May 1952, both in P&D 1951/52 files, Dean of Men's papers, KUA. The rite of the panty raid reemerged almost every spring through the 1960s on college campuses.

2. On the tradition of student riots, see Helen Lefkowitz Horowitz, *Campus Life* (New York: Alfred A. Knopf, 1987). Panty raids clearly embody gendered claims to power. However, and perhaps not surprisingly, gender was not the primary analytic frame at the time. Most discussions and representations emphasize confrontation between the young and their elders, often portraying women as active participants in the ritual sieges of which they were the targets.

3. "Manners and Morals," 27.

4. "Panty Raids," memo, 30 May 1952, "P&D 1951/52 files, Dean of Men's papers, KUA.

5. "Men Students Raid . . . " article. Stories such as this one appeared in national media and also in student newspapers. In virtually all cases, the panty raids began as "copycat" events.

6. "The Rites of Spring," *Time*, 11 May 1953, 82.

7. See my arguments in *From Front Porch to Back Seat: Courtship in Twentieth-Century America* (Baltimore: Johns Hopkins University Press, 1988), especially the chapter "Sex Control." There is a fairly extensive literature on the rise of the psychological and psychoanalytic approach to sexuality and its control. See especially Estelle Freedman, " 'Uncontrolled Desires': The Response to the Sexual Psychopath, 1920–1960," *Journal of American History* (June 1987): 83–106, and Alan Berube, *Coming Out under Fire* (New York: Free Press, 1989).

8. "Youth" were the agents of change in what even people at the time called "the sexual revolution." But in focusing on youth alone, we obscure the larger processes of change of which this specific construction of—even reification of—youth is a part. Both social history and cultural studies have, in different ways, contributed to this blind spot. Social historians' implicit but longstanding assumption that to write about something is to identify with it worked against the production of studies focusing on the "wrong" groups: the white middle class, dead white men, corporate executives, university administrators. We now have sophisticated studies of groups formerly "lost" to history. But in these new histories we have too often accepted a flat, unnuanced—even cardboard—version of those against whom our favored actors struggled. Understanding the creation and exercise of various forms of power is important for historians of all political stripes.

Furthermore, social historians' appropriate sensitivity to the difference between "What Ought to Be" and "What Was" in society worked to deny the importance of convention, prescription, and of culture itself—the force of what more theoretically oriented scholars discussed in the language of cultural hegemony and power. Cultural studies provided an important corrective to some of social history's failings by emphasizing the role of power and the social and historical construction of meaning. Yet sometimes cultural studies approaches (especially in America) become so enmeshed in analyzing and debating the constitutive act, the potential for subversive readings, that scholars lose sight of the extratextual roles of power and of the specific historical context that gives shape to the constitutive acts it analyzes.

9. For a full discussion of my argument on the importance of national culture, see Beth Bailey, "Prescribing the Pill: Politics, Culture, and the Sexual Revolution in America's Heartland," *Journal of Social History*, 30, (Summer 1997):827–856.

10. Dean W. Mallot to Alf M. Landon, 15 July, 1946 [copy], Kansas University Archives (KUA), in Clifford S. Griffin, *The University of Kansas: A History*, (Lawrence: University of Kansas Press, 1974) 634. Enrollment statistics from the letter, p. 617, and from Gwen G. Barstow, "Forty Years of Growth: Student Affairs at the University of Kansas," paper written for History 666, Prof. David Katzman, April 1983, in personal files of Lorna Zimmer, Student Affairs Office, University of Kansas. Enrollment for 1945 was 3,750; for 1946, 8,,947. Administrators had anticipated only 7000 students for 1946. Detailed records of enrollment offer profiles of the changing student population. In the fall of 1947, well over half of KU's 10,282 students are veterans; the student body comes from 104 Kansas counties, 44 states, and the Territory of Hawaii. "Enrollment Statistics, 1866—1957/58," series 14/0/1, KUA.

11. Lawrence C. Woodruff, "Opinions from the Hill," *JW*, 11 March 1963. On changes in the university, see Todd Gitlin, *The Sixties: Years of Hope, Days of Rage* (New York: Bantam Books, 1987), 20—21.

12. Barstow, "Forty Years of Growth" 13. Quote is from Annual Report, 30 June 1958, KUA. This sentiment seems less related to a vision of youth as the bright hope of tomorrow than to a sense that youth, as future citizens, must be carefully managed. There is no rhapsodizing here. Rather, the tone is akin to what Ellen Herman analyzes so well in *The Romance of American Psychology: Political Culture in the Age of Experts* (Berkeley: University of California Press, 1995). Administrators seem concerned about the future of democracy, and desire to create citizens capable of sustaining it. See also Erik Peterson, "Psychological Frontiers: Politics, Culture, and the Redefinition of Democratic Freedom," Ph.D. diss., University of Minnesota, 1996; and, on expectations of maturity, Barbara Ehrenreich, *The Hearts of Men: American Dreams and the Flight from Commitment* (Garden City, N.Y.: Anchor Press/Doubleday, 1983).

13. Lawrence C. Woodruff, "Opinions." It is not that students were unsupervised before; rather, systems of supervision in the smaller prewar colleges and universities were more personal and less rationalized. Housing is an example. In 1946, with more than eight thousand students enrolled, KU had only 455 dormitory rooms. In the prewar years, the smaller student population (under five thousand) had been housed in a loose system of approved boarding houses, fraternities and sororities, and family homes. This system was not tenable with such a large student population. Using funds from state taxes and bond issues, low-cost federal loans, and gifts made by wealthy alumni, the university built dormitories and apartments for married students (Griffin, *University of Kansas*, 635). Students were thus brought into a more standardized and easily regulated system, and were also the beneficiaries or recipients of other university programs, including expanded oversight. The managerial demands of such a large student population required greater levels of specialization on the part of administrators. The possibility of managing students through personal relationships was also significantly reduced, or at least shifted to hierarchical arrangements, with chains of oversight under the deans of men and women.

14. Barstow, "Forty Years of Growth," 4. The Personnel Committee included the deans of men and women, registrar, director of health services, dean of the university, director of the guidance bureau, and director of housing. It was chaired by the dean of students.

15. Council on Student Affairs, no title, 11 January 1966, in Council on Student Affairs, 1966/67, 67/12/AWS, KUA. This document attempts to lay out lines of authority within the university and from whence that authority derives (i.e., the Statutes of the State of Kansas

"vest the responsibility" in the Board of Regents, which in turn "delegated the responsibility to the Chancellor"

16. Interview with Emily Taylor (former dean of women, University of Kansas), Lawrence, Kansas, June 1990; disciplinary case records from the Senior Privilege Board are in Dean of Women, chronological files (DOW) 53/0, box 1, KUA.

17. Emily Taylor served as dean of women at KU from 1956 through December 1974, when she left to become director of the Office of Women in Higher Education of the American Council on Education in Washington, D.C. She had a doctorate from Indiana University. While at KU she began an organization, the "Commission on the Status of Women," and produced and moderated a radio program, "A Feminist Perspective." "Emily Taylor," Personnel files, KUA.

18. "Rules Not Meant to Curb Morals," *UDK*, n.d. (February 1966?), clipping file, KUA; Letter to "Parents of Senior Women" from Emily Taylor, dean of women, fall semester 1966, in DOW 53/0, box 1, 1956/57—70/71, KUA. Parents could withhold permission from their daughters. Some letters of protest from parents are contained in this file, though it seems that few parents refused permission. Interview with Emily Taylor, Lawrence, Kansas, July 1990.

19. Letter to Emily Taylor from Helen Gibson Throop, Kansas City, 11 January 1961, in DOW chronological files, DOW 53/0, box 2, KUA.

20. Lee Byrd, "Student Freedom Movement Gains Momentum at Meeting," *UDK*, 12 November 1965. Cartoon/illustration by Richard Geary.

21. On national SDS, see Gitlin, *The Sixties,* and James Miller, *Democracy Is in the Streets: From Port Huron to the Siege of Chicago* (New York: Simon and Schuster, 1987). Attempts to enact a philosophy stressing participatory democracy and rejecting certain forms of leadership meant that there was little hierarchy—or direction—from the national organization to the local chapters. It is not surprising that KU's chapter would have an independent agenda. The Lawrence SDS chapter did sponsor war-related forums also; in fact, SDS sponsored a discussion about the Vietnam War led by Todd Gitlin in October 1965. However, the parietals issue attracted more campus attention in 1965–66. While the national SDS organization did not mount a campaign on gender issues at this time, Tom Hayden had been very involved in a movement similar to KU's (in goals, not rhetoric) at the University of Michigan in the early 1960s. KU's gender-oriented campaign is an auspicious beginning, but Lawrence's New Left would soon have the same crises over gender inequality that the national organization experienced. Little work has been done on local SDS chapters; for an interesting analysis of a local chapter (very different from Lawrence's), see Douglas Rossinow, "Breakthrough: White Youth Radicalism in Austin, Texas 1956–1973," Ph.D. diss., Johns Hopkins University, 1994.

22. Ibid.

23. John Garlinghouse, "In Loco Deus," *Kansas University Students for a Democratic Society Journal*, issue 2, December 1965, 1–2.

24. Byrd, "Student Freedom."

25. Mrs. Donald Emmons, "Student Responsibility," *KU SDS Journal*, 3. See also Byrd, "Student Freedom."

26. The University Party, "White Paper on Student Rights," March 1966, 5, in Student Protests 1919/20—1968/69, box 1, series 71/18, folder 1965/66, KUA.

27. "Rules Not Meant to Curb Morals."

28. This exchange is described in the following: Eric Morganthaler, "Questions Given to Surface," *UDK*, 25 February 1966; "Text of Questions Handed Provost by Student Group," *UDK*, 25 February 1966; "Policy Probe Gets Answers," *UDK*, 1 March 1966; "SDS Dissatisfied

with Query Result," *UDK,* 2 March 1966; "Provost Sees Loaded Queries," n.d. (mid-March 1966); "Students Want to Know," vol. 1, 25 February 1966, vol. 2, 11 March 1966; all in "Student Protest 1919/20–1968/69 files, 71/18, box 1, 1965/66, KUA. See also the clipping from the *Wichita Eagle and Beacon,* 27 February 1966, titled "KU Students Seek Rule Definition," with UPI as byline, in Student Correspondence file, series 2/12/5, box 11. The clipping was forwarded to Surface by a student's mother. The shift from philosophical to legal language seems to result from increased involvement by other actors. It is, however, another paradigm that makes sense to university administrators, this time those further up the hierarchy than the student life crowd. Universities in the 1960s began to worry not only about the legal limits to their authority over students, but about the liability they assume in claiming in loco parentis authority. For a somewhat later statement of the problem, see "The Legal Relationships between Colleges and Students," *The Editorial Projects for Education 15–Minute Report for College and University Trustees,* 29 May 1968 (in Student Protest files, KUA).

29. Council on Student Affairs, no title, no date (January 1966); letter from Harold R. Fatzer, Attorney General of Kansas, to Mr. Hubert Brighton, Secretary, State Board of Regents, 15 February 1956, this copy stamped with date 21 February 1966; both documents in Council on Student Affairs file, series 67/12/AWS.

30. My account of the AWS convention comes from transcripts of the convention itself, reports from AWS officers, and *UDK* coverage. Documents and clippings in AWS Regulations Convention, 1965/66, series 67/12, KUA. Quotations in the following section will be individually cited.

31. Hayden document in Student Protest files, series 71/18, box 2, KUA; see also Jackie Thayer, "Convention Offers Rare Opportunity," editorial, *UDK,* 9 March 1966.

32. "AWS Regulations Convention" (transcript), 1, 3. Two transcripts of the convention are in this file. Neither is quite complete and the pagination is confused, so it is not possible to sort them out. I use the page number as it appears, without trying to specify which transcript it belongs to.

33. Ibid., 1, 12, 12.

34. Ibid., 12.

35. Ibid., 16.

36. Ibid., combination of pp. 2 and 8, which are clearly the same speech in the same sequence but transcribed slightly differently.

37. There was no sudden end to parietals; instead, the system was altered piecemeal, usually based on votes by dormitory residents. By 1970, most residence halls had twenty-four-hour open visitation.

38. Though the tone of the article itself (Elizabeth Rhodes, "AWS Asks Drop of Most Closing," *UDK,* 14 March 1966, 1) was positive, the front-page article was wrapped around a photograph of a cat, with the caption "catastrophic—A sleepy feline observed most of the demands for liberal women's rules at the AWS convention Saturday."

39. Elizabeth Rhodes, "Student Opinion Varies," clipping, *UDK,* n.d. (probably 17 March 1966).

40. This is discussed in detail in a nine-page report by Cathy Beagle, convention chair, and in a series of four articles by Elizabeth Rhodes in the *Kansan* (*UDK*).

41. "University White Paper on Student Rights," 1, Preface. For more evidence of support from portions of the administration, see the memo from the Mental Health Clinic Staff, "The Relationship of Rules to Mental Health" (67/12/AWS, KUA), which supports the actions of the convention.

42. Chancellor's Office, Correspondence, 1965/66, series 2/12/5, box 11, KUA. The chancel-

lor was politic and polite in his responses, but generally made it clear he supported the student resolutions. He wrote to one parent: "I am one who believes, as the father of a mature young woman who is a student in the University, that when a young woman reaches the age of 20 or 21, she is entitled to some respect and, as well, to some freedom." Letter from Wescoe, 19 April 1966.

43. An interesting comparison can be made to the Port Huron Statement, in which SDS founders speak as youth, but also, quite directly, as members of a privileged class in America. Was youth the primary identity claimed then, or do we read the document with that stress because of the rise of a discourse of youth in the years that followed?

Chapter Twelve

"Birth of a New Symbol"

The Brown Berets' Gendered Chicano National Imaginary

Ernesto Chávez

In January 1967 *Time* magazine declared: "The Man of the Year 1966 is a generation: the man—and woman—of 25 and under."[1] The youth of the sixties, observed *Time*, are "well-educated, affluent, rebellious, responsible, pragmatic, idealistic, brave, 'alienated,' and hopeful."[2] People of color were not well educated and affluent but their desire to be so—and also to eliminate racial and ethnic discrimination in American society—caused them to strike out at that society in ways that were both similar to and strikingly different from the efforts of earlier generations.

For the ethnic Mexican community, as for other communities in the United States, the 1960s proved tumultuous and led to major reconfigurations of identity and culture.[3] One such development was the Chicano movement, which was preeminently a nationalist struggle. By nationalism I mean a culturally constructed ideological movement for the attainment and maintenance of autonomy, cohesion, and individuality for an ethnic group deemed by its members to constitute an actual or potential nation.[4] Chicano nationalism was articulated through "Chicanismo," a predominantly male-dominated political language. This idiom is best understood as a set of words, phrases, and concepts—Aztlán, Chicano, La Raza, La Causa, Huelga, Carnalismo—that individuals used to articulate their political beliefs and press their demands. Fundamentally, Chicanismo called for the creation of Aztlán, a place where Chicanos could exercise self-determination. It was a concept derived from the legendary northern home from which the Mexica (the Aztecs) had journeyed south to Mexico. Yet how this objective would be achieved was up for debate. Chicanismo was also concerned with defining Chicano identity, what it meant to be a Chicano, and how to live a Chicano lifestyle. Chicanismo's amorphous nature allowed for the emergence of varied groups that emphasized different tactics and attracted people with different backgrounds and from distinct regions. Chicanismo also challenged the United States cultural ethos of Americanism and the older so-called Mexican American Generation that had accepted that ethos. As a countercultural idea, Chicanismo was part of a larger critique of the United States, a form of anti-Americanism, that permeated United States society in the 1960s and 1970s.[5]

Anti-Americanism grew in opposition to the older concept of Americanism. Developed in the early twentieth century, Americanism was a political language that is best understood as an idiom, not an ideology. Americanism was a set of words, phrases, and concepts that individuals used, whether by choice or necessity, to express their political beliefs and make known their demands. Growing out of the Americanization campaigns of the First World War, in which the government sought to forge an American identity, it was an unprecedented emphasis on pledging loyalty to American institutions, on defining what it was to be an American, and on elaborating an American way of life. What emerged was a situation in which every group interested in gaining political power had to couch its demands in this language.[6]

Anti-Americanism encompassed a disdain for American institutions and reflected a transition from Americanism to an anti-Americanism that resulted from the turmoil of the 1960s. Critiques of American culture and politics were a reaction to the cold war consensus of the 1950s and accompanied the civil rights movement and the emergence of the New Left. The political generation that was shaped by these events became further disillusioned following the assassination of John F. Kennedy, the failure of Lyndon Johnson's Great Society, and the escalation of the Vietnam War. The social dissonance engendered the Black Power, American Indian, Asian American, antiwar, Women's, Gay, and Chicano movements. These insurgencies questioned the very nature of American society and culture, but their anti-American rhetoric notwithstanding, they were part of the American polity. Their disillusionment with the United States stemmed from their fundamental belief in the promise of America. Thus, in the 1960s and 1970s, the Americanism of an earlier generation came, ironically, to be expressed in anti-American terms.[7]

For Mexican Americans, no group better illustrated the rebellious 1960s and 1970s than the Brown Berets. Examining the Brown Berets provides insight into the construction of a specific style of Chicano nationalism and reveals its gendered dimensions.[8] The notion that a nation is "an imagined community"—a social construct—is well accepted in current scholarship.[9] Not so well acknowledged is the idea that men are privileged within this system. According to Anne McClintock, "explorations of the gendering of the national imaginary are paltry," despite the fact that "all nationalisms are gendered [and] all are invented."[10] Using the Brown Berets as a case study allows us to peer into the workings of both nation and masculinity. The Brown Berets proliferated a highly masculinized view of what it meant to be a Chicano and they practiced this concept in symbolic ways. Its paramilitary structure, which often excluded women from its inner workings, and the recruitment of the "vato loco," or the street thug, point in this direction. The case of the Brown Berets upholds Elleke Boehmer's notion that the male role in the nationalist scenario is typically "metonymic," that is, men are contiguous with one another and with the nationalist whole. She argues that "the idea of nationhood bears a masculine identity."[11] Focusing on the formation of the organization and interrogating its early history uncovers the constructive and masculinist nature of Chicano nationalism and ultimately calls into question essentialized notions of Mexican American culture and identity.

Like other populations in the United States in the postwar era, the ethnic Mexican community experienced a population boom. This is most evident when examining the population figures for the period from 1941 to 1970. The U.S. Bureau of the Census reported that Mexican legal immigration to the United States steadily climbed in these three decades; from 1941 to 1950 it numbered 60,589, from 1951 to 1960 it grew to 299,811 and from 1961 to 1970 it rose again to 453,934.[12] Given that the Mexican American birth-rate was 50 percent higher than that of the general population, Mexican American youths were a force to be reckoned with.[13] This fact was not lost on California authorities following the 1965 Watts rebellion. The McCone Commission, the body which investigated the causes of the South Central Los Angeles uprising, declared in its final report of December 1965 that its "recommendations regarding the Negro problem in Los Angeles apply with equal force to the Mexican-Americans . . . whose circumstances are similarly disadvantageous and demand equally urgent treatment."[14] The post-Watts atmosphere in the City of Angels heightened the concerns of the Los Angeles County Human Relations Commission, which had been formed following the 1943 Zoot Suit Riots, vis-à-vis Mexican American youth. Though the commission had held a Mexican American youth conference in 1963, the aftermath of Watts prompted the commission to sponsor a youth conference for April 1966.[15]

This event, with the prosaic name of the Mexican-American Youth Leadership Conference, became the vehicle for igniting a new generation of Mexican American reformers.[16] The conference, sponsored by Wilshire Boulevard Temple's Camp Hess Kramer in cooperation with the Los Angeles County Commission on Human Relations, was to "examine emotions, feelings, values, identity and the label 'Mexican American.' " Organizers wanted the participants—high school leaders—to discuss what they shared in common in the hope that the students would forge alliances for bringing about positive changes in their neighborhoods.[17] The conference lasted only three days but some of those present continued to meet and talk about issues that troubled them.

In May 1966 seven of them—Vickie Castro, David Sánchez, Moctesuma Esparza, Ralph Ramírez, Rachel Ochoa, George Licon, and John Ortiz—created Young Citizens for Community Action (YCCA).[18] The organizers believed in the principles of Lyndon Johnson's War on Poverty and had faith in the electoral process. With the head-strong eighteen-year-old Roosevelt High School senior Castro as president, they conducted a survey of student needs, met with education officials to discuss school problems, and gathered information about candidates running for election to the Los Angeles Board of Education. Castro and her friends were convinced that the flaws in the school system could be remedied only through political action. Their first move in this direction was to support Julian Nava, a state college professor in the San Fernando Valley, in his successful bid for a seat on the school board. They followed their "Youth for Nava" campaign with service on Los Angeles Mayor Samuel Yorty's Youth Advisory Council. Later some of them served on the California Governor's Youth Advisory Council during the administrations of Governors Gerald "Pat" Brown and Ronald Reagan.[19]

These youths gradually broadened their concerns and began focusing on other issues besides the schools, especially police brutality and the need to improve the quality of life in their communities. They received strong encouragement from Father John B. Luce, the rector of the Episcopal Church of the Epiphany in Lincoln Heights, and worked with the children in his summer day camp. Before moving to Los Angeles, Luce had been assigned to a church in the East Harlem section of New York City, and immediately prior to his move to the City of Angels he had served as rector of Grace Church in Jersey City, New Jersey. In October 1965 he relocated to Los Angeles at the request of the Episcopal Bishop of Los Angeles, who believed that Luce's inner-city experience would enhance the work of the western diocese. Luce's involvement with the youth of the neighborhood stemmed from the Episcopal church's concern with its parish's residents. It was the church's policy, as Luce said, "to try to reach out and work with all sorts of different groups and kids, drug addicts, people that had been troubled with the law."[20] In the late 1960s the Episcopal church's concern with the disadvantaged was evident through its national leader Bishop John Hines's authorization of nine million dollars over three years from 1967 to 1970 for the purposes of supporting organizations that were run for the poor and for self-determination. As Luce further explained, "We feel that the carrying out of this type of work by the church . . . the support of indigenous organizations of the people themselves will build real democracy in this country."[21] Clearly the church saw itself as part of the overall struggle for social change that was so prevalent in the 1960s.

The Church of the Epiphany was part of a large network of urban social groups that helped the YCCA get its start. The California Center for Community Development's Social Action Training Program—a project funded by the Southern California Council of Churches through the Office of Economic Opportunity—established itself across the street from the Church of the Epiphany in the summer of 1967. The Social Action Training Center was affiliated with the Community Service Organization's (CSO) Young Adult Leadership and Community Development Project, a program that ran for ten weeks in the summer of 1966 and sought "to train young adults in East Los Angeles in community action by involving them in neighborhood improvement and community participation projects."[22] The CSO was founded in 1947 and had been initially funded by Saul Alinsky's Industrial Areas Foundation. The organization advocated reformist policies: voter registration and the attainment of U.S. citizenship. By the 1960s it was no longer actively involved in electoral politics; instead it was concerned with social issues in East Los Angeles and had initiated a credit union in 1964 and two years later the Buyers Club, a consumer cooperative that bought items in bulk and offered them to its members at reduced rates.[23] The CSO was operating within an older tradition of politics. Although founded in Los Angeles, it had chapters throughout California. One key former organizer for the organization's San Jose branch was César Chávez. Through its participation with the CSO program, the YCCA met Richard Allatorre, who instructed them in the ways of organizing a community to help itself and introduced them to Chávez.[24] These contacts with CSO, UFW, and Chávez, together with the general reform climate and demand for civil rights, prompted them to take a greater pride in their own ethnicity and to rename their organization Young Chicanos for Community Action (YCCA).[25]

With the help of Father Luce, who provided funds for the rent, the newly renamed YCCA, in October 1967, opened La Piranya, a coffeehouse located on East Olympic Boulevard in an industrial section of unincorporated East Los Angeles. La Piranya served as an office and also a meeting place where prominent civil rights leaders came to express their views to an ever-increasing number of Chicano youth. Among those making an appearance were César Chávez, Reies López Tijerina of New Mexico's Alianza Federal de Mercedes, and African American leaders Hubert "Rap" Brown and Stokely Carmichael of the Student Non-Violent Coordinating Committee and Ron Karenga of United Slaves (US).[26] La Piranya also sponsored "Educational Happenings," designed to encourage youth to get a college education.[27] Usually present on these occasions were representatives from nearby colleges and universities as well as speakers from the United Council Community Organizations, the United Parents Council, and sometimes a political leader or representative from a congressional field office. Though the coffeehouse served many purposes, its most important function was as a place for young people to gather. It had little adult supervision and, according to *La Raza*, a local newspaper published by Chicanos affiliated with the Church of the Epiphany, "Many nights you will hear live music . . . but mostly you will find young Chicanos like yourself."[28]

These gatherings also attracted Los Angeles County Sheriff's deputies, who harassed La Piranya patrons on the grounds that the coffeehouse was a hangout for Chicano "hoodlums." The deputies would frequently drive by and shine their lights into the windows as well as question and illegally search customers as they left the building. Angered by such affronts, the YCCA organized protest demonstrations at the nearby East Los Angeles sheriff's station.[29]

About this time, late 1967 and early 1968, some YCCA members, including several of the founders, began their college studies and gradually drifted away from the group because of the pressure of classes. Along with Licon and Esparza, the two women members, Castro and Ochoa, left the group. Castro's leadership role was assumed by David Sánchez, who had little patience with the continued police harassment and urged a more militant stance. As a symbol of their attitude, around January 1968 the YCCA began wearing clothing that resembled military khaki and changed its name to the Brown Berets. They saw themselves as crusaders for justice, and they soon came to personify the goals of the early Chicano movement: nationalism and the vision of self-determination.

The most distinctive feature of their apparel was the beret and the emblem attached to it, which depicted a yellow pentagon with two bayoneted rifles behind a cross and the words "La Causa" (the cause) above them. One of the new members, Johnny Parsons, recommended the beret and designed the emblem, but others instinctively shared the message he sought to convey. One of those present at the time later recalled:

> We asked him why [are you designing an emblem]? He said, "look, it's like an emblem for guerrillas, . . . a symbol of guerrillas, and in this case like urban guerrillas." He started telling us how there were green berets, how the French guerrillas and the Spanish guerrillas had worn it during the Spanish Civil War and that we should wear a brown beret. So, we thought it was a good idea. So we started wearing the brown beret and

> the khaki jacket—the bush jacket. But we didn't call ourselves the Brown Berets. [Those] who started calling us the Brown Berets were the East L.A. sheriffs . . . and we got pissed off. We would hear it because every time they had us up against the wall we'd hear all the radio messages from the patrol cars, "Brown Berets here" and "Brown Berets over here," and so then it stuck. So, then we just stayed with it.[30]

A new member was responsible for the group's outward symbols but it was a long-standing member, eighteen-year-old David Sánchez who expressed in writing the anger and goals of those attracted to the Berets. Following his arrest on February 20, 1968, for participating in an unlawful assembly, Sánchez was imprisoned for sixty days at the Wayside Maximum Security facility. There he wrote "The Birth of a New Symbol" in a setting reminiscent of Martin Luther King Jr.'s imprisonment in 1963 when he wrote his "Letter from a Birmingham Jail." Instead of the nonviolent philosophy advocated by King, however, Sánchez emphasized that Brown Berets must be ready to use "any and all means necessary." Here too the first glimpses of the Berets masculinist and nationalist ideology first emerged. The document concretely shows McClintock's notion that all nationalisms are gendered and invented. Sánchez's ideas also reflect historian George Mosse's ruminations that "the idea of masculinity" is "basic to the self-definition of modern society."[31] We can read Sánchez's words as his attempt to construct a new society in which the young Chicano man would be the representative subject. Thus in his "imagined community" men are privileged and indeed are metonymic to the idea of nation. "As a Brown Beret," he told his fellow members, "you have been selected to resolve the frustrations of our people." And "because your people have awaited . . . the symbol of change," he announced in a messianic tone, "you are to be considered prophets of [a] disillusioned past" and a "symbol of hope" who should "preach hope." "By merely standing on a street corner, [and] wearing a Brown Beret . . . people [can] observe you and gather information and form an opinion about the Brown Berets." The Berets' mission was to convert Mexican Americans into Chicanos. A Beret should "talk to every potential Chicano who crosses your path. Because every Chicano that you miss is a potential enemy." But avoid "Anglos," he cautioned: "DO NOT TALK TO THE ENEMY, FOR HE IS EITHER A DOG OR A DEVIL. . . . For over 120 years, the Chicano has suffered at the hands of the Anglo Establishment." The only way to combat the injustices and discrimination meted out by "the gavacho" was through the Berets, "an organization that is efficient, disciplined and organized to uncover the [Anglo's] trick."[32]

The goal of the Berets, declared Sánchez, was "to stop discrimination and the many injustices against our people." That would require major social changes, and "in order to motivate someone or something towards change, pressure must sometimes be applied." He identified three stages in exerting pressure. The first was "communication," that is, sending telegrams and letters and making telephone calls directed to elected officials and other authorities. The second was to "embarrass and expose those who are in the wrong." The final stage he described as the use of "alternatives," which he defined as "any and all means necessary." This last option had probably been inspired by similar statements coming from Malcolm X and the Black Panthers.[33]

Success required self-discipline. "Because your people, the land, and the enemy are watching you," declared Sánchez, "you must look good, act right and move with the precision of a clock. . . . [I]f you really believe in your people, you will straighten up for your people."[34] You also had to obey without question your group leader because this person was the "best qualified [individual] to handle any situation." Leadership, Sánchez stressed, was the result of being a good follower and fully aware of Anglo "trickery."[35]

Emphasis was also placed on the need to maintain high standards of personal conduct. Avoid scandal because it will only "reflect upon the organization in a bad way," and always treat one another with respect. The concern with personal behavior reflected Sánchez's conviction that the Berets should avoid doing anything that would alienate them from the community. They should also stay away from "theory and ideology" because "[i]ntellectuals aren't able to communicate with the dude on the street." In addition, wear "simple dress" because "if you dress like the greater part of the community, you will usually be accepted. If you dress different," he cautioned, "and are sloppy or dirty, you usually aren't accepted and your channel of communication is broken." Thus a monolithic character would ensure compatibility between the Berets and the people.[36] Sánchez's emphasis on messianic images (the Berets as "prophets"), on the need for a militaristic organizational structure, on Chicano identity and solidarity, and on Anglos as the enemy permeated all subsequent Beret statements and documents.

"Birth of a New Symbol" articulated gendered notions of nation. In it the Berets ideally were young men that would change the course of, and indeed create, a new history. The colonial manifestation of community would be reconstituted and a new imaginary would emerge. The role of men within the document is reminiscent of Mosse's notion of masculinity in the early modern era in Europe. He states, "The ideal of manliness was basic both to the self-definition of bourgeois society and to the national ideology. Manliness was invoked to safeguard the existing order against the perils of modernity, which threatened the clear distinction between what was considered normal and abnormality."[37] So too was manliness invoked as a safeguard against the normal and the abnormal in Sánchez's rendering of society. The Brown Beret would act as prophet and bring about the "true" nature of Chicano nationalism and identity—the normal—and safeguard it against the infringement of Anglo society—the abnormal.

The Brown Berets' new national imaginary and its symbolic manifestation first gained wide notoriety in March 1968, when they became involved in a student boycott of five East Los Angeles high schools, known as the "Blow Outs." The protest stemmed from the fact that over 50 percent of the Chicano high school community was forced to drop out of school either through expulsion and transfers to other schools or because they had not been taught to read and thus failed their classes. Chicano schools were also overcrowded and run down compared to other schools in the district, and many teachers openly discriminated against Mexican Americans. The students wanted to eradicate these conditions and demanded more Chicano teachers and administrators to achieve this goal.[38] The Berets did not directly participate in the planning of the demonstrations but they did "back up, advise, and assist" those who did. This help began with their allowing students to meet at La

Piranya.[39] As Sánchez later told the *Los Angeles Times*, "The Chicano students were the main action group. The Brown Berets were at the walkouts to protect our younger people [the students ranged in ages from fourteen to eighteen, while the Berets were eighteen to twenty-four years old]. When they [the law officers] started hitting with sticks, we went in, did our business and got out."[40] Such action won wide approval among the students. "Who Are the Brown Berets?" asked the *Chicano Student News* (a newspaper edited by college student Raúl Ruiz with stories written by East Los Angeles high school students). They are people, who "served, observed and protected the Chicano community."

> When the cops moved in, it was the Berets that were dragged behind bars. THE BROWN BERETS became a target for the PLACA [the police], and anyone wearing one [a brown beret] was suspect to be picked up. It is the BROWN BERETS who are presently behind bars or have warrants out for their arrests. You know, *ese*, when you lay it on the line, there are people who mouth about taking care of business, and there are people who TAKE CARE OF BUSINESS. The BROWN BERETS take care of business and leave the "politicking" [*sic*] and mouthing to others. The BROWN BERETS are strictly a defense organization but reserve the right and duty to defend themselves, Chicanos and La Raza wherever and by whatever means necessary. Already many community organizations have found this out and are in full support behind these young Chicanos who stand ready. Their numbers are growing, growING, GROWING. BUENO YA . . . NO SE DEJAN.[41]

Support for the Berets increased when five of them (along with other people who had participated in the Blow Outs) were indicted by a Los Angeles grand jury for engaging in conspiracies to disrupt the public schools, felonies punishable by up to forty-five years in the state penitentiary.[42] Following the arrests, *Inside Eastside* (a student newspaper) protested that "we will not tolerate the felony charges which . . . will prevent the Brown Berets from being effective because its leaders . . . will most likely be jailed."[43] The Berets quickly secured release on bail but it took two years of litigation before the charges against the "conspirators" were dropped.[44] *La Raza* rallied to the defense of the Berets, arguing that Anglo injustices had brought them into existence.

> Because these injustices have existed and the Anglo Establishment shows no sign of changing them, because the cries of individuals have gone unheard and fallen upon deaf ears, a group of young Chicanos have come together under the name of the Brown Berets to demand an immediate end to the injustices committed against the Mexican-American. . . . The Brown Berets are not a gang, car club, or private social group; it is an organization of young Chicanos dedicated to serving the Mexican American community.[45]

The widespread interest in the Berets prompted its leaders to think more deeply about their purpose and to issue public statements about their goals. Like the Black Panthers, whom they admired, the Berets in June 1968 circulated a "Ten Point Program."[46]

1. Unity of all of our people, regardless of age, income, or political philosophy.
2. The right to bilingual education as guaranteed under the treaty of Guadalupe-Hidalgo.

3. We demand a Civilian Police Review Board, made up of people who live in our community, to screen all police officers, before they are assigned to our communities.
4. We demand that the true history of the Mexican American be taught in all schools in the five Southwestern States.
5. We demand that all officers in Mexican-American communities must live in the community and speak Spanish.
6. We want an end to "Urban Renewal Programs" that replace our barrios with high rent homes for middle-class people.
7. We demand a guaranteed annual income of $8,000 for all Mexican-American families.
8. We demand that the right to vote be extended to all of our people regardless of the ability to speak the English language.
9. We demand that all Mexican Americans be tried by juries consisting of only Mexican Americans.
10. We demand the right to keep and bear arms to defend our communities against racist police, as guaranteed under the Second Amendment of the United States Constitution.[47]

The ten points offer a glimpse of what the Brown Berets meant by self-determination. The demands were not revolutionary but reformist. They called for the United States government to grant Mexican Americans their constitutional rights. Throughout their existence the Berets would call for militant change, however the words were used only for effect, as a symbol. Although they implied violence, they never resorted to it.

The Berets accompanied their program with a three-part motto: "to serve, to observe, and to protect." "To serve" meant giving "vocal as well as physical support to those people and causes which will help the people of the Mexican-American communities," while "to observe" required keeping "a watchful eye on all federal, state, city and private agencies which deal with the Mexican American, especially law enforcement agencies." As for the words "to protect," they meant working to "guarantee . . . and secure the rights of the Mexican American by all means necessary." The "means necessary," declared the Berets, depended upon the actions of those in power. If the Anglo establishment accommodated their demands "in a peaceful and orderly process, then we will be only too happy to accept this way. Otherwise, we will be forced to other alternatives."[48]

The officers of the organization were responsible for maintaining order among the Berets. Sánchez served as "Prime Minister," Carlos Montes was "Minister of Information," Cruz Olmeda held the post of "Chairman," and Ralph Ramírez that of "Minister of Discipline." These titles, which reflected the militaristic, masculine, and hierarchical nature of the group, were similar to those adopted earlier by the Black Panthers.[49] The structure implied by the titles, however, never took hold in the Berets and existed only on paper.[50] That the leaders were all men further supports the claim that the organization had a masculinist orientation.

Like the Black Panthers, the Berets expressed a fondness for Marxism, with some of them also seeking guidance in the writings of Mao Zedong and arguing for the need to be "one with the masses of the people." This caused tension within the organization, especially when Cruz Olmeda and several others took Mao's words to heart and insisted that the Berets be transformed into a militia in the service of the community. Sánchez, on the other hand, believed that the Berets should only *appear* to be a military group, projecting the image rather than the reality of a revolutionary cadre. His cold war upbringing had produced in him a deep fear of communism that became so intense that he burned Marxist literature. He also knew firsthand about violent police repression and believed the police would destroy the Berets if they moved in a Marxist direction.[51]

At first, Beret leaders also disagreed about the group's recruitment policies. The approximately thirty members who had joined the Berets by mid-1968 were mostly recruited from local high schools and ranged in ages from fourteen to eighteen.[52] Sánchez wanted to continue the emphasis on enlisting high school students but Olmeda disagreed, arguing that such a policy would prevent the group from reaching a revolutionary takeoff point and relegate it to being just another pacifist organization. These differences were exacerbated by each man's personal desire to control the organization. The conflicts ended only when Olmeda and seven of his followers left the Brown Berets in July 1968 and founded a group called "La Junta," which recruited former gang members and aligned itself with adult leftists, reputed members of the Communist Party.[53] At this juncture the Berets were transformed into "Chicano Boy Scouts." This transformation reveals the group's masculinist orientation once again. If we view the Berets as a Boy Scout-like organization, then we can more clearly see the orientation toward creating the perfect Chicano young man. Mosse argues that "concern with the social function of masculinity was a strong motivating force in setting up the Scouts [in nineteenth-century England]."[54] This male sensibility was further espoused by the media.

Although other periodicals reported on the Berets' activities, the organization initiated its own newspaper, *La Causa*. First published on May 23, 1969, the monthly described itself as "a Chicano newspaper dedicated to serve the Chicano barrio with local and national news" that not only illustrates "the many injustices against the Chicano by the Anglo establishment" but also informs "the Raza of current and coming events" and seeks "to better relations and communications between barrios throughout the country."[55] The paper was preeminently a vehicle for spreading the Brown Beret propaganda and constructing a Chicano male sensibility. The editor, David Sánchez, and his editorial board determined the newspaper's editorial policy. In nearly every issue during the newspaper's three-year existence, Sánchez exhorted the Berets to redouble their efforts on behalf of the community.[56] "Ven, come Chicano prophets—La Raza waits for you," he proclaimed in the first issue.[57] Thereafter he kept coming back to what he called the "8 Points of Attention": "(1) Speak politely to the people; (2) Pay fairly for what you buy from the people; (3) Return everything you borrow; (4) Pay for anything you damage; (5) Do not hit or swear at the people; (6) Do not damage property or possessions of people; (7) Do not take liberties with women; and (8) When working with the people do not get loaded."[58] The monthly featured articles in English and Spanish, covered all important Beret activities, and frequently focused on special topics.

The newspaper was preoccupied with attracting new members. Almost every issue of *La Causa* featured a recruitment appeal, urging readers to "Join Today" and listing meeting dates and times. The appeals were directed primarily to lower-income Mexican Americans who had little formal education and were gang members, the *vatos locos.* Two pages in the April 1970 issue are illustrative of the Berets' efforts to imagine their community and to define that community's representative subject. The first shows a drawing of a Chicano wearing *cholo* garb and apparently drunk and carrying a bottle of beer underneath a banner that proclaims, "Bato [*sic*] Loco Yesterday." This is followed by a sketch of the same man in the Beret uniform with his right arm outstretched and his fist clenched in the power symbol. At his feet are the words "Revolutionist Today, Be Brown, Be Proud, Join the Brown Berets."[59] Thus in this instance the Berets once again function as did the Scouts in England. Like the Scouts, the above shows that the Berets were concerned not only with the national imaginary but also with the creation of clean living—a clean, healthy nation. They contrasted the proper type of young man—the Beret—with his countertype, the *vato loco.* Only through becoming a Beret could the *vato loco* be transformed and become a better person. That the *vato loco* was the Berets' targeted subject is clearly evident in their disparaging depiction of college students. An article on the UCLA student organization, MEChA (Movimiento Estudiantil Chicano de Aztlán), described Chicano students as "bureaucrats" who were out of touch with the community.

> They have never related to the off-campus Chicano community in Venice or the Eastside and have alienated a substantial number of the current Hi-Potential students [a special admissions program at UCLA]. This group used to be on an ultra cultural nationalist kick, affecting the speaking of the Cholo dialect which sounded ridiculous because its pronunciation had a heavy English accent. Most of these people never toked a joint until they came to college—a white hippy undoubtedly taught them how, however they were and are extolling the virtues of the Cholo.[60]

The quotation above once again points to the seeming corruption of Anglo society and exaltation of *cholo* or street thug sensibilities. The Berets emerge as the guardians of a normal Chicano culture as opposed to the abnormal American counterpart.

That the representative subject was male was evident in the way that women were treated in the organization and depicted in the pages of *La Causa.* Though women were welcomed into the organization, their roles were clearly secondary to those of men. Women held none of the more important positions of leadership. They met at different times and in different buildings than the men.[61] Their meetings dealt with such issues as bailing a Beret out of jail, organizing a fund-raiser, or typing the newspaper, while the men focused on what were considered the more weighty questions: planning demonstrations and discussing Beret policies and strategies. *La Causa* stressed that women played a significant role yet the newspaper's description of their activities reinforced traditional gender stereotypes. An example was an article in the

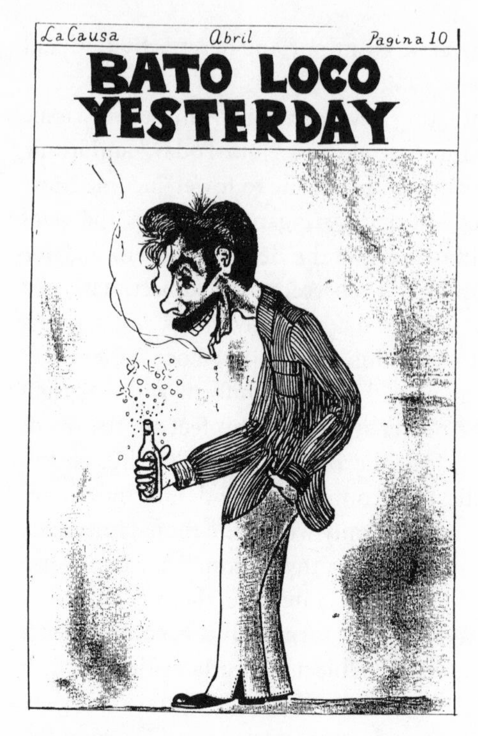

Fig. 12.1. "Bato Loco Yesterday." (Courtesy of Brown Berets, Inc.)

Fig. 12.2. "Join the Brown Berets." (Courtesy of Brown Berets, Inc.)

second issue by Gloria Arellanes. "Beautiful Bronze women all over Aztlán," she wrote, "are beginning to realize how valuable they are in beauty and the movement."

> Your role will be whatever you have to offer your people, whether it be leadership, a good rap, cooking or just to become involved, aware and educated, but find out. Every person has something to offer, every person is valuable. Get your head together, be aware—teach your awareness to those that are lost—teach your awareness to all those around you.[62]

The empowerment of which Arellanes spoke was not as clear in an anonymously written love poem, "Mi Amor," that appeared in a subsequent issue. "To my eyes/ A Chicana is an exotic queen,/ She radiates a glow of exquisite sheen." Certainly these saccharine lines only heightened the objectification of women. Yet the message to women was ambiguous; on the one hand, the organization stressed traditional roles, while on the other it pressed them to break the bonds of tradition. In this imaginary, women played symbolic roles. They were, as Mosse has said of women within other national discourses, "sedate rather than dynamic." They provided the "backdrop against which men determined the fate of nations."[63] This scenario is evident in another article, "Chicanas de Aztlán," which claimed that "women in the Brown Beret organization have left behind the traditional role that the Chicana has held for the past hundreds of years. . . . Of course, we have our duties and assignments to do. And these may be anything from getting a brother out of jail to planning a fund raiser." *La Causa* editor David Sánchez stated that "women can fight just as good as a man, if she wishes," but the women in the organization did not adhere to white feminist ideas. As one woman explained in another article: "We're not talking about women's liberation because, like that's not ours—we're talking about our Raza's liberation and in order to get our Raza liberated we all have to work together within our Raza." Despite articles by women in *La Causa* and their presence on the newspaper's staff, their exact numbers and roles are not clear.[64] The lack of women leaders can be attributed to the masculine and militaristic attitude of the organization and David Sánchez's role as a virtual dictator.[65]

Despite police infiltration and setbacks caused by trials, the Brown Berets persisted in their work on behalf of the Chicano community. A notable achievement was the creation of a free medical clinic in East Los Angeles, which opened in May 1969.[66] Another project that attracted Beret participation was the Chicano antiwar effort. Despite their disparaging attitude toward college students, the Brown Berets joined with them to mount a major campaign against the Vietnam War. Among students the initiative came from a group of Chicanos at UCLA who were particularly upset about the disproportionate number of Chicanos dying in the war, a 3-to-1 ratio when compared to whites.[67] In December 1969 the Berets and a group of college students formalized their alliance against the war by creating the Chicano Moratorium Committee with David Sánchez of the Brown Berets and Rosalio Muñoz, a UCLA student, serving as cochairs. Almost immediately, on December 20, they staged a demonstration against the war that attracted three thousand protesters. They had obviously touched an issue of widespread concern, one that also aroused hundreds of thousands of people of every ethnicity across the nation. But for Chicanos, as *La*

Causa declared, the war was seen as "a matter of survival" and "freedom." The newspaper believed that the "the Vietnam War is the ultimate weapon of genocide of non-white peoples by a sick decadent puto western culture." It viewed the war as "a turning point in the history of mankind" because the "Vietnamese have shown that man's spirit and will to survive can overcome the most brutal punishment ever netted out to any nation." The newspaper went on to show the parallels between the Vietnamese people's struggle for liberation and that of Chicanos. It called for Chicanos to learn from the Vietnamese "that to resist is to survive a free man and to submit is to be a puto and thus a slave."

"Dare to Struggle, Dare to Win—Hasta La Victoria Siempre!"

During the next three years the Brown Berets proclaimed their message in other demonstrations, and other symbolic acts.[68] In an effort to "reconquer [Chicanos'] rights to be treated like people, and not like second-class citizens," the Berets initiated "La Caravan de la Reconquista" (the Reconquest Caravan) and marched throughout the Southwest, covering five states (California, Arizona, Colorado, New Mexico, and Texas) and lasting from October 1971 to August 1972.[69] They also dramatically demonstrated their desire to reclaim the Southwest on August 30, 1972, by "invading" Catalina Island off the southern California coast and remaining there until September 22, 1972. The pretext for the invasion was their contention that the isle, along with the other Channel Islands off the California shore, had not been included in the lands ceded to the United States by the Treaty of Guadalupe Hidalgo following the Mexican War.[70] Both of these events constitute symbolic efforts to create Aztlán, and momentarily realize the national imaginary.

The Catalina Island incident marked the last of the Berets' attention-grabbing exploits. Shortly thereafter bickering among the leaders led to factionalization that robbed the organization of its effectiveness and it gradually disappeared. The bickering seems to have begun because of the ever larger role being played by David Sánchez. He had always been prominent, first because of his inspiring jailhouse writings that galvanized the Berets during their earliest months and, later, because of his role as editor of *La Causa.* Now, however, he was seen as exceeding his authority, writing about Beret policy without first getting permission of the Brown Beret National Headquarters Central Committee. He was also accused of violating basic Beret tenets by killing a fellow member and committing rape. The final insult came when the Central Committee charged him with stealing money from the Berets. The committee fired him on October 21, 1972.[71]

Sánchez responded by calling a press conference and announcing that he was resigning and disbanding the organization. The Berets, he claimed, had a membership of five thousand in ninety chapters but he was dissolving the group because others were using it "as a vehicle for their own purposes" and he feared there would be bloodshed. He also attributed his action to "police harassment and infiltration, internal squabbles and 'hippie-ism' among members, which ruined discipline."[72] As he had done before, Sánchez once again pointed to the destruction of the Chicano national imaginary through corruption by Anglo culture.

Thus the group that burst onto the scene in 1968 was through by 1972. During the Brown Berets' short-lived yet celebrated existence, they depicted themselves as "a new symbol" for challenging the "Anglo Establishment" and reforming society. Like the Black Panthers, they pushed a paramilitaristic form of cultural nationalism that especially captured the imagination of the young. At first they appealed particularly to the youth engaged in the "Blow Outs" and later they caught the attention of a larger audience in their protest of the Vietnam War. Their militant opposition to the war, however, soon escalated into violence and cost them the support of the Mexican American community. Another reason for the waning support may have been their lack of a clear and realistic plan to mobilize communities and create change.

Ultimately the examination of the Brown Berets makes clear the constructive and gendered dimensions of the Chicano national imaginary. In so doing we are able to once and for all dispel the essentialist notions of Chicano culture and identity. Perhaps this knowledge can lead to a clearer understanding of the failure of the Brown Berets, and the Chicano movement in general, to create social change in the 1960s and 1970s. By limiting the representative subject in an effort to create a strong community, the Brown Berets restricted participation in the "imagined community." Consequently they hindered the empowerment of the ethnic Mexican community. Acknowledging the Berets' limited vision of society can perhaps lead to a more liberating and multifaceted vision of what the ethnic Mexican community has been in the past, is in the present, and can be in the future. If history is a dialogue with the past, maybe this conversation will lead to an all-encompassing form of identity politics that empowers rather than disenfranchises. Though the Brown Berets did little to change the status quo, they were not without significance, for ultimately they were engaged in a struggle to define what it meant to be an American in the 1960s and 1970s and gave hope to Chicano youth through their role in the "Blow Outs," their efforts against the Vietnam War and their symbolic ventures aimed at creating Aztlán.

NOTES

1. "Man of the Year: The Inheritor," *Time*, January 6, 1967, 18.
2. Bernhard M. Auer, "A Letter from the Publisher," *Time*, January 6, 1967, 11.
3. Following David G. Gutiérrez's lead in "Significant to Whom? Mexican Americans and the History of the American West," *Western Historical Quarterly* 24 (November 1993):519–39, I employ the term "ethnic Mexicans" when referring to the combined population of all people of Mexican ancestry or descent living in the United States.
4. Anthony D. Smith, "Introduction: The Formation of Nationalist Movements," in Smith, ed., *Nationalist Movements* (London: Macmillan, 1976), 1–30; Benedict Anderson, *Imagined Communities: Reflections on the Origin and Spread of Nationalism*, rev ed. (New York: Verso, 1991), 1–7.

5. My conception of Chicanismo builds on the work of José Angel Gutiérrez in "Ondas y Rollas (Wavelengths and Raps): The Ideology of Contemporary Chicano Rhetoric," in John C. Hammerback et al., eds., *A War of Words: Chicano Protest in the 1960s and 1970s* (Westport, Conn: Greenwood Press, 1985): 121–163; Lloyd Powers, "Chicano Rhetoric: Some Basic Concepts," *Southern Speech Communication Journal* 8, no. 4 (Summer 1973): 340–47; and Michael Victor Sedano in "Chicanismo: A Rhetorical Analysis of Themes and Images of Selected Poetry from the Chicano Movement," *Western Journal of Speech Communication* 44, no. 3 (Summer 1980): 190–202. Conceptually it is modeled on Gary Gerstle's vision of Americanism in *Working-Class Americanism: The Politics of Labor in a Textile City, 1940–1960* (New York: Cambridge University Press, 1989).

6. Gerstle, *Working-Class Americanism*, 9–10.

7. For more on the contestation of what it meant to be an American in this era, see David Farber, *Chicago '68* (Chicago: University of Chicago Press, 1988).

8. Angie Chabram-Dernersesian's "I Throw Punches for My Race, but I Don't Want to Be a Man: Writing US—Chica-nos (Girl Us)/Chicanas—into the Movement Script," in Lawrence Grossberg, Cary Nelson, and Paula A. Treichler, eds., *Cultural Studies* (New York: Routledge, 1992), and Ramón A. Gutiérrez's "Community, Patriarchy and Individualism: The Politics of Chicano History and the Dream of Equality," *American Quarterly* 45, no. 1 (March 1993): 44–72, point to the gendered nature of Chicano nationalism but do not provide a case study of a political group, but survey literary works.

9. Benedict Anderson, *Imagined Communities.*

10. Anne McClintock, *Imperial Leather: Race, Gender and Sexuality in the Colonial Contest* (New York: Routledge, 1995), 352.

11. Elleke Boehmer, "Stories of Women and Mothers: Gender and Nationalism in Early Fiction of Flora Nwapa," in Suheila Nasta, ed., *Motherlands: Black Women's Writings from Africa, the Caribbean and South Asia* (New Brunswick, N.J.: Rutgers University Press, 1992), 6.

12. U.S. Department of Justice, Statistical Yearbook of the Immigration and Naturalization Service, 1983 (Washington, D.C.: U.S. Government Printing Office, 1983), table 2; Bureau of the Census, *U.S. Census of Population, 1960. Subject Reports. Persons of Spanish Surname.* Final Report PC(2)-1B. Washington, D.C.: U.S. Government Printing Office, 1963.

13. Helen Rowan, "A Minority Nobody Knows," *Atlantic* (June 1967), 47.

14. Governor's Commission on the Los Angeles Riots, "Violence in the City—An End or a Beginning?" in Robert M. Fogelson, ed., *The Los Angeles Riots* (New York: Arno Press and the New York Times, 1969), 5.

15. Transcript of Los Angeles Commission on Human Relations meeting, March 21, 1966, 28.

16. Organizing among Mexican American youth was not new. It had happened throughout the twentieth century. The best example of this phenomenon was the Mexican American Movement of the 1940s and 1950s. This Los Angeles-based group focused on educational reform but never included a large following. Like the Brown Berets, it emerged from a youth conference (sponsored by the YMCA). For more on MAM, see George J. Sánchez, *Becoming Mexican American: Ethnicity, Culture and Identity in Chicano Los Angeles, 1900–1945* (New York: Oxford University Press, 1993).

17. Program for Fourth Annual Camp Hess Kramer Leadership Conference for Mexican-American Youth, April 3–5, 1966, 1.

18. Interview with Victoria Castro, Los Angeles, May 24, 1993.

19. Interview with Victoria Castro, May 24, 1993; Gerald Paul Rosen, *Political Ideology and*

the Chicano Movement: A Study of the Political Ideology of Activists in the Chicano Movement (San Francisco: R and E Research Associates, 1975), 73.

20. "Transcript of the John B. Luce Testimony before the Los Angeles County Grand Jury," 397.

21. Ibid., 440.

22. "Community Service Organization: 25th Anniversary Program" (Los Angeles: Community Service Organization, 1972), 8.

23. "Ibid., 8–9.

24. "Transcript of the John B. Luce Testimony before the Los Angeles County Grand Jury," 396–405.

25. Interview with Victoria Castro, Los Angeles, May 24, 1993.

26. *L.A. Times*, June 16, 1969, 24.

27. "It's Happening," *La Raza*, January 15, 1968, 2.

28. *La Raza*, November 15, 1967, 6.

29. "Sheriff's Harass," *La Raza*, January 15, 1968, 1.

30. Interview with Cruz Olmeda Becerra, Alhambra, California, May 15, 1993.

31. George Mosse, *The Image of the Man: The Creation of Modern Masculinity* (New York: Oxford University Press, 1996), 3.

32. "The Birth of a New Symbol," 1.

33. Ibid., 1–2; for more on the Black Panthers' rhetoric, see Phillip S. Foner, ed., *The Black Panthers Speak* (New York: J. B. Lippincott, 1970); for more on Malcolm X, see Malcolm X with Alex Haley, *Autobiography of Malcolm X* (New York: Ballantine Books, 1965); and David Gallen, ed., *Malcolm X: The FBI File* (New York: Carroll & Graf, 1991).

34. "The Birth of a New Symbol," 2.

35. Ibid.

36. Ibid.

37. George L. Mosse, Nationalism and Sexuality: Middle-Class Morality and Sexual Norms in Modern Europe. (Madison: University of Wisconsin Press, 1985), 23.

38. Rodolfo Acuña, *Occupied America: A History of Chicanos*, 3d ed.(New York: Harper and Row, 1988), 336.

39. David Sánchez, *Expedition through Aztlán* (La Puente, Calif.: Perspectiva Press, 1978), 2.

40. Ruben Salazar, "Brown Berets Hail 'La Raza' and Scorn the Establishment," *Los Angeles Times*, June 16, 1969, pt. I, 24.

41. "Who Are the Brown Berets?" *Chicano Student News*, March 15, 1968, 5.

42. Oscar Zeta Acosta, "The East L.A. 13 vs. the L.A. Superior Court," *El Grito*, 3, no. 2 (Winter 1970): 12.

43. Victor Franco, "E.L.A. Raided," *Inside Eastside* 1, no. 15 (June 10–13, 1968): 3.

44. Cruz Olmeda interview.

45. "Brown Berets: Serve, Observe and Protect." *La Raza* 1, no. 13 (June 7, 1968): 13.

46. For the Black Panthers' Ten Points, see "October 1966 Black Panther Party Platform and Program: What We Want and What We Believe," in Foner, ed., *The Black Panthers Speak*, 2–4.

47. "Brown Berets: Serve, Observe and Protect."

48. Ibid.

49. Ibid.

50. Olmeda Becerra interview.

51. Ibid.

52. In May 1969 the Beret newspaper *La Causa* reported that the organization had twenty-eight chapters in cities including San Antonio, Texas; Eugene, Oregon; Denver, Colorado; Detroit, Michigan; Seattle, Washington; Albuquerque, New Mexico; and most major California cities. *La Causa* 1, no. 1 (May 23, 1969): 2.

53. Olmeda Becerra interview.

54. Mosse, *The Image of the Man*, 136.

55. "News for a More Aware Community," *La Causa* 1, no. 1, (May 23, 1969): 8.

56. Ibid.

57. David Sánchez, "To All Brown Berets," *La Causa* 1, no. 1 (May 23, 1969): 8.

58. "Brown Berets: 8 Points of Attention," *La Causa* 1, no. 9 (December 1970): 19; the Brown Berets appear to be modeled after Moa Zedong's 1928 "Eight Rules" for the Red Guard. For more on this, see Zhong Wenxian, ed., *Mao Zedong: Biography, Assessment, Reminiscences* (Beijing: Foreign Language Press, 1986), 60–61. The Black Panthers also had similar "Eight Points"; for these, see Foner, ed., *Black Panthers Speak*, 6. One such recruitment message was entitled "Becoming a Brown Beret: A Reason for Existing," *La Causa* 1, no. 9 (December, 1970).

59. *La Causa* 2, No. 2 (April 1971): 10–11.

60. "Chicanos at UCLA Blow-it," *La Causa* 1, no. 8 (August 29, 1970): 4.

61. *La Causa* 1, no. 4 (December 16, 1969): 7.

62. Gloria Arellanes, "Palabras Para La Chicana," *La Causa* 1, no. 2 (July 10, 1969): 6.

63. Mosse, *Nationalism and Sexuality*, 23.

64. For more on women in the Brown Berets, see Dionne Espinoza, "Pedogogies of Gender and Nationalism: Cultural Resistance in Selected Practices of Chicana/o Movement Activists, 1967–1972" (Ph.D. diss., Cornell University, 1996).

65. "The Adelitas Role En El Movement," *La Causa* 1, no. 10 (February 1971): 10.

66. "Serving the People: The E.L.A. Free Clinic," *La Causa* 1, no. 4 (December 16, 1969): 2.; Salazar, "Brown Berets Hail 'La Raza' and Scorn the Establishment."

67. Though Sánchez claims, in *Expedition through Aztlán*, that he came up with the idea for the group, my research shows that Rosalio Muñoz, a UCLA student, was thinking along the same lines and, along with fellow Bruin Races Noriega, formed an organization, "Chale Con La Draft," to bring awareness on the draft to the Chicano community.

68. Quote in subheading from "Chicano Moratorium: A Matter of Survival," *La Causa* 1, no. 5 (February 28, 1970): 1. For more on the Chicano Moratorium Committee in Los Angeles, see Ernesto Chávez, "Creating Aztlán: The Chicano Movement in Los Angeles, 1966–1978" (Ph.D. diss. University of California, Los Angeles, 1994). For Chicano anti-war activity in other places, see Lorena Oropeza, "La Batalla Está Aquí! Chicanos Oppose the War in Vietnam." (Ph.D. diss., Cornell University, 1996).

69. "La Caravan De La Reconquista Is Coming," *La Causa*, c. 1972, 1.

70. David Sánchez, *Expedition through Aztlán*, 174–81.

71. "National Brown Beret Organization Termination Notice," c. October 22, 1972. CASA Papers, box 25.

72. Dale Torgenson, "Brown Beret Leader Quits, Dissolves Units," *Los Angeles Times*, November 2, 1972, 9; FBI Document, Los Angeles, March 29, 1973, file no. 105-178715-273.

Chapter Thirteen

Art and Activism in the Chicano Movement

Judith F. Baca, Youth, and the Politics of Cultural Work

Jeffrey J. Rangel

In 1973, Chicana artist Judith F. Baca procured funding from the Model Cities Program to paint the *Second Street Mural* with a crew of young Chicanos in the Boyle Heights neighborhood of Los Angeles. By the time she was awarded monies to begin the project, Baca had been an employee with the Los Angeles Department of Recreation and Parks (LADRP) for approximately four years and had generated a reputation for working with East Side gang youth of the barrios. Her success organizing youth in and around community centers and public parks moved city officials to appoint her director of the East Los Angeles Mural Program in 1973, whereby she initiated the *Second Street Mural* as her first project. One day, while working on the mural, the twenty-seven-year-old Baca was approached by Art Torres, a young political upstart running for a seat in California's State Assembly. Baca recalled of the incident:

> They [Torres and staff members] came to see me—on the wall, while I was painting. And I was like kind of, you know, "So you're a candidate?" "Yes." And, "So, what do you want?" "Well, you know. I'm interested in your support." And I said, "You mean you want me to get people to vote for you?" "Well, yeah! Yeah." [Chuckles] I said, "Boy, everybody on this wall is a felon! I don't know. . . . You know, we don't vote!"[1]

Whether or not all the members of her crew were, in fact, felons or abstained from voting for other reasons does not diminish Baca's initial surprise at being courted for an endorsement. Eventually, however, the incident triggered a better understanding of the work she performed with youth as a Chicana artist and activist. She explained:

> At that point I was becoming well known for my connections within the neighborhoods, my communities. But I had no idea that [such work] had any political power, that people would perceive it as political power. And I began to understand the power of the work I was doing, because I developed my concept of imagined power and real power. . . . It was like that whole thing of imagined power to have the connections

> within the communities, the networking ability, that people began to see it as a [real] political force.[2]

As her work with youth progressed, Baca honed her sense of imagined and real power into an artistic and activist career of unmistakable political force. Her combined educational training, steadfast commitment to public art, organizing savvy, and artistic talent expanded her position with the LADRP to director of the City Wide Mural Program in 1974. That same year Baca cofounded SPARC (Social and Public Art Resource Center), a nonprofit community arts center which remains a cornerstone of the Los Angeles cultural infrastructure. The prevailing creative force behind SPARC, Baca gained international recognition for herself and the institution through *The Great Wall* mural project. Approximately seven years in the making and featuring the work of over two hundred youths, the mural stretches through 2,435 feet of the San Fernando Valley's Tujunga Wash. The mural depicts a counternarrative of California history by documenting the struggles against racism, sexism, homophobia, labor exploitation, and anti-Semitism waged by women and people of color. Since directing *The Great Wall* project, Baca has also brought her expertise to university settings, where she has assumed professorships at the University of California at Irvine and the University of California at Los Angeles. All the while, she has remained a seminal figure in developing the visual vocabulary and iconography of Chicano art, particularly its feminist dimensions. Despite her veritable achievements in professional and public art arenas, however, little attention has been devoted to understanding, let alone documenting, the range of cultural work performed by Baca and her peers during the Chicano movement. This is the case predominantly because the Chicano Arts movement and the larger Chicano Power Movement to which it was intimately linked have received but scant attention from scholars and cultural critics outside the fields of Chicana and Chicano Studies.[3] Even within the fields of Chicana and Chicano Studies, scholars have only recently begun to illuminate the ways in which art, culture, and politics merged during the movement.[4] My foremost intent in this chapter is to examine the cultural work performed by Judith Baca and thus build a better understanding of the roles artists played in the Chicano movement. Using Baca's experience as a case study, I seek to offer insights into the imbricated patterns of culture and politics as they were woven throughout the course of the Chicano movement.

Examining the myriad skills Baca cultivated in her work with youth offers insight into some of the multiple ways artists were called upon to serve their communities during this period of heightened political activity. An analysis of Baca's work with youth during the movement reveals that she, in effect, acted as the channel through which various constituencies involved in the process of cultural production negotiated their interactions and concomitant struggles for power. Putting up a single mural, for instance, required that Baca finesse her emerging Chicana feminist vision through a series of interactions with the predominantly Chicano male youth of her crew, community members, other movement artists/activists, and city officials. To run a successful youth art program, Baca also soon realized that she must account for the needs of the youth she solicited and thus became a provider of social services such as on-site counseling and shelters for runaway and abused children. Consequently, Baca developed a system in which the process of mural production yielded not only empowering images, but an educative and politicizing process as well. A more detailed analysis of how Baca developed this political force through her work with youth will be the focus of this chapter. First, however, it is important to understand how the project of organizing youth emerged as a core concern of the Chicano movement.

The Chicano Power movement, roughly marked by the years 1965 to 1 980, witnessed a moment in which ethnic Mexicans in the United States waged an unprecedented campaign for their civil and human rights. Though they drew on a long history of political activity forged by preceding generations, Chicano youth of the 1960s adopted a stance that specifically questioned the political and cultural expediency of assimilation—particularly as it was articulated by the so-called Mexican American generation that came of age during World War II and the cold war.[5] Like many of their contemporaries, young Chicanos also drew inspiration from the civil rights movement and became increasingly politicized amidst rising resistance to the Vietnam War. As such, Chicano youth developed an assertive rhetoric (Chicanismo) and style of politics which constituted an important, if seldom recognized, presence within the 1960s New Left.

And like the New Left, Chicano activists' agenda for change was particularly wide in scope. Inflected as it was by regional concerns and ideological variations ranging from liberal democratic reform, cultural nationalism, and Marxism-Leninism, movement activists nevertheless developed an agenda that sought to create new institutions and reform existing ones across local, state, and national levels. Educational access and reform, workers' and immigrants' rights, police brutality, drug abuse, the Vietnam War, political representation, and assertions of cultural pride were among the primary issues that galvanized Chicano activism during this era.

Though movement participants no doubt understood their activism as benefitting Chicanos as a whole, energies were most consistently directed at those sectors of the community deemed most vulnerable. To this extent, the United Farm Workers Association, with its two charismatic leaders, Delores Huerta and César Chávez, captured the attention and organizing imagination of many as they exposed the plight of migrant farm workers. While the UFW's struggles in the fields brought a degree of national media attention to the Chicano movement, efforts aimed at improving the life chances of Chicano youth were more central to the movement's overall vision and goals. After all, Chicana and Chicano youth were the ones suffering through irrelevant and inadequate education; they were the ones being drafted and killed in disproportionate numbers in the Vietnam War; they were the ones regularly exposed to the dangers of gang violence and drug abuse; they were most often the targets of racist and brutal law enforcement agencies; and, very often, they were the ones initiating activism in resistance to the inequities they faced. In fact, Chicano youth constituted a pivotal presence in three of the movement's most historic events: the 1968 East Los Angeles High School Blow Outs, the 1969 Chicano Youth Liberation Conference, and the 1970 Chicano Moratorium against the Vietnam War.

That concerns facing youth were synonymous with the movement's overall agenda is evidenced in the range of organizations that served as vehicles for their mobilization and political and cultural education. The Movimiento Estudiantil Chicano de Aztlán (Chicano Student Movement of Aztlán or MEChA), for example, was created in 1969 by high school and college students as a means of coordinating their nationwide efforts under the helm of a single organization. Other organizations, such as the Brown Berets, offered Chicano youth a vehicle for community service fashioned after the discipline and paramilitary structure of the Black Panthers.[6] Others still, such as the Centro de Acción Social Autónomo-Hermandad de General Trabajadores (Center for Autonomous Social Action—General Brotherhood of Workers, or CASA), posed a more rigorous ideological base (Marxism-Leninism) for youth committed to international labor and immigration issues.

Artists were forthcoming in their responses to the needs of youth as well. One of the primary means through which artists engaged youth was through the project of cultural reclamation. The project of cultural reclamation was an incredibly diverse phenomenon that permeated all aspects of movement activism and ideology. At its core, however, lay the imperative of creating and expressing new forms of identity that buttressed and furthered the sense of change manifested in other sectors of movement activism. Primarily, this meant replacing dominant cultural constructions of ethnic Mexicans as culturally base and inferior with images of cultural pride and resistance. Artists of the period visually announced the ideological, historical, and cultural components of Chicano identity by drawing genealogical lines through Amerindian societies, Spanish-European conquest and *mestizaje* (the historical process of miscegenation in Mexico), revolutionary Mexico, and the contemporary culture of ethnic Mexicans. Nuclear Chicano families and everyday barrio life were lauded as manifestations and the direct depositories of this line of heritage.

Artistic and cultural production both marked and directed the endeavor of cultural reclamation and, to this end, artists made deliberate attempts at recovering and refashioning certain aesthetic principles. Mandates such as "El Plan Espiritual de Aztlán" (the Spiritual Plan of Aztlán), one of the most important ideological statements to emerge from the Chicano movement, charged artists with the task of "producing literature and art that is appealing to our people and relates to our revolutionary culture."[7] Part of this task, as Tomás Ybarra Frausto has noted, involved creating a bank of visual images and iconography that edified the shift in Chicano consciousness.[8] Consequently, many artists set about creating art that was public, accessible, powerful, and didactic.

Insofar as Chicana and Chicano artists responded to the charge of "El Plan Espiritual de Aztlán" and the overall ethos it articulated, it is clear that their activism affected deep and lasting changes that transcend the simple production and recycling of cultural images. Recognizing cultural organizing and production as interventions not only in the realm of representation, but as a critical catalyst in the chemistry of political and social struggles waged by ethnic Mexicans during the movement, it is perhaps best to think of artists like Judith Baca as cultural workers.[9] Identifying artists as cultural workers takes as its premise one of the fundamental assertions of cultural studies: that culture is a site where power relations are mutually shaped, expressed, and contested. Consequently, recognizing Chicano artists as cultural workers testifies to the melding of art and politics during the Chicano movement by acknowledging the role artists played in leading the movement's rank and file, particularly youth, toward new notions of identity and reinvigorated notions of community.

It is in this context that the cultural work of Judith Baca is best understood. Though scores of artists and arts organizers contributed their skills and leadership abilities to "la causa," examining Baca's organizing efforts with youth provides an opportunity to identify specific qualities embedded in the project of cultural work. And, as mentioned earlier, perhaps the most distinguishing feature of Baca's role as cultural worker involved the demands placed on her as an intermediary between the various groups involved in the processes of cultural production. It is this relationship on which I will now focus my attention.

As a new employee of the LADRP in 1969, Baca was first assigned to teach art classes to children and the elderly at community centers and parks in East Los Angeles. Her attention, however, was immediately drawn to the placas (gang insignias), graffiti, and tattoos generated by the youth who occupied the fringes of these public spaces. Soon realizing that there was no programming for this segment of youth, Baca translated her affinity for their cultural production into a means of organizing. Of this development Baca recalled:

> The kids basically occupied the centers. They occupied those parks. They played dominoes on the exterior, they drank, they did drugs and there was no programming for these kids. So I very fast began to see all the placas on the walls[.] I began to be very interested in the graffiti, was very interested in the tattoos and I started making friends with these people . . . because I was teaching from ten to twelve and from three to five and had all these hours to kill in between. So I would hang out in the parks and I would bring in my paintings [because] they were interested in them. They would bring in drawings on paper bags and, you know, tattoo designs, and I started noticing some of these kids were really hot at making this, doing the spray-can stuff. . . . They would do performances and show me how they did these things and I started to become really good friends with these guys—the so-called criminals, the element that was considered to be the most feared.[10]

Baca's proposal to paint with the "most feared" in her spare time received almost immediate support from city officials at the LADRP. After all, these were the youth that Neighborhood Youth Corps "cool-out" monies were targeting, yet were having little success reaching.[11] Bringing youth from different parks together to paint, however, was another matter, for it meant negotiating longstanding gang turf rivalries. Though it was immediately apparent to Baca that Chicano youth "controlled" the parks and that she "couldn't have put up anything on the East Side without their permission and without their support," she was initially less aware of protocols that restricted the movement of those youth through certain parts of the city.[12] Inspired as she was by movement calls for ethnic solidarity, Baca continued earning the respect and trust of gang members via the exchange of art and ideas and eventually succeeded in forming treaties that allowed for the execution of jointly painted mural projects.

Even when gang treaties were negotiated, they did not always guarantee the safety of those painting on the walls. Thus, as the mural director, Baca had to develop mechanisms to ensure her and her crew's safety. Often this meant tapping into the existing surveillance structures practiced by the youth she organized. For example, when painting the *Mi Abuelita Mural* (*My Grandmother*) on the band shell in Hollenbeck Park, Baca recalled: "And so here I was with this giant group of gang boys who I negotiated treaties with, and who essentially had to place guards around the walls where we were painting. Like in Hollenbeck Park we had to have lookouts, so that we wouldn't get shot up by the neighborhood there, who might be pissed off that I brought somebody [in] from a different territory."[13] Enlisting the help of those who potentially might cause danger was another effective tactic invoked when painting in the street. Such was the case, for example, when Baca and her female assistant arrived at the Hollenbeck site one night to find that her crew had not shown up. Determined to paint anyway, Baca began setting up her scaffolding and projector when a man wearing an overcoat (in the middle of summer) approached. Baca described the incident accordingly:

> All the boys were supposed to show up, and of course, they didn't show up; I think they got drunk instead or something. And finally they did show up late, but this young girl named Rachel Apolloca and I went there. And we drove up the van and put this opaque projector on top of the van, in front of the band shell—and its very dark out there, and very out in the middle of nowhere, with this lake, and, you know, two young women in Hollenbeck Park at night is a, you know, nobody does that. And we started to put this image up, and some man came up with an overcoat—it was midsummer, right? . . . And it was not a good sign. He said, "You guys could get shot out here." And I said, "Oh, really?" Then, "If you think maybe you could help us move this thing?" So he came up on the thing and he took off his jacket to help move the scaffolding, and in his jacket I could feel the weight of his pistol. And I think he was on some kind of drugs or something, but we enlisted his support. And very often that was the case. I mean, there were like potentially difficult situations in which I enlisted the support of the person.[14]

Despite the dangers she and her crews faced, Baca's organizing resulted in murals being painted in several locations including the Casa Maravilla gang rehabilitation center, the Hollenbeck Park band shell (*Mi Abuelita*), and the Wabash Recreation Center (*Medusa Head*). As such, the murals became, as Marcos Sánchez-Tranquilino has demonstrated, "markers of cultural and territorial signification" to the point where Chicano youth from different areas began calling the LADRP and even the mayor's office requesting that the "mural lady" come paint with them as well.[15]

With a growing reputation cultivated through youth response, "splashy press headlines," and a political ethos that prized neighborhood art programs as a "safe" and "expedient" means of occupying youth energies, LADRP general manager, Cy Grieben, appointed Baca director of East Side Murals in 1973 and, in the following year, director of City Wide Murals. For Baca, this constituted "a real major breakthrough" because it allowed her "to work full-time on mural production" with youth including members of the Evergreen, White Fence, and Varrio Nuevo Estrada gangs.[16] And while the city's support of Baca's efforts did, in fact, represent an important development in the Chicano Arts and Chicano Power movements, her successes also animated tensions among Chicano artists and within the larger Chi-

Fig. 13.1. Baca (seated bottom right) and community youth artists applying the first layers of paint for the *Mi Abuelita Mural* located in the band shell of Hollenbeck Park, 1970. The mural was sponsored by the local community and the City of Los Angeles Summer Youth Program. (Courtesy of SPARC)

Fig. 13.2. *Mi Abuelita Mural*, 1970. Though early murals such as *Mi Abuelita* did not exhibit the technical quality of later projects such as *The Great Wall*, Baca's work with the Los Angeles Department of Recreation and Parks as director of East Side Murals was instrumental in her development of a system through which to engage successful community art projects. (Courtesy of SPARC)

cano community. In negotiating these tensions—which generally stemmed from her presence as an artistically and politically competent woman who identified with marginalized youth and their cultural production—Baca continued to hone her skills as an effective cultural worker. Such developments also placed her in a liminal space between the youth she organized, her cultural worker colleagues in the movement, the Chicano community in whose neighborhoods she painted, feminist artists with whom she was becoming increasingly connected, and the city officials who inconsistently supported her work.

Employed full-time as director, Baca orchestrated a system for conducting public arts projects. This system involved tapping into the art talents of gang youth, collaborating with them to come up with a design for a given project, and then soliciting approval/support from members of the particular community in which the mural was to be painted. These meetings, however, often exposed conflicting community perspectives about the youth she was organizing and thus highlighted the degree of diplomacy and determination Baca needed as an effective cultural worker. The first meeting Baca held in preparation for the Wabash Recreation Center project, for example, illustrates some of the community attitudes she was forced to confront.

After an intensive process of devising an image for their mural, Baca and her crew called a community meeting to solicit support (both in terms of approving the image and financing materials for painting) from members of the Boyle Heights community, which the recreation center served. The meeting, Baca remembered, attracted mostly parents of the kids and some local business owners, one of whom donated fifty dollars toward their efforts. Evidencing generational tensions within the meeting and, by extension, those circulating through the larger Chicano community, a woman's voice from the back of the room insisted, "You shouldn't do anything. Don't give them that money. They don't deserve anything. These are the kids who are writing all over the walls and ruining everything in this neighborhood. They're giving Mexicans a bad name."[17] As the woman continued to voice her opinions, Baca recalled that "this woman who stood up was infuriating the gang kids—the boys who were with me—and I was getting very worried that she would go too far. And finally Arturo, who was one of the kids who was a fairly strong leader in the neighborhood, jumped up and said, 'You shut up, Mom.' "[18] Registering the importance of the moment, Baca explained:

> It blew me away, because what was going on basically, was [that it was] the parents of these kids who were so angry at them [for being] rebellious and not [being] good sort of traditional Mexican boys. . . . I kept finding this problem with the police and the community. The boys in the neighborhood gangs were so despised that any attempt to organize them, in a certain way, tainted me as well."[19]

If Baca was "tainted" in the eyes of the police and certain elements of the community, her work with youth also drew mixed support from other Chicano artists and thus evidences another set of conflictual relations she negotiated as a cultural worker. Given that collaboration and the cultivation of "indigenous"[20] art forms were commonly held aspirations within the Chicano Arts movement, it is ironic that Baca, a clear purveyor of both, would incur resistance from among her peers.[21] Neverthe-

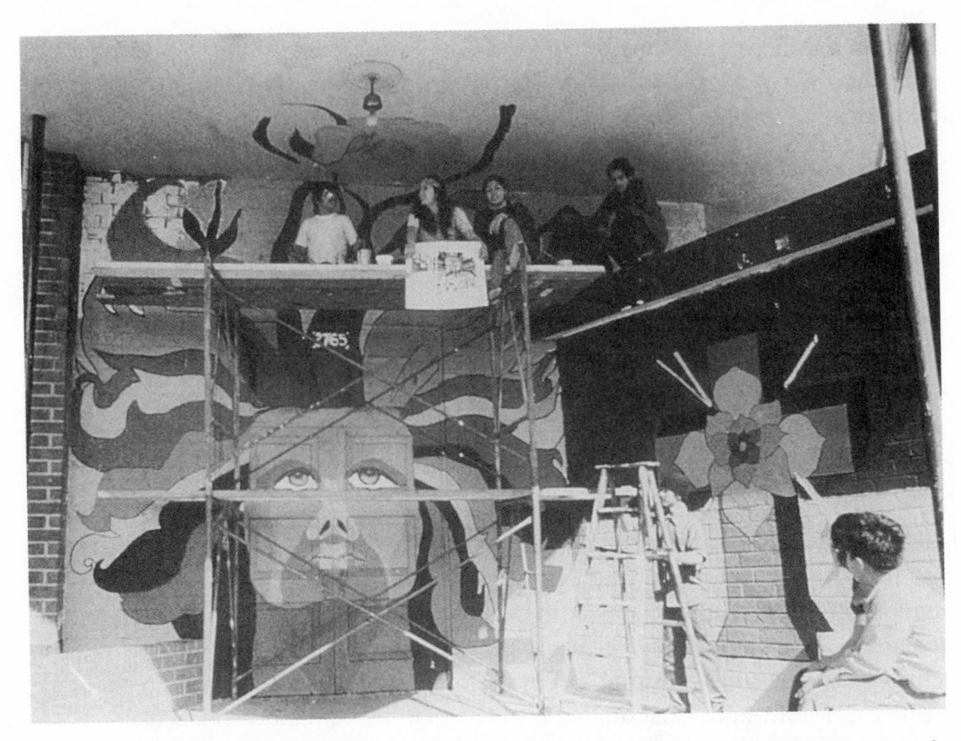

Fig. 13.3. Baca (center, displaying image) and youth on scaffolding while working on the *Medusa Head* mural for the Wabash Recreation Center, 1973. The mural was sponsored by the local community and the Los Angeles Department of Recreation and Parks. (Courtesy of SPARC)

less, the prevalence of patriarchal conceptions of art and culture embedded in the Chicano movement clearly directed Baca's movement toward what might be deemed the "margins" of the Chicano Arts community. More specifically, as an artist, a lesbian, and a feminist organizing street youth in communities she was not immediately recognized as a member, Baca recalled that

> in the East Side, in the area of Latin culture, and Chicano culture—I was really an oddity. I wasn't the girlfriend of one of the men, and I was an artist in myself.... Most of the other Chicanas were only there through the vehicle of a man—either a boyfriend or their husband or their brother—and who were not women who seriously had studied art. So I was a very rare circumstance. I was a very rare person [in that] I have a degree in art.... I was not treated seriously by the men, nor considered a peer. So I wasn't getting the support from them or anything."[22]

While sexism within the Chicano Arts movement immediately placed Baca on unequal footing with her male counterparts, her liberal conception of art and her commitment to Chicano street youth only added to her predicament. For example, as indicated earlier, Baca's work with Chicano youth in the parks of East Los Angeles led her to recognize their graffiti and tattooing as art forms. However, when presenting her views at an anti-graffiti conference hosted by Mechicano Art Center—

one of the busiest centers for Chicano art in the early 1970s—she was "laughed right out of the room." Such humiliation only fueled Baca's conviction however, as she recounted:

> At that point I remember saying, "I'm going to paint. I've organized a group of kids from these different gangs, and I'm going to paint together with them." And I remember being told that was a foolish point of view. So I mean, [Mechicano] was like the seat of Chicano art, and it was like my idea was too radical for them. And that it was like children's art and not really considered serious, and also this graffiti thing was like I was encouraging graffiti in a certain way. . . . And that was a lot of the opinion everywhere at that point, you know, to work with these kids in the community—even though you couldn't have put anything up on the East Side without their permission and without their support—you were, in a way, supporting a negative element. . . . My sense was that I was pretty much out there by myself—particularly organizing kids, in the way I was doing it.[23]

Baca's strong convictions about youth organizing coupled with her access to city and state resources as director of the City Wide Mural Program generated a degree of animosity from certain segments of the Chicano Arts community and thus contributed to her sense of liminality. Such animosities, fellow artist Carlos Almaraz recalled, actually placed her in a position of physical danger since "she worked in the same territory as Mechicano." Elaborating on the situation, Almaraz explained:

> She [Baca] would come all the way to the East Side to work in Lincoln Park and Hollenbeck Park. She was not a well-liked person by certain members [of Mechicano], even to the point of it [being] dangerous for her to be around them. They hated her. Partly because they didn't know her, partly because she did win grants and she did it with all, you know, the savvy of a political person, but there was still a lot of anger, resentment. Mechicano eventually went under, for all those problems that started showing up then. It was male dominated. It tended to be one clique.[24]

While remaining something of an enigma in male-dominated at movement circles, Baca continued her commitment to youth and public art. Of this time in her life, Baca recalled: "Maybe its something about my personality more than about the history of the time—but there was an intense involvement [organizing youth] and nothing else existed."[25] Thus, through a combination of dedication and skills, Baca developed a community art system of power and productivity which began to extend beyond the bounds of the predominantly Chicano communities of East Los Angeles. In her first year as director of the City Wide Mural Program, for example, Baca directed the completion of forty community murals across the city with a budget of approximately $150,000.[26] Such productivity was due in large part to the organizational system she developed, a system in which she integrated her knowledge of local neighborhoods, youth, and city bureaucratic structures with the collaborative methods established by the Chilean mural brigades active during the Popular Unity period of Salvador Allende.[27] Attesting to the system's effectiveness, Baca noted that the contents of the murals became increasingly outspoken as community members developed more articulate means of expressing themselves. As she described it:

> The content of the murals became stronger and stronger. There were pieces on immigration, there were pieces on drug abuse, there were pieces on police brutality, there were pieces on nature, and there were pieces on history. I mean, it was just a whole variety of different types. Children's pieces that were maps of their local area. It was a wonderful and amazing variety of stuff.[28]

So effective were the painting programs in broadcasting a seldom-heard public voice, by her second year as City Wide director, the mayor and city council members were pressuring her to tone down the content of the murals lest program funding be withdrawn. Community members responded with a series of letter-writing campaigns demanding the program's continuation. And while such efforts ultimately succeeded in sustaining the City Wide Mural Program for another three years, Baca recalled eventually having worked herself into an "untenable position" between the city officials who made it increasingly more difficult for her to administer the program and community members who were becoming more aggressive in their public art statements. Baca described the predicament accordingly:

> Suddenly I was hiring over a thousand people in the communities per year, and I was [trying] to figure out how to get them to a location for tuberculosis tests conducted by the city. And, of course, they didn't have any transportation or money. And the payments were taking six to eight weeks, and its very hard to explain to a kid in the gang, he's not going to work today, he's going to get paid in eight weeks. So it was becoming just an untenable position. I was stuck between the city and the community. And at both ends I was despised—the community because they saw me as being part of the city; the city because they saw me being a community person and a radical. So I had this really difficult place to be. And It really took a toll on me.[29]

Such circumstances led Baca to co-found SPARC with her partner Christina Schlesinger in 1974. SPARC was initially conceived as a means of circumventing city control over *The Great Wall* project Baca had designed while still directing the City Wide Mural Program. However, what once constituted a temporary conduit for nonprofit and private monies generated for a single project, by 1977 had grown to a full-scale nonprofit community arts institution. SPARC grew as an institution alongside the rippling growth of *The Great Wall* project. More specifically, through her close experiences working with youth, Baca became intimately aware of the everyday problems they faced as young people, problems which, unchecked, seriously endangered the lives of her crew members, not to mention the successful completion of their mural projects.[30] Consequently, by 1983, Baca's efforts with SPARC on *The Great Wall* generated a network of social services including counseling services, shelters for runaway and battered kids, incest awareness and support, and suicide-prevention hot lines to serve the needs of those who worked on the mural.

Though the system of services she implemented for the project took a number of years to generate and perfect, they provided important spaces for developing the mural's themes of interracial relationships and community solidarity. In conjunction with the crisis-oriented services, Baca also assembled a team of artists, teachers, historians, oral historians, and other cultural workers who worked with the youth

Fig. 13.4. "Origins of the Gay Civil Rights Movement" section of *The Great Wall* mural, pictured in the precolor, undercoating stage, Summer, 1983. Because the site was below ground and secluded from the traffic and interactions normally associated with street mural production, the Tujunga Wash proved an ideal "laboratory" for engaging interethnic and intergenerational exchange and collaboration critical in the mural's conception. Nevertheless, as the sign featured above the scaffolding indicates, Baca's system of painting still deemed community input an integral part of the mural's design and production. (Courtesy of SPARC)

to further solidify the content of the murals. Thus, Baca and her cultural worker counterparts animated a system of public art in which the process of image production was as educative and transformative as the finished product. She described this relationship accordingly:

> What I've had to do is focus increasingly on the support services that will accomplish the goals of the interrelationship between the different cultures, which is the focus of *The Great Wall.* You know, the kind of naive focus was to put alongside of each other the stories of different ethnic groups and the history of those ethnic groups . . . and as we got increasingly better at relating to each another [through the system of services and education], we have also gotten better at relating visually across the boundaries of Chicano history, black history, Jewish history, and Asian history. Its all one piece now, because now we understand in a better way the connection. And *The Great Wall* really then is just the tip of the iceberg. It's just really one part; the image is one part of the whole concept. And the most interesting concept, even, aside from how to orchestrate that application of paint [is that] . . . the imaging is better as we've gotten increasingly better at dealing with our team-building and our interracial relationships.[31]

Though once having expressed doubts about the political implications of her work with youth, Baca's efforts clearly registered as impressive with those who encouraged her to run for City Council, become an educator, or work fulltime as an arts administrator. Nor did it fail to leave a lasting impression on the youth who participated in her projects, for as she related in the interview: "It's amazing, because I get a lot of feedback, and I'm always sort of surprised. I don't think I really get how much it has an impact, how much it changes people."[32] And while this essay has sought to demonstrate the ways in which Baca's cultural work with youth constituted an important facet of activism waged by artists during the Chicano movement, what is perhaps implied throughout is the reciprocity of this relationship. More specifically, while Baca has clearly demonstrated a steadfast commitment to working with youth, it is seldom recognized that such work would have been much more difficult, if not impossible, had the youth not deemed it viable or interesting. Perhaps even less acknowledged is the fact that in tapping into their creative modes of expression (i.e., gang writing, graffiti, tattooing, car customizing, speech, and dress), these same youth also played a constitutive role in shaping the styles, techniques, and sensibilities of the emerging Chicano Arts movement.

If Baca's activism with youth sheds new light on the development of the Chicano Arts movement, then following the channels through which she negotiated her brand of cultural work also draws attention to another strand in the weave of politics and culture during the Chicano Power movement as well. More specifically, Baca's role as an artist, community liason, provider of social services, and administrator exemplifies how specific sites of power were accessed (LADRP) as well as created (SPARC) through activist efforts during the Chicano movement. Such recognitions make a strong case for interpreting the role of Chicano artists as that of cultural workers while simultaneously allowing for the recuperation of some of the most lasting achievements of the movement as a whole.

NOTES

I would like to thank the editors, Joe Austin and Mike Willard, for their enduring patience and incisive editorial skill. I would also like to acknowledge those colleagues and friends who helped me think through various parts of this essay, especially Richard Cándida Smith, Ernesto Chávez, Alejandra Marchevsky, Jason Elias, members of the University of Michigan's Latino Research Collective—Colectiva, and Dita Cárdenas. As is customary, I take full responsibility for the ideas presented here. Thanks also go out to the staff at the Archives of American Art: Paul Karlstrom, Barbara Bishop, Laela Weisbaum, and Marian Kovinick. In addition, I would like to express my gratitude to the staff at the Social and Public Art Resource Center, especially Reina Prado and Debra Padilla, for their professional research assistance and good spirit. Obviously, I owe my deepest thanks to Judith F. Baca for her support, vision, and continued dedication. Finally, props to my sister Jana, Brad Karns, and Grendel for opening their home to me while writing.

1. Judith F. Baca interviewed by Amalia Mesa Bains August 5 and 6, 1986. Archives of American Art, Smithsonian Institution, 32. Subsequent citations will read, "Baca, interview, AAA." Since this interview serves as the main primary resource from which this essay is developed, I am compelled to speak briefly about its contents and the uses of oral history in my work. A tremendously rich historical document, this interview offers countless insights

into the nature of Baca's development as an artist and an activist during the Chicano movement. The interview takes the shape of a life-story narrative and thus presents an opportunity to consider the dual process of documentation and meaning-making. Reading the interview, I have concentrated on both the cultural work performed by Baca as well as the meaning she and Amalia Mesa Bains attributed to it at a later date. At times these processes are nearly indistinguishable since memory and experience are often articulated for the purpose of assigning new meaning to an already layered understanding of the past. Nevertheless, being attentive to the way memory is selectively invoked and continually reshaped by contemporary concerns helps us understand the relationship between individual subjectivity, communal memory, and collective consciousness.

For those interested in the subject of Chicano art and culture, it should be noted that the Archives of American Art houses a collection of several oral histories with Chicana and Chicano artists. The AAA is currently expanding this collection through the Smithsonian Institution's Latino Oral History Project, for which the author is conducting interviews with Gronk, John Valadez, Frank Romero, Gilbert Luján, Roberto de la Rocha, and Elsa Flores.

2. Baca, interview, AAA, 32.

3. Key works in the movement's historiography include Juan Gómez-Quiñones, *Mexican Students por la Raza: The Chicano Student Movement in Southern California, 1967–1977* (Santa Barbara, CA: Editorial La Causa, 1978), and *Chicano Politics: Reality and Promise, 1940–1990* (Albuquerque: University of New Mexico Press, 1990); Carlos Muñoz, Jr., *Youth, Identity, Power: The Chicano Movement* (New York: Verso, 1989); Ignacio García, *United We Win: The Rise and Fall of La Raza Unida Party* (Tucson: University of Arizona, Mexican American Studies and Research Center, 1989); Marguerite Marin, *Social Protest in an Urban Barrio: A Study of the Chicano Movement, 1966–1974* (Lanham, MD: University Press of America, 1991); Ernesto Chávez, "Creating Aztlán: The Chicano Movement in Los Angeles, 1966–1978," Ph.D. diss., UCLA, 1994; David G. Gutiérrez, "CASA in the Chicano Movement: Ideology and Organizational Politics in the Chicano Community, 1968–1978," Stanford Center for Chicano Research, Working Paper Series, no. 5 (1984), and *Walls and Mirrors: Mexican Americans, Mexican Immigrants, and the Politics of Ethnicity* (Berkeley: University of California Press, 1995); Armando Navarro, *Mexican American Youth Organization: Avant Garde of the Chicano Movement in Texas* (Austin: University of Texas Press, 1995); Angie Chabram-Dernersesian, "I Throw Punches for My Race, but I Don't Want to Be a Man: Writing Us—Chica–nos (Girl, Us)/Chicanas—into the Movement Script," in Lawrence Grossberg, Cary Nelson, and Paula Treichler, eds., *Cultural Studies* (New York: Routledge, 1992):81–96; Ramón, A. Gutiérrez, "Community, Patriarchy, and Individualism: The Politics of Chicano History and the Dream of Equality," *American Quarterly* 45.1 (March 1993):44–72; Mario T. García, *Memories of Chicano History: The Life and Narrative of Bert Corona* (Berkeley: University of California Press, 1994); Alma M. García, "The Development of Chicana Feminist Discourse, 1970–1980," in Ellen Carol DuBois and Vicki Ruiz, eds., *Unequal Sisters: A Multi-Cultural Reader in U.S. Women's History* (New York: Routledge, 1990):418–431; F. Arturo Rosales, *Chicano! The History of the Mexican American Civil Rights Movement* (Houston: Arte Público Press, 1996); Edward J. Escobar, "The Dialectics of Repression: The Los Angeles Police Department and the Chicano Movement, 1968–1971," *Journal of American History* 79:4 (March 1993):1483–1514; and Margaret Rose, "Traditional and Nontraditional Patterns of Female Activism in the United Farm Workers of America, 1962–1980," *Frontiers* 11:1 (1990):26–32.

4. See for example, Yolanda Broyles-González, *El Teatro Campesino: Theatre in the Chicano Movement* (Austin: University of Texas Press, 1994); Chabram-Dernersesian, "I Throw Punches for My Race"; José Limón, *Mexican Ballads, Chicano Poems: History and Influence*

in Mexican-American Social Poetry (Berkeley: University of California Press, 1992); Eva Sperling and Holly Barnett-Sánchez, eds., *Signs from the Heart: California Chicano Murals* (Venice, CA, and Albuquerque, NM: Social and Public Art Resource Center and University of New Mexico Press, 1990); Shifra Goldman, *Dimensions of the Americas: Art and Social Change in Latin America and the United States* (Chicago: University of Chicago Press, 1994); Richard Griswold del Castillo, Teresa McKenna, and Yvonne Yarbro-Bejarano, eds., *Chicano Art: Resistance and Affirmation, 1965–1985* (Los Angeles: UCLA Wight Art Gallery, 1991); Tomás Ybarra Frausto, "The Chicano Movement/The Movement of Chicano Art," in Ivan Karp and Steven Levine, eds., *Exhibiting Cultures: The Poetics and Politics of Museum Display* (Washington, DC: Smithsonian Institution Press, 1993):128–150, and "The Chicano Movement in a Multicultural/Multinational Society," in George Yudice, Jean Franco, and Juan Flores, eds., *On Edge: The Crisis of Contemporary Latin American Culture* (Minneapolis: University of Minnesota Press, 1992):207–216; Marcos Sánchez-Tranquilino, "Space, Power, and Youth Culture: Mexican American Grafitti and Chicano Murals in East Los Angeles, 1972–1978," in Brenda Jo Bright and Liza Bakewell, eds., *Looking High and Low: Art and Cultural Identity* (Tucson: University of Arizona Press, 1995): 55–88.

5. As may be expected, historical studies have shown that the Mexican American generation was much more diverse in its political perspectives and organizational agendas. While Chicanos participated in radical labor/political movements, some of the most visible and lasting organizations such as the G.I. Forum, the League of United Latin American Citizens (LULAC), and the Mexican American Movement (MAM) did espouse a brand of politics that asserted that ethnic Mexicans should strive to become part of the United States social fabric. When considering such perspectives, however, it is imperative that one keep in mind the hegemonic power of Cold War anticommunism and Red baiting. George J. Sánchez's *Becoming Mexican American: Ethnicity, Culture, and Identity in Chicano Los Angeles, 1900–1945* (New York: Oxford University Press, 1993); Mario T. García's *Mexican Americans: Leadership, Ideology, and Identity, 1930–1960* (New Haven: Yale University Press, 1989), and Vicki L. Ruiz's *Cannery Women, Cannery Lives: Mexican Women, Unionization, and the California Food Processing Industry, 1930–1950* (Albuquerque: University of New Mexico Press, 1987) are three of the most noted studies of this time period. Gutiérrez's *Walls and Mirrors*; Gómez-Quiñones's *Chicano Politics*; and Chávez's "Creating Aztlán" offer valuable analyses of the era as well.

6. For more on this see Ernesto Chávez's chapter in this anthology, "Birth of a New Symbol: The Brown Berets and the Gendered Construction of the Chicano Nation." For a more general discussion of the masculinist nature of the Chicano movement, see Chabram-Dernersessian, "I Throw Punches for My Race," and Gutiérrez, "Community, Patriarchy, and Individualism."

7. "El Plan Espiritual de Aztlán," quoted from Luis Valdez and Stan Steiner, *Aztlán: An Anthology of Mexican American Literature* (New York: Alfred A. Knopf, 1972):402.

8. Ybarra Frausto, "The Chicano Movement/The Movement of Chicano Art."

9. I have chosen to identify Chicano artists as cultural workers foremost because they identify themselves as such in all the interviews I examined for the larger essay from which this piece is developed. In addition, while I feel the need to distinguish the type of activism that artists engaged in during the movement, I am uncomfortable with viewing their leadership roles as that of organic intellectuals. To my thinking, cultural workers offer a close companion to the Gramscian notion of organic intellectuals. Nevertheless, the designation of cultural worker holds more accurate appeal because it elides the essentializing aspects embedded in the distinction of "organic." Instead, the idea of cultural worker allows for a simultaneous recognition of Baca's (and most of her Chicana and Chicano artist peers) work-

ing-class background as well as her professional training as an artist. The concept also acknowledges how these qualities combined with her passion for working with youth to position her as a de facto leader in the movement. The idea of cultural workers is also attractive because its fluid definition allows for play between the often invoked conception of artists as visionary/creative individuals and the communal responsibility that Chicana and Chicano artists embraced during the movement. Finally, I find the notion of cultural worker attractive because it accounts for a type of cultural activism in which both process and product are important. That is, it acknowledges culture as a site of contestation and artists as both creative and organizing agents on that front. Mario T. Garcia confronts a similar dilemma in his study of the labor leader Bert Corona and opts for the term "community intellectual." See García, *Memories of Chicano History: The Life and Narrative of Bert Corona*. The works of George Lipsitz, especially *A Life in the Struggle: Ivory Perry and the Cultures of Opposition* (Philadelphia: Temple University Press, 1988), also has been helpful in my thinking through this issue.

10. Baca, interview, AAA, 20, 21.

11. Baca briefly touches upon this arrangement in the interview when describing how Neighborhood Youth Corps monies for her first project at the Casa Maravilla gang rehabilitation center were primarily designed to keep youth off the streets in the aftermath of the 1965 Watts civil disturbances. She states: "I was pretty much the first person in the city of Los Angeles to use Neighborhood Youth Corps money, which was being shipped into the *laderas* [slopes/hills] in large amounts because of the fact that they didn't want to have any more riots. So this money was quite abundant and most of the kids would be getting the money by just going to the park and picking up the check. It was sort of buy-off money." Baca, interview, AAA, 24. Joe Austin also brought this issue to my attention. See Joe Austin, "Of Murals and Cool Out Programs: The NEA's support for Community Murals in the 1970s," unpublished manuscript.

12. Baca, interview, AAA, 20, 23, 25.

13. Ibid., 24.

14. Ibid., 25–26.

15. Sánchez-Tranquilino, "Space, Power, and Youth Culture," 78. Baca, interview, AAA, 27.

16. Baca, interview, AAA 26–27.

17. Ibid., 31.

18. Ibid.

19. Ibid.

20. Meaning "everyday" or emerging from within the cultural context of Chicano communities.

21. Not to overstate the case, Baca did collaborate and exchange ideas with scores of artists, including Carlos Almaraz, Leonard Castellanos, Charles "Cat" Felix, Manuel Cruz, Judithe Hernandez, Patssi Valdez, and members of the Mujeres Muralistas.

22. Baca, interview, AAA, 35, 38.

23. Ibid., 23. The irony of Baca's situation at Mechicano is overwhelming since, almost simultaneously, grafitti was recognized as one of the foundational sources for artists developing an expressly Chicano image and iconographic vocabulary. In fact, two of the most celebrated moments in Chicano Art history—ASCO's tagging of the Los Angeles County Museum of Art in 1972 in response to its dismissal of Chicano art, and Los Four's historic exhibit at the same institution in 1974—feature graffiti as a definitive means of Chicano expression.

24. Carlos Almaraz interviewed by Margarita Nieto February 6, 13, and 20, July 31, 1986,

and January 29, 1987. Archives of American Art, Smithsonian Institution, 88. It should be noted that in her interview with the Archives of American Art, Baca recalls having positive collaborations with Leonard Castellanos, a founding member of Mechicano Art Center. Almaraz's observations, however, have been substantiated in other public sources. See, for example, Wayne Alaniz Healy's statement in *Chismearte* (Winter/Spring 1977):53.

25. Baca, interview, AAA, 29.

26. Ibid., 40–41. Shifra Goldman cites city funding at $100,000 for the first year. See, Goldman, *Dimensions of the Americas*, 214–215.

27. Baca relates having learned about the Chilean mural brigades during the early stages of the Chicano movement, when she first began working with the LADRP. During this period she "began to research and study everything [she] could get her hands on" and was particularly impressed by the Chilean muralists' style and efficiency. Consequently, when asked to expand her work in East Los Angeles to a citywide scale, Baca turned to the Chilean method as the model for her painting program. Describing the basic idea the Chileans developed, Baca states in the interview: "I learned about the Chileans, who had formed these brigades of painters, who stood in a line, each with a different color bucket, and within a matter of twenty minutes could put up an image that was a powerful image, politically. One person would go through and make symbols, another person would go through and do the lettering, that they could very quickly get something up." Baca, interview, AAA, 40.

28. Ibid., 41.

29. Ibid., 43.

30. Baca discusses several of the ways in which her work with youth led to the formation of intimate relationships with crew members and their families. For example, she recalled having become a "surrogate mother" to one of the boys on her crew as well as having to help the family of one of her crew members raise money for his burial after he was shot to death in a gang-related incident. Baca, interview, AAA, 29–30.

31. Ibid., 48–49.

32. Ibid., 48.

Chapter Fourteen

Knowing Their Place

Local Knowledge, Social Prestige, and the Writing Formation in New York City

Joe Austin

Why don't young people today know their place? This question is frequently asked of a younger generation by an older one that has conveniently forgotten its own history. "Place" in this question refers to the relative position of young people within the hierarchical social order: "It is not the *place* of young people to question an adult's authority." In this chapter, I will argue that young people do in fact *know their place*, perhaps better than the majority of adults, although I am using "place" in a sightly different sense. Here, "place" refers to a particular *network of localities* that young people might physically occupy: "I know a place we can hang out." These two "places" are closely related for young people; the ambiguity between these two "places" allows meanings to shift from one to the other. That ambiguity challenges the restrictions of one "place" by occupying the other.

The recurring tensions and continuous conflicts surrounding the ambiguous "place" of young people are the result of the historical formation of "youth" during the last century. The *place* of youth has been maintained at a low status within the social hierarchy marked by adult distrust of the "younger generation," increasing surveillance of youth, and the expansion of economic and social dependency on adults.[1] The creation and rapid growth of the "youth market," the centrality of young people as trend-setters and producers of new cultural forms, and the importance of the peer group as the primary arena of social identification have greatly increased young people's relative cultural and social autonomy from adults.[2] These trends, while producing social contradictions, occur simultaneously and synergetically; that is, they are not necessarily in opposition to one another.[3]

Young people's ambiguous and constantly renegotiated autonomy are central points of conflict surrounding their "place" (spatially) in the social world. For adults, these conflicts have been partially contained within *public space* through a haphazard combination of the consumer marketplace, minimally supervised activities, and state-enforced restrictions based on age. The result is that young people may occupy commercial spaces and attend adult-sponsored activities (such as sports), but under the tacit agreement that they are under the surveillance of responsible adults. State policies restrict access to goods, services, basic rights, and spaces deemed "inappropriate" for the age group (alcohol, bars, certain kinds of medical care—including abortion and birth control—driver's licenses, and so forth), which in turn place further constraints on mobility. Local policing authorities[4] function (ideally) to keep young people from "adjusting" their legally defined "place" through their own self-activity. These restrictions are compounded for young people of color and those from less affluent urban neighborhoods: "private" space in the home is less available, commercial spaces are much less inviting, economic resources more scarce, policing forces more hostile, the repercussions of challenge more pronounced.

Conflict arises in part because young peoples' low standing and relatively poor integration into the social order is in contradiction with their abilities and capacities. The restrictions on the lives of teenagers also contradict the ideologies of personal growth and democratic citizenship that are used to motivate their preparations for adulthood.[5] If one can really be anything, do anything, so long as one has the necessary responsibility and drive, then why is there a public curfew after 11 P.M. for all people under the age of eighteen? Thus, the specific ways in which "youth" has been historically shaped has left *young people* without legitimized spaces in which to *live out* their autonomy outside of adult surveillance. Young people are pushed to either "take place" by appropriating nomadic, temporary, abandoned, illegal, or otherwise unwatched spaces within the landscape, or to "hide in the light."[6] As my analysis will demonstrate, maintaining this type of hegemony is hard work, and often quite costly as well.

This chapter examines how local knowledges of the urban landscape were put to use by the writing ("graffiti") formation in New York City. By "knowing their place," writers were able to "claim a place" for themselves within a public order that often renders young people, particularly young people of color, as "invisible" at best and as "outsiders" more typically. In particular, I want to draw the reader's attention to the ways that the writing formation emerged around and through the appropriation of spaces and places that are designed for other purposes, and the importance of constructing a communication network in support of their "taking place."

A Very Brief Overview of a Complex Topic: Writing in New York City

Writing[7] was among the first of a cluster of new aesthetic practices now grouped together as "hip hop" that developed within the multiracial youth cultures of Harlem, El Barrio, the South Bronx, and central Brooklyn during the late 1960s and 1970s.[8] Writing practice is built around spectacularly calligraphied names—ranging from signatures to mural-sized works—written with spray paint and ink markers (often illegally) in public spaces.[9] Since the early 1980s, writing practice has moved out from the East Coast and become a significant international youth art movement, with practitioners in almost every major city in the world. Writing may be the most significant visual art movement of the late twentieth century—but that is another story.[10]

Like most of the new hip hop forms, writing drew upon an older tradition. The street graffiti written by Puerto Rican youths in Spanish Harlem, which consisted of a name or nickname and street number (e.g., JOHNNY of 83), was an important precursor.[11] The new writing practice differed from the older graffiti tradition in four important ways. First, the new writers wrote on the local walls, but they also crossed neighborhood boundaries. This not only helped to spread the practice to other areas of the city, but it also pushed beyond traditional, neighborhood-based notions of "respect," which was based on face-to-face recognition and local familiarity. Second, the new writers realized the potential of writing on a moving surface, including delivery trucks, buses, and subway trains. By writing on these moving surfaces, the name circulated throughout New York City, increasing its exposure. Third, the new writers sought recognition in the mass media and the city at large—"fame"—although the primary audience for their fame remained within their peer cultures, particularly other writers. Finally, the new writing quickly developed an aesthetic sophistication not found in any previous graffiti practice.[12]

Rejecting the alternative offered by territorial street gangs, writers created a new expressive form that both mimicked and mocked the status conventions of elites within the global city. Observing that "the famous" are distinguished from the average citizen by the ubiquity of their names in public space—on billboards, in neon, in magazines, newspapers, and other commercial media venues—writers asserted their "place" in the city alongside them. IBM, Prince, Ronald McDonald, Ronald Reagan, Beaver Cleaver, and Exxon occupy the same space and are forced to compete with KET, PHASE 2, TAKI 183, SAR, and POEM. Explaining their motives, writers often emphasize the conflictual class hierarchy of urban names—a hierarchy that works to circulate the names of "the famous" within the public sphere/public space while ignoring others.[13] Rather than passively observing the spectacle of personality that accompanies the promotion of the "star," writers instead actively entered into that spectacle, crafting their names and initials into striking aesthetic works on the walled streets and subways of the city. Holding little hope that they would be able to gain recognition through the "legitimate" opportunities open to them, writers literally "took the trains" and transformed the city subway system into a kind of communications network that supported an *alternative economy* of recognition and prestige. For those writers living in the South Bronx, Harlem, El Barrio, and central Brooklyn (where writing originated), their names also challenged the social "invisibility" and marginality of their neighborhoods.

The writers' transformation of the subways into a communication system allowed them to broadcast their writing and its claims to social prestige to the entire city and to each other across great distances. Perhaps more importantly, the writers grafted their communication system onto one of the primary structures of circulation that hold the fragmented city together: more than three million people a day ride the trains.[14] But this is not the only system of circulation that writers appropriated. Understanding New York to be a mediated city, constantly under surveillance by the print media, television, and film, writers worked to capture the "mainstream" media's circulation as well. Since the subways are icons of New York City itself, writers' works have appeared in the backgrounds of innumerable television shows, films, news photographs, paintings, and literary representations. On the trains, writers from marginalized neighborhoods "wrote back," asserting their *place* in the city; as the media watched the subways, writers' messages circulated all over the world.

From its inception, writing has been involved with the spectacle of the name and the fame and prestige associated with one's name being known by strangers as well as being respected among peers. That such an art would develop in New York City should come as no surprise. New York City is frequently mythologized in popular literature (and in its own boosterism) as a city where a person can "make a name for him/herself," where the individual can transform him/herself from a "nobody" into a celebrity whose autograph is collected. On the other hand, New York City holds a uniquely concentrated capacity to "make a name." The city is the hub of the global advertising industry, having the highest concentration of major firms and their ancillary support industries of any world city.[15] The commercial signs of New York City (billboards, public advertising, marquees) are almost a national landmark: the flashing neon signs in Times Square or on Broadway (often, corporate logos, brand names, or the names of celebrities and stars) are akin to Old Faithful or Mount Rushmore in the national imagination. Long before "tags" appeared in the urban landscape, New York was a city of the spectacularized name in public space.[16]

Like most urban youths, writers have an incredible "map" of the landscape surrounding them—young people *know their place.* TAKI 183, one of the earliest innovators of the new writing form, aspired to have his name noticed by a journalist or filmmaker and concentrated his writing efforts (while he made deliveries as a bicycle messenger) on the Upper East Side and the downtown business sections of Manhattan, where he knew the elite members of these occupations were likely to live and work. His plan worked. In February 1971, a *New York Times* reporter interviewed TAKI 183 (whose name appeared all over the city) and wrote a short article about him that included a sizable photograph of his writing. The number of names exploded into the hundreds of thousands after TAKI appeared in the *Times* as other urban youths took up the practice. During this period of development, writers typically wrote plainly printed letters, not unlike the printed handwriting taught in schools, with ink markers or spray paint on any easily seen public surface. As the number of names grew larger and larger, writers sought new ways to make their names more distinctive: some added arrows and other designs to the letters, others created unusual (visual or aural) letter configurations, others used different colors of paint. The push to make the presentation of the name unique sparked competition among writers, which in turn became a major impetus for innovation: "style." After about 1972, style and quantity (which value creativity and hard work, respectively) became the primary methods of gaining recognition among writers.[17]

Due in part to the semiautonomy and separation of urban youth cultures from the everyday concerns of adults, most New Yorkers did not initially understand the significance of the new writing that was developing in the public spaces around them. In the newspapers, the new writing was represented as "graffiti," but it was initially less interesting to journalists than the political slogans, obscenities, and prophetic writings on the walls of the late 1960s and early 1970s. But in 1972, the Metropolitan Transportation Authority (the MTA, which oversees the subway system) and Mayor John Lindsay announced that the proliferation of writing on the subways and the public walls was a major "problem." The MTA and the mayor's office represented writing as an insidious juvenile delinquency fad, declaring a "war on graffiti." Lindsay and his allies, with the assistance of the *New York Times* and other city-booster media venues, portrayed writers in ways that drew on popular stereotypes of the moral, ethical, and intellectual degeneracy of urban youth. Together, they attempted to create a moral panic.

Lindsay's antigraffiti campaign worked to pass new laws, design new punishments, and increase enforcement against writing in the early 1970s, but to no avail. During a few months' time in the fall of 1973, the MTA attempted a blitzkrieg and repainted the entire subway fleet, almost seven thousand cars, at a cost of $10 million (public) dollars. The action was taken in the hope of demoralizing the writers; this too proved to be a miscalculation. Lindsay's "war on graffiti" crumbled as he left office in the fall of 1973, the territorial war in public space and the struggle to define writing as a "problem" within the public sphere having utterly failed. The "graffiti problem" more or less disappeared in the commercial press until 1979.[18]

Many older writers now recall the 1973–74 period of the MTA's general repainting nostalgically as a "golden age." Rather than deterring writers, the repainting program provided 14,000 new "canvases" at a crucial turning point in the form's development. Within a year, the size of the names increased from a few feet in length to huge productions that covered the entire side of a sixty-foot subway car. Writers called these larger works "(master)pieces." Rather than simply reproduce the smaller "tags" in larger letters, writers began creating masterpieces that were unique, individual works and rapidly developed several new lettering styles. Writers fractured, peeled, and twisted the letters of their names into abstract shapes that were often illegible to the average reader. To balance the illegibility of their names, elements of representational painting—skylines, urban landscapes, and cartoon characters appropriated from Japanese animation, underground comics, video games, advertising, album covers, or Walt Disney—were added to the backgrounds and margins of a piece.[19]

Writing began in predominantly African American and Puerto Rican American working-class neighborhoods, which tended to be the most socially "invisible" areas of the city. But the practice had spread significantly across class and race lines by the mid-to-late 1970s. Writing culture seems to have been relatively immune to the racial polarization that marked most of the rest of the urban population. Race and class harmony was facilitated by the writers' ethical codes. In many ways, the writers have created a postindustrial artisanal meritocracy, based on the collective evaluation of skill and effort. The similarity with artisanal production extends to its encrypted gender politics: very few young women were welcomed into writers' "crews" (peer groups that frequently wrote together), and the vast majority of writers after 1974 were male.[20]

Although the "graffiti problem" was seldom a news item during the late 1970s, the MTA did not end the territorial "war" in the subway train storage yards during these years. By 1977, the MTA had built a $25 million car wash that smeared and faded (but could not remove) the masterpieces on the trains and had formed an antigraffiti police squad to specifically pursue writers. These efforts did not reduce the amount of writing on the trains, but it did limit the time a work circulated and caused writers to adjust to new structural conditions.

During the early 1980s, Mayor Ed Koch began a second "war on graffiti." Like Lindsay's, Koch's "war" provided the public rhetoric in support of another massive public expenditure, but Koch entwined the second "war" with New York City's efforts to improve its "business image" and "quality of life" after the financial crises of the late 1970s. In this period of neoconservative vision, the argument against the writing on the trains was constructed around writing's symbolic meaning for New York City's "decent" citizens. Articulated by sociologist Nathan Glazer, the new argument was that writing made it appear to the average, middle-class citizen that "no one was in control" of the city, and that its public spaces were unsafe. Writing, it was asserted, perpetuated the image of New York City as dirty, dangerous, and unable to take care of its problems.[21] In an act of postmodern self-parody, the city government built up for another "war on graffiti" but stayed quiet on the topic of how New York City had historically gained this besmirched image. The minor crimes of a contemporary urban youth culture were given a central place in the narrative of New York City's downfall, and thus the removal of graffiti was placed at the center of the city's recovery.

The MTA eventually succeeded in removing the writing from the trains by building medium security prison fences around each of the yards. The $25 million fence construction was included in a $16 billion, decade-long subway rebuilding project. The rebuilding project included the long-delayed replacement of half of the older subway fleet; the new cars were ordered with external shells made of stainless steel so that spray paint would be easier to remove. In 1984, the MTA began methodically removing the writing from the subways train by train, and did not allow a subway train to circulate through the system if it had writing on it. One half of the subway fleet was "graffiti free" by 1986; the "public" subway era of writing in New York City ended in 1989.[22]

Despite the noise of the jubilant victors, writing did not "die" in New York City in 1989, nor did writing on the subways end. But that is another story.

Taking the Trains

Writing style was created from a recombination of borrowed parts from a broad spectrum of cultural practices (advertising, comic books, album covers, corporate logos, television icons, and other visual elements of the urban environment). In much the same way, the institutional spaces of writing culture were created from the available materials at hand. Writers made a place for themselves in New York City by selectively appropriating existing institutions and spaces and rearticulating these into a new physical and cultural network of their own. Several preexisting institutional sites were of major importance to the writing culture. Primary among these was the subway system, including the stations, the trains, and the yards and layups. Writers worked collectively to know these places, sharing their local knowledge with each other.

Public walls were the first writing sites. The walls in the subway stations and the inside walls of the subway cars were important to writers because of the foot traffic that flowed by, and because the subways are the common mode of transportation for young people.[23] Again, for writers, the peer audience was primary. Although some writers were known for boldly writing in the presence of adults, most were not willing to challenge adult authority directly or risk being reported.[24] Stations are periodically abandoned during the rhythm of the daily train schedule, which allowed writers brief periods of time to work on the walls without interference. Writing on the trains required more circumspection. When working on the inside of the trains, writers typically walked through the cars looking for those that were empty. If there were none, then a writer could simply stay on the train until it neared the last station. By that time, several cars were likely to be empty, and a writer could work unimpeded.[25]

The transformation of the subway system into a writers' network took place primarily in the many layups and yards where the trains are stored when not in use. Relatively accessible (some yards are directly across from the high schools that writers attended), the yards were not usually under surveillance at night and on weekends. Almost all of the major work done on the outside of the trains took place in these locations. In taking the trains, writers grafted a new (*unauthorized*) social function onto the largest public rail transportation system in the United States, which stretches over 700 miles in length. Writers appropriated the subways by rearticulating their symbolic ordering, approaching the surfaces of the trains not as the inviolate and finished shells of a transportation system, but as a series of framed, "blank" spaces, like new film, like unfinished canvases, like unused billboards. The trains were hybridized and transformed into a communications network, circulating messages, fame, and aesthetic works among the community of writers and within New York City more generally. The writing on the subways was not only an attempt to grab the public's and the media's attention (although writers were happy to oblige any opportunity), but also an attempt to create an alternative "screen" where the writing community could "take place" and make itself visible to the city and to itself, while maintaining the customary (and tactical) "invisibility" of youth.

The yards and layups are located throughout the city, facilitating the formation of local centers of production.[26] Since the trains circulate across great distances and intersect at several points within the system, these local production centers were integrated into a relatively coherent cultural network across the entire city.[27] Innovations made at one location were quickly recognized and incorporated at another.

The MTA's yards and layups were pressed into service by writers to function as studio, gallery, and classroom. For several hours each night and during the weekends, the majority of the trains are taken out of service and parked.[28] During these windows of opportunity, some yards could have several dozen writers working on the insides and the outsides of the trains at one time. The shared spaces of the yards were important in creating and maintaining a shared writing practice, and served as locations where trusted novices ("toys") and noted "masters" could meet and mix to teach, think through common problems, and experiment with designs and techniques while creating new works for circulation. Although it operated much more informally, writers transformed these spaces into something like craft-guild workshops, with experienced writers providing encouragement and instruction to neophytes and colleagues.

Intimately connected with the development of a new aesthetic practice and its associated economy of prestige is the collective evaluation of individual works.[29] Evaluations are facilitated by shared spaces for observation and discussion. Before the trains became the dominant writing surface, a particular corner on 188th Street in Manhattan, more or less overseen by master writer STITCH 1, was the most famous of these meeting places. Others followed. After writers had grafted their own network onto the subways, similar sites were established at subway stations selected for their strategic location at the interchanges of several different subway lines. The "writers' benches" at these junctions were another principal location appropriated within the subway system. Writers gathered at the benches to critique, compare, and count each others' work on the subway lines that passed through, with the benches at the 149th Street and Grand Concourse in the Bronx, the Brooklyn Bridge station in lower Manhattan, and the Atlantic Avenue station in Brooklyn being among the best known. The benches were useful as a common place to meet up with friends from across town, and as writers' own status hierarchy developed, these benches also became a place where new writers might hang out, hoping to be introduced to the respected masters who were frequently there. In these encounters, the new writer was in the position of an initiate and was likely to be snubbed unless he or she had already gained at least some measure of recognition or knew someone who could make the introductions. Thus, the benches were places where the status hierarchy of writers was established, evaluated, and renegotiated.[30]

The trains, the stations, and the storage areas are under the jurisdiction of the Transit Police, and a kind of cat-and-mouse relationship quickly developed between writers and the cops as each group struggled for occupation of these territories in the early 1970s. There is no doubt that this game was a major contributing factor to writing's development as a distinctive youth culture, but participation in the cat-and-mouse game was never the primary motivation for the writers' involvement. The lack of an autonomous "place" for young people within the urban order/urban space in part re-creates conflictual relationships with policing authorities in all locations. Young people (particularly poor youths and youths of color) are frequently the subjects of police surveillance, and "trouble" offers itself in too many other venues to seriously argue that "the thrill of the chase" alone (or primarily) drew writers into the yards. Nonetheless, the attempts by the Transit Police to patrol the stations, layups, and yards were occasions for writers to publicly taunt them, and many writers did so with glee, often leaving messages for the police as they made their escape.[31] The Transit Police occasionally responded in kind by writing messages over the works of the writers they were pursuing (which ruined them, in writers' eyes), and many writers suspect that the notorious TCO crew (THE CROSS OUTS, who destroyed a large number of well-respected works during the late 1970s) was actually a police squad.[32] The suspicions aroused by TCO created conflict among writers, increasing the likelihood that one writer would turn another over to the police.

The game with the police became part of the survival skills of any experienced writer and constituted an important part of writing culture as well. But there is the question of bodies here: the bodies of young men and of older cops; bodies of local knowledge and bodies of universal laws and standard enforcement techniques (although these were, and are, frequently violated); bodies committed to a peer culture and bodies committed to a wage-earning career that did not necessity depend on their successful apprehension of writers, certainly not a *particular* writer.

Writing has always been practiced with escape routes in mind, a consequence of working within a *place* claimed by another, dominant group. If seen writing in a station, a writer could run away: through one of the entrances (the larger stations have several) and out into the street; across the tracks to the platform on the other side of the station, and then out; or down the tracks into the underground tunnels. Most of the layups are located in these tunnels, where one or a few trains are stored on side tracks while not in use. Writers were familiar with the geography of the tunnel network, knew how to avoid oncoming trains and the electrified third rail, and had memorized the location of the stairways that led to the street through manhole covers.

Most of the yards were surrounded by chain link fencing in various stages of disrepair during the 1970s. Writers cut holes in the fences to make new passageways into the yards, and then cut new holes as the old ones were repaired or were discovered and watched. Despite the writers' efforts, the fences continued to function as barriers in most places. Writers kept the various passageways in mind as they worked; when raided, writers would scatter throughout the yards (a space larger than a football field in most cases), hiding among the parked trains as they made their way back to one of the passageways.[33] Part of becoming a skilled writer was learning how to climb up and down the steel beams that support the elevated yards, layups, and stations. Knowing how to run through the yards without tripping over the rails, particularly the "third" rail which carries the 650-volt electric current that powers the trains, was even more fundamental. The age of writers typically ranged from twelve to twenty-two. Their agility and speed made them difficult prey for most cops over thirty years old; their determination and localized knowledge of the stations, tunnels, and yards made them difficult prey for anyone.

Still, by the mid-1970s the Transit Police claimed to have made over four thousand arrests, and to have a fairly good profile of a writer.[34] The profile allowed the Transit Police to effectively disrupt the writers' benches in the Subway stations as gathering places by the late 1970s. Youths fitting the profile who lingered in these locations were likely to be questioned, asked to leave, or searched and harassed by Transit Police. Despite the thousands of arrests, writing was a relatively insignificant crime in comparison to most others that passed before judges in the overworked juvenile justice system, which made it less likely that the courts would cause a major problem in the writers' lives. Most writers I've interviewed were more worried about beatings from police than being prosecuted by the courts during this period.[35] Although several of the major masters were caught at some time during the late 1970s and early 1980s, a substantial number managed to retain an unblemished record; toys were frequently not arrested at all, but simply scared, questioned, and released. At other times, toys were intimidated and pressed into service as sources of police information, or the police exploited internal rivalries for the same purposes.[36]

Writers' appropriation of the subway system extended to the use of specialized vocabularies borrowed and versioned from the authorized system (MTA) itself. All experienced writers knew and could describe the system's layout and schedule in great detail and had an even more detailed mental map and schedule of the several yards, layups, and stations where they usually worked. They also created a substantial body of knowledge about the trains themselves: how to open doors, how to turn on lights, the different types of cars running on each of the subway lines ("coal miners", "ridgies," "flats"). Keys to all trains were stolen, copied, and traded among writers, as were the reflective orange vests worn by track workers. This camouflage would sometimes allow writers to work in the yards unnoticed, or simply to walk away when raided by police.

The subway system is both a system in time as well as space. Besides the train schedules and routes, the routines of maintenance and cleaning crews in the yards were memorized. Writers learned the characteristic signs of when a train was headed for the repair shed (where it would likely be "cleaned" of writing). These types of knowledges speak to the devotion of writers to their craft and the pleasures that motivate their work; the easy and simple-minded attempts to find a commonsensical pathology behind this practice can only obfuscate the complex negotiations between work, play, adventure, and the pleasure of *taking place*.

Other sites within the city served important functions in writers' cultural geography as well. These locations include the high schools, commercial businesses that catered to young folks, and the private space allotted to some teenagers within their family homes.[37] The possibility of being caught in the yards fluctuated over the twenty-year period that writers took the trains, but never became insignificant. This fact, coupled with the increasing complexity of the works themselves (which often required more than twenty cans of paint in several different colors), meant that entering the yards often required considerable planning beforehand. As masterpieces became a dominant form, writers began to plan their works more rigorously and frequently drew sketches of their work before executing them, carefully planning letter designs, colors, figurative and representational segments, and other compositional elements of their works. Color schemes were compared, discussed, and planned, and the correct colors gathered, rather than work ad hoc with whatever colors were on hand. Sketches were then taken to the yards to assist in the execution of the works. As photography became an important way of recording a writer's work (particularly after the late 1970s, when MTA was more successful in its attempts to remove writing from the trains), these types of spaces were places where photo albums were examined and individual photos exchanged. Writers appropriated commercial, public, and domestic spaces as locations to meet and make such plans, as well as to hang out, talk shop, exchange information, and gossip.[38] These became the alternative to the writers' benches after they were re-taken by the police.

Conclusions

These various appropriated spaces formed a kind of network that remapped the city for writers, constructing a "writers' city," if you will. This "writers' city" emerged from the cracks found in its existing institutional and social structures, which, with the exception of the yards and layups, were often places where writers "hid in the light" of adult surveillance without adults being aware of their purposes.[39] A subculture is always "under" another, more powerful entity. But this has never meant powerlessness or docility. At times, it has not even meant successful domination.

The example of the writing culture in New York City pushes us to ask whether the use of public spaces by young people and other nondominant groups isn't more complex than it first appears. The city is itself a thickly coded (and coated) text that speaks to the social hierarchies that it contains, often announcing the *place* of its inhabitants explicitly in written words. Who is responding? Who is writing back?

NOTES

1. See Joseph F. Kett, *Rites of Passage: Adolescence in America, 1790 to the Present* (New York: Basic Books, 1977); Howard P. Chudacoff, *How Old Are You? Age Consciousness in American Culture* (Princeton, NJ: Princeton University Press, 1989); Viviana A. Zelizer, *Pricing the Priceless Child: The Changing Social Value of Children* (New York: Basic Books, 1985); William Graebner, "The 'Containment' of Juvenile Delinquency: Social Engineering and American Youth Culture in the Postwar Era," *American Studies* 27, no. 1: 81–97; Mike A. Males, *Scapegoat Generation: America's War on Adolescents* (Monroe, ME: Common Courage Press, 1996); James E. Cote and Anton L. Allahar, *Generation on Hold: Coming of Age in the Late Twentieth Century* (New York: New York University Press, 1994).

2. Grace Palladino, *Teenagers: An American History* (New York: Basic Books, 1996) and James Gilbert, *A Cycle of Outrage: America's Reaction to the Juvenile Delinquent in the 1950s* (New York: Oxford University Press, 1986), both speak to this point, as does Kett, *Rites of Passage*.

3. For instance, the segregation of young people from adults in time and space by mandatory schooling extends the surveillance and dependency of youth, while reinforcing the importance of the peer group relative to the family.

4. By "policing authorities" I am referring not only to the police force, but to the entire ensemble of state apparati that regulate youth's "place." This includes the agencies that enforce labor, alcohol, and tobacco restrictions and school attendance, among others

5. This is hardly a new or radical perspective. See James S. Coleman et al., *Youth: Transition to Adulthood* (Chicago: University of Chicago Press, 1974).

6. Dick Hebdige, "Hiding in the Light: Youth Surveillance and Display," in *Hiding in the Light: On Images and Things* (New York: Routledge, 1988), 17–36. See Donna Gaines, *Teenage Wasteland: Suburbia's Dead End Kids* (New York: Pantheon, 1991), for another analysis of youth's use of the metropolitan landscape.

7. I owe a significant debt to the work of several people who began the study of writing in New York City before I did. These include Jack Stewart, "Subway Graffiti: An Aesthetic Study of Graffiti on the Subway System of New York City, 1970–1978." Ph.D. diss., New York University, 1989; Craig Castleman, *Getting Up: Subway Graffiti in New York* (Cambridge, MA:

MIT Press, 1982); Martha Cooper and Henry Chalfant, *Subway Art* (New York: Holt, Rinehart and Winston, 1984); Steven Hager, *HipHop: The Illustrated History of Breakdancing, Rap Music and Graffiti* (New York: St. Martin's Press, 1984). This debt is matched only by the one I owe the writers who so generously and patiently answered questions and helped me to understand this history. In particular, shouts out to Phase 2, Iz the Wiz, Poem, Daze, Crash, Smith, Lady Pink, Futura 2000, Seen, Zephyr, Sar, Cavs, Rated, Death, Nic One, Vulcan, Air, Id, Dash, and Illy.

8. See Phase 2's analysis of the terms "writing" and "graffiti" in Joe Austin, "Re*writing* New York City," in George E. Marcus, ed., *Connected: Engagements with Media* (Chicago: University of Chicago Press, 1996), 277–78, and in Phase 2, "Look at the Myth," *International Get Hip Times*, 8, n.d, n.p.

9. See Stewart, "Subway Graffiti," chapter 5, for a description of writing in Philadelphia. Although Top Cat 126 wrote in both cities, the practice was well established before he arrived in New York. There are no known "migrations" from Philadelphia, where writing appeared first, to New York; it appears that they developed independently.

10. See Joe Austin, *Taking the Train: Youth Culture, Urban Crisis and the "Graffiti Problem" in New York City* (New York: Columbia University Press, forthcoming), for an elaboration of this argument.

11. See Herbert Kohl, photos by James Hinton, *Golden Boy as Anthony Cool* (New York: Dial Press, 1972).

12. Aside from the writers' own testimony, Stewart's work is important in differentiating *graffiti* from *writing*. See chapters 1 through 4 of his dissertation, "Subway Graffiti," for a detailed historical analysis of the elements of graffiti. He covers the origins of writing in New York City in chapter 6. Some of my points here are generated from the observations of Kohl mentioned above, and David Ley and Roman Cybriwsky, "Urban Graffiti as Territorial Markers," *Annals of the Association of American Geographers* 64 (December 1974): 491–505. Armando Petrucci's *Public Lettering: Script, Power, and Culture* (original, 1980; English translation, University of Chicago Press, 1993) offers another historical narrative that can usefully situate writing.

13. See Iz the Wiz and Illy, and Air, quoted in Austin, "Re-Writing New York," 274–75 and 304, respectively.

14. See David Schmidlapp (editor of *International Get Hip Times*), quoted in Austin, "Re-Writing New York," 284.

15. See John H. Mollenkopf's description and analysis of the postindustrial transformation of New York City's economy in *A Phoenix in the Ashes: The Rise and Fall of the Koch Coalition in New York City Politics* (Princeton, NJ: Princeton University Press, 1992), chapter 3. James L. Baughman's article, "Take Me Away from Manhattan: New York City and American Mass Culture, 1930–1990," in Martin Shefter, ed., *Capital of the American Century: The National and International Influence of New York City* (New York: Russell Sage Foundation, 1993), covers the processes and events whereby New York City *lost* the cultural hegemony it enjoyed before the 1950s. However, as Baughman points out, even "if New York no longer dominates mass culture, it is not about to become a Carthage of the popular arts" (p. 131). The city's actual productive capacity cannot be directly correlated with its enduring success myth, in any case.

16. This is clear from the work of any number of urban photographers. See, for instance, Berenice Abbott's photographs published in *New York in the Thirties* (New York: Dover, 1973), particularly the signs and posters in plates 32, 33, and 88.

17. Stewart, "Subway Graffiti," chapters 6 and 7; Castleman, *Getting Up*, chapters 3 and 4.

Howard Becker's *Art Worlds* (Los Angeles: University of California Press, 1982) provides an excellent analysis of collective production of aesthetic works and values.

18. See Austin, "Taking the Train," chapter 2.

19. Castleman, *Getting Up*, chapters 2, 3, and 4; Stewart, "Subway Grafitti," chapters 9, 11, and 12.

20. Castleman, *Getting Up*, chapter 4.

21. See Austin, "Taking the Train," chapters 2 and 4. Glazer's influential article is "On Subway Graffiti in New York," *The Public Interest* 54 (Winter 1979): 11–33.

22. Austin, "Taking the Train," chapter 5.

23. Stewart, "Subway Grafitti," 213–19.

24. Castleman reports that Cool Herc was known to write while others were in the car, even asking some passengers to move so he could reach a particular spot. Cool Herc is an important link between writing culture and rap music; he was a noted writer and among the first to develop the DJ style from which rap emerged.

25. Stewart, "Subway Grafitti," 214 and 246.

26. Ibid., 213.

27. Castleman, *Getting Up*, 85–89; Stewart, "Subway Grafitti," 246.

28. Stewart, "Subway Grafitti," 245–46.

29. See Becker, *Art Worlds*, chapters 2 and 5.

30. Stewart, "Subway Grafitti," 215–20; Hager, *HipHop*, 20. Castleman, *Getting Up*, has an excellent description of the writers' benches on pages 85–89. The quotes by STAN 153, WICKED GARY, and BAMA are particularly revealing about the information network that writers shared.

31. Stewart, "Subway Grafitti," discusses the role of the Transit Police in the culture of graffiti in several places; in particular, see pages 252–258 for the early encounters in the yards, and also see BLADE quoted on pp. 452–55. Cooper and Chalfant, *Subway Art*, have several photos of the taunts; see pp. 27, 50, 89, 98–99, 101. The police were a major source for Castleman's work, *Getting Up*, and the relationships between cops and writers are discussed by each party throughout his book; see chapter 9 in particular.

32. Castleman, *Getting Up*, 46; Stewart, "Subway Grafitti," 463.

33. See STAN 153 quoted in Castleman, *Getting Up*, 107–9. Also, see Stewart, "Subway Grafitti," 252–53.

34. See the Transit Police's "Profile of a Common Offender," reprinted in Stewart, "Subway Grafitti," 203.

35. Ibid., 253–55. Also, see CAY 161 and JUNIOR 161 quoted in Norman Mailer, photos by Jon Naar and Mervyn Kurlansky, *The Faith of Graffiti* (New York: Praeger Press, 1974), n.p.

36. Cooper and Chalfant, *Subway Art*, 99.

37. See the photos and text in ibid., 32–33.

38. Castleman, *Getting Up*, 85.

39. I take this phrase from Dick Hebdige's famous essay and book of the same name, cited earlier. However, writers are a "spectacular" subculture in a very different sense than the subcultures in Britain with whom Hebdige is concerned. It is equally important to follow Michel de Certeau in *The Practice of Everyday Life* (Los Angeles: University of California Press, 1984) and note the *new* and less visible spaces that urban youth appropriate in creating organized communities.

Chapter Fifteen

"... And Tomorrow Is Just Another Crazy Scam"

Postmodernity, Youth, and the Downward Mobility of the Middle Class

Ryan Moore

American youth have wavered in and out of the mainstream media's spotlight for at least the past half century. Today's hype centers around "Generation X," a buzz term which seems to connote little beyond some vague reference to the supposed under achievement, disaffection, and apathy of white middle-class people in their twenties. Yet in part because popular attention has not translated into scholarly investigation, discussion has collapsed into a fruitless antagonism between the mass media's depiction of a relatively homogeneous generation and a growing number of dissenting voices that "defend" twentysomethings by affirming their alleged commitment to hard work, social responsibility, and the American Dream.[1] In what follows I seek to leave behind a debate whose parameters have been set by a "moral panic"[2] surrounding the "character" and ahistorical "choices" of a generation, situating a wide spectrum of contemporary youth culture within the socio-historical conditions faced by America's white middle class.[3] *More specifically, in this chapter, I trace the progressively nihilistic, exhausted, and ironically distanced character of much youth culture and link that "structure of feeling"[4] with the downward mobility of the middle class and the cultural condition we have come to know as "postmodernity."*

Postmodern Culture and the Crisis of Affectivity

In his classic essay, "Postmodernism, or, the Cultural Logic of Late Capitalism," Fredric Jameson laments, among other things, the epochal shift in postmodern art's expression of feeling and emotion.[5] In displacing the notion of centered subjectivity with that of perpetual fragmentation, postmodernism renders inappropriate the kind of "depth models" that presuppose an inner, core self from which one can be alienated. While such surface-level fragmentation thereby offers us the liberation from the modern experience of anxiety and anomie, Jameson warns that it also threatens to act as a "liberation from every other feeling as well, since there is no longer a self present to do the feeling."[6]

Lawrence Grossberg has expanded Jameson's diagnosis beyond art and theory in demonstrating how this postmodern crisis of affectivity has become a dominant "structure of feeling" within everyday life itself.[7] As the line between reality and image seems to implode,[8] one comes to believe that everything and everyone is a fake—a "simulation"—and is therefore best served by an attitude of "aggressive indifference," an ironic detachment from any sort of commitment; as Todd Gitlin remarks, such defensiveness "either mocks the game by playing it or plays it by mocking it."[9] And yet, just as Jameson acknowledges that affect does not disappear entirely but rather is transformed into a "peculiar kind of euphoria",[10] Grossberg recognizes that such ironic distance is, somewhat paradoxically, "coupled with a sense of emotional urgency."[11] In turn, while postmodern subjects may pursue a number of avenues for temporarily locating sources of passion, the fact remains that a fundamental rupture between affect and ideology makes such investment arbitrary at best: "It is not that nothing matters—for something has to matter—but that there is no way of choosing, or of finding something to warrant the investment."[12]

In what follows I trace the increasing predominance of nihilism, cynicism, and cultural exhaustion in white middle-class youth culture as a symptom of the structure of feeling mapped by Jameson and Grossberg. If youthful experimentation is always an unwanted luxury for some, even among the alienated it seems that the rejection of dominant values and identities cannot be matched by an investment in any alternatives. A "seen it all" cynicism predominates whereby all strategies are exhausted and reducible to their simulation. The affective stakes in much postmodern youth culture are such that nothing can be sacred, all styles are exhausted the moment they are born, and, all other things being equal, one does, says, and feels nothing. The dominant "structure of feeling" could thus be summed up by the impossibility of the sentiment expressed in the Doors' song, "Break on Through to the Other Side": even if we could somehow transcend this side of everyday life, it's all too likely that the other side might end up being no different than the one from which we've just escaped.

A fine example of such "aggressive indifference" is Douglas Coupland's *Generation X*, a novel which the author originally imagined as a work of nonfiction but which nonetheless caught the attention of journalists and advertisers searching for a definitive representation of an emerging generation and target market.[13] The story revolves around three people in their twenties who have dropped out of the middle-class rat race and taken up residence in the desert of Palm Springs, California. It is here, between the extremities of wealth (the novel opens with the main character's suspicion that his dogs have been rummaging through the bags of "yuppie liposuction fat" deposited by the nearby cosmetic surgery center) and the ruins of modernity (West Palm Springs Village, a failed housing development that the properly postmodern Coupland describes as "reminiscent of a Vietnam War movie set"), that the characters attempt to gain a narrative foothold on their own lives and discover some source of "real" meaning. Ultimately, however, *Generation X*'s quest for narrative grounding fails, and in the end the characters simply move from Palm Springs to

Mexico in order to fulfill their "terminal wanderlust," in the hope that their next residence will provide the roots and sense of community missing from the last.

Coupland's characters prove unable to adhere to or even locate an alternative because, quite frankly, they've seen it all. They espouse minimalist philosophies without actually acting on them, express a fascination with spectacular situations regardless of their signified content, employ arbitrary superstitions as the only viable means of coping with everyday life, and, of course, incorporate irony into all situations, conversations, and lifestyles, indicating a "refusal to go out on any sort of emotional limb so as to avoid mockery from peers."[14] Thus, though their angst is clear enough, these refugees from the middle class can go no further than to divorce action and belief, thus leaving them to ironically deride the very lifestyles they live; material dissatisfaction aside, our protagonists are left without any grounds to question their aspirations for middle-class existence.

Richard Linklater's 1990 film *Slacker* further attests to the predominance of ironic distance at the expense of affective investment. Documenting the lifestyles of the underworked and overeducated in the bohemian district of Austin, Texas, *Slacker* produces a sense of radical fragmentation by using the camera to follow a succession of characters who wander into a given scene in a seemingly random manner. As the camera pursues one character, it leaves the other behind, never to be heard from again. Douglas Kellner has previously discussed this film as an important text "between the modern and postmodern."[15] While he does recognize the depthlessness and nihilistic tendencies of *Slacker*, Kellner's emphasis on the experience of alienation and the way in which the characters "appropriate media culture for their own ends, turning articles from conservative media into material for radical and social critique,"[16] overlooks some very disturbing aspects of the film's content. To be sure, alienation is ever present, as in one character's affirmation that "withdrawing in disgust is not the same as apathy." Yet there is an important difference between *Slacker* and the 1960s youth films analyzed by Kellner and Ryan in their outstanding book, *Camera Politica*.[17] If, as those authors demonstrate, the protagonists in a film like *Bonnie and Clyde* were alienated from the dominant society, they could also reinvest their affective energies in an admittedly idealized notion of "nature" (or, in others, "youth," "revolution," "self-discovery," etc.). Such solutions are not as readily available in *Slacker*. The way in which the camera quickly pans from one person to the next leaves us with only a rubble of depthless caricatures: a drifter who yells "Every commodity you produce is a piece of your own death!"; a young black man selling "Free Nelson Mandela" tee-shirts while performing cliché-ridden, impromptu raps; and an anarchist who offers an armed intruder some coffee rather than calling the police. These characters appear just as laughable and ridiculous as the man who references the *World Weekly News* to support his tale of government conspiracy regarding the space program and the two youths who note the anti-individualist tropes in the Smurfs and speculate about the way those lovable blue cartoon characters prepare a generation of youth for the coming of Krishna. Indeed, Linklater even pokes fun at himself by including overly enthusiastic student filmmakers in his cast of characters.

Similarly, in *Roadside Prophets* (1992) two factory workers leave their jobs to take a cross-country trip on motorcycles; the older of the two characters is played by the earnest and thoughtful John Doe (from the L.A.-based punk band X), while the bratty Adam Horowitz (a.k.a. AD-Rock from the rap-rock crossover act, the Beastie Boys) portrays the younger of the two. While Doe takes off to properly dispose of a friend's ashes, Horowitz tags along in search of his mother. Road movies and novels, of course, have had a longstanding connection with youth culture because they can serve as metaphors for an ephemeral search for identity and affective investment—the road introduces us to new people and places, only to see us pack up and leave in the morning. In this case, however, Horowitz's encounters with existentialists, peace activists, and LSD gurus inspire nothing beyond the sentiment "wow, that's *crazy*" until Doe finally lambasts him for his indifference.

The flipside of ironic distance and disinvestment is a sense of desperation, a longing for depth and meaning which Coupland himself represented in a series of short stories published in 1994, appropriately titled *Life after God*. For Coupland, *Life after God* provided an opportunity to depart from the self-described cynicism of his first two novels (the second, *Shampoo Planet*, will be discussed later in this chapter). Yet the fundamental problem remains the same: the cover jacket announces "You Are the First Generation Raised without Religion" and the stories revolve around the difficulty of coping not only with anxiety and loneliness, but also with the evaporation of affectivity and faith in pseudoreligious narratives. One passage from a story about a man whose marriage is failing represents this desperation well: "One of my big concerns these past few years is that I've been losing my ability to feel things with the same intensity—the way I felt when I was younger. It's scary—to feel your emotions floating away and just not caring. I guess what's really scary is not caring about the loss."[18]

Even Coupland's more cynical novels turn on moments where an unseen and sudden force proceeds to simultaneously empty out the little worlds of the young middle class and deliver an organically authentic instance of transcendent euphoria. Hence *Generation X* ends with a strange scene in which the main character, standing with a crowd of motorists who are watching what they think is a nuclear cloud, is suddenly swooped upon by an egret and then mobbed by a group of overly affectionate, mentally retarded teenagers. In *Shampoo Planet*, the protagonist Tyler thrusts his hands into a compost pile when facing a crossroads in his life, and the novel itself ends when an upstairs neighbor's floor collapses, bringing a rush of water and small animals down upon Tyler and his girlfriend, Anna-Louise (and ruining all the technology in the room). The fact that these "resolutions" seem rather unsatisfying and symbolically obscure cannot override the simple fact of yearning for *something*, for some "authentic" yet unnamable force that will lift us out of everyday life. After all, Coupland's novels could not produce their sense of torment without the coexistence of desire for the transcendent and the inclination that all accessible strategies are, in the end, exhausted and ineffectual.

Likewise, in *Polaroids from the Dead*, Coupland's look at the Grateful Dead skillfully exposes the ambiguities embedded in what has become—at least until the death of frontman Jerry Garcia in 1996—a staple of contemporary white youth culture. On the one hand, Coupland—perhaps like many other young "deadheads"—is well aware that Dead shows are a commodified simulacrum pure and simple, a kind of Disneyland ride where everyone looks like either Charles Manson or Sharon Tate and, for at least a day, otherwise well-groomed kids born in the 1970s (the "McDead") can put on their tie-dyed tee-shirts and "feel like one of those sixties photographs." And yet we are reminded that a very real sense of dissatisfaction and desperation lurks beneath the spectacle. Seemingly romanticized and commodified beyond recognition, The Sixties and The Dead still represent the last gasp of idealism, an inarticulate longing for an alternative to the suburban rat race, a decayed and rotting (but somehow still dancing) skeleton that carries "a core truth, a germ that refuses to die, an essence of purity and love that is open to abuse."[19] It is here that the young and the middle class—and even the microchip bourgeoisie—seek to shed their skins and achieve a transitory moment of salvation and transcendence while the security they've known and come to expect dissolves at their feet: "At least at a Dead concert you can forget for a few hours that the world is about to go *bang*. You pay your money and you hop on the ride: Fun costumes, tunes as seen on MTV, and afterward you can return to the present."[20]

Alas, perhaps no form of contemporary white youth culture exemplifies the predominance of aggressive indifference—and the corresponding hunger for *something* that matters—better than post-punk rock 'n' roll. As argued by a number of critics and scholars,[21] during the 1970s punk fans and musicians employed the emerging logic of postmodernism—in particular, its androgyny, avant-garde irony and distance, and self-parody—as part of a semiotic assault on what many saw as the growing economic, political, and cultural complacency of rock music and its audiences. The post-punk of today continues such an affinity with postmodernism in its fluidity and self-reflexivity as well as its appropriation of pop culture debris, seemingly schizophrenic tempos and noise making, and depiction of a society irreversibly sitting on the brink of disaster. What is important to note for the purposes of this thesis, then, is that although punks' realization that everything is constructed and therefore mutable allows them to effectively carry out their mission to destroy and "Xpose," it also leaves punk vulnerable to the charge that it too is nothing more than just another style or pose.[22] In short, it seems that we have yet another instance where the rejection of dominant values and identities cannot be matched by an investment in any alternative insofar as punks have unintentionally undercut any stable ground from which they can viably lay claim to reconstructed notions of sincerity and authenticity.

Nonetheless, punk and post-punk can also be seen as sites where the repressed returns with a vengeance, where the yearning for something that matters coexists with playful deconstructionism and aggressive indifference. Indeed, the first generation of punks had in part waged their attack on rock in hopes of restoring its original promises: namely, its populist accessibility, communitarian ethos, and antagonism to the boredom and repetition of "everyday life."[23] Twenty years after the punk revolution, the search for sincerity, meaningfulness, and authenticity continues, and has perhaps even intensified, despite the fact that post-punks' self-conscious, deconstructive impulses suggest that they know better. Among the central manifestations of such longings are the "do it yourself" ethics of small-scale, independent modes of musical production and recording, the imperative of local, personalized communities among fans and musicians, the vastly increased use of a minimalist and/or outdated (and thus somehow more "sincere") recording technology, and, in some cases, the proliferation of "straight edge" scenes that celebrate the purity of the body (no drugs, alcohol, or promiscuous sex) in connection with a vigorous commitment to women's rights, animal liberation, and environmental defense. Largely distrusting ideological content, these youths uphold a perceived purity of form against what many of them see as a hopelessly hypocritical society.[24] If such instances represent the most hopeful examples where young whites have been able to locate *something* that matters, we must also remember that they are less likely to be expressed by way of an investment in the present than in a retrospective mourning of a "lost paradise," a nostalgic mythology about how great a particular scene *used to be* before the media took notice, before the bands "sold out," and before the wrong types of people started coming to the shows.

No single musical artist embodied these affective contradictions of postmodern culture more visibly than the group Nirvana, that popular forebearer of the "grunge" style whose scruffy, unkempt "realism" enjoyed a brief moment of fame as a successor to both the glam rock and pop artists and the symbols of upward mobility that had dominated the previous decade. Musically, Nirvana straddled the line between nihilism and sincerity in alternating between singable pop melodies and abrasive noise and in frontman Kurt Cobain's vocal oscillations from inarticulate rage to monotonous passivity. Indeed, Cobain's own self-description fits such emotional duality: "I'm such a nihilistic jerk half the time and other times I'm so vulnerable and sincere. . . . That's how most people my age are. They're sarcastic one minute and then caring the next."[25] Thus, in beginning their song "Territorial Pissings" with a sickeningly off-key "Come on people now, smile on your brother. Everybody get together try to love one another right now," only to erupt into a fast drum roll and the primitive noise made by plugging a guitar directly into the mixing board, Nirvana saw themselves as both mocking and trying to revive "corny hippie idealism." As bassist Kris Novoselic later recalled, "Maybe it was about lost ideals. Like, what happened to those ideals? . . . Maybe some baby boomers will hear that and wonder, 'Hey, what happened to those ideals?' "[26] Likewise, in contemplating the prospects for a youth revolution in their own time, the hit single "Smells Like Teen Spirit" appears to both embrace and sarcastically dismiss the idea, with Cobain pointing the finger at his apathetic peers while simultaneously acknowledging his own confusion and helplessness.[27] Even as rock stars, Nirvana was able to present both a voice for a more sincere alternative to the music industry and the trappings of stardom and, by virtue of their own "incorporation," testify to the lack of such an oppositional space; the best example of such frustration—and the use of irony to "resolve" these contradictions—was Cobain's appearance on the cover of *Rolling Stone* with a handwritten tee-shirt reading "Corporate Rock Magazines Still Suck."

Downward Mobility, Affect, and Postmodern Narrativity

Having given some examples of the crisis of affect in contemporary youth culture, I now want to address the question of how that structure of feeling connects with the downward mobility of the middle class. In doing so, I assert what I think to be a rather simple point that is nevertheless too often missed by critics of postmodern culture: that is to say, postmodernity is not a monolithic and universal "discursive field" but rather something that is lived very differently and presents different cultural and political opportunities, depending upon one's social position.[28] While I do think that the structural transformation of a particular class has contributed to the cynicism and exhaustion detailed above, I am not prepared to make a simple base-superstructure argument (e.g., postmodern culture is a mere effect of the experience of a particular class) here, either. Indeed, in recognizing that structural processes are always understood through cultural lenses, we must also attend to the fact that the postmodern condition has profound implications for how downward mobility is perceived and acted upon among white middle-class youths.

Let us begin by briefly acknowledging how the American middle class and its young people have been impacted by the kinds of structural transformations that a number of critics have identified as the underlying causes of the condition of postmodernity.[29] In the first place, it is clear that as relatively new entrants into the labor market, "twentysomethings" make up a larger portion of those workers employed in the low-pay, low-benefit, no-security service industries—fast-food restaurants, retail trade, child care, banking, health services, etc.—and/or limited to part-time, temporary work.[30] Meanwhile, the trend toward lower-paying, lower-quality jobs coincides with a contraction of opportunities in the traditional white-collar fields as a result of corporate downsizing and "merger mania," thus leaving today's middle-class youth with less-lucrative opportunities than those from previous generations.[31] Thus, an increasingly large chunk of recent college graduates find themselves on a downward slide with jobs that do not require a four-year degree[32] and dramatic increases in everything from medical services to rents (not to mention new homes!) to education.[33] Moreover, recent economic transformations have led to *qualitative* changes in the nature of middle-class work as well: as argued by Stanley Aronowitz and William DiFazio, traditional professional occupations in the fields of medicine, law, and engineering are being proletarianized as a result of the increasing dominance of labor-saving high technology such that the capacity for relatively autonomous decision making that has historically differentiated intellectual work from manual labor is now eroding.[34]

I think it reasonable to suggest that quantitative and qualitative downward mobility compounds the sense of nihilism, cynicism, and cultural exhaustion characteristic of postmodernity. Sustained downward mobility, after all, represents a threat to what has served as a crucial narrative among the relatively privileged in our society: in postwar America, progress has been tightly bound to the experience of upward mobility such that "we are true optimists, always assuming that the world—or at least our corner of it—will continue to provide more for us than it did for our parents, and more for our children than we have today."[35] Thus, at the risk of nostalgia-induced oversimplification, we might contrast contemporary white, middle-class youth culture with the counterculture and student movement of the 1960s. In short, while many young people were becoming conscious of the fact that the United States was in need of an all-encompassing social transformation, the counterculture and the student movement also managed, at least initially, to reflect the broader cultural optimism of their time.[36] Their faith in progressive renewal and infinite possibilities, in the perfectibility of human nature and the dialectical possibilities presented by postwar society, is indeed striking to the contemporary observer. Such confidence, I believe, was not only driven by the baby boom generation's awareness of its own historical self-importance—they were the impetus behind the widespread migration to the suburban good life, the inheritors of "America's century," the beneficiaries of unprecedented levels of investment in education, and the pride of a nation that had endured the hardships of the Great Depression and could now see nothing but progress and mobility on the horizon[37]—but also by the cushion afforded by a seemingly endless stream of prosperity and affluence. As Marshall Berman remembers:

> It was easy, in those boom years, to live off the fat of the land. This made it easier to experiment, to take risks for the sake of our self-development, for we were secure in the knowledge that it was not only possible, but adventurous and exciting, to move on. Thus the growth and dynamism of the American economy provided for us—for an expanding and energetic new middle class—the same sort of support that Mephisto's money and mobility provide for Faust.[38]

Coming off the heels of Reaganism and the momentary prosperity represented by the likes of *Bright Lights, Big City*, *Less than Zero*, and *St. Elmos' Fire*, many of the aggressively indifferent texts discussed above are indeed littered with references to declining mobility and post-fordist work. In *Generation X*, all three characters work in demeaning service-sector jobs, with Coupland himself delivering blow after blow against the triviality of such employment.[39] Indeed, central to the protagonists' quest for narrative self-comprehension is their attempt to come to terms with their downward mobility: with the sense of betrayal, the suspicion of failure, the resentment of more fortunate generations, and reconciliation with the absence of fulfilling jobs or glamorous lifestyles.[40] Coupland's two other novels, *Shampoo Planet* and *Microserfs*, respectively feature characters who aspire to yuppiedom but can never quite achieve it and leave behind their relatively stable jobs as computer programmers in order to pursue more creative, original work. *Slacker* documents the lives of an array of people for whom fulfilling careers are neither readily available nor an imagined means of realizing identity, and downward mobility was made (ironically) visible by way of tee-shirts produced by the Seattle-based Sup Pop Records inscribed with the word "loser." Even popular television shows like *Friends* spotlight service-sector workers and the chronically unemployed, although the consumerist thrust of that particular show leaves us with the inexplicable contradiction wherein the characters also don first-class wardrobes and reside in state-of-the-art apartments in New York's ultra-gentrified Greenwich Village.

To be sure, such growing economic polarization—"Brazilification," as Coupland labels it—has the potential to disrupt what Barbara Ehrenreich has shown to be a central component of the dominant hegemony in postwar America: namely, the middle class's perception of itself as a social elite that has more in common with the real elites than with oppressed populations.[41] Such a possibility is suggested by the totality of Coupland's fiction, which not only represents the angst of marginal bohemians but also unearths a latent uneasiness among apparently conformist and conservative youths.[42] Nonetheless, one crucial obstacle to such identification and "class consciousness" is the apparent inability to locate oneself or even one's class in a historical, narrative fashion. Indeed, if postmodernity has presented the opportunity for oppressed communities to (re-)discover their "roots," for America's white middle class it seems that this sociohistorical condition has *compounded* its consistent failings with regard to narrative, collective self-comprehension. After all, the dominant ideology of the white middle class includes both a self-congratulatory, liberal individualism derived from the sense of having "made it" by virtue of one's persistence and hard work *and* the collapsing of any number of historical and ethnic differences in the creation of that abstraction we know as "whiteness."[43] The condition of postmodernity exacerbates such crises insofar as its subjects are presented with "a rubble of distinct and unrelated signifiers,"[44] a succession of images and sound bytes that seem to privilege instant amnesia rather than "history" in any sense of the word. As we've seen, such temporal fragmentation is directly related to the crisis of affect in postmodernity insofar as history and narrativity are precisely the type of "depth models" whose apparent evaporation has paved the way for the contemporary liberation from feeling. Lacking a means for mapping their social and personal histories or for grasping the underlying forces that have led to the "broken promises" of downward mobility, family disintegration, and political apathy, many young middle-class whites have latched onto a defensive cynicism that knows that everything is simply a facade—that, in the end, nothing really matters.

"It's not healthy to live our life as a succession of isolated little cool moments," one of the protagonists in *Generation X* proclaims in the opening pages of the novel, "either our lives become stories, or there's just no way to get through them."[45] Yet the futility of such a quest is signaled early and often in both the content and form of *Generation X*. Oscillating between "historical underdosing" and "historical overdosing," of living in an information society where one is barraged by a constant flow of equally insignificant events, the characters' "stories" involve little more than an incoherent amalgamation of everything from the kitsch popular cultures and fashions of the past to disturbingly funny fantasies about nuclear Armageddon to experiences in shopping malls. The novel itself reproduces such a "structure of feeling" through its collection of fragmentary moments and by subordinating its plot to a set of witty and sarcastic slogans ("Nostalgia Is a Weapon") and pseudosociological definitions ("McJob") presented in the margins of the text.

That Coupland himself is all too aware that this crisis of meaning and depth is particularly acute among the white middle class is evident in the narrating character's admission: "It is a feeling that our emotions, while wonderful, are transpiring in a vacuum, and I think it boils down to the fact that we're middle class"; living outside history is thus "the price paid for day-to-day comfort and silence."[46] Similarly, the lack of history and narrativity represented in the popular low-budget film *Clerks* (1994) is most visible in the characters' attempts to come to terms with downward mobility and the sense of betrayal associated with the inability to live up to the promise of middle-class achievement. *Clerks* depicts the day in the life of Dante, a twenty-two-year-old college dropout turned convenience store clerk, and Randall, a fast-talking, wise-cracking young man who works in the video store next door. Their jobs bring them into constant contact with an incompetent and genuinely deranged public that serves as the object of their amusement and direct insults. And yet in the climactic moment of the film when Dante and Randall brawl after the latter's unwanted interventions in the former's love life, the seemingly content Randall erupts with a voice of betrayal and self-pity:

> You like to think the weight of the world rests on your shoulders, like this place would fall apart if Dante wasn't here. Jesus, you overcompensate for having what's basically a monkey's job. You push fucking buttons. Anybody could waltz in here and do our jobs. You're so obsessed with making it seem so much more epic, so much more important than it really is. Christ, you work in a convenience store—and badly I might add. I work in a shitty video store—badly as well. You know that guy Jay [a young drug dealer who hangs out in front of the convenience store] has got it right—he has no delusions about what he does. Us, we like to make ourselves seem so much more important than the people who come in here to buy a paper or, God forbid, cigarettes. We look down on them as if we're so advanced, but if we're so fucking advanced, what are we doing working here?

At the most nihilistic end of the spectrum is MTV's *Beavis and Butt-Head*, which features two futureless losers who, when not in school or at their jobs at a fast-food restaurant, sit on a couch and viscerally respond (i.e., something is either "cool" or it "sucks") to an endless stream of videos and images. To call Beavis and Butt-Head "alienated" would miss the point, for they have no means of identifying with any alternative, of linking their moments of pure elation and refusal into any kind of a coherent response. Central to such a deficiency, of course, is Beavis and Butt-Head's infamous stupidity, much of which revolves around their total lack of historical knowledge and the rather humorous instances where historical figures are confused with pop culture stars and vice versa.

In the place of history understood in the traditional sense, Jameson has observed, postmodern subjects revel in a kind of nostalgia that associates a particular period with "a list of stereotypes, of ideas of facts and historical realities."[47] Within contemporary youth culture, such debased expressions of historicity have returned in everything from the proliferation of nostalgic film to "retro" fashions to the renewed popularity of any number of pop musicians from past decades. While we need to recognize the frequently creative dimensions of reappropriation and restoration and the manner in which the "vintage" sometimes comes to serve as a new model of authenticity,[48] for the most part this type of consumerism intersects with ironic distance insofar as we are not so much fascinated with the object itself but by the sense that someone at some time in the past—perhaps we ourselves when we were younger—could actually take that object so seriously.[49] In other instances, however, nostalgia conveys and in some sense reproduces the disempowerment that many young people feel. To be sure, we can see much evidence supporting Lawrence Grossberg's argument that the difference between categories of youth and adulthood is being deconstructed through "the contradiction between those who experience the powerlessness of their age (adolescents and college students) and the generations of the baby boomers who have attached the category of youth to their life trajectory, in part by defining it as an attitude ('You're only as old as you feel')."[50] In short, young people are routinely reminded that History has passed them by, that they only exist in the shadows of the baby boom generation, that "everything has already been done" and thus "the only time worth living is in the past." The continued popularity of such nostalgia among actual young people is not simply the effect of marketing ploys and generational hegemony, but rather testifies to the longing for the empowerment and freedom associated with the images of the 1960s and 1970s. Such generational envy—which has not only sparked nostalgia but a good deal of resentment as well[51]—is of course compounded by the fact of downward mobility, by the knowledge that the previous generation had more opportunities and, in turn, a larger share of the national spotlight.

Toward a More Optimistic Conclusion

To this point, I have admittedly sketched a very pessimistic political picture and, unfortunately, I am not alone. Notwithstanding the latent uneasiness of the yuppies and nerds portrayed by Douglas Coupland, downward mobility has more often inspired reactionary defensiveness than progressive solidarity within the middle class. Farther down the social hierarchy, the metalheads of Donna Gaines's superb ethnography, *Teenage Wasteland*, imagine suicide to be the only means of transcendence in the face of dismal economic prospects and excessive institutional control. Moreover, the sort of affectlessness and depoliticization that have been surveyed above have, as demonstrated by Lawrence Grossberg, played a crucial role in constructing the conservative hegemony that remains with us today. I want to acknowledge the obvious credulity of these conclusions and, at the same time, offer some more optimistic instances of contemporary youth-dominated cultural practices. After all, one of the fundamental lessons offered by Antonio Gramsci and the cultural studies his writings helped inspire is that both symbolic universes and social orders are full of divergent meanings and political possibilities—in short, we must refuse the temptation to guarantee the course of history.

The first of my two examples concerns the proliferation of "do-it-yourself" micromedia that redirect technology and employment skills toward the production of music, fashion, and underground media. For example, in her extraordinary look at the rise of rap and hip hop in New York City, Tricia Rose reveals that many rappers, DJs, and producers "were 'trained' for jobs in fields that no longer exist" in postindustrial urban America.[52] These poor, inner-city inhabitants, trained to maintain and repair new technologies or for work in recently computerized industries like drafting or printing, proceeded to employ their skills in a creative and unintended manner, "as primary tools for alternative cultural expression."[53] Similarly, Angela McRobbie has shown how British youths looking to break into the culture and fashion industries—with or without the properly "marketable" skills—have played a crucial entrepreneurial role in the development of "ragmarkets" and other small-scale networks of countercultural practice.[54] Within the American middle class, of course, such localized activity has centered on post-punk rock 'n' roll. As we've seen, such subcultures are in large part responses to the dissolution of sources of sincerity and authenticity in postmodern society, but they also serve as an increasingly attractive option among those having trouble breaking into the job market and seeking a kind of meaningful work that may be otherwise unavailable. Though it is unclear exactly what effect newfound corporate interest will have over the long run, such cultural practices not only provide a self-sustained medium for experimentation with "alternative" identities but also allow for the *process* of active collaboration in the creation of underground networks and lines of communication. If the creative content remains largely nihilistic and cynical, we must remember that the participatory form of collective self-empowerment can be appropriated for more explicitly oppositional ends.

Second, if our media-saturated society allows for the appropriation of any number of cultural forms imported from distant places or recycled from previous eras, we must be wary of concluding that such hybrids *only* generate meaningless, ironically distanced "pastiche" and disempowering nostalgia. Let us consider the growing dialogue between post-punk and 1950s-influenced rockabilly.[55] Indeed, many such performers and "scenesters" pose with all-knowing smirks, suggesting that they are simply "putting on" for their audiences in a manner consistent with punk's longstanding use of ironic distance and self-parody. Nonetheless, there is also evidence that such a cultural conversation expresses a really perceived affinity between these two historical forms and provides a type of narrative that recovers rock 'n' roll's cultural opposition at a time when it is included as part of a conservative nostalgia for the innocence and domesticity of the 1950s. As a longtime participant in San Diego's post-punk-meets-rockabilly scene once told me:

> Well, you've got to remember, the media criticism against [punk] was very akin to the media hype against rock and roll. . . . The fact that it was rebellious and it made your parents uptight and worried about you. . . . You read an interview with Mike Ness [of the Orange County-based punk band Social Distortion] and he describes it perfectly. When he thinks of the 1950s, he thinks of fucking dopers, seedy alleyway strippers, the seedy kind of thing. Not this fucking "Rock Around the Clock," Dick Clark bullshit.

Still in its embryonic stage, it remains to be seen whether cultural dialogues such as these can supply young people with the alternative vision they seek and the history and solidarity so desperately needed for a new era of American youth culture.

NOTES

1. See Michael Lee Cohen, *The Twenty-Something American Dream*, and Paul Rogat Loeb, *Generation at the Crossroads*.

2. Stan Cohen, *Folk Devils and Moral Panics*; Jock Young, *The Drugtakers*.

3. Of course, this question of representativeness is not altogether unimportant, and there are some very good reasons for a swelling backlash coming from within the ranks of youth themselves. Advertisers, for instance, have exploited the "Generation X" phenomenon in order to target an important consumer group in the wake of the "aging" of the baby boom generation. Second, the focus on underachievement should be seen partially as the projected anxieties of a class whose parents fear that their children are not succeeding or will not succeed in an increasingly competitive environment because they lack the proper motivation and self-discipline. See Barbara Ehrenreich, *Fear of Falling*. Finally, images of twentysomethings as cynical and apathetic frequently turn out to be inversions of baby boomers' youthful self-images (socially engaged, idealistic) and thus help to reaffirm that which has been so important to the collective identity and life trajectories of the latter. See Lawrence Grossberg, *We Gotta Get out of This Place*.

4. Raymond Williams, *Marxism and Literature*.

5. Fredric Jameson, "Postmodernism, or, The Cultural Logic of Late Capitalism."

6. Fredric Jameson, *Postmodernism, or, The Cultural Logic of Late Capitalism*, 15.

7. Lawrence Grossberg, *We Gotta Get out of This Place*.

8. Jean Baudrillard, *Simulations*.

9. Todd Gitlin, "Postmodernism," 104. Though emphasizing the acceleration of time rather than the transformations of subjectivity per se, David Harvey is similarly pessimistic about the opportunities for feeling and commitment in postmodernity. In Harvey's view, the volatility of post-Fordism generates a "throwaway" society, which means "being able to throw away values, life-styles, stable relationships, and attachments to things, places, people, and received ways of doing and thinking." David Harvey, *The Condition of Postmodernity*, 289.

10. Fredric Jameson, *Postmodernism, or, The Cultural Logic of Late Capitalism*, 16.

11. Lawrence Grossberg, *We Gotta Get out of This Place*, 212.

12. Ibid., 222.

13. Douglas Coupland, *Generation X*.

14. Ibid., 150.

15. Douglas Kellner, *Media Culture*.

16. Ibid., 140.

17. Michael Ryan and Douglas Kellner, *Camera Politica*.

18. Douglas Coupland, *Life after God*, 150.

19. Douglas Coupland, *Polaroids from the Dead*, 62.

20. Ibid., 9.

21. Lawrence Grossberg, "Is There Rock after Punk?"; Dick Hebdidge, *Subculture*; Greil Marcus, *Lipstick Traces*.

22. One persistent symptom of such exhaustion regards an apparent inability to shock audiences in the usual manner. Such a "crisis"—by no means limited to post-punk music—is the product of a media-saturated society where the shocking and the horrifying have become routine aspects of everyday life; not only have apocalyptic and violently terrifying images become commonplace in mainstream popular culture, but they are ironically *sanitized* when received in a context where everything is just an image without any recognizable tie to reality. Jane's Addiction captured this sentiment with their 1988 album *Nothing's Shocking*, whose cover art features two naked, female Siamese twins with their heads on fire and includes the song, "Ted, Just Admit It" ("Camera got them images/ camera got them all/ nothing's shocking/ showed me everybody/ naked and disfigured/ nothing's shocking"). Novelist Bret Easton Ellis has attempted to generalize this condition to the "twentysomething" generation

as a whole: "Since contemporary subversiveness is all on the surface popular culture doesn't, it can't, jolt us in ways it did previous generations. We're basically unshockable. And so culture doesn't play the same role in our lives that it did for previous generations: to liberate, break boundaries, show the unshowable" (quoted in Lawrence Grossberg, *We Gotta Get out of This Place*, 186).

23. Henri Lefebvre, *Everyday Life in the Modern World.*

24. Too often, of course, punk and post-punk's oppositionality is collapsed into differences of form, suggesting that what is presented as anti-corporate resistance is frequently little more than anti-mass culture prejudice. Thus, popular groups like Rage Against the Machine who do profess strong, radical views are regularly dismissed as "hypocrites" because they record for a major rather than independent recording label. While such concerns for authenticity have long been an integral part of rock music and its subcultures, its parallel can be seen in a growing generation of "activists" who distrust ideology in general, maintaining that authentic commitment and concern can only be demonstrated by way of altruistic service work or "environmentally friendly" lifestyle changes and individual choices. See Paul Loeb, *Generation at the Crossroads.*

25. Quoted in Michael Azerrad, *Come as You Are*, 211.

26. Ibid., 175.

27. See ibid., 213–15.

28. For a similar attempt to link postmodernity as an "expressive form" to the "social and material life-experience" of the baby boom generation and professional-managerial class, see Fred Pfeil, "Makin' Flippy-Floppy." Similar results with respect to race, ethnicity, and class are achieved by George Lipsitz, "Cruising around the Historical Bloc," and Tricia Rose, *Black Noise.*

29. In short, many social scientists have recently observed an important shift in the operation of capital since the early 1970s such that the days of standardized mass production, a mostly stable spatial division of labor, and a large, relatively well-paid workforce have given way to the "post-Fordist" era of decentered production processes, greater geographic mobility of capital, higher turnover time via the production of instantly disposable "spectacles," the proliferation of computer-based industries, and large numbers of flexible, temporary, lower-paid workers engaged in the production of services and information. See Ash Amin, "Post-Fordism"; Mark Elam, "Puzzling out the Post-Fordist Debate"; Stuart Hall, "Brave New World"; David Harvey, *The Condition of Postmodernity.*

30. Recent forecasts suggest that "almost all" of the newly created jobs from 1992 to 2005 will be in the service-producing sector ("Employment in Industries" 1993: 20). Service-sector employment will account for an estimated 81 percent of all employment by 2005, a steady increase from 78 percent in 1992, 70 percent in 1979, and just 40 percent in 1959 ("Employment in Industries" 1993: 21; Katherine S. Newman, *Falling from Grace*, 30). It is expected that four-fifths of all new job growth between 1992 and 2005 will come from services (e.g. health, business, and education services, but not including the more lucrative spheres of finance, insurance, and real estate) and retail trade (cashiers, waiters and waitresses, and food preparation workers are among the fastest-growing occupations) ("Employment in Industries" 1993: 22). One-third of all new jobs created in the first half of the 1980s were thought to be of a temporary nature (David Harvey, *The Condition of Postmodernity*, 152) and overall temp work has grown at a rate nine times faster than total employment since 1979 (Katherine S. Newman, "Uncertain Seas," 118).

31. Nearly two-fifths of all workers displaced during the early 1980s were either professionals, managers, or people who held jobs in administrative, sales, and technical fields (Kath-

erine S. Newman, *Falling from Grace*, 25). By 1990, *Business Week* was reporting that 65 percent of the 485,000 newly unemployed workers were managers, professionals, and their clerical employees (ibid., 47). According to the *Wall Street Journal*, cost-cutting, mergers, and takeovers were responsible for some 600,000 middle-management layoffs in 1985 alone (ibid., 34.). Thus, as Katherine Newman has explained, the larger source of trouble is "not simply that people are being laid off from jobs in large numbers," but rather that "the jobs themselves are evaporating" (Katherine S. Newman, *Declining Fortunes*, 25).

32. One year after graduation, more than 40 percent of the class of 1990 were either unemployed or working jobs that did not require a four-year degree (Gary Steinberg, "The Class of '90," 12). While humanities and history majors were the most likely to end up unemployed or in noncollege-level jobs, it is worth noting that 47 percent of business and management majors also found themselves in this dubious position (ibid., 12). While things do tend to get better as a college graduate gets older, about 20 percent of bachelor's degree holders between the ages of thirty and sixty-four were employed in noncollege-level jobs in 1992 (Thomas A. Amirault, "Job Market Profiles of College Graduates in 1992," 24), and this ratio is expected to increase to between 25 and 30 percent for those entering the labor market between 1992 and 2005 (Katherine J. Shelley, "More Job Openings—Even More Entrants," 5; Katherine S. Newman, *Declining Fortunes*, 231.)

33. Whereas 43 percent of persons between the ages of twenty-five and twenty-nine and 61 percent of those between the ages of thirty and thirty-four owned their own home in 1980, a mere ten years later these percentages had dropped to 36 percent for the twenty-five- to twenty-nine-year-olds and 52 percent for the thirty- to thirty-four-year-olds (Katherine S. Newman, *Declining Fortunes*, 30). Overall, the median age of the first-time homeowner leaped from twenty-seven in the early 1980s to thirty-five in 1991 (ibid., 32). The vast majority, then, have had to confront a 28 percent real increase in rents since 1982 (ibid., 53). With regard to education, tremendous and seemingly never-ending increases in tuition at both public and private colleges and universities have coincided with drastic cuts in aid and grants. Thus, not only are more students having to work longer hours at their outside jobs, but they must also now take out larger government loans. Thirty-four percent of graduates from the class of 1977 were in debt eight to twenty months after leaving college and owed an average of just over $4,000 (1990 dollars). Among the class of 1990, on the other hand, 45 percent found themselves owing an average of $7,000 within the same amount of time after graduation (Paul Rogat Loeb, *Generation at the Crossroads*, 406). Young people are also more likely to find themselves owing more as the competition for good jobs heats up and postgraduate degrees become viewed as necessities rather than luxuries. One recent study found that 83 percent of all 1989–90 recipients of bachelor's degrees plan to pursue postgraduate schooling and that more than one-third of these recipients enrolled in graduate programs one year after graduation, a noticeable increase from the mid-to-late 1980s, when less than one-quarter of students immediately enrolled (Gary Steinberg, "The Class of '90," 12).

34. Stanley Aronowitz and William DiFazio, *The Jobless Future*.

35. Katherine S. Newman, "Uncertain Seas," 122.

36. Of course, such widespread optimism rapidly dissipated as a result of defeat, police repression, the continued escalation of the Vietnam War, and numerous drug-related tragedies. For an interesting account of the withdrawal from such Faustian experimentation, see Marshall Berman, "Sympathy for the Devil." Indeed, independently of economic restructuring, I think the events of the late 1960s represent an important turning point within white youth culture and, to complicate matters further, have contributed to the kind of disaffection discussed above. While this is not the place to elaborate upon such an argument, in the future

I plan to examine how such a critical turn of events represents a dialogical reference point for much contemporary youth culture.

37. See Todd Gitlin, *The Sixties.*

38. Marshall Berman, "Sympathy for the Devil," 68.

39. Using a rather humorous, pop-sociological glossary to frame the narrative itself, Coupland defines this type of work in the opening pages of the novel as a "McJob: A low-pay, low-prestige, low-dignity, low-benefit, no-future job in the service sector. Frequently considered a satisfying career choice by people who have never held one" (Douglas Coupland, *Generation X*, 5). Beyond the relatively low incomes and generational inequality, Coupland also frequently refers to the working conditions which we have seen as characteristic of "late capitalism." As Aronowitz and DiFazio have documented the proletarianization of middle-class work, Coupland introduces us to the sacrifice of "recurving," the act of "leaving one's job to take another that pays less but places one back on the learning curve" (Douglas Coupland, *Generation X*, 24). The less than desirable environment of office work is depicted in the "veal-fattening pen: small, cramped office workstations built of fabric-covered disassemblable wall partitions and inhabited by junior staff members. Named after the small preslaughter cubicles used by the cattle industry," while the migration or avoidance of "unhealthy office environments or workplaces" is known as "sick building migration" (ibid., 20).

40. Such sentiments are, of course, very similar to those chronicled in Katherine Newman's interviews with younger, downwardly mobile members of the baby boom generation. In brief, Newman shows us how middle-class explanations of "failure" alternate between the self-blame consistent with the spirit of liberal individualism and the projection of resentment onto more fortunate generations, illegitimate elites (more likely liberal politicians than capitalists), and "parasitic underclasses" who are supposedly unwilling to pick themselves up by their bootstraps and work their way out of poverty. With Coupland, the strong connection between work, material wealth, and self-worth is evident in "ozmosis," "the inability of one's job to live up to one's self-image" (Douglas Coupland, *Generation X*, 25). Reconciliation and/or compensation for loss of prestige are also the source of much of the humor of *Generation X*. Hence we are presented with "lessness," defined as "a philosophy whereby one reconciles oneself with diminishing expectations of material wealth: 'I've given up wanting to make a killing or be a bigshot. I just want to find happiness and maybe open a little roadside cafe in Idaho' " as well as the post-yuppie consumerism of "status substitution," or the use of "an object with intellectual or fashionable cachet to substitute for an object that is merely pricey: 'Brian, you left your copy of Camus in your brother's BMW' " and "conspicuous minimalism," an entire lifestyle based on status substitution (ibid., 54).At other moments, *Generation X* devolves into simple generational resentment. Dag, for instance, is introduced as a former employee of an advertising firm who once aspired to the superficiality of yuppiedom but proceeded to move to the desert when it became clear that the opportunities for such mobility no longer existed. He finally quits his job when his complaints about the poor health conditions of his office place escalate into a verbal attack against his forty-one-year-old, "hippie turned yuppie" boss:

> Or for that matter, do you really think we en*joy* hearing about your brand new million-dollar *home* when we can barely afford to eat Kraft Dinner sandwiches in our grimy little shoe boxes and we're pushing *thirty*? A home you won in a genetic lottery, I might add, sheerly by dint of your having been born at the right time in history? You'd last about ten minutes if you were my age these days, Martin. And I have to endure pinheads like you rushing above me for the rest of my life, always grabbing the best piece of

> cake first and then putting a barbed wire fence around the rest. You make me sick. (Ibid., 21)

41. Barbara Ehrenreich, *Fear of Falling.*

42. In *Generation X*, for instance, the lead character is stunned to learn that his younger brother—a "wannabe yuppie"—is terrified that deep anxieties will peer through his mask of cool indifference:

> I know—it looks as if I enjoy what's going on with my life and everything, but listen, my heart's only half in it. You give my friends and me a bum rap but I'd give *all* of this up in a *flash* if someone had a remotely plausible alternative. . . . And it scares me that I don't see a future. And I don't understand this reflex of mine to be such a smartass about everything. It *really* scares me. I may not look like I'm paying attention to anything, Andy, but I am. But I can't allow myself to show it. And I don't know why. (Douglas Coupland, *Generation X*, 150).

43. Katherine S. Newman, *Declining Fortunes*; George Lipsitz, "The Possessive Investment in Whiteness."

44. Fredric Jameson, "Postmodernism, or, The Cultural Logic of Late Capitalism," 72.

45. Douglas Coupland, *Generation X*, 8.

46. Ibid., 147.

47. Fredric Jameson, *Postmodernism, or, The Cultural Logic of Late Capitalism*, 279.

48. See Angela McRobbie, *Postmodernism and Popular Culture*, and Sarah Thornton, *Club Cultures.*

49. In his second film, *Dazed and Confused* (1993), Richard Linklater transforms such ironically distanced nostalgia into a feature-length film. A portrayal of the last day of high school in Houston, Texas, in 1976, *Dazed and Confused* features a soundtrack of what is now termed "classic rock" and long, aestheticized shots of those signifiers of 1970s youth culture: gas guzzling Novas and Mustangs, puka shells, long feathered hair, skin-tight jeans, and, of course, a seemingly endless supply of pot and pot-smoking paraphernalia.

50. Lawrence Grossberg, *We Gotta Get out of This Place*, 183.

51. This latter can be seen, for instance, in the lyrics of "Against the 70's," performed by Mike Watt and Pearl Jam vocalist Eddie Vedder:

> The kids of today should defend themselves against the 70's!
> It ain't reality, just someone else's sentimentality
> It won't work for you
> Baby boomers selling you rumors of their history
> Forcing youth away from the truth of what's real today
> The kids of today should defend themselves against the 70's!
> Stadium minds with stadium lies gotta make you laugh
> Garbage vendors against true defenders of the craft
> The kids of today should defend themselves against the 70's!

With respect to downward mobility, it seems that many youths take revengeful delight in the image exemplified by Jerry Rubin not because they are conservative ideologues, but rather because they resent both the perceived economic privilege "won in a genetic lottery" and the attention that this affluence helped to both create and subsequently sustain. Such a backlash is perhaps best represented in Ben Stiller's commercially successful counterpart to *Slacker* and *Generation X, Reality Bites* (1993). The opening scene of this film takes us to a college graduation in Houston, Texas, as the valedictory speech is being delivered by the lead female character, Laney (Winona Ryder):

> And they wonder why those of us in our twenties refuse to work an eighty-hour week

just so we can afford to buy their BMWs, why we aren't interested in the counterculture that they invented, as if we did not see them disembowel their revolution for a pair of running shoes. But the question remains—what are we going to do now? [Shot of a graduate with the words "Will Work 4 Food" inscribed on the top of his cap] How can we repair the damage that we inherited? Fellow graduates, the answer is simple.

As we might expect, the joke is that Laney has no answer—she has misplaced the note cards to her speech. She nervously fumbles, repeating "the answer is . . . I don't know," at which time the audience erupts in applause.

52. Tricia Rose, *Black Noise*, 35.

53. Ibid., 63.

54. Angela McRobbie, *Postmodernism and Popular Culture*, 135–154.

55. Such a style centers on slicked-back short hair, long sideburns, and large-collar, Southwestern-design shirts and a kind of music (e.g., the John Spencer Blues Explosion, the Supersuckers, Rocket from the Crypt, and the Reverend Horton Heat) that combines the volume and noise of punk rock with more traditional blues riffs, rockabilly tempos, and/or big horn sections.

REFERENCES

Amin, Ash. "Post-Fordism: Models, Fantasies and Phantoms of Transitions," in Amin, ed., *Post-Fordism: A Reader*, 1–39. Cambridge, U.K.: Blackwell, 1994.

Amirault, Thomas A. "Job Market Profiles of College Graduates in 1992: A Focus on Jobs and Earnings." *Occupational Outlook Quarterly* 38 (Summer 1992), 24–27.

Aronowitz, Stanley, and William DiFazio. *The Jobless Future: Sci-Tech and the Dogma of Work.* Minneapolis: University of Minnesota Press, 1994.

Azerrad, Michael. *Come as You Are: The Story of Nirvana.* New York: Doubleday, 1995.

Baudrillard, Jean. *Simulations.* New York: Semiotext(e), 1983.

Berman, Marshall. "Sympathy for the Devil: Faust, the '60s and the Tragedy of Development," *American Review* 19 (August 1974), 23–75.

Cohen, Michael Lee. *The Twenty-Something American Dream.* New York: Dutton, 1993.

Cohen, Stan. *Folk Devils and Moral Panics: The Creation of the Mods and Rockers.* Oxford: Blackwell, 1980.

Coupland, Douglas. *Generation X: Tales for an Accelerated Culture.* New York: St. Martin's Press, 1991.

Coupland, Douglas. *Shampoo Planet.* New York: Pocket Books, 1992.

Coupland, Douglas. *Life after God.* New York: Pocket Books, 1994.

Coupland, Douglas. *Microserfs.* New York: HarperCollins, 1995.

Coupland, Douglas. *Polaroids from the Dead.* New York: HarperCollins, 1996.

Ehrenreich, Barbara. *Fear of Falling: The Inner Life of the Middle Class.* New York: HarperPerennial, 1989.

Elam, Mark. "Puzzling out the Post-Fordist Debate," in Ash Amin, ed., *Post-Fordism: A Reader*, 41–70. Cambridge, U.K.: Blackwell, 1994.

Gaines, Donna. *Teenage Wasteland: Suburbia's Dead End Kids.* New York: HarperPerennial, 1992.

Gitlin, Todd. *The Sixties: Years of Hope, Days of Rage.* New York: Bantam Books, 1987.

Gitlin, Todd. "Postmodernism: Roots and Politics," *Dissent* 36 (Spring 1989), 100–108.

Grossberg, Lawrence. "Is There Rock after Punk?" *Critical Studies in Mass Communication* 3 (January-February 1986), 50–74.

Grossberg, Lawrence. *We Gotta Get out of This Place: Popular Conservatism and Postmodern Culture*. New York: Routledge, 1992.
Hall, Stuart. "Brave New World." *Marxism Today* 11 (June 1988), 24–29.
Harvey, David. *The Condition of Postmodernity: An Enquiry into the Origins of Cultural Change*. Cambridge, U.K.: Blackwell, 1989.
Hebdidge, Dick. *Subculture: The Meaning of Style*. New York: Routledge, 1979.
Jameson, Fredric. "Postmodernism, or, The Cultural Logic of Late Capitalism." *New Left Review* 146 (July-August 1984), 53–92.
Jameson, Fredric. *Postmodernism, or, The Cultural Logic of Late Capitalism*. Durham, N.C.: Duke University Press, 1991.
Kellner, Douglas. *Media Culture: Between the Modern and Postmodern*. New York: Routledge, 1995.
Lefebvre, Henri. *Everyday Life in the Modern World*. New Brunswick: Transaction, 1984.
Lipsitz, George. "Cruising around the Historical Bloc: Postmodernism and Popular Music in East Los Angeles," in his *Time Passages: Collective Memory and American Popular Culture*, 133–60. Minneapolis: University of Minnesota Press, 1990.
Lipsitz, George. "The Possessive Investment in Whiteness: The 'White' Problem in American Studies." *American Quarterly* 47 (Fall/1995), 369–387.
Loeb, Paul Rogat. *Generation at the Crossroads: Apathy and Action on the American Campus*. New Brunswick, N.J.: Rutgers University Press, 1994.
Marcus, Greil. *Lipstick Traces: A Secret History of the Twentieth Century*. Cambridge, Mass.: Harvard University Press, 1986.
McRobbie, Angela. *Postmodernism and Popular Culture*. New York: Routledge, 1994.
Newman, Katherine S. *Falling from Grace: The Experience of Downward Mobility in the American Middle Class*. New York: Free Press, 1988.
Newman, Katherine S. "Uncertain Seas: Cultural Turmoil and the Domestic Economy," in Alan Wolfe, ed., *America at Century's End*, 112–30. Berkeley: University of California Press, 1991.
Newman, Katherine S. *Declining Fortunes: The Withering of the American Dream*. New York: Basic Books, 1993.
Pfeil, Fred. " 'Makin' Flippy-Floppy': Postmodernism and the Baby-Boom PMC," in his *Another Tale to Tell: Politics and Narrative in Postmodern Culture*, 97–125. New York: Verso, 1988.
Rose, Tricia. *Black Noise: Rap Music and Black Culture in Contemporary America*. Hanover, N.H.: Wesleyan University Press, 1994.
Ryan, Michael, and Douglas Kellner. *Camera Politica: The Politics and Ideology of Contemporary Hollywood*. Bloomington: Indiana University Press, 1988.
Shelley, Katherine J. "More Job Openings—Even More Entrants: The Job Outlook for College Graduates, 1992–2005." *Occupational Outlook Quarterly* 38 (Summer 1994), 5–9.
Steinberg, Gary. "The Class of '90: One Year after Graduation." *Occupational Outlook Quarterly* 38 (Summer 1992), 12–14.
Thornton, Sarah. *Club Cultures: Music, Media, and Subcultural Capital*. Hanover, N.H.: Wesleyan University Press, 1995.
Williams, Raymond. *Marxism and Literature*. Oxford: Oxford University Press, 1977.
Young, Jock. *The Drugtakers: The Social Meaning of Drug Use*. London: Paladin, 1971.

Chapter Sixteen

Dancin' in the Street to a Black Girl's Beat

Music, Gender, and the Ins and Outs of Double-Dutch

Kyra D. Gaunt

Between the gendered assumptions of the maleness of black nationalism or the whiteness of feminism, where do we find an articulation of black-female or "womanist" thought in everyday performance? Though I believe such performance exists in various places, the evidence is difficult to observe within a black popular sphere dominated by hip-hop music—assumed to be a "male" sphere by too many. An answer can be found in a youthful site of musical play. Double-Dutch and the game songs that accompany it demonstrate the formation of certain ideals of black music making that articulate the uniqueness of blackness and femaleness simultaneously.

"I Am Not One Piece of Myself. I Cannot Simply Be a Black Person and Not Be a Woman, Too."

An examination of double-Dutch shows how blackness and femaleness share similar geographies of race/nation consciousness that are conventionally attributed to black male experience.[1] Such performative expression also allows girls to defy the socializing gravity of male hegemony during their youth.

The basis of my claim is the result of an ethnomusicological study that details the musical memories and experiences of African American women who primarily dwelled in urban cities, including Memphis, Detroit, Philadelphia, and New York City. My research suggests that (1) a discernible black vernacular style of music making is learned and manifest in African American girls' play; (2) girls' games are an extension of specific antebellum and early twentieth-century body musicking among African Americans (male *and* female); and (3) the performances of black girls' games are constantly shaped by interpretations of not only race, but gender and sexuality.[2] Given these suggestions, why are black women regularly underrepresented in black popular music making today? The answer appears to be the result of a process that causes black girls' social practices to be read differently in private and public spheres, transforming ideals of black musical play into taboos about female respectability. Freedoms of performance that would be "fair game" in the somewhat exclusively female rhythms and rhymes of double-Dutch are often regulated, and thereby restricted in certain ways, by adults legislating *sportsmanlike* conduct in the mixed racial settings that accompany public performance and competition.

Learning the Ropes of Double-Dutch: Playing with the Popular in Private

At first thought, one might not associate double-Dutch with the stylistic innovations of black popular music, nor with the lived experiences of adult black women who have left the dodging of turning ropes behind. But if one understands popular music as a derivation of black vernacular expression, the relationship is more apparent. But what is double-Dutch?

Imagine that a designated jumper navigates a floating, elliptical space above the pavement defined by two inversely rotating lengths of taut rope. The jumper's feet dance in alternation, leaping above the turning ropes as they pass below. Each rope is navigated by two designated turners who face each other. Their opposing hands grasp each rope and link the turners together in an unusual form of rope play involving rhymes and chants, song and dance, humor and musical gesture, and spectacular kinetic ability.

The primary "rule" or aesthetic ideal of double-Dutch play is to maintain consistency while exploring one's kinetic potential and energy in a span of *musical* time and space. Time and space are linked in the requirement that one keeps the beat or pulse steady, developing an inner sense of a metronomic pulse no matter what movements are performed. This is an ideal found in black dance and music making: keeping the rhythm, not interrupting the meter and the flow of the musical experience. This is a critical skill required for black social musicking. The skill facilitates the learning of new styles of dance, vogue gestures, and vernacular oral expressions all performed in stylized ways.

Liese (pronounced "lee-sah"), a woman in her early thirties from the Bronx, communicated some of these ideals in an interview I conducted:

> Whoever had jump ropes brought 'em out. [Girls] were out in the morning by nine o'clock, you know, eight-thirty, nine o'clock. It's like most of the girls that I would have been hanging out with, we would all be there. Double-Dutch was a game that was . . . predicated on rhythms . . . the longer you could jump meant you were cool, you were fluid. You had rhythm if you could jump [double-Dutch]. . . . [You] jump to patterns. . . . I was never a great double-Dutch person. But I learned. And I worked at

it. Those of us that were not as wonderful would work at it, so that we could be cool. You were *cool* and you had *rhythm*.[3]

Double-Dutch represented a way of authentically experiencing "black-femaleness" as being connected to *black* time, to an ability to express stylized musical movement in ways that were "on time." What happens when you're not "on time"? You get eliminated from play momentarily. Mistakes open up the elliptical stage to the next jumper and/or turner. If a jumper gets the ropes tangled around her feet or one of the circulating ropes is clipped by an arm or a bobbing head, your time is up, but your participation does not end. The concept of "musicking" defined by Christopher Small is useful here; musicking is the act of taking part in ritual performance. Considering music as an act narrows divisions between composer, performer, and listener—all participants are actively involved in the success of black musicking.[4]

If we check out one of the chants that accompanies the characteristic fancy footwork found in double-Dutch, we can glimpse in our imagination the rhythmic complexity, the syncopated coordination of oral and kinetic behavior. The girls must strive to maintain the steady articulation of the pulse sounded jointly by the jumper's feet slapping the pavement and the sound of the ropes skimming its surface. One is bound to hear the recurrent singing of the rhythmic phrase "red hot pepper" accompanying double-Dutch activity. "Red hot pepper," or the individual words "hot," "pepper," or "fire," signify the exciting footwork of double-Dutch. Both the skipping of the ropes and the syncopated footfalls on the pavement or "blacktop" act as a timeline for, and against which, gestures, tuneful melodies, and rhymes are performed in complex musical ways. In an example referred to as "James Brown" (after the "godfather" himself), the accents within the rhymed chant assist the coordination of synchronized movements (i.e., touching the ground or turning around within the undulating ropes). This demonstrates that hip hop is not the only musical context in black culture that samples material from the godfather of soul. James Brown epitomizes the act of shaping music out of, and into, a reflection of the secular experiences found in black social contexts—the sweat of "breaking it down" in a moment of dance, the look and feel of the black dancing body accompanied by gospel-inflected hollers and screams. Why not link Brown's performance to the street performance of double-Dutch by black girls?

In table 16. 1, I have attempted to highlight the measured phrasing of this chant

TABLE 16.1.
"James Brown" Double-Dutch Chant

Downbeats Footfalls	1 r-foot	2 l-foot	3 rf	4 lf	1 rf	2 lf	3 rf	4 lf
	I *went*	down	town	( )	to *see*	James	Brown	( )
	He *gave*	me a	nick-el	( )	to *buy*	a	pick-le	( )
	The *pickle*	was	so-ur	( )	He *gave*	me a	flower	( )
	The *flower*	was	dead	so	*this*	is what	he said:	( )
	Hoppin'	on	one	foot	one	foot	one	foot
	Hoppin'	on	two	foot	two	foot	two	foot
	Hoppin'	on	three	foot	three	foot	three	foot
	Hoppin'	on	four	foot	four	foot	four	foot

SOURCE: Representation of chant based on example found in Cecelia Riddell, "Traditional Singing Games" (Ph.D. diss., University of California, Los Angeles, 1990), 138.

that is synchronized with movement by italicizing certain words. These italicized words highlight the downbeats while certain silent (but internally felt) beats are indicated by an open set of parentheses.

The youthful display of blackness in double-Dutch performance jumps between the rhythm and the rhyme of other game-song performances that also mark the everyday of black girls' play. Most apparent among them are hand-clapping games and "cheers" (performative routines shared by girls away from the sidelines of male sports). All of these games demonstrate the orality of music and social drama that reflects and incorporates popular lyrical themes, tuneful refrains, and vernacular expressions and dances—old and new. The game songs signify social-group identity through everyday musicking that indicates a relationship to popular recordings such as "Shimmy Shimmy Ko-Ko-Bop" and "Rockin' Robin."[5] Black popular culture has reflected a dialogical process between the private and public spheres since at least the 1940s. This process bears witness to the consciousness of black girls and their role in modeling everyday black musicking.

> Songs with references to familiar folk tales and sagas or to everyday speech or street-corner games tended to include listeners in a community of improvisation and elaboration.... [The songs] ritualistically confirmed the commonality of everyday experience.... [They] survived because of their appeal as narratives, but also because they marshaled the resources of the past as part of defining identity in the present.[6]

Double-Dutch, as well as the other types of game songs, are a part of an enculturational process through which the aesthetics of black social musicking and a gendered ethnicity are learned in complex ways. These games help transmit and teach various aspects of black performance, including rhythmic complexity (i.e., syncopation and polyrhythm), coordination of hip rotations and punctuation in musical time, the concept of the break, call and response, and an internal sense of pulse and musical measurement required to choreograph and improvise stylized dances in black social experience.

The construction of a gendered ethnicity and/or an ethnicized gender is defined generation after generation by African American girls as young as age five. This generational tradition seems to go back as far as the mid-1940s, based on the age of those I interviewed. This oral tradition has existed primarily with little or no direct adult intervention. Black girls created unique social arenas of play where they freely extrapolated the musical sound, texture, and movement that defined their cultural experience in racial terms (i.e., the "funky chicken" dance or the body-musicking known as "hamboning"). These games function as a tool of expression that signifies black femaleness in urban, and also rural, contexts. Double-Dutch's origins actually appear to be located primarily in the multiethnic streets of New York City. It has since become prevalent in several other cities, including Philadelphia, New Haven, Detroit, Los Angeles, and Washington, D.C.[7]

The double-rope sidewalk play has evolved into a spotlight for athletic competition in places not conventionally associated with urban experience such as North Charleston, South Carolina—the host of the 1995 World Championships sponsored by the American Double Dutch League. The sport includes practicitioners from beyond the borders of the United States—from Canada, France, and Japan. Other kinds of borders have been crossed in the competition. Once culturally defined gender boundaries "forbade" boys' participation, or at least kept boys from admitting their active participation. As of 1980, the competition allows the limited inclusion of boys: one boy allowed per singles team, two boys per doubles team. The rules of competition limit boys' participation because of the assumption that boys might "overpower" or overwhelm the athletics performed by the girls.[8] Double-Dutch continues to be considered a *girl's* game.

The daredevilish leaps and funky chants that accompany jumping clothesline ropes in the streets continue to reflect, or at least serve, the expressivity of black femaleness through performance of vocal expressivity, gender, and the body. In street play, the expressive forms reflect both the *collaborative* musicking efforts and skillful coordination of play that is stereotypically associated with girls and the *competitive* athletic and acrobatic efforts of play stereotypically associated with boys. This interplay provides a fascinating and overdue avenue of insight into reading black women's participation in hip-hop culture as performers and/or fans from their own vantage point. It also allows a model for rereading women's roles in the histories of black vernacular and recorded musics.

Who "Owns" Soul in the Age of Hip Hop? History, Hegemonic Authority, and Memory

> History is not the past; it is an artful assembly of materials from the past designed for usefulness in the future . . . [It is] the resource out of which people create.[9]

Histories of black popular music and other histories of black music making rarely center female authority and innovation in musicking. As the above quotation suggests, we might assume that such a historical rendering is a construction of the past that informs gender roles and limits expectations about the future. The "artful" assembly of images of black women in contemporary popular music often represents the objectification of femininity and female ways of being. The common stereotype is built from a kind of modern, monolithic myth—black women as part human (they have breasts, variably "colored" brown skin, and locks of human hair) and part four-legged, female dog or "bitch" (most would be offended if an actual four-legged pet were called a "bitch"). The presence of prominent and powerful female artists to counter such objectifications, in hip hop for example, is sadly an exception in the music business. Such "diamonds in the ruff" rarely reap the kind of financial success and control that musicologist Susan McClary (1991) and other feminist critics of popular culture can ascribe to Madonna or Janet Jackson (both artists' success can be attributed to their popularity [read: sales] in more than one commercial music market; they are the business's best crossover artists). Contemporary observations of black popular music place masculine behavior and performance at the center of our collective memory. Women are continually relegated to the margins of hip-hop performance as if the production of recordings or the making of musical sound(s) were a genetic or biological process impossible for the female.

Historian Elsa Barkley Brown's work on political life in the newly evolving black public sphere of Virginia immediately following emancipation from slavery (1863) reveals the active and equitable participation of African American women and children. Brown traces how a shift away from such egalitarian participation soon resulted from black men's struggle for equality with white patriarchs. Recollections of women's (and children's) nineteenth-century egalitarian participation is now a distant, if not incredible, memory in the late twentieth century. Brown concludes that since Emancipation, the politic of "race" (or black culture) in the everyday has been associated with the "masculinization of race," particularly in public settings, leading to the distortion of the collective memory of the past:

> African Americans have come to link a history of repression and racial violence exclusively to challenges to black masculinity [establishing] a notion of freedom and black liberation which bifurcates public discussion and privileges men's history and experiences . . . Those who construct masculine notions of blackness and race progress . . . are remembering a particular history . . . [W]e have some powerful lot of *re*-remembering to do. (Emphasis added)[10]

Though limitations on my space here preclude any full *re*-remembering of the blues queens of the 1920s or key vaudeville stars and company leaders, I hope that the remainder of this chapter will inspire an interest in those black female experiences and forgotten memories as we take a close look at the reinterpretation of a girl's street performance as it moves into the public domain of sports. Whether conscious or unconscious, the "masculinization" of black musical experience in public and popular performance continues to "naturalize" the excorporation of female participation in our collective remembrances of the black musical past. This politicized amnesia limits our vision of a future with women as active agents in culture and history. Double-Dutch highlights the uses of female bodies, their movements, the articulations of their voices, and the expression of a cultural identity that provides a compelling and authoritative oral-kinetic historiography of black secular musicking and intrasocial experience since the emergence of rock 'n' roll in United States popular culture.

The musical mining of space that epitomizes double-Dutch performance was at one time an acknowledged component of the emergence of hip hop in New York City. The musical body of hip hop typically calls to mind break dancers or "b-boys" (a.k.a. break-boys) who broke the horizontal barriers of dance that recall the daredevilish acts of black dancers performing the "lindy hop." Break dancers explored four-dimensional space with back spins, head spins, and aggressive poses. Their moves challenged the eye and mind during the musical breaks or repeated hooks of hip-hop music. The challenge is also remembered as a challenge of male bravado and mock gang warfare—break dancing as a substitute for, or safer version of, real gang fights. The percussive melo-linguistic rhymes of double-Dutch accompanied similar challenges to dimensionality in dance and movement.[11] Just as the complexity of the ethnic identities that actually participated and shaped the earliest years of hip-hop culture are partially remembered (African American, Caribbean, and Latino), so too are non male and non masculine identities and behavior in hip-hop culture overlooked. Let us re-remember the forgotten from 1982, when rap music was making its first splash overseas.

> Rap, graffiti, *double-Dutch rope jumping*, and breakdancing were all part of the same thrilling South Bronx cultural explosion, the [New York City Rap Tour's] bill included Afrika Bambaataa, Fab 5 Freddy, Rammellzee, and Grandmixer DST & the Infinity Rappers (it was DST's scratching that helped to make Herbie Hancock's "Rockit" such a smash the next year). Also aboard were the breakdancing Rock Steady Crew, the *Double-Dutch Girls*, and the graffiti artists. (Emphasis added).[12]

Combining to form a subcultural movement in various boroughs throughout New York City, DJ practice, rapping, graffiti writing, and break dancing reflected aesthetic principles of "flow, layering, and rupture."[13] The public interest in street double-Dutch as a sport arose around 1973 and coincides with the emergence of the unique urban subculture we now recognize as hip hop.[14]

Double-Dutch and other expressive hip-hop forms share an urban aesthetic and way of performing that involve both cooperative and negotiated ensemble interaction and competitive skills. For example, the turners and jumpers in double-Dutch operate in a similar manner to a party DJ spinning records on a turntable through a sound system while rappers flow tunefully inflected rhymes in musical time; collaborative timing, flow, and non stop energy are keys to a "good" double-Dutch or hip-hop performance. These ideals must be practiced, negotiated among the members of the ensemble, and perfected in the moment. Competition between double-Dutch jumpers and turners (or DJs and rappers/emcees) encourages innovation, improvisation, and individual expressivity (and may consequently ignite fierce rivalries). Double-Dutch and hip-hop music may seem to reflect separate expressions because of the separation of males and females. However, these seemingly separate gender performances actually reflect a shared cultural expressivity.

Red Light, Green Light: Playing with Urban Children's Ethnicity and Gender

The transition of double-Dutch from street to sport reveals curious and odd connections. The origin of its name alone highlights its curious association with ethnicity in New York City. Many of its local associations are defined by stereotypical views of immigrants and their language as "foreign" or "alien." According to Amanda Dargan and Steven Zeitlin, ethnographers of city play, the successive waves of immigration in New York heightened concerns about ethnicity and Americanness. The alienation of new immigrants was often manifest in the ridicule of the sounds of "foreign" languages to previous "settlers" of the city who were once, in all likelihood, immigrants themselves. Such prejudices and attitudes about non-English speech and community were passed on by children as well as adults: "Girls jumped in an American style but called it 'double Dutch' or 'double Jewish'. . . . Prejudice insinuated itself into the games of the smallest children."[15] Racial and/or ethnic prejudice is at the heart of the matter whether one is castigating Jewish, Irish, or African American children. Contrary to the racial insinuations of outsiders, double-Dutch play among black girls created an arena where race and gender identity moved from the periphery to the center, sometimes embracing and reinterpreting the very epithets others used to signify inferiority of their race and sex.

In 1973, New York City police officers Ulysses Williams and David Walker organized a local competition of double-Dutch that took place at the mall area in front of Lincoln Center. June Goodwin chronicles the emergence of the sport in a *Christian Science Monitor* article. She quotes former detective Williams as he recalled thoughts about inner-city girls and sports:

> Double Dutch does not have an image of being a *"butch" game*, Williams points out. The idea was to produce a sport that is not a hand-me-down from *men*, so *girls* wouldn't feel second-class. "When I watch *women's* basketball I get ghost vision: I see *men superimposed over the women*." (Emphasis added)[16]

Consciously or unconsciously, Williams asserts that a girls' sport should not be too "masculine" and thereby implying that *sports* are a boys' thing and double-Dutch is a girls' sporty *game*—fun enough for a man, but made for a woman. Implicit here is the notion that there are genetic or biological differences between the sexes that inform the structuring of performance in public and/or institutionalized competition. Though there are certain biological differences, we tend to confuse sex difference with assumptions about gender behavior. Such interpretations privilege assumptions of "natural" gender roles in society and culture—males are "naturally" competitive and aggressive while females are "naturally" cooperative and nurturing. Williams articulates an underlying fear that raises issues about assumptions of male and femaleness. His claim concerning the appropriate gender messages of double-Dutch and his comment about ghost vision and basketball imply that women basketball players are "butch," too masculine, "out of bounds" in a gendered way; in such a case, women can only be viewed as if men were being "superimposed" upon them. This superimposition draws upon the lack of "penetration" we ascribe to female gender and/or sex roles. Women are not allowed to penetrate or interfere with men's spaces, their homosocial realms of play. The uses of history to date have taught us to naturalize, make synonymous certain associations between performing and the sex of the performer. This tangent concerning the perception of gender is important to my thesis because we will see how the culture of double-Dutch is affected because of its shift from the sidewalk to the sports arena. Basketball is not inherently "masculine" and "male" because of its history. Nor is double-Dutch an inherently female social activity. Yet we make choices based on our hegemonic interpretations of history and culture that imply assumptions about authority in the present. Detective Williams's comments ultimately say more about what kind of vision informed his choices in formulating rules about girls' performance in double-Dutch competition.

The Police Athletic League's "Beat" on the Streets

Double-Dutch is a lightning-quick team sport involving two jump ropes, turned eggbeater style around one or two jumpers, testing speed, strength, agility, and creativity. The sport, believed to have originated with Ancient Egyptian, Phoenician, and Chinese rope-makers, has grown in popularity as a competitive sport. Police detective Walker and his partner, Ulysses Williams, had been looking for a new sport like double-Dutch for a long time. Once they found it, they spent months making up rules; they began to dream of having a tournament. It wasn't long before children were jumping double-Dutch to new rules. The two policemen were given a new nickname: "The Double-Dutch Cops."[17]

African American officers Walker and Williams founded the double-Dutch competition as a mission affiliated with the Police Athletic League. The Police Athletic League was founded in 1914 by New York City Police Commissioner Arthur Woods on the premise that police captains would seek out vacant lots to function as supervised play space in an attempt to keep children away from city streets (Dargan and Zeitlin 1990, 158). This was the continuation of a movement to reform children's play that began in the late nineteenth century:

> [The police] saw in organized play and sport ways to ameliorate social ills associated with the effects of new immigration (which crowded New York streets with children), and industrialization. . . . One of the reformers' strategies was to take children off the street and supervise their play in controlled spaces, including parks, playgrounds, and designated "play streets."[18]

Protecting and/or controlling the locus and nature of children's play was an early mission of the community-based league. Street play became a nuisance as cars, buses, and trolleys began to occupy urban streets. Thus the increased mobility of the adult world led to adult intervention in the public space where children once ruled the day. But children "fought back by incorporating cars into their games and continuing to play amid traffic, but eventually they lost."[19] In the early 1970s, amid urban blight and mismanaged infrastructures, the Police Athletic League undoubtedly was concerned about the idle minds and *bodies* of inner-city boys and girls. Their continuing efforts surely confronted newer demands. Juvenile delinquency among both boys and girls was becoming an alarming issue in inner cities (although public attention was focused more on male delinquency in the streets).

In a 1995 telephone conversation, David Walker recalled that his interest in founding the ADDL was piqued while he was working in a Harlem bicycle program. During the program he observed that girls were not attending the programmed events. Walker eventually noticed how black girls in the city liked to "show off their routines" while playing double-Dutch and how they taught each other rhymes. Double-Dutch "was a neighborhood challenge on the streets. Like break dancing."[20] Break dancing and several other street practices in the city have been documented by researchers as if they were exclusively male and masculine expressions of black urban culture. The most remarkable example involves the folklore and performance of "the Dozens" and signifying toasts or raps. "The toasts are a male's genre, not only in performance, but in content: in only a few does one find women included in any purpose other than [the] exercise of male options, male power, and male anger. . . . There is little *romance* here" (emphasis added).[21] Romance symbolized a female or feminine sphere that was not evident in the streets among black males. Therefore, we might assume that female occupation of the street poses a "sexual" risk—posing the "real" possibility of females becoming "butch," acting or performing in masculine ways, in male spaces.

Moving double-Dutch off the streets allowed Walker and Williams the ability to provide an outlet for young inner-city girls because "women are loners, going from toys to boys at an early age."[22] Walker's rhymed explanation—"from toys to boys"—implies that girls are limited to certain kinds of "games" and that the objects of their play cause a certain kind of dependence on boys. Actually, boys go from "toys to boys" as well, given their involvement in exclusively male sports activities. Though Williams and Walker were likely acting in good faith, they were "policing" female behavior and social sensibilities in an increasingly gendered and taboo-conscious public sphere. Their efforts soon precipitated a national organization.

In 1975, Walker and others founded the American Double Dutch League (ADDL), which gained support from the New York City Board of Education, the New York City Police Department, and Mobil Corporation.[23] The ADDL, a not-for-profit organization, is currently headquartered in Washington, D.C. and conducts local, national, and international competitions year-round. Because of their early affiliation with the police department and the Police Athletic League, double-Dutch competitions during the ADDL twenty-year history have often been sponsored locally by police or juvenile-justice officers as well as social and youth advocacy groups, including the 4-H Club, Girl Scouts, and the Salvation Army. The theme of the ADDL's 1995 international competition, held in North Charleston, South Carolina, was "Rope Not Dope," highlighting improvement in the quality of health, education, and recreation.[24] The "policing" of the competition continues to link concerns about delinquency with race, given the overwhelming participation of black girls and boys at the competition. The rules of the "Double-Dutch Cops" ended up policing the bodies and movements of girls who once played the game with not only their athletic abilities but accompanied by oral poetry and musical variations. The verbal expressivity of double-Dutch was *arrested* by official rules and adult interests in creating an authentic sport for girls.

"Ruled" out of Bounds: Gender Roles and Performance in Sport

One of the initial goals in formulating the ADDL was to create a uniform set of rules for the sport. A set of rules and guidelines written by Williams formalized girls' performance in order to define a means for judging the competition.[25] The result was an *official* rule book (which cost thirty dollars in 1995). The size and cost of the rule book clearly privileges adult intervention in a sport that was formerly ruled by the performers themselves. Adult participation, judging, and numerous amendments to the rules are as much a part of the maintenance of the sport as the turning and ticking of the ropes of double-Dutch.

Formal competition requires qualification in three distinct rounds—compulsory, speed, and freestyle. The segmented competition resembles the structure of other sports that feature women or highlight the performance of the voiceless female body, such as ice skating or gymnastics. Teams advance through preliminary rounds through a process of elimination, and points may be deducted for transgressions of certain rules. Competition is divided into age groups from grades four through twelve. There is also an open division for competition among teenagers who have completed high school.

In one of my interviews, a twenty-year-old university student from the Detroit area named Ruqaiijah [ruh-kai-yah] longingly remembered the thrill of "going very fast, keeping the beat" while twirling the ropes of double-Dutch.[26] Ruqaiijah adds, "Most double-Dutch had rhymes. But it's more what you do [in the center of the ropes]. People play off what [movements] went before them and try to bring attention to the game." Obviously, words or verbal expression brings a different kind of attention to the sport that was not desired. Many of the game songs black girls played contain conscious and unconscious articulations about the female body as a source of musical and sexual power:

> *Mail*man, *mail*man, *do* your *du*-ty,
> *Here* come the lady with da *African* boo-ty.
> *She* can do da wah-wah, *she* can do da splits,
> *She* can do *any*thing to make you split, so *split*! [27]

Of all the musical games black girls play, double-Dutch requires the most complex physical ability. Double-Dutch also draws attention to the female body·throughout adolescence, the onset of puberty, and often menstruation—highlighting the development of female sexuality in motion. Perhaps this locomotion explains the absence of the game songs.

I wish to focus on the one segment of the competition that should be most reminiscent of the street aesthetics and flow of double-Dutch—the freestyle rounds of the competition. Freestyle would seem to imply the invention or composition of movements within the ropes, improvisation of style within socially circumscribed expectations. The "freestyle" component of the competition is anything but "free" in its style. But there were a few moments at the 1995 competition in South Carolina that approached the kind of freestyling I had anticipated seeing.

The freestyle rounds were limited by the rules, causing most of the performances to appear routine, to look exactly the same with few exceptions. Each freestyle presentation must not exceed sixty seconds and must include three to five "tricks," a term defined by the cofounders/detectives.[28] Walker and Williams instituted the term "tricks" as a means of identifying and framing the "judged" elements of the competition. Ironically, the use of the term "tricks" for freestyle moves, a term meant to denote the expressive acts performed by females formerly occupying street space, seems quite peculiar. The unintentional association of "tricks" in the street with the "tricks" of prostitution seems unavoidable in my concerns about the policing of female expression in private and public spheres.

In the 1995 World Championship, the tricks appear to be the same turns and jumps required during the "compulsory tricks test":

1. Two right-turn jumps on right foot.
2. Two left-turn jumps on left foot.

3. Two right-foot crisscross jumps (right foot in front of left).
4. Two left-foot crisscross jumps (left in front of right).
5. Ten high steps (alternating jumps in which you lift each knee up to your waist).

Executed by a singles team (two turners + one jumper) in thirty seconds, and by a doubles team (two turners + two jumpers) in forty seconds.[29]

The rule book encourages freestyle tricks that use props, including balls, batons, and short three- to four-foot ropes usually employed in squatting leaps.[30] In the freestyle presentation, as always, the ropes must keep turning without interruption during the entire sixty seconds or deductions will be imposed.

The control of the body appears to be critical to judging the performance in the competition, even in the freestyle rounds. One of the first generations of double-Dutch teams in public competition in New York City was the 1977 championship team known as the "Fantastic Four." Since their performance was still closely tied to street play, a particular incident involving their public performance in the competition illustrates my concern about the reinterpretation of black female participation. The team included African Americans Robin Oakes, Nicki Adams, De'Shone Adams, and Delores Brown. In the book *Double Dutch* (1986), David Walker recalls that a male member of the New York City Board of Education thought that Robin Oakes was "too fat" to compete. In response to the board member's criticisms, Robin invented as many "tricks" as she could the following year of competition and became one of the most innovative performers in the freestyle competition. It was her expressive *skill* that year that ironically earned the Fantastic Four a television spot in a McDonald's commercial for hamburgers.[31] The comments from the member of the Board of Education implied that the ideals of fitness found in other athletic sports required a certain female body type. The board member was monitoring black girls' bodies rather than the unique skills that double-Dutch performance required, particularly in the freestyle competition.

The board member's comments suggest a lack of awareness and understanding about one of the more liberating aspects of street double-Dutch. Any able-bodied girl of any shape or age can "fit" into the ellipsoidal proscenium of double-Dutch play. Double-Dutch is unconditionally a "one-size-fits-all" activity. As Christopher Small has noted in discussing the ideals of musicking in African and African American performance, "it is assumed that everyone is musical," everyone can participate in musicking, and specialization is not sacrificed as a result.[32]

This brings us back to the issue of the game songs that were a significant feature of street performance. What do we make of the curious absence of girls' rhymes and singing practices in the competition? There is little to clearly explain its disappearance. David Walker was unable to offer a sufficient explanation in our conversation in May 1995. He simply claimed the rhymes "died out." During my interactions with Janice Melvin, the president of the ADDL in 1995, I asked several questions about black girls and double-Dutch. Certain responses from Melvin led me to speculate about the reasons behind for excluding the verbal dimensions of street play. My line of questioning also involved explaining my interest in demonstrating a connection between double-Dutch and black musical ideals in popular music and dance, as in hip hop or rap music. Melvin's responses appeared to reflect a lack of appreciation for such a connection; she even seemed to direct her responses away from any such relationship. She stressed that (1) "music is not allowed" (i.e., boomboxes) in the competition, (2) double-Dutch "is *not* dance, it's a sport," and (in an apparent contradiction) (3) double-Dutch is akin to street "ballet"—a respectable art form often associating the female body and its movement with "beauty" and "high" aesthetic ideals. The line and beauty of ballet is also accompanied by anorexic dieting and choreographic control of girls' and women's performance. Melvin's responses elevated double-Dutch from its "low" beginnings in the ghetto of popular music to the height of an "art," disassociating it from its everyday orality and kinetics as well as from the "offensive" boomboxes that serve as the musical accompaniment to dancing double-Dutch in the streets.

I garnered from Melvin's comments a sense of concern about "appropriate" female behavior (and appearance) among young black girls in particular. Melvin, herself a black female long past her youthful days and girlish figure, worked among many female and male justice officers who wish to model high morals rather than street smarts given the problems in inner-cities in the mid- to late twentieth century. Hip hop music and the accompanying gyrating hips and pelvic thrusts are not the kind of expressive behavior that reflects the ideals sanctioned within the competition, where adults and children compete to define space, gender, and acceptable public performance. A possible "double-entendre" of the kinetic behavior found in double-Dutch is the "sexualized" dance that graces the bodies of teenaged girls in other social contexts. Double-Dutch is translated into a sort of "body-English" that when displayed in the public arena of the sport incites a desire among parents and justice officers to ban or censor what may simply be gendered female movement or expression. Yet, is the inherent doubleness of performance within the competition—the public *and* private, the musical *and* athletic, the formal *and* informal, the playful *and* the competitive—that allows girls to remember the street as they compete.

Girls Will Be Girls: Performing Freely and Fully

Although the institutional arms of the ADDL may be legislating various aspects of girls' street performance out of the competition, the actions of the girls themselves demonstrate the "re-remembering" of everyday play, musical expression, and the truer essence of freestyle. Once aware of the ideals of street play, the signature of unconditional cooperation and competition of girls' games and stylized behavior, from hand-clapping games to cheers, becomes apparent. Black girls find ways to reclaim their hidden double-Dutch voices, reinserting the rhyming *and* body-musicking aspects of their street game songs into the marginal spaces of the institutionalized competition itself and the free time that surrounds the judged rounds of competition.

At the 1995 international competition, one could distinctly observe a retention of street elements among the black United States teams, which commonly bear names such as the Hot Peppers, Hot Steppers, and Red Hot Peppers, reminiscent of the lyrics and codes of play in street double-Dutch.[33] The "speed" round was probably formulated from the "hot pepper" element of jumping double-Dutch. Yet the idea of absolute speed (speed-for-speed's sake) was not an aesthetic ideal in playing street double-Dutch. Rather, the adventure and challenge of pushing the collaborative effort and creative ideas to new limits seemed to be ideal (even if it precipitated faster tempos).

If one were to guess, the "freestyle" component of the competition would have been the obvious place for reinserting the use of rhymes, music, cheers, and dancelike expression when the competition was first formulated. As with any arena of publicly displayed freedom, attempts to control the limits of that freedom are never far away. The inclusion of a freestyle round could have served an educative role, nurturing both oral and kinetic literacy and creativity based on ideals prominent in black performance contexts. Had participants been required to develop rhymes as well as the mute and limited "tricks" described earlier, the ability to improvise rhythms, rhymes, and melodies might have become an interesting feature of the sport. But not unlike the improvised social musicking of rhythm 'n' blues or jazz scatting, of partners "cutting a rug" with the lindy, break dancing, or rapping in the public sphere, so little of vernacular black performance is understood and appreciated as a complex musical expression. That which we do not understand is labeled "simple," or an interesting pastime, disregarding the complex skill and craft involved. Hand-clapping games, cheers, and double-Dutch are no exception.

But among the exceptions to rules legislated in the sport of double-Dutch came certain amendments that reflected what I believe to be the ongoing presence of girls' street play in the marginal spaces of the competition. In October 1995, a required choreographic ending was amended to read: "The Freestyle team must demonstrate *T*urning, *A*crobatic, *D*ance and a choreographed *E*nding to the routine (T.A.D.E.). Omitting any one of the four elements will result in point deductions from the Execution Score. The judge in charge of scoring T.A.D.E. will deduct 1 point (not 5 points as noted [earlier]) for omission of a choreographed ending."[34] During the summer competition I observed in North Charleston, South Carolina, moments of expression were clearly emblematic of girls' chants and songs. During idle moments throughout the competition, it was not uncommon to find black girls breaking out into hand-clapping games and cheers.(I never observed any of the non-black girls in such play.) Similar moments of chants, hand claps, and foot stomps were apparent in the choreographed endings of almost every black team, whether from the United States or France. These black girls were reclaiming and recontextualizing their own gendered ways of sporting street double-Dutch. Their stylish hand clapping and body patting, their "old-school" ways of doing gender, race, and authority in play, were remembered through the social interactions that they maintain and continue in their everyday, local play. Some of the choreographic endings presented flashes of contemporary black dances such as the up-and-back, hip-swinging, bowed-legged movements of a dance called the "tootsie roll." The tootsie roll was incorporated into the freestyle performances of a fourth-grade team, Twice as Nice, from Ohio. The dance was also featured during the choreographic ending of a high school division team from Washington, D.C. Tootsie roll—the dance—borrows its name from the well-known chocolate candy. But, the expression may also connote sexual behavior on the dance floor (or in the bedroom; not unlike the use of "jelly roll" in earlier styles of dance music). This street dance was popularized through song in 1994 by a recording group known as the 69 Boyz.[35] Their style of music is recognized as "bass" or "booty-shaking" music. One can clearly imagine the alarm such a dance, the group's name, and the style of music could generate if the patrolling eyes of adults were conscious of their implied meanings.

Watching the daughters of D.C. (known among its black majority as "Chocolate City") or Ohio (a stop on the Underground Railroad) alternately opening and closing bended knees and singing: "up / back / side-ta-side / this is how we tootsie roll" recalls many a dim-light night in somebody's basement partying or "working it out" beyond the gaze of parental control. A kind of work or performance many black parents recognize from their own performance of a sexualized identity of youth. The intertwined meanings of words, movements, and youthful vitalities in the sport of double-Dutch are constantly jumping back and forth, between, and in-and-out of culturally defined expectations. Notions of ethnic and gender identity, the public dis/play of auto-sexuality, and the perceived innocence of same-sex play are being negotiated through performance.

In another special moment, this time not simply a choreographic ending, the all-black French team, Generation Ébène, created quite a reaction from the mostly black audience of kids, parents, and adult sponsors during the preliminary rounds of the freestyle competition. This team of young-spirited black teenagers looked like they had leaped right out of a U.S. rap video with red bandannas, braided hair extensions, baggy gym clothing, and the latest athletic footgear. Ébène elicited the most spectacular moment of the entire competition when they incorporated into the middle of their routine an actual "street ballet" or break dancing (i.e., a back-spin executed as the twirling ropes were momentarily slowed in the air by the turners). The crowd was momentarily mute, and then erupted into screams and applause: Generation Ébène had outdone any expectations of what was possible between the twirling ropes. And they couldn't even speak English! They concluded the routine—which, however, was disqualified because they went over the time limit—with a cheer punctuated with fists held high: "Ébène!" Voilá! The trans-Atlantic conversation among black girls had made its appearance. Many other teams simply employed a choreographic ending that incorporated body musicking, often accompanied by a newly composed, rhymed chant signifying the unique identity of a team while also showing the diasporan unity of black girls' play from New York to Ohio to South Carolina. Here is a stylistic example from Double Forces, a high school division team from Ohio with much attitude (the first two lines end with an *off-beat*, syncopated articulation against the regular ticking of the ropes, the last line concludes emphatically *on* the beat):

> Double Forces has got the beat.
> Cuz' we do it with our feet.
> Cuz' we [five ticks] are [five ticks] BAD!
> [Upon this final word, the ropes are flung into the air and left behind emphatically].

Conclusion

What is most fascinating in tracing double-Dutch from street to sport is how black girls struggle for agency and power within the sport in ways that might be overlooked, especially if one is unaware of the significance of rhymes and musicking in local play. Ironically, music is finally being recognized by one of the "founding fathers" of the sport. Recently, David Walker has been touring the globe with championship double-Dutch teams under the auspices of the International Federation of Double Dutch. In 1991, according to Walker, he and a group of championship double-Dutch teams participated in a prominent dance festival held in southern France entitled "African Dance Rhythms and Music." His observation of the interrelationship between music and dance as featured at the festival led to a revelation on his part: double-Dutch was *missing* a critical relationship with music. He said he realized that "music was not there," yet he acknowledged that the sound of the rope provided a timeline for the possibility of music: "I asked the girls to listen to the drum. The drum is the rope. The rope is the sound of the drum."[36] Since then Walker has been promoting what he calls "fusion double-Dutch," which is often featured at the Apollo Theater in Harlem. Walker sent me a videotape of "fusion" performances by the Dynamic Diplomats of Double Dutch. "Fusion" double-Dutch has taken the freestyle dimensions of the sport and set it to popular black dance music, such as that of Mary J. Blige, a popular hip-hop/R&B artist. Walker noted that music allows the audience to be more involved in the exhibition of double-Dutch but still seems to miss the musicking inherent in double-Dutch itself. This has to do with definitions of music in public culture, particularly relative to black music that features chantlike verbal expressivity. For example, rap is not "real" music because it does not involve singing. Such conceptions are misguided interpretations, for in black culture music is not simply defined by the presence of singing.

I have attempted to reveal the complexity of girls' street play as reflective of urban musicking and play, black social expressivity, and the performance of identity that reflects the intersections of race/ethnicity, gender, and youth. I hope this essay also demonstrates how the relocation and reformation of musical behavior can be partially remembered and thus reinterpreted in ways that highlight certain social assumptions that tend to blur gender and sex. This case study of double-Dutch, tracking its movement from street to sport to fusion double-Dutch, should provide a unique model for analyzing the ways in which both "blackness" and "femaleness" are interpreted in public music performance and may also dispel certain assumptions about gender roles in black music. Ellen Koskoff has suggested that both self- and other-defined sexuality (and interpretations of gender in general) affect music performance in perceivable ways. Cultural beliefs about women's inherent sexuality may limit or negate their participation in musical performance.[37] Many aspects of music making in the everyday culture among blacks are either overlooked, misinterpreted, or "ruled out" from being musical and/or respectable; so, too, has female participation, whether in institutionalized double-Dutch, basketball, or hip-hop performance been treated. But many female voices do attempt to reclaim and *re-member against* hegemonic readings of culture and history. Take, for example, the suave, percussive rhymes of twenty-two-year-old rapper/singer Lauren (a.k.a. "L-Boogie") of the popular, New York-based, hip-hop trio, The Fugees (also known as the "Refugee Camp"). Her rhymes counter masculinist interpretations of power represented by gangster images with the musical revolutions of the "high priestess of soul," the oft-forgotten pianist/composer/singer Nina Simone. Her words and the polysemic meanings of the sounds they combine to create also evoke the "magical" ties to the trio's Haitian ancestry:

> *Who*—do? I can do what *you* do, *ea*-zy.
> Bel*ie*-*ve* me, frontin' niggaz give me heebie *jee*-bies
> So while you *im*ita'in' *Al* Cap*one*
> I be *Ni*na Sim*one*
> And defa*ca*'in' on your *mi*croph*one*.[38]

Girls have been dancing and singing, from ring games to double-Dutch. Their tuneful rhymes and expressive gestures from hand to hip help them claim a black *and* female identity, starting with performances about "Little Sally Walker" and "Mary Mack." The freedom of preadolescence allows black girls to "shake it to the east / shake it the west," divining gender identity and black expressivity with gyrating hips and snarelike hand claps. Their performance of a social/musical identity is *punctuated* by idioms of sexuality and somatic expressivity that are misread in many public settings and lead to the abandonment of such behavior by many adult black females. Such activity in adolescents and adults is read as an abnegation of female respectability. If we could allow a full understanding of the preadolescent behavior located in girls' play, black women's presence in secular musicking and their public performance in sport, music, or play could be viewed in more complex and authoritative ways.

NOTES

1. Subheading quote, Lorde 1983, 262.
2. Gaunt 1996. The women interviewed ranged in ages from eighteen to fifty-six. Analysis of orally transmitted game songs from the women interviewed and from black girls (ages nine to fifteen) also figured prominently in this study. Previous studies of games did not include the subjective understanding of a cultural insider as researcher, nor did they concentrate on the social construction of musical identity relative to race/ethnicity, gender, and sexuality in performance.
3. Liese, interviewed 12 January 1995.
4. Small 1987, 50: "Music is not primarily a thing or a collection of things, but an activity in which we engage."
5. "Shimmy Shimmy" was recorded by Little Anthony and the Imperials (1959) and The Orlons (1964). "Rockin' Robin" was recorded by Bobby Day (1956) and Michael Jackson on his debut solo album (1971). Cooper 1986.
6. Lipsitz 1990, 114–15.
7. Abrahams 1969; Merrill-Mirsky 1988; Riddell 1990.
8. Walker and Haskins 1986, 26.
9. Glassie 1995, 395.
10. Brown 1994, 145–46.

11. I developed the term "melo-linguistics" from my understanding of the concept of "melo-rhythm" (Nzewi 1991, 57), "musical speech" as a retention of African tonal languaging (Wilson 1992, 330), and my own perception of "scatting" and other verbal expressivity and dialogue found in black musicking.

12. Adler 1991, 17.

13. Rose 1994, 21–61.

14. An identifiable culture reflecting a hip-hop aesthetic became apparent between 1971 and 1973, according to information from several primary and secondary sources (George 1988; Toop 1991; and Eure and Spady 1991).

15. Dargan and Zeitlin, 1990, 24.

16. Goodwin, 1980.

17. ADDL 1995b, S.v., "Double Dutch Background."

18. Dargan and Zeitlin 1990, 155.

19. Ibid., 155.

20. From interview with David Walker by author, 14 May 1995. Also see Walker and Haskins 1986, 7–8.

21. Bruce Jackson 1976, liner notes. For sources that suggest exclusivity of males performing this urban verbal art, see Sorenson 1959; Abrahams 1964, 1970, 1983, 1992; Hannerz 1969; Jackson 1976; Dance 1978.

22. Goodwin, 1980.

23. Walker and Haskins 1986, 17.

24. ADDL 1995b.

25. Goodwin 1980.

26. Interview with Ruqaiijah, 16 August 1995. I employ first names only to highlight the emblematic cultural character of black girls' first names, particularly among women born in the 1960s or later. In my experiences within African American culture, calling a woman by her first name rather than her surname (i.e., Miss Joanne) calls attention to her black-female identity in a complex way. It can also signify her communal kinship as a "sister" or "girlfriend" among other black women. Black women often refer to one another by "girl"—reclaiming the youthful cultural difference that often negates their racial and gendered authority as adults.

27. Italics added to mark emphasis or elevated intonation. This chant accompanies a handclapping game song performed by Devonne, age eight, in Los Angeles. The game song was recorded by Carol Merrill-Mirsky (1988, 179, 213).

28. Walker and Haskins 1986, 54.

29. Ibid., 52.

30. Ibid., 54.

31. Ibid., 25. Also see Goodwin 1980.

32. Small 1987, 25.

33. The New York teams that competed at the 1995 World Invitational Championship included Pepper Steppers, Pepper Steppers, Jr., and Hot Steppers. Teams whose names included "hot" and/or "pepper" generally hailed from New York City. Among the few international representatives were Canada's Lincoln Leapers (an all-white team, including one boy) and Jump Energy (an extremely gymnastic team), and the Oriental Peppers from Japan (which included one boy).

34. ADDL 1995a, chapter 6, p. 13, article 3, first sentence.

35. 69 Boyz, "Tootsie Roll," *Tootsie Roll: Hip-hop Mix*, compact disc (date and recording label information unavailable at time of publication).

36. Interview with Walker by author, 14 May 1995.

37. Koskoff 1989, 6.

38. Excerpt from the rap single, "Ready or Not," *The Score* (Ruffhouse Records/ Columbia Records, compact disc CK 67147, 1996).

REFERENCES

Abrahams, Roger D. *Singing the Master: The Emergence of African-American Culture in the Plantation South.* New York: Pantheon Books, 1992.

———. *The Man-of-Words in the West Indies: Performance and the Emergence of Creole Culture.* Baltimore: John Hopkins University Press, 1983.

———. *Positively Black.* Englewood Cliffs: Prentice-Hall, 1970.

———., ed. *Jump-Rope Rhymes: A Dictionary.* Austin: University of Texas Press, 1969.

———. *Deep Down in the Jungle: Negro Narrative Folklore in the Streets of Philadelphia.* Chicago: Aldine, 1964.

Adler, Bill. *Rap! Portraits and Lyrics of a Generation of Black Rockers.* New York: St. Martin's Press, 1991.

Brown, Elsa Barkley. "Negotiating and Transforming the Public Sphere: African American Political Life in the Transition from Slavery to Freedom." *Public Culture* 7/1 (Fall 1994): 107–46.

Cooper, B. Lee. *A Resource Guide to Themes in Contemporary American Song Lyrics, 1950–1985.* New York: Greenwood Press, 1986.

Dargan, Amanda and Steven Zeitlin. *City Play.* Afterword by Barbara Kirshenblatt-Gimblett. New Brunswick, N.J.: Rutgers University Press, 1990.

Dance, Darryl Cumber. *Shuckin' and Jivin': Folklore from Contemporary Black Americans.* Bloomington: Indiana University Press, 1978.

Eure, Joseph D,. and James G. Spady. *Nation Conscious Rap.* Philadelphia: PC International Press, 1991.

Fugees, The (Refugee Camp). "Ready or Not." From *The Score.* Ruffhouse Records/Columbia Records (compact disc CK 67147), 1996.

Gaunt, Kyra D. "The Musical Games African American Girls Play: Understanding Gender and the Black Vernacular in Popular Culture." In *Language, Rhythm and Sound: Black Popular Cultures into the 21st Century.* Pittsburgh: University of Pittsburgh Press, 1997.

———. "The Games Black Girls Play: Music, Body, and 'Soul'." Ph.D. diss., University of Michigan, Ann Arbor, 1996.

———. "African American Women between Hopscotch and Hip-hop: 'Must Be the Music (That's Turnin' Me On)'." In *Feminism, Multiculturalism and the Media: Global Diversities,* ed. Angharad Valdivia, 277–308. Newbury Park, Calif.: Sage Publications, 1995.

George, Nelson. *The Death of Rhythm and Blues.* New York: Pantheon Books, 1988.

Glassie, Henry. "Tradition." *Journal of American Folklore* 108/430 (1995): 395–412.

Goodwin, June. "Double Dutch, Double Dutch: All You Need Is a Clothesline and Jet-Propelled Feet." *Christian Science Monitor* (7 October 1980): B8.

Hannerz, Ulf. *Soulside: Inquiries Into Ghetto Culture and Community.* New York: Columbia University Press, 1969

Hebdige, Dick. "Hegemony." In *The Cultural Studies Reader,* ed. Simon During. London: Routledge, 1993.

Jackson, Bruce, coll. and ed. *Get Your Ass in the Water and Swim Like Me! Narrative Poetry from Black Oral Tradition*. Rounder Records (LP 2014), 1976.

Koskoff, Ellen. "An Introduction to Women, Music, and Culture." In *Women and Music in Cross-Cultural Perspective*, ed. Ellen Koskoff. Urbana: University of Illinois Press, 1989.

Levine, Lawrence. *Black Culture and Black Consciousness: Afro-American Folk Thought from Slavery to Freedom*. Oxford: Oxford University Press, 1977.

Lipsitz, George. *Time Passages: Collective Memory and American Popular Culture*. Minneapolis: University of Minnesota Press, 1990.

Lorde, Audre. "My Words Will Be There." In *Black Women Writers (1950–1980): A Critical Evaluation*, ed. Mari Evans. Garden City, N.Y.: Anchor Press/Doubleday, 1983.

McClary, Susan. *Feminine Endings: Music, Gender and Sexuality*. Minneapolis: University of Minnesota Press, 1991.

Merrill-Mirsky, Carol. "Eeny Meeny Pepsadeeny: Ethnicity and Gender in Children's Musical Play." Ph.D. diss., University of California, Los Angeles, 1988.

Nzewi, Meki. *Musical Practice and Creativity: An African Traditional Perspective*. Bayreuth, Germany: IWALEWA-Haus, University of Bayreuth, 1991.

Riddell, Cecelia. "Traditional Singing Games of Elementary School Children in Los Angeles." Ph.D. diss., University of California, Los Angeles, 1990.

Rose, Tricia. *Black Noise: Rap Music and Black Culture in Contemporary America*. Hanover, N.H.: Wesleyan University Press, 1994.

Small, Christopher. *Music of the Common Tongue: Survival and Celebration in Afro-American Music*. London: Riverrun Press, 1987.

Sorenson, E. Richard, coll. *Street and Gangland Rhythms: Beats and Improvisations by Six Boys in Trouble* (sound recording). Folkways Records (FD 5589), 1959.

Toop, David. *Rap Attack 2: African Rap to Global Hip Hop*. 2d ed. New York: Serpent's Tail, 1991.

Walker, David A., and James Haskins. *Double Dutch*. Hillside, N.J.: Enslow, 1986.

Wilson, Olly. "The Heterogeneous Sound Ideal in African American Music." In *New Perspectives on Music: Essays in Honor of Eileen Southern*, ed. Josephine Wright with Samuel Floyd, 327–38. Warren, Mich.: Harmonie Park Press, 1992.

PRIMARY SOURCES

American Double Dutch League (ADDL). "ADDL Rule Book Changes," booklet. Washington, D.C.: 6 October 1995a.

American Double Dutch League (ADDL). "Souvenir Program, Twenty-Second Annual World Invitational Double Dutch Championship." North Charleston Coliseum, South Carolina, 17 June 1995b.

Liese. B. 1962, Manhattan, raised in Queens. Age thirty-two. Parents from Philadelphia and Cape May, N.J. Occupation: doctoral student and staff at the University of Michigan. Self-designation: Black-American. Interviewed in Ann Arbor, 12 January 1995.

Melvin, Janice. President of the American Double Dutch League. Interview conducted at the World Invitational Double Dutch Championship held at Charleston Southern University in North Charleston, South Carolina, 15 June 1995.

Ruqaiijah. b. 1974, Detroit, raised in Highland Park, Michigan, near Detroit, and New Orleans. Age twenty-one. Mother from Indianapolis. Occupation: undergraduate student in biology at the University of Michigan. Self-designation: African American. Interviewed in Ann Arbor, 16 March 1995.

Walker, David. Co-founder and former president of American Double Dutch League and president of the International Federation of Double Dutch. Telephone interview in Bronx, 14 May 1995.

Chapter Seventeen

Clamor and Community in the Music of Public Enemy

Robert Walser

"My job is to write shocking lyrics that will wake people up," said Chuck D when asked about his goals as leader of the rap group Public Enemy. In only a decade, rap music grew from the local performance practices of a Bronx subculture to a multi-billion-dollar industry mediating a music made and heard around the world. And during the late 1980s and early 1990s, Chuck D's lyrics were at the center of many of the controversies surrounding hip-hop culture—awakening, energizing, and unsettling fans and critics. They helped to make Public Enemy one of the most successful and influential groups in the history of rap, and Chuck D an important spokesperson for the hip-hopcommunity, and even for African Americans more generally.[1]

Chuck D's message exceeds the literal meaning of his lyrics, however; only the musical aspects of rap can invest his words with the affective force that makes people want to wake up or gets them upset enough to call for censorship. Yet despite widespread debates over the meanings and significance of rap, its musical elements have largely escaped all but the most superficial discussion. The infamous *Newsweek* travesty of hip-hop culture, for example, took it for granted that rap couldn't be discussed as music and mentioned only the thumping power of the bass and the noisiness of everything else. More sympathetic and sophisticated analysts typically concentrate on demonstrating rap's verbal complexity and the cultural significance of its lyrics.[2] But the lyrics and reception of rap cannot be detached from the music. Even though many rappers and fans stress the primacy of the message delivered via the lyrics, some, like pioneering rapper Melle Mel, argue that the instrumental parts are actually more important than the rap because they create the mood, set the beat, and prompt the engagement.[3] Chuck D's words would not have reached millions of people as poetry or political commentary; it is the music of Public Enemy that gains them access to channels of mass distribution and underpins their power and credibility. Yet that music has scarcely been mentioned in critical debates over the meanings and importance of hip-hop culture.[4]

Several fine ethnographic and cultural studies have begun to map the social meanings of rap music, stressing its effectiveness in encouraging self-esteem, in building "a sense of community" and serving as "cultural glue," in promoting "interactive dynamics" and participation.[5] Tricia Rose, in particular, has combined ethnographic methods with the theoretical perspectives of cultural studies to produce sophisticated readings of rap as a set of cultural practices.[6] These studies highlight the fact that ethnography in industrial societies poses special difficulties: there is no single "local" to be studied; audiences are diverse and linked by mass mediation; the ethnographer may be included in the target audience of a popular form; the ethnographer's "subjects" may already, as in the case of hip hop, be cultural critics themselves, speaking through rap lyrics, published interviews, and commentary in books and magazines.[7] Their primary achievement, however, is to explain various aspects of a richly nuanced and powerfully coherent hip-hop culture. My concern will be with building upon this work in order to analyze the music of hip hop in more depth. Public Enemy's status in the hip-hop community makes their music especially suitable for a case study.

Yes, But Is It Music?

If music is missing from most discussions of rap, it is partly because so many people do not recognize rap *as* music. Ethnomusicologist John Blacking could casually report that "in Venda, rhythmically recited verse is music, and classed as 'song,' " but similar performances within a more diverse and contestatory society such as the United States may serve as grounds for tense, revealing debates over categories and definitions.[8] Classical musicians and critics often see themselves as guardians of musical culture, and for most of them hip hop is beneath notice, barely worth dismissing. But popular musicians, too—from heavy metal (Lita Ford, Ozzy Osbourne) to jazz (Wynton Marsalis, Henry Threadgill, Al DiMeola)—have characterized rap as simply not constituting "music."[9] These musicians differ greatly in the sounds they produce, yet all share certain fundamental assumptions about what music is: it is based on melody and harmony; it depends on a laborious process of learning to sing or to use a "musical instrument"; it is produced when human beings cause objects to vibrate. People who believe deeply in these premises are sometimes offended by the very idea of rap. For rappers don't "sing" in the usual sense of that word, and hip hop's reliance on sampling, whereby producers extract, manipulate, and reassemble bits of music from many sources, means that the people who make it don't play musical instruments, in the usual sense of that word. Instead, they use sophisticated studio equipment to manipulate sound, often the sounds of others playing traditional instruments.

In many ways, there is nothing new about criticisms of rap that spring from such assumptions, and the debate over rap's status as music should be seen in the light of a centuries-old tradition of cultural authorities and rival musicians missing the point of black music, popular music, rhythmic music, or timbrally complex music, and concluding that such musics are "primitive." The situation is complicated by the recent classification of jazz, which marks a moment when many African American musicians themselves work to interpret and legitimate their music in terms adopted from the musical and analytical priorities of European concert music.[10] Arguments over definitions may seem pedantic and trivial, but in the case of cultural practices as influential as jazz or hip hop, such debates are of great importance because they shape public and official perception of cultural prestige, which in turn affects social prestige, upon which struggles over resources often depend. If we regard a group of people as possessing "music" or, more broadly, "culture," we are more likely to see them as human beings like ourselves and to think them worthy of respect and fair treatment. At issue is the power to define and represent, upon which social contestation often hinges. Debates over rap's status as music thus circumscribe a consequential set of issues.

Objections to including rap in the category "music" typically fall into three categories: hip-hop music is not original; it is not melodious; and it doesn't require "musical" skills. The first of these reflects the assumption that composers who use previously recorded sounds as their raw materials are parasitic; sampling has even been described as "the musical equivalent of shoplifting."[11] Not only is the issue of theft at stake, but also the notion that appropriation is not creative. Yet such accusations seem to take at face value claims made by Romantics and Modernists (and echoed by some jazz musicians and critics) that artists are autonomous creators rather than participants in communal speech acts. Hank Shocklee, head of the production team that assembles rhythm tracks for Public Enemy, disputes this perception: "Let's be realistic here. There are only so many chords you can come up with. Everybody's copying variations anyway. The difference is we're taking it from the record and manipulating it into something else. That's another type of musicianship."[12]

Rap is no more parasitic than other styles of music that quote and vary, and there is in fact a term that is often used to describe the other "type of musicianship" to which Shocklee refers: orality. As Walter Ong has shown, originality in oral cultures—whether represented by Homer's *Iliad* or the blues—arises from the "reshuffling" and inflection of formulas and themes held in common. Henry Louis Gates, Jr., and Dick Hebdige have given us histories of this sort of creativity, sometimes called "signifying" or "versioning," in black music and language, and Tricia Rose and Cheryl Keyes have traced how rap operates within black traditions of verbal virtuosity.[13] Like them, Shocklee is arguing for a view of music as something discursive and social, created out of dialogue with other people in the past and the present rather than through some sort of parthogenesis. Shocklee's compositional method is to combine prerecorded sounds, drawing on his collection of over 19,000 recordings. Like other producers, he must find just the right sounds for each piece, which sometimes requires layering, for example, bass drum sounds from four different records to make one new sound. The samples must be delicately balanced, and the sequences are carefully fine-tuned to simulate the nuances of live performance. All of this means that it is often more work to build tracks out of samples than it would be to compose and arrange for live musicians.[14]

Shocklee's relationship to dominant discourses about "music"—even African American music—is complex and conflicted. On the one hand, it is important for him to reject a categorization of rap that would deny it the prestige of "music." On the other hand, he does not hesitate to differentiate the creators of rap music from other kinds of composers and performers: "We don't like musicians. We don't respect musicians. The reason why is because they look at people who do rap as people who don't have any knowledge. As a matter of fact, it's quite the opposite. We have a better sense of music, of what it can do."[15] Technology is the main issue here, and not for the first time. In blues music, for example, technologies of amplification made available new timbral possibilities and greater volume. But rap's very mode of composition—sampling, sequencing, etc.—marks it off in significant ways from the previous history of black music. Tricia Rose has drawn upon Ong's work to show that hip hop is best seen as a kind of "post-literate orality"; thus, it would be a mistake to regard rap as simply a natural outgrowth of African American oral traditions, for it is deeply technological and it embodies the specificity of its historical and political context.[16]

Another reason for the denial of musical status to hip hop is its noisiness—some listeners perceive only strange sounds piled up into a chaotic, assaultive texture. The noisiness is certainly there—Public Enemy's production crew wasn't called "the Bomb Squad" for nothing—but it is important to examine how and why such noise is crafted, for dissonance and consonance can never be evaluated abstractly, apart from their purposes and meanings. Noisiness is always relative to whatever articulates order in a discourse or a culture, and the noisiness of hip hop contributes to its ability to express dissent and critique, and to articulate the identity of a community that is defined as, or that defines itself as, noise.[17]

Thus the intentionality of hip hop's "noise" is crucial. Gritty timbres have been valued in many kinds of African American music, of course, from Blind Willie Johnson's voice to Miles Davis's Harmon mute. But the significance of such timbres in different contexts requires explanation. "Noisiness" is important in most rap, but Public Enemy became influential and successful in part because of what fans perceived as the extra intensity of their noise and its significance within the context of their lyrics and other aspects of performance. In the high-tech environment of their production studio, the producers of the Bomb Squad often turn their equipment against itself, in search of the rawness that is essential to Public Enemy's conflicted urban soundscape, where sirens and drills punctuate the polytextured layers of modernity. They "misuse" their samplers, hobbling them at very low sampling rates and sometimes resampling samples in order to get a gritty sound, just as grainy photographs are often shot purposely with expensive cameras. And while audio engineers have been working for decades at eliminating tape hiss, considering it an irritating reminder of the artificiality and mediatedness of recorded sound, the Bomb Squad may deliberately add extra hiss to a track. "Hiss acts as glue," Shocklee says; "it fills in cracks and crevices so you get this constant woooooffff."[18]

Public Enemy's producers deliberately placed Chuck D's fluid vocals so as to clash with the key of the backing tracks, to create abrasion. And Flavor Flav's vocals are similarly positioned so they sound out of key, to keep them from being "syrupy," from blending too harmoniously with the backing tracks.[19] In a statement that is reminiscent of John Cage and Edgard Varèse, Hank Shocklee proposed an unconventional definition of music in order to justify his work, suggesting that to marginalize melody and harmony is not to abandon music: "We believed that music is nothing but organized noise. You can take anything—street sounds, us talking, whatever you want—and make it music by organizing it."[20] Shocklee's argument evokes the long history of "nonmusical" sounds eventually coming to be accepted as musical, from polyphony to synthesizers, even as it also resonates with previous defenses of techniques that are perfectly normal within black and popular traditions.

The third common attack on rap's status as music is based on the observation that almost no one involved with hip hop plays a musical instrument or sings, in the usual sense of those terms. Instrumental virtuosity is prized in jazz and classical music alike, and many listeners who are invested in those traditions regard melodic clarity and harmonic coherence as essential to music. Public Enemy's music, as Shocklee argued, is founded on a different kind of musicianship, with its virtuosity dependent on different tools, exercised on a different field, and motivated by different musical and cultural priorities. Its craft shows up not in harmonic complexities, but in how every sample is carefully selected and positioned so as to complement the vocals and contribute to the construction of a specific mood, in how percussive sounds are placed slightly ahead of or behind the beat to create uneasiness or relaxation.[21]

A clash of musicalities is evident in jazz saxophonist Bradford Marsalis's account of being hired by Public Enemy to record a solo used in "Fight the Power":

> They're not musicians, and don't claim to be—which makes it easier to be around them. Like, the song's in A minor or something, then it goes to D7, and I think, if I remember, they put some of the A minor solo on the D7, or some of the D7 stuff on the A minor chord at the end. So it sounds really different. And the more unconventional it sounds, the more they like it.[22]

Even though he is a "real" musician, Marsalis gets the chords wrong, for the song actually moves between D minor and B♭7. Of course, this is only a slip of memory, but the casualness and condescension of his account are revealing. Marsalis understands that the Bomb Squad is deliberately being unconventional, but he doesn't seem fully to comprehend that sampling is a strategy for producing music outside the logic of "trained" musicians. In fact, decontextualization and recontextualization are so fundamental to the compositional process of Shocklee and his associates that even when they commission live performance, they sample and rearrange *that*, layering some of Marsalis's D minor improvisations over the B♭7 groove, and vice versa. The solo in "Fight the Power" has been carefully reworked into something that Marsalis would never think to play, because Shocklee's goals and premises are different from his. Harmonic coherence is not simply a characteristic of "musicality"; it signifies, and it doesn't fit with what Shocklee wanted to signify here.

"Fight the Power" was one of Public Enemy's biggest hits, especially after it was featured in Spike Lee's film, *Do the Right Thing*, and the hard-hitting indictment of racism offered by its lyrics has been much discussed.[23] Thus it has been easy to overlook the music of Public Enemy—if they don't have melody or harmony, if they don't play musical instruments or sing, what is there to analyze? Even some of rap's defenders would resist close scrutiny of musical details; Bruce Tucker warns that "rap, like so many other black musical genres, suffers at the hands of the deeply held formalist assumption that the notes themselves are meaningful."[24] Tucker is right to warn against ahistorical and acultural interpretations of musical discourse, yet it is possible to interpret notes as abstractions of performances with social meanings, and the terms and stakes of current debates over rap suggest that there are important reasons for doing so.

I want to turn to a closer reading of "Fight the Power" in order to draw attention to two neglected aspects of their music: the rhythmic declamation and rhetorical strategies that make up the performative aspect of rapping, and the rhythm track or groove that underpins the delivery of the lyrics. My hope is to explain to some extent the power and meanings of this music, but the analysis should also have the more basic effect of demonstrating the coherence and complexity of music that has been so widely dismissed as monotonous and impoverished. This is itself no small accomplishment, given the shape of recent debates over rap music, which have too often seemed mired in what Paul Gilroy calls "the struggle to have blacks perceived as agents with cognitive capacity and historicity." To redirect the debate requires paying attention to the musical details of a style that many people do not think *has* musical details.[25]

Mapping the Groove

After a brief introduction based on a sample of the band Trouble Funk, a two-measure groove kicks off "Fight the Power." With a few minor changes, this two-bar pattern underpins the entire song, except for the choruses, which switch to a different tonal center and use a somewhat different beat (and a few sections at the end where the fundamental groove is stripped down and chopped up). Composed wholly of samples, the music is based on a combination of drum patterns taken from songs by Funkadelic, Sly Stone, and the Jacksons.[26] On top of this, Hank Shocklee and the Bomb Squad have layered additional sounds from a drum machine, along with sampled vocals, guitar, bass, and synthesizer. The resulting groove, for all its complexity, then provides a stable platform for the rapping.

The "kick" or bass drum pattern is in itself a good introduction to how the producers use rhythm to construct an affect of urgency for this tune.[27] The eighth-notes at the beginning of each measure clearly define the beat, and the pickup to the second bar helps articulate the two-bar pattern. But in the middle of each measure, what might have been a literal repetition of the eighth-note pattern is set with the first note placed one sixteenth-note notch ahead of the beat. Within every bar, the metric pattern is established and then pushed against, creating a dynamic tension even within the line of a single instrument.

The snare drum provides a standard backbeat on beats two and four, but there are several different snare drum sounds being utilized and they vary in pitch, placement, and position in the stereo field. On beat two of each measure we hear a strong, centered backbeat. On four of the first measure, we hear a lower-pitched drum off to the right; on four of the second measure, the same drum along with another, even lower drum, panned to the left. Beat four is prepared in each measure by a different snare's pickup, and a higher-pitched snare in the center answers each backbeat on four, one sixteenth-note later. Timbres, volumes, and placements vary, so that this line too has its own dynamic pattern of interaction, even as these backbeats serve to anchor the entire rhythm track. The cymbals and shaker sounds also steady the groove at the eighth-note level, with additional accents that result from the layering of several drum samples.

The bass plays a repeated pattern that can be heard either as syncopated—it pushes against the metric framework just as the kick drum does—or as polyrhythmic, a layering on of the 3–3–2 pulse (here, in eighth notes) that is known as one version of the "standard pattern" of African and African American music.[28] The bass defines a tonal center on D; its drop to the lower octave on beat four sets the stage for a more emphatic articulation of the downbeat of each measure, grounding the start of each rhythmic cycle regardless of the tensions and ambiguities enacted within the groove. Some sort of sampled noise or scratching can be heard answering each utterance of the bass in the first measure of the pattern, providing a grungy counterpoint. A synthesizer note is one of only two sustaining, nonpercussive sounds in the groove, and its drawn-out B clashes with the D established by the bass. It can be heard as pulling at the tonal orientation, redefining the D as its own third degree, but its fade in each measure weakens this tendency, and the B ends up perched uneasily above, as the unresolved sixth of D.

The guitar sample is so scratchy and percussive that its exact pitches are difficult to discern. Moreover, funk guitar players often lift their fretting fingers just enough to dampen the strings while continuing to pick, creating a bright scratch, an additional sound between pitch and silence. The guitar's pitches are typical of funk harmony, sustaining the minor third of D while playing with the alternation of major sixth and minor seventh degrees; this is a favorite riff because it confirms the mode but creates and releases the tension of the tritone. Rhythmically, the guitar adds to the polyrhythmic mix with a 3–3–3–3–2–2 pattern at the sixteenth-note level. We begin to see that a variety of musical lines operates at different rhythmic levels, remaining within the overall organization of the meter and the two-measure unit, but filling the groove with complex tensions.

The vocal samples drop out when the rapping begins, but during the opening vamp they add further layers of rhythmic direction. One voice articulates nearly the same pattern as the guitar, but placed one eighth-note out of phase; its fragments of the phrase "give it" add urgency to the first measure of each cycle. The second voice answers the first with the syncopated imperative "come on, and get down." And just after the downbeat of the second bar, the third voice's rising line contradicts its text ("down") and anticipates the end of the second voice's phrase. A final set of vocals uses two different samples of James Brown's trademark percussive grunt. One, higher pitched, anchors the downbeat of each two-measure cycle, while the lower-pitched one punctuates the last eighth note of each measure, pushing against metric balance.

Careful attention to the music of even these two measures of "Fight the Power" reveals a solid but richly conflicted polyrhythmic environment in which the rappers operate. If the analytical category of melody seems peripheral, and that of harmony is represented by the sort of static vamp often found in James Brown's music and some earlier blues, the complex interrelationships of rhythm and timbre are paramount. I will return to further discussion of the significance of this musical complexity after discussing the rhythmic performances of the rappers Chuck D and Flavor Flav.

Mapping the Rapping

In his rapping, Chuck D creates the same kind of polyrhythmic flexibility that energizes the rhythm track. Although he is supported by the groove, he refuses to be constrained by it. His phrasing signifies on its regular repetition as he spills over its boundaries, imposes his own patterns over it, or pulls up short to confirm it.[29] In the last eight measures of the first verse, he begins with a repeated pattern marked by rhyme and alliteration. James Snead has analyzed the rhetorical figures most commonly used in black preaching; he would call this "epanalepsis," repetition at the beginning and the end of a clause ("Listen if you're missin', swingin' while I'm singin' ").[30] But just as important, the rhythmic placement of the phrases creates polyrhythmic tension up against the groove. The repeated pattern takes up three beats, while the meter measures out a four-beat framework: 1 2 (rest) 4 1 (rest) 3 4. Chuck's rapping not only overlays a conflicting rhythm at the quarter-note level, but because the pattern internally accents eighth-notes in alternating groups of three articulated and three silent, he creates another layer of rhythmic tension at the same time, a superimposed triple meter: 1&2 (&3&) 4&1 (&2&) 3&4 (&). Similarly, in the chorus of the song, Public Enemy avoids flat repetition by displacing every other "Fight the power!" by one beat. The emphatic repetition of the title serves as a rallying cry for collective struggle, but even here there is flexibility and rhythmic clash, as a different part of the phrase is energized each time: *Fight* the power! Fight the *power*! *Fight* the power![31]

This is what makes rap so different from predecessors such as Gil-Scott Heron or the Last Poets. The music is not an accompaniment to textual delivery; rather, voice and instrumental tracks are placed in a more dynamic relationship in hip hop, as the rapper interacts with the rest of the music. Without the framework of the groove, Chuck D's phrases would simply be parallel utterances. But his rhythmic engagement produces a dialectic of shifting tensions. Because the groove itself is nonteleological, it situates the listener in a complex present, one containing enough energy and richness that progress seems moot. Form and direction are imposed on the song by the rapper through rhetorical fiat, by means of rhythmic patterns, rhyme schemes, the ideas and exhortations of the lyrics, and the verse/chorus alternation.

The second verse begins with more polyrhythms, this time triple patterns at the sixteenth-note level. Rhyme, assonance, and precise rhythmic placement keep Chuck D sounding smooth and coherent, even as the rhythms of his speech are in constant tension with the beat. After the first measure, he moves beyond this strict sixteenth-note pattern into a more complicated rhythmic virtuosity, deftly shifting among syncopation, triplets, and alignment with the meter. He sometimes sticks more closely to the beat, first presenting an idea, "People, people, all the same," then rejecting it: "No, we're not the same cause we don't know the game." The emphasis on the beat in these measures helps portray the first idea as a simplistic platitude and makes Chuck's dismissal seem inevitable. The rhythms thus support his textual argument: pretending that difference doesn't exist won't make injustice go away.

In the third verse, Chuck D works less with the intricacies of each beat or with polyrhythmic tensions, and more with larger-scale rhetorical flow. In measures seven and eight, he directs each phrase toward a landing on beat four, intensifying the sixth measure by shifting to duple rhythms and including more syllables. Black pride and energy in the first phrase parallel a critique of the politics of public representation in the second ("most of my heroes don't appear on no stamps"). Having established a sequence and led us to expect arrivals on beat four, Chuck D then raps straight through measure nine, not cadencing until the fourth beat of measure ten. His precise, undeviating triplets—"Sample a look back you look and find nothing but rednecks for four hundred years if you check"—articulate an anger that draws upon the power of every beat but relentlessly clashes with every subdivision of the groove. Exploiting the rhetorical power of parallelisms, he rolls past the stopping point he had implied in order to deliver a longer, weightier line of text: an indictment of four hundred years of racism.

At the very beginning of his rap, Chuck had already been playing with such rhetorical patterns. In the first measure of the first verse, accent, rhythmic pattern, and overlapping rhymes combine to emphasize the backbeats, beats two and four ("*num*ber," "*sum*mer"). But in the next measure, Chuck skips beat two, hitting three hard ("*sound* of the funky drummer") and accelerating into a sixteenth-note sequence that lands on the downbeat of measure four. He establishes a pattern through repetition, drops in a surprising gap, and then comes upside your head with the answer. By playing with expectations and shifting among rhythmic subdivisions, Chuck presents himself as a willful virtuoso, negotiating the complex groove with ease.[32]

The interaction of Chuck D and Flavor Flav makes the rapping dialogic at strategic places in the song, and during the first verse their exchanges are supplemented by a third voice, which confirms Chuck's downbeat while leaving Flavor Flav free to make his interjection, "brothers and sisters."[33] The end of Flav's comment is overlapped by Chuck's "hey!" which is itself answered by the third voice's "hey!" at the end of the measure. Chuck then goes on to solo for a while, but Flavor contributes both collective affirmation and dialogic counterpoint throughout the song. His interjections support and amplify Chuck's line of thought, but they also constitute a diegetic representation of a broader communal endorsement.

Dialogue and other aspects of rhythmic rhetoric demand social explanations, for notes produce meaning only as they unfold in communities. In the last section of this article, I want to examine certain larger implications of this technical analysis.[34] It is not easy to account for the coherence and cumulative of "Fight the Power" after having isolated its components, for the interactions of groove, rapping, lyrics, and formal trajectory all happen at once, in a real time upon which verbal commentary necessarily drags. But our scrutiny of the musical details of "Fight the Power" does prepare us to ask: What is the attraction of these strategies? Upon what sorts of values and experiences does their efficacy depend?

Rhythm and Sensibility

Historians of rap, along with many hip-hop musicians themselves, explicitly link the verbal and musical styles of rap not only to an African American cultural tradition but, ultimately, to African music itself.[35] This lineage seems all the clearer after a close look at the music of hip hop, for its percussive sounds, polyrhythmic texture, timbral richness, and call-and-response patterns connect it solidly to these antecedents. Moreover, rhythm tracks built up of samples of earlier African American music conjure up collective black experience, past and present, while the rapping combines, as Cornel West argues, "the two major organic artistic traditions in black America," the rhetoric of black preaching and the rhythms of black music. One certainly hears in the music of Public Enemy the "clash of rhythms" that A. M. Jones once singled out as the "cardinal principle" of African music. The polyrhythms in hip hop, like the popularity of James Brown in Africa, demonstrate what Paul Gilroy calls the "diasporic intimacy" and "recombinant qualities" of black culture.[36] But while the ongoing power of African rhythmic concepts to animate many forms of contemporary music is clear, this genealogy does not explain the specific value of such techniques in the present. That is, to trace the origins of a stylistic feature is not to account for its attractions and functions in later contexts.

Scholarship of African music is nonetheless a useful beginning, especially work that furnishes analysis of how rhythmic structures are linked to social values and tensions, such as that of John Miller Chernoff.[37] Chernoff emphasizes that in the African drumming traditions he studied, polyrhythms are heard as multiple rhythmic lines defined with reference to one another; if the listener lacks cultural competence and cannot distinguish these lines and relationships, the result is an experience of monotony or cacophony—terms often used in denunciations of rap. Thus we can begin to understand how rap produces such extremely varied responses among listeners. For example, Tricia Rose has analyzed the characteristic dilemma of a rock critic who personally hears rap as rhythmically "monotonous" and "numbing," but who is frightened and bewildered by the music's demonstrated power to energize and empower youthful black audiences. And David Locke has made much the same point about the reception of Ewe drumming in Ghana.[38]

Polyrhythms make conflicting claims on our attention, since each part is distinct but in tension with the others, and African music exploits this ambiguity: "Musicians put pressure on people's perception by playing with time, by promoting rhythmic dialogue . . . even by challenging their ability to maintain perspective."[39] Like Small, Blacking, and others, Chernoff emphasizes the socializing functions of music in African societies, and he links the music's challenge to unitary perspective to the flexibility valued in African social relationships. In practice, it is bodily motion that establishes the coherence of conflicting polyrhythms, making the music essentially participatory: "The model of community articulated in an African musical event is one that is not held together by ideas, by cognitive symbols or by emotional conformity. The community is established through the interaction of individual rhythms and the people who embody them."[40] Small's concept of "musicking" highlights a similar attitude about the power of musical performance.

My argument is not that polyrhythms mean the same thing in African and hip-hop contexts simply because the same technique is employed, but rather that a variety of factors connects these cases and makes them comparable, and that the comparison is useful for beginning to understand the meaningfulness of rap music. For those who see rap as characteristically "postmodern," the product of a postindustrial society far removed from African contexts, another of Chernoff's observations is provocative: he finds "life in African societies, possibly even more than our own, to be marked by a discontinuity of experience in the encounters and status dramas of daily life."[41] Polyrhythms are one of the ways in which Africans cultivate adaptability and tolerance in the face of a potentially disorienting and alienating world, and the "diasporic intimacy" of black musical traditions suggest that the polyrhythms of Public Enemy deserve parallel explication despite the many differences between these contexts of reception.[42] In much of the music of Africa and the diaspora, repetition cushions fragmentation and helps establish coherence, while polyrhythms articulate a multistranded web of social relationships.[43]

In the music of Public Enemy, repetition is polysemous, suggesting both noise and order, dancing bodies and technological mechanism, resistance and containment: is there joy in this repetition, or only boredom? Is the deliberate noisiness of Hank Shocklee's production to be heard as nihilistic, or as a credible representation of a world filled with struggle and violence? Hip hop's appeal to a variety of audiences, its cultural legitimacy, and its vulnerability to censorship all depend upon reactions to the music: whether its repetition enervates or animates, whether its noisiness alienates or accreditates, whether its complexity disorientates or situates.

As Chernoff notes, there is vitality in rhythmic conflict, and polyrhythmic music offers opportunities to experience power and diversity in ways that are not overwhelming but rather uplifting and strengthening. I have made similar arguments elsewhere about heavy metal, and when I interviewed metal fans I found that significant numbers of them knew former fans who had defected to rap, finding in it compatible experiences of power and freedom.[44] For while Public Enemy often addresses specifically black experiences, the group cultivated and secured a fan base that is half white. So while analysis of rap music must be grounded in the African American context of its creation, its reception is more complex and multicultural.[45]

To be sure, the intensity of the music may provide some listeners with an avenue for reasserting male power or for energizing the defense or claim of some other privilege. That is, for some Public Enemy fans, "Fight the Power" might not mean much more than "Annoy Your Parents." But differences in reception cannot simply be drawn along racial lines. Declining expectations, the injuries of deindustrialization, the growing disparity of wealth, the disruption of communities, and the dismantling of social-support programs are not limited to black communities, although they have been hit hardest; Public Enemy's lyrics articulate anger and protest that many other people find resonant with their own experiences. Rap has both achieved widespread popularity among white fans and "Africanized" many white musical traditions because the values it embodies have been found so attractive by so many. As George Lipsitz has pointed out, in a world where more and more people feel dislocated and disenfranchised, the culture of people who have historically lived with the contradictions of being outsiders becomes increasingly relevant to everyone.[46]

The music of Public Enemy enacts survival in a complex, dangerous world; however oppressive and dissonant that world, it is made to seem negotiable through dialogue and rhythmic virtuosity. The dancing body seizes and rearticulates the power of the music, in contexts of reception that are communal even when they depend upon mass mediation. Many fans seem to be attracted to the flexibility and multiple perspectives of hip-hop, to its embrace of contradictory values, such as an emphasis on building community that coexists in tension with individualism. In the groove and the rhythmic virtuosity of the rapping, more than in the lyrics, they find experiences that are available nowhere else yet seem highly relevant to the lives they lead. While the pro-black rhetoric of rap is often perceived as promoting separatism, in fact many white youth develop black friends and reject their parents' racism because of the respect they have developed for black rappers.[47] Although the importance of Public Enemy's verbal critiques and other messages should not be minimized, their success with black and white audiences depends just as much upon the kinds of musical experiences they offer their fans.

Public Enemy's lyrics became the subject of so much controversy in part because some listeners find Public Enemy's music assaultive and alien, the figuration of experiences they do not want to have or understand. They hear complexity as chaos, noise and power as the signs of a nihilistic threat; for them, polyrhythms are disturbing because they inscribe multiple patterns that refuse the discipline of an overriding rhythmic hierarchy. Others hear such rhythms as their own, as part of a cultural history they value or as a social model to which they are attracted, particularly since the samples hip-hop musicians use are overwhelmingly drawn from previous African American music and thus bring a sedimented history into their new contexts. But at the same time that such grooves offer a dialogic, polyphonic environment, they also present these possibilities in noisy, technological, urban terms, making this social ideal seem relevant to the specific historical situation of many fans. In the terms of Tricia Rose's analysis, the polyphonic layering and repetitive flow create continuity, while rhythmic ruptures teach participants to find pleasure in and develop creative responses to social ruptures.

Music, as Christopher Small has argued eloquently, is one of the most important media through which social relationships are explored, affirmed, and celebrated, through which identities and subjectivities can be altered, shored up, or tried on for size.[48] Hip hop contains many raps, many grooves, and many meanings. Its musicians compose rich, complex music that makes rap more than protest—makes it, as Cornel West says, a "paradoxical cry of desperation and celebration."[49] If we are to understand why rap is so important to millions of people and why it stands at the center of debates over culture and affects struggles over resources, analyzing lyrics is not enough—any more than is purely formalist musical analysis, or sociological analysis that accepts the music industry's dehumanizing assumptions about its "product." We need to begin to hear not only what these rappers are saying, but also what these musicians are composing—how they are using rhythm, rhyme, and rhetoric to enact survival and celebration, clamor and community.

NOTES

This essay is an abridged and slightly revised version of "Rhythm, Rhyme, and Rhetoric in the Music of Public Enemy," *Ethnomusicology* 39:2 (Spring/Summer 1995), 193–217. I am grateful for Tricia Rose's invigorating criticism and support, and for the challenging and helpful comments offered by Reebee Garofalo, Jeff Titon, Larry Polansky, Susan McClary, and the anonymous reviewer for *Ethnomusicology*. I am fortunate to have had opportunities to present versions of this paper to the Center for the Study of Black Literature and Culture at the University of Pennsylvania, the Center for Twentieth-Century Studies at the University of Wisconsin-Milwaukee, and the InterArts Consortium at the University of California-San Diego; I thank Ron Radano, Houston Baker, Jr., Carol Tennessen, Kathleen Woodward, and Jann Pasler for those invitations.

1. Mark Dery, "Public Enemy: Confrontation," *Keyboard*, September 1990, 94. In another interview, Chuck D argued that the purpose of all music is to raise dialogue; see ABC News, "Nightline," Transcript #2781, January 20, 1992, 4. Following normal usage within the hip-hop community, I use "rap" as a general term that refers to a kind of music, and more specifically to designate a style of vocal performance, "rapping." "Hip hop" embraces more cultural terrain, including styles of clothing, dancing, and graffiti art, among other things. See David Toop, *Rap Attack 2: African Rap to Global Hip Hop* (New York: Serpent's Tail, 1991); Tricia Rose, *Black Noise: Rap Music and Black Culture in Contemporary America* (Hanover, N.H.: Weslyan/University Press of New England, 1994). Public Enemy included several members who had a variety of functions: on their recording of "Fight the Power," which will be discussed below, Chuck D and Flavor Flav are the rappers; Terminator X is the DJ, who mixes and scratches records; Hank Shocklee, Eric "Vietnam" Sadler, Carl Ryder, and Keith Shocklee are members of the Bomb Squad, the production crew that assembles the instrumental tracks. At the time of the recording, Professor Griff was considered a member of the group, with the function of "Minister of Information," but he is not heard on record.

2. Jerry Adler et al., "The Rap Attitude," *Newsweek*, March 19, 1990, 56–59. See also that issue's companion article, less virulent but no less vague about the music: Daved Gates et al., "Decoding Rap Music," *Newsweek*, March 19, 1990, 60–63. Many similar examples could be cited, including *The New Yorker*'s genial assurance to its readers that "rap isn't music": Ethan Mordden, "A Critic at Large: Rock and Cole," *The New Yorker*, October 28, 1991, 113. For sympathetic analyses of lyrics, see, for example, Elizabeth A. Wheeler, " 'Most of My Heroes Don't Appear on No Stamps': The Dialogics of Rap Music," *Black Music Research Journal* 11: 2 (Fall 1991), 193–216; and Cheryl Keyes, "Verbal Art Performance in Rap Music: The Conversation of the 80's," *Folklore Forum* 17:2 (1984), 143–52.

3. Cheryl Keyes, "Rappin to the Beat: Tap Music as Street Culture Among African Americans" (Ph.D. diss., Indiana University, 1991), 199.

4. John Blacking made a similar point in a different context: "The effectiveness of the South African Freedom songs has been discussed chiefly in terms of their words, but it was their music which made the deepest impact, especially on those who did not speak the language in which the sentiments of the songs were expressed. The combination of the triads

and cadences of European hymn-tunes and the rhythms and parallel movement of traditional African music expressed the new solidarity and values of urban groups: the sound of the music conveyed as clear a message as the words of the songs." John Blacking, "The Value of Music in Human Experience," *Yearbook of the International Folk Music Council* (1969), 36.

5. Venise Berry, "Rap Music, Self Concept and Low Income Black Adolescents," *Popular Music and Society* 14:3 (Fall 1990), 89–107; Rose, *Black Noise*; Madeline Slovenz, " 'Rock the House': The Aesthetic Dimensions of Rap Music in New York City," *New York Folklore* 14:3–4 (1988), 151–63; Keyes, *Rappin to the Beat.*

6. Tricia Rose, "Orality and Technology: Rap Music and Afro-American Cultural Resistance," *Popular Music and Society* 13:4 (Winter 1989), 35–44; " 'Fear of a Black Planet': Rap Music and Black Cultural Politics in the 1990s," *Journal of Negro Education* 60:3 (1990), 276–90; "Never Trust a Big Butt and a Smile," *Camera Obscura*, May 1991, 108–31; and *Black Noise.*

7. Such books would include Joseph D. Eure and James G. Spady, eds., *Nation Conscious Rap* (New York: PC International Press, 1991). Rap magazines are legion; perhaps the most seriously analytical of the widely distributed publications is *The Source: The Magazine of Hip-Hop Music, Culture, and Politics.*

8. John Blacking, "The Structure of Musical Discourse: The Problem of the Song Text," *Yearbook for Traditional Music* 14 (1982), 18.

9. J. D. Considine, "Fear of a Rap Planet," *Musician*, February 1992, 41. In an interview with Cheryl Keyes, Wynton Marsalis asserted that rap represents a "decadent and degenerate culture" and that it therefore does not qualify as legitimate music (*Rappin to the Beat*, 2). On the other hand, a few jazz musicians, notably Max Roach and Miles Davis, have publicly hailed hip hop as a worthy heir to jazz's legacy of virtuosity and rhythmic complexity. Overall, though, rap has had few defenders outside of the hip-hop community.

10. See Robert Walser, " 'Out of Notes: Signification, Interpretation, and the Problem of Miles Davis," *Musical Quarterly* (Summer 1993), 343–65; and Gary Tomlinson, "Cultural Dialogics and Jazz: A White Historian Signifies," in *Disciplining Music: Musicology and Its Canons*, ed. Katherine Bergeron and Philip V. Bohlman (Chicago: University of Chicago Press, 1992), 64–94. On the politics of cultural prestige, see, for example, Pierre Bourdieu, *Distinction: A Social Critique of the Judgement of Taste* (Cambridge, Mass.: Harvard University Press, 1984).

11. Dery, "Public Enemy," 84.

12. Tom Moon, "Public Enemy's Bomb Squad," *Musician*, October 1991, 69.

13. Walter Ong, *Orality and Literacy: The Technologizing of the Word* (New York: Methuen, 1982); Henry Louis Gates, Jr., *The Signifying Monkey: A Theory of African American Literary Criticism* (New York: Oxford University Press, 1988); Dick Hebdige, *Cut n' Mix: Culture, Identity, and Caribbean Music* (New York: Methuen, 1987); Rose, *Black Noise*; Keyes, *Rappin to the Beat.*

14. See Mark Dery, "Rap," *Keyboard*, November 1988, 32–56; Dery, "Public Enemy"; Moon, "Public Enemy's Bomb Squad"; Jon Young, "P. M. Dawn Sample Reality," *Musician*, June 1993, 23–24.

15. Dery, "Public Enemy."

16. Rose, "Orality and Technology."

17. Compare Jacques Attali, *Noise: The Political Economy of Music* (Minneapolis: University of Minnesota Press, 1985).

18. Dery, "Public Enemy," 86; Moon, "Public Enemy's Bomb Squad," 76.

19. Dery, "Public Enemy," 83; Moon, "Public Enemy's Bomb Squad," 72. A new production crew worked with Public Enemy on *Apocalypse 91 . . . The Enemy Strikes Black* (1991); I will be writing throughout about the sounds created for the earlier three albums, as exem-

plified by "Fight the Power," which was released as a single in 1989 and as part of the album *Fear of a Black Planet* in 1990.

20. Dery, "Public Enemy," 83.

21. Moon, "Public Enemy's Bomb Squad," 70.

22. Considine, "Fear of a Rap Planet," 42. The sax solo appears on the single release of "Fight the Power," but not on the album cut.

23. Some of Public Enemy's lyrics have been much more controversial, and Chuck D has sparked a great deal of dialogue about whether sexism, homophobia, anti-Semitism, and black racism are useful responses to white racism. See, for example, Greg Tate, "Public Enemy: The Devil Made Them Do It," *Village Voice*, July 19, 1988, 71; Frank Owen, "Public Service," *Spin*, March 1990, 57; Harry Allen and Chuck D, "Black II Black," *Spin*, October 1990, 67. While anti-Semitic statements cannot be defended or excused, it is important to note that such statements tend to receive much more media coverage when uttered by black rappers than when attributable to white rock musicians or Christian fundamentalists; see *Rock and Roll Confidential* 90 (July-August, 1991), 4. Public Enemy wrestled with problems that are among the most serious and pressing in contemporary politics, and their responses were affected by the ways in which those problems are commonly framed. For example, Chuck D accurately diagnosed links between racism and economic exploitation:

> The Chinese over here, the whites over here, Jews here, you know it's broken up like that. Capitalism does that. They'll tell you capitalism sees no color, but at the same time the ones that all feel they have something in common with each other become the most powerful block right there, and it stomps upon those that don't fit that mold. And the only way that you can exist within that mold is that you have to put together a "posse," or a team to be able to penetrate that structure, that block, that strong as steel structure that no individual can break. . . . Public Enemy, number one, tries to tell the black man and woman in America that we as a constituency have to stick together and realize that we all have something in common with each other. (Eure and Spady, *Nation Conscious Rap*, 330–31)

Public Enemy has indeed been successful in raising dialogue, and to his credit, Chuck D has been willing to reverse himself and admit he was wrong in response to public controversies over his lyrics.

24. Bruce Tucker, "Review of Public Enemy, *It Takes a Nation of Millions to Hold Us Back*, and De La Soul, *3 Feet High and Rising*," *American Music* 10:4 (Winter 1992), 497.

25. Paul Gilroy, "Cultural Studies and Ethnic Absolutism," in *Cultural Studies*, ed. Lawrence Grossberg, Cary Nelson, and Paula Treichler (New York: Routledge), 187–88; see also Paul Gilroy, *There Ain't No Black in the Union Jack: The Cultural Politics of Race and Nation* (Chicago: University of Chicago Press, 1991). A few writers have transcribed hip-hop music: Cheryl Keyes (*Rappin to the Beat*) used notation in order to demonstrate the existence in rap music of certain techniques, such as word stresses, hocket, "trading phrases," and interlocking rhythms; and Mark Costello and David Foster Wallace's transcription of Eric B. and Rakim's "Paid in Full" labels the samples that were used to construct the piece; see their *Signifying Rappers: Rap and Race in the Urban Present* (New York: Ecco Press, 1990). Here, I will discuss musical details as evidence for interpretations of affect and social meaning. For the transcriptions that originally illustrated my analysis, see the fuller version of this essay (cited above).

26. Dery, "Public Enemy," 92.

27. References to the "kick" drum are common among musicians to avoid confusion between bass guitar and bass drum.

28. See Hafiz Shabazz Farel Johnson and John M. Chernoff, "Basic Conga Drum Rhythms in African American Musical Styles," *Black Music Research Journal* 11:1 (Spring 1991), 67; and Robert Kauffman, "African Rhythm: A Reassessment," *Ethnomusicology* 24:3 (September 1980), 393–415.

29. Dwight D. Andrews has analyzed a similar kind of virtuosic self-empowerment in Ray Charles's performances, as he plays around with the beat, affirming or subverting it at will; see his "From Black to Blues," in *The Blues Aesthetic: Black Culture and Modernism*, ed. Richard J. Powell (Washington, D.C.: Washington Project for the Arts, 1989), 37–41. For discussions of two very different kinds of willful virtuosity in popular music, see Robert Walser, "Eruptions: Heavy Metal Appropriations of Classical Virtuosity," *Popular Music* 11:3 (1992), 263–308; and Walser, " 'Out of Notes.' " I use the word "signify" here in the sense attributed to it by Henry Louis Gates, Jr.

30. James Snead, "Repetition as a Figure of Black Culture," in *Black Literature and Literary Theory*, ed. Henry Louis Gates, Jr. (New York: Methuen, 1984), 70. Compare also Gerald L. Davis, *I Got the Word in Me and I Can Sing It, You Know: A Study of the Performed African American Sermon* (Philadelphia: University of Pennsylvania Press, 1985). Measures 9–11 of this section utilize the rhetorical strategy of anaphora, repetition at the beginning of a clause.

31. The lyrics I have quoted are taken primarily from the printed version that accompanied the album release. However, in two places where the actual delivery of the lyrics varied from what was printed, I have made minor changes in the text to match what appeared on the recording.

32. Few rappers work at Chuck D's level of rhythmic virtuosity, but the rhetorical practices he uses are ubiquitous. Queen Latifah is another rapper who has an especially powerful and ingenious rhythmic style.

33. For further discussion of the dialogic aspects of rap music, see Wheeler, " 'Most of My Heroes.' "

34. As Christopher Small has pointed out, an analytical focus on internal relationships too often displaces attention from external (social) relationships; the closer we analyze, the more impoverished our sense of what it all means. See Christopher Small, *Music of the Common Tongue: Survival and Celebration in Afro-American Music* (New York: Riverrun, 1987), 289.

35. See especially Toop, *Rap Attack 2*. For an overview of discussions of African retentions in African American music, see Portia K. Maultsby, "Africanisms in African American Music," in *Africanisms in American Culture*, ed. Joseph E. Holloway (Bloomington: Indiana University Press, 1990), 185–210. See also Olly Wilson, "The Significance of the Relationship between Afro-American Music and West African Music," *Black Perspective in Music* 2:1 (Spring 1974), 3–22; and Lee Cronbach, "Structural Polytonality in Contemporary Afro-American Music," *Black Music Research Journal* (1981–82), 15–33. As important as such work is, it seems imperative to begin to take up newer critical projects, such as explaining how people of diverse origins come together and find cultural common ground (see Johnson and Chernoff, "Basic Conga Drum Rhythms," 63).

36. Cornel West, *Prophetic Fragments* (Grand Rapids, Mich.: William B. Eerdmans, 1988), 186. On collective memory in popular culture, see George Lipsitz, *Time Passages: Collective Memory and American Popular Culture* (Minneapolis: University of Minnesota Press, 1990); A. M. Jones, "African Rhythm," *Africa* 24 (1954), 27; Gilroy, "Cultural Studies," 193, 197. See also Wilson, "Significance," and Edmund John Collins, "Jazz Feedback to Africa," *American Music* 5:2 (Summer 1987), 176–93.

37. See John Miller Chernoff, *African Rhythm and African Sensibility* (Chicago: University of Chicago Press, 1979), and "The Rhythmic Medium in African Music," *New Literary History*

22:4 (Autumn 1991), 1093–1102. While it is important to recognize differences among African musical traditions, analytical recognition of significant pan-African similarities can be productive; see Kauffman, "African Rhythm." On the general problem of the relationship of sound structures to cultural logics, see the symposium in *Ethnomusicology* 18:3 (September 1984), featuring papers by Steven Feld and Marina Roseman.

38. Rose, "Fear of a Black Planet," 276–90; David Locke, "Principles of Offbeat Timing and Cross-Rhythm in Southern Ewe Dance Drumming," *Ethnomusicology* 26:2 (May 1982), 244.

39. Chernoff, "Rhythmic Medium," 1101.

40. Ibid., 1095. See also Blacking, "Value of Music"; Small, *Music of the Common Tongue*; and Blacking, *How Musical is Man?* (Seattle: University of Washington Press, 1973).

41. Chernoff, *African Rhythm*, 156. Compare Richard Shusterman's attempt to connect rap with postmodernism and American pragmatism—in the process reducing rap's African American dimension to "roots"—in order to invigorate an attack on modernist aesthetics: "The Fine Art of Rap," *New Literary History* 22:3 (Summer 1991), 613–32.

42. This is, of course, very different from how musicologists and music theorists tend to discuss rhythm. Not only is it customarily assumed to be cognitive and disembodied, but Western music theory's traditional emphasis on harmony has led many music theorists to conceive of rhythm through harmonic metaphors. Terms like "metric dissonance" and "dissonant strata" suggest that rhythmic conflicts must always be resolved, whether in performance or analysis. There seems to be no place for tensions that remain unresolved, differences that can coexist. See, for example, Barbara R. Barry's relentlessly cognitive model in *Musical Time: The Sense of Order* (Stuyvesant, N.Y.: Pendragon Press, 1990); her title signals the foregone conclusion that underpins much of what is done in the name of "music theory." For "rhythmic dissonance," see Murray Yeston, *The Stratification of Musical Rhythm* (New Haven: Yale University Press, 1976), and Grosvenor W. Cooper and Leonard B. Meyer, *The Rhythmic Structure of Music* (Chicago: University of Chicago Press, 1960); the latter credited Curt Sachs with having originated the concept of "metric dissonance" (108). Wye Jamison Allanbrook achieved a significant advance by linking rhythm with bodily postures and human character, in her *Rhythmic Gesture in Mozart* (Chicago: University of Chicago Press, 1983). But generally, uneasiness about rhythm has caused musicologists and other devotees to etherealize canonic musicians such as J. S. Bach, whose physical engagement with his music is well documented. See, for example, a letter of 1738 by Johann Matthias Gesner that describes Bach as "full of rhythm in every part of his body" as he conducted; see Hans T. David and Arthur Mendel, eds., *The Bach Reader*, rev. ed. (New York: W. W. Norton, 1966), 231. Such distortions of music history enable the mind/body split to be mapped onto the high/low cultural split, or the Western/non-Western dichotomy, remaking the past in order to stabilize the hierarchies of the present. See Susan McClary, "Music, the Pythagoreans, and the Body," in *Choreographing History*, ed. Susan Leigh Foster (Bloomington: Indiana University Press, 1995), 82–104.

43. See Frances R. Aparicio's forthcoming work on salsa, and Veit Erlmann's *Nightsong: Performance, Power, and Practice in South Africa* (Chicago: University of Chicago Press, 1996).

44. See Robert Walser, *Running with the Devil: Power, Gender, and Madness in Heavy Metal Music* (Hanover, N.H.: Wesleyan University Press, 1993). Further evidence for this compatibility is provided by the collaborations of Public Enemy with the metal band Anthrax, and by Ice-T's band, Body Count. However, in heavy metal, power and freedom are usually articulated through a dialectic between the rhythm section and the solo guitar or vocal, rather than through polyrhythms.

45. See Cronbach ("Structural Polytonality"), who argues for a more general recognition of this fact in the study of African American music.

46. See Lipsitz, *Time Passages.*

47. Greg Tate, "Manchild at Large," *Village Voice*, September 11, 1990, 77.

48. Small, *Music of the Common Tongue*, 46.

49. West, *Prophetic Fragments*, 186. The specific techniques I have discussed in the music of Public Enemy are deployed by other rap musicians to other ends, although a shared discursive system keeps their meanings related. For example, Queen Latifah's style of performance is very similar to that of Chuck D, but she is much more interested than he in speaking to and for women, about issues of gender and power. Sister Soulja's concerns are closer to those of Public Enemy, yet her rapping style features nearly arrhythmic declamation, utterly unlike the rhythmic rhetoric of Queen Latifah and Chuck D.

Chapter Eighteen

Hmong American Youth

American Dream, American Nightmare

William Wei

"Tough" is the word that Thai Xiong uses to describe his people, the Hmong.[1] It is apt, given their long history of rebellion and repression. In their quest to remain Hmong, they have experienced a diaspora that started in China, spread to Southeast Asia, and is ending in America.[2] Ironically, it is in America, the "land of liberty," that the Hmong (literally, "free") may lose their identity as a people. Indeed, many in the Hmong community fear that in their struggle to survive, their most valued and distinctive traditions will be lost.

Hmong Americans trace their ancestry to China, where they lived for two millennia before suffering a fate like that of American Indians. In carrying out their "Manifest Destiny," the Han Chinese expanded from their homeland in North China, conquering the Hmong and other indigenous peoples in their way. Calling them by the derogatory term "Miao" and stereotyping them as a barbaric tribal people, the Han Chinese persecuted the Hmong for their resistance to Confucian culture and drove them into remote mountainous areas, where they lived as "slash-and-burn" agriculturists. Nevertheless, from 400 to 900 A.D. the Hmong were able to establish a federation of clans stretching from Henan to Hunan province. In their historical memory, this is their original homeland, where they lived in peace and prosperity. Eventually, the Hmong Camelot fell to the more numerous Han Chinese, scattering them to the frontiers of the Chinese empire, west to Guizhou and Sichuan provinces and south to Guangxi and Guangdong provinces. Ever since, the Hmong have dreamed of establishing another homeland.

Under the Qing dynasty (1644–1911), the Manchus intensified the repression of the Hmong, forcing many of them to seek refuge in the mountainous regions of Southeast Asia. By the mid-nineteenth century, about 750,000 Hmong had migrated there, with at least 350,000 settling in the highlands of northern Laos,[3] where they constituted 10 percent of the country's population and lived much like the people of Appalachia, eking out a living as subsistence farmers. Unlike the so-called hillbillies of West Virginia, the Hmong cultivated upland rice rather than corn and harvested opium rather than distilling "moonshine" as a source of cash. Like the West Virginians, the Hmong would eventually become rural-to-urban migrants, though it would be many times more difficult for them since their migration would be to cities in a foreign land.

Despite occasional conflicts among themselves and with their lowland neighbors, on the whole the Hmong lived peacefully until the mid-twentieth century. During World War II, they joined the French to oppose the Japanese; afterwards, they fought the French to end colonial domination of Laos. When Laos became independent in 1954, many of the Hmong clans supported the Royal Lao government, though a few supported the Communist Pathet Lao. Because of their role in its emergence as an independent nation, many older Laotian Hmong identify Laos as a symbolic homeland where they developed a political presence and were able to maintain their cultural identity.

In 1960, the Central Intelligence Agency persuaded the Hmong to join the Armée Clandestine to assist the United States in the Vietnam War. Superb guerrilla fighters, the Hmong conducted covert counterinsurgency operations against the North Vietnamese and Pathet Lao, interdicting the flow of men and materiel down the Ho Chi-minh Trail and rescuing American pilots downed in enemy territory. Hmong soldiers were considered one of the most effective fighting forces in the region because of their knowledge of the terrain and their ferocity in combat. In the course of the conflict they suffered a staggering 30,000 casualties.[4] By the end of the war, their ranks had been reduced to the point where boys aged ten to fourteen were being recruited to fight America's secret war in Laos.[5]

In return for their service the Hmong believed the Americans would assist them in establishing an autonomous state in northern Laos, a homeland where their people could finally be free to be Hmong.[6] While it is unclear whether the United States government or any of its representatives ever made such a commitment, the Hmong, especially the older generation, believed that it had. They also believed that the Americans had agreed to evacuate them in case of defeat. Whether or not there was an agreement, it is painfully evident that when the Americans retreated from Southeast Asia in 1975, they abandoned the Hmong to their enemies. Over 100,000 Hmong refugees were forced to flee to western Thailand. Half of them died of starvation and disease or were killed by their enemies along the way. Those who survived languished in Ban Vinai and other squalid refugee camps along the Mekong River until they could be resettled in a third country. The country of choice was and still is the United States, where at least 90,082 Hmong Americans live today.[7]

"War is hell," an American general once said, and many of the Hmong still bear its physical and psychological scars. Hmong veterans suffer from posttraumatic stress syndrome and depression. And there are other casualties of war. For example, one Hmong woman suffered multiple family losses during the war; resettled in Denver, Colorado, she tried to keep her teenage daughter a prisoner at home out of fear of losing her, too.[8] In response, the daughter became a truant at school, a runaway from home, and, from the Hmong community's perspective, a whore (that is, she engaged in promiscuous sex). The personal fate of such Hmong is a tragic testimony to the continuing effects of America's policy of intervention in Indochina.

In the United States another threat awaited the Hmong—cultural assimilation. In the past, they had moved from one Asian agrarian hinterland to another where they could minimize the amount of change they had to endure.[9] Now, they have migrated from a preindustrial country in the Far East, inhabited by a racially homogeneous and culturally complementary Asian people, to a postindustrial nation in the Far West, populated by diverse races and cultures and dominated by English-speaking Euro-American "giants." Without their agrarian base, the Hmong would in any case have been hard put to continue their traditional way of life and in the face of an ideology of Americanization as overwhelming as the Sinicization of the Han Chinese, it is nearly impossible. It is as if the Hmong had encountered the Borg, that powerful race of cyborgs in the *Star Trek* episode "The Best of Both Worlds," who demoralized their enemies with the dictum, "Resistance is futile, your life, as it has been, is over.... Your people will be assimilated."

The older Hmong generation realizes that the struggle for their people's cultural identity depends mainly on their young. Hmong American youths make up the majority in their communities. In Minnesota, for example, nearly three-fifths of the local Hmong population is under eighteen, and half of these youths were born in the United States. What the older generation fails to appreciate is that the battle may be largely lost. Indications are that the youths are rapidly surrendering what their parents fought so hard to retain—the right to be Hmong. The only issue left is what identity will replace the old one.

To the Land of Giants

The circumstances of the Hmong's resettlement in the United States contributed to the erosion of their culture. Arriving in 1976, they entered a monocultural American society that expected immigrants and refugees to adapt to its dominant Euro-centric culture, with its Judeo-Christian traditions and Anglo-American institutions. The society the Hmong were encouraged to adapt to was entering the "Greedy Eighties," when an extreme version of the capitalist ethic took hold. Though the Hmong have their own version of this ethic, in the context of their Asian culture it serves group rather than individual interests. Making money is considered a virtue because it allows a man to support his family and to pay the bride price necessary to acquire a wife. In the United States money is equated with personal achievement and is important because it allows personal independence. Accordingly, young Hmong Americans are becoming more independent and less committed to their community's interest; they show little concern for the welfare of others. With its emphasis on materialism, consumerism, and individualism, America's commodified culture is having a corrosive effect on the holistic Hmong culture.

Underlying the United States government's resettlement policy was an assumption that immigrants would eventually lose or abandon their ethnic characteristics. Of course, for Hmong Americans and other people of color this has never happened because racial differences continue to prevent them from integrating fully into mainstream society. To prevent ghettoization and accelerate assimilation, the government consciously dispersed Hmong refugees throughout the country. For some Hmong, this practice did promote acculturation and facilitate learning English. For most, however, it led to social isolation and psychological depression. Consequently, the majority of them have chosen to leave their initial place of settlement in the United States to join kin or simply to be with other Hmong.

This secondary migration has led to the establishment of major Hmong communities in California, Minnesota, and Wisconsin and minor ones elsewhere. These are usually dispersed communities, organized around families and clans rather than the physically concentrated urban enclaves characteristic of some Asian ethnic groups, such as the ubiquitous Chinatowns in U.S. cities. However, in major urban centers, the Hmong often live in public housing projects located in the poorer sections among other people of color. In such a multicultural milieu, it is hardly surprising that young Hmong Americans "talk the talk" and "walk the walk" of Afro-American and Latino adolescents in their neighborhoods. Appropriating the style of so-called Third World people allows them to participate in American society at its cultural margins.

For the first immigrant generation, finding a Hmong community to belong to has proven the best way to reduce culture shock and increase social stability. As with other ethnic groups, the second generation of Hmong Americans, particularly the well educated, will probably move out of the Hmong community in search of employment in yet another diaspora. Meanwhile, the Hmong community tries to follow traditional values and customs, restore kinship networks, and promote mutual support on the basis of a common ethnic identity. They expect their children to know the history of their people and to carry on its culture as previous generations have done.

What Is America Doing to My Children?

Initially, Hmong Americans were more concerned about their elderly than their young. They expected their children to do better than they did, especially those who were born in the United States. After all, their children had been spared the ravages of war and enjoyed the material comfort of an American life. Moreover, they would be socialized into American culture at an early age and would acquire an American education, enabling them not only to survive but to prosper. It was all a dream. Only recently have they awakened to the fact that some of their young are doing poorly in schools or even joining hoodlum gangs. They are asking, What is America doing to my children?

Hmong American youths may be divided into two groups: those born overseas, either in Laos or another Southeast Asian nation or in one of the Thai refugee camps; and those born here. Most of those born abroad speak some Hmong and have internalized traditional values, with primary allegiance to their families and an identity defined in terms of their position in their ethnic community. As a matter of course, they respect their parents and elders for their age, experience, and wisdom. They have personal memories of being refugees and appreciate being in the United States. Many of those born in the United States feel alienated from both Hmong and American cultures and have difficulty functioning in either. At home, they are not Hmong enough; in school, they are not American enough. They feel culturally despised by everyone, including the Hmong community, and materially deprived in an affluent American society.

Both groups face the challenge of defining who they are and who they want to become, a process that involves coming to terms with the legacy of their past and the circumstances of their present. In this self-examination, their people's participation in the Vietnam War looms large.

Most of those born overseas are steeped in the history and culture of their people. They take particular pride in the heroism of their parents, who fought as loyal allies of the Americans during the Vietnam War and struggled to survive the persecution of the communists afterwards. They feel that by virtue of their fathers' participation in the war, their people have earned the right to be in the United States. So far as they are concerned, their fathers were soldiers in the American army. Hence, they support the Vento amendment to the Immigration Reform Bill, which would waive the language requirements for naturalization for Hmong, citing earlier precedents of aliens whose war service made them eligible for naturalization. In particular, a provision in the 1990 Immigration Bill waived the residency requirement for Filipino Scouts who served during World War II.[10]

Many of their younger siblings, however, feel ambivalent about the war years. Some feel that the United States betrayed the Hmong: first, by tricking them into fighting against the communists with false promises of an autonomous Hmong kingdom; second, by stranding them in Laos after retreating from Southeast Asia in 1975. Some believe that their people were used as "cannon fodder." At the 1996 Hmong Youth Conference at Georgetown University, after Dr. Jane Hamilton-Merrit's tribute to the selfless heroism of Hmong soldiers who suffered enormous casualties rescuing two downed American pilots, the same incident was decried by a young Hmong American student as an example of the callous disregard by Americans for Hmong lives.[11] In effect, this student was delivering an Asian American critique of the Vietnam War. As David L. Moore has put it, "The question was, were the Hmong being used, abused and ultimately abandoned in order to fight someone else's war?"[12]

To its shame, the United States government has essentially disavowed the Hmong who fought in the Vietnam War. Its official position is that the Hmong were part of the Royal Lao Army rather than soldiers in a Central Intelligence Agency secret army, despite the fact that the agency recruited them, paid them, and provided them with military equipment, medical care, and provisions. Noam Chomsky, a critic of the Vietnam War, spoke for many when he observed that the "American policy of sacrificing the [Hmong] for America's anti-Communist crusade must be regarded . . . as one of the most profoundly cynical aspects of the American war in Indochina."[13]

Considering how much their people sacrificed for America and how little America has given in return, it is understandable that some young Hmong Americans are disenchanted with their own people for being foolish enough to be involved with Americans, and with Americans for using their people so badly.

Generation Gap

The alienation felt by some young Hmong Americans may be traced to three factors: the disintegration of family cohesion, the loss of self-esteem in school, and the racism experienced in the United States. Instead of supplying the support and security of familiar customs, the Hmong family in America has become a battleground where customary assumptions are challenged. At its base is the difficulty of language. Like most immigrants and refugees, Hmong parents speak English only at an elementary level, for basic communication purposes, rather than at a higher cognitive level. Many are not fluent enough to conduct business transactions or deal with government bureaucracies. Having to ask English-speaking children to help with even the most ordinary tasks, such as shopping for food and paying bills, diminishes the father's authority as head of the household. The father's role as protector of the family all but disappears when he must rely on children in interactions with the dominant society, such as negotiating the rent with the landlord and filling out job applications. Family roles are reversed, with Hmong American youths functioning prematurely as adults thrust into awkward positions of power and responsibility. As negotiators between their families and the world, they feel a great deal of pressure: a mistake in English translation or misinterpretation of American customs could cost their families dearly. Yet they are treated by their families and society as youngsters. This situation fosters disrespect and deception, as when children misinform their parents about their progress in school. It is a short step from mediation to manipulation.

Even with honest intentions, family members may fail to communicate. Because many parents barely speak English and many children barely speak Hmong, misunderstandings and arguments often arise. Children who were born overseas and have a better grasp of the native language have to mediate between their parents and younger siblings who were born in the United States. There is little meaningful intergenerational dialogue; parents are reduced to issuing orders and children to obeying them. Among other things, lack of a shared, nuanced, abstract language makes it difficult for the older generation to explain Hmong ways and for the younger generation to explain American ways to their parents. As one Hmong father, Nu Yeng Yang, observed sorrowfully, "Our children do not respect us. One of the hardest things for me is when I tell my children things and they say, 'I already [know] that.' When my wife and I try to tell my son about Hmong culture, he tells me people here are different, and he will not listen to me."[14]

Life at home becomes particularly problematic during the adolescent years, since the phenomenon of the teenager is alien to Hmong parents. In Laos, at age thirteen or fourteen, the young begin working as farmers (or during wartime as soldiers). In other words, they go from childhood to adulthood without an adolescent stage. But Hmong American youths, like other American youths, do go through this intermediate age, a "rebellious" period when they seek acceptance by emulating the behavior and appearance of their peers, especially adolescents of color with whom they share common experiences. In contemporary society, this means wearing baggy hip-hop clothes and Reeboks, speaking slang, giving and receiving "high-fives," and wanting to go out with their friends or to date members of the opposite sex. Parents, in contrast, want their children to dress more conservatively and to stay at home to help out as members of a Hmong cooperative household united by common interests. They certainly expect more than the fleeting answers they get whenever they ask teenagers what they are doing or where they are going. As for Hmong parents' attitude toward dating, "forget it," the teenagers complain. To Hmong parents, dating is tantamount to an engagement; the only question left is when and where the marriage will take place. And, of course, the casual sex of American teenagers is anathema. In traditional culture, the acceptable way to meet someone of the opposite sex is to play the "Ball-Tossing" game during the annual Lunar New Year Celebration.[15] Back in Laos, this courtship ritual worked well enough, but from the perspective of Hmong American teenagers, it is a tradition better remembered than practiced.

Further undermining the authority of the parents has been the poverty of the Hmong community. Hmong refugees, of course, arrived impoverished, requiring public assistance. Unfortunately, their impoverishment persists because of widespread unemployment and poorly paid occupations, which can be traced, in part, to the deindustrialization and downsizing that have occurred in the United States since the Hmong began arriving in the mid-1970s. In Minnesota, for instance, 65.3 percent of Hmong Americans report that they are unemployed, with 42 percent of adults reporting that they have never been able to find employment in the United States.[16]

As former subsistence farmers, the Hmong have few marketable skills and have had a difficult time integrating into a modern economy, which itself is in the process of change. Almost 90 percent of the Hmong Americans who went to California's Central Valley to engage in farming have abandoned the idea.[17] Those fortunate enough to find other employment in the country's stratified labor market have usually taken low-wage blue-collar jobs in factories and in the service industry, jobs that, in America, are usually occupied by people of color. Often, both parents must work in order to make ends meet, a necessity that clashes with the tradition of Hmong women remaining at home to raise their children. Hmong American youths, like other latch-key children, fend for themselves after school, relying for guidance on television, or on peers who are in a similar situation.

In sum, communication difficulties and unemployment have significantly eroded filial respect for and the self-esteem of Hmong men accustomed to being the unchallenged patriarchs of their households and providers for their families. In an effort to assert control over rebellious and recalcitrant children, they have resorted to corporal punishment, only to be told that this is a violation of the law.[18] To make matters worse, children have often embarrassed their parents by informing the police of such beatings. Nu Yeng Yang was speaking for a generation of Hmong parents when he said, "We have lost all control."[19] At a loss as to what they can and cannot do, they have been forced to rely on American schools to instill discipline in their children.

Anti-Model Minority Student

Recognizing that education is the ladder of success in America, Hmong parents have wanted their children to do well in school. In fact, there are excellent Hmong American students, individuals who have met and often exceeded parental and community expectations. They unwittingly reinforce the stereotype of Asians as the "model minority," an image that is often invoked to make invidious comparisons with other students of color. Hmong Americans who came to the United States as young children have fared better than their older siblings, experiencing fewer difficulties in school and having higher retention and graduation rates. Many of them have even been able to attain a college education, bringing honor to their families even while they escape the authority of their parents and their parents' working-class lifestyles.

Because they know both English and the Hmong dialect spoken at home, they have become the most effective intermediaries between cultures. This is the group from which the Hmong social service professionals will most likely be drawn. Their ability to move easily from one culture to the other is the key to their success in America. Sia Lo, for example, learned that accepting herself as a Hmong was the best thing she could do for herself: "This was a very big part of me getting valedictorian and a lot of the steps I took, I learned a little at a time, that's why I am so well adjusted between the two cultures."[20]

But successful Hmong American youths like Sia Lo are outnumbered by those who are failing and dropping out of the school system. Older children born overseas had no previous education in Southeast Asia, having spent most of their young lives in the midst of war or in refugee camps. In the United States, they found themselves in an unfamiliar, often hostile environment and in schools indifferent to their needs. Ignorant of Hmong culture and unable to provide adequate bilingual instruction, schools simply enrolled Hmong students in classes according to their age rather than according to their needs. And their parents, not themselves formally educated, are unable to give their children much academic support and have inadvertently handicapped them with heavy family obligations, effectively limiting their educational opportunities. As Theexa Vue notes:

> The pressures . . . are so different than for the typical Boulder Valley students with a family whose focus is on high academic achievement, getting into good colleges and going on to exciting careers before having families . . . it's hard for Hmong students to find friends and teachers who understand their lives. They're only living one life. . . . We're really living in two worlds: the Hmong culture and the American culture.[21]

The situation is especially difficult for Hmong American girls, who are under considerable parental pressure to marry and bear children. In keeping with their custom of early marriage, they say to their children, "Go get married because we want you to be taken care of if we die." As Pang Yang, recipient of an "I Have a Dream Foundation" award, notes, it makes school particularly hard for them.[22] Like other American girls who marry early and get pregnant, they usually drop out of school to raise their families. By the time their classmates are seniors in high school, they will have been married and given birth to a child or two.

The school dropout rate for Hmong American adolescents is extraordinarily high, about 50 percent nationwide and as high as 80 to 90 percent in some places.[23] Those who cannot do well in school believe that they can at least achieve a modicum of pride by being respectable members of the Hmong community, which for men means attaining gainful employment and for women marrying a good Hmong man. Predictably, these youths enter the low-paying sector of the economy, finding employment in factories, often where their parents work, and establishing families that become their main source of satisfaction.

Schools have proven to be a double-edged sword for the Hmong community. As schools are supposed to do, they have opened new horizons, liberating children from the confines of their communities and providing them with an entrée into mainstream society. They have also constituted alternate sources of authority, competing with Hmong parents for the affection and allegiance of their children, and even challenging parental prerogatives to decide what is best for them. Naturally, such a situation has sowed further discord in Hmong families.

To Be Young and Hmong in America

Of the three reasons contributing to the alienation of Hmong American youth, racism is probably the most significant. It has certainly been the most systematic and structural factor that the Hmong have had to cope with in America. As a people of color in the United States, the Hmong have been exposed to the usual stereotyping, discrimination, harassment, and violence, giving rise to feelings of fear and inferiority. In their schools and in their neighborhoods, they have had to endure racial epithets and physical abuse, being "beaten up for no reason other than for being Asian."[24] The problem is manifest in essays on the topic "Who Am I?" from the sixth-grade Hmong boy who says proudly, "I like being Hmong no matter . . . what white people say about my color," to the eighth-grade Hmong boy who says simply, "We fought with two white boys and I hit one three times. A week later they chased us in a car while we were on our bikes."[25]

Hmong American parents have been of little help. Unfortunately, they blame their children for the harassment and violence, believing that the children must have done something to cause it or that they should have avoided the situation somehow. Or they rely on traditional methods of protection as when a father tied bands made of string on to his children and sacrificed a cow for them.[26] Local authorities have been equally ineffectual, being either unable or unwilling to protect Hmong American youths from local hoodlums.

As generations of immigrants before them have done, Hmong American youths have responded by gathering together for mutual protection, making up for their smaller size with greater numbers. When numbers proved insufficient, they have resorted to firearms, as did the young Hmong American in Lafayette, Colorado, who fired a sawed-off shotgun at his tormentors.[27] Evidently, they feel that they "need guns to intimidate the football players."[28] They have been so successful that their enemies no longer give them the finger, lest it get shot off.[29] As one might expect, violence has been fetishized by these marginalized individuals. For them, self-defense has been an empowering experience.

Unlike the self-defense formations of previous immigrants, those of Hmong American youth have produced a subculture with self-destructive, nihilistic tendencies. This warped development can be traced to the Hmong's star-crossed relationship to the Central Intelligence Agency, their abandonment after the war in Indochina, and subsequent settlement in the United States.

Disaffected Hmong American youths take pride in belonging to an adolescent group that is obviously estranged from both their own ethnic community and the larger American society. They identify themselves as Hmong even though they are ashamed of being Hmong, rejecting such cardinal Hmong values as respect for elders and education. They have a profound distrust of authority, any authority—parents, teachers, police. Consciously dressing and behaving in a manner that challenges authority, they display Crip and Bloods gang colors as "gangbanger wannabes" and revel in their "outlaw" status. About the only thing they find meaningful is being "tough," modeling themselves on peers in school or in the neighborhood who have a reputation for being "macho." It seems to be the one quality that they find worth retaining from their ethnic culture. As part of this cult of "toughness," they sometimes have a need to test their mettle against a rival ethnic youth group that is similar to themselves, becoming involved in a cycle of violence.

From this Hmong American youth subculture have emerged hoodlum gangs such as the DRG (Dirty Rotten Gooks, so called in defiant acknowledgment of the racism that gave rise to this particular group). Increasingly, Hmong American "gangbangers" are involved in crimes ranging from shoplifting to car theft to murder. They are motivated primarily by money, which allows them to engage in the kind of conspicuous consumption encouraged in America's capitalist economy and thus to acquire the status and self-esteem that American society denies them. Like other Asian gangs, Hmong gangs are prepared to engage in violence, though usually to achieve group goals rather than for personal reasons.[30]

For deracinated young Hmong Americans a gang serves as a surrogate family that provides them with the understanding and support they miss at home. Indeed, it seems in many cases that they have transferred their primary allegiance from their natural family to a gang, trading in their feelings of isolation and rejection for fellowship and acceptance. Perverting some Hmong social practices, they abide by codes of behavior such as loyalty to the gang and secrecy about its activities, and rely heavily on ethnic solidarity to maintain discipline. According to David Yang, a St. Paul, Minnesota police officer and an expert on Asian gangs, they follow a simple creed, the "Four Ways": (1) Knowledge is the key, (2) Money is the way, (3) Patience is a virtue, and (4) Death is beautiful.[31] With the fourth way, their nihilism is complete.

In the gang members' "us versus them" mentality, the "them" includes the Hmong community, which has been one of their major targets. To the extent that they have a territory, it conforms to wherever the Hmong are located. Hmong gangs are highly mobile groups willing to travel long distances, to other states if necessary, to commit crimes. Their deterrent effect on non-Hmong gangs is of little solace to

Hmong victims, who consider these gangs no better than terrorists. As former soldiers, older Hmong leaders have considered vigilante reprisals against the gangs, but they fear that the judicial system would treat them, not the gang members, as the criminals.

An Asian American Identity

Fortunately, a few alienated young Hmong Americans have begun to explore an Asian American alternative to the "gangbanger" identity. They too are motivated by the racism they have experienced in the United States but they express their opposition through a variety of progressive means, including popular culture. Tou Ger Xiong, Hmong American rap artist and recent graduate of Carleton College, is an example par excellence.[32] He and his family fled Laos in 1975 and were incarcerated in a refugee camp in Thailand for four years before coming to America. The remainder of his youth was spent in a St. Paul inner-city public housing project dominated by Afro-Americans and Mexican Americans.

Highly conscious of his ethnicity, Tou realizes that he is a product of two cultures and two generations, a member of "generation one and a half."[33] Rather than becoming lost in the space between, Tou has developed his own sense of self, which he expresses musically and dramatically. Indeed, he uses his talents to help others bridge these cultural and generational gaps.[34] Besides telling traditional folktales through interactive dramatization, he has appropriated Afro-American rap music as a performance vehicle for teaching young Hmong Americans and others about "Asian/Hmong American issues": "Rap music appeals particularly to youth. Thus, I use rap as a medium to educate. In a street-language style, I rap about coping with racism, balancing a bicultural identity, building self-esteem, and liberating oneself."[35]

While distinguishing himself racially from Afro-Americans, he consciously uses the oppositional voice that they popularized to implicitly critique American culture.

> As you can see
> I'm Asian
> Yeah, I'm not black[36]

Comfortable with a public persona that incorporates an Afro-American style, Tou even equates himself with the white rapper Vanilla Ice, creating a multicultural identity as well as an Asian American one. He informs his audience that this transformation is possible because it is based on a Hmong culture that sings and dances too, implicitly challenging his audiences' stereotype of Asian Americans as passive, apolitical nerds.

> You may think its weird
> To see that I'm Asian
> Busting some rhymes
> On such an occasion
> Let me tell you how
> I came to be

I was born in Laos in '73
In my culture
We sing and dance
But I'm gonna start rapping
And take my chance
Even though
It's my first rap
You don't have to like it,
You don't have to clap
To those of you listening
It might be nice
To think this Hmong boy's kicking it like Vanilla Ice.

Tou seeks to nurture self-esteem, telling his audiences, "You have something that is already there. You just have to realize that it's something valuable."[37] By embracing the popular media stereotype of Asian Americans as martial arts experts (Bruce Lee is one of his role models), he seeks to connect with young Hmong Americans who place a high value on toughness, hoping to get their attention long enough to consider Hmong history and culture.

Yeah, I know kung-fu
And martial arts,
You try to go against me,
Man, I'll tear you apart.
Yeah, I'm bad,[38] mean
And tough is my game
They call me the master,
Yeah, that's my name.

Some Hmong Americans are acting on this newfound pan-Asian consciousness to mobilize their community to engage in collective action necessary to improve their lot in America, as other marginalized groups have done before them.[39] Moreover, they are exploring ways to go outside the Hmong American community to participate in inter Asian coalitions based on an Asian American identity and interethnic coalitions opposed to racism to achieve racial equality, social justice, and political empowerment in a culturally pluralist America. Opposition to police brutality against Hmong American youth has catalyzed coalition building.[40] On November 15, 1989, in Minneapolis, Minnesota, Ba See Lor and Thai Yang, two teenagers, were fatally shot in the back as they fled in an abandoned stolen car. The police officer said he thought Yang had a gun. However, the Lor and Yang families believe that the killings were racially motivated. Because of racial harassment and death threats, the two families had to move out of the area. Meanwhile, a black, white, and Asian American progressive coalition has initiated a letter-writing campaign to reopen the investigation.

More recently, on October 12, 1993, also in Minneapolis, Minnesota, Bruce Teng Thao and Kai Lor, two teenagers, were shot and killed by a security guard during an attempted robbery. The guard said he fired in response to gunfire. Thao had two gunshot wounds and a gun that had never been fired; Lor, who was never claimed to have had a gun, suffered two entrance wounds in the back of the chest and neck. A Hmong Social Justice Committee has raised questions about the inconsistencies surrounding the incident. Thao and Lor's deaths may not have been in vain.

Conclusion

For the Hmong, the diaspora to America has been a disillusioning experience, forcing them to endure inexorable change. The most difficult part of their odyssey has been to watch helplessly as many of their young struggle to negotiate the transition from Hmong to American culture. Some young Hmong Americans have been able to succeed by balancing both, or, to use Daisy Ngialah's metaphor, by tying a bow with the two cultures.[41] They meet different people's expectations by acting "Hmong" at home and "American" in society. As time goes by, they will become less Hmong and more American, though by reason of race they cannot become fully "American," at least not Euro-American.

Many other young Hmong Americans have undergone a profound identity crisis that has alienated them from both Hmong and American cultures. In reconstructing their identity in the racially hostile American environment, a few have chosen to become criminal gang members, living violent and lawless lives. In assimilating into the worst sector of society, they have realized their parents' worst fears, transforming an American dream into a nightmare.

It is encouraging that there are signs that some Hmong American youths have discovered another resolution of their identity crisis. Among ethnically conscious Hmong, an Asian American identity is emerging. Developing such an identity involves integrating aspects of Hmong culture and American culture, specifically those elements that allow them to maintain a high level of self-esteem, and also to understand how the Hmong experience fits into the broader patterns of American history and culture. It is a process that requires Hmong American youth not only to remember Hmong history as their parents have transmitted it, but also to mediate it through the prism of their own experience. Becoming Asian American will allow them to assert, on their own terms, their right to belong to American society and to be treated as respected and responsible members in it. In claiming America as their own, they will finally end the Hmong diaspora.

NOTES

I would like to thank the editors, Michael Willard and Joe Austin, for their insightful comments on an earlier draft. I owe a debt of gratitude to Susan Cherniack for serving as a sounding board during the research and writing of this article. Needless to say, none of them are responsible for the opinions expressed in it or the imperfections that mar it.

1. Thai Xiong, interview, Westminster, Colorado, January 26, 1996. Unless otherwise noted, this essay is drawn from my interviews with the following people: Leo Carrillo, Mim Campos, Kevin Her, Nick Her, Pasia Her, Richard Her, Xong Her, D. J. Ida, John Lamb, Julie Lor,

Eda Moua, Paia Daisy Ngialah, Shuayie Xiong Ngialah, Rose Richman, Gao Vue, Chee Xiong, Kao Xiong, Leng Xiong, Lor Xiong, Michael Xiong, Tou Ger Xiong, Yer Bee Xiong, David Yang, Sieng C. Yang, and Xao Yang.

2. Keith Quincy, *Hmong: History of a People* (Cheney, Wash.: Eastern Washington University Press, 1988), provides a comprehensive history of the Hmong.

3. Tricia Knoll, *Becoming Americans: Asian Sojourners, Immigrants, and Refugees in the Western United States* (Portland, Oreg.: Coast to Coast Books, 1982), 237.

4. Ibid., 241.

5. Noam Chomsky, *At War with Asia: Essays on Indochina* (New York: Vintage Books, 1969), 255.

6. D. Gareth Porter, "After Geneva: Subverting Laotian Neutrality," in *Laos: War and Revolution*, ed. Adams and McCoy, cited in Sucheng Chan, ed., *Hmong Means Free: Life in Laos and America* (Philadelphia: Temple University Press, 1994), 239. Also see Daisy Ngialah, "Visions of Utopia," in *Rebels without a Clue: Young Hmong Speak Out* (Boulder, Colo.: Boulder Mental Health Center, 1994), 9.

7. Asian Week, *Asians in America: 1990 Census* (San Francisco: Grant Printing House, 1991), 6. This figure may be a significant undercount. Pai Yang and Nora Murphy, *Hmong in the '90s: Stepping towards the Future* (St. Paul, Minn.: Hmong American Partnership, 1993), 7, estimate that there are 125,000 Hmong in the United States.

8. Dr. D. J. Ida, Director, Child/Adolescent Services, Asian Pacific Development Center, interview, Denver, Colorado, January 2, 1996.

9. Gary Yia Lee, "Culture and Adaptation: Hmong Refugees in Australia," in Glenn L. Hendricks et al., eds., *The Hmong in Transition* (Center for Migration Studies of New York, Inc. and the Southeast Asian Refugee Studies Project of the University of Minnesota, 1986), 55, discusses the Hmong way of life and the changes that it has undergone.

10. Pang Thao, "Amendment Would Extend Citizenship to Vets," *Hmong Free Press*, April 1996.

11. Author was present during this incident.

12. David L. Moore, "Georgetown University," *Hmong Free Press*, May 1966.

13. Noam Chomsky, *At War with Asia*, 256.

14. Seth Mydans, "Laotians' Arrest in Killing Bares a Generation Gap," *New York Times*, June 21, 1994.

15. This activity is usually held in a public place where Hmong American youths gather to toss a tennis ball to each other, providing them an innocuous way to introduce themselves to a member of the opposite sex and engage them in conversation. In Laos the Hmong used heavy hand-made cloth balls for this purpose. Barbara Taylor, "Hmongs Celebrate New Year through Traditions," *Daily Camera*, Boulder, Colorado, December 2, 1992.

16. Pai Yang and Nora Murphy, *Hmong in the '90s*, 26.

17. John Finck, "Secondary Migration to California's Central Valley," in Glenn L. Hendricks et al., *The Hmong in Transition*, 186.

18. The medicinal use of opium, the ritual slaughter of animals, and the kidnapping of brides are some other Hmong customs that have contravened American laws.

19. Mydans, "Laotians' Arrest in Killing Bares a Generation Gap."

20. Thai Xiong, "An Interview with Sia Lo: Culture, Modernization, and Where I Stand," in *Rebels without A Clue: Young Hmong Speak Out*, 20.

21. Barbara Taylor, "Trust Fund Helps 'Dreamers' Meet Educational Goals," *Sunday Camera*, Boulder, Colorado, May 26, 1996.

22. Ibid.

23. Wendy Walker-Moffat, *The Other Side of the Asian American Success Story* (San Francisco: Jossey-Bass, 1995), discusses the Hmong American youths' educational experience.
24. Pai Yang and Nora Murphy, *Hmong in the '90s*, 1.
25. From essays written by Hmong American students at Angevine Middle School and Broomfield Middle School, Colorado, Spring 1996.
26. John Lamb, interview, Boulder, Colorado, September 27, 1996.
27. Leo Carrillo, Chief of Police, interview, Lafayette, Colorado, January 8, 1996.
28. David Yang, interview, Washington, D.C., April 6, 1996. He notes that 90 percent of the gunshop burglaries in the Minneapolis-St. Paul area are perpetrated by Hmong American gangs.
29. Ibid.
30. *"L.A. Style": A Street Gang Manual of the Los Angeles County Sheriff's Department* (n.d, n.p.).
31. David Yang, "Youth Delinquency: Rebuilding Hmong Family Structure," Hmong Youth Conference, Georgetown University, Washington, D.C. , April 4–6, 1996.
32. Unless otherwise noted, the comments about Tou Ger Xiong are based on Trevor Roberts, producer and director, "A Profile of Tou Ger Xiong," International Cable Channels Partnership, Ltd., 1996, and Tou Ger Xiong, interview, September 27, 1996.
33. Yee Chang, "Rap, Folktales, Comedy Gives One Message," *Hmong Free Press*, December 1995.
34. Yee Chang, "Tou Ger Xiong Receives Grant," *Hmong Free Press*, May 1996, says that Tou Ger Xiong has received a one-year, $15,000 Echoing Green Foundation fellowship to fund and expand his one-person service project called "Respectism."
35. Tou Ger Xiong, "Respectism: A Universal Thing," pamphlet, December 1995.
36. Rap music excerpts are from Trevor Roberts, "A Profile of Tou Ger Xiong." Besides using rap to appeal to young Hmong Americans, Tou uses it as a way of defining himself as an Asian American and to contest the way mainstream society has demeaned him and his people. In the ongoing "culture war" against monoculturalists, he has joined the ranks of the multiculturalists, promoting a broader interpretation of American culture that recognizes the contributions that the many racial and ethnic groups have made to the culture, transforming it in significant ways.
37. "Carleton Student Working to Bridge Hmong and American Cultures," *Northfield News*, January 3, 1996.
38. With his use of "bad," which means "good" in the black street lexicon, Tou continues to cross ethnic boundaries to define himself as a unique individual but from within American youth culture.
39. William Wei, *The Asian American Movement* (Philadelphia: Temple University Press, 1993), provides a study of Asian American activism.
40. Both cases from a display mounted by Asian American students at the University of Colorado during spring 1996 to protest anti-Asian violence.
41. Daisy Xiong Ngialah, "Reflections on Being Hmong," in *Rebels without a Clue*, p. 36.

Fig. 19.1. Shoeshine man Joe V. "Borrego" Rodriguez gives up his seat (and place of work) to watch Daewon Song's boardslide bring the truth to power, as they and photographer Socrates Leal become urban planners exploring the multipurpose variations of a single-use "bum-proof" bench. These benches form the first line of defense against the homeless along Hill Street, which separates Bunker Hill from old downtown Los Angeles. (Photo by Socrates Leal)

Chapter Nineteen

Seance, Tricknowlogy, Skateboarding, and the Space of Youth

Michael Nevin Willard

In much of Los Angeles, the casual pedestrian was an oddity—or a walking threat to the civic order.

—Edward Soja, Rebecca Morales, and Goetz Wolff, "Urban Restructuring," *Economic Geography* 59, no.2 (1983)

[If I won the lottery] I'd like to help people who really need it. Like, I'd give to a homeless person before I'd give to a relative or something.... Some people think the homeless deserve to be where they are because they could just get up and get off the street if they wanted it bad enough. But I don't think that way.

—Daewon Song, skateboarder, in *Transworld Skateboarding* 12, no. 9 (1994)

Angles of History in the City of Angels

Wing Ko and I stand on the corner of Third and Broadway, once-downtown Los Angeles, loitering in the shadows of postmodernism. Behind our backs to the west the new downtown skyline of eclectic history, glass, and aluminum grows upon itself as it piles skyward. Hovering over us from atop Bunker Hill, and announcing Los Angeles as a global city, it melts into air.

Wing is a filmmaker and skateboarder. We are waiting for Rodney Mullen, a professional skateboarder, and Socrates Leal, a video maker and skateboarder, who have been on Broadway all day shooting footage for Rodney's segment of the next Plan B skateboard company video.[1] "Soc" works with Rodney on the skateboarding segments of the video. Wing films the segments for the "feeling" and storyline of the video. Later Rodney tells me that the "feeling" of a skate video is crucial these days when there aren't as many contests to differentiate skaters.[2] The tricks that win contests often aren't as good as the tricks in the videos. What with so many good skateboarders all of whom can do the most difficult tricks, it becomes even more important that each skater in a video have an "identity."

Today Wing will shoot footage of Rodney carrying his skateboard and walking among the dense crowds who fill the sidewalks along Broadway: families, youth, elderly, mostly working-class, mostly Latino; fewer Asian and Black shoppers; present though much fewer still, lunch-hour, predominantly Anglo business people, though almost never shoppers; equally diverse, all-adult homeless people; and civil servants from the Ronald Reagan office building located a block away on Spring Street.[3]

Across Third Street, on the corner opposite from Wing and me, stands the renovated Bradbury building, anchor of the redevelopment project sometimes known as "Bunker Hill East," which appears to be fulfilling Mike Davis's predictions for this corner of Broadway. In his 1990 book *City of Quartz*, he identified Community Redevelopment Agency (CRA) strategies for recolonizing the northern end of Broadway, this "two way street" that runs south culturally and transnationally all the way to Mexico and back.[4] Along with the Bradbury, the Grand Central Square Market[5] and Apartments and the Million Dollar Theater[6] anchor owner Ira Yellin's Grand Central Square redevelopment plan.[7] Over the last thirty, years corporate tenants and urban renewers have abandoned Broadway in favor of insular citadels of higher finance built on the razed and renewed, formerly Filipino, Mexican American, and working-class neighborhoods of Bunker Hill. Now some of these "off-world" corporate privateers are beginning to return, lured back down to the ground, as lunch-hour tourists[8]—to consume the more diverse, if not more public and democratic, street life of Mexican Americans and immigrant Latinos who have reclaimed Broadway as their own.

While Wing and I wait for Rodney and Soc, I point to the Bradbury building and ask him if he has seen the movie *Blade Runner*. Of course he has. I tell him that the scenes of the toymaker's house were shot here. Wing accesses his memory bank and registers a sudden flash of illumination. The sign above the door reads 1893. We enter. From the dim bottom of a well of shimmering daylight we marvel at the intricate wrought-iron work on landings and exposed elevator shafts silhouetted in the illumination from the arcaded glass ceiling that squints down from five stories above and a century ago. We leave the building and chance upon Rodney and Soc.

Rodney has to get something from the car. While we wait, I follow Wing as he shows Soc inside the Bradbury. Taking his turn as tour guide, he tells Soc that *Blade Runner* was filmed here. This time the security guard, who is used to tourists, notices Soc's skateboard, and with quick sidewards glances—awkward in their practiced nonchalance—makes a concerted effort to casually drift toward us from the other side of the lobby. Apparently a skateboard is not one of the cultural codes that identifies people as harmless tourists and grants them access to this building—not even as tourists of Los Angeles's dystopian present/future. We take this as our cue to leave and head out the door.

Further down the street, Wing and Rodney find a good location where the crowd is somewhat thicker. Rodney has chosen this street because of the crowds and the urban feeling of "the city" that it imparts on film. Broadway has the densest concentration of pedestrians anywhere in Southern California. While Wing and Rodney work, Soc and I talk about the street. Soc and I watch and talk about the Mexican bullfight and rodeo videos playing in one of the open storefronts that face onto the sidewalk. Soc tells me about how in Mexico, where his family is from, he once got on TV. When visiting, he had given his friend a video of himself skateboarding. Soc's friend knew someone at a local TV station, and since they didn't have enough programming to fill their airtime they played Soc's video.

Later that week, back on Broadway on a Sunday morning with Wing and Rodney to get the last bits of footage. As we pass the Bradbury on our way down the street, Wing shows Rodney into the building. When Wing tells him, "*Blade Runner* was shot here," Rodney looks at us and replies, "That's exactly the feeling I'm going for [in my video]." His comment reminds me of the scenes of crowded, multilingual street life in the movie. We thank the security guard, who has already completed the first few steps of the security guard boogie, his dance of feigned inattention. We evacuate the building—emptying it of space—for the more industrious sidewalks.

On Sunday afternoons, the bustle and hustle remind me of what I think New York must be like, though I imagine that the recently immigrated Latino shoppers may find more similarities to shopping districts in their native countries. The stores on Broadway open right onto the sidewalk, many of them wedged and retrofitted into the abandoned lobbies of the many palatial two thousand-seat movie palaces of early twentieth-century Los Angeles that line Broadway. Now, with *banda* and *ranchera* recordings trumpeting out pop and disco "*ritmos Latinos*" from banks of three-foot-tall speakers positioned on the sidewalks in front of the music and audio equipment shops that dot the street at half-block intervals, shopping on Broadway is less formal than in the early twentieth century. Now Sunday shopping on Broadway is more like a celebration. Families doing their shopping after church are dressed up, but they mix unconcernedly with less formally dressed homeless people and other Sunday strollers, all of whom soak in the music and commotion.

On this day Wing and Rodney work to get a few more shots of Rodney among the crowds of shoppers that will establish his "identity."[9] Wing has told me, and I have also learned from reading magazine interviews and watching videos, that Rodney is sometimes known in the skateboarding subculture as a mad scientist, a "brainiac" who finds more entertainment in doing calculus problems than in hanging out on the beach. All skaters exhibit a high degree of intellectual expertise when they skate. Rodney's is incredibly technical and uniquely inventive.[10]

For example, most skaters execute boardslides using the underside of their decks to slide along the edge of benches, down staircase handrails, or down the slides of concrete that are sometimes built alongside staircases. Rodney, on the other hand, rolls up to the sloped concrete on the side of a staircase and as he ollies onto it, in a pique of inspiration, he flips his board upside down to theorize a version of his trademark "darkslide" down the concrete. Standing on what is normally the underside of the board to either side of the wheels that now face up, he slides topside down, descending the sloping incline of concrete on the "dark" black grip tape, only to flip the board over at the last nanosecond of the slide, to land topside up and roll away.[11]

Back on Broadway Wing and Rodney discuss their objectives in these shots. They work to construct an image of Rodney appropriate to the persona of the introverted, solitary genius—whose inspiration borders on madness and spirituality—that he expresses in his skating and his trademark "darkslide." Rodney walks up the block and disappears into the crowd. He returns sometimes as much as five minutes later. Wing films him as he comes into view. Every time Rodney emerges from the crowd, he is walking a few steps behind one of the frequent homeless men whose spatial privation is so visually communicated through his clothing, mussed hair, and bodily posture. Nevertheless, the homeless prefer the relatively greater freedom of Broadway to what can be found on Bunker Hill or in other shopping districts in the city. At first I don't notice this, but after watching Wing and Rodney repeat this shot a few times and listening to them talk between shots, I realize that the delays between Rodney walking up the street and coming back into view are due to his waiting to find a homeless person to walk behind. When I ask Rodney why he chose to shoot on Broadway, he tells me that his video segments usually show him skating alone at the beach. This time he wanted to be seen skating in the city, among many people, but still alone.

While Rodney cultivates his image of the lone intellectual, in this instance by juxtaposing his sense of isolation with similarly isolated homeless men, his identification with the homeless is not unique. Scenes of homeless people talking to skaters and expressing enthusiasm for their tricks are common in skate videos. Shooting in urban settings brings skaters into close contact with the homeless. While many of these scenes occur as chance encounters during skate sessions or during the work of making videos, it is important to note that skaters use the chance documentation of these moments of everyday urban life to call attention to the similarities of spatial exclusion that both skaters and the homeless experience.

In the process of making a skate video, the camera also inevitably documents encounters between skaters and security/police forces or irate adults. Inclusion of such scenes in skate videos is also common. Such scenes of both the police and the homeless suggest that skaters create relationships of affinity with the homeless to intentionally dramatize their own kind (but not degree) of spatial poverty. I have witnessed both on video and on the street that, unlike most urban pedestrians, the homeless often stop to watch and express interest in skaters' activities.

In sharp contrast to Broadway, Bunker Hill is coated with redundant kevlar layers of high-tech security. As Mike Davis explains, "The occasional appearance of a destitute street nomad . . . in front of the Museum of Contemporary Art sets off a quiet panic; video cameras turn on their mounts and security guards adjust their belts."[12] Increasingly in most urban areas, multiple levels of cooperation and coordination between private and public police forces, building security guards, video surveillance cameras, computer databases, and, in Los Angeles, barrel-shaped, bum-(in both senses of the word)-proof,[13] bus-stop benches define space as a prec(ar)ious material (and cultural) condition of urban life.[14] In L.A. this security apparatus effectively sweeps undesirables off Bunker Hill and further reduces the geographical scale of urban space available to people without homes.

By comparison the physically crumbling yet culturally recycled, vibrant, and retrofitted Broadway seems humanitarian. But for the present—until gentrification remakes Broadway in the image of rehistoricized shopping districts and tourist bubbles such as Old Town Pasadena or the more tolerant, though still vigilant, Third Street Promenade in Santa Monica, where the homeless and "idle" youth are permitted to occupy public benches and pedestrian space for hours on end—Broadway is well within the space of downtown Los Angeles that has been cordoned off to contain and limit the mobility of the homeless, Latino transnationals, and sometimes even skateboarders.

What I come to understand more fully later is that both skaters and downtown redevelopment agencies employ images of "the urban" to generate cultural coherence among their respective constituents. Sharing similar images of "the urban" within structures of their respective communities and corporations enables skaters and downtown developers to construct space to match their value-producing activities—as profitable historical nostalgia and a simulated "public" for developers; and as variable, in-constant space for skaters. The restructuring of urban space—which makes the global scale of transnational capitalism possible—also makes a new status of "youth" possible. On the level of a global scale, skateboarders (youth) and business/development coalitions coincide and constitute each other; at the level of the production of scales of the body and the urban, skaters (youth), corporate redevelopers, and municipal officials often conflict. I will elaborate on this point below.

When I ask Rodney whether the cops have ever hassled him while he was on Broadway shooting his video, he says that they never said a word: "And we [Rodney and Soc] were really in the way. Sometimes for thirty minutes in one spot."[15] For skateboarders space is something temporary, but their use of the media "constructs" larger spatial scales that help to overcome such a transient and transitory existence.

Jumping Scale

It may be an unusual comparison to draw parallels among the homeless, immigrants of Latin American diasporas, and skateboarders. The vast dissimilarities of class privilege, opportunity, and access to media and social infrastructures among these groups are more important than the similarities. However, the very same processes of global economic restructuring that have dislocated entire communities from Bunker Hill to "renew" it[16] have also fundamentally restructured the social and spatial conditions of youth. "In the wake of the Watts rebellion" in 1965, businesses abandoned Broadway for fear of the "Black and Mexican poor." Now in the wake of Proposition 187 and despite the presence of sales-tax-paying immigrant shoppers—whom Southern California businesses are happy to employ, but along with most California voters would deny citizenship, let alone basic human services such as health care and education—real estate developers and gentrification have returned to Broadway to inoculate and pacify it.[17] The way that skateboarders interact with the forces of gloabal restructuring is the subject of the rest of this essay.

It is significant that Rodney, Soc, and Wing were never hassled by cops and security guards while they were shooting on Broadway. So often, skaters must contend with security guards in practically every place they find to skate. During the past thirty years of urban renewal, Broadway has been spatially cut off from newer downtown Los Angeles. Despite the unexpected comparison, it becomes especially important to recognize the significance of a moment where socially dissimilar groups who share the experience of spatial exclusion occupy the same space.

The possibilities for these groups to assert their presence beyond tightly controlled and partitioned urban spaces such as Broadway, has much to do with their ability to jump scale, to expand the spatial range and scope of their self-activity—beyond the limits imposed by external organizations of power—to larger internally defined extensions of community and affective experience.[18]

Geographer Neil Smith explains scale as a social and geographical "contest to establish boundaries between different places, locations and sites of experience." Whenever a place is constructed—both architecturally and socially—scale is also produced. When real-estate developers build plazas to project an image of public space they also produce multiple scales. For example, they produce a scale of the body that organizes and limits mobility (walking vs. running), postures (sitting, leaning, standing), and appearance (the quality of one's clothing or the color of one's skin, which catches the attention of surveillance cameras).

Scale is open-ended and extends in an indefinite series of nested levels from the smallest scale of the body to the largest scale of the global. For Neil Smith, "scale is the criterion of difference not so much between places as between different kinds of places."[19] A single place is made up of multiple (if not infinite) scales. In Smith's formulation, both places and people have and produce scale. "Scale both *contains* social activity, and at the same time provides an already partitioned geography within which social activity *takes place*. Scale demarcates the sites of social contest, the object as well as the resolution of contest."[20]

Skaters, like their Latino and homeless counterparts on Broadway, experience scale as separation, as the attempt by those with greater power to produce scale that limits the extent of their social activity and everyday life. Smith's explanation of scale jumping in regard to the homeless is useful for understanding the implications of skaters' movement on the urban landscape: "The importance of 'jumping scales' lies precisely in [the] active social and political connectedness of apparently different scales, their deliberate confusion and abrogation."[21] Skaters' similar experience of the imposition of scale is likewise overcome by their ability to connect apparently different scales.

Jumping scale is a process of circulating images of self and community that can be cast broadly to the rest of the social hierarchy. This is the basis for the production of larger scales that insure continued inclusion in, and ability to shape, urban spaces. For skateboarders the production of "translocal" community within mass-mediated networks of subcultural skills/knowledge has become the most significant scale of identity formation.[22] One of the first steps that the spatially marginalized can take to counter the spatial limitations of their identity is to call attention to the fact that space is socially constructed according to specific imaginings of who may occupy it and who may not.

In the rest of the essay I will focus on the production of some of the many scales that skaters jump whenever they skate. In each case the geographical production of scale functions as common knowledge among skaters that is circulated among them to establish the existence of "translocal" subcultural community, one of the larger scales that has become available to skaters through global economic restructuring, economies of information, and resultant changes in the status of youth.

First, as they construct a scale of the body (as well as "local" community) that is radically different from the scale of the body produced by urban planners and built into "public" spaces, skaters teach us about the social construction of space. Second, skaters teach us about the history of the spatial construction of youth. Third, I will consider how skaters reproduce the global scale of youth itself, according to values created through skating.

Big Trees Small Acts

> Gaps, blocks, handrails, benches, ramps, street. I like to skate things that are not built for skateboarding.
> —John Reeves, interviewed by Kien Lieu in *Transworld Skateboarding* 12, no. 9 (1994)

We have all noticed, perhaps dismissed as "boys' stuff," but definitely marveled at, the clatterous, noisy moments of skateboarding that have become a predictable part of the everyday urban landscape. Skaters interact spectacularly with the built environment in a way that denaturalizes its fixity, wears its welcome "out," embellishes the functional, operationalizes the ornamental, disobeys architectural modifications of behavior, re-bounds decency in a single leap, liberates the strictures of structure, and breaks out of the channeled flows (commerce, transportation) of city life.[23]

Whenever skaters perform their "tricks" they make their own meanings, critiques of power, and interpretations of urban life. When a skater ollies into a frontside tailslide down a thirteen-stair handrail, the genius of such tricknowlogy is that it makes the unexamined assumptions of otherwise inconsequential architectural elements become strange, and stand out in stark relief. Is a handrail *only* for safety, or is it also intended to keep people off the grass? Is a bus-stop bench barrel-shaped because it is meant to be aesthetically pleasing?

The basis of skaters' alchemical estrangement of urban space and critique of urban life is the ollie. As the skater nears the object (bench, fire hydrant, curb, handrail, staircase, planter box, trash can) the ollie begins by thrusting the back foot down and quickly slapping the tail of the skateboard on the pavement, while at the same time unweighting the front foot and raising the front wheels off the ground. At the full extension of the back foot's downward thrust, the skater quickly jumps off the same foot, bending the knees and quickly pulling them up, allowing the tail to rebound from the force of the tailslap. Rear wheels follow front wheels into the air so that board and skater are spectacularly airborne—sometimes four or five feet above flat ground, or even "phatter" yet, ten to fifteen feet above a flight of stairs, off a wall or building. Reversing this sequence, first thrusting the nose of the board down to elevate the tail followed by the nose rebounding into the air, is known as a "nollie" (nose ollie).

Increasingly difficult ollie variations include kick-flipping and/or spinning the board, once airborne, so that board and rider are momentarily separated in midair. Riffs on these ollie variations proliferate further when a skater rides switch-stance, reversing the original foot placement to execute ollies, nollies and kick flips with back foot forward. When a skater learns to skate, foot placement is determined with similar left- or right-handed preference exhibited when learning to write or play a guitar. Executing a complex switch-stance trick is comparable to playing a Jimi Hendrix solo in the first-learned, right-handed position, then flipping the guitar over and playing the solo left-handed with equal virtuosity. Skaters' revision of urban space calls into question the seeming fixity of distance and the directional stability of forward and backward, right and left, perhaps even of up and down.[24] By producing their own body scale, skaters create variable space.

When a skater ollies, without any banked transition, from horizontal sidewalk to the vertical wall of an office building, the social construction of space changes radically. In these moments skaters become urbanologists with perhaps as much "expertise" and facility for the construction of space according to concepts of "multiple use" as architects or urban planners. What may seem, to passersby, to be repetitious tricks performed by different skaters are, to the eyes of other skaters, variations on one another's techniques. Through the mutual enjoyment and recognition of variations between these tricks as they are inventively planned (as opposed to childishly played) on the urban landscape, skaters' ability to understand these variations allows them to create local and translocal subcultural communities.

One Sunday morning I witnessed moments of variable space creation. Passing the Arco Plaza in new downtown L.A., I heard telltale tailslaps and boardslides. In the recesses of this plaza—one of the first statements of L.A. "public" space resulting from downtown urban removal/renewal—I witnessed objects such as benches and handrails become transformed. While skaters were using them, the architectural elements of the plaza could no longer be seen and assigned a place within a stable set of elements according to urban planners' or corporate tenants' definitions of "public space." A bench was no longer an invitation to inclusion through the act of sitting, nor was a sculpture intended as a shared viewing experience.

On this strategically chosen Sunday morning there were no security guards to chase the skaters away. In both their after-hours timing of this skate session and in other instances when security guards do eject them, skaters reveal the limits of "the public" that postmodern architecture and shopping zones typical of new-downtown L.A. project. If it were really a diverse "public" space there would be reason for people to make multiple use of the Arco Plaza during and after business hours. Every day. Moments when undesirables such as skaters or the homeless are ejected from such places also show that the "public inclusion" projected so invitingly by postmodern plazas of high finance, in fact, is a "public illusion" limited to narrow definitions of who may enter and how they may participate in this fiction of public space. Skaters reveal spatial artifice, but they also bring their own social meaning to their constructions of space.

During any instance of skateboarding, as on that Sunday morning, the technology of vision at the interface between skateboard, human body, and built environment is linked to the group of skaters who created space "up close," more tactilely according to perceptions of foot placement on the board and board placement on the object than according to optical perceptions and overall organizing vision employed by architects or planners who create space to communicate a visual definition—as well as a limitation—of "the public."

The urban jazz contests that groups of skaters enter into when a they play versions of the same trick on built space allows them to constitute a coherent subculture by their very ability to understand the "intrinsic variations on the division of a single distance." Each subsequent performance and kick-flipping, spinning, and switch-stancing of a trick produces variable space.[25] Space is seen not from far away, but up close. What skaters see and others miss are the ways that each skater uses the same space differently.[26] The space that skaters produce is relational, between skaters who can see the multitude of possible relationships between skater and object. See, for example, Steve Berra's and Swift's (photographer) crooked grind down a bench placed between the roofs of two school buildings on the cover of the April 1997 issue of *Transworld Skateboarding*. The skaters' ability to see alternate possibilities in common places provides them with a knowledge of urban space that they can circulate among other skaters for the formation of subcultural community.

An ethic of cooperation is shown by the skaters' formation of a "local" community by repeating one another's tricks, and by the constantly shifting and instantaneous relations between the skaters themselves. Architect Ken Wormhoudt, a designer of skate parks, tells the story of watching a kid trying to learn a trick until he "nearly killed himself." When he finally landed the trick, the rest of the skaters cheered and clapped him on the back. Immediately the kid went over to another kid and started teaching the trick to him.[27] Sports sociologist Becky Beal identifies such cooperation as a value that is alternative to the win-at-all-costs competitive values of more traditional sports.[28]

In such instances the body scale produced by skaters is not identical to that of developers and planners, whose plans may limit bodies as fixed points within the static relations of architectural objects in a public plaza. Skaters' production of body scale overlaps developers' and becomes a kind of knowledge that in place- specific instances of skateboarding produces a "local" community, which in turn also allows skaters to jump the local scale of place contained in the developers' narrow definitions of "the public" to produce a translocal community.

Rather than simply ollieing over the dead space between objects, ollie variations fill gaps with social relations constituted through shared knowledge of variable space. Frozen on film in magazine or video, but circulated among translocal communities, the impossibly chaotic angles of board and body that "take place and make space" during ollie variations provide a theorization of space simultaneous to and independent of theorizations advanced by philosophers and critical theorists of space in 1970s France and in 1980s–1990s America and Britain.[29]

While most of the photos in skateboard magazines primarily produce the scale of the body through detailed sequences of body movement captured with high-speed film advance motors, this is not the only scale that skateboard magazines produce.[30] Two such pictures are worth more than the brief description I give them here. The

Solar clothing ad in the February 1997 issue of *Thrasher* features skater Jackson Taylor ollieing over a five foot high, closed (and locked?) wrought iron gate. The photo is labeled "surveillance image h5;Tx1l1" and calls attention to both the limits of scale imposed on skaters as well as an increasing trend toward gated communities that lock in their own scale through active policing of their borders. In the Gullwing ad in the April 1997 issue of *Slap*, Malcolm Watson and photographer Chris Otiz construct Los Angeles urban space as collective memory by juxtaposing two generations of youth: the Black Panther mural on Jefferson Boulevard in the Jefferson Park neighborhood, and Malcolm Watson ollieing over a fire hydrant in the foreground.

What skaters explain if we know how to see it is that space is not absolute, not a "field, container, [or] co-ordinate system of discrete and mutually exclusive locations."[31] If French, American, and British theorists and urban planners such as Henri Lefebvre, Edward Soja, Doreen Massey, and Neil Smith use concepts of scale and variable space to argue for more inclusive constructions of public space, skate-urbanologists' argument for the same is no less valuable[32]—though communicated in a vocabulary of gesture and image that is less comprehensible to those outside their subcultural communities.

A Handrail Is Not a Toy

So far, skaters have shown us how the "uses" of space are socially constructed and accepted as self-evident. A handrail is not a toy; it is only for safety; but we aren't meant to know that it is also a mechanism of discipline and separation. Even here, once skaters have shown the artificiality of the built environment, we also catch glimpses of other processes at work, here the spatial construction of the social. By "the social" I mean the commonsense understandings of, for example, "the public" or of "youth."

As geographer Doreen Massey puts it, "Society is necessarily constructed spatially, and that fact—the spatial organization of society—makes a difference in how it works. . . . All social (and indeed physical) phenomena/activities/relations have a spatial form and relative spatial location."[33] "Space" is created "out of the vast intricacies, the incredible complexities, of the interlocking and the non-interlocking, and the networks of relations at every scale from local to global. What makes a particular view of these social relations specifically spatial is their simultaneity."[34]

If a handrail is not a toy, then stairs are not a place where skateboarders should be, and because skaters use handrails for pleasure—as "toys" in the eyes of local authorities—their actions are constru(ct)ed as expressions of youth, but youth defined as people who need supervision and warnings, people who cannot take care of themselves and who must be limited in their spatial mobility.

Skateboarders show that city planners, architects, and corporate members of redevelopment agencies may often construct urban spaces according to rather narrow principles of multiple use. What is important for the purposes of this essay is that historically, youth have been limited in their spatial mobility according to a logic that says that a handrail is not a toy. Historically youth have been located within

Fig. 19.2. Urban historian Malcolm Watson ollies a fire hydrant to add a chapter to the history of Los Angeles's African American youth. Like the artwork of the mural depicting the history of the Black Panthers in the background, the skate work of skateboarders also tears down walls intended to keep in or keep out, and rebuilds them for a sense of shared space and shared history. (Photo by Chris Ortiz)

spaces that are safe, where it is O.K. to "play," the assumption being that when they grow out of playing with toys they can leave such enclosed spaces of containment. Historically, "youth" has been located within a logic of moral reform.

The corresponding assumption built into this spatial production of youth is that, if left unsupervised, youth will become immoral or delinquent, because every young person has within him the potential to become delinquent and within him or her the potential to become immoral. The history of spaces constructed according to the logic of moral reform is a history of spaces constructed to limit youth to the geographical scale of the home and to stay within parental control.[35]

In Beth Bailey's article in this volume, the policy of parietals that women students at the University of Kansas fought against is a useful example of the spatial construction of youth. Students were contained within residence halls and were required to report to dorm "mothers" who enforced the rules of containment and enclosure so that students would not engage in sexual relations.[36] Students were assumed to be incapable of controlling their own sexuality.

Similarly, moral reform, supervision and containment often inform city officials' attitudes toward skateboarders specifically and youth generally; and they are often derived from the past, from a historical period that constructed the space of youth according to a conception of youth based on the logic of moral reform. A significantly different concept of youth is now emerging from global economic restructuring.

Whosoever Diggeth a Pit: Skateboarding and the Status of Youth

Skateboarding is one of the most spectacular forms of urban cultural expression to emerge in postindustrial America. Along with hip-hop culture, punk rock, graffiti, heavy metal, gangsta' rap, riot grrrl, and low riding, skateboarding provides an important record of, and insight into, the history of youth and urban space. This youth-produced history is quite often absent from the "public" record produced by more powerful adults.

This absence is doubly reinforced when youth's expertise and their complex interpretations of the urban hierarchy are constructed by police, media, and city officials as "juvenile." Such trivialization fails to recognize that these popular-culture practices express a complex, insightful, and sophisticated understanding of history, power, and the structuring of urban space. Too often authorities are quick to locate the source of urban problems in what they perceive to be questionable morals of the youth culture. Given the spatial outcomes (containment, enclosure, supervision) of the history of youth and moral reform, it is worth suggesting, given the topic of this essay, that dismissal of youth on the basis of moral disapproval may be more than a simple misunderstanding, it may be evidence of the desire to contain and enclose youth in spaces over which they have little control.

The images of urban density, of the homeless, and of Latino ethnicity that Rodney, Soc, and Wing created in order to give Rodney's five-minute video sequence an "identity" may echo relationships of tourists visiting a foreign culture for a photo opportunity. However, we can also see that they were using communication and information technology to create unexpected (though not without differences of power and privilege) relationships of affinity. These can call attention to similarities of spatial positioning and exclusion. These relationships are gaining increasing importance within economies of global urban restructuring.

In her brilliant study of British Rave culture, Sara Thornton points out that the subcultures that youth create within information societies can exist only because of the availability of niche-, micro- and mass media.[37] Thornton's explanation is useful because it shows precisely the (im)material basis of the new youth status. The status of youth has changed from a life stage to be contained and protected—as a reserve army of labor—until they assume adult status, to one where coming of age matters much less because youth already engage in labor that, in addition to producing subcultural values, is already a highly sophisticated form of techno-scientific, information management, and value-producing labor within the global information economy. The circulation of situated knowledges such as skateboarders' critiques of urban space allows youth to reproduce the global scale of immaterial (because its products are images and information) labor, as a little-remarked result of the same processes that have deindustrialized central and south-central Los Angeles, replaced manufacturing jobs with automation, and replaced desk jobs with computers.[38]

When youth produce a global scale, through the immaterial labor of media and information circulation, they have explicit permission to form translocal communities on the basis of values produced *within* such networks of knowledge. Thornton further points out that most often the formation of a subcultural community is based on the ability of young people to exploit the moral panic that adults are still prone to when they encounter the alternative values of internally coherent youth subcultures. Skateboarders show us that their exploitation of moral panic—as is evident in a magazine titled *Thrasher*—or, to adult eyes, monstrous and terrifying graphics on the bottom of a skateboard, is not simply rebellion for the sake of rebellion.[39] At the same time that skaters use the impetus to moral reform, which is still espoused by some adults, against itself, their sometimes shocking statements also express profound, sophisticated, but highly coded understandings of the spatial relations that global capitalism has produced.[40]

Outsiders often cannot understand skaters' production of the scale of the body as an intimate expression of variable space. This works to the skaters' advantage because their ability to differentiate between a nollie and a fakie ollie is one way to gain control of the boundaries of "local" and translocal scales of community.

On another day of filmmaking with Wing, this time in Huntington Beach, Phil of Clockwork Skateboards tells me something similar: every skateboard company has to have its own image, or icon, in order to get kids to buy their products; but because skateboarding is "punk rock," it is very difficult to keep an icon and one's image fresh. I take "punk rock" to mean anti-commercial and anti-sellout, but more importantly D.I.Y. (do-it-yourself) and "anti-mass culture." Within micromarkets of the skateboarding subculture, processes of distinction and style are intense. Many skaters carefully choose ensembles of shoes, everyday clothing, and brands of skateboard decks, trucks, and wheels. Important in this process are brand logos and the ubiquitous decals that skaters use to code and recode their decks, cars, and skate spaces. A collage of stickers on the bottom of a board can become, in the hands of a skilled applicator, an important form of subcultural expression. Like the underground of the British Rave culture that Sara Thornton discusses, Phil's (and skaters') concern is "popularization." To paraphrase Phil, "If too many kids have the same board [or brand of shoes, clothes] it will become stale and they won't want it anymore, because everyone has it." Skateboards, or "decks," feature amazing graphic art—movable micromurals—on the underside of the deck. A majority of skaters are themselves self-trained and awesome graphic artists, and as of this writing a traveling exhibit of skateboard art has been organized in Southern California.

Because skateboarding is punk rock, it creates opportunities for skaters to form clothing, graphics, and equipment companies (usually all of the above), and, at least for the youth involved in these microbusinesses, to move beyond—while still perpetuating—the primarily cultural economy of subcultural distinction to a subcultural "career," a means of economic survival. However, because skateboarding is punk rock, companies are limited, and it becomes difficult to sustain the business as a means of cultural survival without growing too big and becoming stale.[41]

Skaters are often misunderstood in their production of the scale of translocal community. Because their subcultural activities are sanctioned by global economic restructuring and because the status of youth is much less stringently defined by the logic of containment and moral reform, skateboarders have been able to participate in urban restructuring to demand that municipalities build spaces for them. Planners and developers have listened to skaters' demands, but they have usually missed the fact that economies of information and global economic restructuring have changed the status of "youth." Some of these spaces are organized, if not according to the logic of moral reform and containment, then still according to the logic of organized sport. This organization also functions as a means of control by making skateboarding conform to more mainstream values of individual competition.

Recently, in the California state legislature, assembly bill 2357 was introduced to add skateboarding to the state's list of "hazardous recreational activities."[42] Declaring skateboarding a hazardous sport would absolve municipalities of liability for injury. In anticipation of the passage of this bill, cities around the state have begun to build skate parks. While legislation has given cities the confidence to build parks, all have done so as a means of alleviating the spatial crisis between skaters, business people, and property owners. The cities of Huntington Beach, Temecula, Glendale, and Ventura have all built skate parks in the last five years.

Because skateboarding exists at the global scale of immaterial labor, skaters have gained the means to jump previous scales of youth, to form translocal communities. As they have become both subcultures defined by the circulation of sophisticated understandings of urban space and corresponding productions of scale, skaters have also produced their own institutional stability. Herein small skater-run businesses also construct a market equal in expanse to the scale of the subcultural community, because skateboarders exist as a coherent community held together through the circulation of style, products, and most important, translocal community-producing knowledge. I would argue that this new status of youth is as much responsible for the recent construction of municipal skate parks as is the more often cited "public nuisance" that skaters create.

While it is beyond the scope of this essay to detail the ways in which scale has been contested in city officials' explanations of their reasons for building skateparks, a brief comparison of the ways in which the actual parks themselves has been organized is instructive for what it reveals about the new status of youth.

The cities of Santa Cruz, Palo Alto, and Marin in northern California have had skate parks for a number of years when skateboarding was in relative decline. These cities chose simply to risk the threat of liability. Since it opened, the Derby Park skate track in Santa Cruz has had one serious injury and one liability suit, which the plaintiffs lost.

What is more significant for the purposes of this essay is that these skate parks have permitted skaters to construct the meanings of their activities according to the values that result from their use of the built environment. For example, graffiti is permitted on the concrete of the skate parks, and the parks are free. Parks built in the cities of Temecula and Glendale, on the other hand, have chosen instead to try to reform skateboarding and, to varying degrees, contain it within the legitimacy of sport. Both cities have taken a zero tolerance approach to graffiti, maintaining that it would be impossible to control the kinds of messages that skaters would write and that it would be impossible to keep graffiti only on skateboarding surfaces. By comparison, derby skate track designer Ken Wormhoudt maintains that the cities of Santa Cruz, Palo Alto, and Marin have had no problems with the spread of graffiti. Temecula runs its skate park on a per hour fee basis, and with the police department it cosponsors a skateboard club at the high-school. The club cleans the park on weekend mornings in exchange for free skate time.[43]

What is most significant about these two different attitudes toward graffiti is that they suggests two different understandings of skateboarding. While all of the parks mentioned here are administered by recreation departments, Glendale and Temecula have organized their skate parks according to an older perception of youth where the elders must save young people from themselves while carrying out a program of moral reform.

I realize that I have not given voice to the views of planners and city officials regarding urban space. In the book-length version of this article I will. Perhaps some would agree that skaters have something to teach us about concepts of multiple use and the ways that the social can be spatially constructed to make the production of variable space more possible. Those who disagree with skaters' (and my own) explanations and critiques of space-as-power and argue that the spatial exclusion of skateboarders from urban space has more to do with issues of functionality, vandalism, and public safety and liability only prove my (and the skaters') point. First, they misunderstand youth, especially now when youth have an amplified and expanded ability to comment on the conditions of urban life. Second, they can only say this if they assume that space is static and universally perceived by all people in the same way. It should be possible to plan and build spaces for skateboarding that are not segregated according to older histories of youth or spaces of separation and enclosure, but rather that coexist with and are next to places of public gathering.

As global restructuring reconfigures the potentials of youth, and as youth, in the coded language of a translocal community, critique the present spatial order and demand spaces of their own, the possibility remains that spaces configured to contain youth may not work. On the other hand, one of the most spectacular instances of skaters' taking control of urban space occurred in Portland, Oregon, in 1989, when Mark Scott and Brett Taylor took space into their own hands: they excavated and cemented a skate bowl under a city-owned highway overpass. They continued to build more bowls until this space became known as the Burnside Project. The choice between skate parks built according to containment and enclosure or governed by the formation of a translocal community seems obvious. If you dig a pit, you can fall in it, or skate it.[44]

NOTES

This article has benefitted immeasurably from the wisdom, seance, and tricknowlogy of Mary Kay Van Sistine, Joe Austin, Michael Steiner, Alejandra Marchevsky, Jason Elias, Linda Maram, Jonathan Sterne, Carrie Rentschler; Rodney Mullen and Socrates of Plan B Skateboards; Julie Pelletier, Scott Reese, Ken Wormhoudt; and the all-terrain-vehicle, cross-training, hybrid, vert-street-cope-slope you-name-it-we'll-skate-it, super morphin' skaters of Clockwork Skateboards: Brian Patch, Christian, Jeff Patch, and Phil. Edward Soja commented on an earlier version of this essay delivered at the meetings of the American Studies Association in 1992. Special thanks go to Joe Austin, Joe Austin, Joe Austin; and Jeff Rangel for conversations about skateboarding and surfing. Martin Wong (and *Giant Robot* magazine) got me skating after years away and knew all the right people at exactly the right times; Jason Loviglio read drafts of this essay and offered indispensable criticism and rare insight; Wing Ko, skater with a camera and the Sergei Eisenstein of skate filmmakers, patiently answered my endless questions, listened to me propound my theories of skateboard discourse, and taught me much as I watched him at work. Socrates Leal and Daewon Song, who work tirelessly to redesign Los Angeles every day, came through on the shortest notice.

1. At thirty years of age and having skated professionally since the age of thirteen, Rodney is semiretiring from professional skateboarding. This video montage will be his farewell tour. For the last year Rodney has been working on his five-minute segment to come up with a montage of his best tricks. He tells me that it takes most pro skaters a year to get enough "really good" tricks together to make a good five-minute segment. Soc works with the teams of three skateboard companies and shoots video all the time.

2. Now that skating—including in-line, skateboarding, and roller hockey—is the fastest-growing sport in America, it seems inevitable that more contests will be organized. Rodney also remarked that contests have been increasing. On the popularity of skating, see Marilyn Martinez, "Plan Approved for Temporary Skating Park," *Los Angeles Times*, Home Edition, October 18, 1996, Metro Section, 5; "Gravity Schmavity," *Los Angeles Times*, Orange County Edition, August 1, 1996, Life and Style Section, 4.

3. The Reagan building was completed after the publication of Mike Davis's *City of Quartz: Excavating the Future in Los Angeles* (London: Verso, 1990). As has happened so often with his book, Davis's analysis of Los Angeles has proven to be prophetic, the rebellion and civil unrest of 1992 being only the most obvious example. Based on my own observations I am convinced that Davis's prophecy about the Reagan building has become reality. In his book Davis explained that the Los Angeles Community Redevelopment Agency spent

$20 million inducing the State to build the "Ronald Reagan Office Building" a block away from the corner of Third and Broadway, while simultaneously bribing the Union Rescue Mission $6 million to move its homeless clientele out of the neighborhood. The 3,000 civil servants from the Reagan Building are intended as shock troops to gentrify the strategic corner of Third and Broadway where developer Ira Yellin has received further millions in subsidies from the CRA to transform the three historic structures he owns (the Bradbury Building, Million Dollar Theater and Grand Central Market) into "Grand Central Square." The 'Broadway-Spring Center' . . . provides 'security in circulation' between the Reagan Building and Square." (Davis, *City of Quartz*, 261, n. 8)

4. Such processes of redevelopment are not totally predictable. When I called the Grand Central Square Apartments I found out that the CRA has required the owner of the building to rent half of the one- and two-bedroom apartments to "income qualified" people at roughly half the market rate. For example, a one-bedroom apartment rents for $460 to renters with an income of less than $17,000 a year, and slightly above $500 for those with an income between $17,000 and $20,000. Two-bedroom apartments also go at approximately half the market rate, depending on level of income.

5. A large Spanish-language produce, meat, and seafood market, where local residents do their daily shopping and browse among the many stalls.

6. At present, a Spanish-language evangelical church.

7. Much of the urban history of Los Angeles that informs my physical and written wanderings on Broadway comes from Davis, *City of Quartz*, 230–31, 261n.8. See also Margaret Crawford, "The Fifth Ecology: Fantasy, the Automobile, and Los Angeles," in Martin Wachs and Margaret Crawford, eds., *The Car and the City: The Automobile, the Built-environment, and Daily Urban Life* (Ann Arbor: University of Michigan Press, 1992), 233.

8. Pedestrians are now carried up and down Bunker Hill by the recently refurbished Angels' Flight incline railroad. This incline railroad, a formerly much-used vehicle that facilitated movement between Bunker Hill and the old downtown shopping district, has been re-created for use mostly as a trendy tourist route. There are, however, high-rent, high-rise apartment buildings on Bunker Hill, and it is possible that their occupants may also be using the railroad to gain somewhat easier access to Grand Central Square.

9. Identity is usually created through the skater's choice of music that accompanies his video segment.

10. See, for example, Rodney Mullen, interviewed by Thomas Campbell, *Transworld Skateboarding* (December 1993); Plan B, advertisement, *Transworld Skateboarding* (September 1996). See also Plan B Videos, *Questionable* (1992), *Virtual Reality* (1993), *Second Hand Smoke* (1995).

11. *Virtual Reality*, Plan B Video (1993).

12. Davis, *City of Quartz*, 231.

16. Robert Morrow, " 'Bum-Proof' Bus Bench Hill Street Downtown," photograph in Davis, *City of Quartz*, 235.

14. I use nested and parenthetical words such as "prec(ar)ious" primarily for economy, and not proliferation, of mean(der)ing.

15. In interviews with recreation officials from the cities of Glendale and Temecula, I learned that the police hate to "bust" skaters. The police come out looking like villains when skaters are not really doing anything seriously wrong. In the cities of Temecula and Glendale, the police were the most vocal and ardent supporters of the skaters' repeated requests that the city provide them with a place to skate.

16. For a more developed angle on the history of urban renewal and the disastrous "civic

development" of "big league" cities that characterized the widespread clearance and renewal projects of the 1950s and 1960s, including the clearance of Mexican American neighborhoods in Chavez Ravine in order to build Dodger Stadium, which is only minutes to the northwest of Bunker Hill, see George Lipsitz, "Sports Stadia and Urban Development: A Tale of Three Cities," *Journal of Sport and Social Issues* 8, no.2 (Summer/Fall 1984). Sports stadia become one of the elements in a larger pattern of faux-public-foe tourist attractions anchoring contemporary downtown developments that Dennis Judd refers to as "tourist bubbles." See Dennis R. Judd, "Enclosure, Community, and Public Life," *Research in Community Sociology* 6 (1996), 230.

17. On developers' fears of "the Black and Mexican poor" in the wake of the 1965 civil unrest, see Davis, *City of Quartz*, 230. Many scholars and politicians see proposition 187 as the first salvo in a concerted effort to create two tiers of citizenship. See Leo R. Chavez, "Immigration Reform and Nativism: The Nationalist Response to the Transnationalist Challenge," *The New Nativism* (New York: New York University Press, 1996). On the relationship between global-economic urban restructuring and anti-immigrant attitudes, see Alejandra Marchevsky, "The Empire Strikes Back: Globalization, Nationalism, and California's Proposition 187," *Critical Sense* 4, no.l (Spring 1996), 8–51.

18. I am not arguing that the ability to "jump scale" constitutes the new status of youth. Young people have always jumped scale. See, for example, David Nasaw, *Children of the City: At Work and Play* (New York: Anchor/Doubleday, 1985). Instead, I am arguing that the horizon for jumping has expanded.

19. Neil Smith, "Contours of a Spatialized Politics: Homeless Vehicles and the Production of Geographical Scale," *Social Text*, vol. 10, no.4 (1992), 64.

20. Ibid., 66.

21. On the spatial politics of scale, the homeless, and the "strategic political geography" of scale jumping, see Neil Smith, "Homeless/Global: Scaling Places," in Jon Bird, Barry Curtis, George Robertson, and Lisa Tickner, eds., *Mapping the Futures: Local Cultures, Global Change* (New York: Routledge, 1993), and idem, "Contours of a Spatialized Politics." On Latin American immigrants and citizenship in Southern California, see Chavez, "Immigration Reform and Nativism"; S. Pincetl, "Challenges to Citizenship: Latino Immigrants and Political Organizing in the Los Angeles Area," *Environment and Planning* A 26 (1994), 895–914. The source of the phrase "translocal community" is Brenda Bright's essay (chapter 25) in this volume.

22. For Latino immigrants, expanding the geographical scale of daily life to the scale of the nation and the rights of citizenship has become one of the most significant scales. For the homeless, the scale of community has become one of the most significant scales of spatial and identity formation.

23. Iain Borden, a former Skatopia (a Southern California skate park built in the late 1970s) denizen and now urban planner, explains skateboarding similarly: "Skateboarders threaten accepted definitions of space, [by] taking over space conceptually as well as physically and so striking at the very heart of what everyone else understands by the city." Iain Borden, "Beneath the Pavement, the Beach: Skateboarding, Architecture and the Urban Realm," in Iain Borden et al., eds., *Strangely Familiar: Narratives of Architecture in the City* (London: Routledge, 1996), 85. For a much more developed discussion of the relationship between architecture, power, knowledge, and the possibilities for the kinds of "freespaces" that skateboarders produce, see Lebbeus Woods, "The Question of Space," and Michael Menser, "Becoming-Heterarch: On Technocultural Theory, Minor Science, and the Production of Space," in Stanley Aronowitz et al., eds., *Technoscience and Cyberculture* (New York: Routledge, 1996).

24. This and the following paragraph are influenced by the analysis of space in Gilles Deleuze and Felix Guattari, *A Thousand Plateaus: Capitalism and Schizophrenia* (Minneapolis: University of Minnesota Press, 1987), especially their discussion of nomad art, pp. 492–500.

25. Ibid., 493. For more on technologies of vision, see Donna Haraway's important essay, "A Cyborg Manifesto: Science, Technology, and Socialist-Feminism in the Late Twentieth Century," in *Simians, Cyborgs and Women: The Reinvention of Nature* (New York: Routledge, 1991), 149–81.

26. I want to repeat this point in two different ways. On that Sunday morning, skaters produced place-bound scales of "local" community through their ability to critique the commonplace understanding of space as universally self-evident. To reiterate: skaters produce scale not by the fact that they share a common perception of any built object or space, but because they share a common awareness of the many possibilities for seeing space differently.

27. Phone interview, Ken Wormhoudt, March 1997.

28. Becky Louise Beal, "The Subculture of Skateboarding: Beyond Social Resistance" (Ph.D. diss., University of Northern Colorado, 1992).

29. For discussion of French spatial theorizations by Henri Lefebvre and Michel Foucault, see Smith "Contours of Spatialized Politics," and Soja, *Postmodern Geographies*; also Michel deCerteau, *The Practice of Everyday Life* (Minneapolis: University of Minnesota Press, 1988); Gilles Deleuze, "Postscript on the Societies of Control," *October* 59 (1992); and Deleuze and Guattari, *A Thousand Plateaus*. For more-recent work by Americans and Britons see Smith, "Contours of a Spatialized Politics" and "Homeless/Global"; and Neil Smith and Cindi Katz, "Grounding Metaphor: Towards a Spatialized Politics," in Michael Keith and Steve Pile, eds., *Place and the Politics of Identity* (New York: Routledge, 1993); Soja, *Postmodern Geographies*; and Doreen Massey, "Politics and Space/Time," in *Place and the Politics of Identity*.

30. See, for example, the covers of *Transworld Skateboarding*, for June 1996, April 1997, and June 1997, which are highly staged commentaries on the urban location of the photos in addition to showing the action in them. Such photos required an incredibly creative and sophisticated understanding of the multiple possibilities for using any space.

31. Smith and Katz, "Grounding Metaphor," 75.

32. While skaters align themselves with the homeless and advance critiques of "public" space, at the same time they also reproduce spaces of masculinity. In her ethnography of skateboarding, Becky Beal asserts that, when considered in relation to the masculinity of organized sports, skaters exhibit a cooperative form of masculinity that is not included in the values of competition and performance of more "legitimate" sports. Beal also considers moments of contradiction when skaters' masculinity can be seen as a situational construct that reinforces traditional, competitive masculinity. To supplement my argument I cite Beal's explanation here to point out that often skaters' challenges to power and security forces reproduce the kind of masculinity that informs constructions of space that do not account for the subjectivity of women. See Beal, "The Subculture of Skateboarding: Beyond Social Resistance"; "Disqualifying the Official: An Exploration of Social Resistance through the Subculture of Skateboarding," *Sociology of Sport Journal* 12 (1995), 252–67, and "Alternative Masculinity and Its Effects on Gender Relations in the Subculture of Skateboarding, *Journal of Sport Behavior* 19, no.3 (August 1996). For a very useful consideration of the ways that masculinity gets produced in contestations between urban governments and male youth subcultures, see Joe Austin, "Taking the Train: Youth Culture, Urban Crisis, and the 'Graffiti Problem' in New York City, 1970–1900" (Ph.D. diss., University of Minnesota, 1996). See also Rosalyn Deutsche, "Men in Space," *Strategies: A Journal of Theory Culture and Politics* 3 (1990);

Mary Jo Deegan, "The Female Pedestrian: The Dramaturgy of Structural and Experimental Barriers in the Street," *Man-Environment Systems* 17 (1987), 79–86.

33. Massey, "Politics and Space/Time," 146.

34. Ibid., 155–56.

35. On the history of constructions of youth, see Susan Ruddick, *Young and Homeless in Hollywood: Mapping Social Identities* (New York: Routledge, 1996). Ruddick finds the origins of the status of youth as the subject of moral reform in the formation of the juvenile-care system at the beginning of the twentieth century.

36. See Beth Bailey's essay (chapter 11) in this volume.

37. Sara Thornton, "Moral Panic, the Media and British Rave Culture," in Andrew Ross and Tricia Rose, eds., *Microphone Fiends: Youth Music and Youth Culture* (New York: Routledge, 1994); Sara Thornton, *Club Cultures: Music, Media and Subcultural Capital* (Hanover, N.H.: Wesleyan/University of New England Press, 1996).

38. On immaterial labor, see Michael Hardt and Antonio Negri, *Labor of Dionysus: A Critique of the State-Form* (Minneapolis: University of Minnesota Press, 1994).

39. Now graphics have expanded beyond heavy-metal-influenced terror and horror imagery to include cartoon kid figures. This is an important recuperation of "kid" status by linking it to the serious work of subcultural formation. On terror imagery as a means to symbolically challenge the imbalance of power that youth experience see Robert Walser, *Running with the Devil: Power, Gender and Madness in Heavy Metal Music* (Hanover, N.H.: Wesleyan/University Press of New England, 1993).

40. On the mediation and construction of "opposition" as a strategy for the formation of youth culture and subcultural capital, see Thornton, "Moral Panic, the Media and British Rave Culture"; Thornton, *Club Cultures: Music, Media and Subcultural Capital*; Dick Hebdige, *Hiding in the Light: On Images and Things* (London: Comedia/Routledge, 1988), 17–36.

41. For more on the subcultural dynamics of being "punk rock," see Steve Duncombe's essay (chapter 26) in this volume. On youth culture, selling out, and cultural economies of distinction, see Thornton, "Moral Panic, the Media and British Rave Culture"; Thornton, *Club Cultures*. On the dangers of overexposure in the surfing and skateboarding industries, see Mary Ann Galante, "Surfwear Firms Jump on the Skateboard Bandwagon," *Los Angeles Times*, April 17, 1988.

42. Bill Billiter, "Council Endorses Skateboarding Bill," *Los Angeles Times*, Orange County Edition, July 23, 1996, Metro Section, 3.

43. Interview, Julie Pelletier, Temecula Recreation Department, March 1997.

44. Mark Scott, "Burnside Project," *Transworld Skateboarding* 10, no.9(September 1992), 52–55.

Chapter Twenty

Teens at Work
Negotiating the Jobless Future

Susan Willis

"I can't wait 'til I can work because then I'll have something to do all day." Charlotte's comment knocked me for a loop. We were in the bank where her older sister, who had a summer job, was opening an account. In the context of the bank and her sister's income, I expected Charlotte to say, "I can't wait 'til I can work because then I'll have money to spend." Granted Charlotte is young, nine years old, and likely to regard work as one more thing that teens "get" to do and therefore something to be desired. However, I took her comment as something to ponder and explore. Perhaps young people, bombarded with consumer advertising since toddlerhood and sated on leisure time possibilities yearn for something else and thus conceptualize work as a positive antithesis to their exploitation as consumers.

Charlotte's comment was a catalyst to an informally organized year-long ethnographic investigation of teens as workers. This is not an extensive economic or social survey, but rather an attempt to analyze both the ideological functions of teen attitudes toward work as well as their actual work in the context of what Stanley Aronowitz and William DiFazio aptly term *The Jobless Future*.[1] Today's fourteen- to nineteen-year-olds will not be downsized out of jobs they already hold, as is the case for many adult workers. Rather, they enter the job market as an already de-skilled and downsized labor pool. They are the ones who learn to labor on minimum and below-minimum wages. They are the ones who work part time or hobble together full-time weeks out of part-time jobs. They are, by definition, occasional employees, ineligible for benefits, whose only clout is the power to quit.

My research draws on informal interviews with middle and high schoolers and some teens not currently in school in my hometown of Durham, North Carolina. The research is skewed as I tended to gravitate toward kids who expressed strong opinions about themselves as workers or who demonstrated imaginative or innovative approaches to their job situations. While I began by talking to equal numbers of black and white teens, I found more openness to me on the part of white teens, and so the majority of the informants represented here are white. I also observed that black youths—either by choice or lack of opportunity—predominantly work in fast-food restaurants and have less employment mobility across a variety of jobs than their white peers. My final research sample also includes more young women than men. As companions in gender, they too were more willing to be frank with me. However, I suspect that in economic terms this sector of the teen population has the most job mobility. As the recipients of the ideological gains that feminism has generated in the culture generally, white female teens manifest the most ardent desire for autonomy and the most innovative approaches to employment.

Finally, my research base does not include teens who see themselves preparing for college and a professional future. Such teens conceive of themselves primarily as students. They may gripe about their summer and part-time jobs, but they do not conceptualize themselves as workers. To get a picture of teen workers (and a sense of a potential workforce in formation), I chose to talk to teens who had dropped out of school (some with the intention of returning), had graduated but were uncertain about going to college, or were in school aiming at a technical or job-training program or a year or two off.

Many of the teens I spoke with reported seeing Richard Linklater's film, *Slacker*, as representative of their lives, or at least how they feel about their lives. When pressed to be more specific, they explained that, like the characters in the movie, they tend to float from job to job and moment to moment. Many characterized themselves as "bored" or described their lives, town, friends, schools, or jobs as "boring." None suggested a cure for boredom, but all gave the impression that they see their current situations as temporary, in the same way they see their jobs and schools as temporary. The fact that they were describing themselves to me (a middle-aged professional) tended to inform our conversations with a quality best described as "Let's patronize the anthropologist by letting her think we'll turn out like she is." Most probably this attitude does not pertain to young people when they confide in each other.

What recommends *Slacker* to its intended audience is its unhurried ambience, the casual pointlessness of all encounters, and the pleasant tedium of daily existence. The movie features a hundred or more players who never become a cast of thousands as they would in a Hollywood spectacle. This is because there are no heroes, let alone protagonists, in *Slacker*. No plot, except in the loosest sense of the term. No beginning, middle, and practically no end. Nor is there any emotionally high or low point in the entire movie. Contrary to mainstream feature films and the sort of narrative expectations they instill in audiences, *Slacker* is constructed episodically on a series of anecdotal vignettes that never involve more than three people. It is the consummate example of narrative parataxis, first identified by Erich Auerbach as the defining characteristic of the epic.[2] Like the *chansons de geste*, *Slacker* presents a series of events and individuals strung together by the implied repetition of the conjunction "and" between each of its vignettes. However, unlike the medieval versions where parataxis allows the expression of both history and social hierarchy, *Slacker* depicts a flow of events whose only history is their sequence and a cast of characters whose social equality matches their narrative neutrality in the denial of any sort of social hierarchy. For example, in the *Cantar de Mio Cid*, parataxis is a vehicle for tracing the hegemonic consolidation of Spain's Catholic monarchy in the tale of its hero's exploits and for depicting the complexities of class and race in the portrayal of the Cid's relationship to enemies, aristocracy, and comrades in arms. This is not the case in *Slacker*, whose characters are interchangeable, narrative integers and where the differences between black and white, young and old, male and female have more to do with decor than social meaning.

All of *Slacker*'s anecdotal vignettes depict two characters engaged in an activity or conversation. What moves the movie to its next anecdotal vignette is the arrival of a third character whose addition brings about the redefinition of the existing situation. This causes the removal of one of the participants and the formation of a new anecdote around the remaining two characters. For instance, two young people (a woman and a man) are chatting about an upcoming concert. They are joined by a third, a young woman who attempts to sell one of them a vial said to contain Madonna's Pap smear. Showing neither amazement nor shock, the woman who figured in the original couple casually saunters off. The anecdote re-forms around the young man and the would-be entrepreneur. Thus, the movie rolls along for two or more hours. Viewers can see *Slacker* from start to finish or join the narrative at any point, doze on and off, or wander in and out. I imagine one might run the video tape backwards from finish to start and derive the same sense of the movie as someone who sees it from start to finish.

True to its title, no one works in *Slacker*. With the University of Texas-Austin as its off screen epicenter, the movie's population might best be characterized as a reserve army of intelligentsia rather than labor per se. Indeed, *Slacker* depicts the common lot of many of the students I see graduate who rationalize their postgraduation joblessness by saying they've decided to "take a year or two off." This syndrome also affects students midterm who, out of a sense of angst or aimlessness, take their year or two off before graduation. Conveniently, many universities have formulated the "junior year abroad" to give students a sense of being off and at the same time placate middle-class parents' fears over their children's purposeful adhesion to their education and their parents' expectations.

In *Slacker*, no one is instrumentalized or "bent to purpose"[3] in the terms that Theodor Adorno uses to describe daily life in capitalism. In his book, *Minima Moralia*, Adorno condemns the way the productive ends fundamental to capitalism deform society and dehumanize individuals. Because nothing is produced in *Slacker*—not even a thesis—social exchange is most often based on the interchange of words in conversation or the exchange of goods and services. Very seldom does anyone engage in consumption or commerce. However, it would be wrong to characterize *Slacker* as an attempt to imagine a society of leisure—at least not as we know it. This is because consumerism is minimal. Besides beer, coffee, cigarettes, and Coke, the movie lacks the glut of commodities that commonly designate leisure for us: the video games, roller blades, designer sunglasses, customized kites, Walkmen, boom boxes, VCRs, and Ben and Jerry's ice cream—everything that makes daily life a vacation.

This is not to say that *Slacker* is devoid of commerce. Besides the young woman hawking Madonna's Pap smear, other episodes feature a group of kids who sell the cans of Coke that they kick out of a vending machine and a pair of auto mechanics who attempt to get the right part for their car. However, on the whole, *Slacker* strives to imagine a world of unmediated social relationships, a world where people meet and correspond with one another as equals.

Indeed, Linklater's loose assemblage of University of Texas marginals suggests a striking resemblance to the neolithic hunter-gatherers described by Marshall Sahlins in his study that coalesced utopian analysis with a model for countercultural practice, *Stone Age Economics*. Characterizing hunter-gatherers as "the original affluent society,"[4] Sahlins reevaluates what other economists and anthropologists have stigmatized as societies of scarcity. According to Sahlins, wealth and access to leisure are based on the inability to accumulate. This is because excess requires care, guardianship, and maintenance. Similarly, in *Slacker* no one has more than can be carried in a backpack or on a bicycle. The lack of possessions appears to free the movie's characters to live their relationships rather than clutter their lives with things.

Sahlins goes on to describe societies organized around gift giving: the potlatch, in terms of social parataxis much like the community presented in *Slacker*. According to Sahlins, gifting societies are segmented societies whose individuals constitute the group as links in a chain. Their point of articulation is the moment of exchange: the giving of the gift, which does "not organize society in a corporate sense, only in a segmentary sense."[5] This is because the gift prevents accumulation and distributes wealth evenly among the group's members. Such societies are not apolitical, but rather practice the politics of reciprocity. As Sahlins puts it, "Reciprocity is a 'between' relation. It does not dissolve the separate parties within a higher unity, but on the contrary, in correlating their opposition, perpetuates it."[6]

On the surface, as a society defined by segmented and reciprocal relationships, *Slacker* appears to be a postindustrial reenactment of *Stone Age Economics*. However, *Slacker*'s utopia is based on a fallacy. It erases economics, whereas Sahlins recognizes that social reciprocity requires a rigorous economics of nonaccumulation. In *Slacker*, economics is presented as so tangential to social life as to be trivial or inexplicable. For example, one episode depicts a bored young woman who suggests to her boyfriend that they get out of bed and do something other than have sex. "Let's play frisbee." He, lazy and loath to move, reminds her that she doesn't have a frisbee. "You'll have to buy one; and to do that, you'll have to go to the drugstore and cash a check." Like manna from heaven, the unexplained facility to cash a check immediately redefines what appeared to be unmediated reciprocal social relationships by placing them in the larger context of banking and the implied necessity to labor and accumulate. Linklater attempts to imagine the social divorced from the economic as if this were remotely possible in an advanced capitalist state. Then, in a Baudrillardian move, he hyperrealizes the social. However, where Baudrillard would accelerate the nonproductive aspects of society to achieve implosion, Linklater happily creates a blissfully bored community of vignettes. *Slacker* exists as the erasure of the necessary capital accumulation that has to exist in order to facilitate the free-floating lifestyle of its teens and twentysomethings. While U of T, Austin, appears on the horizon of many of the film's episodes, the university's relationship to its economic environs is never stated. On the whole, universities tend to stifle the economic health of a community because the broad mass of employees in universities are most often not unionized and receive low wages. However, universities do stimulate some ancillary economic development aimed primarily at students as paying customers, such as coffeehouses, ice cream shops, T-shirt emporiums, take-out pizza restaurants, book stores, and used CD and tape stores. The youth in *Slacker* inhabit this environment without participating fully in it. Nevertheless, to inhabit it requires some access to cash—derived either from parental subsidies or the sale of labor power.

In erasing the economics of daily life, *Slacker* presents a utopia born of the bourgeois imagination that wishes social interaction to be uncontaminated by economic reality. This vision cannot comprehend social equality and reciprocity connected to and facilitated by economic exchange. In its portrayal of young people in a world seemingly divorced from economic constraints and only minimally related to commerce, *Slacker* diverges from the lives of real teens for whom the economics of daily life in a consumerist society is an ever present and primary concern. Teens may give the appearance of living blithely from happenstance to happenstance. They hang out in malls, storefronts, and sidewalks. They parlay a dozen refundable cans into an afternoon's snack. They borrow from friends to come up with the cash for entertainment or gas. Or they tap their parents for a couple of bucks. Notwithstanding their laid-back appearance, teens are constantly and consciously negotiating their restricted means. Getting through the day in an advanced consumer society requires a flow of consumptions. These indicate that the individual is not only alive and participating, but clued in to the prevailing identity-shaping cultural trends. A great many teens may not have a clue about their futures or the larger world, but the ones I spoke with are very clear on what constitutes a good job and what they aim for when they seek employment.

My conversations with middle and high schoolers in the Durham area very quickly yielded a set of attitudes toward work that challenge both bourgeois and working-class ideologies. Bear in mind that my research focuses on teens who said they don't plan to go to college or who thought they wanted some time off before considering a career. Those teens who perform well in high school and aim to pursue higher education are also often ambivalent about their futures, but they don't share the attitudes of the teens expressed here.

Among all the teens I interviewed, the most strongly held notion about work is that horizontal mobility through a variety of meaningless jobs constitutes autonomy. From my informants' point of view, the particulars of a job matter less than their ability as employees to move across a field of jobs. One might stock shelves in a supermarket, work the counter in a fast-food restaurant, or service video rental customers—"there's not much difference, a job's a job." In mouthing this clichéd colloquialism, a teen demonstrates how teen employment parallels and approximates a consumerist society. Jobs, like the brand-name items on the supermarket shelf, are really no different from one another. Consequently, things like working conditions and hours are akin to the details of a product's packaging. Neither is significant—not worth fighting over.

In an open market of casual youth employment, many teens move from one job to the next in a matter of weeks. As one sixteen-year-old boy put it, "Independence is having a pointless job that I can quit any day." This bold statement negates the yuppie brainwashing that some ten years ago permeated our culture (and may well have seeped into this young man's childhood) with images of besuited businesswomen toting briefcases and sporting running shoes for those between-deal jogs.

Where professional ideology imagines autonomy somewhere at the top of the corporate hierarchy, teens situate it in the loopholes between jobs. And rather than lapping up stress as a fuel for success as young yuppies were told to do, most teens today cite stress as ample reason for quitting a job.

Marcus, an eighteen-year-old who lives independently but whose father is a professional, stipulates, "Freedom is not having to take your work home with you." Where professional ideology preaches the benefits of the collapsing distinction between public and private spheres with its concomitant flood of work into the home, Marcus defiantly argues for the separation of work and home life or leisure. "When I leave here (the work site) I don't want anything that reminds me of this place. I mean, I'm outta here!" Marcus purposefully chooses a job he won't like so as to heighten his experience of freedom during his hours away from the job. His attitude not only represents a rejection of yuppie ideology, but also a reaction against the way new forms of technology and entrepreneurial businesses in the service sector have introduced work into the homes of many in the working class. Menial information processing as well as a whole array of marketing strategies have turned many homes into workplaces. The desire to maintain the private sphere as separate and autonomous includes nostalgic references to a world no longer available to many in either the working or professional classes. While that world was born at a time of bourgeois privilege and is mired in the patriarchal division of labor, it now haunts the imagination as a site for utopian longing.

"I want a job I don't have to think about. You know—like sleepwalking." Bryan prints photos from negatives in a one-hour photo processing shop. His job looks technical; but, he says, "The machine does all the work." Bryan's somnambulist approach to his job allows him to interpret the repetitiveness of his job and his redundancy as a worker as indications that he is not really working. When I asked if his job is boring, Bryan responded, "Yeah, but that's how I want it." His reverse logic exemplifies the extreme of minimalist thinking. As long as he doesn't break a sweat or have to think, he feels he's getting paid for doing nothing. Of course he doesn't sully his victory over the job by factoring in the time spent sitting at his fully automated photo finisher. As far as Bryan is concerned, he's not really there. This would be a horrifying example of alienation were it not for the resistant aspects of Bryan's zombie-like approach to his highly taylorized job.

The pursuit of autonomy in horizontal mobility also represents a reaction against traditional working-class attitudes that preach the American Dream as a lifelong march up the job ladder, which translates into upward social mobility from one generation to the next. From this point of view, worker loyalty (whether to company or union) is traded for increments in status or wages. Born into the downward turn of industry and labor, none of the teens I spoke with had any interest in factory work. Nor did they see themselves entering a company and working their way up to a supervisory position. "It's all the same," said one. "You get laid off before you get anywhere."

When I presented some of my findings at a meeting of the Association of American Historians, I was reminded by a labor historian in the audience that the ardent desire to "take this job and shove it" that I found among teen workers might have something to do with the Southern base of my research sample. Indeed, the less strongly unionized South has a history of occasional work and a workforce accustomed to using the power to quit a job as a means for addressing abuse. It may be that today's postindustrial economy has incorporated an earlier form of labor control—namely, horizontal mobility among nonunionized labor—and developed this particularly with regard to the job categories typically filled by teens. Young people in turn interpret their mobility as a sign both of their precarious futures and their temporary autonomy.

Many of the teens I spoke with clearly choose jobs they know they will not like in order to have a built-in excuse to quit. This greatly differentiates the youth in my sample from many college-bound teens and eighteen- and nineteen-year-olds already in college. College students often work in the expanding field of internships (both paid and unpaid) and see their labor as integral to career preparation. For instance, Dave, a former student, worked through three internships during the course of his summer vacations: an unpaid stint at MTV, a paid internship also at MTV, and finally a paid internship at *Entertainment Weekly*, where he was hired upon graduation. Dave's parents are social workers whose modest incomes weighed heavily on Dave's decision to take unpaid employment. However, Dave realized that the time spent as an intern would balance against the long-term benefits of a career. In contrast, the youth in my sample reported wanting immediate earnings and the possibility of rapid job turnover. When faced with the choice between waitressing at Shoney's, a chain family restaurant perched on the exit ramp of the interstate, and a more upscale restaurant downtown, Heather chose Shoney's. When I asked her why she turned down the posh ambiance of the downtown restaurant, Heather responded, "This is not a career, it's not even a life." She went on to say, "I don't want anything that ties me down." Heather concluded by explaining that during past stints at Shoney's she had occasionally made sixty dollars a day in tips. This seemed the equivalent of winning a scratch and win lottery.

Vickie, an eighteen-year-old who recently graduated from high school, demonstrates how the philosophy of "take this job and shove it" underscores a contradictory relationship between the possibility of being free and not free. When I met Vickie, she had a full-time job as a salesperson/counselor at a fitness gym. She also worked afternoons and some evenings as a drugstore clerk. She topped off her employment with a weekend job at Blockbuster Video. In describing her employment, Vickie expressed a curious blend of pride in the fact that she had three jobs and worked close to sixty hours a week and a desperate appeal for sympathy for her inhuman schedule. She complained of fatigue and accentuated her victimization by wearing a vampire hue of makeup and a deep mauve lipstick.

About three weeks later, I rediscovered Vickie. She was working as a checkout clerk at a chain supermarket. She had quit the job at the gym as well as her drugstore job; but she still worked at Blockbuster on the weekend. Vickie was all smiles—not because her new job arrangement was any better, but because she had just "had a week off. It was a blast." Apparently Vickie had given herself a week's vacation between the time she quit her previous jobs and started her new ones. Rolling her eyes, she said she had "spent a bundle." Vickie's work pattern is not unlike a bulemic eating disorder: binging on excessive work punctuated by excessive leisure.

Vickie's situation characterizes practices and attitudes that I found throughout my teen informants. Like many, she emphasized that she does have long-range goals. She affirmed proficiency in French and German; and said she wants to get back to school in order "to do something with languages." However, Vickie, like a great many teens I spoke with, said she doesn't seem to be able to save any money "even though I'm working all the time." Being able to "take this job and shove it" gives Vickie an instantaneous rush of independence—even while it signifies the unlikelihood of ever breaking the circuit of excessive employment balanced against excessive leisure.

The practice of "shoving" a job combines the same elements of defiance and self-destruction that Paul Willis documents in his book *Learning to Labor*,[7] a study of British working-class youth. Observing the antagonistic behaviors that working-class youths practice in school against teachers, administrators, counselors, and the entire process of learning, Willis points out that such behaviors represent a dramatic rejection of middle-class ideology that equates learning with the possibility for advancement. He also makes it clear that the failure to learn cancels all possibility of self-fulfillment. Willis urges a progressive alternative to the way education functions to integrate the working class into low-level supervisory positions, holding individuals hostage to wages, benefits, and payments. Extending Willis's findings, it's clear that learning is instrumentalized to meet the needs of production in the same way that binging on work and leisure ensures a replaceable workforce and avid consumers.

Vickie's situation might also be considered in the light of Michel DeCerteau's analysis of *The Practice of Everyday Life*. DeCerteau demonstrates how the underclass either "copes"[8] with or negotiates the dominant structures that seek to contain their activities and aspirations. Where the forces of domination maintain power through oppressive "strategies,"[9] the underclass develops "tactics"[10] that subvert or undermine the aims of the dominant factions. One such tactic is the "perruque,"[11] that is, a practice that bends a job definition to suit personal aims. (Here DeCerteau gives the example of a secretary who uses office time and her typewriter to write letters to her boyfriend.) Another tactic is "poaching"[12] or stealing the boss's time by idling or loafing while on the job.

Vickie's practice manifests the impulse to break the structures that define her as occasional labor. However, rather than poaching by deaccelerating her labor, Vickie overaccelerates in a frenzied attempt to break the system by maximizing it. From Vickie's point of view, if the system ties the worker to the eight-hour work day, then the adept guerrilla worker takes on a twelve-hour day in order to wrest week-long blocks of vacation time out of a system that niggardly allows workers only two weeks out of a year. As is clear in DeCerteau's work, such guerrilla tactics don't change or even impede the larger system. But they afford individuals a degree of control over their lives and a sense of having beat the system on its own terms.

In its exaggerated proportions, Vickie's work pattern sheds light on a widespread practice among teens who seek short-term employment to meet immediate consumerist goals. However, in a larger sense, Vickie's erratic employment and her consequent fluctuations in income point to a communality with the plight of many workers today. As reported in the *New York Times*,[13] a great many workers, who not too long ago could count on a fixed income and predictable increases, now find themselves having to deal with income volatility. Suspension of overtime or fluctuating weekly hours are but two of the factors that contribute to variations in take-home pay. According to the *Times*, over 50 percent of U.S. workers are currently experiencing the negative effects of roller-coaster incomes. This is another instance where the factors that have typically characterized teen employment now inform the system more generally. One of the repercussions of variable income is the inability to make long-term plans and commitments to long-term purchases. It's not inconceivable that more mature workers are in the process of developing work and spending patterns similar to Vickie's.

Besides interpreting horizontal mobility as independence, the teens in my sample demonstrated another tactic as a more direct response to their sense of an impending "jobless future." As Chrissy puts it, "I want to get certified as a cosmetologist because then I can live anywhere." Chrissy translates horizontal mobility into a desire to move from place to place supporting herself by plying a certified trade. More and more teens seek certification as a necessary entrée into specific jobs and as a means for substantiating the idea—if not the reality—of job security. Lifeguards and aerobic instructors also carry certification, as does the enterprising teen who posted this Xeroxed notice all over town: "Certified In-Line Skate Instruction." The flier included a phone number and the guarantee of satisfaction.

Certification is not self-authorized—except, perhaps, in the case of the rollerblade entrepreneur. Most often certification requires the successful completion of a course involving practical and written tests. These can be community sponsored, as is the case with some swim instruction certification programs as well as the burgeoning number of CPR classes that many teens are required to pass for employment as camp counselors and baby sitters. There are also a great many private certification enterprises such as IDEA, whose first-level aerobics certification course lasts a day and costs one hundred dollars. Because most gyms offer their instructors free memberships, certification provides a means for parlaying unlimited workouts into the job package.

My discussions with teens revealed a surprising number of certification options, which suggests an overall linkage between businesses and the insurance industry. I suspect a great many policies stipulate the need for "certified" employees. Certification has long been associated with certain professions such as elevator installers and air-conditioning specialists. What's interesting is the spread of certification into jobs most often held by teens. Youth in turn redefine a job requirement as a ticket to freedom. The relationship of teens to certification reveals the contradictions of their relationship to class and labor generally. On the one hand, the teens in my sample reject the professional route through school and into careers. But in seeking certification and attempting to use it as a ploy for freedom, they recycle professional ideology to suit their down-graded possibilities and expectations.

During the course of my informal interviews with teens I was most struck by their sense of themselves as simultaneously oppressed and free. Their desire not to fall into what they see as bankrupt working-class patterns or dehumanizing professional life-styles fills their comments about themselves with both a strong yearning for some sort of alternative as well as a great deal of ambivalence toward the future. The teens in my sample all said they "had to work." They had either dropped out or graduated from high school. Or they were still in school and needed to support their cars and social lives. Very few of my informants said they liked their jobs. Those who described their jobs as "the pits" did so with their eyes on another job that promised to be less stressful, boring, or demanding. All agreed that the time between jobs is the best. However, as one young woman put it, "It's hard to party when everyone else is working." Clearly, a job action would involve massively coordinating the between-job period so that all teens agree to quit at the same time. When I mentioned this idea, my informant expressed agreement as well as amazement.

It occurred to me that even though teens hang out together and commiserate about their work, they function on the job and in the job market as individuals unaware of any sort of collectivity they might represent as workers. The atomization of the teen workforce is a consequence of expanded part-time and service-sector employment coupled with diminished job security. Teens cope by inventing individual solutions to their job situations and collective solutions to their culture. They float from job to job, binge on work and leisure, hedge their bets with certification scams, all the while channeling their desire for community into music and fashion styles associated with subcultural affiliation. The dramatic separation between the individual practices that teens develop to cope with employment and the collective practices that they invent in their off-the-job cultural lives underscores the desire expressed by many of my informants to preserve themselves and their leisure as somehow "free." The teens I spoke with say they don't mind being anonymous integers on the job so long as they can see themselves as autonomous off the job and in their ability to quit a bad job. They trade their isolation as individual workers against the satisfaction they feel in cultural pursuits. And no one mentions changing any of this because to do so would break the charmed aura of the illusion of freedom in culture.

NOTES

1. Stanley Aronowitz, and William DiFazio, *The Jobless Future* (Minneapolis: University of Minnesota Press, 1994). The authors don't focus specifically on teen workers; however, their survey of the consequences of global capitalism suggests strong parallels between the sorts of jobs and employment conditions generally associated with teens and a growing number of older employees—particularly women—who have been downsized or de-skilled into part-time or service sector work.

2. Erich Auerbach, *Mimesis* (Princeton: Princeton University Press, 1968) 99–121. Auerbach characterizes the *chanson de geste* as reflecting a rigidly horizontal relation to God. This meant that earthly events did not require explanation, but might relate to one another in a simple

relationship of juxtaposition. Linklater's film is a banal version of the *chanson de geste*, one that no longer believes in God and whose characters are less heroically memorable. Imagine the trivial in the place of Auerbach's comments on the *Chanson de Roland* and you will have *Slacker*: "The single event is filled with life. That is why this style is so rich in individual scenes of great effectiveness, scenes in which only a very few characters confront one another, in which the gestures and speeches of a brief occurrence come out in sharp relief. The characters facing one another at close quarters, without much room for movement" (120).

3. Theodor Adorno, *Minima Moralia* (London: Verso, 1914). "Technology is making gestures precise and brutal, and with them men. It expels from movements all hesitation, deliberation, civility. It subjects them to the implacable, as it were ahistorical demands of objects" (p 40).

4. Marshall Sahlins, *Stone Age Economics* (Chicago: Aldine, 1972) 1–39.

5. Ibid., 170.

6. Ibid.

7. Paul Willis, *Learning to Labor* (New York: Columbia University Press, 1997).

8. Michel DeCerteau, *The Practice of Everyday Life* (Berkeley: University of California Press, 1988), 29–44.

9. Ibid., 34.

10. Ibid.

11. Ibid. 34.

12. Ibid., 165–76.

13. "A New Era of Ups and Downs: Volatility of Wages Is Growing," *New York Times*, August 18, 1996, A1.

Chapter Twenty-one

What to Make of *Wiggers*

A Work in Progress

David Roediger

The well-paid worrier about the alleged "black underclass," Charles Murray, frets these days too about those white kids described by the "popular neologism *wigger*," that is, white niggers. Taking in U.S. society from his comfortable viewpoint at the far-right tail of the bell curve of I.Q., Murray argues, "If the dominant culture deems you a misfit, then you plug away." But, he adds, "If there is an alternative culture that says, 'Who needs that shit?' then dropping out becomes an option. And that alternative culture is the black underclass." Female-headed households among the white population and the very presence of the Black poor produce a spate of *wiggers*—the dominant culture that brands kids as misfits could hardly get the blame—who "mimic black dress, walk or attitudes." But such mimicry, largely male, masks a deeper reality that what wiggers are "really imitating is black-underclass attitudes toward achievement."[1]

Fashion writer Robin D. Givhan likes wiggers. Pronouncing them, as of the early 1990s, "perhaps the fastest growing group among teenagers," she finds these "white kids who want to be black" open to "new worlds and different ideas." Her informant, a youth marketing consultant, whom "companies such as Pepsi pay big bucks," describes wiggers as white kids "wearing Cross Colors and oversized baggy jeans . . . watching Spike Lee movies, 'Soul Train' and 'Yo! MTV Raps.'" Givhan holds that "these folks have absorbed" Black culture, making it "their own." Their interest in "what makes some African Americans groove can only be helpful to improved race relations." Wiggers "are crossing cultural lines. And that's a lot more stylish than anything you can buy off the rack."[2]

In the inaugural 1992 issue of *VIBE*, the slick magazine of "hip-hop culture," James Ledbetter dismissed or perhaps just dissed wiggers. They were "desperate . . . parodies," "rip-offs," and "suckers." They had failed, wrote Ledbetter in the same issue of *VIBE* in which Greg Tate denounced rappers for having failed to denounce "commodity fetishism," to do more than "play at being black." They had not been "willing to renounce, up front, the systemic abuses of the white order."[3]

Neil Bernstein, writing in *West Magazine*, world-historicizes wiggers. They, along with "white cholitas," "white skaters and Mexican would-be-gang-bangers [who] listen to gangsta rap and call each other 'nigga' as a term of endearment," "blond cheerleaders" who stress their Cherokee ancestry, and "children of mixed marriages [who] insist that they are whatever race they say they are," are the world. They are "facing the complicated reality of what the 21st century will be" and "inching toward . . . the dream of what the 21st century should be" each and every time that they treat racial identity as a voluntary claim rather than a biological or cultural inheritance.[4]

My own notes on wiggers, which follow, can claim nothing like the clarity of any of these journalistic accounts. In these pages, wiggers will not be marching toward dystopia or toward utopia, toward irrelevance or toward an integrated and corporate-sponsored community. They will not be seen as reincarnating minstrelsy nor as miraculously waving away centuries of racism and current inequalities in money and power. They will not be seen as just more of the same old past nor as the guides in our safe passage to a multicultural future. They will be seen as complex and contradictory, as parts of a terrible past and of what is bound to be a long struggle to transcend it. Their presence will be taken as an occasion to reflect on that past, on that complexity, and on how to find grounds for guarded optimism in the very long run.

What I have called the "Ellison question" frames my remarks. It provides a sharp reminder that, in a society in which an imagination of Blackness so thoroughly frames both what attracts and repulses whites, white identity will as often turn on a question as an answer. Two decades ago, Ellison posed that question as extremely and precisely as anyone has yet done: "What, by the way, is one to make of a white youngster who, with a transistor radio, screaming a Stevie Wonder tune, glued to his ear, shouts racial epithets at black youngsters trying to swim at a public beach?"[5] In the early 1990s, while I was first trying to research the word *wigger* and come to grips with its larger meanings, life in mid-Missouri caused me to see the phenomenon very much in terms of Ellison's question. The first sign of wiggerdom I could see in that area was the backwards "X" cap white kids began to wear. Some of them had another "X," the Confederate flag, on their belt buckles, T-shirts, or trucks. As part of a larger pattern in which racism seems to be getting chronically better and worse simultaneously, such jarring images suggest that Ellison has asked a question not only of profound cultural ramification but also of literal political import: What *can* be "made of" the impulses that at once and often in the same person lead to tremendous attraction toward "nonwhite" cultures and toward hideous reassertions of whiteness as what the theorist and activist A. Sivanandan has called a "political colour"?[6]

The brief sketch of the varied uses and explanations of origin of the word *wigger* that follows is not meant to answer exactly how and where the word was coined or what its most common meaning has become. Instead, the argument is that *wigger* is of interest precisely because of the messiness surrounding its meanings and because of the ways this messiness gives us some entry into the tragic and dramatic complexities of Ellison's question.

Wigger first came to my attention as a slur used at Cabrini High School in a Detroit suburb in about 1989. When white Detroiters enrolled at the school, bringing with them "black-influenced" styles and friendships with African Americans, some of the suburban white students caused a stir at the school by calling the newcomers "wiggers," meaning "white niggers," or whites acting "too black." Similar recent uses of *wigger* as a slur against whites by whites have been reported in Madison, Wisconsin; Warren, Ohio; and most dramatically, in Morocco, Indiana, where the hip-hop fashions and musical tastes of young, rural white women recently resulted in their being called "wiggers," suspended from school, spat upon, and threatened with death by white male students who demanded that they "dress white."[7]

This sense of *wigger* is consistent with uses of "white nigger" as a white-on-white epithet (like "smoked Irishman," "guinea," "black Dutch," "nigger lover," "Black Republican," et cetera) that date back at least to the nineteenth century. But it was at that time more likely to be applied to a white accepting "nigger work," or politically breaking with what was seen as proper behavior for whites, than to a suspected cultural dissenter from whiteness. Closer to modern uses was the branding of Johnny Cash as a "white nigger" during his rockabilly days. *Wigger* as a culturally based white-on-white slur existed in Buffalo in the early 1970s. The white rapper MC Serch, of 3rd Bass, heard it in the early 1980s when classmates reacted to his adoption of hip-hop clothing by calling him a "wigger" or a "black wanna-be."[8]

However, at the same time that Serch was derisively called a "wigger" by whites, another young East Coast hip-hopper, Gary Miles, was being called "wigger" affectionately by African Americans. Miles, self-described as only "phenotypically white," is a University of California-Los Angeles graduate student who forcefully argues that *wigger* originated among African Americans to name whites seriously embracing African American cultural forms and values, in contrast to "wanna-be" dabblers in the externalities of rap. The meaning was still "white nigger," but *nigger* in the rehabilitated sense proliferating in rap. Often pronounced "wigga," the term signals the same sort of inclusion as a greeting "That's my nigga" might. In this sense *wigger* would echo earlier African American uses of words like *hillbilly cat* in early rock and roll and the friendly reception of being called "Black" that Jerry Lee Lewis remembered. Miles allowed that the implied approbation could sometimes change on short notice, however.[9]

In Milwaukee, another usage of *wigger* appears. Although one young white informant there sees it as used in his inner-city high school as a flat (neither friendly nor pejorative) description of those whites who "want to identify with black culture," another account finds Black Milwaukee high schoolers using it to discuss with contempt white suburban school kids who "wear the jackets . . . and tried to talk black but who wouldn't last a minute" in the city. This comports with long-standing African American uses of *white nigger* as a derogatory term for "a white person with Negro affectations."[10]

The case for *wigger* as a coinage of African Americans—this does not rule out that whites also independently created the term at another place and time—is buttressed by two further considerations. As both Miles and Sundiata Cha-Jua have pointed out, using *w* or *wh* as a substitute beginning to create new words describing whites or white institutions is frequent in African American speech—thus *witch* for "white bitch" and *whitianity* for "white Christianity." Secondly, and here the tremendous hybridity of American slang complicates easy racial distinctions, *wigger* clearly gestures toward earlier uses of *wig* and *wigged out* by both black jazz musicians and beat poets and by white jazz musicians and beat poets. *Wigged*, contradictorily meaning overstimulated, intellectualized, laudably crazy and stressed, could hardly have failed to strike Black-influenced musical subcultures as an apt cousin for *wigger*.[11]

Yet other variations exist. Where my son went to junior high school, *wigger* was concurrently acceptingly applied by Blacks to whites, disparagingly applied by racist whites to other whites, dismissively applied by whites adopting Black styles to whites seen as doing so inauthentically, and used approvingly by white would-be hip-hoppers to describe one another. One high schooler in the north suburbs of Chicago, who had recently moved there from the city, proudly saw herself as a wigger—as one of the white students who "wished they were black"—but had never thought of the term as derived from *nigger*.[12]

This is not the place to evaluate the political importance of wiggers, let alone their wisdom. The broader white hip-hop audience is rather easily ridiculed. Hip-hop magazines, marketed in large part to white audiences, who now buy half of the rap tapes sold, often ridicule wiggers and wanna-bes as middle-class, superficial, voyeuristic, apolitical, consumerist, "dumb," and even racist. There is little reason to doubt these charges or to suppose that white fans are underrepresented among those whom Greg Tate derides as "all the B-boy wannabes who like to say *ho*!"[13] When Italian American youth in New York City choose to identify themselves with elements of African American style, they at times proudly call themselves *guineas*. In doing so, they rehabilitate a term used earlier in the century to slur Italian immigrants and to connect Italians with Blacks. But these *guineas*, as Donald Tricarico writes, "resist identification" with African Americans on other levels and may "bite the hand that feeds them style." Whites appropriating a form of *nigger* is likewise fraught with difficulties. Being a wigger is, moreover, often an adolescent phase, calling to mind Leslie Fiedler's remark that white American males spend their early years as imaginary Indians and their teens as imaginary Blacks before settling into a white adulthood (not to mention Janis Joplin's bizarre hope that "being black for a while will make me a better white").[14]

While wiggers are, as the courageous high schoolers of Morocco, Indiana, show, by no means all male, they often are aggressively so and identify with violence, scatology, and sexism in rap rather than with Black music and culture more broadly. Indeed, Robin D. G. Kelley's fine work on hip hop reminds us that one impulse toward sexual violence in the lyrics is precisely that it plays well to white adolescent males. Consumerism, sexuality, and male supremacy can hardly be separated in either the music or in the fan magazines, not when Benetton uses the center spread of the inaugural issue of *VIBE* to gesture toward both *Playboy* and *National Geographic* with a large photo of topless African women, including one albino to make the advertisement somehow antiracist.[15]

But the very matters that warn us against romantically mistaking wiggers for the vanguard of antiracism ought also to allow us to see that the proliferation of *wiggers* illuminates issues vital to the history of what Albert Murray has called the "incontestably mulatto" culture of the United States The dynamics of cultural hybridity have long featured much that is deeply problematic on the white side. From minstrelsy through *Black Like Me*, from the blackfaced antebellum mobs that victimized African Americans to the recent film *Soul Man*, the superficial notion that Blackness could be put on and taken off at will has hounded hybridity. Aggressive male posturing, sexual and otherwise, accompanied the fascination with Black culture long before rap. Surely no wigger has gone further over the top in this regard than Norman Mailer's loathsome "The White Negro," which squarely premised an admiration for Black culture on that culture's capacity to produce orgasms in white males.[16] Nor is the commodification of Black cultural forms by white promoters, artists, and audiences new. A century and a half ago minstrels likened themselves to slavers on the African coast, joking that both made money by "taking off the niggers." Not only have individual Black artists been impoverished in the process the minstrels began, but also whole genres. When Elvis "discovered" Big Mama Thornton, Amiri Baraka reminds us, she was "dis'd" and her music "covered."[17]

Hybridity, in a highly unequal society, has as often been the product of tragic, tawdry, and exploitative forces as of romantic ones. Whether we judge the beauty and solidarity created by the crossing of cultural color lines in the interstices of racial capitalism to outweigh the associated slights and tragedies is on one level immaterial. The process goes on, superficially and at times deeply. If to abdicate studying it were only to abdicate understanding that mythical thing called "white culture," the consequences would be bearable. But such an abdication also entails giving up on understanding American culture and African American culture, the latter having as one of its essential elements the ability to borrow creatively from others and to create hybrid forms.[18]

The scholarly literature that positions us to understand both the drama and the tragedy of the wigger, and of his or her ancestors, is growing in both style and sophistication. At its best, in the works of Eric Lott, Michael Rogin, and others, this scholarship is often deeply wary of the intentions of some whites pushing the process of hybridization forward and of the results of that process. But this suspicion is not allowed to stand in for analysis—often highly concrete and historicized analysis. The specific perils, and the openings, created by white interest in (and identification with) Black culture change profoundly even amid continuities. In the case of wiggers, for example, the tendency toward essentializing views of Black culture as male, hard, sexual, and violent are likely more pronounced than was the case in earlier white attraction to rhythm and blues and to soul. The physical separation of the races combines with the seeming intimacy of video culture to give a large field to adolescent fantasies. Late capitalism has, moreover, never been so quick to fashion ads and commodities out of rebellious styles or, perhaps, so effective at using sex and violence to sell those commodities.[19]

On the other hand, the 1990s also differ from the 1950s and 1960s in far more hopeful ways. The close contact with African American communities that produced a few "white-Negro women," in the words of Calvin Hernton in 1965, was born often of interracial marriages and the long pattern of African American communities incorporating the children of those marriages more consistently.[20] The significant increase of such marriages and the generally greater mixing of Black and white youth have ensured that not all identifications with African American culture by whites are based on projected images of that culture. Large and critical aspects of popular and not-so-popular culture are now significantly shaped directly by Black artists, not by white artists drawing on black creativity. These include not only music and sport but also literature and, increasingly, poetry, cinema, and cultural studies. (This open secret is one context for shrill defenses of the canon.) Except perhaps among the very young, white hip-hop consumers do not seek out the music by white artists. Wigger or wanna-be, the consumer preference is for "authentic" Black artists. There is little cultural space for a Pat Boone (though the problems raised by the influence of market shares among white consumers and of corporate profits over deciding what is "authentic" are great). To an unprecedented extent, white youth are listening to an explicit critique, often an unsparing critique, of "white" society. This fact and the widespread adulation of Malcolm X by white as well as Black hip-hoppers caused as tough-minded an observer as the Cincinnati-based criminologist Zaid Ansari to raise the possibility of whites "becoming X"—that is, losing that quality in whiteness that "keeps them accepting oppression, including their own oppression."[21]

Whether or not we believe that wiggers are part of anything that is as grand a future transformation as that envisioned by Ansari, we ought to realize that the little things that they do in the present fully reflect the racialized dramas that have so shaped the past of U.S. culture. In identifying with hip hop, for example, white rap fans drew unconsciously on an African heritage. The *hip* in *hip hop*, and in so much else in modern U.S. culture, was put there by Africans. As the extraordinary research of David Dalby and others has shown, enslaved Wolof speakers, from what is now Senegal, carried *hipi*, meaning "to open one's eyes" and "be aware of what is going on," to the New World perhaps as early as the late seventeenth century. In the welter of African ethnicities that slavery and Black creativity melded into an African American culture, *hip* survived and prospered. Nearly three centuries later, it was still there for the white mainstream to pick up from the jazz subculture. Even the beatnik/jazz insider ideal of the "hep cat" echoed the Wolof *hipi-kat*, meaning "someone with his eyes open." When the name *hippie* came to be applied to masses of young people who sought out eye-opening experiences in the 1960s, it did so because those young people grew up in a culture steeped in African influences, although they seldom knew it.[22]

A striking number of wiggers (and Black hip-hoppers) sport oversized T-shirts and backwards baseball caps featuring Bugs Bunny as the hippest, not to mention the hopping-est, figure in American popular culture. Sometimes it is a dark Bugs with rasta braids and hip-hop clothes. Sometimes it is the standard issue Warner Brothers Bugs. Some kids wear a "black" Bugs one day and a gray one the next. The crossing of colors on Bugs Bunny shirts is perfectly, albeit unconsciously, in tune with the dramas of American cultural history, for Bugs's heritage is anything but white. The verb *bug*, meaning "annoy" or "vex," helps name the cartoon hero. Its roots, like those of *hip*, lie partly in Wolof speech.[23] Moreover, the fantastic idea that a vulnerable and weak rabbit could be tough and tricky enough to menace those who menace him enters American culture, as the historian Franklin Rosemont observes, largely via Brer Rabbit tales. These stories were told among various ethnic groups, especially those along the West African coast. They were further developed by American slaves before being popularized and bastardized by white collectors like Joel Chandler Harris. They were available both as literature and folklore to the white Southerner Tex Avery, whose genius so helped to give us Bugs. Joe Adamson's forceful connection of African folklore and Bugs cuts in two ways. Brer Rabbit inspired creators of Bugs *and* prepared audiences for his arrival.[24]

Hipness and Bugs Bunny are obviously nothing but sideshows or short subjects in American cultural history. Neither, for all the obvious marginality of triracial guineas and full-fledged wiggers, do the stories of *guineas* and *wiggers* belong in the wings of historically based cultural studies. These words, and the people behind them, remind us that race, although itself a social construction, has also dramatically constructed American lives. They further suggest that race has been a source of drama, contestation, and tragedy not only for the minority of "nonwhites" but also for the "white" majority.

NOTES

1. Tad Friend, "The White Trashing of America," *New York* 27 (August 22, 1994), 30, quoting Murray. Portions of this essay originally appeared in David Roediger, "*Guineas, Wiggers* and the Dramas of Racialized Culture," *American Literary History* 7 (Winter 1995), 654–68. Reprinted with permission.

2. Robin D. Givhan, "Wiggers See Style a Way into Another Culture," Detroit *Free Press*, June 21, 1993, 1–D.

3. James Ledbetter, "Imitation of Life," *VIBE*, Special Preview Issue, September 1992, 114; Greg Tate, "The Sound and the Fury," *VIBE*, Special Preview Issue, September 1992, 15.

4. Neil Bernstein, "Goin' Gangsta, Choosin' Cholita," as reprinted in *UTNE Reader*, March-April 1995, 87, 88, 89, and 90, from *West*, a Sunday Supplement to the (San Jose) *Mercury News*. Bernstein uses *cholita* as a stand-in for "Mexican gangsta' girl" (86); one of the "white cholitas" Bernstein interviews longs to acquire "a big enough attitude to be a black girl" (86).

5. Ralph Ellison, "The Little Man at Chehaw Station," in *Going to the Territory* (New York: Vintage, 1987), 21.

6. A. Sivanandan, *Communities of Resistance: Writings on Black Struggles for Socialism* (London: Verso, 1990), 66.

7. Telephone interview with Terry Moore in Detroit, October 25, 1992; Denise Sanders, "Black Is In," *Isthmus* (Madison), October 29, 1993, 1 and 20; Letter to the author from Tom Sabatini in Warren, Ohio, November 7, 1993; Richard Roeper, "Fashion Statement Gets an Ugly Reply," *Sun Times* (Chicago), November 29, 1993, 11; "Wiggers Attacked," MTV News, November 24, 1993.

8. On these usages, see David R. Roediger, *The Wages of Whiteness: Race and the Making of the American Working Class* (London and New York: Verso, 1991), 68 and 145; and "*Guineas, Wiggers* and the Dramas of Racialized Culture," *American Literary History* 7 (Winter 1995), 654–58; Steve Pond, "The Hard Reign of a Country Music King," *Rolling Stone*, December 10, 1992, 122; Serch quoted in David Samuels, "The Rap on Rap," *New Republic*, November 11, 1991, 24–29.

9. Telephone interview with Gary Miles in Los Angeles, November 15, 1992; Alice Echols,

" 'We Gotta Get Out of This Place': Notes Toward a Remapping of the Sixties," *Socialist Review* 22 (1992), 9–34; Bryant Gumbel, "Interview with Jerry Lee Lewis," NBC *Today Show*, March 24, 1993. Gumbel: "You've been called a white man with a black man's soul." Lewis: "I took that as a great compliment."

10. Telephone interview with Steve Meyer in Milwaukee, November 29, 1992; Abra Quinn, "Field Notes from Milwaukee on *Wigger*," December 1992; Clarence Major, *From Juba to Jive: A Dictionary of African-American Slang* (New York: Viking, 1994), 122.

11. Miles interview and interview with Sundiata Cha-Jua in Columbia, Missouri, January 25, 1993; Clarence Major, *Dictionary of Afro-American Slang* (New York: International Publishers, 1970), 122; "Notes on *Wigged*," Peter J. Tamony Collection, Western Historical Manuscripts Collection, Ellis Library, University of Missouri at Columbia.

12. Interview with Brendan Roediger in Columbia, Missouri, March 16, 1993; interview with name withheld in Cambridge, Massachusetts, February 20, 1993.

13. Ledbetter, "Imitation of Life," 112–14; William Upski Wimsatt, "We Use Words Like 'Mackadocious,' " *The Source*, May, 1993, 64–66; Tate, "Sound and Fury," 15. See also Wimsatt, "*Wigger*: Confessions of a White Wannabe," *Reader* (Chicago), July 8, 1994, 1.

14. Leslie Fiedler, *Waiting for the End* (New York: Stein, 1964), 134; Janis Joplin quoted in Ledbetter, "Imitation of Life," 114; Donald Tricarico, "Guido: Fashioning an Italian-American Youth Style," *Journal of Ethnic Studies* 19 (1991), 56–57.

15. Robin D. G. Kelley, "Straight from Underground," *The Nation*, June 8, 1992, 793–96; Barbara Ransby and Tracye Matthews, "Black Popular Culture and the Transcendence of Patriarchal Illusions," *Race and Class* 35 (1993), 57–68; Leerom Medovoi, "Mapping the Rebel Image," *Cultural Critique* 20 (1991–92), 153–88; *VIBE* Special Preview Issue, September 1992, centerspread. On nudity in *National Geographic*, see Catherine A. Lutz and Jane L. Collins, *Reading National Geographic* (Chicago: University of Chicago Press, 1993), esp. 172–78.

16. Albert Murray, *The Omni-Americans* (New York: Vintage, 1983), 22; Norman Mailer, "The White Negro," in *Advertisements for Myself* (New York: Putnam's, 1959), 341 and 349; on *Soul Man*, see Margaret M. Russell, "Race and the Dominant Gaze: Narrative of Law and Inequality in Popular Film," in Richard Delgado, ed., *Critical Race Theory: The Cutting Edge* (Philadelphia: Temple University Press, 1995), 59–63.

17. Roediger, *Wages of Whiteness*, 119; Nelson George, *The Death of Rhythm and Blues* (New York: Pantheon, 1988); Amiri Baraka in William J. Harris, ed., *The Le Roi Jones/Amiri Baraka Reader (New York*: Thunder's Mouth Press, 1995), xiii.

18. On "white culture," see Roediger, *Towards the Abolition of Whiteness* (London and New York: Verso, 1994), 1–17; on hybridity in Black culture, see Lester Bowie's remarks in Dave Marsh, "Grave Dancers Union," *Rock and Rap Confidential*, September 1993, 7; Stuart Hall, "What Is This 'Black' in Black Popular Culture?" *Social Justice* 20 (1993), 104–14.

19. Eric Lott, *Love and Theft: Blackface Minstrelsy and the American Working Class* (London and New York: Oxford University Press, 1993); Michael Rogin, "Blackface, White Noise: The Jewish Jazz Singer Finds His Voice," *Critical Inquiry* 18 (1992), 417–53.

20. Calvin Hernton, *Sex and Racism in America* (New York: Grove Press, 1965), 51.

21. Zaid Ansari, on *Tony Brown's Journal* (Public Broadcaster Company), March 1993.

22. David Dalby, "The African Element in American English," in Thomas Kochman, ed., *Rappin' and Stylin' Out: Communication in Urban Black America* (Urbana: University of Illinois Press, 1972), 180–81; Major, *Juba to Jive*, 234.

23. Dalby, "The African Element in American English," 180–82.

24. Franklin Rosemont, "Bugs Bunny," in Rosemont et al., eds., *Surrealism and Its Popular Accomplices* (San Francisco: City Lights Books, 1980), 55; Joe Adamson, *Bugs Bunny: Fifty*

Years and Only One Grey Hare (New York: Owl-Holt, 1991), 50. Sterling Stuckey's brilliant *Going through the Storm: The Influence of African American Art in History* (New York: Oxford University Press, 1994), 165–67, places Senegal, home of Wolof speakers, at the center of the creation and elaboration of Brer Rabbit tales. On Harris and Brer Rabbit, see Alice Walker, "Uncle Remus, No Friend of Mine," *Southern Exposure* 9 (1981), 29–31.

Chapter Twenty-two

Virtually Out

The Emergence of a Lesbian, Bisexual, and Gay Youth Cyberculture

Joanne Addison and Michelle Comstock

Actually, over the Internet was when I had my first close encounter . . . there was this bisexual woman on the rave net. And she was very persuasive, and that was like when I was, 'This is safe. This is the Internet. And I can do this—I can talk to her, and no one has to know.' So that's when I started experimenting with the idea that maybe it's okay to accept all these feelings after all. And that's how it all started to come out, and that's when I started to come out . . . I would go to the library and look up stuff on les-bi-gay issues, then I would go to the Internet and look it up. So it turned from just wanting to escape . . . by this time I had friends I could talk to . . . from like a sheltered kind of area to becoming a place where I found knowledge . . . information about stuff I wanted to know. And it was a safe way to do it too.

—interviewee's response to the question: "How did you find out about the different Internet sites that you log onto?"

QUIRX
the gay generation-X youth MOVEment
It's about us. I look at our generation, that being gay youth, in 1995, and I smile. I went to Stonewall in New York last year with my friend Ernie, and when I was marching alongside my peers, I felt a wave of what they call 'pride.' I had heard that term tossed around, a gay cliché, I suppose, but I never felt it before. We all are busting with so much potential, and I see the winds of change everywhere I look. It fills me with hope for the future, you know. That we recognized our potential, and more importantly, our worth, and that we move on, in spite of differences, in spite of the chaos around us. We are honest with ourselves, and with our lives. . . . And so

it begins, the start of something big, the initiation of a movement that will no longer go unseen, and more importantly, unfelt. Think of Quirx as nothing more than a record of this, an electronic scroll-sealing the past, feeling the present, and anticipating the future.

—homepage of the les-bi-gay youth cyberzine Quirx

Responses to the question: "What do you think of mainstream definitions of [queer]?
I think they fuck it up like the mainstream fucks everything up by making it something that's either a cartoon of itself or something to be capitalized on.

kinda good and kinda bad. sometimes i don't mind being thought of as a freak, drag, drunk, fool or whatever other thing the mainstream fantasy make us. sometime, like when people die of aids just because we're "gay"—i hate it.

—from "Silly Questions," edited by Steph, *Square Pegs*, February 1996

Introduction

In *Common Culture*, Paul Willis claims: "Young people are all the time expressing or attempting to express something about their actual or potential cultural significance" (1990:1). This is especially true of oppressed youth groups whose significance, and more importantly whose existence, is continually questioned not only by the culture at large, but by the youths' parent and peer culture as well. Such is the case with most lesbian, gay, and bisexual youth. A population largely ignored not only in current research on youth but also in political debates concerning homosexuality on both the Right and the Left, les-bi-gay youth are often isolated and lack the means by which to articulate their subject position in society.[1] As a result of this isolation and increasing access to the Internet and World Wide Web, it seems that more and more les-bi-gay youth have begun to employ technology in order to understand and express their experiences and demand that they be considered culturally significant members of society.

The discursive moments that served as the above epigraphs stand as partial articulations of an emerging lesbian, gay, and bisexual youth subculture situated in the intersections between cyberspace and "real" space, or between on-line life and off-line life. This les-bi-gay youth cyberculture is composed of multiple real, virtual, and imagined identities and realities that are actualized on various levels at different times and places. These different times and places, or developing histories and spaces, are informed by and engage the material conditions and lived experiences of many of today's les-bi-gay youth.

However, as the above discursive moments suggest, studying les-bi-gay youth on-line carries many risks, as well as benefits. Giving more attention to these already heavily censored sites risks further regulation and adult surveillance (most notably the Communications Decency Act of 1995 and its regulatory right wing anti-youth, anti-access effects). Yet, it is important to argue for the existence of this cyberculture because of its ongoing contributions by youth to larger anti-homophobic political and social efforts. As Donna Gaines, a longtime advocate of youth, states, "Young people have experienced an erosion of their cultural prestige, their impact as a social force has diminished, they are losing ground in their rights and civil liberties" (1994: 227). Les-bi-gay youth organizations are especially undersupported and over-regulated, as legislators touting "family values" continue to limit youths' access to both real and virtual queer communities, as indicated in the state of Utah's recent legislation banning les-bi-gay student groups from meeting on public school property. Chris Thomas, in the May 1996 issue of the e-zine *Oasis*, writes, "For too long, adults, gay and otherwise, have ignored the problem of gay and lesbian youth—problems ranging from isolation to AIDS and suicide. Now, via the youth-dominated technology of the future, young gay people are finding one another on-line and staking their claim for attention and recognition." In response, les-bi-gay youth Internet sites such as Youth Action Online have emerged. As Christian Williams (age nineteen), one of the founders of Youth Action Online, explains, "For youth who have been abandoned by their families or, worse, thrown out for who they are, YAO can serve as both a resource of agencies and services to turn to for help, as an alternative to the streets, and as a place to receive the emotional healing and support—the understanding that comes from another young person" (Thomas 1996).

In the following essay, we will discuss the challenges of doing research on-line in relation to the significance of the emergence of a les-bi-gay youth cyberculture. This will involve building effective geographical as well as historical frameworks through a discursive mapping of les-bi-gay youth Internet sites, as they are being constructed by their founders and participants.

Part I

Any attempt to map cyberspace (meaning here the Internet and World Wide Web) has to take into account its fluid, ever-changing multiplicity. Sites and links shift and change according to where, when, and how one logs on, leading on-line participants to often experience alternating feelings of vertigo and euphoria.[2] At the same time, cyberspace is often characterized in terms of fixed, concrete spaces: "netizens" talk about the various places they have visited, they enter specific chat rooms to engage in discussions of interest, and they meet each other at virtual restaurants, swimming pools, and sex clubs. These on-line experiences often cross over into off-line experiences. It is the intersections between on-line and off-line experiences that we must strive to account for when conducting research on the Internet and World Wide Web because it is these intersections that reveal the complexities and possibilities of a les-bi-gay youth cyberculture.[3]

Doing so requires moving outside of academia's obsession with and reliance on "history" as our basis for critique and interpretation.[4] Instead, we base our understanding of cyberspace and the formation of cybercultures on Soja's notion of spatiality as "actually lived and socially created spatiality, concrete and abstract at the same time, the habitus of social practices. It is a space rarely seen for it has been obscured by a bifocal vision that traditionally views space as either a mental construct or a physical form" (Soja 1993:143). This is not to argue solely for spatial critiques of the Internet, but rather to argue for viewing it not only in terms of a history, but also in terms of a geography that frustrates any attempts at locating some Archimedean point from which to offer a centered historical map. The notion of spatiality is an important one to consider not only as a way of breaking out of current temporal frameworks in order to deepen our understandings of social life, but also so that in the process of doing research on the Internet and World Wide Web, we do not fall into simplifying it in terms of a concrete physical space that can be observed or historicized in the ways that we are familiar with.

Further, representing cyberspace, particularly the les-bi-gay youth cyberculture, as dialectical also challenges early efforts to map or partition off lesbian and gay subcultures. These often racist and homophobic mappings argued for the existence of "gay ghettos," where lesbian and gay men led "lifestyles" that were distinct and separate from more mainstream lifestyles.[5] Our mapping not only resists ghettoizing les-bi-gay youth, but works to take into account the complexity of their lives—their participation in a variety of on- and off-line mainstream and countercultural activities. As cultural theorist Ann Balsamo discovered in her work on the Internet and cyberpunk culture, many youth who identify as cyberpunks also participate in other youth countercultural activities like raves and body piercing (1996). Angela McRobbie, in *Postmodernism and Popular Culture*, also refuses to position the youth rave music movement in simple opposition to either mainstream culture or other music countercultures of the past and present. She claims, "[T]he old model which divided the pure subculture from the contaminated outside world, eager to transform anything it could get its hands on into a sellable item, has collapsed" (1994:161). It is time, according to McRobbie, for cultural theorists to begin noting the subculture's wider social connections to "otherwise conceptually separate spheres like the media and higher education" (165). Electronic networks make it especially difficult and inadvisable to draw fixed borders between on-line and off-line cultures and subcultures. Thus, like Balsamo and McRobbie, we have taken care not to isolate or ghettoize the emerging les-bi-gay youth cyberculture, but have instead positioned it in a mutually constituting dialogue with often homophobic mainstream cultures as well as other anti-establishment subcultures.

Positioning this les-bi-gay cyberculture in dialogue with and in relationship to other cultures challenges claims that the Internet is purely a bourgeois space controlled by the military-industrial establishment. On one level our research takes issue with arguments such as that of cultural critic Donald Morton. Morton suggests that cyberspace is just another "bourgeois designer space in which privileged Western or Westernized subjects fantasize that instead of being chosen by history, they choose their own history" (1995:375). Instead of dismissing les-bi-gay youth websites as just more examples of corporate exploitation and surveillance, we view them as important sites for resistance, reproduction, and pleasure. And although many queer Internet and websites sometimes appear to serve as large cyberclosets for an elite class of mostly white, gay, politically disengaged males, we have found that these sites can also provide powerful opportunities for resistance and political organization.[6] It is this establishment of politically effective "social selves," a process both enabled and shaped by Internet technology, which marks les-bi-gay youth on the Internet as a subculture.

Constructing these Internet and websites as spaces for political and social resistance is not the same as denying their investments in elitist corporate structures and dominant cultural narratives. In delineating this cyberculture's prominent features, such as its reliance upon and use of computer technology, its "coming out" narratives and statements of identity, its anti-homophobic political positions, and its utopian fantasies of a world without shame and homophobia, we will discuss how these features are informed by social, cultural, and political conditions. Our approach also takes into account how subjectivities—raced, classed, gendered, sexualized—are articulated and experienced by youth participants, a question largely ignored by early subcultural theorists. Finally, instead of offering just one, totalizing vision—an adult researcher's perspective—we are engaging multiple views and alternate mappings of the cyberculture, based on how a variety of participants have experienced interfacing with it.

Engaging multiple perspectives, however, has been complicated by academic bureaucratic strictures on research in general. Research guidelines that are meant to prevent the exploitation of "under-age" survey respondents (a protective measure we both agree and disagree with) also serve to isolate youth and deny them the opportunity to speak for and contribute to the accounts of their communities that are being constructed by others. Further, in the case of les-bi-gay youth, it is generally not an option to obtain parental permission for them to be part of a research project, since most of them are not "out" to their parents or guardians.

In light of these concerns, the Internet offers an interesting research opportunity. Many of these under-age youth are establishing cyberzines, discussion groups, and support services through the Internet. In studying these public sites, we can gain insight into an emerging les-bi-gay youth cyberculture that we would not otherwise be able to engage. We have chosen our study sites based on high levels of activity (the number of "hits" or the number of people who visit and/or contribute to the site), as well as their founding, construction, and maintenance by youth instead of adults. Our analysis of these highly active sites will be intermixed with on-line and face-to-face interviews with les-bi-gay youth between the ages of eighteen and twenty-one who are actively involved in the Internet, as well as our own experiences as lesbian- and queer-identified women under thirty years of age.

Part II

In what follows, we will be marking and positioning many of the sites that constitute what we are calling a les-bi-gay youth cyberculture. While there are a number of sites that deal with issues affecting les-bi-gay youth, very few of these were founded and are being maintained *by* les-bi-gay youth. We have limited our focus to the most widely used of these youth-moderated sites. The sites we will explore include four cyberzines (*Square Pegs*, *Elight!*, *Oasis*, and *Blair*), which are the most popular type of youth Internet site; an IRC (Inter-Relay Chat) Channel (#gayteen); and one on-line les-bi-gay youth services site (Youth Action Online).

As emphasized in the previous section, our study focuses on two broad aspects of this emerging cyberculture: (1) how its members articulate and situate themselves politically in relation to heterosexist mainstream adult cultures and other youth subcultures (including utopic visions of the future); and (2) how the sites represent and actualize a variety of gendered, raced, classed, and sexualized subjectivities and/or identities. We can begin to explore these aspects in terms of a les-bi-gay youth cyberculture by exploring the "home page" or welcome page of the sites listed above. The home page of any site is the first direct experience that a person has with that site and often contains a purpose or mission statement. From the home pages, potential participants can determine much about the types of discourses and action that are allowable or deemed appropriate by the sites' moderators (who, again, are themselves les-bi-gay youth). For example, YAO's home page reads:

> Youth Action Online is a service, run by volunteers, created to help self-identifying gay, lesbian, bisexual, and questioning youth. YAO exists to provide young people with a safe space on-line to be themselves. This organization was formed to provide for the needs of queer youth; the need for a rare opportunity to express themselves, to know that they are not alone, and to interact with others who have already accepted their sexuality.

These mission statements represent not only what the site wants to be or do, but also what the site doesn't want to be or do. It is important for YAO, for example, to state that it is "run by volunteers" and not by corporations seeking to build marketing databases. YAO also represents itself as a youth-only space, a "safe space on-line." From what threatening forces YAO is protecting its youth participants is only implied. Adults? Homophobia? On-line and off-line sexual harassment? According to its mission statement, YAO's utopic intention is not only to provide and achieve a "safe space" for youth (a space that must be reclaimed again and again in the face of on-line and off-line regulations and harassment), but to help participants reach a point where they can "accept" their own sexuality. It is this intention that marks YAO as a provider of personal emotional support for youth, an act that is just as much political as personal in its resistance to homophobia and ageism.

Relatedly, moderators of these sites, often in response to participants' requests, have become responsible for articulating not only what type of activities are allowed between les-bi-gay youth at specific sites, but who is allowed to participate. Staking out a "safe space" becomes tricky when posts are often anonymous and emerge from undisclosed locations (a typical chat group sender line reads "nobody@nowhere"). Recently, when a number of users of the IRC channel #gayteen started to receive mail of a sexual nature, the moderator posted a statement elaborating on the fact that #gayteen is not a sex-chat line and should not be used for those purposes as it threatens the safety of the users. One #gayteen participant we interviewed appreciated attempts at this type of moderation, saying, "I mean, it's [#gayteen] a pure issues thing. You don't have the problems that you have on gaynet where you get people posting for sex and stuff that's really inappropriate. It's just talking to people about dealing with parents, coming out, losing a boyfriend. I like to read that just to remind myself that there are a lot of people that are going through what I went through."

In contrast to YAO, the home page for the cyberzine *Blair* reads: "Hey there supahfreak, welcome to blair #3. blair is a web-only superzine for kooks and retards such as yrself! come on in! viva la yoplait! we ate all the fruzen gladje." *Blair* markets itself as the magazine for "modern fags," "cyberfags," and "fashionauts." While YAO's purposes may seem more explicit than *Blair*'s, in fact the use of terms such as "supahfreak" and "kooks," as well as the name of the cyberzine itself (Blair was a teen-aged character in the TV series *The Facts of Life*), point to a specific group of teenagers who have appropriated and "queered" retro pop culture (such as the iconization of Pippy Longstocking in the third issue) in terms of fashion, politics, and technology. Although it may not be overtly political, *Blair*'s queer appropriation of pop, skater, and club culture works toward a refashioning of a queer youth self or image, albeit a gay, white, male image, in conjunction with and in resistance to these other youth cultures. When *Blair* provides links to "straight" alternative rock sites, like Verruca Salt and Lollapalooza, they are not only paying tribute to the sites and their attending countercultural values, they are, in effect, repositioning the sites in a new and irreverent context. For example, when links to the website for the Smashing Pumpkins (a popular alternative rock band) appear in *Blair*'s fashionzine *Sissy* (a spoof on *Sassy*, a fashion magazine marketed to young female teens), a reframing and queering of both the straight-identified site and band known as the Smashing Pumpkins occurs.

Most of *Blair*'s articles focus on those fashion codes which mark a person as gay or straight. An ongoing discussion entitled "gay or eurotrash?" opens with the following narrative: "i swear . . . some smiling guy comes walking thru soho in some tight Bundeswear ribbed t-shirt and like . . . red jeans, and a caesar hairdo . . . and your mind starts going *blip* *blip* and then all of a sudden your NEW BOYFRIEND starts talking german and hugging his girlfriend! what a mindfuck! it's so not fair" (richard 1996). *Blair*'s resistance to mainstream adult heterosexist culture is also evidenced in its numerous narratives of "irreverence" to and "deviance" from dominant adult regulatory codes. *Blair* editor, richard, marks the zine's birthdate as the moment he was fired from his web job for downloading gay porn (richard and bryan 1996).

Deviance from adult culture, both gay and straight, is also articulated in *Oasis*, another popular les-bi-gay youth cyberzine, which features articles on the "Queercore" and "Outpunk" music movements. In a recent article, *Oasis* editor Jeff Walsh described Brian Grillo, the self-identified queer punk lead singer of Extra Fancy, as "the anti-Christ to Judy Garland fags." Walsh goes on to write, "This bare-chested rock stud bangs away those stereotypes harder than he bangs his 50-gallon oil drum in concert; as if to say 'Sorry honey, it's the 90's, no more wallowing in victimization allowed. Get with the program' " (May 1996). The desire to mark themselves as different from adult and more mainstream les-bi-gay artists is articulated repeatedly in articles by members of the "queercore" music movement. In an earlier *Oasis* article, guest columnist Midol writes: "As larger bands and media take on more and more queer presence, the impetus of queercore gets lost in the perceived acceptance of homosexuality in popular culture. Even as gay people get more attention in general, the queercore movement is more concerned with making great music and spreading new ideas than, say, attending an Ivy League college or appearing in a fitness infomercial" (1996). Unlike *Blair*, however, *Oasis* provides, along with its articles on fashion and music, extensive coverage of news and events that have direct relevance to les-bi-gay youth, such as the recent stand by the Coalition of Concerned Women (a Religious Right organization run by Beverly LaHaye) against the celebration of Pride Month in schools. Walsh, the zine's current editor, also provides ample webspace for youth to respond to articles and to interact with one another as readers are encouraged to write and submit letters and opinion pieces, poetry, fiction, humor, and coming-out stories, as well as personal columns.

Another cyberzine committed to providing web space and a web presence for young les-bi-gay writers is *Elight!*, whose mission is to "provide a literary freelance publishing forum for gay teens" (Jace, "*Elight!* Philosophy"). Providing space for participants to articulate their positions is central to many of these sites. This insistence on providing a space/forum where les-bi-gay teens have the opportunity to articulate their experiences *as* les-bi-gay teens points not only to the insignificant subject position our culture has assigned these members of our society, but also to the invisibility demanded by our culture of les-bi-gay youth as well as the dangers involved in articulating coherent social selves. Thus, many of the sites we explored talked about their aim of creating an environment where teens feel safe and of claiming space on the Internet where les-bi-gay teens can express their emotions, opinions, and issues as well as gather to take political action. The need to articulate social selves through the Internet, however conflicted they may be, points not only to a lack of opportunity for les-bi-gay youth to do so by other means, but also to their desire to differentiate themselves from the adult les-bi-gay culture as it has been popularly constructed (as discussed earlier). Further, creating this space for one another evidences the ability of les-bi-gay youth with Internet access to resist this positioning as insignificant subjects through the use of current technologies. This is not to suggest that this resistance exists only "on-line." As our opening quotations and numerous coming-out narratives on the net reveal, these virtual experiences lead to resistance in other environments as well. Indeed, even the most personal coming-out stories on the 'net are stories of political activism, reinforcing the notion that coming out as a lesbian, gay, or bisexual youth often means coming out as a youth activist.

Many of the on-line youth participants describe the Internet as a virtual stage—a space and time to safely rehearse the coming-out process. For them, there is no clear distinction between their "net selves" and "real selves." One informs the activities of the other. For other participants, the Internet is one of the only places where they can be "out." An anonymous contributor to a recent edition of *Oasis* writes: "Because I'm closeted, it would be very difficult for me to be active for gay-rights. I really don't want to come out. Only about 5 of my closest friends know I'm gay. Anyway, I WANT TO HELP!! :) So . . . if there is anything you can suggest, or anything I can do for Oasis/OutProud, please tell me!" Many participants like this one are careful to note the divisions and difference between their on-line and off-line lives, claiming that being out on-line is not as real as being out at school or at home. For them, the consequences of being out on-line are not perceived to be as great as those of being out off-line. One participant we interviewed said he didn't want to join any on-line discussion groups at first for fear of becoming "one of those cyberjunkies" who spends all of his or her time at the computer. Because he was "busy coming out and meeting all kinds of people," he "didn't need to depend on the net for [his] social life." On the other hand, on-line participants, like Eric Wilcox, do depend on the Internet as a place to share or record their ongoing coming-out process. In a recent edition of *Oasis*, Wilcox narrates his crush on the guy down the hall, as well as his frustration with not being out. He uses his monthly column to speculate on and fantasize about the various ways he might ask someone out as well as become an active advocate of gay rights at his school (Wilcox 1996).

What may induce so many youth to share their coming-out stories and their experiences as activists and as victims of abuse is the cyberculture's promise of "community." Just the names "*Oasis*" and "*Elight*" connote escape, nurturing, and shared knowledge. One participant we interviewed used the Internet primarily to escape her parents: "At the time [when she found the queer youth chat groups], I was living at my parents' house, and I didn't want to be there. I used to say, 'I have to go check my e-mail Mom, I'll be back in a couple hours.' And she'd be like, 'Okay.' And that was my escape." Walsh, editor of *Oasis*, describes his early experiences on-line in similar terms: "I remember it being such a rush to finally talk to other gay people on my home computer. I'll also never forget how alone I used to feel after I shut off my computer because that was the only place my gay community existed" (April 1996).

While "community" is a highly contested term, it is appropriate for us to take our definition of community from one offered in the cyberzine, *Square Pegs*: "Community exists where 'we' (people who have relations with people of the same sex-sex outlaws) converge" (Steph 1996). The use of the word "converge" (from "com" meaning "together" and "vergere" meaning "to bend") is interesting here as it suggests a coming together of different people at the same point in order to take action. This is, in fact, what happens as many les-bi-gay youth make their way through the Internet maze to find a point of community with others in order to take action on one level or another. For example, in the section of their cyberzine titled "revolution," the *Square Pegs* editors have provided links and/or addresses for the president, vice-president, and many of the Senate and House of Representatives members.

But an aspect that stands out in many of these sites is the express attempt at constructing an inclusive community, despite the reality of exclusiveness based on gender, race, class, and sexuality. The images and subjectivities represented on most of these sites, in both graphic and textual form, are exclusively those of white gay males. In fact, unless one indicates otherwise (i.e., "I am a 15 year-old black gay male" or "I am a 16-year old white lesbian"), it is assumed participants are gay white males. This bias is especially evidenced in "personal ad" pages, where people can hook up with each other electronically as friends or "something more" ("*Elight!*—Personal Ads"). Out of the sixty-seven youth who sent in personal ads to *Elight!*, only seven identified themselves as women and only one identified himself as a black male. This situation mirrors the current social and material conditions of most females and minorities in relation to their access to and knowledge of technology.

It seems editors and participants do see gender exclusiveness as a problem on many of the sites. Walsh answered a recent *Oasis* opinion letter complaining about the zine's "boysey content" with the following statement: "*Oasis* has tried to increase the girl content on many occasions, and each attempt brings letters of interest, but none that follow through. We're trying." Also, the moderator of #gayteen concludes his welcome page with what seems like both a response to criticism and a plea for more female participants: "I just want to stress that #gayteen is NOT just for gay males. We have quite a few lesbian/bisexual females on the channel, and any more are welcome to be a part of the channel as well." The women we talked to about their on-line experiences spoke of gravitating from general "queer" and "queer youth" sites, which are dominated by males, to women-only sites, like Sappho, where they were likely to read about experiences more closely resembling their own. But even at these sites lesbian and female bisexual youth do not have space of their own, as these sites include women of all ages and thus seldom focus on issues specific to lesbian and female bisexual youth. Tellingly, our search thus far has not turned up any exclusive lesbian and/or female bisexual youth sites, although it has turned up exclusive gay male youth sites (e.g., BOY2BOY). As one young lesbian wrote in her Letter to the Editor: "I am a 16 year old lesbian, and you are right, it is hard for us to find people to talk to and information to help us. Very little is done for gay youth and people on gay chat lines won't even talk to me because they say I am too young" (Shannon 1995). Perhaps because it focuses exclusively on participant short stories and poems, *Elight!* appears to be the only site able to balance "boy" and "girl" content. None of the sites, however, seems willing to address the race and class inequities inherent in both the cyberculture and in the culture at large—exclusionary forces that determine not only who participates or who is represented in the cyberculture, but also who gets access to the technology and information necessary for participation.

Conclusion

Earlier in this essay we stated: "It is this establishment of politically effective 'social selves,' a process both enabled and shaped by Internet technology, which marks [this specific group] . . . as a subculture." In concluding this essay we would like to reflect further on this statement. Following Rosi Braidotti (1992), Angela McRobbie claims that "the postmodern subject . . . is a subject in process, organized by a will to know and a desire to speak" (1994:67). It is an urgent will to know and desire to speak on the part of les-bi-gay youth on-line that has ultimately driven our exploration and causes these youth to converge at different Internet sites. Within these sites they are positioned by others but are also allowed to articulate their subjectivity as part of an emerging les-bi-gay cyberculture that is, and can continue to be, politically effective in the fight for recognition and social change in the lives of lesbian, gay, and bisexual youth. While our exploration has suggested a number of inequalities within this emerging cyberculture, inequalities that are largely rooted in issues of class and gender in relation to access to technology, it is our own utopian vision that these youth continue to struggle against these inequalities despite the cultural and material forces working against them.

NOTES

1. One indication of the low status of les-bi-gay youth is the lack of scholarship in this area. Following is a bibliography of work in this area:

Chandler, Kurt. *Passages of Pride: Lesbian and Gay Youth Come of Age.* New York: Toner Books, 1995.

DeCrescenzo, Teresa. *Helping Gay and Lesbian Youth: New Policies, New Programs, New Practice.* New York: Haworth Press, 1994.

Due, Linea. *Joining the Tribe: Growing up Gay and Lesbian in the 90's.* New York: Anchor Books, 1995

Herdt, Gilbert. *Children of Horizons: How Gay and Lesbian Teens Are Leading a New Way Out of the Closet.* Boston: Beacon Press, 1993.

Herdt, Gilbert, ed. *Gay and Lesbian Youth.* New York: Haworth Press, 1989.

Bernstein, Robin, and Seth Siberman, eds. *Generation Q.* Los Angeles: Alyson, 1996.

2. The Internet is a gateway for the network of computers linked throughout the world via various means (e.g., telephones and fiber optics). Through the Internet a connection can be made to the World Wide Web which works as a hypertext and multimedia interface. People who have access to computers equipped with modems and telecommunications software can link to many of the les-bi-gay youth sites through Internet search engines, such as "yahoo" and "Veronica," which then provide links and descriptions of the more popular sites, like the Youth Action Online home page. Each home page or web page is composed of "hypertext" (text, graphics, sound effects, moving images, links, etc), which can be characterized as a "body of discourse existing in computer memory as an open-ended matrix to which new components and linkages may continually be added" (Moulthrop 1991:254). However, a number of technological as well as social and political factors determine how users read, respond to, and experience hypertext.

3. We are aware of the artificial boundaries between on-line and off-line experiences for many people and thus will position our research in a dialectical relationship between the two as much as is possible within discursive limits.

4. As Edward Soja states the case: "An essentially historical epistemology continues to pervade the critical consciousness of modern social theory. . . . This enduring epistemological presence has preserved a privileged place for the 'historical imagination' in defining the very nature of critical insight and interpretation. . . . Space still tends to be treated as fixed, dead,

undialectical; time as richness, life, dialectic, the revealing context for critical social theorization" (1993:136–37).

5. David Bell and Gill Valentine, both postmodern geographers, critique some of the first geographical works on homosexualities in their recent collection, *Mapping Desire: Geographies of Sexualities* (1995). This early work, which sought to map "gay regions and neighborhoods," has been heavily criticized and largely rejected out of hand because of its 'racist' and hetrosexist assumptions" (Bell and Valentine 1995:4). Some of these early studies include Lyod and Rowntree's 1978 attempt to map lesbian and gay migration to urban centers; Harry's 1974 study of "gay life in the big city," and Barbara Weightman's 1981 study in which lesbians are "categorized along with criminals, ethnic minorities, and down-and-outs as neglected marginalised groups within the inner city" (Bell and Valentine 1995:4).

6. Gay Chicano activist Max Padilla argues in a recent *Village Voice* article that the "World Wide Web has turned out to be nowhere near as diverse as the number 7 train" (1995). After subscribing to the soc.motss (members of the same sex) discussion list, Padilla discovered that virtual queers are "mostly straight up and very white and male." He writes, "I still use the Internet, but I'm wary of its claims. This is not netopia, but an all-too-painful reflection of the real world."

REFERENCES

Balsamo, Ann. *Technologies of the Gendered Body*. Durham, N.C.: Duke University Press, 1996.

Bell, David and Gill Valentine, eds. *Mapping Desire: Geographies of Sexualities*. London: Routledge, 1995.

Braidotti, Rosi. "On the Feminist Female Subject or from She-self to She-other." In *Beyond Equality and Difference: Citizenship, Feminist Politics and Female Subjectivity*, ed. G. Bock and S. James, 176–92. London: Routledge, 1992.

Gaines, Donna. "Border Crossing in the U.S.A." In *Microphone Fiends*, ed. Andrew Ross and Tricia Rose, 227–34. New York: Routledge, 1994.

McRobbie, Angela. *Postmodernism and Popular Culture*. London: Routledge, 1994.

Midol. "Queercore." *Oasis*, May 1996.

Morton, Donald. "Birth of the Cyberqueer." *PMLA* 110 (1995): 369–81.

Moulthrop, Stuart. "The Politics of Hypertext." In *Evolving Perspectives on Computers and Composition Studies: Questions for the 1990s*, ed. Gail Hawisher and Cynthia Selfe, 253–71. Urbana, IL: NCTE and Computers & Composition, 1991.

Padilla, Max. "Affirmative Access: A Gay Chicano Lost in Cyberspace." *Village Voice*, 26 September 1995, 21.

Richard. "gay or eurotrash?" *Blair* #3, 1996.

Richard and bryan "blair #3: letter from the editors," 1996.

Shannon "Letters to the Editor" *Oasis*, May 1995.

Soja, Edward. "History: Geography: Modernity." In *The Cultural Studies Reader*, ed. Simon During. New York: Routledge, 1993.

Steph. "Silly Questions." *Square Pegs*, February 1996.

Thomas, Chris. "Gay Youths' Internet Safe Home." *Oasis*, May 1996.

Walsh, Jeff. "Extra Fancy's Brian Grillo: Saint or Sinnerman?" *Oasis*, May 1996.

Walsh, Jeff. "Logging On. Coming Out." *OutProud!*, April 1996.

Wilcox, Eric. "Personal Column." *Oasis*, June 1996.

Williams, Christian. "Gay Youths' Internet Safe Home." *Youth Action Online*, May 1996.

Willis, Paul. *Common Culture*. Boulder, Colo.: Westview Press, 1990.

Chapter Twenty-three

Gender and Generation down the Red Road

Rachel Buff

Colonial Optics: The Photo Opportunity

July, 1994. Powwow at the Mille Lacs Band Ojibwa Casino in Hinckley. The powwow is taking place in a new open-air amphitheater right next to the casino. There is a band shell, a stage, and rows of benches that climb a small incline up to a row of concession stands. On other weekends, this arena features country singers and comedians, open-air entertainment for casino goers. The powwow MC jokes about how much money his wife has lost already, but encourages people to go try their luck at the machines next door anyway.

Admission to both the casino and the powwow is free; you only have to pay to eat or to gamble. The only thing separating the two places is a specially marked-off parking lot for powwow participants. Here vans and older cars cluster, from as far away as Oklahoma, Louisiana, and Oregon; as close as the nations of Leech Lake, Red Lake, White Earth, and Mille Lacs in northern Minnesota.

A steady stream of people crosses over between these two worlds. People from the powwow take breaks at the glowing slots and cheap buffet of the casino. People up here to gamble wander into the powwow, sometimes accidentally, lost; sometimes to get a breath of fresh air and watch the dancers.

Sunday morning of a weekend long powwow. Few people have left yet, because the final rounds and judging of important events, like the grass dance, fancy dance, and jingle dress, has not yet taken place. Casino powwows offer prize purses fattened by this new source of revenue for some Indian bands.

I have been waiting to interview the current Comanche tribal princess, Karel Ann Coffey, who waited up late last night and most of this morning for her contest dance event, Women's Southern Style Straight. The dancing and drumming went on until past one in the morning; they pick up again just after noon.

Finally, Coffey's event takes place. One of the drums does a lighter, southern-style song to accompany this dance. About ten young women, fewer than for traditional northern events like jingle dress and women's fancy shawl, move into the circle. They dance slowly, dipping gracefully around the circle. Faster powwow dances, like fancy-dancing, originated in North Dakota, while slower dances permeated northern powwow culture from their original base in Oklahoma.[1] *Southern Straight dancing, though, is slower than any dances now commonly performed at powwows in the north.*

After the Southern Straight, we meet at the edge of the circle where the dance competitions are taking place. Together with Coffey's friend and traveling companion, DaLynn Alley, Little Miss Shawnee Nation, we walk up the slightly dusty incline away from the circle of drum groups, dancers, and spectators.

The two young women, aged eighteen and eleven, respectively, are dressed in carefully crafted traditional outfits. Each has a long, fringed buckskin dress, beautifully beaded jewelry, feather headbands. These represent long hours of work and dedication for powwow royalty. Coffey has already held five different titles in five years. She is carefully made up, her hair held back in a long braid.

As we walk up the incline, looking for a place to sit and talk, an older white man comes up, seemingly out of nowhere. Without looking at us, he quickly puts his arm around Coffey. A second: he poses. Someone—his wife?—snaps a picture, and he is gone without a word. Rewinding, the woman comes up to us. "Did you make that, honey?" she asks, friendly. "So lovely." She leans to finger Coffey's skirt. The couple leaves, headed for the casino.

Being a powwow princess makes a young woman used to this kind of attention. Coffey spoke during our interview in the confident public voice of one used to talking to members of the curious media. Alley, though younger, is also a veteran of royalty competitions, and she acts in local television commercials in her native Oklahoma. When I asked her if the incident with the camera had bothered her at all, Coffey responded with practiced charm:

> *If people see us, and they think it's beautiful, then good. Come on, come talk to me, and see what I am, not just on my outside, but on my inside. An Indian princess isn't just her looks, it's her mentality. It took her a lot to get where she is. And it's good that people recognize that.*
>
> *As far as people putting their arms around me, they better be good looking!*[2]

This chapter explores postcolonial inventions like the figure of the powwow princess. These figures serve not only as "goodwill ambassadors," translating alterity into a language that tourists can understand, but as powerful signs and actors in the landscape of contemporary Indian culture. Like the powwow grounds at Hinckley, this culture is crucially intersected by the myriad processes of national and international capitalist culture. At the same time, Indian people draw on an arsenal of memory and reinvented traditions to negotiate their positions as dual citizens of Indian and U.S. nations and cultures.

In this ongoing negotiation, young women like Coffey and Alley play an important role. Tradition and cultural survival are intimately involved with and implicated in the category of "youth" and the practices of young people. Young native people draw on the cultural narratives conveyed to them by Indian elders, role models and teachers to make sense of their experiences, to create something that sustains them. As denizens of hybrid social contexts on reservations, in rural communities and in cities, they must mediate the everyday occurrences of racism and sexism, modifying the stories and practices that shape their identity as they go.

Rayna Green argues that "(I)n order for anyone to play Indian successfully, real Indians have to be dead."[3] Certainly the way that the photo snapping couple treated the Comanche tribal princess was closer to the playful way one might treat a cigar store Indian or a cardboard cutout of Ronald Reagan than a typical interaction with a stranger. A five-hundred-year history of displacement, administration, migration, and appropriation prepared all of us for that moment: the photo opportunity. The optics of colonialism[4] here operate as a mirror in which live young women look like dead artifacts. A product of a stray tourist moment, the photo will become a relic of a dying culture rather than a moment in a long powwow weekend of many moments in years of creative invention, retention, and struggle. But these young people, the subjects of the tourist artifact, will remember, and represent, the weekend quite differently.

For the young people who participate in powwows, this optics of colonialism is an assumption: racism and sexism would condition their lives, regardless of their choice to pursue royalty crowns or advanced degrees. Young women, for example, use the role of powwow princess to negotiate their dual identities—as young Indian people with a claim to a specific history and culture, and as minorities in a nation that sees them as culturally extinct and calls on them to assimilate. For example, Miss Indian South High School, Lisa Doucet, talked about her desire to compete in the Miss Indian World Pageant, but she was uncertain if she would qualify. While both of her parents are Indian, she does not have enough ancestry from one specific tribe to meet the standards of blood quantum that would qualify her for official enrollment. Though she has relatives whom she visits on reservations, Doucet would not be able to compete for the many tribal princess titles that require enrollment. The princess competition at South High, she explained, emphasizes a different idea of tradition. Contestants are nominated on the basis of their knowledge of Indian tradition and dance and must meet a minimum grade point average to be chosen.[5] This notion of tradition, clearly reinvented in a historical context, accommodates both the hybrid nature of urban life and the legacy of migration and intermarriage that have resulted in a population of mixed ancestry, many of whom are culturally Indian but not able to enroll in Federally recognized tribes due to the standards established by Indian nations.

As internal transmigrants within a nation that has consistently displaced them from the ground on which they stand, these young people operate within the claims and restrictions of at least two institutional logics, both of which operate through discourses of race, ethnicity, and gender. They are socialized and reared in the logics of contemporary pan-Indian culture as well as in the logic of the dominant culture. Linda Basch, Nina Glick Schiller, and Cristina Szanton Blanc write: "By living their lives across borders, transmigrants find themselves confronted with and engaged in the nation-building processes of two or more nation-states. Their identities and practices are configured by hegemonic categories, such as race and ethnicity, that are deeply embedded in the nation-building process."[6] While transmigration often describes the movement of people between nations whose political boundaries are indisputable, my argument here is that contemporary Indian people are cultural transmigrants, moving between an "Indian country" of reservations and urban enclaves and a dominant culture that seeks to transform and assimilate them as national citizens.

Because of their dual socialization, young people are particularly important in the process of cultural transmigration. By law and by cultural proxy, citizenship is at least partially a matter of inheritance. And Indian young people inherit both the rights of citizenship guaranteed to their people in this country since 1924, and a more contested, less litigated citizenship in the sovereign communities of contemporary Indian country.

At the same time that powwow princesses suggest an iconography of conquest, they also play a role, along with dancers and drummers, powwow bums and campers, in the massive pan-Indian political and cultural revival that began in cities as a response to the culturally genocidal programs of Termination and Relocation in the 1950s and 1960s. Contemporary native youth are the children and grandchildren of this revival. As such, they inherit both the transforming work of cultural invention and a gap caused not only by the process of generational change, as in dominant Euro-American society, but by the constant pressure on Indian people to assimilate and forget. Powwows are transmigrant institutions that pass on the political and cultural project of renewal; as such, they are key sites of generational transmission and conflict.

Invented Traditions: Heartbeat of a Nation

In this chapter we look at the "invented traditions" of contemporary powwow culture.[7] Powwows are places where Indian elders speak about historical continuity with the past; where Indian youth find a place to hang out and express themselves as denizens of reservations and urban Indian communities, and as the "seventh generation" that will rise to inherit a legacy of pride and continuity with the past. The contemporary pan-Indian institutions that host powwows are a direct response to the history of relocation and urbanization in the post-1945 period. These survival schools, social service agencies, and Indian centers emerged in the 1970s as native responses to the oppressive policies of the Termination period, where federal policy sought to resolve the "Indian problem" once and for all by assimilating Indians into the national family and compelling them to accept "full citizenship" by abandoning their lands and cultures.

Control over the education and socialization of Indian youth has long been a central arena of conflict between Indian people and the federal government. Federal boarding schools preceded the program of forced relocation during the post-World War II period. Boarding schools and migration have crucially shaped the landscape of postwar urban native communities. The first generation of postwar Indian migrants to settle in cities like Minneapolis and St. Paul came previous to Relocation, largely as a consequence of wartime and immediate postwar economy. These people had often been educated in the federal boarding school system. Moving to cities for war work in the 1940s, or returning after military service, they had often left younger siblings or children behind them on the reservations, to be raised by aunts, uncles, or grandparents. This first generation of semipermanent urban denizens, with their limited knowledge of Indian languages and traditions, began to hold small urban powwows. Back home, according to Ron Libertus, their children and younger siblings were being raised by an older generation, elders who still often spoke in their native languages and remembered the better days of large powwows and open religious practices. These children, a "skip generation" in the processes of forced assimilation and necessary urbanization, came to the cities in the 1950s and 1960s to join urban-dwelling family members. This generation of Indian migrants would transport with them more substantial memories of language and culture, along with the more recent, graphic memories of reservation struggles against Termination policy and local poverty.[8]

In Minneapolis and St. Paul, this second generation of postwar transmigrants struggled to assert control over their children. Nationally, Native legal activists worked for the passage of the Indian Child Welfare Law in 1974, which stipulates that Indian children must be adopted into culturally appropriate, Native families. Title IV of the Indian Education Act amended the 1936 Johnson-O'Malley Act to provide for bilingual and bicultural education, allowing for the opening of Native Survival Schools, such as the Heart of the Earth School and the Red Schoolhouse in the Twin Cities. Locally, activists and community organizers worked to form Indian Centers. Survival schools, Indian Centers, and the Indian Social Service infrastructure, in turn, have sponsored powwows as places for people to converge, socialize, and educate their children.

The development of community institutions was closely tied to the struggle to maintain some control over the socialization of Indian youth. Dorene Day, a member of the "skip generation" that came of age during the 1970s, remembers how closely these issues were tied to political mobilization and community solidarity:

> The American Indian Movement *was* the community. It wasn't just a bunch of rough guys trying to cause radical problems. It was every age of people. Of Indian people. And that's what I remember. So that when we talk about how the [urban] Indian community began, and how Indian people corralled together to address these issues, it was the community. And, so that the powwows when they began, were even some very small celebrations that were a direct result of what kind of battle we won. If we kept some Indian kids out of juvenile because their parents were being harassed by the public school system, because they weren't going to school, because they were being discriminated against. I mean that, in itself, was a little victory. So that those victories, as they got bigger, then the powwows got bigger, to salute those victories. We just wanted to have fun, because there was a real purpose, meaning behind that.[9]

Powwows, then, were reinvented in urban communities as spaces to celebrate the struggle for native self-determination in the cities. The "skip generation" that Day remembers as holding powwows that were closely connected to political activism reached back in time and partially created, partially remembered "traditional" festivals. Powwows were a logical place for such invention, because they have been spaces of intercultural meeting and exchange since before Native contact with Europeans. In a quite traditional manner, then, they provide a place for negotiations between the new and the familiar.

"Invented traditions" offer the inventors a link to a long past and a response to the exigencies of the current situation. Through them, contemporary native people negotiate what George Lipsitz provocatively talks about as a "dangerous crossroad," a place that "encompasses both danger and opportunities," and that calls for "new forms of social theory capable of explaining new connections between culture and politics, as well as for new forms of cultural criticism suited to seeing beyond the surface content of cultural expressions to understand and analyze their conditions of production."[10] In another frame, outside of the one provided by the optics of colonialism, powwows offer exactly this kind of transmigrant social theory.

Homi Bhaba calls this use of colonial forms by colonized peoples "mimicry." Rereading Franz Fanon, he suggests that this use of colonial hierarchies and symbols "almost but not quite—suggests that the fetished colonial culture is potentially and strategically an insurgent counter appeal."[11] In mimicry, he argues, the colonized come close to subverting imperial ambition. Certainly the racial logic of colonialism is problematized by the adoption of imperial signifiers in an anti-imperialist performance like the powwow. As Bhaba well knows, however, this is a dangerous game. Imperial forms depend for their power on complicated constructs of race, gender, caste, and class. And fragments of these forms can detonate unexpectedly, like landmines from some abandoned struggle for imperial control, with the results being no less damaging for being residual and accidental.

Aware of these contradictions, Indian people debate their own continuous "invention of tradition." With a stake in their creation and insistence on a long history that links contemporary pan-Indian revival to both the long struggle against colonization and a proud precolonial past, Indian people define the best interpretation and practice of this history multiply. These debates are divided by gender and generation, and more rarely in the 1990s, by Indian nation, reservation, and band.

In this chapter I focus on arguments about powwow forms and practices along lines I can identify as generational and gendered. My focus on gender and generation comes out of my increasing conviction that these are the terrains on which transmigrant peoples struggle for their right to be dual citizens—to be entitled with respect to the dominant nation, as well as to their narratives of homeland, exile, and return. As Paul Gilroy so eloquently argues, gender is the modality in which race is lived.[12] Further, as Riv Ellen Prell's important scholarship points out, conflicts over the demarcation of identity and the possibility or desirability of assimilation and upward mobility very often take the form of struggles between genders and generations.[13] I focus on these struggles in part because they are what is clearest to me, what people spoke to me about most often and most saliently, and what I am, as an outside interpreter, most qualified to interpret and to report. Finally, issues of gender and generation are modalities in which aggrieved communities speak about their persistence and survival. These conflicts are the cracks that break the glassy mirror of colonial optics, that alter the representation of native traditions as "static" and "surviving." Powwows are places where young and old people, men and women, dancers, drummers, and spectators create their own kind of postcolonial social theory, insisting on the complexity and multiplicity of their survival.

Practicing Tradition: Contest Powwows, Traditional Powwows

My research has focused primarily on urban powwows, which are held during the winter months in Indian centers and schools, as well as in rented space at local colleges, civic centers, and the state fairgrounds. These powwows are a component of a more extensive "powwow circuit" that expands in the summer to include weekend-long powwows on reservations and at casinos throughout the Midwest and West. A Cherokee woman from Indiana told me at the Shakopee Mdewakanton Dakota Community Twenty-Fifth Anniversary Powwow that she and her family travel every weekend of the summer to powwows as far away as Montana and Connecticut.[14] Like many contemporary Indian people, they travel the powwow circuit in the summer to see friends, watch grandchildren and other relatives dance and drum, and see the country. Though most of the Minnesota summer powwows I went to were, by my license plate count, primarily attended by residents of the upper Midwest, each powwow also had about a 15 per cent attendance of cars from outside the immediate area.

The "powwow circuit" has developed and expanded since the 1950s, when the combined forces of urbanization and the proliferation of automobile and bus travel made Indian people much more mobile and likely to travel between reservations and cities. As Jim Clermont of the Porcupine Singers remembered, this new mobility allowed Indian people in the 1950s and 1960s to travel between reservations. The Pine Ridge-based singing group traveled to reservations throughout the United States and Canada, popularizing their drumming and singing style, which had earlier been restricted to the districts of the reservation.[15]

The dissemination of Plains Indian dance songs through the travels of groups like the Porcupine Singers changed local styles. A new style of singing and songwriting that used identifiable words to make songs easier to learn became popular at powwows. Amplifiers allow audiences to hear small sounds, replacing the longstanding necessity for singers to be loud and clear and powwow grounds to be small and quiet. George P. Horse Capture writes: "Unlike the Sioux songs of long ago whose words told a story of honor or bravery, today's songs in this category tell no logical story, but like the Beach Boys, urge one to 'dance, dance, dance.' "[16] Songs became quicker and more dance-oriented in the cities, and powwows became a form of weekend entertainment and sociality that Indian people used to ground themselves in the new environment. These invented social forms were facilitated by the very nontraditional context of automobile travel and popular music.

Powwows migrated with Indian people to cities, becoming there an important center of pan-Indian political and cultural revival. As with drumming, this revival also changed the culture of the powwow. A "powwow circuit" that links Indian people in southern New Mexico with those in eastern Canada has allowed new forms to permeate Indian country. As drum lyrics have become more dance-oriented, dances have become faster and flashier. Traditional grass dancing, which moved from Oklahoma to the northern plains with the last great diffusion of pan-Indian culture in the late nineteenth century, was revived and reinvented in the 1940s to include faster, more athletic moves and brighter costumes whose grassy fringes are often made from a psychedelic array of bright yarns.[17] At large powwows in the 1970s, the pace of Grass Dancing, Fancy Dancing, and Fancy Shawl dancing picked up, as drums became ever faster.[18] These changes paralleled the exposure of Indian transmigrants to urban mass culture, which, at least in dominant white society, segments leisure consumers by generation and gender. But, as powwows grew to incorporate flashier costumes, more athletic dances, and faster drum beats, they remained essentially intergenerational spaces, alternatives to the divided peer culture of dominant social life.

By definition, the building of institutions is an intergenerational process. Survival schools and OICs set out to train young people in maintaining their sense of identity as Indians and in successfully negotiating the social and economic hierarchies of the dominant culture. Other Indian agencies, like Indian Family Services and the American Indian Center, facilitate ties between generations by providing spaces and activities where young people can benefit from the knowledge of their parents' and grandparents' generations. In a culture where mention of "elders" is charged with tradition and respect, this intergenerational aspect of urban institutions is extremely self-conscious. At the same time, however, some aspects of contemporary urban Indian culture challenge static definitions of tradition, replacing them with new forms and celebrations that are understood differently in different parts of the community.

A central innovation in powwow culture in the late 1960s was the contest powwow, which offered cash prizes to top dancers and drum groups.[19] The distinction between these contest and "traditional" powwows, which offer small gifts to all participants, is the single most controversial issue among the people I spoke to. Particularly the people currently in their thirties and forties—the "skip generation" who remember the struggle to organize Indian institutions along with pieces of the stories and languages of their grandparents—often worry about the effects of cash in the contemporary powwow circuit. Often, their urban children take the size and flash of contest powwows for granted. These two visions, while not always divided strictly along generational lines, point to tensions in contemporary Indian culture about how the past is remembered and what kinds of bargains are to be struck between traditional practices and the capitalistic values of the dominant culture.

The contrast between traditional and contest powwows involves the story of Indian revival in the cities. Though they are sometimes staged in urban arenas, traditional powwows more often take place during the summer on reservations. They now tend to be smaller, the costumes are less elaborate, fewer drum groups are invited, and fewer categories of dance events are included. Contest powwows are held in the winter at Indian centers and schools as well as in the huge rented spaces of civic arenas. In the summers, bands with casinos sponsor lucrative contest powwows, as do some reservations. In large part, contest powwows are a product of the success of Indian people in generating and maintaining their own institutions. At the same time that a revived powwow circuit links urban and rural Indians to a constantly maintained and re-created past, contest powwows offer a new means of facilitating participation, extending the ability of Indian people to travel, and furthering the development of contemporary pan-Indian culture.

Many of the adults I spoke with were ambivalent about the effects of the contest powwow on Indian traditions and values. They supported the idea of these powwows because of their ability to attract participants and revenue, but many questioned this expansion of commercialism into native culture. Many felt that contest powwows were suspect, that the intersection of commercialism and culture somehow impacted negatively on culture. Quite a few said that they attend contest powwows but dance only in traditional powwows. Many adults expressed their ambivalence about contest powwows by showing concern for what their children would learn there. Dorene Day explained it in terms of her respect for traditional forms and showed concern about what cash and competition does to native values:

> On one hand, we should realize the things that are valuable and meaningful to us to better our conditions. In other words, if the Heart of the Earth School has a contest powwow to increase the funding so that they can provide quality and culturally appropriate education for Indian children, then that's a good thing. But, on the other hand, in a general view, that is the powwow with the monetary value placed into it, that is really not our value.

On the other hand, Johnny Smith, who has been teaching Indian music and dance since the 1960s, saw no conflict between traditional values and contest powwows. Acknowledging that contest powwows are a fairly recent innovation, he said that they are consistent with traditional Indian games and competitions. A teacher of urban Indian youth, Smith sees tradition as continuous, in whatever ways it is currently expressed. He dismissed the concerns of his contemporaries as overly finicky, not committed enough to the reality of traditional practices:

> People who are always looking down at powwows are not the powwow people, otherwise, why are they putting down what belongs to them? . . . Where were these people at when our culture almost died out? . . . Besides, the people who can't dance at contest powwows are the ones who can't take the competition.[20]

Smith's view allows for ongoing transformations in form and practice. In this view, it is what Indian people *do* in struggling to maintain a dynamic culture that is traditional. Because contest powwows are vital at the current time to Indian culture, they become "tradition," in Hobsbawm's sense. This vitality, Smith argued, speaks for itself; contest powwows attract the most vibrant costumes, the best dancers, the drum group with the best sound. On this point, Day concurred:

> Well, the contest ones are glitzier, they're more exciting. You know, they're probably more famous drums that will come. . . . For example, my son is a singer, so if he idolizes Stony Park or Black Lodge, and Black Lodge will be there, yeah, he should have the opportunity to hear, and physically go up to that drum and hear that drum sing, and that's gonna be good for him, if those are his idols, you know.

The star-system aspect facilitated by contest powwows keeps Day's son interested, helping him to progress as a musician and a powwow participant. In other words, they speak to him through the valences not necessarily of contemporary native culture alone, but of a contemporary native *youth* culture that combines elements of mass culture, an urban youth culture that has aspects of a contemporary, reinvented, pan-Indian tradition.

This kind of mass culture appeal is, on one level, distinct from and threatening to the grassroots powwow form. The mass culture industry can eviscerate the communal appeal of popular forms, or evacuate them of native peoples, as the history of western rodeos clearly shows.[21] Mass culture can replace the transmission of alternative values that take place at powwows, threatening to substitute community with commerce, participation with representation. But powwow culture has long been entangled with colonial power and commercial capital. Exactly how distinct are categories of tradition and invention, folk and mass here?

The fluidity and dynamism among these categories are, in part, what has allowed Indian culture to survive five hundred years of genocidal warfare, so that it exists to be revived in postwar U.S. cities. Concerns about the effects of contest powwows on contemporary Indian life, however, are also important. Preserving a culture means always having an acute sense of what is being lost and created: what can be salvaged, whether meaning inheres in form, or whether meaning continues to speak through the voices of invented traditions. And questions of forms and practices, traditions and inventions are political questions. They ask how people will learn to be Indians; who will have the power to teach them these skills; how they will resist the considerable pressures to cave in to assimilation; and how they will combat the force of the widespread racism that would silence them.

"Powwow Bums!": Generation and Tradition

In part, contest powwows grow out of the tradition of giving food and money to participants in powwows, particularly those who had traveled some distance to attend. Contest powwows also evolved as fund-raisers for institutions like survival schools. But the prizes of contest powwows now facilitate another development in powwow culture: economic autonomy for the participants. Norene Smith, whose agency sponsors contest powwows, was ambivalent about the idea of a group of people who are able to make enough money through the powwow circuit. "That's all they do," she commented, looking at the record of prize-winning drummers and dancers, "is go to powwows." She expressed deep ambivalence about letting her daughter, who was just finishing college, go on the powwow circuit and become a "powwow bum" for a summer. For her, the middle-class status she has struggled to achieve in her life, and which she wants to pass on to her children, was threatened by the values of the powwow circuit. "I'm a real workaholic, so it's real hard for me to think somebody just wants to go do that."[22]

Smith's concern about contest powwows combines a definition of Indian traditions as outside a cash-oriented economy with a focus on the class mobility that she has achieved through hard work and discipline. Contest powwows, for her, provide a distraction from the focus that her daughters and other Indian youth need to succeed in a competitive economy that places them, as people of color, at the bottom. Traditions, in this view, are part of a past that should be preserved by hard-working urban citizens as they struggle for upward mobility. It was easier for this particular woman to show me carefully beaded leggings and dresses made by her daughters, than it was for her to think of them as "powwow bums," even for one summer.

Julie Bealieu, a neighborhood activist deeply opposed to contest powwows, worried about the ways that Indian youth are exploited by cultural exhibitions that pay them to demonstrate their drum and dance skills to non-Indian audiences. Contest powwows and paid exhibitions, to her, are a long way from the communal solidarity and exchange offered by powwows. Both Bealieu and Day spoke of their own experiences at contest powwows in terms of losing themselves and their spirituality in their concern for winning and performing well. Both were able to "make that transition back through myself",[23] to separate their Indian values from feelings of competition and nervousness, but both worried that the engagement with contests threatened the power of tradition in the lives of young Indians. For these women, contest powwows challenge the Indian values that have allowed them to become powerful community figures. While they are not preoccupied with upward mobility in the same sense that Smith is, their concerns about tradition focus on the use of values to negotiate the complex work of urban Indian life.

How do young Indian dancers and drummers deal with the dual pressures of competition and tradition present at contest powwows and commercial exhibitions? For one thing, many of the younger generation of Indian people I spoke with had a different view of Indian institutions than the generation that so clearly remembers the rapid change and struggle associated with urbanization. For them, survival schools are an option that removes them from racist teachers and name-calling white peers; cultural programs at school help them travel to powwows and maintain drum and dance skills that most of them remembered learning as soon as they could walk; and the cash prizes of contest powwows and cultural exhibitions facilitate, rather than inhibit, their participation in a vast and exciting powwow circuit. This generation of urban Indians, like their inner-city contemporaries across the nation, confronts a city profoundly stratified by race and class. Their negotiations with this landscape utilize and reinvent the traditions and institutions that have been passed down to them through the active struggles of their elders.

For the Boyz drum group, the realities of drugs and violence that surround them are much more of a problem than the commercialization of contest powwows. The cash prizes available to them through the contest powwow circuit supplement the money they get through part-time jobs and from Indian institutions that facilitate their continual travel and performance. For the ten- to twenty-year-old members of the Boyz, being "powwow bums" constitutes a choice to work hard at the drum, to perform at powwows, and to follow a "Red Road" of sobriety and respect for tradition.

> Either you choose the drum, and you choose to follow that route, to be straight and sober and be respectful, or, we figure, you choose the other road, and you choose to do whatever you want. Don't gotta answer to nobody, don't have to answer to the drum, you don't have to think about, "Well, if I use [drugs], what are the people on the drum gonna think," because they aren't gonna be there. So it really is a big decision, almost a life decision, it is a life decision.[24]

The members of the Boyz expressed a lifetime commitment to their decisions about the drum. The two oldest members, at ages eighteen and twenty, saw their relationship to the drum surviving, and sometimes superseding, the demands of marriage and family, work and school. Whereas Beaulieu was ambivalent about Indian cultural exhibitions, the Boyz see their participation in the Mystic Lake Dance Troop as a chance to travel and to maintain their connection to one another, to the drum, and to a life of traveling and performing on the powwow circuit.

Both young men and young women can be called "powwow bums." While I do not have statistics to show how many of them actually support themselves from summers on the powwow circuit, almost everyone I spoke with under the age of twenty-five talked with admiration about legendary drum groups and dancers who were able to travel endlessly on their winnings. These heroes were much more likely to be men, but young women also spoke to me about the pleasures of the powwow circuit, including far-flung circles of friends, and "snagging" or "cruising" those of the opposite sex.

The translations made between generations are sometimes mutually unrecognizable. Though the adults concerned about commodification and appropriation clearly remembered the struggle for Indian institutions in Minneapolis, the younger generation had a much less clear vision of their recent history, one that does not correlate with the careful accounts of their elders. Most of the younger people I spoke with identified the importance of drumming and dancing in their lives and the role of these forms in the life of contemporary Indian nations. They expressed a passionate commitment and connection to their culture and a deep appreciation of the institutions, such as survival schools, that facilitated their strong identity as Indian people. But few knew the derivation of these forms or clearly understood the history of institutions such as survival schools and Indian centers. When I asked the younger dancers, powwow royalty, and drum group members about the history of powwows in Minneapolis, they were vague. A group of girls at Heart of the Earth School thought that the jingle dress, a nineteenth-century Ojibwa invention, was probably invented before white people came to the Americas; a powwow princess at South High School could only identify powwows as "very old"; some drum group members knew that veterans' songs went back even before their fathers' generation, but could not say more than that about the songs' history.

Countering, in some ways, the very legitimate concerns of adult Indians about the younger generations, Angela McRobbie wrote: "Youth cultures, in whatever shape they take, represent to me a staking out of an investment in society. It is in this sense that they are political."[25] What young urban Indians stake out is a place for themselves to be Indian, to claim an identity. In the baggy pants of b-boy and b-girl chic, Indian teenagers ally themselves with an urban youth culture that is crucially in dialogue with the commodification and exploitation confronted by young people of color. They cut their straight hair into the high-top fades popularized by African American youth, wear the below-hip baggy pants and team jackets of urban notoriety, and they have insisted in all of my interviews that they listen to homemade tapes of famous drum groups and store-bought tapes of rap with equal enthusiasm. At a time when their elders in the American Indian Movement are organizing against the use of Indian mascots and team names, young Indian men often sport Redskins football jackets with defiant flair at powwows, and sometimes also at political rallies held to protest the appropriation of native culture and naming practices. Young Indians, then, inherit a hybrid social context of tradition and invention, the moving engine of urban cultural crossover. Their use of these forms is both conscious and dynamic.

Their practices are made possible by the creation of Indian institutions, but at the same time, they are not always in harmony with what their elders imagined for them. While they do not always know dates and time lines, young Indians identify the significance of the cultural forms they do practice. Young girls who can't explain a linear history of dance know the story of the jingle dress, its healing power, and feel the difference between the jingle dress and the comparatively newer fancy dance. The same young woman who had trouble placing the dance forms in time spoke about the significance of different kinds of dances: "Jingle, it's not as free as you are when you're a fancy dancer. Jingle . . . it's kind of like a spiritual dance, but not really. Jingle, you have to do certain things, we have to be really light on our feet. And when you hit the floor, you have to be slow, not stomping on the ground."[26]

Contest powwows facilitate some of the connections made by this generation of Indians between their experiences as urban minority youth and their bond to a native past they recognize as both ancient and sustaining. The Mdewakanton Dakota anniversary powwow featured performances both by Dixie Harris, a Native country singer, and Litefoot, an Indian rap artist from Oklahoma. After a long day of contest and intertribal dancing, of "specials" and drumming, the affluent Mdewakanton band provided entertainment for its guests. Dixie Harris entertained a generation whose musical tastes were nurtured in rural Midwestern contexts, and Litefoot performed the next night for young Indians whose daily experiences as urban youth familiarize them with hip-hop styles and whose historical heritage prepares them to hear him "teach" them about their history:

> It's been years since we walked
> the trail of tears
> But you still instill fear for speakin'
> about what happened here.[27]

Combining traditional forms like the powwow with non-Indian popular styles is not new. The adult generation's current preference for country music was different from that of *their* parents, who often danced waltzes and fox trots along with grass and traditional dances at small reservation powwows during the 1930s. And it was this older generation, which learned to manage the fancy footwork of popular dance, who conveyed so many fractured memories of language and tradition to their children and grandchildren, making contemporary Indian revival possible.

The political act of creating, struggling for, and maintaining an Indian culture does not look the same from generation to generation. The experiences of young people, and particularly of young people of color, often do not reduce along the lines of the ideologies held by their elders or by chronicles like this one. What people with one experience of fighting for economic and cultural survival sees as threatening, another generation embraces. Not all practices are equal, and no individual is exempted from the intersections of pleasure and danger so deeply inscribed in the history of popular culture. But invented traditions establish their links to the past through practice and memory. Contemporary contest powwows, with their large winnings and their ability to draw people from around the country to dance, drum, and socialize, are a part of this ongoing invention of Indian tradition.

Conclusion: Colonial Optics, Postcolonial Options

The Indian princess is a cultural myth that emanates from the myopia of cultural contact and the myriad oppressions of colonial control. The princess comes from nowhere in precontact history, yet becomes a standard feature at the powwow, a hybrid postcolonial performance. Winning a princess title represents fluency with various conceptions of tradition, as discussed above. It can also represent popularity for young women who are crucially involved in the economies of sexuality and dating. Some of the princesses I talked with emphasized this aspect of holding a title; they explained that other girls were jealous of them, while boys tended to be more solicitous. Some young women I talked with at powwows did not hold titles but wished that they did. And, when their daughters cried over a lost title or crowed over a new one, some mothers questioned the similarity of princess pageants and beauty contests, wondering what exactly this particular invention of "tradition" was preserving.

In her analysis of girls' magazines and dance culture, McRobbie has suggested that contemporary femininity is fluid, that young women may assert power through practices that look to their feminist elders in order to be dangerously engaged with patriarchy and cultural commodification.[28] Young Indian women confront a dangerous field of race and gender hierarchies; on one level, the princess as a myth looks like an engagement with the mythologies that have sponsored generations of degradation of native women.

As Tricia Rose insists, however, it is also crucial that young women, particularly young women of color, stake out a place in public to speak and be heard.[29] After the photo opportunity passed, Coffey and Alley, the Comanche Tribal Princess and the Junior Miss Shawnee Nation, finished talking to me. Coffey wants to attend law school; she sees her experience as a princess, in addition to getting her dates and travel opportunities and attention, as a prelude to a career of defending the rights of her people:

> I think that being a princess allows you to see all different sorts of people and meet different people and the way things are. Being a lawyer is kind of out of the rank of being a princess, but still it is very helpful in that area. You talk in public, meet Indian people, get to see what kind of people I like, you get to hear about different tribes and their problems.
>
> Now with water rights, tribal sovereignty, and our own religious freedom. They take it away from us. And I'm not gonna allow that to happen for my children. And I have

the right to do it, and my children have the rights to do it, and same with my grandchildren. (1994)

The position of Indian princess, reinvented in the contemporary powwow circuit, here allows a young Indian woman to speak in a voice that simultaneously claims tradition and insists on the struggle for justice. Coffey speaks in a voice that is at once feminine—claiming the rights for her children and grandchildren—and feminist, aspiring to work as a lawyer for her people. The position she outlines straddles claims of tradition and the exigencies of the present, using the culture that Indian people have brought together in this most recent revival to protect the self-determination of future generations.

NOTES

1. William Powers, *War Dance: Plains Indian Musician Performance* (Tucson: University of Arizona Press, 1990), 59.
2. Coffey and Alley, interview, Hinckley, Minnesota, July 1994.
3. Rayna Green, "The Tribe Called Wannabee: Playing Indian in America and Europe," *Folklore* 99, no. 1 (1988): 30–55.
4. The phrase *colonial optics* in the subhead is taken from the writings of Ranajit Guha, whose excellent analysis of the semiotics of colonialism sets the tone for much of my thinking here. See "The Prose of Counter-Insurgency," in Ranajit Guha and Gayatri Chakravorty Spivak, eds., *Selected Subaltern Studies* (Oxford: Oxford University Press, 1988).
5. Gina Artishon, Carol's Diner, Minneapolis, July 1994.
6. Linda Basch, Nina Glick Schiller, and Cristina Szanton Blanc, *Nations Unbound: Transnational Projects, Postcolonial Predicaments, and Deterritorialized Nation States* (Amsterdam: Gordon and Breach, 1994), 22.
7. Eric Hobsbawm, *The Invention of Tradition* (Cambridge, U.K.: Cambridge University Press, 1983).
8. Ron Libertus, interview, University of Minnesota, October 1994.
9. Dorene Day, interview, Indian Family Services, Minneapolis, January 20, 1994.
10. George Lipsitz, *Dangerous Crossroads: Popular Music, Postmodernism and the Poetics of Place* (New York: Verso, 1994), 19.
11. Homi Bhaba, *The Location of Culture* (London: Routledge, 1994), 91.
12. Paul Gilroy, *The Black Atlantic: Modernity and Double Consciousness* (Cambridge, Mass.: Harvard University Press, 1993), 85.
13. Riv Ellen Prell, "Rage and Representation: Jewish Gender Stereotypes in American Culture," in Faye Ginsburg and Anna Tsing, eds., *Uncertain Terms: Negotiating Gender in American Culture* (Boston: Beacon, 1990).
14. Melinda Hanell, Mdewakanton Dakota Powwow Grounds, Shakopee, Minnesota, August 1994.
15. Jim Clermont, American Indian Center, Minneapolis, June 1994.
16. George P. Horse Capture, *Powwow* (Cody, Wyo.: Buffalo Bill Historical Center, 1989), 10.
17. Ibid., 36.
18. Libertus, 1994.

19. The Indian Health Board sponsored a contest powwow in 1992. Cash prizes were as follows:

Drum Contest: 1st—$1,000; 2d—$800; 3d—$600; 4th—$400; 5th—$300. *Adult (18–44) Dance Events* (10 events: Men's Senior Traditional, Men's Traditional, Ladies' Senior Traditional, Ladies' Traditional, Jingle Dress, Ladies' Buckskin, Ladies' Cloth, Men's Grass Dance, Men's Fancy Dance, Men's Straight/Southern): 1st—$700; 2d—$600; 3d—$500; 4th—$400; 5th—$300; 6th—$200). Junior Categories (11–17): 1st—$300. (Source: Indian Health Board Powwow Notebook, Courtesy of Norene Smith, Director, Indian Health Board.)

20. Bob Larson, Ft. Snelling State Park, September 5, 1994.

21. Marilyn Burgess, "Canadian 'Range Wars': Struggles over Indian Cowboys," *Canadian Journal of Communications* 18. (1993): 351–64.

22. Norene Smith, Indian Health Board, Minneapolis, November 1994.

23. Day, 1994.

24. Opie Day and Hokie Clermont, the Boyz Drum Group, Red School House, St. Paul, Minnesota, June 1994.

25. Angela McRobbie, "Shut Up and Dance: Youth Culture and Changing Modes of Femininity," *Cultural Studies* 7:3 (October 1993): 407.

26. Debbie Ironshield, Heart of the Earth School, Minneapolis, April 1994.

27. Litefoot, "Seein' Red," in *Seein' Red* (Red Vinyl Records, Tulsa, 1994).

28. McRobbie, "Shut Up and Dance," 409.

29. Tricia Rose, *Black Noise: Rap Music and Black Culture in Contemporary America* (Middletown, Conn.: Wesleyan University Press, 1994), 163.

Chapter Twenty-four

The Hip Hop Hearings

Censorship, Social Memory, and Intergenerational Tensions among African Americans

George Lipsitz

In 1994, Representative Cardiss Collins of Illinois, a member of the Congressional Black Caucus, presided over hearings on the detrimental effects of "gangsta rap" on the Black community. Called in response to a request by C. Delores Tucker of the National Political Congress of Black Women, the hearings revealed deep divisions among Blacks, not only about the lyrics of gangsta rap songs, but also about the general conditions confronting African Americans. Although the sponsors of the hearings, key witnesses, and committee members all insisted that their efforts were directed against youth music rather than against the youths themselves, the hearings and the circumstances that brought them into being in the first place offer clear evidence of a deep chasm across generational lines.

Many witnesses at these hearings blamed gangsta rap lyrics for encouraging disrespect for women and for glorifying crime, while the music's defenders stressed the importance of gangsta rap as a register of the social disintegration that inner-city youth see all around them. Largely absent from this debate was an appreciation of how these debates worked to detach gangsta rap from the context that gave birth to it—i.e., how arguments over song lyrics obscure the ways in which deindustrialization, economic restructuring, and neoconservative politics have driven a wedge between generations, not just among African Americans, but among youth and their elders in other ethnic groups as well. Seemingly a debate about censorship and crime, these arguments about gangsta rap actually advanced the agenda of the enemies of the Black community by assisting in the suppression of social memory, by attacking the most public and visible record of the devastation enacted upon young people over the past two decades by neoconservative economics and politics, deindustrialization, and economic restructuring.

It is my contention that efforts to censor gangsta rap stem less from actual outrage about the lyrics of rap songs than from the ways in which gangsta rap emerges in the neoconservative cosmology as the only plausible explanation for the ruptures between genders and generations that are, in fact, the consequence of neoconservatism, deindustrialization, and economic restructuring. The pain caused by these divisions is real, but efforts to silence their expression in commercial culture cannot heal the wounds they open up. Indeed, censorship serves largely to obscure the social causes and consequences of historical change, rendering as individual and personal experiences that have broad-based collective origins and effects.

Invited to present her views as the first witness at the hearings, C. DeLores Tucker invoked the moral authority of Martin Luther King, Jr., on behalf of her cause, alleging that if he were alive today, the civil rights leader "would be marching and demonstrating against the glamorization of violence and its corrupting influence, which has now become a part of our culture in the name of freedom. This freedom, freedom from responsibility and accountability, is not the kind of freedom that Dr. King, Medgar Evers, John Lewis, James Farmer, Rosa Parks and so many others risked their lives for."[1] Tucker claimed that for four hundred years African Americans had maintained a sense of humanity and morality that enabled them to survive the middle passage and slavery, but that "today, however, our morality, which has been the last vestige of our strength, is being threatened" by "lyrics out of the mouths of our own children."[2] Describing gangsta rap as "pornographic smut," Tucker alleged that this music provoked "our youth" to violence, drug use, and mistreatment of women. "This explains why so many of our children are out of control and why we have more black males in jail than we have in college," she charged.[3]

In his testimony at the hip hop hearings, syndicated talk show host Joseph Madison also invoked the legacy of the civil rights movement ("I was twenty-three years old when I became the executive director of the Detroit NAACP") as a justification for his attack on gangsta rap as the cause of intergenerational antagonisms within Black communities. "When radio stations bombard the airwaves with these messages of hate, killing, and self-destruction, it will cause a conflict even within those families that may have taught other values," he claimed. Citing the case of his own fourteen-year-old son, Madison told the committee that images of thugs and criminals projected by gangsta rap turned his son from a young man who had been on the school honor roll and a star athlete into someone who began dressing like gangsta rappers and who told his father in one conversation that time in jail would be preferable to life in his middle-class home.[4]

Madison took pains to say that "this is not a confrontation with young people," but then his subsequent testimony took up that very theme. After detailing how he had "educated" his son that "the pants had to come off the hip and the shoe strings had to go back in, and the language had to be cleaned up and the fascination with guns had to end," he referred derisively to young rappers for saying that "the older generation, the black leaders have done absolutely nothing. The black politicians have done nothing for this generation." Madison answered that charge by taking it personally, asserting:

> Well, we obviously have more opportunities than we had 30, 40, 50 years ago and it was because many of us sitting here today sacrificed and gave our lives to see to it that this young generation has at least the opportunity to do what they need to do. Have we completed it all? No. And there is a lot of work to do, but this is not because we do not love our young people. It is just the opposite.[5]

Although often completely unaware of even the most elementary facts about the lyrics, artists, and music they condemned, Tucker, Madison, and other witnesses at the hearings were not incorrect in their perception of a generation gap among African Americans, nor were they completely off-base in detecting a certain contempt and resentment among young Blacks for the civil rights movement and its record. Young people interviewed by a reporter for the *Pittsburgh Courier* about holiday celebrations commemorating Dr. King's birthday in 1996 expressed this disdain clearly. "Ours is not the same kind of struggle," one explained. "We really don't know what it was like back then. All we know now is that the only thing that counts in this world is money, power, and material wealth." Another opined: "Dr. King believed in righteousness, but that's not something you can take to the bank or to the grocery store. To survive in this society today, you've got to be the firstest with the mostest."[6] These young people clearly do not know enough about the civil rights movement, about Dr. King's Poor People's March, about his support for striking sanitation workers in Memphis at the moment when he was assassinated, or about the broad-based struggle for jobs, education, and housing that accompanied efforts to secure access to public accommodations. On the other hand, Tucker, Madison, and contemporary critics of African American youth do not know enough about the circumstances facing young people today, about the ways in which every significant institution in our society makes it clear to them that they do not count, that their parents are losers, and that their communities are places where no one would live if they were not forced to do so. Each side in this argument blames the other for problems both have in common because of deindustrialization, economic restructuring, and neoconservative politics. Gangsta rap does not cause this division, although it is an interesting and important symptom of it, but the campaign to censor and suppress gangsta rap is, nonetheless, enormously important because it serves as a prototypical example of the ways in which conservative cultural and political mobilizations operate to obscure public understanding of who has power in our society and what they have done with that power for the last twenty years.

During the 1980s, the number of children living in poverty increased by 2.2 million. Among European Americans, child poverty rose from 11.8 percent in 1979 to 14.8 percent in 1989; for Latinos, child poverty went from 28 percent to 32 percent; and the percentage of African American children who were poor increased from 41.2 percent to 43.7 percent. Most experts predict that the 1996 "welfare reform" laws enacted by Congress alone will drive a million more children into the ranks of the poor by 1998. Neoconservative commentators blame these increases in poverty on the mental deficiencies of minorities (see Charles Murray and Richard Hernstein, *The Bell Curve*) or on their cultural deficiencies (see Dinesh D'Souza, *The End of Racism*); but, in fact, the fastest-growing segments of the poverty population have been young white families with children, families headed by married couples, and families headed by high school graduates.[7]

The effects of deindustrialization have been particularly devastating to entry-level workers beginning their careers. In 1979, 23 percent of male workers between the ages of eighteen and twenty-four received wages below the poverty line, but by 1990, that number had risen to 43 percent. Only 6 percent of full-time workers between the ages of twenty-five and thirty-four received poverty-level wages in 1979, but 15 percent did so by 1990. The impact of these changes fell most harshly on communities of color: between 1965 and 1990, Black family income fell by 50 percent, while Black youth unemployment quadrupled.[8] While most devastating to communities of color and to those with little education, deindustrialization, economic restructuring, and neoconservative economics and politics have also hurt the life chances and opportunities of college graduates. By 1993, the real wages received by college graduates lagged 7.5 percent behind those received by similarly educated workers in 1973, and a Department of Labor Study predicted that close to 30 percent of college graduates between 1992 and 2005 would be unemployed or underemployed for significant periods of time.[9]

Under these circumstances, one could well understand congressional committees and mass media outlets engaged in anxious debates about infant mortality, child nutrition and health care, or youth education and employment. These discussions do take place, but they attract less attention and play smaller roles in academic and public policy debates than do cultural controversies about mass media images and their imputed influences and effects. The reasons for this imbalance are multiple and complex, but one aspect of the problem stems from the strategic utility of questions about censoring commercial culture in suppressing social memory and silencing social theory at the grass roots. The controversy over gangsta rap is only the latest in a long line of historical moral panics about mass media and social relations that have almost always stemmed from the same sources and produced the same results.

During the Great Depression of the 1930s, for example, motion picture censors took aim at gangster films because they made crime seem like a logical response to social conditions rather than a matter of personal morality. As Jonathan Munby has shown in his pathbreaking research, sound films enabled Edward G. Robinson and James Cagney to bring the actual speech of an ethnic urban underclass before a broad audience, and their tremendous popularity (many theaters had Robinson and Cagney "imitation" shows before screenings) disclosed a broad desire to register the suffering and express the resentments of those who suffered most from the Depression.[10]

Gangster films defamed Italian, Irish, and other ethnic Americans by reinforcing the association between ethnic identity and urban crime that had been disseminated by nativists and eugenicists as a reason to curtail immigration during the 1920s. These views were implicitly conservative because by grounding the plight of the lower classes in their biological makeup, they portrayed efforts at social reform as futile. Yet many viewers of these films drew directly opposite conclusions, identifying with the "gangsters" as symbols of their own desire for upward mobility, as emblems of suppressed ethnic and class anger, and as icons who escaped the humiliating stigma of ethnic and class subordination through daring action and stylish consumption.[11] Aware of the oppositional potential of such narratives, some representatives of Catholic groups participated in censorship efforts enthusiastically, because they viewed the "glorification" of the gangster as ammunition for their enemies. Consequently, the understandable desire to disrupt the link that connected ethnic identity to criminal behavior also served to mute collective memories and to suppress social analyses about the conditions that immigrant and ethnic communities confronted. Disconnected from social causality, the gangster became an individual aberration whose "deviance" could be addressed only by repressive state power or by individual psychological treatment rather than meliorative social reform.

Similarly, during the post-World War II period, the House Un-American Activities Committee held repeated hearings into alleged Communist subversion in Hollywood. Committee counsel repeatedly asked actors of Jewish ancestry to disclose their original names—as if Emmanuel Goldenberg became Edward G. Robinson or Morris Carnovsky became Chester Morris because of a secret Communist plot, rather than in response to American anti-Semitism. Witnesses were asked to spell out their non-Anglo Saxon names, even though the Committee knew perfectly well how they were spelled, because emphasizing the foreign and often Jewish origins of the witnesses enabled the Committee to create the impression that challenges to capitalism could not originate in America. As part of a larger conservative ideological assault, HUAC wanted to brand the New Deal itself as subversive, to portray its thought and culture as foreign to America, to transform anti-fascism into pro-communism. The premise that only something outside of the United States could account for anti-capitalist attitudes led an otherwise largely cooperative and compliant Clifford Odets to protest to the Committee that he had not been radicalized by anything said to him by members of the Communist Party, but because his mother "worked in a stocking factory in Philadelphia at the age of eleven and died a broken woman... at the age of forty-eight."[12] Odets's efforts to bring historical memory and social analysis back into the discussion proved futile. The success of HUAC came not from any discoveries about Communist influence in Hollywood, but rather from the articulation and dissemination of the idea that analyses of unequal and unjust social relations in the United States stemmed from the malicious actions of unruly individuals rather than from honest observation of social conditions.

Attempts to silence, regulate, and even criminalize rap music in the United States in recent years have followed this same trajectory. They emerge clearly in the context of what Leola Johnson calls "one of the most sustained censorship drives in United States history."[13] By examining the origins and evolution of these censorship efforts, we can see the influence of the neoconservative agenda in the hip hop hearings and analyze the ways in which they evaded the connection between gangsta rap and social conditions.

In 1989, the assistant director of the Federal Bureau of Investigation, Milt Ahlerich, sent a letter to Priority Records in Los Angeles to complain about "a song," which he did not name but was obviously "Fuck the Police," on the label's album *Straight Outta Compton*, by the group NWA. Hiding behind the passive voice to disguise agency, Ahlerich explained that this song "has been brought to my attention," and that he was writing "to share my thoughts and concerns with you," although later in the letter he claimed more strongly that he was expressing "the FBI's position relative to this song and its message." Complaining that the song expressed "violence and disrespect for the law enforcement officer," the letter went on to state that "we in the law enforcement community take exception to such action."[14] Ahlerich later admitted to reporters that the FBI had never before taken an official position on any piece of music, literature, or art, that nobody in the Bureau had actually purchased *Straight Outta Compton*, and that he could not explain how the song came to his attention except by citing "responsible fellow officers" whom he did not name.[15]

Directly or indirectly, the Bureau's letter about "Fuck the Police" encouraged police officers around the country to set up an informal fax network designed to prevent public appearances by NWA. Police officers withheld concert security services from the group, making it impossible for promoters to secure insurance for NWA appearances.[16] Police harassment jeopardized or canceled the group's shows in Washington, D.C., Chattanooga, Milwaukee, and Tyler, Texas. They played in Cincinnati only because members of the Cincinnati Bengals professional football team (including City Council member Reggie Williams) spoke up for them. When members of the group sang a few lines from "Fuck the Police" in Detroit, officers rushed the stage, fought with arena security staff, and followed N.W.A. to their hotel, where they detained the group for fifteen minutes. "We just wanted to show the kids," one officer explained to a reporter, "that you can't say 'fuck the police' in Detroit."[17]

The next year, the crusade against hip hop emerged within local politics in Florida, when a federal district court judge in Fort Lauderdale agreed with the complaint of conservative activist Jack Thompson and declared the rap album *As Nasty as They Wanna Be* by 2 Live Crew to be obscene. Two years earlier, Thompson had been a candidate for the position of prosecuting attorney in Dade County, Florida, on the Republican Party ticket against the incumbent, Janet Reno. At one campaign appearance, Thompson handed Reno a prepared statement and asked her check the appropriate box. The statement read, "I, Janet Reno, am a ____ homosexual, ____ bisexual, ____ heterosexual." It continued, "If you do not respond . . . then you will be deemed to have checked one of the first two boxes." Luther Campbell, known as Luke Skywalker, the leader of 2 Live Crew, had supported Reno and conducted voter registration drives in her behalf during that race.[18] Six weeks after the election, Thompson wrote letters to Reno and to Florida governor Bob Martinez demanding an investigation of 2 Live Crew for possible violation of state obscenity statutes and racketeering codes because of *As Nasty as They Wanna Be.*[19]

Two days after the federal court ruled that *As Nasty as They Wanna Be* was obscene, a Broward County sheriff arrested Charles Freeman, a twenty-eight-year-old Black man and owner of a music store for selling a record and tape version of the album to an adult undercover deputy. Officers put Freeman in handcuffs and took him to the police station; he was later convicted of a first-degree misdemeanor. Sheriff's deputies also arrested two members of 2 Live Crew later that week for singing lyrics from the album to an adults-only concert.[20] An Appeals Court later overturned the District Court's ruling and declared that *As Nasty as They Wanna Be* was not obscene, but Thompson's efforts did persuade the Musicland stores with 752 outlets and the Trans World Stores with 450 branches to drop 2 Live Crew's album from their inventories.[21] At the same time, United States Marine Corps officials announced that base stores in Yuma, Arizona; Beaufort, South Carolina; Jacksonville, North Carolina; and Oceanside, California, had removed the group's album from their shelves.[22]

The videotaped beating of Rodney King by members of the Los Angeles Police Department in March 1991, and the mass violence directed against persons and property when the Simi Valley jury found the officers accused of the beating "not guilty" on April 29, 1992, set the stage for the next wave of attacks against rap music. For many rap artists, fans, and critics, the Los Angeles Rebellion demonstrated the broad community consensus behind the claims of police misconduct and the desire for justice expressed in NWA's "Fuck the Police" and many other rap songs, validating the claim made by Ice Cube when he was still with NWA that rappers were "underground street reporters."[23] But others saw the riots as a partial consequence of the views and attitudes popularized by rap music. In May 1992, then presidential candidate Bill Clinton scolded rap artist Sister Souljah for commenting that she understood the "logic" behind attacks on whites during the rebellion, especially from Black people who had had no compunction about attacking other Black people before the riots. Less than a month later, a group calling itself the Combined Law Enforcement Association of Texas (CLEAT) denounced the song "Cop Killer," released several weeks before the riots on Ice-T's successful album with his speed metal band, *Body Count*. Even though "Cop Killer" is not a rap song, Ice-T's long history as a rap artist and his visibility in films as an actor playing roles about inner-city life led many critics of the song to refer to it as "gangsta rap." CLEAT called for a boycott of all products by Time-Warner, the conglomerate distributing *Body Count*, in order to secure the removal of the song and album from stores.

Two days after CLEAT announced its campaign against "Cop Killer," Los Angeles City Council member Joan Milke Flores, a Republican, joined the Los Angeles Police Protective League and the Fraternal Order of Police in asking the City Council to demand that Time Warner stop selling the song. Vice-President Dan Quayle attacked Ice-T at a national convention of radio talk show hosts, while President George Bush denounced the rap artist at a national police association conclave. Sixty members of Congress declared "Cop Killer" to be "vile and despicable." Oliver North's Freedom Alliance urged the governors of all fifty states to bring criminal charges against Time Warner for distributing the song, and North hired Jack Thompson to represent these concerns at Time Warner's annual stockholders meeting.[24]

The National Association of Black Police opposed the boycott of Time Warner and the attacks on "Cop Killer." They identified police brutality as the cause of much anti-police sentiment, and they proposed the creation of independent civilian review boards "to scrutinize the actions of our law enforcement officers" as a way of ending the provocations that caused artists such as Ice-T "to respond to actions of police brutality and abuse through their music." Their statement noted that "many individuals of the law enforcement profession do not want anyone to scrutinize their actions, but want to scrutinize the actions of others."[25]

Time Warner initially stood behind the song on free speech grounds, and Ice-T announced his intention to defy the pressure against him and his song. But as the complaints mounted, both the artist and his label caved in. In Greensboro, North

Carolina, police officers delivered the ultimatum to the management of one retail store that if they kept selling "Body Count," the police would not respond to any emergency calls at the store. The management removed the song from the store's inventory.[26] Time Warner severed relations with Paris, a San Francisco Bay Area rapper best known for his political lyrics attacking capitalism and celebrating the history of Black activist groups like the Black Panther Party.[27] Police departments around the country began requesting their pension funds to divest themselves of Time Warner stock. Ice-T had difficulty securing performing or speaking engagements because of police harassment. By August, Ice-T announced "his" decision to remove "Cop Killer" from the *Body Count* album. When Time Warner executives asked Ice-T to make changes in the cover of his new album, *Home Invasion*, early in 1993, the artist severed his ties with the company completely.[28]

Starting in 1993, African American individuals and groups joined the campaign against rap music. Calvin Butts, pastor of the Abyssynian Baptist Church in Harlem, condemned rap music from the pulpit and attempted to drive a steamroller over a pile of compact discs and cassette tapes.[29] Los Angeles attorney Eric Taylor charged that African Americans like himself had just begun to realize the dreams of Frederick Douglass, Malcolm X, and Martin Luther King, Jr., when "another movement was emerging within the same community that quickly began tearing away at epic civil rights advancements. It labeled many blacks who have endured systemic obstacles to take part in the American Dream as 'sell-outs.' Ironically this movement has found a voice, and to some, legitimacy in gangsta rap music."[30] Detroit ministers James Holley and Wendell Anthony called for a boycott, decrying rap music as "immoral, racist, and decadent."[31] In October 1993, the National Urban League and the National Association for the Advancement of Colored People started to host youth forums attacking "gangsta rap," while the National Political Congress of Black Women launched demonstrations at retail record outlets against the sale of "obscene" rap songs.[32]

Early in 1994, Senator Carol Mosley Braun and Representative Cardiss Collins, both Democrats from Illinois, responded to entreaties by C. Delores Tucker of the National Political Congress of Black Women to hold legislative hearings about rap music. As Leola Johnson astutely notes, Mosley Braun and Collins shifted the focus of attacks on rap music away from its supposedly seditious stance toward the police, and instead critiqued the music as obscene, misogynous, and a threat to decency within Black communities. Although the legislators denied any intention to promote censorship, they did remind record industry executives of the power of Congress to pass legislation affecting their financial position, such as the Audio Home Recording Act, implying that some form of self-censorship would secure future cooperation from them.[33]

In her opening remarks to the hip hop hearings, C. Delores Tucker testified on behalf of the National Political Congress of Black Women that rap music glamorized violence, degraded women, exposed children to "pornographic smut," incited violence, and seduced young people into lives of crime. She argued that freedom of speech was not an issue because rap lyrics were obscene and "it was never intended by the Founding Fathers of this Nation that First Amendment rights be for the protection of obscenities."[34] Unlike Representative Collins, who seemed to favor an improved parental advisory rating system for popular music, Tucker argued that rap music should be banned because of the harm that it does to Black communities.

Committee member Clifford Stearns, a Republican from Florida, cited Joe Madison's testimony at a later hearing but gave it a slightly different spin. Attempting to reconcile Tucker's and Madison's views on misogyny, pornography, and intergenerational tensions among Blacks with the broader conservative agenda embodied in the attacks on "Fuck the Police," *As Nasty as They Wanna Be*, and "Cop Killer," Stearns noted Madison's remarks about his son's expressed preference for jail over his middle-class home and existence, and then concluded, "For this reason, I am greatly disturbed by the proliferation of a music, a style, and class, and type that advocates the killing of police officers, the denigration of women, and the need for violent revolution."[35] Conservative spokesperson and former secretary of education William Bennett followed Stearns's logic in 1995 when he teamed up with C. Delores Tucker in a joint public attack on "hate and sexism in rock and rap music and its corporate sponsors."[36] At the same time, Senator Bob Dole of Kansas launched his campaign for the Republican presidential nomination with a spirited condemnation of motion picture violence and gangsta rap music.[37]

The systematic and sustained attack on rap music by white conservatives and black liberals, by the FBI and police officers' associations, by local prosecutors and state governors, by members of the House of Representatives and the Senate, by presidential candidates and presidents, might indicate that rap music does pose a threat to public decency and safety. Yet the bad faith, cynicism, and opportunism of rap's opponents indicates something less than sincere concern for public morality. The FBI might have had more credibility in its complaints about NWA's "Fuck the Police" if it had a better record responding to the 47,000 police brutality cases reported to the Department of Justice between 1986 and 1992, of which only 15,000 were investigated and only 128 designated for prosecution.[38] Alabama's governor, Guy Hunt, one of the first public figures to attack Ice-T's "Cop Killer" in 1992, would have been a better spokesperson for law and order had he not looted his inaugural fund to pay his personal expenses, a felony offense for which he was convicted and sentenced to a $211,000 fine and ordered to perform one thousand hours of community service in 1993.[39]

Similarly, Oliver North would have been a more convincing spokesperson for law and order in the campaign to punish Time Warner for "Cop Killer" had he not himself defied the law against covert aid to the "contras" in Nicaragua as a White House aide, a crime for which he was convicted before an appeals court overturned the verdict as a result of one of those legal technicalities that conservatives always complain about when they are not the direct beneficiaries of them. Jack Thompson would have been a more convincing opponent of *As Nasty As They Wanna Be* had he not targeted an entertainer who supported his opponent in the previous election, and Bob Dole would have been a more convincing crusader against motion picture and music violence had he not singled out only the products of firms whose executive officers donated money to Democrats while expressly exempting from his critique films by Arnold Schwareznegger, a Republican whose *Terminator* films portray every bit as much fantasy violence against the police as any song by NWA or Ice Cube. Singer Dionne Warwick, a co-chair of the National Political Congress of Black Women and a witness against gangsta rap at the hip hop hearings, would have been a more credible defender of "our children" from the alleged damages done to them by commercial popular music if she were not also the official on-camera spokesperson for a "psychic friends hot line" that encourages children and adults to spend three dollars a minute on a telephone service that connects callers to "psychics" who purport to have special insights into their personal problems and dilemmas.

The chair of the National Political Congress of Black Women, C. Delores Tucker, would have had more credibility in her campaign against the immorality of rap music had she not been fired as Pennsylvania's commonwealth secretary in 1977 for running a private for-profit business at state expense, had she not used state employees to write speeches for which she received $66,931, had she and her husband not been found in 1973 to owe close to $25,000 in real estate taxes on twelve properties that she and her husband owned in the North Philadelphia ghetto, and had she not set up a meeting in August 1995 where she proposed that Time Warner create a record distribution company for her and give her control over the highly profitable Death Row Records label. When executives from Death Row Records filed suit against her for trying to interfere with their contracts with Time Warner, Tucker explained to a reporter that "whatever they accuse me of doing, it would be worth it to protect children"—a comment that Dave Marsh notes "is markedly different than 'not guilty.' "[40]

Bad faith, personal hypocrisy, and political opportunism have been important features of the campaign against rap music, but they do not explain why the campaign exists or why it has largely succeeded. Like most conservative mobilizations over the past two decades, the crusade against rap music identifies real problems in people's lives—hostility between men and women, disintegration of family and community networks, urban violence, intergenerational tensions, and the materialism, vulgarity, and scopophilia of much popular culture and advertising. But the crusade against rap music takes these social realities out of history, hiding their causes and consequences by making them matters of personal and private morality. The crusade against rap music suppresses social memory by claiming that only culture counts, that history—in this case deindustrialization, economic restructuring, white backlash against the civil rights agenda, and neoconservative politics—has nothing to do with social disintegration in our society. Criticizing rap music enables conservatives and their allies to run away from their own responsibility for today's social problems, to blame cultural responses to intolerable conditions for the conditions themselves. But the attack on rap not only suppresses social memory; it also silences social theory. Because conservatives have a theological faith in the infallibility of "the market" to convert private greed into public good, they can explain systemic social breakdown only in terms of the deficient actions of individuals. As a result, Dan Quayle can attribute the Los Angeles rebellion to "a poverty of values in the inner city," while Pat Buchanan and Bruce Hershensohn argued that a return to prayer in the schools would address the root causes of the riots. The attack on rap music grows logically from that denial of history and of social theory. If we have bad conditions, it must be because of bad people and their private decisions, not because of the systematic structuring of privilege and advantage for a few through the systematic exploitation and disadvantage for the many that is crafted out of economic restructuring, through the role of low wage labor and unemployment in the new transnational economy, through disinvestment in social institutions and the social wage, and through the neglect to enforce civil rights laws and principles.

Rap music not only makes a convenient target for this crusade, but it is also a practice and an institution offering an alternative to the suppression of social memory and social theory. Early in the Reagan years, a White House aide announced the administration's goal as "defunding the Left," a phrase used routinely by Pat Robertson and others to explain the philosophical agenda uniting diverse activities from attacks on the NEA to campaigns for school vouchers. As much as any institution in our society, hip hop culture and rap music have been repositories of social memory through their basic musical techniques of sampling songs from the past as well as their lyrical concern for Black history, their specificity in detailing the devastation of inner cities, and their eloquence in expressing the feelings and experiences of people that mainstream media and institutions ignore.

Throughout the sustained censorship campaign against hip hop, rap artists and their defenders have conceded that the music's lyrics are sometimes obscene, sometimes celebratory about violence, and sometimes sexist and misogynist. They do point out, however, that critics often forget that rap lyrics use metaphors—that Ice-T's "Grand Larceny" is actually about "stealing" a show, and that his "I'm Your Pusher" is an anti-drug song celebrating "dope beats and lyrics" with "no beepers needed."[41] Yet while conceding the presence of obscene, violent, and misogynist elements, they contend that these features are incidental to the music's main purpose—telling the truth about the conditions experienced by young people, especially those in inner-city ghettos and barrios. "This is our voice," argues Vinnie Brown of the group Naughty by Nature. "If it wasn't for rap, you would never know that these horrors are going on in the community."[42] Chuck D of Public Enemy explains, "Hip hop is not exactly a music. It's damn near real life."[43]

Rap music creates a discursive space open to young people who have little access to any actual physical space. They are largely not wanted as workers, as students, as citizens, or even as consumers. Police officers, private security guards, electronic gates, and gang violence constrain their access to public spaces, while politicians and the mass media demonize them as criminals responsible for the poverty of their own neighborhoods. Through rap music, they tell the story as it appears to them. Bushwick Bill of the rap group The Geto Boys stressed the material dimensions of hip hop as a response to ghetto conditions in his answer to Senator Dole's attack on violence in rap music.

> Dole, who opposes affirmative action, has now bashed rap, which is the number one form of jobs to be had for a lot of inner city youths, as even if you don't rap, engineer, or produce, you can get paid to put up posters, pass out fliers, distribute promotional tapes, work on music video sets, do security, promote a club, just all kinds of things

> you can get paid to do. Not only is Dole's attack another attempt to censor us because this is our creative art form talking about what's going on, but also rap has been a way to get out of the ghetto without violence or selling drugs.[44]

Television personality and *Soul Train* host Don Cornelius describes rap music fans as young people who realize that they have been given the worst of everything that this society has to offer.

> They are people who nobody really has spent much money on or spent much concern on. They are part of a more or less forgotten community. Along comes these young rappers with all of this negative commentary who are saying, "we know that you are there, we know what your problems are, we not only know what they are, we are willing to dramatize and comment on these problems in our records."[45]

A study by the California legislature in 1982 revealed that deindustrialization, capital flight, and neoconservative economic restructuring in the late 1970s produced a 50 percent rise in unemployment in South Central Los Angeles, while purchasing power there dropped by one-third.[46] In Los Angeles at the time of the 1992 rebellion, the African American poverty rate reached 32.9 percent, Black unemployment hovered between 40 and 50 percent, and 40,000 teenagers (20 percent of the 16–19-year-olds) were both unemployed and out of school.[47] Nationwide, 43 percent of young workers received poverty wages, nearly 18 percent of full-time workers earned less than a subsistence income. Between 1965 and 1990, Black family income fell by 50.[48] In one study, nearly 5 percent of all Blacks reported being unjustly beaten by the police. Civilian deaths resulting from police force have long been at least nine times more likely for Blacks than for whites.[49] Contrary to C. Delores Tucker's claim that violence promoted by rap music is the source of "the greatest fear" in Black communities, environmental hazards, on-the-job injuries, and inadequate access to medical care remain the sources of the greatest physical threats to Black people and to other exploited and aggrieved populations. Even in respect to violence, the definitive sociological study in the field shows that "socioeconomic inequality between races, as well as economic inequality generally, increases rates of criminal violence," and that "aggressive acts of violence seem to result not so much from lack of advantages as from being taken advantage of."[50]

Rap music chronicles the devastation of inner cities and the demise of jobs, services, and opportunities during twenty-five years of neoconservative contraction of the industrial economy and the welfare state. Moreover, rap artists and their defenders understand that many of the attacks on rap are aimed at obscuring these realities. Rap artist Michael Franti, formerly a member of Disposable Heroes of Hiphoprisy and currently the leader of Spearhead, argues:

> Rap didn't start the phenomena of people killing each other or mistreating women in our community. Education and welfare cuts and a buildup of jails has more to do with it. . . . Nobody got mad when Eric Clapton sang "I Shot the Sheriff." You've got *The Terminator*, a whole movie about blowing cops to bits, and there's Arnold Schwarzenegger posing with George Bush. It's hypocrisy.[51]

Representative Maxine Waters, a Democrat from California, speaks bluntly about the attack on rap:

> Let's not kid ourselves. There are those who have a political agenda in seeking to distract people from other issues. Sometimes our friends, the conservatives, are having a field day. They have always believed blacks cause most of the crime in America. After all, they say, look at the inordinately high number of blacks in prisons and on death row. Now their evil propaganda stands virtually unopposed in today's public debate over rap music.[52]

In a similar vein, David Harleston, a music industry executive associated with a popular hip hop label, Def Jam Recordings, claims that

> it is increasingly apparent that certain opponents of hip hop music are of the misguided view that if we do not hear about the issues raised and addressed in the music, then those issues will not exist. In fact, one could argue that efforts to suppress hip hop artists are efforts to ignore unpleasant realities that exist in America's back yard. Such a view simply denies reality. Silencing the messenger will not extinguish the problem.[53]

Tricia Rose, author of the best book on hip hop, *Black Noise*, described the 1994 hearings chaired by Senator Mosley Braun and Representative Collins as "a form of empty moral grandstanding, a shameful attempt by politicians to earn political favors and ride the wave of public frenzy about crime while at the same time remaining unable and often unwilling to tackle the real problems that plague America's cities and their poorest black children."[54]

Members of the civil rights generation are not wrong to detect resentment of themselves within gangsta rap, but their interpretation of the causes of the chasm between them and today's inner-city youths is misdirected. In a brilliant chapter on gangsta rap in his indispensable book *Race Rebels*, Robin D. G. Kelley argues that the use of the word "Nigga" by gangsta rappers is an attempt to speak to "a collective identity shaped by class consciousness, the character of inner-city space, police repression, poverty, and the constant threat of intraracial violence."[55] In short, it is a form of what Kelley calls "ghettocentricity," a moral choice to identify with the poorest and most aggrieved part of the collective community while rejecting individual solutions predicated on a personal upward mobility premised upon forgetting the suffering one leaves behind for others to face. As Michael Eric Dyson explains,

> Gangsta rap is largely an indictment of mainstream and bourgeois black institutions by young people who do not find conventional methods of addressing personal and social calamity useful. The leaders of those institutions often castigate the excessive and romanticized violence of this music without trying to understand what precipitated its rise in the first place. In so doing, they drive a greater wedge between themselves and the youth they so desperately want to help.[56]

In their desire to be seen, to wield the symbolic and material currency of American society, some rappers do rely on misogyny, abusive language, and eroticized brutality. How could it be otherwise given the social relations and reward structures of our society? But in a subculture that has made an art form out of talking back, the best rebukes of these rappers will come from within, from women rappers like Queen Latifah and M. C. Lyte, from politicized male rappers like Public Enemy and KRS-1. In addition, artists and intellectuals have utilized other media to provide important metacommentaries on hip hop that evade the facile condemnations that dominated the hip hop hearings. For example, rap artist Sister Souljah's book, *No Disrespect*, combines a moving memoir and a searing indictment of sexism, while Michael Eric Dyson's *Between God and Gangsta Rap* eloquently explores the ambivalence toward the genre felt by a man who is a father of a teenage son, an ordained Baptist minister, a university professor, and a knowledgeable and discerning fan of hip hop.[57]

Government censorship and regulation or private mobilizations and moral panics cannot cure the ills they misidentify and misattribute to rap music. But nurturing the social memory and social theory found in some rap music might lead us to a more mature and more responsible understanding of our problems and their solutions. Representative Maxine Waters of California, whose district encompasses many of the neighborhoods from which gangsta rap emerged, offered an example of precisely that kind of analysis in her testimony before the hip hop hearings. Pointing out that hip hop emerged from the bottom up, from children who created an art form in their garages and basements, Waters praised the success of rap artists in communicating their experiences to a wider world. "For decades, you and I and so many others have talked about the lives and the hopes of our people," she told the committee, "pain and the hopelessness, the deprivation and abuse. Rap music is communicating that message like we never have. It is, indeed, as was described, the CNN of the community causing people from every sector, including black leadership, to listen and pay heed."[58]

Conceding that gangsta rap often contained lyrics that offended her, Waters related that she had grown up in a Black community in St. Louis and heard those words many times before she ever heard them used by gangsta rappers, that she remembered them uttered by adults held in highest esteem in the churches on Sunday morning. "I don't say to people, you should use them. I don't encourage them, but we had better stop pretending like we are hearing them for the first time."[59] Most important, Waters detailed her efforts to work with, rather than against, young rap artists—bringing them to Washington to meet with the Congressional Black Caucus and the Black Women's Forum, and sponsoring a program, "L.A. 17 to 30," designed to attract ghetto youths into vocational training as well as into high school and community college courses, and to place them in gainful employment.

The silencing of social memory and the suppression of grass roots social theory within hip hop is not a matter of concern for African Americans exclusively; it is a process that harms our whole society. For in erasing history from public debate, we unduly constrain our understanding of the present. The demonization of Black people in general, and of inner-city youth in particular, often proceeds through an argument that claims that poverty does not cause crime, that Depression-era Americans endured hardships nobly, and that the problems facing aggrieved racial minorities today stem solely from the internal moral and cultural failings of those groups. But in the 1930s, when white people were among the poorest parts of the population, many of today's dynamics also prevailed. The humiliating subordinations and indignities of poverty ripped families apart then as they do now. Despair and rage over inequality provoked criminal behavior then as it does now, and it gave rise to popular preferences for sadistic and vengeful representations of social life then, the same as now. C. L. R. James shows in *American Civilization* that during the 1930s the gangster film, violent comic strips like Dick Tracy, and detective stories and motion pictures gave voice to popular desires for representation of what the Depression had done to them, for expression of the anger they felt—and feared. Writing about the plays of Clifford Odets during that decade, Robert Warshow later zeroed in on the intergenerational tensions between parents disappointed in their children and children who thought that their parents evaded the central fact of American life—"without a dollar you don't look the world in the eye." Warshow sees the young people in Odets's plays and the entire generation they depicted as internalizing cynicism but nonetheless engaging in the strongest subversion—"taking capitalism without sugar."[60] Young rap artists and their listeners today are taking capitalism without sugar. More than anything, they seek an art that refuses to lie, that refuses to run from the hard facts and harsh realities of our own time. A politics based on their perceptions, on honest engagement with the suppression of social memory and the silencing of social theory might enable us to see our place in history, and our potential for a different future.

NOTES

1. Subcommittee on Commerce, Consumer Protection, and Competitiveness of the Committee on Energy and Commerce, House of Representatives Hearings, February 11, 1994, 5.
2. Ibid., 6.
3. Ibid., 5.
4. Ibid., 24.
5. Ibid., 31.
6. Reginold Bundy, "The Great Divide," *Pittsburgh Courier*, January 13, 1996, A1, A3.
7. Holly Sklar, *Chaos or Community: Seeking Solutions Not Scapegoats* (Boston: South End Press, 1995), 69.
8. Noel J. Kent, "A Stacked Deck," *Explorations in Ethnic Studies* 14, no.1 (January 1991), 12, 13. Richard Rothstein, "Musical Chairs as Economic Policy," in Don Hazen, ed., *Inside the L.A. Riots* (New York: Institute for Alternative Journalism, 1992), 143.
9. Sklar, *Chaos or Community*, 25, 26.
10. For a detailed account of the extent and significance of censorship efforts aimed at the gangster film, see the brilliant dissertation by L. Jonathan Munby, "Screening Crime in the USA, 1929–1958: From Hays Code to HUAC: From Little Caesar to Touch of Evil," Ph.D. diss., University of Minnesota, 1995, especially 46–52.
11. In *Inventing the Public Enemy: The Gangster in American Culture, 1918–1934* (Chicago and London: University of Chicago Press, 1996), David E. Ruth presents an important discussion of gangster films that delineates the centrality of misogyny, material acquisitions, and style to that genre. This discussion holds some important parallels to the internal properties of the "gangster" image and ideal that emerges within gangsta rap as well.
12. Brian Neve, *Film and Politics in America: A Social Tradition* (London: Routledge, 1992), 12.
13. Leola Johnson, "Silencing Gangsta Rap: Class and Race Agendas in the Campaign against Hardcore Rap Lyrics," *Temple Political and Civil Rights Law Review* 3, no.19 (Fall 1993/Spring 1994), 25 .
14. Quoted in Houston A. Baker, "Handling 'Crisis': Great Books, Rap Music, and the

End of Western Homogeneity (Reflections on the Humanities in America)," *Callaloo* 13 (1990), 177.

15. Tricia Rose, *Black Noise* (Hanover, N.H.: Wesleyan/University Press of New England, 1994), 128.

16. Johnson, "Silencing Gangsta Rap," 29–30.

17. Dave Marsh and Phyllis Pollack, "Wanted for Attitude," *Village Voice*, October 10, 1989, 33–37, quoted in Rose, *Black Noise*, 129.

18. Chuck Phillips, "The 'Batman' Who Took on Rap," *Los Angeles Times*, June 18, 1990, F1.

19. Chuck Phillips, "The Anatomy of a Crusade," *Los Angeles Times*, June 18, 1990, F4.

20. Associated Press, "Rap Group Members Arrested over 'Nasty' Lyrics," *St. Paul Pioneer Press*, June 11, 1990, 2.

21. Amy Binder, "Constructing Racial Rhetoric: Media Depictions of Harm in Heavy Metal and Rap Music," *American Sociological Review* 58 (December 1993), 753. Chuck Phillips, "The Anatomy of a Crusade," *Los Angeles Times*, June 18, 1990, F4.

22. Chuck Phillips, "Boss Apparently Oks Crew's Use of 'U.S.A.,' " *Los Angeles Times*, June 26, 1990, F10.

23. Robin D. G. Kelley, *Race Rebels* (New York: Free Press, 1994), 190; Rose, *Black Noise*, 183.

24. Johnson, "Silencing Gangsta Rap," 31; Rose, *Black Noise*, 183.

25. Quoted in Johnson, "Silencing Gangsta Rap," 33.

26. Dave Marsh, "The Censorship Zone," *Rock and Rap Confidential* 100 (August 1992), 5.

27. Dave Marsh, "The Censorship Zone," *Rock and Rap Confidential* 123 (April-May 1995), 7.

28. Johnson, "Silencing Gangsta Rap," 33.

29. Rose, *Black Noise*, 184.

30. Eric Taylor, "Gangsta Rap Is Deferring the Dream," *Los Angeles Times*, March 7, 1994, F3.

31. Johnson, "Silencing Gangsta Rap," 34.

32. Ibid.

33. Subcommittee on Commerce, Consumer Protection, and Competitiveness, Committee on Energy and Commerce, House of Representatives, Hearings, February 11, 1994, 4.

34. Ibid., 5–6.

35. Ibid., May 5, 1994, 75.

36. Marlene Cimons, "Outrage over Lyrics Unites Unlikely Pair," *Los Angeles Times*, July 5, 1995, A1.

37. Dave Marsh, "Cops 'n' Gangstas," *Nation*, June 26, 1995, 908.

38. Jesse Jackson, "A Call to Bold Action," in Don Hazen, ed., *Inside the L.A. Riots* (New York: Institute for Alternative Journalism, 1992), 149.

39. Dave Marsh, "The Censorship Zone," *Rock and Rap Confidential* 108, (August 1993), 7.

40. Mark Landler, "Label Tied to Time Warner Sues a Critic of Rap Lyrics," *New York Times*, August 16, 1995, C5. Jeffrey Trachtenberg, "Interscope Records Sues Activist Critic, Alleging Distribution Pact Interference," *Wall Street Journal*, August 16, 1995, B8. Chuck Phillips, "Interscope Files Lawsuit against Rap Music Critic," *Los Angeles Times*, August 16, 1995, D1. Dave Marsh, "We Told You So," *Rock and Rap Confidential* 127 (September 1995), 7.

41. Kelley, *Race Rebels* 190.

42. Dave Marsh, "Doug and the Slugs," *Rock and Rap Confidential* 125 (July 1995), 4.
43. Edna Gunderson, "Rap against Time Warner," *USA Today*, October 2, 1995, 4d.
44. Dave Marsh, "Cracked Rear View," *Rock and Rap Confidential* 125 (July 1995), 2.
45. Subcommittee on Commerce, Consumer Protection, and Competitiveness of the Committee on Energy and Commerce, House of Representatives, Hearings, February 11, 1995, 21.
46. Kelley, *Race Rebels*, 192.
47. Maxine Waters, "Testimony before the Senate Banking Committee," in Don Hazen, ed., *Inside the L.A. Riots* (New York: Institute for Alternative Journalism, 1992), 26.
48. Kent, "A Stacked Deck," 12, 13. Rothstein, "Musical Chairs as Economic Policy," 143.
49. Bernard D. Headley, "Black on Black Crime: The Myth and the Reality," *Crime and Social Justice* 20(n.d.), 53.
50. Judith R. Blau and Peter M. Blau, "The Cost of Inequality: Metropolitan Structure and Violent Crime," *American Sociological Review* 47 (February 1982), 114, 126.
51. Gunderson, "Rap against Time Warner," 4D.
52. Subcommittee on Commerce, Consumer Protection, and Competitiveness of the Committee on Energy and Commerce, House of Representatives, Hearings, February 11, 1994, 65.
53. Ibid., 38–39.
54. Tricia Rose, "Rap Music and The Demonization of Young Black Males," *USA Today* Magazine, May 1994, 35–36.
55. Kelley, *Race Rebels*, 210.
56. Michael Eric Dyson, *Between God and Gangsta Rap: Bearing Witness to Black Culture* (New York: Oxford University Press, 1996), 185.
57. Sister Souljah, *No Disrespect* (New York: Times Books/Random House, 1994). Dyson, *Between God and Gangsta Rap.*
58. Subcommittee on Commerce, Consumer Protection, and Competitiveness of the Committee on Energy and Commerce, House of Representatives, Hearings, May 5, 1994, 65–66.
59. Ibid., 65.
60. Robert Warshow, *The Immediate Experience* (New York: Atheneum, 1971), 64.

Chapter Twenty-five

Nightmares in the New Metropolis

The Cinematic Poetics of Low Riders

Brenda Jo Bright

The use of nightmare film images such as Freddy Kruger and the Joker on the car murals of Chicano low riders in Los Angeles raises provocative questions concerning the uses of popular icons in the poetics and politics of identity, space, and place: What does it mean when people choose to inhabit the persona of a film's nightmare character rather than the nightmare's traditionally bourgeois hero? How do such images circulate in the metropolis? Why would Chicanos draw iconography from a source that seems so removed from Chicano culture?

Nightmare murals are in marked contrast to those seen on Chicano low riders in the 1970s when the Chicano movement's poetics of cultural nationalism provided the basis for the resistive and affirmative poetics embodied in the figures of the Virgin of Guadalupe, Aztec warriors, and others. Increasingly, as economic restructuring and its attendant moral panics demonize Blacks and Latinos, low rider and hip hop cultures converge in shared visions of metropolitan experience that eclipse the optimism and activism of 70s Chicano nationalism. Instead of cultural warriors fighting for space and equity through the imaginary of a cultural past, nightmarish figures howlingly confront the horrors of a rigidifying and bleak system of race and class inequity. In Los Angeles, the monstrous cinematic imaginary has become a key tool for reimagining cultural locations in low rider car murals. These murals move away from the nostalgia of earlier forms of nationalism toward the rage of having one's dreams invaded.

The question of how to conceptualize low rider aesthetics has developed out of my ethnographic research project on Chicano low riders. The research project investigates three regionally distinct places, two that are urban—Los Angeles and Houston—and one that is rural yet semi-urban, the Española area of northern New Mexico. Of the three, Los Angeles is historically the most central site, and its practices, media production, and image creation have influenced the other two sites. The broader comparative project traces the creation of identity through low rider practices. But because the project is comparative, it also examines the significance of locality for cultural productions that are in some sense mediated (through mass-produced commodities and media), widely distributed (films, cars, magazines, etc.), and hence inherently translocal. While most work in Chicano studies focuses on one medium or one location, this project focuses on cultural practices that cross geographical and cultural regions and asks how such practices are simultaneously infused with local and extralocal concerns.[1] Here I examine how film poetics influence low rider poetics.

Low Riding's Two Mediations

Contemporary low rider practices have been heavily influenced by two mediations. The first mediation was the publication of *Low Rider Magazine* beginning in 1977 with its combined emphasis on cars, popular *Chicanismo*, and the poetics of self and community construction in urban contexts. While low riding has a long history in Los Angeles and the Southwest, the publication and regional distribution of *Low Rider Magazine* expanded and organized its practice to focus on car club participation, car show competition, and other car-based events. These events often incorporated other popular forms, such as break dancing in the mid-eighties.

The second mediation was the emergence of hip hop music, especially West Coast, Los Angeles-based gangster rap in the late 1980s as represented on television and in films. For example, Music Television (MTV) became influential as a national disseminator of hip hop when it began airing "Yo MTV Raps" in August 1988. While African American low riders date back at least to the 1960s, they were not broadly associated with low riding until the emergence of gangster rap. Many gangster rap music videos feature African Americans in low riders, cruising in Los Angeles street scenes. Hip hop emphasizes cultural style and urban critique. Low rider cars serve as mobil embodiments of both, enabling participation in the city as a scene itself. Conversely, West Coast rap and hip hop's attention to the way the music sounds in cars has influenced Chicano music, as seen on the recently released compact disk, *Latin Lingo*, which features photographs of low riders on its cover. Through music and its ideologies, this second mediation links low riding to the popular practices and urban cultural critiques of African Americans, and has enabled the spread of low riding to rap and hip hop aficionados.[2]

These two mediations can be seen in Houston, whose low riding scene began in 1978 after *Low Rider Magazine* began regional distribution. A primarily Chicano phenomenon, it thrived until the bust in Houston's oil-based economy in the mid-1980s. After the bust, organized low riding almost died out. Low rider car shows disappeared for a time, as low riders found it necessary to attend mixed-style customized car shows. But eventually the economy improved and with it the low riding scene. However, the reemerging scene coincided with the second mediation of low riding as a component of hip hop. In 1995, Los Magnificos Car Club—now the oldest low rider car club in Houston—co-sponsored a low rider car show and concert at the Astrohall Arena with KBXX, "the Box," which plays hip hop and "light" rap. The show was attended by thirty thousand viewers, who were almost evenly Latino and African American in number. The traffic was backed up on all nearby freeway ramps with people trying to get in. The show featured over two hundred low riders. Performances by hip hop artists Ecstasy, Kid Frost, and Ice Cube alternated with those by Tejano bands, including the popular Home Town Boys. The convergence of these two currents—low riding and hip hop—suggests a need to rethink how Chicano popular practices are linked with those of other groups. They emerge not just as the cultural practices encoding memory and history of a specific ethnic group, but as hybrid forms representing mutual influence and locally shared experience, with the media enabling translocal as well as transcultural recreations.

Images and Narratives

Within the metropolis of Los Angeles, low rider practices and representations frequently exhibit concerns with place. For example, many car clubs begin with a core group from the same neighborhood, perhaps the same street or family. But these clubs quickly become populated with members from outside of the original area. For some, place is a point of origin and pride. For others, it may present limitations they wish to transcend. Indeed, many low riders join clubs to widen their social networks. In contrast to gangs, low rider clubs often replace a geographically based identity with a practice-based identity, relishing the freedom of mobility and expanded social networks that are enabled through car culture.

An example of expanded social mobility through low rider participation can be seen in the work of photographer Kathleen Estrada. At the Los Angeles Public Library in October 1996, Estrada showed her photographs of low rider George Luna, alternating them with photos of more traditional Mexican practices in order to highlight the continuities between low riders and other Mexican forms. Following a cruising scene, she showed a photograph of a group of *charros* (Mexican horsemen with ornate costumes and saddles) directing the audience to the striking similarities of these two forms of "cruising" and their decorative motifs.

After her photo presentation emphasizing the continuities, she showed a five-minute video of Luna. In the video, Luna tells how he ran away from Texas as a young boy and ended up in central Los Angeles. There he joined a gang and led a street life for many years. But eventually he was shot, and while he was recovering in the hospital, he vowed to change his life. Ending his participation in the gang, he began to put his life together by putting his car—a low rider—together. In the video he contends that before he made his car, he was nobody. Through the building of his car, he became somebody. On his trunk is a beautiful airbrushed rendering of the Sacred Heart of Jesus, to whom he attributes the opportunity for living his life.

Estrada's presentation employed a common strategy in representing low riders, pointing out their penchant for tradition. Yet absent from Luna's own account were representations of his activities as "traditional." Instead, what emerged was the way in which the car was linked to complicated narratives about life, opportunity, and aesthetics. His account emphasized the car as an opportunity, and the image of Jesus as a kind of *ex voto*—it was because of Jesus that Luna believed he had such an opportunity in his life. Luna's narration of his car and experiences are in accord with interviews I have conducted with other low riders. Their stories indicate that whenever images are located on cars, they are linked with narratives that are at once personal, social, and cultural—even those images, such as the Sacred Heart, that seem the most "traditional." The challenge is how to account for the complexity of the images in ways that account for cultural continuities, but that also account for the dialogue that subjects maintain with their surroundings. These dialogues are not simply the products of cultural traditions, but the complex and ongoing lived experiences of the low rider subjects. The variety of images in low riding, including traditional ones, are themselves inflected with contemporary conditions and, as a result, are highly mediated. Importantly, they are produced through the intersection of a number of narratives that must be considered in interpreting the images themselves.

Cars and Social Life

When earlier writers have looked at low riding, they have limited their examination to cultural influences that can most clearly be typed as "Chicano," such as religion and music, and have ignored more complicated low rider narratives.[3] For example, Calvin Trillin noted some low riders' pared-down aesthetics in an early article on low riders in East Los Angeles. *Cholos* did not ordinarily go in for "fancy lacquer paint jobs or crushed velvet interiors or even hydraulic lifts." Usually they would lower a car (at that time an old Chevy), install a tape deck, and etch the name of a song, preferably an "oldie," in the back-seat quarter window. Similarly, Diego Vigil attributes the *cholos'* taste for "a more or less informal" casual run of stock cars, especially their love for customized models from the 1940s and 1950s, to "their penchant for tradition." But just exactly what this penchant for tradition is needs to be specified. As the following examination of low rider aesthetics will indicate, their penchant for tradition is not easily reduced to practices of cultural difference associated with Chicanoness, especially as they incorporate hip hop culture, urban-themed films, television, and comic books. Rather, low rider practices underscore the experiences and the conditions of their production. Instead of simple nostalgia or tradition, low riders produce cultural images of institutional relationships, where, as Willis states, "the cultural is part of the necessary dialectic of reproduction."[4]

In Compton, the hard life of the gangbangers—in terms of material difficulty and in terms of institutional and interpersonal violence—is the thematic material for popular music as well as for customized vehicles. Hardcore gangster rappers such as Ice-T, Ice-Cube, and NWA are all from Compton. NWA's Easy-E asserted, "We're telling the real story of what it's like living in places like Compton. We're giving [the fans] reality. We're like reporters. We give them the truth."[5] Yet hip hop productions, in contrast to low riders, are characterized in public discourse not as traditional, but as bearing the maladies of our larger society. For example, Mike Davis is critical of Los Angeles's hardcore gangster rappers' version of social realism because, he contends, "In supposedly stripping bare the reality of the streets, 'telling it like it is', they also offer an *uncritical* mirror to fantasy power trips of violence, sexism and greed."[6] Davis implies a straightforward "reflection" of reality in the music. Cultural products do not straightforwardly mirror greed, violence, and sexism. Nor are they simply traditional. They may indeed *reproduce* larger social maladies just as they

Fig. 25.1. Young low riders with low rider bicycles, Houston, 1984. (Photograph by Brenda Bright)

draw on tradition for making meaning, but they do so through a process of cultural dialogue and transformation that is important to understand.

It is through the dialectics of social life that cars emerge as a canvas for personal and cultural representation. Differently from many other youth culture phenomena, low riding begins as a youth enthusiasm but carries beyond the teenage years. Low riders typically range in age from fifteen to forty-five. The longevity of their interests demonstrates the importance of understanding how youth culture practices are connected to broader life histories. Some low riders begin by constructing low rider bikes in their early teenage years before they are old enough to drive (fig. 25.1). Most begin their first car when in high school, often working in conjunction with a family member such as a father or uncle. Car purchases at this time are very important as a means of developing autonomy, craft proficiency, and prestige. For many, becoming a low rider is a path that influences other choices of friends, peer groups, and activities.

Low rider ownership during high school has its own social logics. Because of the violence and intergang conflicts in many Los Angeles high schools, cars become the targets for hits and retaliations. To destroy a car is to hurt someone in two ways. It wounds his pride which is invested in producing his car. It is also expensive. Currently, cars belonging to low riders in their teens to early twenties are "lowered" with "paint," rims, and a stereo. Few of them have hydraulics, fancy paint jobs, or murals, all of which require large investments of money. Potential violence, then, coupled with the expense of producing a car, produces the pared-down aesthetics noted by both Trillin and Vigil.

After high school, low rider aesthetics become more elaborate. As the demands of work and family life tend to overshadow the demands of one's peer group, peer life often "chills out" and becomes more social. In the confluence of work life and, for some, decreased gang participation, the automobile becomes an increasingly important site for cultural production, peer interaction, and socializing. A number become low riders upon entering the workforce, primarily in working-class jobs. As truck drivers, mechanics, and computer processors, low riders often find greater pleasure and satisfaction in the creative, expressive, and social opportunities provided by their cars than they do in their jobs. The car often becomes the canvas, as it were, for a range of significations that are "answers of the real." Working from the experiences of ghetto, gang, and working-class life, the outsider aesthetic of the cars is meant to be interpretive of, not reflective of, the conditions of the owner's life and creative of his identity.

Cinematic Poetics

Central Los Angeles car murals display unique and complex images that narrate metropolitan experience. Many of them feature film and comic-book anti-heroes. I first encountered these "nightmare" murals in 1989 at a South Gate car show. They are an emergent genre of low rider murals. According to Jesus Mata, the muralist who painted a number of such images, the more difficult the circumstances of the owner's life, the more complex the imagery. Central Los Angeles car murals tend to combine images from a variety of sources. These murals, both with and without explicit cinematic references, suggest the idea of a cinematic poetics. At the simplest level, many murals use references to films. But they also use references to cultured geographic places as well as references to contested social locations. Cinematic poetics provide ways for low riders to narrate complex social locations and urban experiences.

The narration and negotiation of social locations is exemplified by the car, "La Vida Loca y el Corazón Sangrante." In the car's mural (fig. 25.2), the car appears as a character invoking personal, religious, and civic narratives. The beautiful car is parked in a liquor store parking lot amid drug dealers, gamblers, and *cholos*, depicting the wickedness of contemporary life. Integrated into the liquor store wall is a mural of the Sacred Heart of Jesus, looking beneficently upon the scene below. In deploying the signs of *la vida loca* under the purvey of *el corazon sangrante*, the mural incorporates two gazes—that of the public and that of God, while shifting the focus of civic discourse from urban demons to the cultural authority of Jesus. The image functions as a visual *testimonio*, narrating from personal experience in the face of the more prevalent demonizing public narratives typically attached to such ghettoites. The image is an appeal for Jesus' beneficence and a sympathetic public audience. His presence has the iconographic effect of lending empathy to the scene of decadent ghetto experience. It also holds out the possibility of redemption. The image embodies the owner's hope of the healing possibility of traditional authority.[7]

Even though this mural is without an explicit film reference, the "cinematic"

Fig. 25.2. "La Vida Loca y El Corazón Sangrante," Los Angeles, 1990. (Photograph by Brenda Bright)

device is its use of *mise-en-scène*, or putting Chicano urban experience into the scene. Here the urban Chicano *mise-en-scène* is created through montage, or piecing together narratives of urban experience, public discourse, and cultural authority. Unlike film, with its juxtapositions and multilayered images, a mural must work through static images. Hence, many murals work like this one, juxtaposing and layering images rich in narrative meaning into a single melodramatic image.

The layerings of meaning in a single image can be seen as well in "Joker's Revenge" (fig. 25.3) where there is no image on the car itself. Instead, the credits board that accompanies the car (a cinematic device denoting credit for image production) features the Joker, from *Batman*. Owned by Mario Saavedra, an aerospace machinist, this car's aesthetics are typical of the Lifestyles car club to which Saavedra belongs. He uses a single image, the Joker, and the title, "Joker's Revenge," to communicate a complicated narrative of outsider aesthetics. This mural appeared shortly after the 1989 film, *Batman*. The Joker in *Batman* is a diabolical character who was "created" at the hands of vigilante justice. Originally just a two-bit hood, Jack Napier became the demented Joker as a result of being double-crossed by his boss, a chemical plant owner who set him up to be busted by the police. Disfigured after being dumped into a chemical vat by Batman, the Joker takes over the chemical plant and begins producing disfiguring cosmetics. He calls himself an artist promoting a new aesthetic. In naming his car "Joker's Revenge," Saavedra represents the idea of an outsider's ability, as a product of the metropolitan-industrial system, to thwart that same system by promoting a new aesthetic. The Joker evokes the conflicts, experiences, and visions inherent in the industrial metropolis. In this, as in other murals, aesthetics emerges as a means of struggle. Through a cinematic reference attached to a film narrative about power, belonging, and revenge, the owner is able to "locate" himself in social terms, as is further exemplified by "Gangster of Love."[8]

The images on the 1939 Chevrolet in figure 25.4 uses both cinematic and geographic references. It is covered with murals on the trunk, the hood, under the hood and on the quarter panels. Each large mural portrays a gangster theme through movie references. On one side appears a scene of "bombs" under the sign, "Al Capone's Bank." On the other side is an East Side scene with gangster cars cruising the boulevard under a sign reading *Aztlán*. The cars are driving past a movie theater featuring *East Side Story*. These two signs, *Aztlán* and *East Side Story*, reference Chicano Los Angeles as the East Side and play on the notions of territory and conflict in the movie *West Side Story*.[9]

The gangster motifs and cinematic references on the car are diverse. The image of "Al Capone's Bank" links the car to the narratives of gangsters, cars, and movies. *East Side Story* references the specificity of Latino urban experience. This car does not limit itself to a single image. Rather, here the images function as a kind of montage, drawing a number of film references and narratives together to create an image of an alternative city. The images of cars, *vatos*, money, guns, and "dolls" stage the man as belonging to a society with its own map—a geography of place and desire—of the city. In the mural, the culture of money has been reinvisioned in a Chicano city and *la vida loca* is legitimated. The hallmark of gangster life is that while it lies outside of the bounds of bourgeois rationality, it is nevertheless preoc-

Fig. 25.3. "Joker's Revenge," Los Angeles, 1990. (Photograph by Brenda Bright)

Fig. 25.4. "Gangster of Love," Los Angeles, 1992. (Photograph by Brenda Bright)

Fig. 25.5. "Freddy's '3," Los Angeles, 1989. (Photograph by Brenda Bright)

cupied with the theoretical rewards of the bourgeois all-American life. The gangster, in truly American fashion, strives to achieve many of the goals—power, fame, money, status—that are regarded by society as symbols of success. Yet, at the same time, the gangster is both a villain and a hero.

Freddy Martinez's "Freddy's '3" perhaps best illustrates a low rider's employment of a movie character to create a powerful anti-subject. "Freddy's '3" (fig. 25.5) is a beautiful red 1963 Chevy convertible that features Freddy Kruger in a hellish setting manipulating a group of blonde women.[10] He is gigantic in size, while the women are miniatures. "Freddy" is the dead character from the movie series *Nightmare on*

Elm Street, a janitor and alleged child murderer himself killed by a group of vigilante middle-class parents. He returns to haunt the dreams of his murderers' children, attempting to kill them in their dreams. Never buried, he operates in the phantom social space of his victims' dreams. Like the Joker, he is disfigured, this time by the furnace fire that consumed him. As a result, he is terrifying in both looks and deeds.

In Freddy Martinez's fantasy, "Freddy" is the sexual nightmare of a trio of beautiful, barely dressed women. A pair of ominous dark hands caresses and constrains each of the women, who appear to be sharing in his dream and writhing in passionate pleasure. This mural allegorizes Freddy Martinez's fantasy powers to control the staging and evoking of desire, in this case symbolized as women's sexual desire on the surface of a beautifully customized car.[11] The threat of violent power stands above them in the form of Freddy's razor-fingered glove.

"Freddy's '3" uses of a popular fantasy figure to narrate a class-based subjectivity relative to ruling metropolitan forces and fictions. The film's Freddy was created through a "liberating" death at the hands of vigilante justice.[12] This so-called justice was itself based upon the bourgeois myths that poor people are criminals out to rob them of their hard-earned way of life, that good people are victimized by criminals, and that the justice system allows criminals to go free. Therefore, an important if controversial low rider mural theme is depicting oneself as the nightmare of bourgeois dreams. One becomes terrifying at the hands of a system that disfigures some in the name of a beautiful life for others. To the extent that it is "dreams" that the petit bourgeois pursue, it is dreams that must be disrupted, punctured by a nightmare character like Freddy Kruger.

In the Realm of the Gaze

Low riding activities and aesthetics exhibit strategies for creating identities that both are products of and reflections on metropolitan experience. Mobility for the owner, the pleasures of the moving car and its images, and the sociality of communal interactions provide the foundational premises of low rider participation. In order to participate in the larger dialogues surrounding them, low riders use *mise-en-scène* for "locating" themselves. They do this through the use of nightmare characters like Freddy Kruger, the Joker, and gangsters—through the use of movie references such as *West Side Story*, *Nightmare on Elm Street*, and *Batman*, and through representations of locality itself. They also use montage to situate themselves simultaneously in spatial and social locations. For example, montage juxtaposes images of experience and fantasy with narratives of redemption or of satisfaction, as in "Sacred Heart" and the "Gangster of Love." It relocates narratives to particular geographical places, in particular the *West Side Story* to East Los Angeles on the "Gangster of Love." Montage creates readily identifiable social locations for the owner, as through Kruger as a victim of the middle class and subsequently its nightmare.

As a cinematic device that enables the simultaneity of narratives, the use of mural *montage* enables personal identity to be inserted in public discourse. The use of movie references as narratives of metropolitan experience enables the owner to communicate complicated experience. In cinematic poetics, popular representational practices are not simply resistive to metropolitan power, nor are they simply folk art that reinforces the "traditional" qualities of low riders. Instead, cinematic poetics conceives of popular practices as combining visual and narrative strategies. Therefore, a cinematic analogue provides a means of labeling low rider aesthetic strategies. Cinematic poetics includes the influence of postmodernity, particularly film as a form of public discourse, in the creation of popular aesthetics. Low rider murals incorporate multiple resources through cultural dialogues that are popular, class-based, and Chicano. Through murals, low riders re-create and resituate the varieties of metropolitan experience, and in so doing, narrate the lived politics of culture.

Objects and Narratives

Previous accounts of low riding have elided the lived politics of culture, simplifying the way low riders employ narrative. In contrast, low riders' own accounts and imagery draw on a range of sources to create complicated narratives. In this way they operate in ways similar to Chicano literature. Ramón Saldívar has argued that the function of Chicano narrative is "to produce creative structures of knowledge that allow its readers to see, to feel and to understand their social reality."[13] Through the use of multiple approaches that foreground the importance of narrative—ethnographic, anthropological, cultural, and literary studies—it is possible to see not only how low riders are "Chicano," but also how, through acts of representation, they are grappling with issues of class and the realities of being postmodern subjects.

The works of Susan Stewart and Slavoj Zizek are particularly helpful in considering how cars become the focus for self-representation. In her work on the relation of objects to narratives, Susan Stewart makes a series of assertions relevant to analyzing the cultural meanings of modified car bodies and their relationships to men's bodies. First, she says, "The body presents the paradox of contained and container at once,"[14] in which, "[T]he fetishized object must have a reference point within the system of the exchange economy—even the contemporary fetishization of the body in consumer culture is dependent upon the system of images within which the corporeal body has been transformed into another point of representation."[15] Second, she argues that "kitsch and camp, as forms of metaconsumption, have arisen from the contradictions implicit in the operation of the exchange economy." Third, Stewart explains that these forms "mark an anti-subject whose emergence ironically has been necessitated by the narratives of significance under that economy."[16]

Low rider cars embody Stewart's three themes in ways that illuminate the creation of identity out of what Hebdige calls the blocked identities of race and class.[17] First, they engage in culturally constructing their own bodies through their cars. Second, inasmuch as their bodies and their car bodies are already represented in a system of images (media, advertising, and policing) having to do with civic value and participation, they must enter into those discourses in order to transform the effects of representation. And finally, to the extent that low-rider cars and men appear as anti-subjects indicated through the creation of an outsider aesthetic, their engagement is necessitated by the "narratives of significance" of our social system. While these narratives of commodities, media, popular images, and policing are crucial to an understanding of low rider practices, the question remains as to how low-rider aesthetics use images to intercede in them.

In *Looking Awry*, cultural critic Slavoj Zizek examines film to reveal the ways popular culture is invested with an excess that is predicated upon "experience." He posits what he calls the "answer of the real,"[18] which creates a "surplus enjoyment that has the same paradoxical power to convert things into their opposite."[19] Accordingly, low riders use film themes, images, and characters to stage fantasy in relation to public narratives. As Zizek argues, "What fantasy stages is not a scene in which our desire is fulfilled, fully satisfied, but on the contrary, a scene that realizes, stages, the desire as such."[20] In the preceding murals, we see low riders' desires staged in the realm of the city through the use of film and other cultural narratives.

NOTES

I would like to thank Tiffany Ana Lopez, Tricia Rose, Susan Phillips, David James, Joe Austin, and Thomas Dumm for offering important insights and suggestions at different stages of this essay. Any mistakes are mine alone. A fellowship from the Getty Research Institute for the History of Art and the Humanities supported me during the writing of this essay and enabled me to present it at the 1996 American Studies Association annual meeting and at the 1996 Conference on Latin American Popular Culture. A slightly modified version of this essay first appeard in *Studies in Latin American Popular Culture*, Volume 16, 1997. Thanks to Charles Tatum, the editor, for permission to reproduce it here.

1. Two critical perspectives on Chicano popular culture emerge in my research project. The first is an historical perspective on the transformations of low riding practice over a forty-five year period (1950–1995). The second is a transcultural translocal perspective that examines the complexity of popular practice in view of circuits of circulation and practice. See Brenda Jo Bright, "Remapping: Los Angeles Low Riders" in Brenda Jo Bright and Liza Bakewell, eds., *Looking High and Low: Art and Cultural Identity* (Tucson, AZ: University of Arizona Press, 1995) and Brenda Jo Bright, *Low Rider: Culture in the Time of the Automobile* (Berkeley, CA: University of California Press, forthcoming).

2. Rap producer Dr. Dre explains that he makes music for people to play in their cars because that is where they do the most listening. See "Dr. Dre," in Brian Cross, *it's not about a salary: rap, race + resistance in Los Angeles* (London: Verso, 1993). *it's not about a salary* documents rap in Los Angeles, including African American and Chicano practices. For a comprehensive look at the music and themes of rap, and debates surrounding it, see Tricia Rose, *Black Noise: Rap Music and Black Culture in Contemporary America* (Hanover: Wesleyan University Press, 1994). See also William Eric Perkins, *Dropping Science: Critical Essay on Rap Music and Hip Hop Culture* (Philadelphia: Temple University Press, 1996).

3. A notable exception is Michael C. Stone, "*Bajito y Suavecito*: Low Riding and the 'Class' of Class" in *Studies in Latin American Popular Culture* 9 (1990), 85–126.

4. Calvin Trillin, "Our Far-Flung Correspondents: Low and Slow, Mean and Clean" in *The New Yorker Magazine* 54 (1978), 70–74. Diego Vigil, *Barrio Gangs: Street Life and Identity*

in Southern California (Austin, TX: University of Texas Press, 1988). Paul Willis, *Learning to Labor: How Working Class Kids Get Working Class Jobs* (New York, NY: Columbia University Press, 1977).

5. Hillburn, Robert, "Striking Tales of Black Frustration and Pride Shake the Mainstream," *Los Angeles Times*, Calendar Section, April 2, 1989, 7.

6. Mike Davis, *City of Quartz: Excavating the Future in Los Angeles* (London: Verso, 1990), 87, emphasis mine.

7. This scene replicates the melodrama staged in the movie, *Boyz in the Hood*. Here, life in South Central is presented as an ever present struggle for daily life against poverty, drugs and joblessness. The hope presented in the movie lies in the figure of the responsible, politically aware and street savvy father who is willing to guide his son to manhood through his teachings and discipline. The mural is accompanied by the panel images of naked women in Mexican wear which serve as emblems of desire, masculinity, and identity. As Linda Williams reminds us, "there is inevitably power in pleasure." See Linda Williams, *Hard Core: Power, Pleasure, and the Frenzy of the Visible* (Berkeley: University of California Press, 1989).

8. The bottom of the credits board reads, "Thanks, Julie for this Nightmare."

9. East Side is also the name given to a rich collection of Los Angeles music issuing out of performance venues on the East side. The El Monte stadium was a particularly important site of music performances after the Los Angeles Police Department shut down mixed-race audience venues within Los Angeles city limits.

10. *Low Rider Magazine*, June 1990, 24.

11. It might be argued that this mural provides a men's analogue to the vision of the devil discussed by José Limón, *Dancing with the Devil: Society and Cultural Poetics* (Madison: University of Wisconsin Press, 1991). In Mexican American women's folklore in South Texas, the devil appears to them in the form of a handsome, desirable Anglo man who upon closer inspection has the hands and feet of a beast. His appearances occur largely in sexually charged settings such as bars and dances. Limón suggests that these visions are twofold: provoking/suggesting guilt born from desires, and teaching the woman that, like Eve, she may not have the freedom and the pleasure she dreams of, thereby replicating the Mexican American woman's place in the political economy.

12. When the Joker returns to confront the owner of the chemical plant, who set him up as the subject of a police bust, he says, "I've already died. I found it quite a liberating experience!"

13. Ramón Saldívar, *Chicano Narrative: The Dialectics of Difference* (Madison: University of Wisconsin Press, 1990).

14. Susan Stewart, *On Longing: Narratives of the Gigantic, the Miniature, the Souvenir, the Collection* (Philadelphia: University of Pennsylvania Press, 1984), 104. For the purposes of this essay, "the body" can be interpreted broadly to refer to the body in both of its forms—the human body (here the racialized, class-ified body) and the car body.

15. Stewart, 1984, 163.

16. Stewart, 1984, 169.

17. Dick Hebdige, *Subculture: The Meaning of Style* (London: Methuen and Company, Ltd., 1979), 86.

18. Slavoj Zizek, *Looking Awry: An Introduction to Jacques Lacan through Popular Culture* (Cambridge, Mass.: Massachusetts Institute of Technology Press, 1991), 34.

19. Zizek, 1991, 12.

20. Zizek, 1991, 6.

Chapter Twenty-six

Let's All Be Alienated Together
Zines and the Making of Underground Community

Stephen Duncombe

> Let's all be alienated together in a newspaper.
>
> —John Klima, editor of *Day and Age*, interview (1993)

"This country is so spread out," twenty-one year old Arielle Greenberg tells me, "people my age . . . feel very separate and kind of floating and adrift . . . I feel like that myself."[1] Looking for roots, a way to feel connected and supported in a world where her ideas and ideals seem out of place, Arielle and other misfits have created what she calls "a community." The community they've imagined and fashioned is an odd one, not situated in a region or specific place, but spread out across the country, often invisible from the outside. It's a community brought together and defined primarily through a medium of communication that Arielle and her fellow citizens make themselves: *zines.*

Zines are noncommercial, nonprofessional, small-circulation magazines that their creators produce, publish, and distribute by themselves. Most often laid out on plain paper and reproduced on common Xerox machines, zines are sold, given away, or, as is common custom, swapped for other zines. They're distributed mainly through the mail and are advertised through the grapevine of other zines and in the pages of zines containing reviews of other zines such as *Factsheet Five.* Filled with highly personalized editorial "rants," "comix," stories, poems, material appropriated from the mass press, hand-drawn pictures, and cut-and-paste collages, the zine world is vast. Subjects range from the sublime (for example, the travelogue entries and philosophical reflections of a wandering outcast in *Cometbus*) to the ridiculous (*8-Track Mind,* a zine devoted to eight-track tape-player enthusiasts), and make a detour through the unfathomable (pictures of bowling pins in different settings in *Eleventh Pin*). The printruns of these zines are small, averaging about 250, though the phenomenon, while hidden, is much larger. Anywhere from 10,000 to 50,000 different zine titles circulate in the United States at any moment. They are produced by individuals—primarily young people, raised with the "privileges" of the white, middle class—who feel at odds with mainstream society and feel that their interests, voice, and creativity are unrepresented in the commercial media.

As far back as the 1930s, *fanzines* were created by science fiction fans as a way to exchange ideas and passions for a literature deemed worthless by the literary world. In the 1970s, this zine stream was joined by punk rockers who created their own publications to celebrate bands and music that were by and large ignored by the commercial and journalistic arbiters of rock music. Today, individuals reveal the intimacies of their lives in *perzines*, gays and lesbians vent in *queerzines*, and anarchists denounce the state and capitalism in their zines—forging distinct communities through their communication. But central to the greater community and connecting all zines is *The Scene*: the loose confederation of self-consciously "alternative" publications, bands, shows, radio stations, cafes, bookstores, and people that make up modern bohemia.

The Scene

The name "bohemia" conjures up images of Paris cafes, cold-water New York City walk-ups, and San Francisco poetry readings. Certainly bohemia still exists in these locales and zines help to weave the scene together there. But more common than a New York or San Francisco "scene zine" is a zine like the one written by Eric, who publishes to "rave on and on about the scene back home" in Pennsylvania's Lehigh Valley; or the "scene reports" from Huntsville, Alabama.[2] These are bohemias in backwater towns and suburbs scattered throughout the United States.

Today bohemia is first and foremost not *a* bohemia—it is many bohemias and they are widely dispersed. As C. Carr has coined it, it is a "bohemia diaspora," and "for the first time in 150 years, bohemia can't be pinpointed on the map."[3] The reasons for this dispersal are manifold, not the least of which is that bohemia followed in the shadow of the rest of society, spreading out of the cities and into the suburbs. But this dispersal is also linked to more recent phenomena: gentrification and a superheated culture market.

While the Beats of the 1950s and the counterculturists of the 1960s benefitted from the cheap urban quarters left in the wake of middle-class white flight to the suburbs, hipsters of the following decades were priced out of established bohemian locales by the return of the middle class. Young professionals, sometimes veterans of the sixties' counterculture themselves, wanted the excitement and cultural vitality of bohemian neighborhoods, and they had good-paying jobs that ensured they could live where they pleased.

Priced out of traditional bohemias, new bohemians moved elsewhere . . . and were soon followed by yuppies, the process repeating itself, ad infinitum. This gentrification cycle was so well established in the 1980s that the president of the art school I attended heralded this practice as one in which "[t]he presence of the arts and artists can work in mysterious ways as an economic force." In an annual report to the New York state bureaucracy, he outlined this "mysterious . . . force," arguing that

> despite the stereotype of the starving artist, the artist as tenant improves the real estate market. It was the artist who generated the increasing valuation of property in Greenwich Village, and then, after being priced out of that area, did the same in Soho. As artists are forced out of Soho by rents they can no longer afford, they settle [elsewhere] . . . in every case stimulating the renewal of decayed areas.[4]

When one added into this equation the superheated high art market of the 1980s and the ever-growing importance of the cultural industry to the American economy—by now its second largest export—the consequences for bohemia became disastrous. At first, cultural innovations and their creators were thrown under the spotlight and feted and dined in Soho or on Wall Street; then they were bought up and moved out, or discarded as worthless and unprofitable. The impact of these two forces on the cultural world that traditionally populates bohemia was severe: up and out or down and out; instant stardom or the inability to pay your ever-increasing rent. Either way, the result was an exodus. For the old bohemia and the healthy discontent and creativity it fostered, this exodus was lethal. "Dissent cannot happen in a vacuum," argues Carr. "Nor can social or aesthetic movements grow in one. Community is the fabric that sustains experiment, stimulating that leap into the void and maybe even cushioning a fall."[5]

For some critics this disappearance of physical locale is irreplaceable. Russell Jacoby, bemoaning the death of the public intellectual, writes:

> Fragile urban habitats of busy streets, cheap eateries, reasonable rents, and decent environs nourish bohemias. . . . When this delicate environment is injured or transformed, the "surplus" intellectuals do not disappear, but disperse; they spread out across the country. The difference is critical: a hundred artists, poets, and writers with families and friends in ten city blocks means one thing; scattered across ten states or ten university towns, they mean something else.[6]

And for Jacoby that something else signals the death of bohemia.

But bohemia has been declared dead and buried too many times for anyone to take such pronouncements too seriously. And it is not completely true that geographical bohemias don't exist anymore. The Mission in San Francisco, the Lower East Side of Manhattan, the unfortunate Williamsburg in Brooklyn (unfortunate because it is heralded as the "New Bohemia" every couple of years in the real estate section of the *New York Times*) still exist. Seattle, Olympia, Portland, Austin, Minneapolis, Chapel Hill, Richmond: all these locales have bohemian scenes. But the fact remains that there is no longer a Paris—no longer one unified and coherent geographical bohemia.

Marigay Graña in the preface to a monumental anthology of writings, *On Bohemia*, writes:

> In reviewing the literature for this anthology we were able to come up with only two characteristics of bohemianism which appear to hold constant over the century-and-a-half of its recognized existence: (1) an attitude of dissent from the prevailing values of middle-class society—artistic, political, utilitarian, sexual—usually expressed in life-style and through a medium of the arts; and (2) a cafe.[7]

In this new bohemian diaspora, place no longer plays the important part it once did. When cafes are renamed coffee bars, and a nationwide chain—Starbucks—is profiled in the *Wall Street Journal* as one of the fastest-growing and most profitable businesses of the year, the cafe as a locus of bohemia is in its death throes.[8] One hundred and fifty years of geographical bohemia may indeed be coming to an end. And perhaps that is only to be expected. The world in which we live is an increasingly mobile one and becoming ever more decentralized across space. Besides, there was always something contradictory about nailing a word that is synonymous with Gypsies and vagabonds to a fixed location.

If the latter condition of place no longer holds, the former characteristics—those of bohemian ideas, practice, and creativity—live on through nonspatial networks. Webs of communication can offer the community, support, and feeling of connection that are so important for dissent and creativity. One of these networks, these virtual spaces where bohemia still exists, is the network of zines.

Asked to characterize her zine, *Slug & Lettuce*, Christine Boarts uses rare instrumental terms, describing it as "providing space for communication and networking within underground music and political scenes."[9] In other words, *S&L* is a virtual cafe. In issue no. 29 Chris is the hostess who greets scenesters with "Some Thoughts": a long personal editorial about living in New York City and feeling like "a faceless body in a crowd." Inside, entertainment is provided by photos of punk shows and reviews of zines and records. Back pages are given over to armchair philosophers who opine on subjects from information on AIDS to the imprisonment of Native American activist Leonard Peltier to the enduring question, "What is punk?" And the free classified ads that make up the bulk of *S&L* are voices of the patrons looking for company: "Oi, Everyone. Interested in Philippine stuff? Send me your stuff list and I'll send you mine . . . "; or, "I'm a poor little punk girl in search of someone to share thoughts with . . . I'm chemfree, I hate homophobics, conformity, bimbos, and many other things." Places to stay, spaces to play shows, zines looking for contributors, bands looking for members, homemade T-shirts for sale—*S&L* makes space for it all.[10]

The idea of zines holding a scene together is not new. In the science fiction scene, "for almost forty years Fanzines were the net, the cement which kept fandom together as an entity," writes longtime sci-fi fanzine writer Don Fitch.[11] And in many ways The Scene, in terms of community structure, is a lot closer to the nongeographical community of science fiction fandom than to the traditional spatial bohemia. With coffeehouses owned by corporations and traditional bohemian neighborhoods populated by middle-class professionals, zines like *S&L* offer an invaluable service, acting as a cafe, community center, and clubhouse that help connect these bohemians to one another, providing the "cement" that holds together a dispersed scene.[12]

But if zines like *Slug & Lettuce* bind The Scene together by providing *virtual* cafes, others do it by providing tour guides to the bohemia diaspora scattered across the *terra firma*. This function explains the almost ubiquitous presence in punk zines of the Band Tour Diary. In these diaries the zine writer takes the reader on a day-by-day tour with the band: riding in vans, playing at clubs, eating bad food, crash-

SLUG & LETTUCE

A few notes on Recycling: With little effort, you can make a considerable difference. One simple thing you can do is reduce the amount of bags you take when shopping. If making a small purchase (esp. a soda or something you will consume immediatly) just don't take a bag. If you plan on shopping take a bag with you, either a cloth bag, or one you've already collected. If you stop and think if you really need it (bag or whatever xtra packaging) you can make a difference. There is an unbelievable amount of waste, on unnecessary things. Locate either a recycling center in your neighborhood or check into curbside recycling. Newspaper,glass & cans can be recycled easily (jsut clean them), but it dosen't have to stop there, find out what items your neighborhood recycles, there is probably more that you realize. Therefore you can help preserve resources, prevent excess garbage that will be dumped in landfills and extra garbage floating on the streets. Pre cycling is another thing to consider. When buying things check for overpackaging. By purchasing items in bulk or getting fruits, veggies/ deli loose rather than prepackaged in plastic you can reduce what you will throw away. There is a lot that can be done with out a lot of effort. if you just stop and think about what you're using. Every little bit helps!! -Chris

Start Recycling Today!

NEGAZIONE AT CBGB'S 8/28/90

Christine
Slug and Lettuce
Peter Stuyvesant Sta.
PO BOX 2067
New York NY 10009-8914

#18 FREE Nov. 1990
Donations Appreciated

All Photos: Chris Boarts

Welcome to another issue of Slug and Lettuce. S&L is still free, but **donations** are greatly appreciated to help with printing costs. For those unfamiliar w/ my 'zine', the purpose is to bring together contacts for communication, especially DIY (Do it yourself) projects and people. So if you have a project and have not been in touch, please write w/ more info. **Classifieds are Free,** but please keep them short and to the point. Each issue is avaliable for a SASE (Self addressed stamped envelope) also send a SASE w/ classifieds if you want a copy of the issue. S&L is printed bi-monthly, 1000 copies. **Advertising:** is nned to help cover printing costs, if interested please write. Rates are $15 for 2½" x 5" down ad. Send any material you would like reviewed or to trade for S&L. Feedback is always welcome, and anyone that just wants to write, that's cool too! -Chris

CITIZENS ARREST at CBGB'S 8/28/90

Fig. 26.1. The Virtual Coffeehouse of *Slug & Lettuce.* (Courtesy of Christine Boarts)

ing on couches.[13] A member of Born Against chronicles his band's tour in *I, Yeast Roll*:

Baltimore, MD
March 4, 1993

Spent last night here at Brooks' house, marinating in my own uselessness. Spent the night before that in a parking lot of a Louisville Taco Bell, sleeping in the loft of my van, after

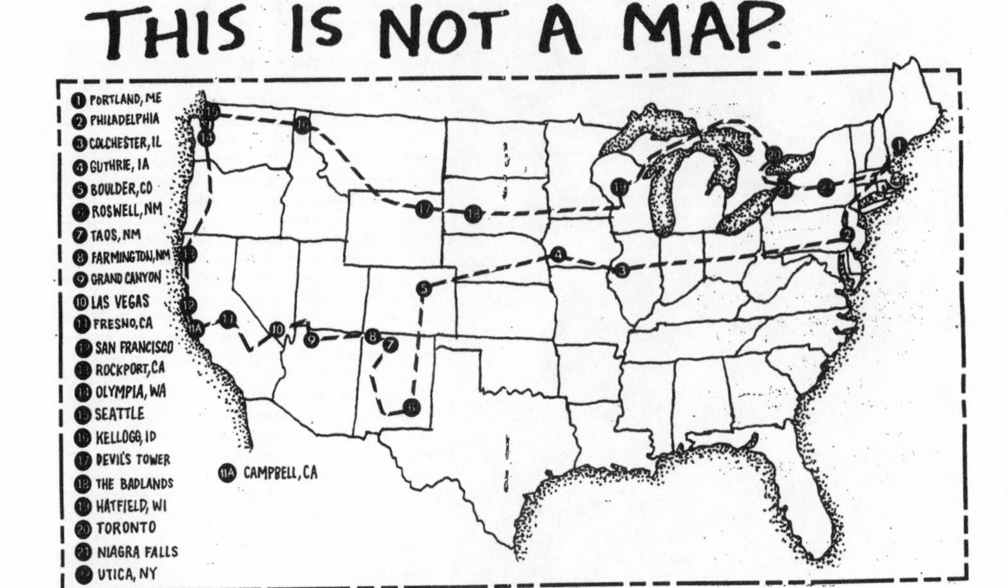

Fig. 26.2. Bohemia's map in *Po.* (Courtesy of Mike Wolstat)

having arrived many hours too late for our show with Agent Orange. I am eating reheated pasta and drinking some old Fresca . . . a coca-cola beverage, making me guilty in global corporate fascism.[14]

A slight variation on the tour diary theme is the "Road Trip," where much the same happenings are chronicled, minus the band. In *Gogglebox,* Jennifer takes her reader with her as she bums rides from New York City to San Francisco;[15] in *Po,* the editor produces a map of his road trip;[16] and in the January 1993 issue of *Crash,* after chronicling their own road trip, the writers invite readers to "Join the Crash Network!," a network of people looking for places to crash and others offering up their floor to be crashed on.[17]

One way to look at this regular feature of the zines is as a modern extension of the great American directive: Go West, young man! Following in the footsteps of Woody Guthrie, Jack Kerouac, the Merry Pranksters, and Thelma and Louise, rebels hit the road. "Freedom from school, freedom from [boyfriend] Brian, freedom to live for nothing except my own desires and curiosities," writes Jenn of *Gogglebox,* about to embark on her road trip.[18] Shaking the dust from your heels, beholden only to circumstance, is a deeply American dream.

In the long boho road trip tradition, chroniclers always present *their* America. Zinesters are no different. Rarely, if ever, are the Grand Canyon, Walt Disney World, the Washington Monument, or other sanctified sites of the tourist trail mentioned. Instead, the landmarks are the individuals whom the zine writers meet, the clubs where the bands play, the underground bookstores they visit—in brief, the people

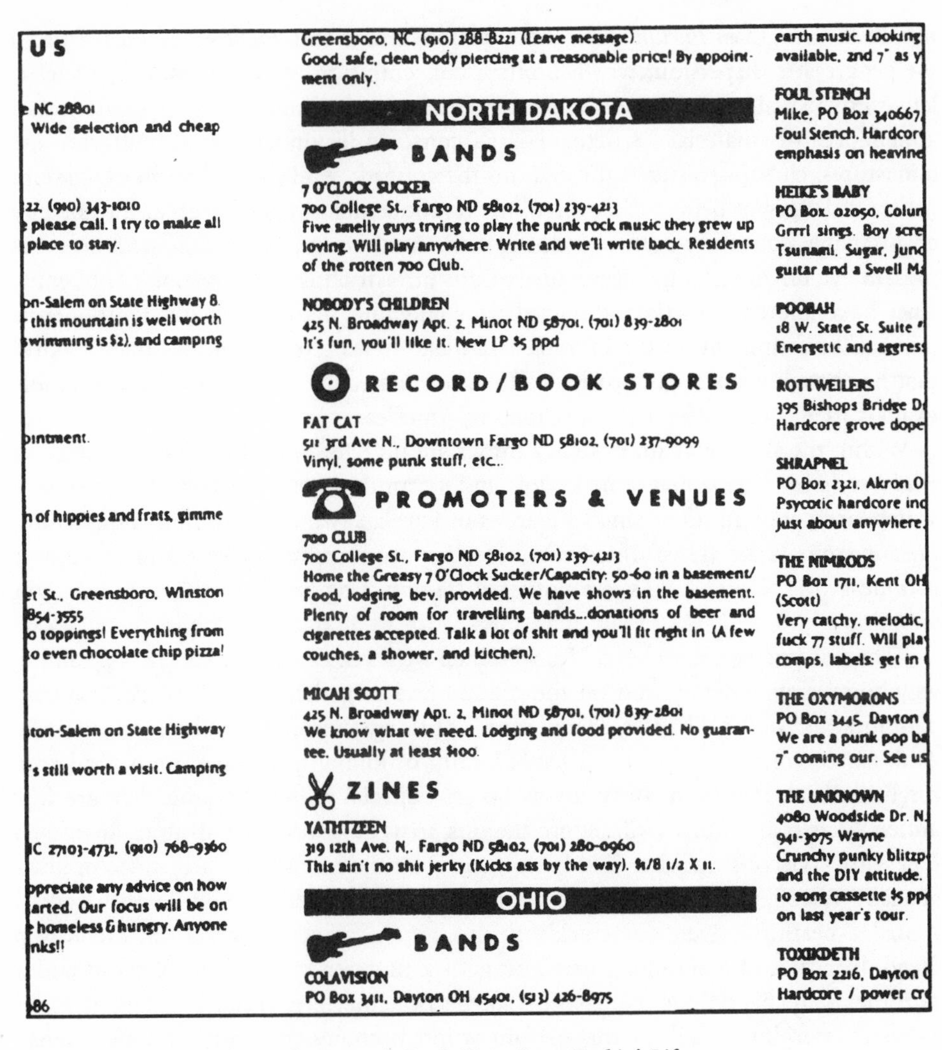

US

e NC 28801
Wide selection and cheap

22, (910) 343-1010
e please call. I try to make all
place to stay.

on-Salem on State Highway 8.
r this mountain is well worth
swimming is $2), and camping

pintment.

n of hippies and frats, gimme

et St., Greensboro, Winston
854-3555
o toppings! Everything from
to even chocolate chip pizza!

ton-Salem on State Highway

's still worth a visit. Camping

IC 27103-4731, (910) 768-9360

ppreciate any advice on how
arted. Our focus will be on
e homeless & hungry. Anyone
nks!!

86

Greensboro, NC (910) 288-8221 (Leave message)
Good, safe, clean body piercing at a reasonable price! By appointment only.

NORTH DAKOTA

BANDS

7 O'CLOCK SUCKER
700 College St., Fargo ND 58102, (701) 239-4213
Five smelly guys trying to play the punk rock music they grew up loving. Will play anywhere. Write and we'll write back. Residents of the rotten 700 Club.

NOBODY'S CHILDREN
425 N. Broadway Apt. 2, Minot ND 58701, (701) 839-2801
It's fun, you'll like it. New LP $5 ppd

RECORD/BOOK STORES

FAT CAT
511 3rd Ave N., Downtown Fargo ND 58102, (701) 237-9099
Vinyl, some punk stuff, etc..

PROMOTERS & VENUES

700 CLUB
700 College St., Fargo ND 58102, (701) 239-4213
Home the Greasy 7 O'Clock Sucker/Capacity: 50-60 in a basement/ Food, lodging, bev. provided. We have shows in the basement. Plenty of room for travelling bands...donations of beer and cigarettes accepted. Talk a lot of shit and you'll fit right in (A few couches, a shower, and kitchen).

MICAH SCOTT
425 N. Broadway Apt. 2, Minot ND 58701, (701) 839-2801
We know what we need. Lodging and food provided. No guarantee. Usually at least $100.

ZINES

YATHTZEEN
319 12th Ave. N., Fargo ND 58102, (701) 280-0960
This ain't no shit jerky (Kicks ass by the way). $1/8 1/2 X 11.

OHIO

BANDS

COLAVISION
PO Box 3411, Dayton OH 45401, (513) 426-8975

earth music. Looking
available, 2nd 7" as y

FOUL STENCH
Mike, PO Box 340667,
Foul Stench. Hardcor
emphasis on heavin

HEIKE'S BABY
PO Box. 02050, Colur
Grrrl sings. Boy scre
Tsunami, Sugar, Jun
guitar and a Swell M

POOBAH
18 W. State St. Suite "
Energetic and aggres

ROTTWEILERS
395 Bishops Bridge D
Hardcore grove dope

SHRAPNEL
PO Box 2321, Akron O
Psycotic hardcore in
just about anywhere.

THE NIMRODS
PO Box 1711, Kent OH
(Scott)
Very catchy, melodic,
fuck 77 stuff. Will pla
comps, labels: get in

THE OXYMORONS
PO Box 3445, Dayton
We are a punk pop b
7" coming our. See us

THE UNKNOWN
4080 Woodside Dr. N.
941-3075 Wayne
Crunchy punky blitzp
and the DIY attitude.
10 song cassette $5 pp
on last year's tour.

TOXIKDETH
PO Box 2216, Dayton
Hardcore / power cr

Fig. 26.3. Guide to the underground: *Book Your Own Fuckin' Life.*

and places of The Scene. The tour diaries and road trips in zines bring to life the landscape of a dispersed bohemia.

The underground is not a tight, formalized, and coherent social grouping with firm boundaries; instead, it is a nongeographical sprawl that must be mapped out. Zine publications like *Book Your Own Fuckin' Life: Do-It-Yourself Resource Guide* provide state by state lists of the zines, cafes, radio stations, alternative clubs, and so forth that make up this underground diaspora. "We have shows in the basement," advertises the 700 Club in Fargo, North Dakota. "Plenty of room for traveling bands . . . donations of beer and cigarettes accepted. Talk a lot of shit and you'll fit right in (A few couches, a shower and a kitchen)."[19] Through the narrative of road trips and tour diaries, zine writers draw connections between these scattered sites, charting a map of the underground.

But even with the impressive list of institutions and connections listed in guides like *Book Your Own Fuckin' Life*, modern bohemia is extremely precarious. Due to the geographic dispersion, which limits a concentration of resources, and a speculative urban real estate economy, which curtails investment, there is simply not an abundance of material structures—self-consciously underground coffeehouses, bookstores, clubs—scattered throughout the country. And those that do exist are in constant danger of being "discovered" by nonbohemians: gobbled up and ruined by an insatiable consumer-culture industry and an all-consuming public with an ever-present eye for the new thrill. Because of this infrastructural deprivation of bohemia, zines have another function: the road trips and tour diaries map out the bohemia that can be found within the everyday. The narratives give keys to decipher a world that lies below the straight world, in front of "normal" society's eyes but invisible to their gaze. Zines offer a shadow map of America.

Within the shadow map, ordinary things are invested with different meanings. In *Pool Dust*'s road trip, abandoned pools and storm drain culverts become temporary skateboard parks. In other zines, Veterans of Foreign Wars halls become punk clubs, or laundromats are transformed into cafes for impromptu poetry readings. And in countless zine tales, Kinko's is a potential free printing press if you know the right scam.[20]

"There is poetry everywhere," Rob Treinen writes in *Cramped and Wet*, explaining why he reprints letters found on the ground and in garbage cans.[21] Marc Arsenault describes his *Andy's Chair* as "The journal of things missed . . . Things forgotten."[22] And, as recounted in Aaron's *Cometbus* story of killing time while on a road trip, forgotten back streets in dusty towns become special merely because they are forgotten. "I had an hour to kill before the bus arrived, so I looked around downtown Janesville [Wisconsin], where I'd been assured by the locals that there was "nothing at all"," Aaron writes. "As usual, 'nothing at all' turned out to be pretty cool. I passed a beautiful river, old crackly neon signs, a farmer's market, an old 'Chop Suey' district, and a shopping cart guy with a tiny general store junk stand and a sign that said 'Everything You Need Can Be Bought Here.' Yeah, nothing at all."[23] What is "nothing at all" to the straight world becomes something for the underground. Even mundane items like a children's science experiment book from the 1950s takes on a different meaning when recontextualized through different eyes and repackaged in a zine.[24] As *William Wants a Doll*'s Arielle Greenberg elliptically yet accurately defines it, "The Scene is a network of things that people who don't know The Scene wouldn't necessarily know are cool."[25]

In addition to reinvesting the everyday with shadow values, out of the ordinary events and places are often highlighted and joyfully recounted as testament to the depth and breadth of America's weirdness that lurks just below the patina of normality. Adam Bregman, editor of *Shithappy*, tells tales of his travels with The Cacophony Society as they tour the Great Western Gun Show, visit booths that sell Nazi armbands next to little toy bunnies, and play the game "Guess Who's a Serial Killer" while watching the crowd (at about the time the accused Oklahoma City bomber was making his gun show rounds, too). On another field trip, Adam & Co. have lunch at the Los Angeles Police Training Academy, sitting beneath the LAPD's brass knuckle collection.[26]

SMELL EXPERIMENT

YOU WILL NEED: your friend, and something pleasant for her to smell

NOW DO THIS. Hold it in front of her nose and *keep it there.* Tell your friend to keep sniffing away. What happens?

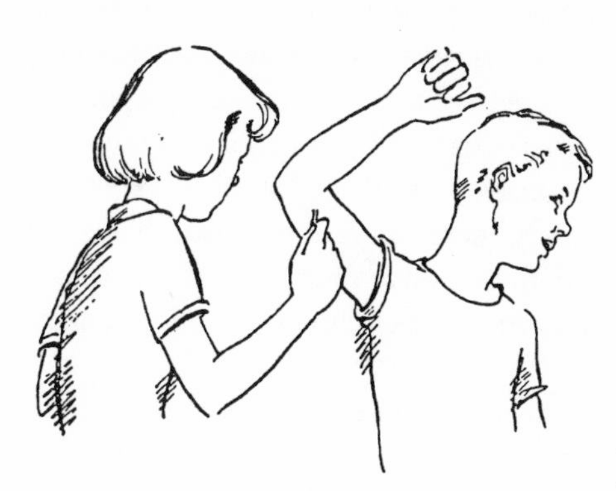

Look at the gentleman in the picture. As you might guess, he is queer.

Reading in queer positions is hard work for the muscles that move your eyeballs as you follow the words. They have been trained to do their work with your head in an upright position.

Fig. 26.4. In the shadows of innocence with *You Own a Wonderful Machine: Your Body.*

The shadow map is the property of people who possess very little. What they do possess, however, is the ability to give things they don't own *new meanings.* As Dick Hebdige and others in the early days of the Centre for Contemporary Cultural Studies in Birmingham have argued, this "semantic rearrangement of components of the objective world" gives the materially impoverished material with which to fashion their subcultures.[27] Dispersed geographically without the resources to build their own physical spaces, zinesters chart out a world of bohemianism, overlaying the straight world with one of their own. While these new bohemians do not command significant material resources, what they do have is a vast communication network and thus the ability to build, combine, and spread this bohemian shadow map of America. Combined with the network of people and institutions that do exist, and virtual community centers like *Slug & Lettuce,* the bohemian diaspora holds together. The Scene may not be a place, but it is a community.

No Rules

> The next time I hear someone define "A REAL PUNK," I'm gonna shit rabbit turds and hop down a fucking hole!
>
> —Wolfboy, in a letter to *Maximumrocknroll* (1985)

Bohemia is the home of the libertine. At the same time, bohemia, like all communities, has rules. Most often these rules are those of definition: What is bohemian? What is not bohemian? "The foreigner fails to understand that the laws of Bohemia are not the same as his native country, and so he believes that Bohemians are of necessity unconventional," wrote Edwin Irwin in 1906, "when the fact is that the Bohemian is merely living in accordance with the laws of his own country."[28]

The virtual "country" of The Scene has laws as well. And as was the case with institutions, these laws may be more important to this modern bohemia than they were to the old ones. As The Scene is dispersed across space, rules and traditions are the only things that can draw boundaries between the bohemian and straight worlds. Living within a modern consumer society that celebrates lifestyle choice and stylistic differences, it is also more difficult to mark yourself as a cultural rebel than it was in Irwin's day—strict criteria of bohemian inclusion and exclusion helps. But there's a conflict. For as much as they need these conventions to exist and hold together, those who make up The Scene, true to their bohemian lineage, honor above all individuality, originality, and freedom.

As being "punk" is one of the prime identities of The Scene, nowhere is this conflict between individual expression and community allegiance argued more vehemently than around the definition of what actually is "punk." And nowhere has this argument taken place with more heat—and sometimes light—than in the letter pages of *Maximumrocknroll.* Started in 1982 by Tim Yohannan as a way to bring together and politicize a then burgeoning punk music scene, *Maximumrocknroll* is one of the most venerable institutions of The Scene. Not everybody likes it. Tim and *MRR* are often slagged for being too political (or PC), for being too authoritarian, for trying to dominate The Scene, or simply for being too big. But these criticisms highlight *MRR*'s success: it has, more than any other institution, helped to define—and continually redefine—what is "punk." This definition takes place in editorials by Tim, in columns by other regular writers, and in scene reports and articles sent in by readers. But the war of definition happens primarily in *MRR*'s extensive letters section.[29] For fifteen years, and close to one hundred and fifty issues, punks have been slugging it out in the trenches of *MRR*'s letters column, setting up and tearing down the rules of being punk.

One of the flash points for debating the rules of the subculture is whether the markers of this particular bohemian identity are external or internal; that is, is punk what you are on the inside to yourself, or outside to the world? "I come from a very small town of maybe 1000 people," writes Planet Boy of North Dakota in a 1983 issue of *MRR*, "I try to make the people around here realize that Punk is not dead . . . I had my ear pierced 3 times and [put] color in my hair."

The prime directive of punk is individuality. This is what straight society lacks, and this is what being a punk expresses. If upstanding members of straight society dress conventionally, then as an individual you dress in an opposite way. Like Planet Boy, you dye your hair and pierce your ear (remember, this is North Dakota in 1983). But as a punk you're also part of a community. "I hope someone at Max RNR is reading this," Planet Boy continues. "I wrote this . . . to let you know that there are punks in N.D. . . . at least one anyway (That'll change!)."[30]

In the next issue someone from this "community," John Hurt, another reader, responds:

MAXIMUMROCKNROLL

august 93. #123. $2.00. newsprint for life.

Fig. 26.5. What is a Punk? *Maximumrocknroll.* (Courtesy of Martin Sprouse and Tim Yohannan)

> I can identify with what [Planet Boy] is saying, but I also think he needs to re-examine some of his ideas about punk. . . . He boasted that he's had his ear pierced three times and has colored his hair . . . I think [that's] trendy. Punk is thinking for yourself, and *being* yourself. . . . Perhaps you don't realize it, but you are acting just like the phony society jerks you're supposed to be against.[31]

For John, dressing like a punk is a betrayal of punk: it is a symbol of conformity to a group ideal—just like that of phonies "you're supposed to be against." But in giving his opinion, John is also defining an ideal of what it is to be punk, a contradiction pointed out in the next issue of *MRR* when another reader, Mike Impastato, joins the fray: "Who the fuck does John think he is? Some divine god who gets to call someone trendy for dyeing their hair and piercing their ears. Personally I think it takes a lot of guts to look that wild and take all the shit people have to give, and not bowing to peer pressure to look 'right.' I think Planet Boy is being himself."[32] Mike takes us back to Planet Boy's argument: dressing punk is "being himself," because it is not bowing to "peer pressure." But in doing this publicly, Mike too is defining punk, implicitly arguing a standard for the community. Reading through hundreds upon hundreds of letters, I've seen the same argument countless times. Read enough of them and you begin to realize that the debate about how one dresses, how one thinks, is it punk?, is really a debate about something else: the conflict between rebellious individualism and group identity.

Punks are in a predicament: being a punk means you define yourself against society as an individual, but it also means that you define yourself as being part of a group, adhering to community standards. But the mix of authentic individuality and communal solidarity is a rough one. "What the fuck is going on?" asks Carlos Fernandez, "Here I am, new to the scene . . . hoping to be accepted without having to compromise my individuality, and what do I see? A flood of self-righteous, overbearing assholes pushing their views on me. . . . I thought I could be a punk without having to follow anyone's idea of punk."[33] What sort of a community do you have if everybody has to have his or her own idea of that community? Answer: an unstable one.

This inherent instability perhaps explains another trope in *MRR* and in other punk zines: the Golden Age of Punk. Two years ago, three years ago . . . pick any time in the past two decades, and you'll see that just a few years ago The Scene was different. Invariably it was better. For some the Golden Age was an era of unbridled individuality. "I think it's time somebody speaks up. I can't believe what's happening with the idea of punk," Steve Stepe writes as early as 1983. "Punk started out as an idea for us to break out of the mold we've been placed in. A way to do what you want; a right to be yourself and not what someone else wants you to be." *But*, "Now the complete opposite has happened. Instead of falling into the confines of 'normal' people, punks are trapped into being punks. At the next show you go to, look around. Everybody looks the same. . . . They all think the same."[34]

For other letter writers what's gone is the opposite. Whereas Steve remembers the days of true individuality, Javi writes to reminisce on the former unity of the scene: "Fuck this Peace Punx vs. Nazi Skins deal. When is this shit gonna stop? . . . Make the scene what it used to be . . . let's get it together brothers and sisters."[35] John

Fig. 26.6. What happened to The Scene? In *Flipside*. (Courtesy of Lee and Al)

Jankowski writes in another plea for past harmony: "Dear MRR, I'm writing to you because I'm afraid punk is dying fast. . . . Punks today just seem thoughtless and uncaring and unfriendly."[36] This "what's happened to The Scene?" complaint is such a standard feature in punk zines that *Flipside*, a long-standing Southern California punk zine with an extensive letters column, pokes fun at it on their cover, projecting the conflict into punk's distant future.[37] Like all nostalgia, that for the Golden Age of The Scene is based on trying to escape the realities of the present. In all societies there is conflict between the individual and the community. But because The Scene is a self-conscious construction fashioned in rebellion against the dominant model of society, these tensions between individual and community, which would otherwise be buried in tradition and convention, are laid open and bare. This explains why absolute acts of kindness and support like catching someone diving blind off a stage can exist in the same scene where spitting on the performer—and vice versa—was considered de rigueur. How a letter written by a punk to his community can conclude with the deeply contradictory "Individuals all have something in common—THEIR INDIVIDUALITY!!! UNITE, FUCKHEADS."[38] Or why month after month punks brutally slag each other in the pages of *MRR*, *Flipside*, and countless other zines, yet month after month they keep writing back.

The tension in the punk scene between the individual and community, between freedom and rules, is a microcosm of the tension that exists within all of the networked communities of the zine scene. Zines are profoundly personal expressions, yet as a medium of participatory communication they depend upon and help create community. This contradiction is never resolved. It's one of the things that keeps the underground dynamic and fresh, but it is also debilitating, a morass that leads Viktim Joe to conclude, in all earnestness, that "anyone who calls themselves a punk is definitely not one."[39] If community never goes farther than the pages of a zine or the floor of a club, this contradiction matters little. But if this community is to be the basis for collective action or the model for a new society, it matters a great deal.

Revolution Grrrl Style Now!

> You don't need to be a punk.
> You don't need our permission.
> There are no rules.
> No leader.
> Every girl is a Riot Grrrl.
> —Riot Grrrl, D.C.[40]

In a 1983 issue of *Maximumrocknroll*—while men were busy defining punk in the letters section—a group of women published the results of an informal poll surveying the feelings of women in the punk scene. The anonymous replies from different women revealed a deep discontent with their place in The Scene:

- When I flip through these American punk zines, all I see are pictures after pictures of what looks like the same guy with an almost-shaved head, leaping and grimacing with a microphone and no shirt. . . . God, it gets boring! Just once, I'd like to see a photo of a girl playing a guitar and really working at it.

- There are so few girls into hardcore here and they are totally into their boyfriends more than anything. I'm tired of living through someone else!

But the women also came up with some solutions:

- How about a women's caucus of punk music?
- I feel that if women want to be more involved, do it! Write for a fanzine, start a fanzine, set up gigs
- There are no easy answers, but I do know that women should be there for each other and talk, and most important listen. If we don't help ourselves, who will?[41]

Less than a decade later, in Olympia, Washington, Riot Grrrl was founded. Bringing together the radical critique of patriarchy and a desire for the female community of past feminist movements, and the in-your-face, rebellious individualism of punk rock, Riot Grrrl became a network of young women linked by zines and bands . . . and by their anger, dedicated to "putting the punk back into feminism and feminism into punk."[42]

But while punk and feminism were their influences, "Riot Grrrl is about *not* being the girlfriend of the band and *not* being the daughter of the feminist," as Emma explains in *Riot Grrrl #5*.[43] "We're tired of being written out—out of history, out of the 'scene,' out of our bodies," write the editors of *Riot Grrrl #3*. "For this reason we have created our zine and scene."[44] For young feminist punk rockers, Riot Grrrl was founded as a space of their own, though perhaps "founded" is not the best term. For while there are (or were) Riot Grrrl chapters in a number of cities and hundreds of zines produced by women who identify themselves as Riot Grrrls, Riot Grrrl had no founding convention, no structure, and little formal organization outside of local meetings and zine exchanges. "There is no particular agenda or pledge or motto," states Ne Tantillo in *Riot Grrrl #6 1/2*. "There is no singular allegiance to any one's thought. There is no structure to follow, only what you build yourself."[45]

What these women built is a forum for self-expression, "a MEDIUM for grrrls to say what's on their minds."[46] And what's on their minds is the personal effect of growing up as a girl in a man's world. Included in almost every Riot Grrrl zine is at least one—and usually more than one—poem, rant, experiential scream about having been sexually abused, often by a male friend or relative. Diana's from *Riot Grrrl #5* is typical.[47]

Sexual abuse is an all-too-common problem for young women, with approximately one in three girls a victim before the age of eighteen.[48] One of the most damaging effects of such abuse is the shame girls feel, that it's somehow their fault, or, because they often know the attacker, that it isn't *really* abuse. Sharing their stories with comrades and pointing their fingers at the accused, these young women express their rage, relieve their shame, and overcome the isolation that accompanies such an experience.

Another issue Riot Grrrls commonly address is self-image. In a study commissioned by the American Association of University Women, girls in elementary school, when asked how often they felt "happy the way they were," responded "always" 60

Fig. 26.7. Riot Grrrl Revolution sticker.

Fig. 26.8. "It felt like rape . . ." *Riot Grrrl,* New York City.

Fig. 26.9. Arguing image in *Riot Grrrl, Huh?*

percent of the time. By high school this number dropped to 29 percent, leading the researchers to conclude that "girls emerge from adolescence with a poor self-image, relatively low expectations from life and much less confidence in themselves than boys."[49] Bombarded with idealized mass media images of what a girl "should" look like, and solicited by lipstick, mascara, perfume, deodorant, and weight loss advertisements whose purpose is to convince a girl that she is—sans product—incomplete, it's no surprise that girls develop a poor self-image of themselves. In angry response, Riot Grrrl zines offer a forum to talk back to the demands of the media and men, about how a woman ought to look, or how a woman ought to be.[50] In answer to the implicit question, "Why Riot Grrrl?," *Bikini Kill*'s Kathleen Hanna et al. answer: "BECAUSE we are angry at a society that tells us Girl = Dumb, Girl = Bad, Girl = Weak."[51]

Riot Grrrl zines, like all zines, are "continually re-rehearsed self-definition[s]."[52] They are a way to reject definitions given by the dominant society and replace them with one's own, a means of "taking over the means of production in order to create our own meanings," as one Riot Grrrl statement puts it.[53] This partially explains another archetypal feature of these zines: the manifesto explaining what Riot Grrrl is. No Riot Grrrl zine is complete without one, or as is likely, without a dozen. A flier handed out by members of Riot Grrrl NYC at a show explaining "Who—What—Why" lists sixteen individual responses in answer to this question. These multiple statements are not rooted in indecisiveness, but in a philosophy. "We want the definition of Riot Grrrl to be whatever anyone who wants to use the term wants it to be," Lisa Wildman of Riot Grrrl NYC explains. "We feel that over-organization would cost us the individuality we spend too much of the time fighting the rest of the world for."[54] And so it is not unusual to see in *Riot Grrrl Newsletter One* a defining manifesto prefaced with the title: "RIOT GRRRL (to me)."

As Lisa explains, this individualization is a product of rebellion against dominant definitions of what it is to be a woman. Working hard to free themselves from one definition, Riot Grrrls are understandably reluctant to adopt another. Their second-hand experience with the codification of the feminist movement of the early 1970s into set "feminist" roles makes them doubly suspicious of group definitions. "RIOT GRRRL (to me)" is surrounded by rants on date rape (to me), demeaning images (to me), sexual inequality (to me). The authors and contributors go out of their way to stress that what follows is only their point of view. As in all zines, the politics in Riot Grrrl are personalized. Lists of women's resource groups, herbal remedies, and statistics on sexual abuse can be found in Riot Grrrl zines, but these are dwarfed by personal testimonials. And this is an integral part of the Riot Grrrl (anti)line. "I encourage girls everywhere to set forth their own revolutionary agendas *from their own place in the world*," writes one of the founding mothers of Riot Grrrl, Kathleen Hanna, in her *Bikini Kill #2*, for Riot Grrrls should "embrace subjectivity as the only reality there is."[55]

Context is important. Kathleen's dictum is at the end of a discussion of what she sees as a danger in Riot Grrrl. "Have you noticed," she writes, "that there is this weird phenomenon that happens to do with naming something and having it turn into something else." Riot Grrrl, a repository of individual voices, is becoming a community of shared ideas, and Kathleen is aware of the problems this will cause. "It is too easy for our doctrines to turn into dogma and . . . recitations rather than meaningful interactions," and thus "new standards arise when the whole thing was to shatter the old and replace it with action."[56]

Others share Kathleen's concern. "The whole idea of Riot Grrrl in the beginning was that you sat around and told your *own* story," Arielle Greenberg explains, mourning the passing of the Golden Age of RG. Now, she elaborates, Riot Grrrl has turned into "a few different formulas and you have to follow them: You do drawings of women, you do a little ranting about some guy who harassed you at one point in your life. And once you've seen them enough it seems like . . . they're just regurgitating material that someone else told them. And that doesn't seem too real to me."[57] Both Kathleen and Arielle are pointing out the problems associated with the necessary "routinization" of community, the move from innovation to tradition, from individual experience to shared realities.

Like punks, Riot Grrrls are more than just individuals, they are a community. And group function is stressed even more with Riot Grrrls than in the punk scene. "RIOT GIRL (to me)," Dawn describes paradoxically, is "GRRRLS getting together and standing up for their rights and empowering each other, knowing we are not alone."[58] Grrrl community is underscored in reaction to the competition that women often feel toward one another in the dominant society. In the face of this division, Riot Grrrl solidarity is the answer: "Riot Grrrl Loving Riot Grrrl" reads the back cover of *Riot Grrrl Olympia*.[59]

Solidarity is also important because Riot Grrrls see themselves as a political force. As it was for their feminist sisters in the 1970s, the "consciousness raising" of personal testimonials is ostensibly not meant solely as an end in itself. "Riot Grrrl is," writes Ne, "a river of ideas and perspectives flowing through our minds; a tributary with a swift current rippling over and around obstacles, poring into an ocean, not to become part of the tide, but to change the tide."[60] The question is: How does one change the tide if you are against becoming a common, communal countertide yourself?

Riot Grrrls, like punks and zinesters writ large, are trying to construct a new model of community. No Leaders, No Rules, No Permission Asked. The new community will be based not in common understandings, but in shared dialogue. The new community will not be based in traditions or laws, but in re-creating the community anew with each act of communication between individuals. This model is an exciting one, offering both liberty and connection at the same time—it also may not work outside of the realm of communication and culture.

"This is our revolution—it's right here in these pages,"[61] proclaim the editors of *Riot Grrrl #8*. And this spells the limitation of Riot Grrrl as a political force. It is very hard to translate the individual expression and personal subjectivity that are the trademark of Riot Grrrl communication into a lasting political movement. Riot Grrrl politics, like all zine politics, are based in the existential act of creative rebellion, "creat[ing] revolution in our lives every single day by envisioning and creating alternatives to the christian capitalist way of doing things," *Bikini Kill #2* reads.[62] But with so much emphasis on individual expression and creativity, zines are less a means to an end than the ends in themselves: the revolution itself—a virtual revolution in the realm of culture and individual consciousness that leaves the material world of structures and power very much intact.

Riot Grrrl breathes new life into feminism. By mixing the politics of feminism with the culture of punk rock, it takes the ideas of feminism past and translates them into a modern language. By producing zines and networking with one another, Riot Grrrls become producers instead of merely consumers, creating their own spaces rather than living within the confines of those made for them. But some crucial political questions still remain: How does cultural action translate into political change? And how do you build a movement when you are afraid to coalesce as a community? Because these problems are routinely neglected by Riot Grrrls, zinesters, and bohemians throughout history, a more appropriate question might be: Do these rebels really want to change the greater society at all?

Communities against Society?

"Americans of all ages, all stations in life, and all dispositions are forever forming associations."[63] So wrote Alexis de Tocqueville, impressed by this distinctive feature of America as he traveled through the country in the early nineteenth century. Voluntary associations, he pointed out, are constituted to govern towns, build churches, promote morals, discuss ideas, throw parties . . . for seemingly everything. He believed that Americans formed these alliances so readily because democracy renders the individual citizen independent, and thus, in his opinion, weak. Only by coming together in association do individuals have presence. Tocqueville also understood associations as a force that mitigated the individualistic tendencies in American society. Coming together in purposeful unions, citizens were no longer isolated individuals.

However, Tocqueville also observed another result of these voluntary associations. The multiplicity of associations could turn people's attention inward toward the business of the group and away from more general concerns, the result being a dizzying array of associations with few shared meanings and little interest in greater social change. To quote Tocqueville: "Civil associations . . . far from directing public attention to public affairs, serve to turn men's minds away therefrom."[64] Focused on the immediate businesses of their own individual group, association members could forget that they were also citizens of a larger society.

The world of zines share the characteristics—both positive and negative—of these free associations.[65] There is no doubt that zines foster community, but because zine writers privilege personal experience and subjective realities over broader, public concerns, the tendency is for this community to fragment into microcommunities as each group turns inward to concentrate on what is real (to me).

For many individuals, being able to define what is real for them is critical as they feel that *their reality* is ignored by the rest of society. Queer punk rockers, for example, feel unrepresented in both predominantly straight punk zines and in the liberal assimilationist gay and lesbian press. Therefore they use zines like *Homocore*

Fig. 26.10. The network of *Factsheet Five.*

and *J.D.s* as a virtual meeting place, a space to define and communicate who they are and remind themselves and others that they are not alone.[66] "Dear Homocore," a reader from Montana writes in. "I am a seventeen year old gay punk. Life in Missoula sux. Thank god for Homocore."[67] In an issue that carried fifty-one letters (totaling almost a third of the zine), letter after letter reads the same.

Gay punks aren't the only ones who want a place for their own voice. *Skinned Alive* is a zine for racist skinheads who feel their idea that rock-n-roll is an Aryan invention is an underrepresented viewpoint, while the zine *Color Blind* is put out by skinheads who vehemently denounce racism.[68] These endless divisions and subdivisions of different realities are such a part of the zine and underground scenes that a joker writes to *Maximumrocknroll*:

> You know how there are a lot of fights and stuff between Skins into Straight Edge, Skins into Skating, and Skins into Surfing. Well—they just got another group to fight with: SKINS INTO SOAPS! We believe that Soap Operas rule! We are pretty much united against nonsoap Skins, but we have a lot of fights among ourselves . . . like which channel's Soaps rule.[69]

Ideally the individuals who make up the network of microcommunities of the zine world communicate to one another, sharing their differences, and speaking across voids, materializing the vision of the networked community sketched on the cover of *Factsheet Five* #35, where a punk with spiked hair hands a comic to a young black man, a bearded hippie picks up a poetry zine from a soldier in uniform, an older beatnik gets an album from a straight-looking young woman, an older gypsy passes a zine to a trendy girl, and a businessman with a tie shares a film with a space alien.[70]

There is plenty of evidence that this sort of cross-fertilization does happen. But there is also a tendency to move in the opposite direction: hunkering down in your microcommunity, surrounded by only your own reality. For every zinester like Janet Fox who "reads almost all the reviews," in *Factsheet Five*, because "if somebody has reached a new level of consciousness raising hogs in Idaho, I certainly want to know it," there are also individuals like Ann Wilder, who writes that when selecting zines to network with, she "scan[s] the whole review section—looking for keywords—political, gay, sf, punk, whatever—to decide whether or not to read the review."[71] While Ann's keywords suggest an impressive breadth of interest, her comments point to a problem in the zine world: there's no necessity to integrate.

In the virtual world of zines, creators and readers can pick and choose whom to call on and whom to entertain. This means you can visit and be visited by people who have interests and experiences far outside your own. But it can also mean that you can limit interaction to people *just like you.* In our society this is a luxury available only to the very rich sequestered in their gated communities. In the zine world, as with other virtual communities like the Internet, this dubious privilege has been democratized. This is the battle in the new virtual communities. Armed with the tools of communication, one can construct a wide network of connected voices, differing in timbre and substance, yet sharing in a love of communication, forging primary bonds with strangers that seem otherwise impossible in a mass society. Or, if one chooses, it is possible to never meet, never speak, and never understand those whom you don't want to, and spend your days living in a virtual ghetto.

NOTES

This chapter, slightly expanded, appears in my book, *Notes from Underground: Zines and the Politics of Alternative Culture* (London: Verso, 1997).

1. Arielle Greenberg, personal interview, August 25, 1993, New York City.
2. Eric, "Why Publish?" *Factsheet Five*, #22, 1987, Rensselaer, NY, 47; Dommie Sharp and Greg Skalka, "The South," *Maximumrocknroll*, #6, May-June 1983 San Francisco.
3. C. Carr, "Bohemia Diaspora," *The Village Voice*, February 4, 1992, 27.
4. President Sheldon Grebstein, SUNY-Purchase, "Institutional Overview and Program Plans, 1987–88," cited by David Tomere, "Shock Troops of Gentrification," *The Load*, October 15, 1986, 5.
5. Carr, "Bohemia Diaspora."
6. Russell Jacoby, *The Last Intellectuals: American Culture in the Age of Academe* (New York: Basic Books, 1987), 28.
7. Cesar and Marigay Graña, *On Bohemia*, (New Brunswick, N.J.: Transaction, 1990), xv.

8. Starbucks Coffee Company, with its chain of coffee bars, saw its net income increase 71 percent in 1992, to $4.1 million. Charles McCoy, "Entrepreneur Smells Aroma of Success in Coffee Bars, "*Wall Street Journal*, January 8, 1993, sec. B, 2.

9. Chris Boarts, personal interview, July 12, 1993, New York City.

10. Chris Boarts, *Slug & Lettuce*, #29, February-March 1993, New York City.

11. Don Fitch, personal letter, April 22, 1994.

12. By providing this service, zines can actually help to *create* The Scene as well. As Claude Bessey, editor of *Slash*, an early Los Angeles-based punk zine, explains: "We were pretending there was an LA scene when there was no scene whatsoever. The magazine was it. . . . Then all these disaffected loonies started focusing on the mag and decided 'We can be it, too.'" Within a few months there was a self-conscious L.A. punk scene. Claude Bessey, quoted in Jon Savage, *England's Dreaming* (New York: St. Martin's Press, 1992), 437.

13. The tour diary is such a part of punk zine tradition that the editor of *Minions of Evil* writes a five-page "Generic Band Tour Diary" poking fun at the genre. Anon., *Minions of Evil*, 1992(?), Middletown, Conn.

14. S. McPheeters, *I, Yeast Roll*, #78, October 1993, Richmond, Va., 8.

15. Jennifer, *Gogglebox*, #4, Winter 1995, New York City.

16. Mono, *Po*, #14, 1993, Portsmouth, N.H.

17. Miles Poindexter and John Labovitz, *Crash*, 1993, San Francisco.

18. Jennifer, *Gogglebox*, #4, Winter 1995, New York City, 28.

19. *Book Your Own Fuckin' Life*, #1, Maximumrocknroll and Profane Existence, 1992; *Book Your Own Fuckin' Life*, #2, Maximumrocknroll and Underdog Records, 1993; *Book Your Own Fuckin' Life*, #3, Maximumrocknroll and Rocco Publishing, 1994.

20. Jack Patten, *Pool Dust*, #20, 1993, Seattle; Laundromat cafe: Adam Bregman, *Shithappy*, #3, 1993, Los Angeles, 15; Kinkos scam: Aaron, *Cometbus*, #31, Spring 1994, Berkeley, Calif., 28.

21. Rob Treinen, *Cramped and Wet*, "completely disjointed issue," no date, Sioux City, Iowa, 19–20.

22. Marc Arsenault, telephone interview, December 12, 1993.

23. Aaron Cometbus, *Cometbus*, #31, early 1990s, Berkeley, Calif., 72.

24. Michael Dixon, *You Own a Wonderful Machine, Your Body*, 1992, Chicago.

25. Arielle Greenberg, personal interview, August 25, 1993, New York City.

26. Adam Bregman, *Shithappy*, #3, 1993, Los Angeles, 12–13. The Cacophony Society is also mentioned in "Tales from The Zone," *Iron Feather Journal*, #11, 1991, Boulder, Colo.

27. Dick Hebdige, "The Meaning of Mod," in *Resistance through Rituals: Youth Subcultures in Post-War Britain*, ed. Stuart Hall and Tony Jefferson (London: Unwin Hyman, 1976), 93.

28. Edwin P. Irwin, "In Quest of Bohemia," 1906, in Graña, *On Bohemia*, 314.

29. Issue #23 (March 1985) listed thirty-seven letters, #63 (August 1988) had thirty-two. Even though the number has slipped recently, in issue #120 (May 1993) to twenty-one, and in #129 (February 1994) to eighteen, most of the letters are still seven to ten paragraphs long.

30. Planet Boy, "Letters," *Maximumrocknroll*, #5, March-April 1983, San Francisco.

31. John Hurt, "Letters," *Maximumrocknroll*, #6, May-June 1983, San Francisco.

32. Mike Impastato, "Letters," *Maximumrocknroll*, #7, July-August 1983, San Francisco.

33. Carlos Fernandez, "Letters," *Maximumrocknroll*, #85, June 1990, San Francisco.

34. Steve Stepe, "Letters," *Maximumrocknroll*, #7, July-August 1983, San Francisco.

35. Javi (John Souvadji), "Letters," *Maximumrocknroll*, #23, March 1985, San Francisco.

36. John Jankowski, "Letters," *Maximumrocknroll*, #7, July-August 1983, San Francisco.

37. Illustration by Lee, *Flipside*, #44, 1984, Whittier, Calif.

38. Thomas Pluck, "Letters," *Maximumrocknroll*, #88, September 1990.

39. Viktim Joe, "Letters," *Maximumrocknroll*, #62, July 1988, San Francisco.

40. Cited in Lisa K. Wildman, "Where the Boys Aren't: Riot Grrrl NYC," *SUNY Purchase Free Press*, March 4, 1994, 7.

41. All responses anonymous, "Annihilate Sex Roles, Survey for Women—Poll Results," compiled by Ruth S., Erikka, Lynn, and Anna. *Maximumrocknroll*, #7, July-August 1983, San Francisco.

42. Liberty, "What Riot Grrrl Means to Me," *Riot Grrrl*, #5, March 1993, New York City.

43. Emma, "What Riot Grrrl Means to Me," *Riot Grrrl*, #5, March 1993, New York City, (emphasis mine).

44. Jen Devosb et al., *Riot Grrrl*, #3, May 1992, Amherst, Mass.

45. Ne Tantillo, *Riot Grrrl*, #6 1/2, December 1991, Arlington, Va., 3.

46. Ibid., 8.

47. Diana, *Riot Grrrl*, #5, March 1993, New York City.

48. D. E. H. Russell, "The Incidence and Prevalence of Intrafamilial and Extrafamilial Sexual Abuse of Female Children," *Child Abuse and Neglect* 7 (1983), 133–46.

49. Suzanne Daley, "Little Girls Lose Their Self-Esteem on Way to Adolescence, Study Finds," *New York Times*, January 9, 1991.

50. R. F., *Riot Girl, Huh?*, 1991, Olympia, Wash.

51. Kathleen Hanna et al., "Riot Grrrl is . . .", *Bikini Kill*, #2, Washington, D.C. Kathleen Hanna, in addition to being one of the founding mothers of Riot Grrrl, is the lead singer of a punk band, also named *Bikini Kill*.

52. Joanne Gottlieb and Gaye Wald, "Smells Like Teen Spirit," in *Microphone Fiends: Youth Music and Youth Culture*, ed. Andrew Ross and Tricia Rose (New York: Routledge, 1994), 253.

53. Hanna et al., "Riot Grrrl is. . . ."

54. Wildman, "Where the Boys Aren't" 7.

55. Kathleen Hanna, "OO69," *Bikini Kill*, #2, 1992, Washington, D.C.

56. Ibid.

57. Arielle Greenberg, telephone interview, March 28, 1994.

58. Dawn, *Riot Grrrl Newsletter One*, 1991, Newbury Park, Calif.

59. R.F., *Riot Grrrl, Huh?*

60. Ne Tantillo, *Riot Grrrl*, 3.

61. "Riot Grrrl Intro," *Riot Grrrl*, #8, 1992, Washington, D.C.

62. Hanna et al., "Riot Grrrl is . . ."

63. Alexis de Tocqueville, *Democracy in America*, trans. George Lawrence, ed. J. P. Meyer (New York: Harper and Row, 1988), 513.

64. Ibid., 523. Marshall Berman suggested that I consider the dialectics of Tocqueville's views on voluntary associations.

65. Tocqueville felt that *both* these attributes were positive ones—the former for the same reasons as I, and the latter because distraction from public affairs led to an implicit support of the status quo and as such was a politically stabilizing force.

66. Tom Jennings, *Homocore*, #1–7, September 1988–February 1991, San Francisco; Bruce LaBruce and G. B. Jones, *J.D.s*, #8, 1991, Toronto, Ontario; Factsheet Five Collection, New York State Library, Albany.

67. Steve Ackert, "Letters," *Homocore*, #7, Winter-Spring 1991, San Francisco; Factsheet Five Collection, New York State Library.

68. *Skinned Alive*, #1, 1987, Murrieta, Calif; *Colorblind*, #1, 1989, Chicago; Factsheet Five Collection, New York State Library.

69. Ivory-Snow Dial, "Letters," *Maximumrocknroll*, #5, March-April 1983, San Francisco.

70. Drawing by David Lee Ingersoll, *Factsheet Five*, #35, Rensselaer, N.Y., 1990.

71. Janet Fox, "Letters," *Factsheet Five*, #23, 1987, Rensselaer, N.Y., 67; Ann Wilder, "Letters," *Factsheet Five*, #22, 1987, Rensselaer, N.Y., 65.

Index

Abbott, Berenice, 251n. 16

Abeyta, Narcisco, 77. *See also* Native American youth

Acland, Charles, 16 n. 1

Acosta, Oscar Zeta, 221 n. 42

Acuña, Rodolfo, 221 n. 38

Adams, Arvil V., 19 n. 19

Adams-Gonzáles, María Elena (Gina Terry), 166, 172 n. 49

Adamson, Joe, 364, 365–66 n. 24. *See also* Wiggers

Addison, Joanne, 7, 13–14

ADDL. *See* American Double Dutch League

Adler, Herman, 27

Adolescence, 2–3, 9, 21, 23, 27, 30–31, 32 n. 3, 40; child labor laws and, 21; and education, 95–96; psychology and, 22–27; sociology and, 22–30. *See also* Hall, G. Stanley; Juvenile delinquency

Adorno, Theodor, 349, 357 n. 3; *Minima Moralia*, 349. See also *Slacker*

Adults, 7, 240–41; cyberzines and adult culture, 373–74. *See also* Lesbian, bisexual, and gay youth

African American girls and young women, 272–92. *See also* Double-Dutch; Double-Dutch performers; Bay Ridge High School

African American Music, 299. *See also* Double-Dutch; Double-Dutch Performers; Gangsta' rap; Hip hop; Hip hop performers; Rap music

African American youth, 6–7, 10–11, 15, 95–117, 136–56, 152 n. 8, 161–62; bebop music, 142–43; Black popular music making, 272–92; clothing styles, 162; cultural politics, 150; development of graffiti writing, 244; double-Dutch, 272–92; hairstyles, 140–41; hipster subculture, 7, 137–38, 140, 142–43, 145–48; interracial dating, 164; low rider culture and, 413–14; Malcolm X as cultural icon, 150–51; musicking, 274, 287, 302–3; manipulation of white racial ideology, 147; unemployment, 398; World War II, 137; young men and high school sports, 98; young women and high school newspapers, 99; zoot suiters and World War II draft, 144; zoot suiters and servicemen, 144–45. *See also* Double-Dutch; Double-Dutch performers; High schools; High school students; Malcolm X; Youth

African Americans, 138, 158–59, 163, 167, 169; African American culture and white emulation of, 358–66; Blacks and employment opportunities, 145; Black Power movement, 206; class tensions among, during World War II, 139, 141–43, 149; conceptions of sexuality, 61 n. 7, 62 n. 15; and criminality, 145, 155 n. 25, 158, 395–411; masculinization of race, 277; in Miami, 174; and opposition to World War II draft, 144, 154 nn. 20, 22; presence of African culture in American culture, 363–64, 365–66 nn. 22–24; and social autonomy, 53; young women and employment opportunities, 53. *See also* African American girls and young women; African American music; African American youth; Double-Dutch; Double-Dutch performers; Femininity; Gangsta' rap; Hip hop; Hip hop performers; Malcolm X; Masculinity; Music; Music performers; Rap music; Wiggers

Age of Consent, 50

Age-formation, 3–6, 15. *See also* Youth formation

Ahlerich, Milt, 399–400. *See also* Gangsta' rap

Aikman, Duncan, 135 n. 63

Alameda County, Calif., 53; Superior Court, 50, 56, 59–60, 61 n. 2

Albers, Patricia, and William James, 69

Alexander, John L., 38

Alinsky, Saul, 208

Allanbrook, Wye Jamison, 309 n. 42

Allatorre, Richard, 208. *See also* Young Citizens for Community Action (YCCA)

Allen, Harry, and Chuck D, 307 n. 23. *See also* Chuck D; Gangsta' rap; Hip hop; Hip hop performers; Public Enemy; Rap music

Almaraz, Carlos, 232, 238 nn. 21, 24. *See also* Baca, Judith F.; Chicano Arts movement

Almirol, Edwin B., 132 n. 8

Alsaybar, Bangele, 130–31 n. 4

Altruism, 37, 39–40, 42–43, 45; biological theories of, 40, 47 n. 25; nature writing and, 40. *See also* Boy Scouts of America (BSA); Carnegie Hero Fund; Heroism

American Double Dutch League (ADDL), 9, 275, 280–81, 284–85, 289 nn. 17, 24, 34; Janice Melvin, 283–84. *See also* Double-Dutch

American Indian Movement. *See* Native Americans

Amin, Ash, 266 n. 29

Amit-Talai, Vered, 18 n. 8

Amott, Teresa L., 62 n. 17

Anderson, Benedict, 171 n. 21, 219 n. 4, 220 n. 9

Anderson, Jervis, 154 n. 16
Andrews, Dwight D., 308 n. 29
Ansari, Zaid, 363, 365 n. 21. *See also* Wiggers
Anti-Semitism: in Miami, 174, 180
Antiwar movement, 206
Antolin, Bob, 133 n. 17
Aparicio, Frances R., 309 n. 43
Aquino, Valentin R., 132 n. 14
Arcadia, Calif., 164
Arcaráz, Luis, 159
Arellanes, Gloria, 217, 222 n. 62. *See also* Brown Berets
Ariès, Phillipe, 31 n. 3
Arnett, Jeffrey Jensen, 19 n. 17
Arnold, Fred, 130–31 n. 4
Aronovitz, Abraham, 176–77
Aronowitz, Stanley, 67–68, 259, 344 n. 23
Aronowitz, Stanley, and William DiFazio, 259, 267 n. 34, 268 n. 39, 347, 356 n. 1
Asher, Robert, and Charles Stephanson, 132 n. 8
Asian American/Pacific Islander Youth, 162
Asian Americans/Pacific Islanders, 158, 162, 167, 169; social movements, 206
Assimilation, 95–96, 312–13; high school students and, 104, 113–14; racial differences and, 313. *See also* Bureau of Indian Affairs (BIA); Hmong American youth; Hmong Americans; Native American boarding schools; Native American youth
Attali, Jacques, 306 n. 17
Auerbach, Eric, 348, 356–57 n. 2
Austin, Joe, 10, 13, 251 nn. 8, 10, 13, 252 nn. 18, 19, 21–22, 345 n. 32
Austin, Texas, 255. *See also* Linklater, Richard; Postmodern youth culture
Azores, Tania, 130–31 n. 4, 132 n. 14
Aztlán, 205

Baca, Judith F., 6, 12, 223–39, 235–36 n. 1, 236 n. 2, 238 nn. 12–19, 21–24, 239 nn. 25–32; and City Wide Murals project, 228, 232; and conflict over content of murals, 233; as cultural worker, 226–27, 228–30, 235, 237–38 n. 9; and development of system for mural production, 230, 232–34, 239 n. 27; East Los Angeles Mural Program, 223; and East Side Murals, 228; and gang youth, 227–28, 230; and graffiti/tattooing as an art form, 227; and *The Great Wall* mural project, 224, 233–35; and *Medusa Head* mural, 228, 231; and *Mi Abuelita Mural*, 228, 229; oral history, and, 236; parents, youth artists, and, 230; and *Second Street Mural,* 223; and tensions with Chicano Arts movement artists, 230–32, 238 nn. 21, 23; Wabash Recreation Center project, 230–31. *See also* Chicano art; Chicano Arts movement; Chicano movement; Mexican American youth
Bach, J. S., 309 n. 42
Baden-Powell, Lord, 37, 46 n. 5. *See also* Boy Scouts of America (BSA)
Baderman, Gail, 17 n. 5
Bagwell, Beth, 61 n. 5, 63 n. 19
Bailey, Beth, 9, 201 n. 9, 346 n. 36
Baker, Houston, 409–10 n. 14
Balsamo, Ann, 370
Baltes, Paul B., 18 n. 8
Banham, Reyner, 170 n. 20
Baraka, Amiri, 362, 365 n. 17. *See also* Wiggers
Barker Benfield, G. J., 61 n. 6
Barry, Barbara R., 309 n. 42
Basch, Linda, Nina Glick Schiller, and Christina Szanton Blanc, 381, 393 n. 6. *See also* Native American powwows; Native Americans
Basie, Count, 157
Baudrillard, Jean, 265 n. 8
Baughman, James L., 251 n. 15
Bauman, Richard, 170 n. 14
Bay Ridge High School, 97, 99; Black young women, 111; ethnic mixing, 113; Italian young women, 110; Jewish young women, 110. *See also* High schools; High school students; Youth
Bayor, Ronald H., 117 n. 18
Beal, Becky Louise, 335, 345 n. 28, 345–46 n. 32. *See also* Skateboarders
Bealieu, Julie, 389. *See also* Native American powwows
Beard, Daniel Carter, 38; Sons of Daniel Boone, 38. *See also* Boy Scouts of America (BSA)
Beavis and Butt-Head, 262. *See also* Coupland, Douglas; Postmodern culture; Postmodern youth culture
Beck, Earl R., 154 n. 19
Becker, Howard, 251–52 n. 17, 252 n. 29
Bellah, Robert, Richard Madsen, William M. Sullivan, Ann Swidler, and Steven M. Tipton, 44, 49 n. 52
Belle, Deborah, 17 n. 8
Bello, Madge, and Vincent Reyes, 130–31 n. 4
Bello, Vincent, 123, 133 n. 18. *See also* Filipino American youth
Bender, Charles Albert, 70
Benjamin, Walter, 16
Bennett, James, 35 nn. 42, 44
Benson, Thomas, 151 n. 2
Berman, Marshall, 260, 267–68 n. 36, 268 n. 38, 450 n. 64
Bernard, L. L., 34 n. 32
Bernstein, Neil, 358, 364 n. 4
Berrol, Selma Cantor, 17 n. 8
Berry, Richard, 162
Berry, Venise, 306 n. 5
Berthoff, Werner, 151 n. 2
Bérubé, Allan, 185 n. 1
Best, Joel, 16 n. 1, 19 n. 17
Betz, Betty, 16 n. 2

Bhaba, Homi, 384, 393 n. 11
BIA. *See* Bureau of Indian Affairs
Bishop, Jeff, and Paul Hoggett, 88, 91, 94 nn. 19, 31, 33
Blacking, John, 302, 305 n. 4, 306 n. 8, 309 n. 40
Bloom, John, 8–9
Bocock, Sarane Spence, 17 n. 6
Boehmer, Elleke, 206, 220 n. 11. *See also* Brown Berets; Chicano movement
Bogardus, Emory, 130 n. 2
Borden, Iain, 344 n. 23
Boston, Mass., 138; Malcolm X and, 139; Roseland Ballroom, 141–142. *See also* African American youth; Dancehalls; Malcolm X
Bottles, Scott L., 170–71 n. 20
Bourdieu, Pierre, 19 n. 21, 89, 91, 94 n. 25, 306 n. 10
Bowers, Norman, 19 n. 19
Bowler, Alida C., 134 n. 39
Bowler, Peter J., 47 n. 25
Box, Steven, 155 n. 27
Boy Scouts of America (BSA), 9, 36–37, 42, 44, 48 n. 48; *Boys Life Magazine*, 36; character building, 44; and crisis of masculinity, 38; *Handbook for Boys*, 36, 38; *Handbook for Scoutmasters*, 40; and heroism, 36–37, 39; honor medals, 36–37, 39. *See also* Altruism; Heroism
Braidotti, Rose, 376
Brake, Michael, 18 n. 8; 93 n. 18
Breines, Wini, 16 n. 2
Breitman, George, 152n. 3, 154 n. 20, 155 n. 24
Bright, Brenda Jo, 11, 344 n. 21
Bright, Brenda Jo, and Liza Bakewell, 236–37 n. 4, 425 n. 1
Bronner, Augusta, 24–25, 27–28, 30–31, 32 n. 13, 33 n. 17, 33 nn. 22–23; Freudian explanation of juvenile delinquency, 26. *See also* Juvenile delinquency
Bronner, Simon J., 46 n. 8
Brown Berets, 206, 209–19; and goals of, 212–14; and invasion of Catalina Island, 218; and La Caravan de la Reconquista, 218; *La Causa* newspaper, 214–15; and masculine nationalism of, 210–13, 215, 217, 219; recruitment policies, 214–15; and representations of women, 215–17, 222 n. 64; and symbols/iconography of, 209–10; and Vietnam war, 217–18. *See also* Chicano movement; Chicano youth; Mexican Americans
Brown, Elsa Barkley, 277, 288 n. 10
Brown, Gerald "Pat," 207
Brown, Hubert "Rap," 209
Brown, James, 274
Brown, Les, 157, 159
Broyles-González, Yolanda, 236 n. 4
Bruno, Frank J., 33 n. 27
BSA. *See* Boy Scouts of America
Buaken, Manuel, 127, 130–31 n. 4, 134 n. 54, 135 n. 62
Buff, Rachel, 2, 12, 15, 16 n. 3
Bugs Bunny, 363–64
Bulmer, Martin, 35 n. 43
Bulosan, Carlos, 127, 134 n. 51
Bureau of Indian Affairs (BIA), 65, 67, 69, 76–77; assimilationist policies, 77; ban of boxing in boarding schools, 75; Willard W. Beatty, 75; Ryan W. Carson, 65, 69; John Collier, 65, 69–70, 76, 79; ethnic memory and, 77–78; Fred Foard, 75; and Native American collegiate football, 70. *See also* Native American boarding schools; Native American powwows; Native American youth
Burgess, Ernest W., 34 n. 40
Burnham, John C., 32 n. 14

Cahan, Emily, Jay Mechling, Brian Sutton-Smith, and Sheldon H. White, 48 n. 46
California Center for Community Development Social Action Training Program, 208. *See also* Brown Berets; Community Service Organization (CSO)
Callvori, Raymond A., 18 n. 8
Capeci, Dominic J., Jr., 153 n. 9
Car culture, 161–62, 163, 170–71 n. 20, 171 n. 23
Carillo, Leo, 323–24 n. 1, 325 n. 27
Carmichael, Stokely, 209
Carnegie, Andrew, 40–42, 45, 47 n. 29
Carnegie Hero Fund, 40–42, 44, 47 n. 30, 48 n. 44; Wilmot, F. M., 48 n. 43. *See also* Altruism; Boy Scouts of America (BSA); Heroism
Carr, C., 428–29, 448 nn. 3, 5. *See also* Zine culture
CASA. *See* Centro de Acción Social Autónomo-Hermandad de General Trabajadores
Castellano, Jerry, 160, 163, 165–67, 170 nn. 11, 14, 17, 171 nn. 28, 30–31, 172 nn. 40–43, 46, 50–52. *See also* Dancehalls; Mexican American youth; Music
Castello, Lou, 159. *See also* Mexican American youth; Music
Castillo, Toribio, 121, 132 nn. 10, 18, 20; 133 n. 18
Castillo-Tsuchida, Adelaida, 134 n. 38
Castleman, Craig, 250–51 n. 7, 251 n. 17, 252 nn. 19–20, 24, 27, 30–32, 38. *See also* Graffiti; Graffiti writers
Castro, Vickie, 207, 209, 220 nn. 18–19, 221 n. 25. *See also* Mexican American youth; Mexican American Youth Leadership Conference; Young Citizens for Community Action
Catapusan, Benecio T., 130–31 n. 4, 132 n. 8, 133 nn. 23, 25
Cavan, Ruth, 34 n. 23
Cayton, Horace, and St. Clair Drake, 155 n. 29
Centro de Acción Social Autónomo-Hermandad de General Trabajadores, 226
Chabram-Dernersesian, Angie, 220 n. 8, 236 nn. 3–4, 237 n. 6
Cha-Jua, Sundiata, 360, 365 n. 11. *See also* Wiggers
Chambers, Jack, 154 n. 17
Chan, Sucheng, 130–31 n. 4
Chang, Yee, 325 nn. 33–34
Charles, Don C., 18 n. 8

Chastity, 50–52
Chauncey, George, 185 n. 1
Chávez, César, 208, 209, 225
Chávez, Ernesto, 6, 9, 222 n. 68, 236 n. 3, 237 nn. 5–6
Chavez, Leo R., 344 nn. 17, 21
Chernoff, John Miller, 302–3, 308–9 n. 37, 309 nn. 39–41
Chibnall, Steve, 153 n. 8
Chicago: juvenile court, and, 26–27; Native American boxing and, 71–72
Chicago Social Scientists, 22–27. *See also* Juvenile delinquency
Chicago Woman's Club, 32 n. 8
Chicana youth, 162, 217; "white cholitas," 358, 364 n. 4. *See also* Wiggers
Chicana/o studies, 224
Chicanismo, 205; anti-Americanism and 205–6, 220 n. 5, 225; popular Chicanismo, 413
Chicano art, 223–39. *See also* Chicano Arts movement
Chicano Arts movement, 12, 226, 412; and cultural reclamation, 226; tensions among artists, 228–29, 230–32; sexism within, 231. *See also* Baca, Judith F.; Chicano movement; Low rider culture
Chicano movement, 205–22, 223–39, 225–26, 228, 236 n. 3; Chicano Arts movement, 223–39; Chicano Moratorium Committee against the Vietnam war, 217–18, 225; Chicano Youth Liberation Conference, 225; East Los Angeles High School "Blow Outs," 211, 225; "El Plan Espiritual de Aztlán," 226; and nationalism, 205–6, 237 n. 7; and social construction of masculinity, 205–22, 237 n. 6. *See also* Baca, Judith F.; Brown Berets; Chicano Arts movement; Masculinity
Chicano youth, 6, 11–12, 152 n. 8, 160–62, 205–22, 225; and Chicana fashion, 162; and Chicano Arts movement, 224; Chicano popular culture, 425 n. 1; low rider culture, 412–26; pachuco youth culture, 153 n. 8, 171 n. 28; and generational differences, 160, 162, 165–66. *See also* Baca, Judith F.; Mexican American youth; Low rider culture
Child, Brenda, 66. *See also* Native American boarding schools; Native American boxing
Chomsky, Noam, 315, 324 nn. 5, 13
Chuck D, 293, 305 n. 1, 307 n. 23; dialogics, 301, 308 n. 33; lyrics, 293; racism, 307 n. 23; vocals, 296; vocals and polyrhythms, 300–301, 308 n. 32. *See also* Gangsta' rap; Hip hop; Hip hop performers; Rap music
Chudacoff, Howard P., 17 n. 6, 31 n. 2, 250 n. 1
Cinel, Dino, 62 n. 14
CIO. *See* Congress of Industrial Organizations
Civil rights movements, 208, 396–97; Black Panthers, 210, 212–13, 221 nn. 33, 46, 222 n. 58; and Chicano Power movement, 225; Mexican American movements, 237 n. 5; and Mexican American youth, 220 n. 16; Pan-Africanism and, 137
Clark, B. H., 34 n. 34
Clark, Kenneth B., 144
Clark, Kenneth B., and James Barker, 153 n. 11, 154 n. 21
Clarke, John Henrik, 152 n. 3
Clarke, Kenny, 142
Clasby, Nancy, 151 n. 2
Class: American films and, 84–85
Clinton, Bill, and Sister Souljah, 401. *See also* Gangsta' rap
Clothing. *See* Fashion
Cobain, Kurt, 258. *See also* Music; Postmodern youth culture
Cochran, Thomas, C., 44, 48 n. 49
Cohen, Michael Lee, 264 n. 1
Cohen, Ronald, 32 n. 4
Cohen, Stanley, 16 n. 1, 265 n. 2
Coleman, James S., 18 n. 8, 250 n. 5
College administrators, 188, 190–92, 195–96, 198–99, 201 nn. 12–13, 203–4 n. 28; administrators of "student life," 189, 191–92, 201 n. 14; and debates about youth sexuality, 189, 193–99, 200 n. 8. *See also* College campuses; College students; University of Kansas; Youth
College Campuses: Carleton College, 321; Princeton University, 188; University of Alabama, 187; University of Indiana, 187; University of Kansas, 187, 190; University of Oklahoma, 187; University of Michigan, 202 n. 21; University of Texas-Austin, 349–50; University of Wisconsin, 187; Westminster Choir College, 188. *See also* College students; Postmodern youth culture; *Slacker*; Youth
College students, 9, 187–204; and debates about youth sexuality, 189, 193–99, 200 n. 8, 202 nn. 21, 25; panty raids, 187–88, 199, 199–200 nn. 1, 4–6; socialization of, 190–91; student activism, 188, 190. *See also* College administrators; Universities; University of Kansas; Youth
Collins, Cardiss, Rep., 395. *See also* Gangsta' rap
Collins, Edmund John, 308 n. 36
Coloma, Casiano, 132 n. 6
Coloma, Frank, 124–25, 132 n. 13, 133 nn. 30, 37. *See also* Filipino American youth
Commercial leisure, 54, 118–35; Filipino youth, 122, 123, 126; teenage girls and working class parents, 50–64. *See also* Teenage girls
Commons, John, 32 n. 11
Community Service Organization (CSO), 164, 208, 221 nn. 22–23
Comstock, Michelle, 7, 13
Cone, James, 152 n. 3
Congress of Industrial Organizations: and Black workers, 138
Congressional Black Caucus, 395. *See also* Gangsta' rap
Connelly, Mark, 63 n. 23
Considine, J. D., 306 n. 9, 307 n. 22
Consumerism, 12, 38, 41, 45, 347–57; impulsiveness and, 44; short-term employment and, 355; work

and, 347. *See also* Postmodern culture; Postmodern youth culture; Teenage workers; Zine culture
Coontz, Stephanie, 20 n. 22
Cooper, Grosvenor W., and Leonard B. Meyer, 309 n. 42
Cooper, Martha, and Henry Chalfant, 250–51 n. 7, 252 nn. 31, 36–37. *See also* Graffiti; Graffiti writers
Cordasco, Francesco, 115 n. 3
Cordova, Dorothy, 130–31 n. 4
Cordova, Fred, 130–31 n. 4
Cordova, John May T., and Alexis S. Carillo, 133 n. 26
Corello, Leonard, and Guido D'Agostino, 117 n. 24
Cornelius, Don, 406. *See also* Gangsta' rap
Corona, Bert, 171 n. 34, 237–38 n. 9
Corpus, Ray Edralin, 133 n. 17
Corpus, Severino F., 130–31 n. 4, 132 nn. 7–8, 14, 134 n. 41
Corpuz, Ray, 122
Correll, L. E., 65, 76
Cosgrove, Stuart, 153 nn. 8–9, 155 n. 24
Costello, Mark, and David Foster Wallace, 307 n. 25
Cote, James E., and Anton L. Alahar, 17 n. 7, 250 n. 1
Cott, Nancy, 61 n. 6
Coupland, Douglas, 254–55, 256–57, 260–61, 263, 265 nn. 13–14, 18–20, 268 n. 39, 268–69 n. 40, 269 nn. 45–46; *Generation X*, 254–56, 260–61, 269 n. 42, 269–70 n. 51; *Life After God*, 256; *Microserfs*, 260; *Polaroids from the Dead*, 256–57; *Shampoo Planet*, 256, 260. *See also* Economic restructuring and youth cultures; Postmodern culture; Postmodern youth culture
Courage, 37–38. *See also* Altruism; Boy Scouts of America (BSA); Carnegie Hero Fund; Heroism
Cravens, Hamilton, 32 n. 4, 34 n. 31
Crawford, Margaret, 343 n. 7
Cremin, Lawrence, 115 n. 1
Cressy, Paul, 134 n. 34
Cronbach, Lee, 308 n. 35, 310 n. 45
CSO. *See* Community Service Organization
Cubberly, Elwood, 95–96, 115 n. 4. *See also* High schools
Cultural studies, 2, 200 n. 8

Dalby, David, 363, 365 nn. 22–23. *See also* Wiggers
Dalfiume, Richard, 152 n. 4
Dameron, Tadd, 142
Dance, 285; break dancing, 277, 286, 413; double-Dutch, 272–92; Lindy hop as youth style, 137, 139, 141–42, 277; mambo, 167, 168; powwow culture, 379–94; tootsie roll, 285, 286, 289 n. 35. *See also* African American girls and young women; Dancehalls; Double-Dutch; Fashion; Femininity; Filipino American youth; Hairstyle; Immigrants; Malcolm X; Middle class; Music; Music performers; Native American powwows; Native American powwow performers; Working class; Youth; Zoot suit
Dancehalls, 13, 12–24, 164; American Legion Stadium (Pomona, Calif.), 158, 161–64, 167–68, 171 n. 22, 425 n. 9; Filipino immigrants and, 123; inter-ethnic working-class culture, 124–25; Long Beach Municipal Auditorium, 169–70 n. 7; in Los Angeles, 122–24, 167, 169–70 n. 7; Majestic (Oakland), 54; multi-ethnic audiences, 164–66; Orange Show (San Bernardino, Calif.), 169–70 n. 7; Paramount Ballroom (East Los Angeles), 169–70 n. 7; Rainbow Gardens (Pomona, Calif.), 158–161, 164, 166–68, 170 n. 14; Rhythm Room (Fullerton, Calif.), 169–70 n. 7; Roseland (Boston), 41–42; Savoy Ballroom (Harlem), 141, 150, 154 n. 16; taxi, 118–35, 127–28, 129; taxi, and Mexican immigrants, 124; Valley Ballroom (San Bernardino, Calif.), 169–70 n. 7; working class men and women, 142, 150; Zenda Ballroom, 169–70 n. 7. Los Angeles: Danceland, 122; Hippodrome Palace, 122–24, 126; Liberty, 122; Orpheum, 122, 126; Palladium, 169–70 n. 7; Red Mill, 122; Roma, 122; Solomon's Dancehall, 57; Virginia's, 168. *See also* African American youth; Filipino American youth; Intercultural communication; Malcolm X; Middle class; Music; Popular culture; Teenage girls; Working class; Zoot suit
Dangaran, Alfronso Perales, 135 n. 59
Darwinism, 38, 40
Dating, 164; interethnic, 164; Filipino youth and interracial dating, 125. *See also* Filipino American youth; Intercultural communication; Malcolm X
David, Hans T., and Arthur Mendel, 309 n. 42
Davidson, Bill, 16 n. 2
Davis, Gerald L., 308 n. 30
Davis, Mike, 172 n. 54, 343 nn. 7, 16, 415–16, 425 n. 6; *City of Quartz*, 328, 342–43 n. 3, 344 n. 17. *See also* Low rider culture; Skateboarders
Day, Dorene, 387, 389, 393 n. 9, 394 n. 23. *See also* Native American powwows
Deanna Durbin fans, 10–11, 81–94; Deanna Durbin Devotees, 81, 83, 87–92, 94 n. 26; Deanna Durbin Society (Great Britain), 82; *Deanna's Diary*, 88–92, 94 n. 26; *Deanna's Journal*, 82; fan-produced texts, 89–92; Universal Studios and fan clubs, 82–83. *See also* Zine culture
DeCerteau, Michel, 18 n. 11, 252 n. 39, 345 n. 29, 357 n. 8; *perruque* tactic, 354
Deegan, Mary Jo, 345–46 n. 32
Degler, Carl, 33 n. 17
deLauretis, Teresa, 93 n. 9
Deleuze, Gilles, 345 n. 29
Deleuze, Gilles, and Felix Guattari, 345 nn. 24–25, 29
Demarest, David, 151 n. 2
D'Emilio, John, 61 nn. 6–9; 185 n. 1
Demos, John, 17 n. 6
DeRobles, Eddie, 163. *See also* Mixtures, The
Dery, Mark, 305 n. 1, 306 nn. 11, 14–15, 18–19, 207 nn. 20, 26
DeTocqueville, Alexis, 446, 450 nn. 63–65. *See also* Zine culture; Zines and zinesters

Detroit: double-Dutch, 272; World War II interracial violence, 140
Deutsche, Rosalyn, 345–46 n. 32
DeWitt, Howard A., 130–31 n. 4, 132 n. 8
Dick Tracy comic strips, 408. *See also* Gangsta' rap; James, C. L. R.
DiLeonardo, Micaela, 62 n. 13
Ditton, Jason, 155 n. 27
Doane, Mary Ann, 83, 93 n. 9. *See also* Feminist film criticism
Doe, John, 256
Double-Dutch, 9, 272–92; Black masculinity, and, 277, 279, 289 n. 21; Black popular culture in private and public spheres, 275; boys' participation, 276; chants and rhymes, 274–75, 285, 287, 289 n. 27; competitive innovation/improvisation, 278; cooperative urban aesthetic, 278; development of, in New York City, 275, 279; development of hip hop and, 277–78, 289 n. 14; "the Dozens," 280–81; female body, 282–84, 286; female music making in Black music history, 276–77, 287; formal competition, 281–84, 285; freestyle competition, 282–83, 284–85; origins of, 279–80; Police Athletic League, 279–81; regulation of female performance, 273, 279, 281–84; social construction of Black femaleness, 274–75, 289 n. 26; social construction of ethnicity, 278–79; stereotypical gender roles and, 276, 279; street performance, 282–85; vernacular oral expression, 273–74, 281–82, 285, 289 n. 11. *See also* African American youth; Dance; Femininity; Gender; Hip hop; Music
Double-Dutch performers: De'Shone Adams, 283; Nicki Adams, 283; Delores Brown, 283; Double Forces, 286–87; Fantastic Four, 283; Generation bène, 286; Hot Steppers, 289 n. 33; Liese, 273–74, 288 n. 3; Lincoln Leapers, 289 n. 33; Robin Oakes, 283; Oriental Peppers, 289 n. 33; Pepper Steppers, 289 n. 33; Pepper Steppers, Jr., 289 n. 33; Ruqaiijah, 282, 289 n. 26; Twice as Nice, 285
Drucker, A. P., 34 n. 34
D'Souza, Dinesh, 397. *See also* Gangsta' rap
Duarte, Calif., 164
Duberman, Martin, 185 n. 1
DuBois, Ellen Carol, and Vicki Ruiz, 62 n. 15, 236 n. 3
Duggan, Lisa, 185 n. 2, 186 n. 19
Dummer, Ethel Sturges, 23–24, 32 nn. 10–12. *See also* Juvenile delinquency
Duncombe, Stephen, 14, 346 n. 41; *Notes from Underground*, 448. *See also* Zine culture; Zines and zinesters
Dunn, M., and Alex Stepick, 185 n. 3
Durbin, Deanna (Edna Mae), 81; attitude toward fans, 88; Charles Henri David, 82; film characterizations and social construction of femininity, 10, 86; films and feminist film criticism, 83–87; filmography, 92 n. 3; *It Started with Eve*, 82; Henry Kosters and, 81; *100 Men and a Girl*, 82, 84–86; *Three Smart Girls*, 81, 82; Universal Studios and, 81. *See also* Deanna Durbin fans
Durham, N. C.: teen workers, 347–57

East Los Angeles, 227–28; Boyle Heights, 223, 230; Hollenbeck park, 228; Lincoln park, 232; Wabash Recreation Center, 228. *See also* Baca, Judith F.; Chicano Arts movement; Los Angeles
Easton Ellis, Bret, 265–66 n. 22
Echols, Alice, 364–65 n. 9
Eckert, Charles, 93 n. 11
Economic Restructuring and youth cultures: gentrification, 428–29; hip hop and, 395–411; low riders and, 412–26; white middle class youth and, 253–71; skateboarders and, 326–46; teenage workers and, 347–57. *See also* Graffiti; Postmodern youth; Skateboarders; Teenage workers; Youth; Zine culture
Eder, Donna, 18 n. 12
Ehrenreich, Barbara, 201 n. 12, 261, 265 n. 3, 269 n. 41
Eisenstadt, S. N., 18 n. 12
El Monte, Calif., 158. *See also* Dancehalls; Intercultural communication; Music
Elam, Mark, 266 n. 29
Elder, Glen H., John Modell, and Ross D. Parke, 18 n. 8, 48 n. 46
Elequin, Vicente, 125, 134 n. 38. *See also* Filipino American youth
Ellison, Ralph, 137, 149, 150; on white youth's imitation/incomprehension of Black culture, 359, 364 n. 5. *See also* Malcolm X; Wiggers
Emmons, Mrs. Donald, 194, 202 n. 25. *See also* College students; University of Kansas
Enstad, Nan, 20 n. 22
Erenberg, Lewis, and Susan E. Hirsch, 93 n. 10
Erlmann, Veit, 309 n. 43
Escobar, Edward J., 236 n. 3
España-Maram, Linda Nueva, 9, 11, 130–31 n. 4, 135 n. 68
Esparza, Moctesuma, 207, 209. *See also* Mexican American youth; Mexican American Youth Leadership Conference; Young Christians for Community Action (YCCA)
Espina, Marina, E., 130–31 n. 4
Espinoza, Dionne, 20 n. 22, 222 n. 64
Espiritu, Augusto Fauni, 132 n. 14
Essien-Udom, E. U., 155 n. 22
Estrada, Kathleen, 414. *See also* Low riders
Ethnicity: American films, and, 84–85, 398–99; assimilation, 69; ethnic neighborhoods, 127; high school students and, 95–117; situational aspects of, 69; youth and, 8
Eubanks, Bob, 163
Eure, Joseph D., and James G. Spady, 306 n. 7
Evander Childs High School, 98–100, 107–8; Black students, 107–8, 111; Italian students, 107–8; Jewish students, 107–8; white students, 108. *See also* High schools; High school students; Youth
Evans, Catherine Colleen, 18 n. 12

Evans, Sara, 19 n. 16
Evers, Medgar, 396
Ewen, Elizabeth, 62 nn. 14, 18

Faderman, Lillian, 185 n. 1
Family: patriarchal structure of, 51
Fanon, Franz, 384
Fans. *See* Deanna Durbin fans; Rap music; Zine culture
Farber, David, 16 n. 4, 220 n. 7
Faris, Robert E. L., 31 n. 1, 34 n. 32, 35 n. 43
Farmer, James, 396
Fashion, 123, 125, 129–30, 162; gay/straight, 373; Hmong American youth, 316–17; skateboarders and, 339–40; teenage workers and, 356; youth fashion, 162–63, 171 n. 25; Zoot suit, 136–56. *See also* African American youth; Consumerism; Filipino American youth; Lesbian, bisexual, and gay youth; Zoot suit
Fass, Paula S., 8, 17 n. 8, 32 n. 3, 116 n. 7, 117 n. 22
Fear, 37–38, 42; socialization of masculinity and, 39; Victorian socialization of, 39. *See also* Altruism; Boy Scouts of America (BSA); Carnegie Hero Fund; Heroism
Feld, Steven, 308–9 n. 37
Female impersonators/drag queens, 176, 181–82, 183
Femininity: African American young women and double-Dutch, 272–92; Deanna Durbin fans and, 81–94; Riot Grrrl, 440–46, 450 nn. 42–62. *See also* Deanna Durbin fans; Double-Dutch; Gender; Riot Grrrl; Teenage girls; Zine culture; Zines and zinesters
Feminist film criticism, 83–88
Fernald, Grace, 24
Fiedler, Leslie, 361, 365 n. 14. *See also* Wiggers
Filipino American youth, 11, 118–35; attitudes toward women, 125–26; dancehalls, 123–24; clothing styles, 123, 125, 129–30; interracial dating, 125; Los Angeles Police Department and, 119, 129; and Mexican immigrants, 124–25; performance of heterosexual masculinity, 124–25, 128; tensions with Anglo laborers, 128–29. *See also* Commercial leisure; Dancehalls; Fashion; Popular culture
Filipino immigrants, 118–35, 130 n. 4, 315; in California, 120; class tensions among, 119, 123–24, 127–28; history of, in U. S., 120; immigration policy toward, 120; in Los Angeles, 328; migrant labor, 121; segregation and living conditions, 127. *See also* Filipino American youth
Films: *Batman,* 419; *Black Like Me,* 362; *Bonnie and Clyde,* 255; *Boyz in the Hood,* 425 n. 7; *Clerks,* 262; *Nightmare on Elm Street,* 422–23; *Reality Bites,* 269–70 n. 51; *Roadside Prophets,* 255–56; *Soul Man,* 362, 365 n. 16; *West Side Story,* 419, 423. *See also* Coupland, Douglas; Low rider culture; Postmodern culture; Postmodern youth culture; *Slacker;* Wiggers
Finck, John, 324 n. 16
Fine, Benjamin, 16 n. 2
Fine, Gary Allan, 46 n. 6
Finkle, Lee, 152 n. 4
Fisher, Carl, 174
Fiske, John, 89–90, 94 nn. 25–26
Fitzhugh, Percy Keese, 43; 48 nn. 47–48. *See also* Altruism; Boy Scouts of America (BSA); Carnegie Hero Fund; Heroism
Flavor Flav. *See* Public Enemy; Rap music
Florida: lesbian youth, and, 173–76. *See also* Lesbian, bisexual, and gay youth
Flynn, George Q., 154 n. 22
Fogelson, Robert M., 61 nn. 4–5
Foley, Douglas, 68
Foner, Anne, 17 n. 6
Foner, Philip, 152 n. 5, 221 nn. 33, 46, 222 n. 58
Foucault, Michel, 345 n. 29
Frank, Henriette Greenbaum, 32 n. 8
Franklin, Delbert, 163. *See also* Mixtures, The
Fraser, Al, 154 n. 20
Freedman, Estelle, 200 n. 7
Freedman, Samuel G., 116 n. 4
Fretwell, Elbert K., 115 nn. 1, 4–5
Freud, Sigmund, 25, 33 n. 22; *Three Contributions to the Sexual Theory,* 25. *See also* Juvenile delinquency
Friday, Chris, 130–31 n. 4
Furstenberg, Frank F., 18 n. 8
Fusfield, Daniel R., and Timothy Bates, 152 n. 5

Gaines, Donna, 19 n. 17, 250 n. 6, 369; *Teenage Wasteland,* 263
Gallalee, John, 187
Gangsta' rap, 338, 358, 395–411; African American campaign against, 395–97, 402–3, 410 nn. 29–34; Black youth and disregard for civil rights movement, 397, 407, 409 n. 6; censorship of, 395–96, 399–403; context/conditions of production, 395, 404–5; debate over lyrics as sexist and glorifying crime, 395–96, 402, 405; deindustrialization, economic restructuring, and neoconservative politics, 395, 398, 404–5, 406, 409 nn. 7–9, 411 n. 46–49; Bob Dole and, 403–4, 405; Michael Eric Dyson and, 407, 408; FBI and, 399, 403; gangsta' rap hearings, 395, 409 n. 1, 410 nn. 33–35, 411 nn. 45, 47, 52, 58–59; generational differences among African Americans, 395, 396–97; Ice-T/*Body Count,* censored, 401–2, 403, 410 nn. 24–26; low rider culture and, 413–14, 425 nn. 2, 4, 5; N.W.A. censored, 399–400, 403, 410 nn. 14–17; National Urban League and, 402; NAACP and, 402; Oliver North and, 401, 403; 2 Live Crew, censorship of, 400–401, 403, 410 nn. 18–23; Maxine Waters and, 406–7, 408, 411 n. 47. *See also* Economic restructuring and youth cultures; Hmong American youth; Hip hop; Hip hop performers; Low rider culture; Madison, Joseph; Moral panics; Rap music; Tucker, C. Delores

Gannon, Michael, 185 n. 3
García, Alma M., 236 n. 3
Garcia de Vera, Arleen, 130–31 n. 4
García, Ignacio, 236 n. 3
Garcia, Johnny, 123, 133 n. 27. *See also* Filipino American youth
García, Mario T., 171 n. 34, 236 n. 3, 237 n. 5, 237–38 n. 9
garcia, matt, 7, 13
Gardner, George, 32 n. 13, 33 n. 20
Garfinkel, Herbert, 152 n. 4
Garland, Judy, 81
Garlinghouse, John, 193–94, 202 n. 23. *See also* College students; University of Kansas
Gates, Henry Louis, Jr., 295, 306 n. 13, 308 nn. 29–30
Gaunt, Kyra, 6, 9, 11, 288 n. 1
Gelder, Ken, 18 n. 8
Gender, 7, 10; and lesbian, bisexual, and gay cyberculture, 376; Native American young women, 379–94. *See also* African Americans; Brown Berets; Chicano movement; Deanna Durbin fans; Double-Dutch; Durbin, Deanna; Filipino American youth; Graffiti; Lesbian, bisexual, and gay youth; Low rider culture; Masculinity; Malcolm X; Riot Grrrl; Teenage girls
Generation X, 11, 253–54, 265 n. 3; lesbian, bisexual, and gay youth, 367–68
Genovese, Kitty, 48 n. 42
Gentrification, 13, 14. *See also* Economic restructuring and youth cultures; Social space; Zine culture
George, Nelson, 365 n. 17
George, P., 185 n. 3
George Washington High School (New York City), 98–100, 104–7; Jewish students, 104–5; Italian students, 106; white students, 106; class status and extra curricular participation, 113. *See also* High schools; High school students; Youth
German American youth, 95–117; high school sports and young women, 98; young women and high school newspapers, 99
Gerstle, Gary, 220 nn. 5–6
Gesner, Johann Matthias, 309 n. 42
Getis, Victoria, 8
Gilbert, James, 19 n. 17, 93 n. 14, 250 n. 2, 16 n. 1
Gill, Gerald R., 154 nn. 19, 22
Gillespie, Dizzy, 142, 150, 154 n. 20; and evasion of World War II draft, 144
Gillis, John R., 17 n. 8, 31 n. 2
Gilroy, Paul, 154 n. 18, 169, 172 n. 58, 302, 307 n. 25, 384, 393 n. 12; on dance as opposition to wage work, 143
Girl Scouts, 45 n. 3
Gitler, Ira, 154 n. 17, 154 n. 19
Gitlin, Todd, 201 n. 11, 202 n. 21, 254, 265 n. 9, 268 n. 37
Givhan, Robin D., 358, 364 n. 2
Gladden, George, 48 n. 44
Glazer, Nathan, 245, 252 n. 21
Glendale, Calif., 341, 343 n. 15
Glendon, Mary Ann, 48 n. 42
Glenn, Susan, 61 n. 8, 62 n. 14
Global Economic Restructuring, 12. *See also* Economic restructuring and youth cultures
Goddard, H. H., 24; intelligence tests, 24. *See also* Juvenile delinquency
Goldberg, David Theo, 154 n. 18
Goldman, Peter, 152 n. 3
Goldman, Shifra, 236–37 n. 4
Gómez-Quiñones, Juan, 236 n. 3, 237 n. 5
Gonsalves, Theodore Sanchez, 130–31 n. 4
Gonzalo, D. F., 130 n. 2
Goode, Erich, and Nachman Ben-Yehuda, 16 n. 1
Goodheart, Lawrence B., 151 n. 3
Gordon, Jay, 82, 92 nn. 5–6, 94 n. 29. *See also* Deanna Durbin fans
Gordon, Linda, 62 n. 15
Gordon, Michael, 61 n. 6
Gorn, Elliott, 72. *See also* Native American boxing
Goulet, L. R., 18 n. 8
Graebner, William, 16 n. 2, 250 n. 1
Graffiti, 10, 13, 238 n. 23, 240–53, 278; anti-graffiti campaigns, 244, 245; artisanal work ethic, 244, 247; and "fame," 242; gender, 244; history of, in New York City, 241–45, 250–51 n. 7, 251 nn. 8–14, 17; interracial communication, 244; knowledge of urban space, 249; (master)pieces, 244; New York City subway system, 242–43, 245–49; in Philadelphia, 251 n. 9; skateboarders and, 338, 341; tags, 244; transit police, 247–49, 252 nn. 31, 34; writing style, 244, 245. *See also* Baca, Judith F.; Economic restructuring and youth cultures; Graffiti writers; Hip hop; Low rider culture; Masculinity; MTA; Skateboarders; Youth
Graffiti writers, 250–51 n. 7, 251 nn. 8–14, 17, 252 nn. 24, 30–31, 33, 35; Air, 250–51 n. 7, 251 n. 13; BAMA, 252 n. 30; BLADE, 252 n. 31; Cavs, 250–51 n. 7; CAY 161, 252 n. 35; Cool Herc, 252 n. 24; Crash, 250–51 n. 7; Dash, 250–51 n. 7; Daze, 250–51 n. 7; Death, 250–51 n. 7; Futura 2000, 250–51 n. 7; Id, 250–51 n. 7; Illy, 250–51 n. 7; Iz the Wiz, 250–51 n. 7, 251 n. 13; JUNIOR 161, 252 n. 35; KET, 242; Lady Pink, 250–51 n. 7; Nic One, 250–51 n. 7; Phase 2, 242, 250–51 n. 7, 251 n. 8; Poem, 242, 250–51 n. 7; Rated, 250–51 n. 7; Sar, 242, 250–51 n. 7; David Schmidlapp, 251 n. 14; Seen, 250–51 n. 7; Smith, 250–51 n. 7; STAN 153, 252 nn. 30, 33; STITCH 1, 247; TAKI 183, 242, 243; Top Cat 126, 251 n. 9; TCO crew, 247–48; Vulcan, 250–51 n. 7; WICKED GARY, 252 n. 30; Zephyr, 250–51 n. 7. *See also* Graffiti; Hip hop
Gramsci, Antonio, 263
Graña, Marigay, and Cesar Graña, 429, 448 n. 7. *See also* Zine culture
Grange, Red, 98
Gray, Herman, 19 n. 17
Greater Mexico, 170 n. 14

Green, Rayna: on playing Indian, 381, 393 n. 3. *See also* Native Americans
Greenberg, Cheryl, 153 n. 11, 155 n. 26
Grendysa, Peter, 170 n. 16
Grieben, Cy, 228. *See also* Baca, Judith F.; Chicano Arts movement; Los Angeles Department of Recreation and Parks
Griffin, Christine, 17 n. 7
Grillo, Brian, 373–74. *See also* Lesbian, bisexual, and gay youth
Griswold del Castillo, Richard, 62 nn. 11, 14
Griswold del Castillo, Richard, Teresa McKenna, and Yvonne Yarbro-Bejarano, 236–37 n. 4
Grossberg, Lawrence, 20 n. 22, 94 n. 20, 254, 263, 265 nn. 7, 11–12, 265–66 n. 22, 269 n. 50
Grossberg, Lawrence, Cary Nelson, and Paula Treichler, 153 n. 8, 220 n. 8, 236 n. 3, 307 n. 25
Guevara, Rubén, 172 n. 44
Guha, Ranajit, 393 n. 4
Gunn, J. Brooks, 32 n. 3
Gutiérrez, David G., 219 n. 3, 236 n. 3, 237 n. 5
Gutiérrez, Jose Angel, 220 n. 5
Gutiérrez, Ramón, 61 n. 61, 62 n. 11, 220 n. 8, 236 n. 3
Gutowski, Thomas, W., 115 n. 5, 8

Haas, Lisabeth, 170 n. 14
Hager, Steven, 250–51 n. 7, 252 n. 30. *See also* Graffiti; Graffiti writers
Haggerty, Timothy, 39
Hairstyle, 137; conk, 136, 137, 140–41. *See also* African American Youth; Fashion; Filipino American youth; Malcolm X
Hall, G. Stanley, 2–3, 16 n. 5, 21–23, 30, 33 n. 19, 40; *Adolescence,* 23, 40. *See also* Adolescence; Juvenile delinquency
Hall, Stuart, 93 n. 18, 133 n. 16, 266 n. 29, 365 n. 18
Hall, Stuart, and Tony Jefferson, 16 n. 1, 93 n. 17
Halpern, Sydney, 17 n. 6
Hamilton-Merrit, Jane, Dr., 315
Hampton, Lionel, 143
Hanna, Kathleen, 444–45, 450 nn. 51, 53, 55–56. *See also* Zine culture; Zines and zinesters
Hantover, Jeffrey, P., 46 n. 9
Haraway, Donna, 345 n. 25
Hardt, Michael, and Antonio Negri, 346 n. 38
Hareven, Tamara K., 17 n. 8
Harlem, 138, 280; and World War II interracial violence, 140; Savoy Ballroom, 141–42; Small's Paradise, 145
Harper, Frederick, 151 n. 3
Harris, Joel Chandler, 364. *See also* Wiggers
Harris, William H., 152 n. 5
Harvey, David, 265 n. 9, 266 n. 30
Hata, Donald Teruo Jr., and Nadine Ishitani Hata, 134 n. 50
Hawes, Joseph M., 17 n. 8, 31 n. 2, 32 n. 4, 33 n. 19
Hayden, Tom, 202 n. 21
Haynes, F. E., 34 n. 36
Hazzard-Gordon, Katrina, 154 n. 18
Healy, William, 21, 23–25, 27–28, 30–31, 32 n. 13, 33 nn. 16–18, 23–27, 29; Freudian explanation of juvenile delinquency, 26; *The Individual Delinquent,* 24–25; *Mental Conflicts and Misconduct,* 25; sociology of juvenile delinquency, and, 25–26. *See also* Bronner, Augusta; Juvenile delinquency
Healy, William, and Augusta Bronner, 34 n. 30
Hebdige, Dick, 16 n. 1, 19 n. 13, 93 n. 18, 153 n. 13, 250 n. 6, 252 n. 39, 295, 306 n. 13, 346 n. 40, 424, 426 n. 17, 435, 449 n. 27
Helper, Laura, 20 n. 22
Henderson, Charles R., 33 n. 15; 34 n. 34
Hendrickson, Robert, Se n., 176
Herman, Ellen, 201 n. 12
Herman, Melvin, 19 n. 19
Hernton, Calvin, 362, 365 n. 20. *See also* Wiggers
Heroism, 9, 38; Boy Scout novels and, 43; commodity capitalism and, 37; everyday heroism, 39, 41–42; impulsive, 37, 42, 44; instincts, 40–42; Gustav Kobbe and, 41, 47 n. 31; psychology and, 45. *See also* Altruism; Boy Scouts of America (BSA); Carnegie Hero Fund
Herrera-Sobek, María, 172 n. 45
Hershberg, Theodore, 18 n. 8
High School of Commerce, 98, 99, 100, 110; German students, 111; Irish students, 111; Jewish students, 111–12; white students, 111–12. *See also* High schools; High school students; Youth
High school students, 8, 95–117, 178–80, 211–12; academic activities and ethnicity, 101–4; class status and extra curriculur activities, 113; ethnic mixing, 113; ethnicity and, 95–117; extra curricular activities, 96; gender and extra curricular activities, 113; imitation of white students, 114; newspapers and ethnicity, 99, 103–4; performance clubs and ethnicity, 103–4; science clubs and ethnicity, 102, 103–4; service clubs and ethnicity, 103–4; sports and ethnicity, 98–99, 103–4; student celebrities and ethnicity, 100–101, 103–4; student politics and ethnicity, 99–100, 103–4; teen workers, 347–57; yearbook and ethnicity, 99, 103–4. *See also* Bay Ridge High School; Brown Berets; Chicano movement; Evander Childs High School; George Washington High School; High School of Commerce; Lesbian, bisexual, and gay youth; New Utrecht High School; Seward Park High School; Theodore Roosevelt High School
High Schools, 8, 95–117. *See also* High School students
Hill, Joseph A., 62 n. 16
Hinant, Mary H., 93 n. 16
Hiner, N. Ray, 17 n. 8, 31 n. 2, 32 n. 4
Hip hop, 263, 338; censorship of, 395–411; culture, 242, 305 n. 1, 405; development of, 277–78, 289 n. 14; double-Dutch, 272–92; gangsta' rap hearings, 395, 409 n. 1, 410 nn. 33–35, 411 nn. 45, 47, 52, 58–59; magazines, 306 n. 7, 361; and Malcolm X, 150–

Hip hop *(Continued)*
51; multiethnic and multigendered origins of, 277–78; style and Hmong American youth, 316; style and Native American Youth, 390–91; white hip-hoppers, 360–62; women performers, 276. *See also* African American girls and young Women; Chuck D; Double-Dutch; Economic restructuring and youth cultures; Graffiti; Graffiti writers; Hip hop performers; Hmong American youth; Low rider culture; Moral panics; Music; Music performers; Public Enemy; Rap Music; Wiggers

Hip hop performers: Vinnie Brown/Naughty by Nature, 405; Bill Bushwick/The Geto Boys, 405–6; Chuck D, 293, 405; Cool Herc, 252 n. 24; De La Soul, 307 n. 24; Dr. Dre, 425 n. 2; Easy-E, 415; Ecstasy, 413; Eric B. and Rakim, 307 n. 25; Michael Franti/Disposable Heroes of Hiphoprisy, 406; Ice Cube, 401, 413, 415; Ice-T, 309 n. 44, 401, 410 nn. 24–26, 415; Kid Frost, 413; KRS-1, 407; Lauren (Fugees), 288; Litefoot, 391, 394 n. 27; M. C. Lyte, 407; MC Serch, 360, 364 n. 8; Melle Mel, 293; NWA, 399–400, 410 nn. 14–17, 415; Public Enemy, 293–310, 405, 407; Queen Latifah, 308 n. 32, 310 n. 49, 407; Sister Souljah, 310 n. 49, 401, 408, 411 n. 57; 69 Boyz, 289 n. 35; 2 Live Crew, 400–401, 410 nn. 18–23; Tou Ger Xiong, 321–22. *See also* Double-Dutch performers; Hmong American youth; Graffiti writers; Native American powwow performers; Public Enemy; Rap music; Wiggers

Hmong American youth, 15, 311–25; Afro American culture and, 314, 321; and dating, 317, 324 n. 15; expression of pan-Asian, Asian American identity, 315, 321–23, 325 n. 36; girls, 318; foreign-born, 314–15, 318; hip hop style and, 316; Hmong Youth Conference, 315; Latino culture and, 314; gangs, 314, 320–21; rap music, 316, 321–22, 325 n. 36; stereotype of model minority, 318; students, 315, 318–19; U. S.-born, 314–15. *See also* Hmong Americans

Hmong Americans, 311–25; and CIA, 312, 315, 320; concept of the "teenager," 316; cultural assimilation, 312–14; family structure of, 316–17; generational tensions, 313, 316–17; history, 311–13, 324 nn. 2–7; maintenance of traditional values, 314; parents, 314, 316, 319; resettlement in U. S., 313–14; Vietnam War, 312; work ethic, 313. *See also* Hmong American youth

Hobsbawm, Eric, 393 n. 7

Hodges, John, 151 n. 2

Hollinger, Richard and J. P. Clark, 155 n. 27

Homeless, 328, 330–32, 338–39, 344 nn. 21–22, 345 n. 32. *See also* Skateboarders

Homophile movement, 179, 184

Homophobia: and coldwar conservatism, 175; in Miami, 175–76; police harassment of lesbian and gay youth, 183–84. *See also* Lesbian, bisexual, and gay youth

hooks, bell, 156 n. 39

Horn, Margo, 17 n. 6

Horse Capture, George P., 385, 393 nn. 16–17. *See also* Native American powwows

Houston, Texas, 412, 413. *See also* Low rider culture; Low riders

Howard, John, 185 n. 2

Hudson, Julius, 155 n. 28

Huerta, Dolores, 225

Hunter, Tera, 154 n. 18

Huxley, Thomas Henry, 40

Hyer, Sally, 66. *See also* Native American boarding schools; Native American boxing

Ibañez, Rosemarie D., 132 n. 14

Iceberg Slim (Robert Beck), 156 n. 34

Ida, D. J., Dr., 324 n. 8

Immigrant youth: and high school curriculum, 95–117; teenage girls and sexuality, 50–64. *See also* Filipino American youth; German American youth; High School students; Hmong American youth; Irish American youth; Italian American youth; Jewish American youth; Mexican American youth; Teenage girls; Sports; Youth

Immigrants: Norwegian, 69; sexuality, 50–64, 61 n. 7. *See also* Filipino immigrants; Teenage girls

Indian Child Welfare Law, 383. *See also* Native Americans; Native American powwows

Individualism, 9, 37, 44–45

Industrial Areas Foundation, 208

Intercultural communication, 158, 161, 163–65, 167, 168–69; graffiti writers, 244; high school students and ethnic mixing, 135; wiggers, 358–66. *See also* Dancehalls; Graffiti writers; Mixtures, The; Public Enemy

Internet, 14, 377 n. 2; gay male youth sites, 376; Inter-Relay Chat (IRC), 372; social/spatial dimensions, 369–71; women-only sites, 376. *See also* Lesbian, bisexual, and gay youth; Social space; Zine culture

IRC. *See* Internet

Irish American youth, 95–117; young men and high school sports, 98; young women and high school newspapers, 99. *See also* High schools; High school students; Youth

Italian American youth, 95–117; and African American style, 361; young men and high school sports, 98; young women and high school newspapers, 99. *See also* High schools; High school students; Youth; Wiggers

Jackson, Jackie, 176, 181. *See also* High school students; Lesbian, bisexual, and gay youth

Jacoby, Russell, 429, 448 n. 6

James, C. L. R., 408

James, C. L. R., George Breitman and Edgar Keemer, 155 n. 24

James, Harry, 157, 159

James, William, 22, 40–41, 44, 47 n. 38; and child study, 23

Jameson, Fredric, 253–54, 262, 265 nn. 5–6, 10, 269 nn. 44, 47
Jankowski, Martin Sanchez, 16 n. 1
Jenkins, Henry, 93 n. 9
Jensen, Joli, 88, 94 n. 20
Jerome, Amalie Hofer, 32 n. 8
Jewish American youth, 95–117; young women and high school newspapers, 99; lesbian youth in Florida, 173–86
Jewish youth, 178, 184
Jews: in Florida, 174; in Miami, 175; in rock 'n roll, 163. *See also* Jewish American youth
Jezer, Marty, 16 n. 2
Johnson, Autry, 163. *See also* Mixtures, The
Johnson, Hafiz Shabazz Farel, and John M. Chernoff, 308 nn. 28, 35
Johnson, Leola, 399, 402, 409 n. 13, 410 nn. 16, 24–25, 28, 31–32. *See also* Gangsta' rap
Johnson, Marilyn S., 61 nn. 4–5
Jones, A. M., 302, 308 n. 36
Jones, Galen, 115 n. 4
Jones, Jacqueline, 62 n. 17
Jones, LeRoi, 153 n. 9
Joyce, Richard E., and Chester L. Hunt, 130–31 n. 4
JPI. *See* Juvenile Psychopathic Institute
Judd, Dennis, 343–44 n. 16
Judge Baker Foundation, 26–27
Julian, Don, 162
Juster, Susan, 32 n. 3
Juvenile court, 26–28, 50–64; Chicago, 27; Cook County, Ill., 28–29; Los Angeles County, 50, 56, 60, 61 n. 2; statutory rape, 50–51, 54, 56, 60. *See also* Juvenile delinquency
Juvenile delinquency, 8, 21–22, 27, 29, 82, 280; class status and, 30; double-Dutch and, 280; environmental theory of, 27–28, 29–31; feeble-mindedness, 23; Freudian analysis and, 26, 31; juvenile court and, 21; juvenile delinquency hearings in Miami, 176–77, 186 nn. 10–11; Juvenile Protective Association, 23; psychology and, 24, 26, 30–31; psychology of the individual and, 25, 27, 31; race and, 281; social use of Gestalt psychology and, 28; science and social sciences as mechanisms of discipline, 31; sociology of, 25–26, 30–31; theories of causation, 26; theories of the family and, 28. *See also* Hmong American youth; Double-Dutch; Gangsta' rap; Graffiti; Graffiti writers; Moral panics; Skateboarders
Juvenile Psychopathic Institute (JPI), 24–25, 27

Kagan, Sharon Lynn, 17 n. 8
Kagnoff, Nathan M., and Melvin I. Urofsky, 185 n. 3
Kant, Immanuel, 22
Kaplan, Louise J., 32 n. 9
Karenga, Ron, 209
Kater, Michael H., 154 n. 19
Katz, Jonathan, 185 n. 1
Kauffman, Robert, 308 n. 28, 308–9 n. 37
Keller, Betty, 46 n. 6
Kelley, Robin D. G., 5, 7, 11, 126, 133 n. 16, 134 n. 48, 361, 365 n. 15, 410 nn. 23, 41, 411 n. 46; on gangsta' rap, 407, 411 n. 55. *See also* African American youth; Gangsta' rap; Malcolm X
Kellner, Douglas, 255, 265 n. 15. *See also* Postmodern youth culture
Kellogg, Peter J., 152 n. 4
Kennedy, Elizabeth Lapovsky, and Madeline Davis, 185 n. 1
Kessler-Harris, Alice, 63 n. 20, 63 n. 39
Kett, Joseph F., 16 n. 5, 21, 31, 31 n. 3, 47 n. 22, 93 n. 13, 115 n. 1, 250 nn. 1–2; *Rites of Passage*, 21. *See also* Juvenile delinquency
Keyes, Cheryl, 295, 305 nn. 2–3, 306 n. 9, 307 n. 25
Kim, Sojin, 19 n. 22
Kimmel, Michael, 47 n. 33
King, Martin Luther, Jr., 210, 396, 402
Kinsey, Alfred, 187
Kinsey report on women, 188
Kitano, Harry H. L., and Roger Daniels, 132 n. 6
Klein, Norman, and Martin J. Schiesl, 134 n. 50
Klugman, Edward, 17 n. 8
Knoll, Tricia, 324 nn. 3–4
Koch, Ed, 245
Kochman, Thomas, 155 n. 28, 365 n. 22
Kofsky, Frank, 154 n. 17
Kohl, Herbert, 251 nn. 11–12
Kohli, Martin, 18 n. 8
Korstad, Robert, and Nelson Lichtenstein, 152 n. 4
Koskoff, Ellen, 287
Kozol, Wendy, 74
Krisberg, Barry, 33 n. 24
Kropotkin, Peter, Prince, 40, 47 n. 24. *See also* Altruism; Boy Scouts of America (BSA); Carnegie Hero Fund; Heroism
Krout, Maurice, 34 n. 36

La Questa, Celedonio, Jacinto Sequig, and Florentino Mendoza, 132 n. 11
La Questa, Celendo, 121
Laboe, Art, 161, 170 n. 18, 171 n. 22
LADRP. *See* Los Angeles Department of Recreation and Parks
Lamb, John, 325 n. 26
Landon, Alf, 190
Laos (Cambodia), 15. *See also* Hmong American youth; Hmong Americans
Lasch, Christopher, 37, 45 n. 2
Laslett, Peter, Karla Oosterveen, and Richard M. Smith, 62 n. 10
Lassonde, Stephen, 115 n. 2
Latino Youth, 139; and indifference to World War II, 144
Latinos, 158–59, 167–69; immigration, 328, 331, 344 nn. 17, 21–22; in Los Angeles, 327, 328
Lawagan, Miguel, 124, 133 n. 31. *See also* Filipino American youth

League of United Latin American Citizens (LULAC), 237
Lears, T. J. Jackson, 46 n. 8
Ledbetter, James, 358, 364 n. 3, 365 n. 13. *See also* Wiggers
Lee, Gary Yia, 324 n. 9
Lee, Spike, 297
Lefebvre, Henri, 266 n. 23, 336, 345 n. 29
Lerner, Richard M., 32 n. 3
Lesbian, bisexual, and gay youth, 7, 13–14, 173–86, 368–78; beach dances, 182–83; *Blair* cyberzine, 372, 373, 374; computer technology and "coming out" narratives, 371, 375; cyberculture and multiple identities/realities, 368–69, 372–76; *Elight!* cyberzine, 372, 374, 375–76; feelings of isolation and the Internet, 368, 374, 377 n. 1; female impersonators/drag queens, 176, 181; high school students, 178–80; Inter-Relay Chat (IRC), 372–73; male impersonators, 181–82; Miami gay bars and, 180–82; Merril Mushroom, 178–84; *Oasis* cyberzine, 372–76; queercore and outpunk music movement, 373–74, 446–47, 450 nn. 66–67; queering straight culture, 373; queerzines, 428; *QUIRX*, 367–68; race and lesbian, bisexual, and gay cyberculture, 376, 378 n. 6; research complications, 371, 377 n. 1; social/spatial dimensions of cyberculture, 369–71, 375–76, 377–78 nn. 3–5; *Square Pegs* cyberzine, 368, 372, 375; white gay males, 376; Youth Action Online (YAO), 372–73. *See also* Music; Music performers; Youth; Zine culture; Zines and zinesters
Lesbian, bisexual, and gay history, 173, 185 n. 2
Lesbian, bisexual, and gay Southerners, 173–86
Levine, Lawrence, 153 n. 13, 156 n. 36
Levine, Murray, and Adeline Levine, 33 n. 26
Levine, Susan, 62 n. 15
Lewis, Jerry Lee, 161
Lewis, John, 396
Lewis, Lisa, A., 19 n. 20, 89–91, 93 n. 9, 94 nn. 20, 27, 30
Ley, David, and Roman Cybriwsky, 251 n. 12
Libarle, Marc, 19 n. 20
Libertus, Ron, 383, 393 n. 8, 394 n. 18. *See also* Native American youth
Libre, Bonifacio, 121
Lichtenstein, Nelson, 152 n. 5
Licon, George, 207, 209. *See also* Mexican American youth; Mexican-American Youth Leadership Conference; Young Citizens for Community Action (YCCA)
Liebow, Elliot, 156 n. 32
Limón, José, 236–37 n. 4, 426 n. 11
Lindsay, John, 244. *See also* Graffiti; Graffiti writers
Linebaugh, Peter, 155 n. 27
Linklater, Richard, 255, 269 n. 49, 350, 357 n. 2; *Dazed and Confused*, 269 n. 49. *See also* Postmodern culture; Postmodern youth culture; Skateboarders; *Slacker*; Teenage workers
Lipsitz, George, 2, 10, 14, 16 n. 4, 69, 77–79, 135 n. 64, 152 n. 5, 158, 169 n. 4, 170 n. 13, 171 nn. 28–29, 34, 153 n. 16, 172 n. 44, 266 n. 28, 288 n. 6, 308 n. 36, 310 n. 46, 343–44 n. 16, 384, 393 n. 10
Little Richard (Richard Penniman), 159
Littlefield, Alice, 66–68. *See also* Native American boarding schools; Native American boxing
Lo, Sia, 318, 324 n. 20
Locke, David, 302
Lomawaima, Tsianima, 66, 71, 73. *See also* Native American boarding schools; Native American boxing
Lombroso, Cesare, 24
Lopez, Sammy R., 124, 134 n. 35. *See also* Filipino American youth
Lor, Ba See, 322
Lor, Kai, 322–23
Loranger, Joyce, and Mary Tyler, 62 n. 16
Lorde, Audre, 288 n. 1
Los Angeles, 7, 13, 51, 53, 55, 59, 153 n. 8, 174, 50–64, 339; Boyle Heights, 223, 230; Broadway, 327, 328–32, 342–43 n. 3, 343 nn. 4–8; Bunker Hill, 326–30, 343 n. 8; Chavez Ravine, 343–44 n. 16; commercial leisure in, 54, 50–64; Community Redevelopment Agency (CRA), 328, 343 n. 4; double-Dutch, 275; Filipino districts, 127, 132 n. 14; Filipino immigrants, 121–22, 127; greater Los Angeles, 157–72, 161, 168, 169 n. 2; Rodney King and 1992 rebellion, 401; low riders, 412–26; new downtown, 327; old downtown, 132 n. 14, 327; redevelopment, 328, 343–44 n. 16; Ronald Reagan office building, 328, 342–43 n. 3; South Gate, 417; suburbs and youth music, 157–72; taxi dancehalls, 11, 118–35; zoot suit violence, 144, 153 n. 8. *See also* Brown Berets; Chicano Movement; Economic restructuring and youth cultures; Dancehalls; Filipino American youth; Los Angeles County; Skateboarders
Los Angeles County, 50, 53, 157; Dancehalls, 118–35, 157–72; Filipino immigrants, 120, 328; Long Beach, 58; San Pedro, 58
Los Angeles Department of Recreation and Parks, 223–24, 227–28, 235; East Side Murals, 228; City Wide Murals, 228. *See also* Baca, Judith F.; Chicano Arts movement
Lott, Eric, 153 n. 9, 154 n. 16, 362, 365 n. 19. *See also* Wiggers
Low rider culture, 161–62, 338, 412–26; bikes, 416; cars of, and men's bodies, 424–25; cinematic poetics, 413, 417–24; commentary on, 415–16, 425 n. 3; convergence with hip hop culture, 412–14, 415, 425 nn. 2, 4, 5; cultural nationalist murals, 412; economic restructuring, 412; locality and translocal cultural production, 412–14, 417–23; nightmare/horror murals and, 412; tradition and lived experience, 414–17, 424. *See also* Baca, Judith F.; Chicano Arts movement; Economic restructuring and youth cultures; Gangsta' rap; Hip hop; Low riders; Moral panics
Low Rider Magazine, 413, 426 n. 10

Low riders, 412–26; Kathleen Estrada, 414; "Freddy's '3," 422–23, 426 n. 11; "Gangster of Love," 419, 421, 423, 426 n. 9; "Joker's Revenge," 419–20, 425–26 nn. 8, 12; Los Magnificos Car Club, 413; George Luna, 414; Freddy Martinez, 422; Mario Saavedra, 419
Lowrey, Lawson G., 32 n. 12, 34 n. 30
Loza, Steven, 158, 169 n. 4, 169–70 n. 7, 135 n. 68
Lubove, Roy, 33 n. 16
Luce, Father John B., 208, 221 nn. 20–21, 24
LULAC. *See* League of United Latin American Citizens. *See also* Civil rights movements
Lunbeck, Elizabeth, 33 n. 24
Lutts, Ralph H., 47 n. 27
Lynd, Robert S., and Helen Lynd, 86–87, 93 n. 13
Lyon, F. Emory, 34 nn. 38, 39

Macleod, David I., 46 n. 4
Madison, Joseph, 396–97, 403. *See also* Gangsta' rap; Hip hop; Tucker, C. Delores
Madrid-Barela, Arturo, 153 n. 8
Madrigal, Romy, 121
Mailer, Norman, 252 n. 35, 362, 365 n. 16. *See also* Wiggers
Major, Clarence, 365 nn. 10, 22
Malcolm X, 7, 136–56, 151 n. 1, 152 n. 7, 153 nn. 8, 12–13, 154 nn. 19, 20–21, 154 n. 22, 155 nn. 24, 28, 30, 156 nn. 35–36, 38, 40, 210, 221 n. 33, 402; and attitude toward wage labor, 145–48; autobiography of, as literary construction, 131, 151 n. 2; *The Autobiography of Malcolm X,* 136, 137, 151 n. 2; biographies of, 145–47, 150, 151 nn. 2–3; class tensions, 139, 149; and conk hairstyle, 137, 140–41; evasion of World War II draft, 143–44; as icon for African American youth, 150–51; as icon for white youth, 359, 363; and masculinity within hipster subculture, 146–47; perception of his own youth, 148–49; teenage years, 150; and view of capitalism, 148; and understanding of criminality, 148; and zoot suit, 136–37, 144–45
Males, Mike A., 16 n. 1, 250 n. 1
Mallot, W., 190, 201 n. 10. *See also* College campuses; University of Kansas
MAM. *See* Mexican American Movement
Mangum, Garth, L., 19 n. 19
Marable, Manning, 152 n. 5
Marchevsky, Alejandra, 344 n. 17
Marcus, Eric, 185 n. 1
Marcus, George E., 251 n. 8
Margon, Arthur, 48 n. 45
Mariano, Honorante, 134 n. 53
Marin, Calif., 341
Marin, Marguerite, 236 n. 3
Marriage, 52, 53
Marsalis, Branford, 297
Marsh, Dave, 410 nn. 26–27, 37, 39, 411 nn. 42, 44
Marshall, Victor W., 18 n. 8
Martin, Linda, 19 n. 17
Martínez, Rubén, 170 n. 14
Masculinity, 7, 9, 39, 40, 46 n. 9, 205–22, 237 n. 6; Black, 277, 279; graffiti writers and, 244; heroism as proof of manliness, 42; gay male youth cyberculture, 376; late nineteenth-century crisis of, 38; low rider cars and men's bodies, 424; Malcolm Little (Malcolm X) and, 146–47; mythopoetic men's movement, 46 n. 9; skateboarders and, 345–46 n. 32; whites and Black masculinity, 362. *See also* African Americans; Altruism; Boy Scouts of America (BSA); Brown Berets; Carnegie Hero Fund; Chicano Movement; Double-Dutch; Fear; Filipino American youth; Gender; Graffiti writers; Heroism; Malcolm X; Skateboarders; Wiggers;
Massey, Doreen, 336, 345 n. 29, 346 nn. 33–34
Mathiews, Franklin K., 48 n. 48
Maultsby, Portia, K., 308 n. 35
May, Lary, 84–85, 93 nn. 10, 12, 169 n. 4
May, Martha, 62 n. 15
Mazon, Mauricio, 153 n. 8, 155 n. 24
McBeth, Sally, 66. *See also* Native American boarding schools; Native American boxing
McBride, David, 20 n. 22
McClary, Susan, 276, 309 n. 42
McClintock, Anne, 206, 210, 220 n. 10. *See also* Brown Berets, Chicano movement
McCone Comission, 207
McDonald, Dwight, 16 n. 2
McIntosh suit, 129. *See also* Zoot suit
McKay, Henry D., 35 n. 41
McRobbie, Angela, 16 n. 1, 88, 93 n. 17, 263–64, 269 n. 48, 270 n. 54, 376, 390, 392, 394 nn. 25, 28; *Postmodernism and Popular Culture,* 370
McRobbie, Angela, and Jenny Garber, 19 n. 13, 93 n. 18
McWilliams, Carey, 63 n. 19, 124, 133 n. 28
Mead, George Herbert, 49 n. 52
MEChA. *See* Movimiento Estudiantil Chicano de Aztlán
Mechicano Art Center, 231–32, 238 n. 23, 238–39 n. 24. *See also* Baca, Judith F., Chicano Arts movement
Mechling, Elizabeth Walker, and Jay Mechling, 46 n. 9
Mechling, Jay, 9, 46 nn. 6, 8, 47 n. 28, 48 n. 46, 49 n. 54
Medovoi, Leerom, 20 n. 22, 365 n. 15
Mejia, Cynthia, 134 n. 35
Melendy, H. Brett, 130–31 n. 4
Memphis: double-Dutch, 272
Mendoza, Candelario, 157–59, 161, 167, 171 n. 28, 172 n. 52, 172 n. 56
Mendoza, Steve, 163, 169 n. 1, 170 n. 9. *See also* Mixtures, The
Meñez, Hermina Quimpo, 132 n. 8
Mennel, Robert M., 34 n. 38
Menser, Michael, 344 n. 23
Mercer, Kobena, 153 n. 13

Metropolitan Transit Authority (New York), 244–47, 249. *See also* Graffiti; Graffiti writers
Mexican American Movement (MAM), 237 n. 5. *See also* Civil rights movements
Mexican American youth, 9, 68, 162; and rock 'n roll music, 159–160, 161, 162; and zoot suit riots, 207. *See also* Chicano youth; Filipino American youth; Hip hop; Hip hop performers; Latinos; Latino youth; Low rider culture; Low riders; Music; Music performers; Young Centers for Community Action (YCCA); Wiggers
Mexican-American Youth Leadership Conference, 207
Mexican Americans, 157–172, 158, 159, 163, 167, 168, 205; in Los Angeles, 327, 328; population growth 206–7, 237 n. 5. *See also* Baca, Judith F.; Chicana youth; Chicana/o studies; Chicano art; Chicano Arts movement; Chicano youth; Chicanismo; Filipino American youth; Hip hop; Hip hop performers; Latino Youth; Latinos; Low rider culture; Low riders; Mexican American youth; Music; Music performers; Wiggers
Meyerowitz, Joanne, 62 n. 18, 171 n. 34
Miami, 174–75
Miami Daily News: and homosexuality moral panic, 177–78. *See also* Moral panics
Middle class, 38; families and adolescence, 21; ideology of sexual restraint, 51; parents and fear, 39; purity reformers, 50, 56, 59; sexuality, 61 n. 7. *See also* Altruism; Boy Scouts of America (BSA); Carnegie Hero Fund; Heroism; White middle class
Miles, Gary, 360, 364–65 n. 9, 365 n. 11. *See also* Wiggers
Miller, James, 202 n. 21
Milner, Christina and Richard Milner, 156 nn. 32, 36
Min, Gap Pyong, 130–31 n. 4
Minneapolis, Minn., 382–83, 429
Mitchell, Alice, 184
Mitchell, S. Weir, 41–42, 47 nn. 34–36, 48 n. 40
Mitterauer, Michael, 17 n. 8
Mixtures, The, 163–64, 165, 169, 171 nn. 32–33. *See also* Intercultural communication; Mexican American youth; Music performers
Modell, John, 32 n. 3
Modell, John, Marc Goulden, and Magnusson Sigurdur, 152 n. 4
Modernization, 38, 42
Mollenkopf, John H., 251 n. 15
Monk, Thelonious, 142
Monrovia, Calif., 164
Montes, Carlos, 213. *See also* Brown Berets
Moon, Tom, 306 nn. 12, 14, 18–19, 307 n. 21
Moore, David L., 315, 324 n. 12
Moore, Deborah Dash, 116nn 15, 17, 185 n. 3
Moore, Ryan, 11
Moore, William, 152 n. 3
Moral panics, 1, 10, 14, 244, 245, 253; depression era gangster films, 398–99, 409 nn. 10–11; gangsta' rap and, 395–411; Hollywood and House Un-American Activities Committee, 399, 409 n. 12. *See also* Economic restructuring and youth cultures; Gangsta' rap; Hip hop; Low rider culture
Morales, Royal, 130–31 n. 4
Moran, Gerald, 32 n. 3
Mordecai, Abraham, 174
Moreland, Dick, 163, 164, 171 n. 32
Morin, Edgar, 94 n. 21
Morrow, Robert, 343 n. 16
Morton, Donald, 371
Mosse, George, 210, 217, 221 nn. 31, 37, 222 nn. 54, 63
Motz, Marilyn F., 49 n. 54
Movimiento Estudiantil Chicano de Aztlán (MEChA), 215, 226
MTA. *See* Metropolitan Transit Authority (New York)
Muhammad, Elijah, 155 n. 22
Mulvey, Laura, 83, 92 n. 8. *See also* Feminist film criticism
Muncie, Indiana, 86–87
Muñoz, Carlos Jr., 236 n. 3
Muñoz, Rosalio, 217, 222 n. 67. *See also* Brown Berets
Murray, Albert, 361, 365 n. 16. *See also* Wiggers
Murray, Charles, 358, 364 n. 1, 397. *See also* Gangsta' rap
Murray, Charles, and Richard Hernnstein, 397. *See also* Gangsta' rap
Mushroom, Merril, 178–84, 186 n. 18. *See also* Lesbian, bisexual, and gay youth
Music, 6–7, 157; bebop, 142–43; big band, 158–59, 166; British rave culture, 339, 340, 346 n. 37; commercialization of, and Los Angeles youth culture, 166–67; *conjunto*, 157, 159, 170 n. 10; *corrido* and rock 'n roll, 165, 172 n. 45; double-Dutch, 272–92; "Eastside Sound," 165, 167; heavy metal, 303, 309 n. 44, 346 n. 39; jazz, 361, 363; Latin American music, 157–61, 166, 168, 170 n. 14; Mexican American/Chicano, 160, 165; Nirvana, 258; *norteño*, 170 n. 10; *orquesta*, 157, 170 n. 10; punk rock, 257–58, 264, 266 n. 24, 338–40, 346 n. 41, 428, 430, 435–46, 449 n. 13; queercore and outpunk, 373–74, 446–47, 450 nn. 66–67; Riot Grrrl, 440–46, 450 nn. 42–62; rock 'n roll, 159–61, 163, 165; San Diego punk scene, 264, 270 n. 55. *See also* African American youth; Dancehalls; Double-Dutch; Graffiti; Hip hop; Lesbian, bisexual, and gay youth; Male impersonators; Mexican American youth; Music performers; Skateboarders
Music performers: Handsome Jim Balcolm, 165; Hank Ballard, 163; Bikini Kill, 444; Pat Boone, 363; The Boyz drum group, 389; James Brown, 274, 300, 302; John Cage and Edgard Varèse, 296; Lou Castello, 159; Ray Charles, 161; El Chicano, 167; Jim Clermont, 385; Sam Cooke, 161; Cool Herc, 252 n. 24; Miles Davis, 142, 155 n. 32, 296, 306 n. 9; Bobby Day, 288 n. 5; Al DiMeola, 294; John Doe,

256; Elvis, 362; Extra Fancy, 373–74; Lita Ford, 294; Funkadelic, 298; Kathleen Hanna, 444–45, 450 nn. 51, 53, 55–56; Gil-Scott Heron, 300; Chuck Higgins, 171 n. 28; Home Town Boys, 414; Adam Horowitz, 256; Janet Jackson, 276; Michael Jackson, 288 n. 5; Jane's Addiction, 265–66 n. 22; Blind Willie Johnson, 296; Janis Joplin, 361, 365 n. 14; Last Poets, 300; Lauren/Fugees, 288, 290 n. 38; Jerry Lee Lewis, 360, 365 n. 10; Little Anthony and the Imperials, 288 n. 5; Los Lobos, 167; Machito, 159; Madonna, 276, 349; Malo, 167; Branford Marsalis, 297; Wynton Marsalis, 294, 306 n. 9; Charles Mingus, 155 n. 32; The Mixtures, 163–64, 165, 169, 171 nn. 32–33; Porcupine Singers, 385; the Orlons, 288 n. 5; Ozzy Osbourne, 294; Public Enemy, 293–310; Rage Against the Machine, 266 n. 24; Max Roach, 306 n. 9; Veruca Salt, 373; Nina Simone, 288; 69 Boyz, 289 n. 35; Smashing Pumpkins, 373; Sly Stone, 298; Big Mama Thornton, 362; Henry Threadgill, 294; Tongueston Trio, 181–82; Trouble Funk, 298; Ritchie Valens, 159, 160–61, 163; Watt, Mike and Eddie Vedder, 269 n. 51; The Velveteens, 160, 166, 172 n. 43; WAR, 163, 167; Brenton Woods, 162. *See also* African American youth; Dance; Dancehalls; Double-Dutch; Double-Dutch performers; Filipino American youth; Graffiti; Graffiti writers; Hip hop; Hip hop performers; Intercultural communication; Low rider culture; Low riders; Lesbian, bisexual, and gay youth; Male impersonators; Mexican American Youth; Mixtures, The; Music; Native American powwows; Native American Powwow performers; Public Enemy; Wiggers

Mydans, Seth, 324 nn. 14, 19

NAACP. *See* National Association for the Advancement of Colored People

Nasaw, David, 17 n. 6, 344 n. 18

National Association for the Advancement of Colored People (NAACP), 402. *See also* Gangsta' rap

National Child Labor Committee, 23

National Political Congress of Black Women, 395, 404. *See also* Gangsta' rap

Native American boarding schools, 65–80, 70, 382; Albuquerque Indian School, 70; autonomous youth culture at, 66, 69, 76, 78–79; BIA control of youth leisure time, 76–77; Carlisle Indian School, 65–66, 70, 72; Chilocco Indian School, 65–66, 69, 71, 73, 75–76; gendered curriculum, 74; Haskell Institute, 66, 69–70 72, 74; Meriam Commission Report, 69–70; Mt. Pleasant Indian School, 67; policies of assimilation, 72; regulation of females student sexuality, 74; Santa Fe Indian School, 71, 72, 74–75, 77–78; vocational curriculum, 75–76

Native American boxing, 8, 65–66; 69–79; Amateur Athletic Union and, 71–72; and organizaion of amateur boxing in the 1930s, 71–72; origins of and Chilocco Indian School, 70; as social event, 73–75; as source of racial pride, 72. *See also* Native American boarding schools; Native American youth; Sports

Native American powwow performers: DaLynn Alley, 380, 392; The Boyz drum group, 389–90, 394 n. 24; Jim Clermont, 385, 393 n. 15; Karel Ann Coffey, 379–80, 392–93, 393 n. 2; Lisa Doucet, 381; Dixie Harris, 391; Litefoot, 391, 394 n. 27; Mystic Lake Dance Troop, 390. *See also* Native Americans; Native American powwows; Native American youth

Native American powwows, 15, 379; contest powwows, 388–92, 394 n. 19; dance styles, 385–86; drumming, 385–86; history of, 385–88; as invented tradition in urban communities, 383–84; powwow princesses, 380, 381, 392–93; tradition and, 388–92. *See also* Native Americans; Native American powwow performers; Native American youth

Native American youth, 8, 65–80; African American youth styles and, 390–91; assimilation and, 65, 73; boarding school sports, 66–69, 73; and generational/cultural interaction with elders, 380, 382–83, 386–88, 389–92; girls' attitude toward boxing, 73–75; powwow princesses and negotiation of identities, 381, 392–93; "skip generation," 383; socialization of, 382, 383; transmigrant identity, 381–82. *See also* Native American boarding schools, Native American boxing

Native Americans, 65–80, 379–94; American Indian Movement, 206, 383, 390–91; and assimilation, 66, 67; commodification of Native American culture, 77; football teams, 70; Indian agencies, 386; Native American boxing, 65–80; pan-Indian identity, 73, 381–82, 385, 386; Leonard Peltier, 430; policies of Termination and Relocation, 382–83; powwow culture, 379–94; Santee (Sioux), 69; survival schools, 382, 383; white claims to Native American ancestry, 359; white imitation of, in "playing Indian," 361, 381

Nava, Julian, 207

Navarro, Armando, 236 n. 3

Nelson, Ricky, 160, 163, 170 n. 16

Nestle, Joan, and John Preston, 186 n. 18

New Haven, Conn.: double-Dutch, 275

New Utrecht High School, 99, 100, 107–8; Black students, 107–8; class status and extra curricular participation, 113; Italian students, 107–8; Jewish students, 107–8; white students, 108. *See also* High schools; High school students; Youth

New York City, 10, 13, 240–53, 251 n. 15; Brooklyn, 241–42, 429; development of double-Dutch, 275; double-Dutch, 272–92; El Barrio, 241–42; Harlem, 138, 141, 150, 154 n. 16; high schools and ethnicity in, 95–117; mythology of, 243; South Bronx, 241–42, 293; Spanish Harlem, 242. *See also* African American youth; Bay Ridge High School; Double-Dutch; Evander Childs High School; George Washington High School; Graffiti; Graffiti writers;

New York City *(Continued)*
High School of Commerce; Malcolm X; New Utrecht High School; Theodore Roosevelt High School
Newman, Katherine S., 266–67 nn. 30–31, 35, 268 n. 40, 269 n. 43
Newman, Morris, J., 19 n. 19
Ngialah, Daisy Xiong, 323, 325 n. 41
Ngialah, Paia Daisy, 323–24 n. 1
Noonan, John T., 61–62 n. 9
Novoselic, Kris, 258. *See also* Music; Postmodern youth; Postmodern youth culture
Nybatten, Elizabeth I., 17 n. 8

Oakland, Calif., 51, 53, 55; commercial leisure in, 54; Idora Park, 54–55, 58; Lincoln Park, 57
Ochoa, Rachel, 207, 209. *See also* Mexican American youth; Mexican American Youth Leadership Conference; Young Citizens for Community Action (YCCA)
Odem, Mary, 7, 12, 14, 61 n. 1
Odets, Clifford, 399, 409
Ohmann, Carol, 151 n. 2
Olmeda, Cruz, 213–14, 221 nn. 30, 44, 50–51, 222 n. 53. *See also* Brown Berets
Olympia, Wash., 441
Omatsu, Glenn, and Augusto Espiritu, 130–31 n. 4
Omi, Michael, and Howard Winant, 4–5, 18 n. 9
Ong, Walter, 295–96, 306 n. 13
Oring, Elliott, 49 n. 54
Oropeza, Lorena, 222 n. 68
Ortiz, John, 207. *See also* Mexican American youth; Mexican-American Youth Leadership Conference; Young Citizens for Community Action (YCCA)
Ostrow, James M., 19 n. 21
Ottley, Roy, 138, 152 n. 4
Ow, George Jr., Geoffrey Dunn, and Mark Schwartz, 132 n. 11
Owen, Frank, 307 n. 23
Owens, Jesse, 98

Palladino, Grace, 19 n. 18, 93 n. 13, 94 n. 24, 250 n. 2
Palo Alto, Calif., 341
Paredes, Américo, 170 n. 14
Parents, 198–99, 202 n. 18, 203–4 n. 28; Black parents, 286; of Chicano youth, 230; Hmong parents, 314, 316; of lesbian, bisexual, and gay youth; 371; working class, 55. *See also* Baca, Judith F; Chicano Arts movement; College administrators; College students; Hmong Americans; Hmong American youth; University of Kansas
Paris, Shirley Jacoby, 116 n. 16
Parker, Charlie, 142
Parker, Stephan, 18 n. 12
Parks, Rosa, 396
Parsons, Johnny, 209. *See also* Brown Berets
Pasadena, Calif., 165, 169 n. 2
Pascoe, Peggy, 171 n. 34
Pascua, Felix, 123–24, 133 nn. 19, 29. *See also* Filipino American youth
Patten, Simon, 32 n. 11
Paz, Octavio, 153 n. 8
Peiss, Kathy, 62 n. 18, 63 nn. 19, 40, 75, 133 n. 16
Pelletier, Julie, 346 n. 43
Peña, Manuel, 170 n. 10
Penelope, Julia, and Sarah Valentine, 186 n. 18
Peristany, John G., 62 n. 11
Perry, Bruce, 151 n. 3, 152 n. 7, 154 n. 20, 155 nn. 25, 29–31, 156 n. 37; and biography of Malcolm X, 145
Pet, Catherine Ceniza, 130–31 n. 4
Peterson, Anne C., 32 n. 3
Peterson, Erik, 201 n. 12
Petrucci, Armando, 251 n. 12
Pettiford, Oscar, 142
Pfeil, Fred, 266 n. 28
Philadelphia: double-Dutch, 272
Pickford, Mary, 81
Pierce, Charles, 181. *See also* Female impersonators/drag queens
Pilkington, Hilary, 18 n. 8
Pincetl, S., 344 n. 21
Pitt-Rivers, Julian, 62 n. 11
Pizzo, Peggy, 17 n. 8
Playboy, 188, 361
Pollock, Dan, 163. *See also* Mixtures, The
Pomona, Calif., 157, 158, 169 n. 2
Popular culture, 90; Bugs Bunny, 363–64; double-Dutch, 272–92; Gangsta' rap, 395–411; popular novels, 42; reform of commercial leisure, 119, 129; taxi dancehalls, 118–35; working class, 75; working class Filipino youth, 127, 129. *See also* Dancehalls; Deanna Durbin fans; Filipino American youth; Gangsta' rap; Graffiti; Hip hop; Low rider culture; Middle class; Music; Postmodern youth culture; Public Enemy; Rap music; Skateboarders; Sports; Teenage girls; Zine culture
Portes, Alejandro, and Alex Stepick, 185 n. 3
Portuguese American youth, 59
Posadas, Barbara M., 130–31 n. 4, 132 n. 8
Postmodern culture, 253–59; and crisis of affectivity, 253–54; cultural exhaustion among white middle class youth, 254, 265–66 n. 22; post-Fordism, 266 n. 29. *See also* Coupland, Douglas; Linklater, Richard; Postmodern youth culture; Skateboarders; *Slacker;* Teenage workers
Postmodern youth culture, 253–71; compared to counterculture of 1960s, 260; cynicism, 254; downward mobility, 259–63. *See also* Coupland, Douglas; Economic restructuring and youth cultures; Linklater, Richard; Postmodern youth culture; Skateboarders; *Slacker;* Teenage workers
Powell, Bud, 142
Powers, Lloyd, 220 n. 5
Powers, William, 393 n. 1
Powwows. *See* Native American powwows; Native American powwow performers

Prado, Dámaso Pérez, 159–60, 170 n. 16
Pratt, Richard Henry, 66. *See also* Bureau of Indian Affairs (BIA); Native American boarding schools; Native American boxing
Prell, Riv-Ellen, 384, 393 n. 13
Preston, Richard E., 169 nn. 2, 5
Psychoanalysis 31; Freudian, 33 n. 24, 49 n. 52; and youth sexuality, 188. *See also* Juvenile delinquency
Psychology, 38, 40; anthropometric school, 24; feeble-mindedness, 24; heroism and, 45; moral philosophy and, 22; youth and, 8. *See also* Juvenile delinquency
Public Enemy, 11, 293–310; Bomb Squad, 296, 298; "Fight the Power," 298–302; Flavor Flav, 296, 301; lyrics, 303–4, 307 n. 23, 308 n. 31; multicultural, multiracial fan base, 303–4; Professor Griff, 305 n. 1; Carl Ryder, 305 n. 1; Eric "Vietnam" Sadler, 305 n. 1; Hank Shocklee, 295–97, 303; Keith Shocklee, 305 n. 1; Terminator X, 305 n. 1; vocals, 296. *See also* Chuck D; Hip hop; Hip hop performers; Intercultural communication
Puente, Tito, 159
Puerto Rican youth, 242; and development of graffiti writing, 244

Quincy, Keith, 324 n. 2

Race, 7; American films and, 84–85; and deindustrialization, 398, 412–26; and lesbian, bisexual, and gay cyberculture, 376; and poverty, 397–98, 406, 411 n. 46–49; wiggers, 358–66. *See also* African Americans; Economic restructuring and youth cultures; Harlem; Intercultural communication; Zoot suit
Racial Diversity, 163–64, 168; interracial marriage, 362–63
Racism, 307 n. 23, 359; colonialism, 384; Filipino immigrants and, 120, 124, 126; Hmong immigrants, and, 316, 319–20; Native American youth and, 380, 381
Radio, 160, 167; and Mexican American youth, 160; and dissemination of rock 'n roll music, 160–61, 163, 168. *See also* Dancehalls; Intercultural communication; Mexican American youth
Radway, Janice, 93 n. 9
Railey, H., and L. Polansky, 185 n. 3
Rallonza, Johnny P., 121, 122 n. 12. *See also* Filipino American youth
Ramírez, Ralph, 207, 213. *See also* Mexican American youth; Mexican American Youth Leadership Conference; Young Citizens for Community Action (YCCA)
Randolph, A. Philip, 138
Rangel, Jeffrey, 6, 12
Rap music, 10–11, 14–15, 293–310; African polyrhythms and, 302–3, 308–9 n. 37; censorship of, 395–411; debates over musical status of, 294–98, 305 n. 2, 306 n. 9, 307 n. 25; heavy metal fans and, 303, 309 n. 44; Hmong American youth, 316, 321–22, 325 n. 36; lyrics, 305 n. 2; musical aspects of, 293–305; noise, 296–97, 306 n. 17; orality, 295, 296; magazines, 306 n. 7, 361; reception/audiences, 303–4; sampling, 295, 297; study of, 293–94, 306 nn. 5–6. *See also* African American youth; Chuck D; Double-Dutch; Gangsta' rap; Graffiti; Hip hop; Hip hop performers; Hmong American youth; Low rider culture; Low riders; Music performers; Public Enemy
Reagan, Leslie, 64 n. 50
Reagan, Ronald, 207
Recinos, Luis Felipe, 134 nn. 36, 40
Redford, Polly, 185 n. 3
Reese, William, 115 n. 1
Reisner, Robert, 154 n. 17
Remington, B., 185 n. 2
Reno, Janet, 400. *See also* Gangsta' rap
Revitalization movements, 44
Rhoades, Mabel Carter, 28, 34 n. 35
Rice, Stuart, A., 34 n. 39
Ringgold, Gene, 92 n. 4
Riot Grrrl, 338, 440–46, 450 nn. 42–62. *See also* Femininity; Gender; Postmodern youth culture; Zine culture; Zines and zinesters
Roberts, John Storm, 170 n. 8, 172 n. 57
Roberts, Trevor, 325 n. 36
Robeson, Paul Jr., 104
Robinson, Cedric J., 151 n. 3
Robinson, Cyril, 155 n. 27
robles, al, 118
Rodriguez, Joe V. "Borrego," 326
Rodríquez, Richard, 161–65, 171 nn. 22–28, 35–37, 172 n. 38
Roediger, Brendan, 365 n. 12
Roediger, David, 7, 364 nn. 1, 8, 365 nn. 17, 18
Rogin, Michael, 362, 365 n. 19. *See also* Wiggers
Ronnie and the Casuals, 166
Rosales, F. Arturo, 236 n. 3
Rose, Margaret, 171 n. 34; 236 n. 3
Rose, Tricia, 18 n. 8, 263, 266 n. 28, 270 nn. 52–53, 294–96, 302, 306 nn. 5–6, 13, 309 n. 38, 392, 394 n. 29, 407, 410 nn. 15, 17, 23–24, 425 n. 2
Roseman, Marina, 308–9 n. 37
Rosemont, Franklin, 363, 365–66 n. 24. *See also* Wiggers
Rosen, Gerald Paul, 220–21 n. 19
Rosen, Marjorie, 93 n. 15
Rosenberg, Bernard, 19 n. 19
Rosenthal, Michael, 46 n. 5
Ross, Andrew, and Tricia Rose, 18 n. 8, 346 n. 37, 450 n. 52
Ross, Dorothy G., 16 n. 5, 32 n. 5, 40, 47 n. 23. *See also* Boy Scouts of America (BSA); Heroism; Juvenile delinquency
Ross, E. A., 32 n. 11
Rossinow, Douglas, 202 n. 21
Rothchild, John, 185 n. 3

Rothman, Ellen K., 62 n. 12
Rotundo, E. Anthony, 47 n. 33
Rowan, Helen, 220 n. 13
Royals, The, 160, 163. *See also* Castellano, Jerry; Mexican American youth; Mixtures, The
Rubin, Jerry, 269 n. 51
Ruddick, Susan M., 17 n. 7, 346 n. 35
Rugg, Earle, 115 n. 1
Ruiz, Raúl, 212
Ruiz, Vicki L., 63 n. 20, 237 n. 5
Ryan, Mary P., 17 n. 6
Ryan, Michael, and Douglas Kellner, 255, 265 n. 17. *See also* Kellner, Douglas; Postmodern youth culture

Sachs, Curt, 309 n. 42
Sadofsky, Stanley, 19 n. 19
Sahlins, Marshall, 350, 357 n. 4
Salazar, Ruben, 221 n. 40
Saldívar, Ramón, 424, 426 n. 13
Salem, Dorothy, 62 n. 15
Salisbury, Harrison, 16 n. 2
Sammons, Jeffrey, 72. *See also* Native American boxing
Samuel, Raphael, 133 n. 16
San Buenaventura, Steffi, 135 n. 56
San Diego, 264, 270 n. 55
San Francisco, 55, 429, 432
San Gabriel Valley, Calif., 157, 161, 164–65, 169 n. 2, 170 n. 14
Sánchez, David, 207, 209, 210–14, 217–19, 221 n. 39, 222 nn. 57, 67, 70; "Birth of a New Symbol," 210–11, 221 nn. 32–33, 34–36. *See also* Mexican American youth; Mexican American Youth Leadership Conference; Young Citizens for Community Action (YCCA)
Sánchez, George J., 62 nn. 13–14, 63 n. 19, 133 n. 32, 220 n. 16, 237 n. 5
Sánchez-Tranquilino, Marcos, 153 n. 8, 228, 236–37 n. 4, 238 n. 154
Sánchez-Tranquilino, Marcos and John Tagg, 153 n. 8
Sando, Joe, 73, 75. *See also* Native American boarding schools, Native American boxing
Santa Cruz, Calif., 341
Santos, Bienvenido, 130–31 n. 4
Scharf, Lois, 134 n. 45
Scharlin, Craig, and Linda Villaneuva, 130–31 n. 4
Schecter, Hope Mendoza, 171 n. 34
Scheiner, Georganne, 10, 11
Schlesinger, Christina, 233. *See also* Baca, Judith F., Social and Public Resource Center (SPARC)
Schmidlapp, David, 251 n. 14. *See also* Graffiti; Graffiti writers
Schneider, Jane, 62 n. 11
Schultz, April, 68
Scott, James, C., 133 n. 16
Sears, James T., 13, 14, 185 n. 2, 186 n. 20
Sedano, Michael Victor, 220 n. 5
Seeman, S., 185 n. 3
Segrave, Kerry, 19 n. 17
Segregation, 158, 164, 167–68, 172 nn. 54–55; against Jews, 174–75; against Filipinos, 127
Segrest, Mab, 185 n. 2
Seligson, Tom, 19 n. 20
Seninger, Stephen, F., 19 n. 19
Seton, Ernest Thompson, 37–38, 40, 46 n. 5, 47 n. 26; Woodcraft Indians, 37–38
Seward Park High School, 98, 100, 104–7; Jewish students, 104–5, 107. *See also* High schools; High school students; Youth
Sexism: Native American youth and, 380, 381
Sexuality, 52
Shank, Barry, 19 n. 22
Shapiro, Herbert, 152 n. 4
Shaskolsky, Leon, 48 n. 42
Shaw, Clifford R., 29, 31, 35 nn. 41, 40, 44–46; *The Jack Roller*, 29; *Delinquency Areas*, 29
Shocklee, Hank. *See* Public Enemy
Shumsky, Neil Larry, 134 n. 50
Shusterman, Richard, 309 n. 41
Sidran, Ben, 153 n. 9, 154 n. 17, 155 n. 22
Singer, Stan, 134 n. 47
Sitkoff, Harvard, 152 n. 4
Sivanandan, A., 359, 364 n. 6
Sizer, Theodore, 115 n. 1
Skateboarders, 12, 326–46; and affinity for the homeless, 330–31, 332, 338–39; Steve Berra and Swift, 335; clothing styles, 339; formation of subcultural communities, 335, 339; formation of translocal community, 335, 339–41; geographical and social production of scale, 331–33, 335–36, 339, 344 n. 18; global economic restructuring and, 338–42; graffiti, 338, 341; immaterial labor of, 338–40, 346 n. 38; Wing Ko, 327–31, 338–39; Socrates Leal, 326–29, 331, 338–39, 342 n. 1; Rodney Mullen, 327–31, 338–39, 342 nn. 1–2, 343 n. 10; punk rock aesthetic/ethic, 339–40, 346 n. 41; John Reeves, 333; Mark Scott, Brett Taylor and Burnside Project, 342, 346 n. 44; and security guards, 329–31; skateparks, 340–41; social construction of space, 333–36; Daewon Song, 326–27; spatial construction of the social, 335, 336–38; spatial construction of "youth," 336–38, 338–42; Jackson Taylor, 336; tricks, 329–30, 333–34; variable space, 334–35, 345 n. 26, 345 n. 30; Malcolm Watson and Chris Ortiz, 336; white skaters, 358. *See also* Economic restructuring and youth cultures; Graffiti; Graffiti writers; Social space
Skateboarding, 13, 326–46, 434
Slacker, 11, 255, 260, 269–70 n. 51, 348–51, 357 n. 2; and college students, 349; economics of daily life, 350–51; University of Texas at Austin, 349–50. *See also* Linklater, Richard; Postmodern youth culture; Skateboarders; Teenage workers

Slide, Anthony, 92 n. 2, 94 n. 22
Slovenz, Madeline, 306 n. 5
Small, Christopher, 274, 288 n. 4, 289 n. 32, 302–4, 308 n. 34, 310 n. 48
Smart, Christopher, 62 nn. 10, 12
Smelser, Neil J., 17 n. 6
Smith, Anthony D., 219 n. 4
Smith, Dennis, 34 n. 32
Smith, Johnny, 387. See also Native American powwows
Smith, Lillian, 185 n. 2
Smith, Neil, 332, 336, 344 nn. 19–21, 345 n. 29. *See also* Skateboarders
Smith, Neil, and Cindi Katz, 345 nn. 29, 31
Smith, Norene, 388, 394 n. 22. *See also* Native American powwows
Smith, T. V., and Leonard D. White, 35 n. 40
Snead, James, 300, 308 n. 30
Snodgrass, Jon, 35 n. 41
Social and Public Art Resource Center (SPARC), 224, 233. *See also* Baca, Judith F.; Chicano Arts movement
Social history, 200 n. 8
Social space, 158, 240–53, 405; cyberspace, 369–70; low riders and locality, 412–26; and radio, 161, 168; skateboarders and, 326–46; zine culture and new bohemias, 427–51
Sociology: Chicago school, 30, 31; youth and, 8
Soja, Edward, 13, 158, 169 n. 4, 336, 345 n. 29
Soja, Edward, Rebecca Morales, and Goetz Wolff, 327
Soto, Zag, 163. *See also* Mixtures, The
SPARC. *See* Social and Public Art Resource Center
Spaulding, Edith R., 33 n. 16
Sperling, Eva and Holly Barnett-Sánchez, 236–37 n. 4
Sports, 8, 67–68: and assimilation, 68; ethnic youth and basketball, 98; boxing, 65–80; boxing and race, 72–73; ethnic youth and track and field, 98–99; high school football, 68. *See also* High school students; High schools; Native American boarding schools; Native American boxing; Skateboarders
St. Paul, Minn., 321, 382–83
Stacey, Judith, 84, 93 n. 8. *See also* Feminist film criticism
Stack, Carol B., 155 n. 27
Staiger, Janet, 93 n. 9
Stansell, Christine, 61 n. 7, 63 n. 40, 64 n. 51
Stearns, Clifford, 403. *See also* Gangsta' rap
Stearns, Peter, 39, 46 n. 18, 46 nn. 17, 19–20
Stevens, David A., 18 n. 8
Stewart, Jack, 250–51 n. 7, 251 nn. 9, 12, 17, 252 nn. 23, 25, 28, 30–35. *See also* Graffiti, Graffiti writers
Stewart, Susan, 424, 426 nn. 14–16
Stone, Lawrence, 61 n. 9
Stuckey, Sterling, 365–66 n. 24
Subcultural formation, 5, 7, 12; lesbian, bisexual, and gay youth, 371, 376
Surface, James, 195, 203–4 n. 28. *See also* College administrators; College campuses; College students; University of Kansas
Susman, Warren, 44, 48 n. 50

Takaki, Ronald, 130–31 n. 4, 135 n. 55
Tate, Greg, 307 n. 23, 310 n. 47, 358, 361, 364 n. 3
Taylor, Barbara, 324 nn. 15, 21–22
Taylor, Emily, 192, 202 nn. 17–19. *See also* College administrators; University of Kansas
Teenage girls: chastity, 51; challenge to myth of sexual innocence, 56–57; chaperonage of, 52, 54; independence, 55; and pregnancy, 59; pregnancy out of wedlock and working class parents, 55; and prostitution, 56; rape, 60; runaways, 54–55; sex for promise of marriage, 58–59; sexual autonomy, 50, 56; treating, 58, 63 n. 40; and working class recreation, 53. *See also* Commercial leisure; Double-Dutch; Femininity; Gender; High school students; High schools; Popular culture
Teenage workers, 11–12, 347–57; binge-purge work ethic, 354; Black teens, 347; boredom, 348; compared to students and ethic of professionalism, 348, 351–52, 353, 356; employment as parallel of consumerism, 351; ethic of certification, 355; horizontal mobility and sense of autonomy, 351, 352, 355; identification with film *Slacker*, 348; individual jobs and collective culture, 356; intentional choice of unpleasant jobs, 351–52; leisure, 352; poaching, 354; possibilities for organizing as workers, 356; the South and history of occasional work, 353; white, 347; white female, 348; working class ethic and the American Dream, 352, 356. *See also* DeCerteau, Michel; Economic restucturing and youth cultures; Linklater, Richard; Postmodern youth culture; Skateboarders; *Slacker*
Teenagers, 188. *See also* Hmong Americans; Teenage girls; Teenage workers; Youth
Television, 160, 168; and Mexican American youth, 160
Temecula, Calif., 341, 343 n. 15
Temple, Shirley, 81, 85, 93 n. 11. *See also* Deanna Durbin fans
Tentler, Leslie, 63 n. 39
Terkel, Studs, 154 n. 19, 173
Terry, Gina. *See* Adams-González, María Elena
Tewanima, Louis, 70. *See also* Native American boarding schools; Native American youth
Thao, Bruce Teng, 322–23
Thao, Pang, 324 n. 10
Thee Midnighters, 163, 165
Theodore Roosevelt High School, 99–100; Black students, 111; Irish students, 109–110; Jewish students, 109–10, white students, 109. *See also* High schools; High school students; Youth
Thomas, Chris, 369. *See also* Lesbian, bisexual, and gay youth
Thomas, Gertie, 157–58, 167. *See also* Dancehalls; Mexican American youth

Thomas, Jim, 34 n. 32
Thomas, Keith, 62 n. 10
Thomas, Ray, 157–58, 167. *See also* Dancehalls; Mexican American youth
Thornton, Sara, 18 n. 8, 339–40, 346 nn. 36, 40–41
Thorpe, Jim, 70. *See also* Native American boarding schools; Native American youth; Sports
Thorpe, Margaret, 92 n. 6
Thrasher, Frederic, 28–31, 34 nn. 37, 38–39; *The Gang*, 29. *See also* Juvenile delinquency
Tiffin, Susan, 17 n. 6
Tijerina, Reies López, 209
Tilly, Louise A., and Joan Scott, 61 nn. 8, 12
Todd, Arthur J., 34 n. 39
Tomlinson, Gary, 306 n. 10
Toop, David, 305 n. 1, 308 n. 35
Torres, Art, 223
Tosti, Don, 171 n. 28
Touzet, Ray, 159
Tricarico, Donald, 361, 365 n. 14. *See also* Wiggers
Trillin, Calvin, 415, 425 n. 4. *See also* Low Rider Culture
Troupe, Quincy, 155 n. 32
Tucker, Bruce, 297–98, 307 n. 24
Tucker, C. Delores, 395–97, 402–4, 406. *See also* Gangsta' rap; Hip hop
Turner, Jonathan, H., 34 n. 32
Turner, Ralph H., 44, 49 n. 52
Turner, Ralph H., and Samuel J. Surace, 153 n. 8
Tyler, Bruce M., 153 nn. 8, 9, 154 n. 19, 155 nn. 23, 24

UFW. *See* United Farm Workers
United Farm Workers (UFW), 208, 225
United Negro College Fund, 138
United States Childrens Bureau, 87, 125
Universities: management/administration of, 189; postwar growth of, 189–90, 201 nn. 12–13; student activism in midwest, 190. *See also* College administrators; College campuses; College students; University of Kansas; Youth
University of Chicago, 21, 27, 31. *See also* Juvenile delinquency
University of Kansas, 9, 190–204; administrators, 191–92, 195–96, 198–99, 201 nn. 10–15, 202 nn. 16–17, 203 n. 41, 203–4 n. 42; Students for a Democratic Society (SDS), 193–95, 202 n. 21, 204 n. 43; women students and parietal rules, 192–94, 196–99, 203 nn. 30–40. *See also* College administrators; College campuses; College students;

Valens, Ritchie, 159–61, 163
Valentine, Betty Lou, 155 n. 27
Vallangca, Roberto V., 133 n. 30
Vedder, Clyde Bennett, 134 n. 33, 135 n. 65
Victoria, María, 159
Vietnam War, 312, 315. *See also* Brown Berets; Hmong Americans; Hmong American youth
Vigil, James Diego, 415, 425 n. 4. *See also* Low rider culture
Villa, Beto, 157, 158
Villa, Raul, 20 n. 22
Vinovskis, Maris A., 32 n. 3
Vue, Theexa, 318

Wadland, John Henry, 46 n. 6, 47 n. 27
Walcott, Rinaldo, 20 n. 22
Walker, Alexander, 92 n. 6
Walker, David A., 279–81, 283, 287, 288 n. 8, 289 nn. 20, 23, 28–31, 290 n. 36. *See also* Double-Dutch
Walker-Moffat, Wendy, 325 n. 23
Wallace, Anthony F. C., 46 n. 8
Walser, Robert, 11, 306 n. 10, 308 n. 29, 309 n. 44, 346 n. 39
Walsh, Jeff, 373–74, 376. *See also* Lesbian, bisexual, and gay youth
Ward, Freda, 184
Ward, Lester, 32 n. 11
Warshow, Robert, 409, 411 n. 60. *See also* Gangsta' rap; Moral panics
Washington, D. C.: double-Dutch, 275
Watsonville, Calif., 129
Watts rebellion, 207, 220 n. 14
Wechsler, Harold S., 117 n. 23
Weeks, Jeffrey, 62 n. 15
Wei, William, 12, 15, 325 n. 39
Wells, Johnny, 163. *See also* Mixtures, The
Welter, Barbara, 61 n. 6
West, Cornel, 302, 304, 308 n. 36, 310 n. 49
West, Elliott, and Paula Petrik, 17 n. 8, 134 n. 46
Wheeler, Elizabeth A., 305 n. 2, 308 n. 33
Whelihan, Peter, 16 n. 2
White, Frank Marshall, 48 n. 41
White middle class, 253–71; downward mobility, 253, 259–63, 266–67 nn. 29–31, 267–68 nn. 32–36; narrative self-comprehension, 261; whiteness, 261; youth, 11. *See also* Postmodern culture; Postmodern youth culture; Zine culture
White, Sheldon H., 32 n. 6
White youth, 95–117, 161–62, 253–71; cultural dissent from whiteness, 360; middle class and zines, 428; young men and high school sports, 98; young women and high school newspapers, 99. *See also* Postmodern youth culture; Wiggers; Zine culture
Whites, 158–59, 163, 167, 169
Whitfield, Stephen, 151 n. 2
Whitmore, Allan Richard, 46 n. 7
Whyte, William H., 16 n. 2
Wicke, Peter, 172 n. 53
Wiggers, 7, 358–66; African heritage and, 363–64; Black popular culture, 363, 365 n. 15; construction of Black culture as essentially male, 362; cultural hybridity, 361–62, 365 n. 18; Italian American youth and African American style, 361; Malcolm X, 359, 363; origins/variations of the word "wigger," 359–61; MC Serch of 3rd Bass, 360; "white

cholitas," 358. *See also* African Americans; Malcolm X; Race; Hip hop; White middle class
Wilcox, Eric, 375. *See also* Lesbian, bisexual, and gay youth
Willard, Michael, 12, 13, 134 n. 42
Williams, Christian, 369. *See also* Lesbian, bisexual and gay youth
Williams, Mary Lou, 142
Williams, Raymond, 265 n. 4, 48 n. 51
Williams, Ulysses, 279–81. *See also* Double-Dutch
Willis, Paul, 354, 357 n. 7; *Common Culture,* 368; *Learning to Labor,* 354
Willis, Susan, 12, 18 n. 11
Wilson, John, 154 n. 17
Wilson, Olly, 308 nn. 35–36
Wimsatt, William Upski, 365 n. 13
Withers, Jane, 81
Wolfenstein, 152 nn. 6, 7, 153 n. 13, 155 nn. 28, 29, 31
Wolfenstein, Eugene Victor, 151 n. 3
Wollons, Roberta, 17 n. 6
Women's Movement, 206
Wood, James Earl, 133 n. 15; 135 nn. 57, 60
Woodruff, Lawrence C., 191, 201 n. 13. *See also* College administrators; University of Kansas
Woods, Lebbeus, 344 n. 23
Working class, 138–39; Black employment, 145; Black workers and World War II, 138–39; Black youth, 137; and chastity of teenage girls, 51; and cultural politics of Black workers, 149–50; and dancehall leisure, 141–42; Filipino youth, 118–35; popular amusements, 72; skilled laborers and standards of sexual responsibility, 52; sexuality, 61 n. 7; teenage girls' recreation, 53–54. *See also* African American youth; Filipino immigrants; Filipino American youth; Teenage girls
Working class families, 50; chaperonage, 54; and family wage, 53, 62 n. 15; and ideology of sexual restraint, 51
Working class youth, 136–56, 347–57. *See also* African American youth; Filipino American Youth; Malcolm X; Teenage workers
Works Progress Administration (WPA), 145
World War II: and African Americans, 137–39; African Americans and the draft, 143–45; Latinos and, 137, 139; and interracial violence, 140
World Wide Web, 368, 377 n. 2, 378 n. 6; social/spatial dimensions, 369–71. *See also* Lesbian, bisexual, and gay youth; Internet
Wormhoudt, Ken, 335, 341, 345 n. 27. *See also* Skateboarders
WPA. *See* Works Progress Administration
Wrathall, John, 20 n. 22
Wulff, Helena, 18 n. 8
Wynn, Neil A., 152 n. 4

Xiong, Thai, 311, 323 n. 1, 324 n. 20
Xiong, Tou Ger, 321, 325 nn. 32, 34–35, 37–38

Yang, David, 325 nn. 28–29, 31
Yang, Nu Yeng, 316–17
Yang, Pai and Nora Murphy, 324 nn. 7, 16, 325 n. 24
Yang, Thai, 322
Yans-McLaughlin, Virginia, 61 n. 8, 62 nn. 11, 13, 116 n. 12
YAO. *See* Youth Action Online
Ybarra Frausto, Tomás, 226, 236–7 n. 4, 237 n. 8
YCCA. *See* Young Citizens for Community Action. *See also* Brown Berets; Chicano movement; Chicano youth
Yeston, Murray, 309 n. 42
YMCA. *See* Young Men's Christian Association
Yorty, Sam, 207
Young Citizens for Community Action (YCCA), 207–9; La Piranya coffee house, 209
Young, Jock, 265 n. 2
Young, Jon, 306 n. 14
Young, Kimball, 34 n. 39
Young Men's Christian Association, (YMCA), 20 n. 22, 38
Young Women: dancehall employment, 126. *See also* African American youth; German American youth; Irish American youth; Italian American youth; Jewish American youth
Youth, 240; adolescent girls and film industry, 87; Americanization, 8; art making and, 12; autonomy, 240–41; challenges to hierarchies of power in 1950s and 1960s, 187–88, 190; child-rearing advice manuals, 39; clothing styles, 123, 125, 129–30, 162; consumerism, 7–8, 12, 87–92; contested sexuality, 187–90, 193–96, 200 n. 8; courts, 54; cultural work and, 12; ethnic young women and high school activities, 99; family dependence, 7; gender and, 14; girls during great depression, 81–94; girls during World War II, 81–94; historical formation of, 240; impulsiveness of, 44; *in loco parentis,* 9, 189, 191, 195, 196; invisibility of youth self-organization, 13; movements, in late nineteenth-century, 36–38; naturalization of generation conflicts, 14; peer groups, 5–6, 13; peer mediated ethnicity, 114; preindustrial societies and sexual behavior, 52; play and conservatism of organized sports, 67–68; progressive reformers and, 21; postindustrial economy and, 11, 253–71, 326–46, 347–57, 395–411; postmodern culture and, 253–71; queer adolescents, 184, 373–74, 446–47, 450 nn. 66–67; regulation of sexuality in large cities, 53; rural societies and sexual behavior, 52; self-organized institutions, 13; service industries and, 12; social construction of, 1–3, 188–89, 199, 200 n. 8, 240; social space, 240–52, 250 n. 4, 326–47; socialization of, 37–38, 39; subcultures, 87–92, 93 n. 18, 356; sports and social construction of youth, 67–68; urban amusements, 54, 56, 57, 58; working class, 50–64, 64 n. 51. *See also* African American youth; Chicano youth; College administrators; College campuses; College students; Filipino American youth; High school students;

Youth *(Continued)*
Immigrant youth; Lesbian and gay youth; Mexican American youth; Native American youth; Puerto Rican youth; Teenage workers; Universities; University of Kansas
Youth Action Online (YAO), 369, 372. *See also* Lesbian, bisexual and gay youth
Youth Culture, 10–12; in southwest Texas, 68. *See also* Coupland, Douglas; Postmodern youth culture
Youth formation, 3; family and, 14–15; identity and, 4, 6–8; institutions and, 4, 8–9; popular culture and, 10–12; social space and, 13–14
Youth gangs, 38, 227–28, 416; Evergreen, 228; style of, 358; White Fence, 228; Varrio Nuevo, Estrada, 228. *See also* Gangsta' rap; Hmong American youth; Moral panics
Youth Market, 240

Zamora, Pedro, 184
Zamorano, Dodo, 121
Zappa, Frank, 166
Zelizer, Viviana A., 17 n. 6, 47 n. 37, 250 n. 1
Zierold, Norman, 92 n. 4, 94 n. 23
Zigler, Edward F., 17 n. 8
Zimmerman, Gereon, 16 n. 2
Zine culture, 14, 427–51; band tour diaries, 430–33, 449 n. 13; fanzines, 430; "new" bohemian cities, 429; punk identity, 435–40, 449 n. 13; Riot Grrrl, 440–46, 450 nn. 42–62; The Scene (bohemias), 14, 428–35; Starbucks, 430, 449 n. 9; zines and community, 446–48, 450 nn. 63–65; zines defined, 427–28. *See also* Deanna Durbin fans; Economic restructuring and youth cultures; Lesbian, bisexual, and gay youth; Music; Postmodern youth culture; Zines and zinesters
Zines and Zinesters: *Andy's Chair*, 434; Marc Arsenault, 434, 449 n. 22; Claude Bessey, 449; *Bikini Kill*, 444–45; *Blair*, 372–74; Christine Boarts, 430, 449 nn. 9–10; *Book Your Own Fuckin' Cometbus*, 434; *Color Blind*, 447; *Cramped and Wet*, 434; *Crash*, 432; Dawn, 445, 450 n. 58; *8–Track Mind*, 427; *Eleventh Pin*, 427; *Elight!*, 372, 374, 375, 376; *Factsheet Five*, 427, 447–48; Carlos Fernandez, 438, 449 n. 33; *Flipside*, 439–40; *Gogglebox*, 432; Arielle Greenberg, 427, 434, 445, 448 n. 1, 449 n. 25, 450 n. 57; Kathleen Hanna, 444–45, 450 nn. 51, 53, 55–56; *Homocore*, 446; John Hurt, 436, 438, 449 n. 31; *I, Yeast Roll*, 431–32; Mike Impastato, 438, 449 n. 32; *J. D. s*, 447; John Jankowski, 438, 440, 449 n. 36; *Life: Do-It-Yourself Resource Guide*, 433; *Maximumrocknroll*, 435–38, 440, 447; *Minions of Evil*, 449 n. 13; *Oasis*, 372–76; Planet Boy, 436, 438, 449 n. 30; *Po*, 432; *Pool Dust*, 434; *Riot Grrl*, 441–42, 445; *Riot Grrrl, Huh?*, 443; *Riot Grrrl Newsletter One*, 444; *Riot Grrrl Olympia*, 445; *Shithappy*, 434; *Skinned Alive*, 447; *Slash*, 449; *Slug & Lettuce*, 430–31, 435; *Square Pegs*, 368, 372, 375; Steve Stepe, 438, 449 n. 34; Ne Tantillo, 441, 445, 450 nn. 45–46; Rob Treinen, 434; Ann Wilder, 448; Lisa Wildman, 444, 450 n. 40; *William Wants a Doll*, 434; Wolfboy, 435; *You Own a Wonderful Machine: Your Body*, 435. *See also* Lesbian, bisexual, and gay youth; Music performers; Zine culture
Zinsser, William, 16 n. 2
Zizek, Slavoj, 424–25, 426 nn. 18–20
Zoot suit, 136, 137, 139–40; Chicano zoot suiters, 153 n. 8; civil unrest, 207; Filipino youth, 130; politics of fabric rationing, 140; servicemen and, 144–45; work clothes and, 141–42; World War II German youth subcultures, 154 n. 19. *See also* African American youth; Fashion; Filipino American youth; Hairstyle; Dance; Malcolm X; McIntosh suit